The PRI Directory

Charitable Loans and Other Program-related Investments by Foundations

Second Edition

Compiled by
THE FOUNDATION CENTER

Jeffrey A. Falkenstein, Editor

The Foundation Center
New York • 2003

CONTRIBUTING STAFF

Senior Vice President for Information Resources and Publishing	Rick Schoff
Director of Foundation Database Publishing	Jeffrey A. Falkenstein
Vice President for Research	Loren Renz
Director of Research	Steven Lawrence
Senior Database Editor	Margaret Mary Feczko
Senior Editor	Francine Murray
Editor	David G. Jacobs
Director of Grants Processing	Rebecca MacLean
Assistant Manager of Grants Processing	Denise McLeod
Grants Indexing Specialist	Ben McLaughlin
Manager of Bibliographic Services	Sarah Collins
Assistant Librarian	Jimmy Tom
Coordinator of Information Control	Yinebon Iniya
Assistant Editor	Regina Judith Faighes
Editorial Associates	Elia S. Glenn Joey W. Guastella
Publishing Database Administrator	Kathye Giesler
Programmer	Crystal Mandler
Database Operations Assistant	Emmy So
Production Coordinator, Publications	Christine Innamorato

The Editor gratefully acknowledges the many other Foundation Center staff who contributed support, encouragement, and information that was indispensable to the preparation of this volume. Special mention should also be made of the staff members of the New York, Washington, D.C., Cleveland, San Francisco, and Atlanta libraries who assisted in tracking changes in foundation information. We would like to express our appreciation as well to the many foundations that cooperated fully in updating information prior to the compilation of *The PRI Directory*.

ISBN 1-931923-49-3
Printed and bound in the United States of America.

Contents

INTRODUCTION

Only a tiny number of the many thousands of foundations in *The Foundation Directory* or *Foundation Directory, Part 2* report that they make program- related investments (PRIs), and of these, fewer still make them on an annual basis. Nevertheless, PRIs, in the form of loans, equity investments, and guarantees of projects can be an important tool for grantmakers and nonprofits alike. Increasingly, they are viewed as an alternative to a grant when the circumstances are right, e.g., when the organization seeking capital has the potential to repay it. In an era of shrinking public resources, they are valued by many in the nonprofit field as a means of leveraging precious philanthropic dollars.

In the early 1990s, information was not available about the field of PRI makers and recipients. To remedy this, in 1994 the Foundation Center initiated the first PRI database, modeled after the Center's grants database. In the first year, 550 historical records of the 100 largest providers were added to the database, covering activity from 1990 to 1992. In 1995, the Center published *Program Related Investments: A Guide to Funders and Trends.*[1] The *Guide* included a directory of 189 PRI providers, an indexed listing of the 550 PRI records from the PRI database, and a trends analysis for 1990 to 1992. The *PRI Guide* was developed with support from the Ford Foundation. In 1997, *The PRI Index* was produced as an update.[2] The *Index* listed PRIs made by the largest providers from 1993 to early 1995 and included an updated trends analysis. In 2001, the Foundation Center released the first edition of *The PRI Directory: Charitable Loans and Other Program-Related Investments by Foundations.* The *Directory* contained information on 192 foundations making PRIs from 1997 to 2000 and provided detailed analysis of 581 individually indexed PRIs made from 1998 to 1999.[3]

1. Renz, L., and C. Massarsky. *Program-Related Investments: A Guide to Funders and Trends,* New York, Foundation Center, 1995.
2. *The PRI Index: 500 Recent Foundation Charitable Loans and Investments,* New York, Foundation Center, 1997.
3. See *The PRI Directory: Charitable Loans and Other Program-Related Investments by Foundations,* New York, Foundation Center, 2001.

What's in *The PRI Directory?*

The second edition *PRI Directory* lists 1,137 program-related investments of at least $10,000 with a total value of $776,839,142 made by 183 foundations between 1999 and 2002.

The PRI Directory is compiled using the latest information from the foundations themselves or from public records. To identify organizations for inclusion in *The PRI Directory,* Foundation Center staff monitor IRS information returns for private foundations (Form 990-PF), journal and newspaper articles, press releases and news services related to foundation activities, and foundation publications such as newsletters and annual reports. Entries are prepared from the most recent information available and sent to the individual foundations for verification.

How to Use *The PRI Directory*

The PRI Directory is one of the first tools grantseekers should use to identify foundations that might be interested in providing PRIs (program-related investments) to their project or organization. It provides basic descriptions and current fiscal data for the nation's largest PRI-providing foundations—those with assets of $1 million or more or annual giving of at least $50,000. In addition, indexes help to identify foundations that may have giving interests in particular subject fields or geographic areas, or that provide specific types of support.

Researchers, journalists, grantmakers, and others interested in the philanthropic field may use *The PRI Directory* to get a broad overview of current foundation activities nationally or within a particular geographic region, or to gather facts about one or more specific foundations.

When using *The PRI Directory* to identify potential lending sources, PRI seekers are urged to read each foundation description carefully to determine the nature of the PRI maker's interests and to note any restrictions on giving that would prevent the foundation from considering their proposal. Many foundations limit their lending or investing to a particular subject field or geographic area. Even when a foundation has not provided an explicit limitations statement, restrictions on giving may exist. This is often the case with entries updated from public records. Further research into the giving patterns of these foundations is necessary before applying for PRIs.

Overview of PRI Activity for All Foundations

In 2000, the nation's nearly 57,000 active private and community foundations made charitable distributions totaling over $30 billion. Grants of $27.5 billion accounted for the vast share of these distributions.[4] Nonetheless, for some foundations, grantmaking was not their only charitable activity. Among the alternatives to grantmaking, foundations reported $225.6 million in charitable loans and other program-related investments (PRIs). These asset-based funds provided low- or no-interest loans to organizations, capitalized community loan funds and venture capital funds, or were invested in charitable use assets.

In 2001, over 61,000 active foundations paid $30.5 billion in grants, an increase of over 10 percent over the prior year despite a decline in asset values. During the same period, foundations reported a 3 percent increase in new program-related investments, from $225.6 million to $232.9 million.[5]

Although the level of PRI financing grew only modestly compared with the late 1990s, the number of active PRI funders has increased despite the current economic environment. The new *PRI Directory* includes descriptions of 255 PRI providers, up substantially from the number identified in the Center's first PRI publication, which was published in 1995. The field has undergone dramatic changes since the early 1990s: several new—including recently established— PRI providers have developed formal programs or have made PRIs on an occasional basis; the number of PRI providers reporting PRI transactions of $10,000 or more has grown; and several major new PRI funders have emerged. Counterbalancing these positive developments, several foundations that reported PRI activity earlier in the decade were not active in later years. In a few cases, these funders had made major PRIs in response to specific national or regional initiatives and then indicated that they did not expect to continue the practice.[6]

4. See Lawrence, S. et al., *Foundation Yearbook: Facts and Figures on Private and Community Foundations,* New York: Foundation Center, 2002.
5. Total 2001 PRI amount for all foundations is based on data compiled for the PRI Directory, 2003. Figures reflect distributions paid in circa 2001 do not precisely match new authorizations in the PRI database.
6. In the early to mid-1990s, a few large funders provided one-time support for the National Community Development Initiative (NCDI), a collaborative effort of major foundations, corporations, HUD, and local public and private organizations seeking to significantly increase urban community revitalization activities regionally and nationwide.

Trends in PRI Financing: 2000–2001

The following trends analysis reviews the PRI activity of a sample of 135 leading PRI providers. A subset of the 255 foundations listed in the PRI Directory, these funders reported individual PRI transactions of $10,000 or more, which are indexed in the Foundation Center's PRI database (see box on page viii.) Since many foundations do not make PRIs on an annual basis, the trends analysis examines a cumulative two-year period.

Dimensions of PRI Financing

In the period 2000–2001, 135 leading PRI providers authorized 667 charitable loans and other PRI investments exceeding $421 million. PRI activity was not consistent across years. After declining in 2000, the level of PRI authorizations jumped from $174.9 million in 2000 to over $246 million in 2001.

During 1998–1999 (the last two-year period analyzed by the Foundation Center), a sample of 133 top providers authorized 581 program-related investments totaling $426.9 million. Since 1998–1999, the value of PRIs authorizations has remained relatively steady at $421 million, while the number of PRIs increased by almost 15 percent to 667 (Figure 1). The sample of foundations reporting PRIs of $10,000 or over also remained relatively stable. (For information on the annual growth of PRIs for foundations in the PRI database, see Table A in "The Foundation Center's Historical PRI Database.").

Profile of PRI Providers by Foundation Type and Size

In 2000–2001, over 85 percent of funders in the PRI database sample were independent foundations and they accounted for 79 percent of all PRI dollars and 83 percent of PRIs (Table 1). Only 5.2 percent of the leading providers were corporate foundations, but they accounted for roughly 9.7 percent of PRIs. By dollar amount, however, corporate funders provided only 4.6 percent of PRI financing. This suggests that, on average, their charitable loans and investments were smaller than the PRIs of independent foundations. Community foundations also represented 5.2 percent of the leading providers. Yet they were responsible for only 2.5 percent of the number of PRIs and 2 percent of the total dollar value of PRI financing. Compared with 1998–1999, community foundations' share of PRI financing has remained steady. Corporate foundations' share of PRI dollars decreased slightly and their share of number of PRIs has also decreased.

Although foundations in the sample represented all asset sizes, they tended to be larger relative to all foundations (Table 2). Fifty-seven percent of leading PRI providers held assets of $50 million or more, and they accounted for 80.3 percent of new charitable loans and investment dollars in 2000–2001.

Still, among the very largest U.S. foundations, many do not have PRI programs. For example, only 7 of the 43 U.S. foundations with assets of $1 billion or more reported PRI transactions of $10,000 or more in 2000–2001. This finding suggests that asset size is not the principal determinant for making PRIs.[7] Even foundations with significant resources, and therefore greater capacity to manage loans and charitable investments, have not opted to do so.

The number of smaller foundations in the PRI database has not grown substantially since 1998–1999. Still, 58 foundations with assets of less than $50 million made PRIs totaling nearly $83 million in 2000–2001 and were responsible for nearly two-fifths of the total number of PRIs in the sample.

7. For a discussion about incentives and disincentives to PRI making, see "Capturing the Experience of Funders and Recipients" in *Program-Related Investments: A Guide to Funders and Trends,* New York: Foundation Center, 1995.

Large vs. Small PRI Providers

Although 135 funders made charitable loans or other PRI transactions in 2000–2001, the largest providers were responsible for a disproportionate share of the total financing. The top ten funders provided 60 percent of all distributions, while the top 56—those authorizing at least $1 million in new financing during the two-year period—accounted for 92.5 percent of the total funds (Table 3).

Compared with 1998–1999, the listing of top ten providers reveals very dramatic changes. Seven of the largest funders—University Financing Foundation, Inc. (GA), Presbyterian Health Foundation (OK), AVI CHAI Foundation (NY), Lincy Foundation (CA), Libra Foundation (ME), Fannie Mae Foundation (DC), and Otto Bremer Foundation (MN)—were new to the top ten in 2000–2001.

FIGURE 1. Changes in PRI Financing Between 1998–1999 and 2000–2001*

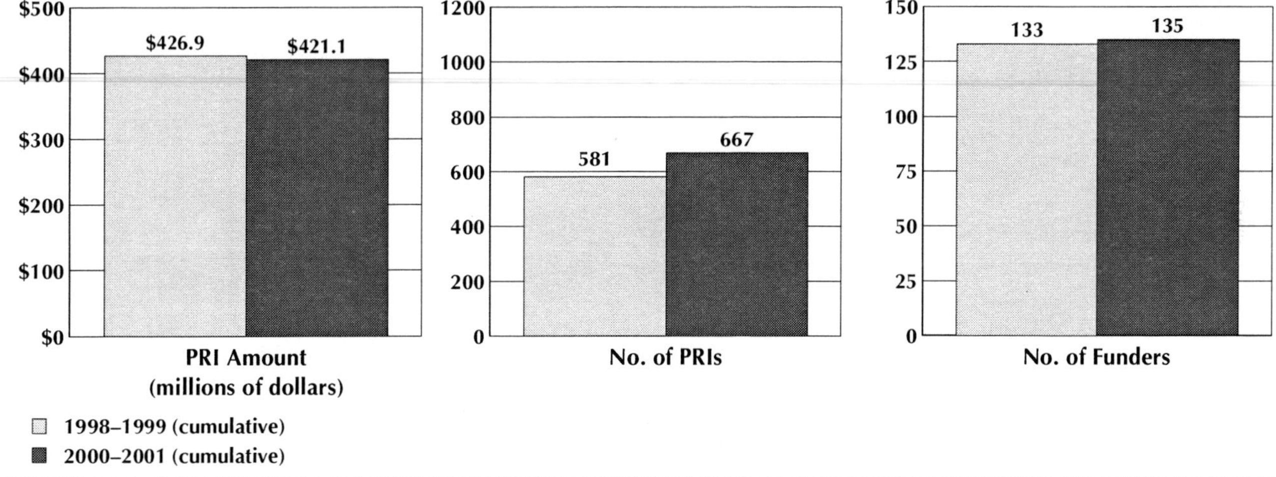

Source: *PRI Directory,* 2003.
*Based on PRI transactions of $10,000 or more of a sample of larger PRI funders.

TABLE 1. PRI Financing by Foundation Type, 2000–2001*

Foundation Type	No. of Foundations	%	Dollar Amount of PRIs	%	No. of PRIs	%
Independent	115	85.2	$333,053,530	79.1	554	83.1
Corporate	7	5.2	19,271,748	4.6	65	9.7
Community	7	5.2	8,553,869	2.0	17	2.5
Operating	6	4.4	60,258,881	14.3	31	4.6
Total	**135**	**100.0**	**$421,138,028**	**100.0**	**667**	**100.0**

Source: *PRI Directory,* 2003
*Based on PRI transactions of $10,000 or more made in 2000 and 2001 by a sample of 135 larger PRI funders. Figures may not add up due to rounding.

The number of larger PRI providers has greatly expanded over the past few years. Table 4 shows that in 2000–2001, 53 foundations distributed at least $1 million. In contrast, in 1998–1999, just 35 met the $1 million criteria. These larger providers represented more than 41 percent of the sample in the latest period, compared with roughly 27 percent two years ago.

The Foundation Center's Historical PRI Database

The Foundation Center's PRI database includes more than 3,000 individual records of program-related investments (PRIs) of $10,000 or more made between 1990 and mid-2002 by a diverse sample of larger independent, corporate, community, and operating foundations. These unique records provide the basis for detailed investigations of financing patterns. They are also a primary source of information for anyone seeking to find out who makes and who gets PRIs, and which fields benefit.

The sample of leading PRI funders—those making individual charitable loans and other charitable investments of $10,000 and over—has increased steadily since the early 1990s. For 1990–1992, the period analyzed in the Foundation Center's inaugural study of PRIs, the sample size was 100 funders.[1] The number of larger funders increased to 116 for the period 1993–1994, which was examined in an updated trends report released in 1997.[2] In 1998–1999, the sample grew to 133 funders.[3] In the latest study period, 2000-2001, the sample increased slightly, to 135 foundations.

The Foundation Center's PRI database is modeled after its grants database. Individual PRI records include foundation name and state; recipient name, city, and state (or country); PRI amount; and year of authorization or payment. If available, additional information provided in the record includes loan term, interest rate charged, and a description of the project financed by the PRI. For purposes of retrieval and to facilitate trends analysis, individual PRI records are coded to track institutional or programmatic fields, recipient auspices, type of financial vehicle, type of support, and beneficiary groups. Institutional or programmatic codes were adapted from the National Taxonomy of Exempt Entities (NTEE), a comprehensive coding scheme developed by the National Center for Charitable Statistics to classify nonprofit activities, and used by the Foundation Center since 1989 to classify and track grants.

Records of PRI activity were gathered from lists of PRIs provided by funders, foundation publications, survey questionnaires, and IRS information returns (Form 990-PF) filed by foundations. A few leading PRI providers, especially those with cash flow loan programs, report only summary or cumulative PRI figures, instead of data on individual loans and their recipients. For lack of information from which to create discrete searchable records, the activities of those providers are not included in the PRI historical database. Nevertheless, those funders were researched, and entries describing their activities have appeared in both of the directories of PRI funders published by the Foundation Center.

Table A presents summary information on the PRI database sample from 1990 to 2002. This database

TABLE A. PRI Activity for Funders in the PRI Database by Year Authorized*

	No. of Foundations	Dollar Amount of PRIs	No. of PRIs
1990	57	$ 91,919,366	161
1991	76	130,028,751	202
1992	74	117,714,091	181
1993	93	103,655,127	215
1994	69	72,893,253	173
1995	69	94,530,363	180
1996	62	76,575,398	197
1997	70	143,868,571	268
1998	89	148,067,104	341
1999	117	260,779,909	348
2000	100	174,983,668	327
2001	105	246,154,360	340
2002[1]	31	94,909,205	121
Total		**$1,756,079,166**	**3,054**

Source: *PRI Directory*, 2003.
*Based on PRI transactions of $10,000 or more of a sample of larger PRI funders.
[1]Data incomplete for 2002.

1. See Renz, L. et al., *Program-Related Investments: A Guide to Funders and Trends*, New York: Foundation Center, 1995.
2. See Mandler, C., *The PRI Index: 500 Recent Foundation Charitable Loans and Investments*, New York: Foundation Center, 1997.
3. See *The PRI Directory: Charitable Loans and Other Program-Related Investments by Foundations*, New York, Foundation Center, 2001.

The number of providers in the middle distribution ranges has decreased as a result. Thirty-six foundations (27.9 percent of the sample) distributed between $250,000 and $1 million in PRIs in 2000–2001, down from 53 foundations (41 percent) in 1998–1999.

The number and share of providers making PRI distributions totaling less than $250,000 has remained steady. Foundations authorizing less than $250,000 in PRI distributions represented less than one-third of the sample of all providers in 2000–2001 (31 percent). Two years earlier, they accounted for 32 percent of providers.

State and Regional Distribution of PRI Providers

PRI providers in the sample were located in 44 states and the District of Columbia. Nevertheless, 87 providers in 15 states provided the vast majority (90.3 percent) of PRI dollars distributed to recipients in 2000–2001, and 51 funders in just five states provided nearly 70 percent of all PRI support (Table 5).

California again led the nation by amount of PRI financing. With its 12 PRI makers, led by the Packard Foundation, the state provided nearly 30 percent of all PRI dollars ($102.7 million), yet 9 percent of the number of PRIs (58). New York, which towered above all other states in PRI financing in the early 1990s (due largely to the preeminence of the Ford Foundation), ranked second by PRI amount ($83.1 million or 23.7 percent) in 2000–2001. Still, it exceeded California by number of providers (22), and distributed more than twice as many PRIs (140 or 21.7 percent). Illinois ranked third by PRI amount ($26.5 million) and by number of providers (9). Maine, with only one PRI funder in the state, ranked fourth by PRI amount, due mainly to the Libra Foundation's exceptionally large PRIs. District of Columbia ranked fifth by PRI amount ($12.8 million), but it placed second by number of PRIs (71), and fourth by number of PRI providers (7).

State and Regional Distribution of PRI Recipients

States in which foundations provided the largest share of PRI funding generally also attracted the largest share of PRI dollars (Table 6). This finding reflects either the localized focus of most foundation support and/or the concentration of borrowers, especially financial intermediaries, in particular states. Exceptions included Virginia, Massachusetts, Ohio, and Hawaii. Although they did not report many large PRI providers, these states received relatively large PRI amounts, directed either to intermediaries or to local or regional development agencies, community groups, or larger institutions (such as universities).

FIGURE 2. Analysis of PRI Activity by Assets Loaned or Invested vs. Assets Held as Charitable Use Assets, 2000–2001*

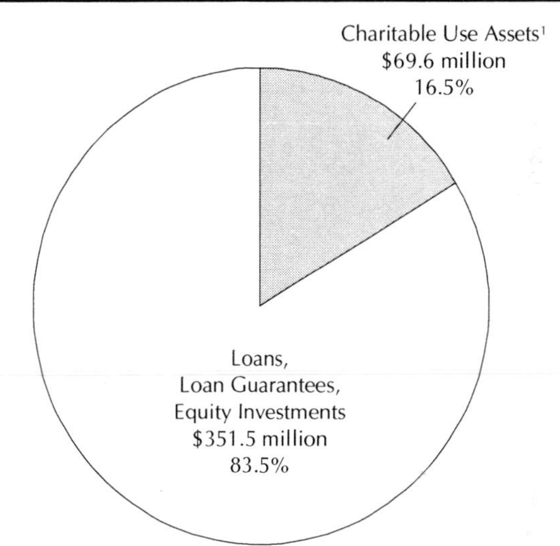

Percent of PRI Dollars
Total PRI Activity = $421.1 million

Source: *PRI Directory,* 2003.
*Based on PRI transactions of $10,000 or more made in 2000 and 2001 by a sample of 135 larger PRI funders.
1 Program-related investments in assets (e.g. property) that is used for charitable purposes.

TABLE 2. Distribution of PRI Funders in 2000–2001 by Asset Size*

Asset Range[1]	No. of Foundations	%	Dollar Amount of PRIs	%	No. of PRIs	%
$1 billion+	7	5.2	$125,680,934	29.8	57	8.5
$250 million–$1 billion	20	14.8	89,706,022	21.3	161	24.1
$50 million–$250 million	50	37.0	122,785,240	29.2	187	28.0
$10 million–$50 million	34	25.2	63,396,530	15.1	126	18.9
Under $10 million	24	17.8	19,569,302	4.6	136	20.4
Total	**135**	**100**	**$421,138,028**	**100.0**	**667**	**100.0**

Source: *PRI Directory,* 2003
*Based on PRI Transactions of $10,000 or more made in 2000 and 2001 by a sample of 135 larger PRI funders. Figures may not add up due to rounding.
[1]Based on market value of assets reported to the Foundation Center as of June 2003. Fiscal year of most foundations was 2001–2002.

TABLE 3. 56 Largest PRI Providers, 2000–2001*

	Foundation Name	State	Dollar Amount of PRIs	%	No. of PRIs
1	The David and Lucile Packard Foundation	CA	$ 63,030,934	15.0	23
2	The University Financing Foundation, Inc.**	GA	43,917,025	10.4	10
3	The Ford Foundation	NY	33,000,000	7.8	14
4	John D. and Catherine T. MacArthur Foundation	IL	23,550,000	5.6	13
5	Presbyterian Health Foundation**	OK	20,131,140	4.8	4
6	The AVI CHAI Foundation	NY	18,675,000	4.4	22
7	The Lincy Foundation	CA	15,871,280	3.8	2
8	Libra Foundation	ME	15,711,453	3.7	3
9	Fannie Mae Foundation	DC	10,316,551	2.4	31
10	Otto Bremer Foundation	MN	9,110,445	2.2	37
11	Media Development Loan Fund**	NY	8,283,654	2.0	31
12	Layne Foundation	CA	8,264,196	2.0	13
13	Walton Family Foundation, Inc.	AR	7,160,124	1.7	4
14	Conrad N. Hilton Foundation	NV	7,000,000	1.7	2
15	Everlasting Private Foundation	CA	6,873,405	1.6	1
16	Pleasant T. Rowland Foundation, Inc.**	WI	5,839,670	1.4	1
17	The Prudential Foundation	NJ	5,735,000	1.4	22
18	The F. B. Heron Foundation	NY	5,252,500	1.2	16
19	Kalamazoo Community Foundation	MI	5,250,000	1.2	3
20	Righteous Persons Foundation	CA	4,970,387	1.2	2
21	The Frist Foundation	TN	4,900,000	1.2	2
22	Open Society Institute	NY	4,000,000	0.9	3
23	McCune Charitable Foundation	NM	3,965,286	0.9	3
24	Michigan Capital Fund for Housing Non-Profit Housing Corporation	MI	3,606,451	0.9	13
25	The Bullitt Foundation	WA	3,600,000	0.9	6
26	Marty and Dorothy Silverman Foundation	NY	3,241,750	0.8	15
27	Eula Mae and John Baugh Foundation	TX	3,000,000	0.7	1
28	Development Credit Fund, Inc.	MD	2,803,285	0.7	43
29	Claude Worthington Benedum Foundation	PA	2,771,000	0.7	3
30	Geraldine R. Dodge Foundation, Inc.	NJ	2,600,000	0.6	2
31	The Cleveland Foundation	OH	2,500,000	0.6	2
32	Pearl M. and Julia J. Harmon Foundation	OK	2,421,550	0.6	6
33	Nelson Puett Foundation	TX	2,415,898	0.6	2
34	Ewing Marion Kauffman Foundation	MO	2,400,000	0.6	1
35	T. L. L. Temple Foundation	TX	2,326,921	0.6	2
36	The Abell Foundation, Inc.	MD	2,129,154	0.5	12
37	McCune Foundation	PA	2,000,000	0.5	1
38	The Winthrop Rockefeller Foundation	AR	2,000,000	0.5	2
39	The Cafesjian Family Foundation, Inc.	FL	1,985,634	0.5	4
40	Joe W. & Dorothy Dorsett Brown Foundation	LA	1,931,920	0.5	10
41	Hutton Foundation	CA	1,916,665	0.5	6
42	The Anonymous Fund	NC	1,750,000	0.4	1
43	MetLife Foundation	NY	1,660,884	0.4	3
44	Eugene and Agnes E. Meyer Foundation	DC	1,552,798	0.4	33
45	The Atlantic Foundation of New York	NY	1,500,000	0.4	2
46	The Jon and Karen Huntsman Foundation	UT	1,447,581	0.3	2
47	The CARLISLE Foundation	MA	1,362,000	0.3	3
48	Gebbie Foundation, Inc.	NY	1,300,000	0.3	1
49	Hansen Foundation	PA	1,300,000	0.3	1
50	The Highland Street Connection**	MA	1,149,623	0.3	2
51	Alavi Foundation	NY	1,063,360	0.3	10
52	The Samuel Roberts Noble Foundation, Inc.	OK	1,057,867	0.3	3
53	Ervin G. Houchens Foundation, Inc.	KY	1,052,000	0.2	29
54	The Faith Foundation, Inc.	OR	1,025,688	0.2	4
55	Gordon Lovejoy Foundation	WA	1,000,000	0.2	1
56	The Rockefeller Foundation	NY	1,000,000	0.2	2
	Subtotal		**$389,481,164**	**92.5**	**441**
	All other foundations		31,656,864	7.5	226
	Total		**$421,138,028**	**100.0**	**667**

Source: *PRI Directory,* 2003
*Based on PRI transactions of $10,000 or more made in 2000 and 2001 by a sample of 135 largest PRI funders.
2001 data is incomplete for a few providers. Figures may not add up due to rounding.
**PRI distributions by these foundations represent, either in part or full, expeditures for charitable use assets.

Domestic vs. International PRI Financing

Most PRIs were invested with U.S. organizations. As shown in Table 7, however, there was a dramatic increase in PRI-related activity overseas. In 2000-2001, 64 PRIs totaling nearly $44 million as compared with 40 PRIs valued at $14.7 million in 1998-1999. This represented an increase of over 50 percent in the number of PRIs and almost triple the amount of loans and other investments distributed to overseas recipients. This increase can be attributed largely to 4 PRIs totaling $17.3 million to the government of Armenia, including 2 PRIs totaling $15.9 million from the Lincy Foundation.

An additional 19 PRIs totaling $15.6 million (2.9 percent) were made to U.S.-based organizations in support of international programs. Examples of recipients included Survivors of the Shoah Visual History Foundation and Organic Commodity Project.

TABLE 4. Distribution of PRI Providers by Range of PRI Financing, 2000–2001*

PRI Activity Range	No. of Foundations	%	No. of PRIs	%	Dollar Amount of PRIs	%
$25 million+	2	1.6	37	5.7	$ 96,030,934	27.3
$10 million–$25 million	5	3.9	71	11.0	84,124,284	23.9
$5 million–$10 million	9	7.0	125	19.3	61,542,135	17.5
$1 million–$5 million	37	28.7	245	37.9	85,098,438	24.2
$500,000–$1 million	21	16.3	63	9.8	14,522,694	4.1
$250,000–$500,000	15	11.6	33	5.1	5,237,639	1.5
Under $250,000	40	31.0	72	11.1	4,927,738	1.4
Total	**129**	**100.0**	**646**	**100.0**	**$351,483,862**	**100.0**

Source: *PRI Directory*, 2003
*Based on PRI transactions of $10,000 or more made in 2000 and 2001 by a sample of 129 larger PRI funders. Excludes PRI distributions for charitable use assets. Figures may not add up due to rounding.

TABLE 5. Top 15 States by PRIs Reported, 2000–2001*

State	No. of Funders	%	Dollar Amount of PRIs	%	No. of PRIs	%
California	12	9.3	$102,685,069	29.2	58	9.0
New York	22	17.1	83,129,284	23.7	140	21.7
Illinois	9	7.0	26,583,598	7.6	34	5.3
Maine	1	0.8	15,711,453	4.5	3	0.5
District of Columbia	7	5.4	12,844,349	3.7	71	11.0
Minnesota	4	3.1	10,456,445	3.0	51	7.9
Texas	7	5.4	9,664,756	2.7	14	2.2
Arkansas	2	1.6	9,160,124	2.6	6	0.9
Michigan	4	3.1	9,098,951	2.6	18	2.8
New Jersey	3	2.3	8,345,000	2.4	25	3.9
Nevada	1	0.8	7,000,000	2.0	2	0.3
Pennsylvania	7	5.4	6,835,658	1.9	10	1.5
Maryland	3	2.3	5,432,439	1.5	56	8.7
Washington	3	2.3	5,370,000	1.5	9	1.4
Tennessee	2	1.6	4,930,650	1.4	4	0.6
Subtotal	**87**	**67.4**	**$317,247,776**	**90.3**	**501**	**77.6**
All other states	42	32.6	34,236,086	9.7	145	22.4
Total	**129**	**100.0**	**$351,483,862**	**100.0**	**646**	**100.0**

Source: *PRI Directory*, 2003
*Based on PRI transactions of $10,000 or more made in 2000 and 2001 by a sample of 129 larger PRI funders. Excludes PRI distributions for charitable use assets. Figures may not add up due to rounding.

TABLE 6. Top 15 States by PRIs Received, 2000–2001*

State	Dollar Amount of PRIs	%	No. of PRIs	%
California	$ 67,039,080	20.9	64	11.0
New York	37,891,494	11.8	58	9.9
Maine	18,711,453	5.8	4	0.7
Virginia	18,590,266	5.8	11	1.9
District of Columbia	18,522,367	5.8	43	7.4
Massachusetts	13,901,680	4.3	13	2.2
Michigan	12,398,951	3.9	21	3.6
Texas	12,263,540	3.8	22	3.8
Maryland	12,071,173	3.8	72	12.3
Minnesota	11,419,000	3.6	33	5.7
Ohio	9,649,173	3.0	19	3.3
Pennsylvania	8,760,158	2.7	10	1.7
New Jersey	8,677,500	2.7	28	4.8
Hawaii	7,023,405	2.2	2	0.3
Arkansas	6,530,000	2.0	5	0.9
Subtotal	**$263,449,240**	**82.2**	**405**	**69.5**
All other states**	56,995,027	17.8	178	30.5
Total	**$320,444,267**	**100.0**	**583**	**100.0**

Source: *PRI Directory*, 2003
*Based on PRI transactions of $10,000 or more made in 2000 and 2001 by a sample of 129 larger PRI funders. Excludes PRI distributions for charitable use assets. Figures may not add up due to rounding.
**Figures include 18 PRIs totaling $2,665,000 made to recipients based in unspecified locations or U.S. territories.

Size of Individual PRIs

Although many local PRI funders tailor their loan programs to provide small amounts—especially for interim financing and emergency loans—Table 8 shows that close to two-thirds (61.9 percent) of the PRIs invested with recipients were in amounts of at least $100,000, and these larger PRIs accounted for over 97 percent of PRI financing. The most typical PRIs were for amounts between $100,000 and $500,000. More than 36 percent of PRIs (233) fell into that size category. Looking at the largest PRIs, 106 (16.4 percent) were in amounts of at least $1 million, including 10 PRIs of $5 million or more.

The sample confirms that PRIs are on average far larger in dollar value than foundation grants. For example, of the nearly 125,000 grants of $10,000 or more reported in the Foundation Center's grants database for 2001, less than 2.0 percent were valued at $1 million or over, compared with 16.4 percent of PRIs, and less than 23 percent of grants were in amounts of at least $100,000, compared with almost 62 percent of PRIs.

TABLE 7. Domestic and International PRIs, 2000–2001*

Focus of PRIs	Dollar Amount of PRIs	%	No. of PRIs	%
Domestic	**$307,550,313**	**90.1**	**582**	**87.5**
International	**43,933,549**	**9.9**	**64**	**12.5**
Overseas Recipients	28,374,595	7.0	45	8.1
U.S.-based Recipients	15,558,954	2.9	19	4.4
Total	**$351,483,862**	**100.0**	**646**	**100.0**

Source: PRI Directory, 2003 +

*Based on PRI transactions of $10,000 or more made in 2000 and 2001 by a sample of 129 larger PRI funders. Excludes PRI distributions for charitable use assets. Figures may not add up due to rounding.

TABLE 8. Distribution of PRIs by Size Range, 2000–2001*
(All dollar figures expressed in thousands)

PRI Range	No. of PRIs	%	Dollar Amount of PRIs	%
$10 million and over	2	0.3	$ 24,911	7.1
$5 million–under $10 million	8	1.2	51,225	14.6
$1 million–under $5 million	96	14.9	176,747	50.3
$500,000–under $1 million	61	9.4	36,567	10.4
$100,000–under $500,000	233	36.1	52,491	14.9
$50,000–under $100,000	95	14.7	5,795	1.6
$25,000–under $50,000	76	11.8	2,549	0.7
$10,000–under $25,000	75	11.6	1,199	0.3
Total	**646**	**100.0**	**$351,484**	**100.0**

Source: *PRI Directory,* 2003

*Based on PRI transactions of $10,000 or more made in 2000 and 2001 by a sample of 129 larger PRI funders. Excludes PRI distributions for charitable use assets. Figures may not add up due to rounding.

FIGURE 3. PRI Financing by Major Program Areas, 2000–2001*

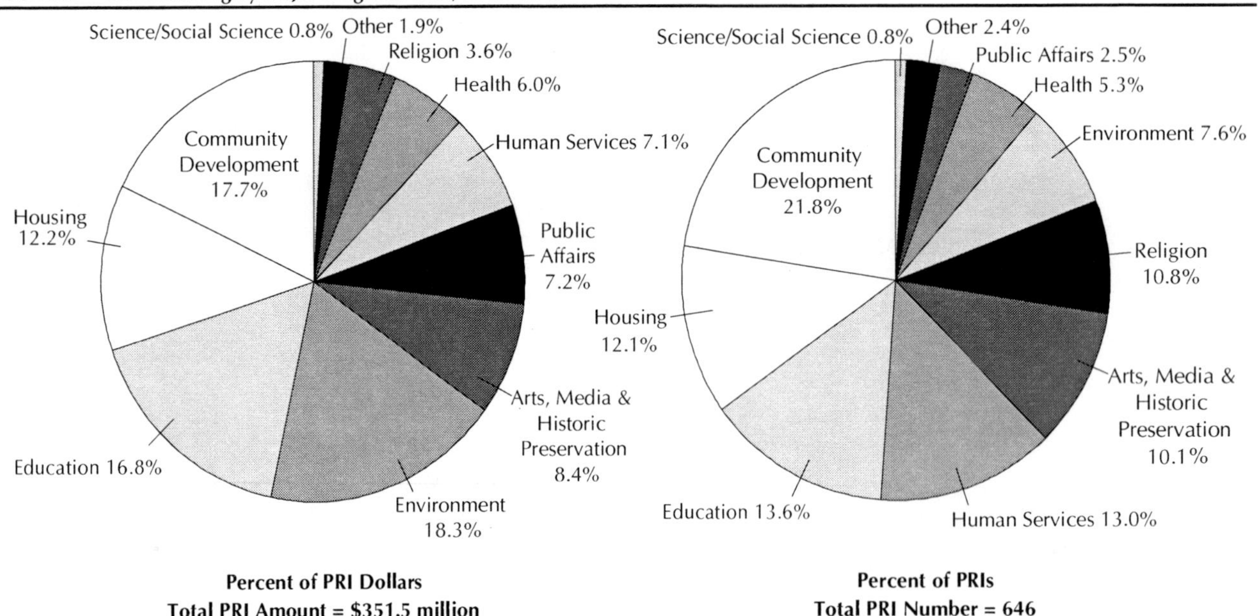

Source: *PRI Directory,* 2003.

*Based on PRI transactions of $10,000 or more made in 2000 and 2001 by a sample of 129 larger PRI funders. Excludes PRI distributions for charitable use assets.

Programmatic Focus

The Foundation Center reports broad funding trends within ten broad major subject divisions and 24 field areas. These institutional/subject classifications derive from the National Taxonomy of Exempt Entities (see page xxi). The individual PRI records included in this sample may be accessed by subject in the "Index to PRIs by Subject" section of this volume.

Although PRI financing remains closely associated with community development and housing, the practice of making, and using, no- or low-interest charitable loans and investments has spread to nearly all fields. In 2000–2001, two-thirds of PRIs and roughly 69.9 percent of PRI dollars financed projects and organizations in fields other than development, especially education, the environment, arts and culture, human services, public affairs, health, and religion (Figure 3).

Who Receives PRIs?

Table 9 lists the top recipients of PRIs, each receiving at least $2 million in financing in 2000–2001. Together these 49 organizations received $210.1 million, representing 60.2 percent of all PRI support.

Most organizations received only one or two PRIs over the two-year period. Exceptions included Women's Capital Corporation (seven PRIs), Trust for Public Land (five PRIs) and the Government of Armenia (four PRIs). In addition, four organizations received three PRIs each.

TABLE 9. Largest PRI Recipient Organizations, 2000–2001*

Recipient Name	State/Country	Dollar Amount of PRIs	%	No. of PRIs
1. Armenia, Government of	Armenia	$17,318,861	4.9	4
2. Nature Conservancy	VA	17,000,000	4.8	2
3. Trust for Public Land	CA	16,060,000	4.6	5
4. Freshway, Inc.	ME	14,211,453	4	2
5. Ohana Foundation for Technical Development	HI	6,873,405	2	1
6. Womens Capital Corporation	DC	6,175,000	1.8	7
7. Big Sur Land Trust	CA	6,038,000	1.7	2
8. School Futures Research Foundation	CA	5,480,124	1.6	1
9. Audubon Society, National	NY	5,000,000	1.4	1
10. Perkins School for the Blind	MA	5,000,000	1.4	1
11. Survivors of the Shoah Visual History Foundation	CA	4,970,387	1.4	2
12. Frist Center for the Visual Arts Foundation	TN	4,900,000	1.4	2
13. Enterprise Foundation	MD	4,750,000	1.4	3
14. National Housing Trust Enterprise Preservation Corporation	DC	4,500,000	1.3	2
15. Danco Laboratories	NY	4,200,000	1.2	1
16. Kalamazoo Aviation History Museum	MI	4,000,000	1.1	1
17. Southern Development Bancshares	AR	4,000,000	1.1	2
18. Historic District Improvement Company	NM	3,745,286	1.1	2
19. Low Income Housing Fund	CA	3,500,000	1	2
20. National Federation of Community Development Credit Unions	NY	3,500,000	1	2
21. Baylor University	TX	3,000,000	0.9	1
22. Coastal Enterprises	ME	3,000,000	0.9	1
23. Focus: Hope	MI	3,000,000	0.9	1
24. Mercy Housing	CO	3,000,000	0.9	1
25. TRF Urban Growth Partners	PA	3,000,000	0.9	1
26. Open Space Institute	NY	2,850,000	0.8	3

TABLE 9. (continued)

Recipient Name	State/Country	Dollar Amount of PRIs	%	No. of PRIs
27. Michigan Capital Fund for Housing	MI	$2,685,009	0.8	1
28. Construction Management Alliance (Europe)	England	2,500,000	0.7	2
29. Housing Partnership Network	MA	2,500,000	0.7	1
30. Rocky Mountain Mutual Housing Association	CO	2,500,000	0.7	1
31. Southern Financial Partners	AR	2,500,000	0.7	2
32. Project Home	TX	2,415,898	0.7	2
33. Community Builders of Kansas City	MO	2,400,000	0.7	1
34. First United Pentecostal Church	CA	2,400,000	0.7	1
35. River Network	OR	2,255,000	0.6	2
36. Local Initiatives Support Corporation (LISC)	NY	2,250,000	0.6	1
37. Shelter Network of San Mateo County	CA	2,250,000	0.6	1
38. Napa County Land Trust	CA	2,200,000	0.6	1
39. Methodist Retirement Services	TX	2,100,000	0.6	1
40. Shorebank Enterprise Group Cleveland	OH	2,032,108	0.6	3
41. Aldea Global	Guatemala	2,000,000	0.6	3
Community Loan Technologies	MN	2,000,000	0.6	1
Council for Adult and Experiential Learning	IL	2,000,000	0.6	1
Ecotrust	OR	2,000,000	0.6	1
Neighborhood Capital Corporation	OH	2,000,000	0.6	1
Neighborhood Progress	OH	2,000,000	0.6	1
Organic Commodity Project	MA	2,000,000	0.6	1
Saint Johns Hospital and Health Center	CA	2,000,000	0.6	1
Strategic Regional Development	PA	2,000,000	0.6	1

Source: PRI Directory, 2003

*Based on PRI transactions of $10,000 or more made in 2000 and 2001 by a sample of 129 larger PRI funders. Excludes PRI distributions for charitable use assets.

Arrangement of *The PRI Directory*

The PRI Directory is arranged alphabetically by foundation name. Each descriptive entry is assigned a sequence number and at the end of each entry a list of PRIs identified by the foundation's sequence number and its own sequence number as it falls within the PRI list; references in the indexes are to these entry numbers.

What's in an Entry?

There are 23 basic data elements that could be included in a *PRI Directory* entry. The content of entries varies widely due to differences in the size and nature of foundation programs and the availability of information from foundations. Specific data elements that could be included are:

1. The full legal **name of the foundation.**
2. The **former name** of the foundation.
3. The **street address, city, and zip code** of the foundation's principal office.
4. The **telephone number** of the foundation.
5. The name and title of the **contact person** of the foundation.
6. Any **additional address** (such as a separate application address) supplied by the foundation. Additional telephone or FAX numbers as well as E-mail and/or URL addresses also may be listed here.
7. **Establishment data,** including the legal form (usually a trust or corporation) and the year and state in which the foundation was established, as well as when its PRI activities began, if available.
8. The **donor(s)** or principal contributor(s) to the foundation, including individuals, families, and corporations. If a donor is deceased, the symbol (‡) follows the name.
9. **Foundation type:** community, company-sponsored, independent, or operating.
10. **General financial activity** may include:

    The **year-end date** of the foundation's accounting period for which financial data is supplied;

    Assets: the total value of the foundation's investments at the end of the accounting period. In a few instances, foundations that act as "pass-throughs" for annual corporate or individual gifts report zero assets;

    Asset type: generally, assets are reported at market value (M) or ledger value (L);

    Gifts received: the total amount of new capital received by the foundation in the year of record;

    Expenditures: total disbursements of the foundation, including overhead expenses (salaries; investment, legal, and other professional fees; interest; rent; etc.) and federal excise taxes, as well as the total amount paid for grants, scholarships, and matching gifts;

    The total amount of **qualifying distributions** made by the foundation in the year of record. This figure includes all grants paid, qualifying administrative expenses, loans and program-related investments, set-asides, and amounts paid to acquire assets used directly in carrying out charitable purposes;

    The dollar value and number of **grants paid** during the year, with the largest grant paid **(high)** and smallest grant paid **(low)**. When supplied by the foundation, the average range of grant payments is also indicated. Grant figures generally do not include commitments for future payment or amounts spent for grants to individuals, employee matching gifts, PRIs, or foundation-administered programs;

    The total dollar value of **set-asides** made by the foundation during the year. Although set-asides count as qualifying distributions toward the foundation's annual payout requirement, they are distinct from any amounts listed as grants paid;

    The total amount and number of **grants made directly to or on behalf of individuals,** including scholarships, fellowships, awards, and medical payments. When supplied by the foundation, high, low, and average range are also indicated;

    The dollar amount and number of **employee matching gifts** awarded, generally by company-sponsored foundations;

    The total dollars expended for **programs administered by the foundation** and the number of foundation-administered programs. These programs can include museums or other institutions supported exclusively by the foundation, research programs administered by the foundation, etc;

    The dollar amount and number of **charitable loans and other program-related investments** made to organizations by the foundation. These can include bridge loans, emergency loans to help nonprofits that are waiting for grants or other income payments, loan guarantees of lines of credit and equity investments, etc. When supplied by the foundation, high, low, and average range are also indicated;

The number of **loans to individuals** and the total amount loaned. When supplied by the foundation, high, low, and average range are also indicated; and/or,

The monetary value and number of **in-kind gifts;**

11. The **Cumulative PRI activity** statement provides the **year-end date** of the foundation's accounting period for which PRI information is provided, as well as the **amount and number of outstanding PRIs** in the portfolio; the **high, low,** and **average outstanding PRI;** the **longest, shortest,** and **average PRI term;** and/or the **high, low,** and **average PRI interest rate.**
12. The **general purpose and activities,** in general terms, of the foundation. This statement reflects funding interests as expressed by the foundation or, if no foundation statement is available, an analysis of the actual grants awarded by the foundation during the most recent two-year period for which public records exist. Many foundations leave statements of purpose intentionally broad, indicating only the major program areas within which they fund. More specific areas of interest can often be found in the "general fields of interest" section of the entry.
13. The **general fields of interest** reflected in the foundation's giving program. The terminology used in this section conforms to the Foundation Center's Grants Classification System (GCS).
14. The **general international interests** of the foundation (if relevant).
15. The **program-related investment (PRI) activity** statement provides more specific data on a foundation's historical, current, and future PRI fields of interest and types of support.
16. The **types of PRI support** (loans/promissory notes, interim financing, lines of credit, etc.) offered by the foundation. Definitions of the terms used to describe the forms of support available are provided in the Glossary.
17. Any stated **limitations** on the foundation's giving program, including geographic preferences, restrictions by subject focus or type of recipient, or specific types of support the foundation cannot provide. It is noted here if a foundation does not accept unsolicited applications.
18. **Publications** or other printed materials distributed by the foundation that describe its activities and giving program. These can include annual or multi-year reports, newsletters, corporate giving reports, informational brochures, grant lists, etc. It is also noted whether a foundation will send copies of its IRS information return (Form 990-PF) on request.
19. **PRI program information,** including the preferred form of application, the number of copies of proposals requested, application deadlines, frequency and dates of board meetings, and the general amount of time the foundation requires to notify applicants of the board's decision.
20. The names and titles of **officers, principal administrators, trustees, or directors,** and members of other governing bodies. An asterisk (*) following the individual's name indicates an officer who is also a trustee or director.
21. The number of professional and support **staff** employed by the foundation, and an indication of part-time or full-time status of these employees, as reported by the foundation.
22. **EIN:** the Employer Identification Number assigned to the foundation by the Internal Revenue Service for tax purposes. This number can be useful when ordering microfilm or paper copies of the foundation's annual information return, Form 990-PF.
23. A list of **recipients of program-related investments** of at least $10,000 authorized between 1999–2002, sorted by recipient name, year, and PRI amount. If the full amount authorized is not available, the PRI amount "paid" during the year is shown.

Note: The PRI amount reported in section 10 "General Finacial Activity" represents the total paid in the latest period as reported in the foundation's 990-PF Tax Return. This amount may differ from the total of individual PRIs reported for the same period in Section 23, which sometimes represents PRIs authorized.

Indexes

Eight indexes to the descriptive entries are provided at the back of the book to assist grantseekers and other users of *The PRI Directory:*

1. The **Index to Donors, Officers, Trustees** is an alphabetical list of individual and corporate donors, officers, and members of governing

boards whose names appear in *PRI Directory* entries. Many loanseekers find this index helpful in determining whether current or prospective members of their own governing boards, alumni of their schools, or current contributors are affiliated with any foundations.

2. The **Geographic Index** references foundation entries by the state and city in which the foundation maintains its principal offices. The index includes "see also" references at the end of each state section to indicate foundations that have made substantial PRIs in that state but are located elsewhere.
3. The **PRI Recipient Location Index** provides the locations of those organizations listed in the *Directory* that received program-related investments. Recipients are separated by domestic and foreign locations. Domestic recipients are listed alphabetically by state, city, and name. Foreign recipients are listed alphabetically by country, city (if available), and name. Each recipient name is followed by an entry number, then a PRI number within the foundation entry for easy reference.
4. The **Index to PRIs by Subject** provides information on the specific subject focus of each individual PRI listed in the *Directory.* Within each subject term, PRIs are listed by foundation entry number and then by individual PRI number. For a more general foundation PRI subject index, see the Index to Foundations by Fields of PRI Interest.
5. The **Index to Foundations by Fields of PRI Interest** is a listing of the PRI making foundations in the *Directory* sorted by their very broad fields of interest categories. PRI makers are sorted within each field of interest category by state. Within each state, foundations are listed alphabetically by an abbreviated name. Each name is followed by a corresponding entry number, referring directly to the foundation's listing within the *Directory.*
6. The **Index to Foundations by PRI Types of Support** categorizes foundations by their general PRI making types of support. PRI makers are sorted within each type of support category by state. Within each state, foundations are listed alphabetically by an abbreviated name. Each name is followed by a corresponding entry number, referring directly to the foundation's listing within the *Directory.*
7. The **Foundation Name Index** is an alphabetical list of all foundations appearing in *The PRI Directory.* Former names of foundations appear with "see" references to the appropriate entry numbers.
8. The **Recipient Name Index** is an alphabetical listing of the names of all the organizations listed as recipients of PRIs in the *Directory.* Each recipient name is followed by an entry number and a PRI sequence number within the foundation's entry.

Researching PRI Makers

Foundations commonly make PRIs as a supplement to their existing grant programs when the circumstances of a request suggest an alternative form of financing, when the borrower has the potential for generating income to repay a loan, and as a last resort when an organization—in most cases a charitable nonprofit but in a few cases a commercial venture—has been unable to secure financing from traditional sources. To decide whether you should seek a PRI and to learn more fully about what the PRI request and administration process entails, see "Seeking and Securing Alternative Financing: Advice from Experts."

Using the PRI Index to Identify Prospects

If you have determined that your organization is eligible to seek and manage a charitable loan or investment from a foundation, *The PRI Directory* can help you identify potential funding sources. In developing a prospect list, you should scan the PRI listings in the category or categories closest to your field, or alternatively look broadly at those funders who have been active in your geographic area. Once you have scanned the broad categories, you should use the four indexes to identify more precise examples of PRI transactions similar to your own project and needs. Depending on the nature of your search, you will add to your list of possibilities the names of those foundations whose recent PRIs seem to indicate a potential interest in your organization or project. You should be looking for foundations that have funded an organization or project like yours, that are located or seem to award PRIs in your geographic area, that award the type of PRI you are looking for, and/or have made PRIs in the dollar amounts similar to the amount you are seeking.

In seeking potential funding sources, you should keep in mind that many foundations place limitations on their giving, including the types of programs or organizations they are willing to fund, the kinds of support they provide, and the geographic area in which they fund. As in grantseeking, you must pay attention to these restrictions when researching PRIs. If your organization does not fall within a funder's specified guidelines, do not seek a PRI with that foundation. You should also bear in mind that some foundations who made PRIs in 1999 through 2002 and who appear in this *Directory* may not accept unsolicited requests for PRIs or may no longer make them.

Expanding Research Using Other Resources

The PRI Directory is an excellent starting point for identifying prospects but it cannot stand alone. Nevertheless, you will need the *Directory* to review a prospective funder's purpose statement, its detailed PRI program or activity statement, information about the types of PRI financial vehicles it has used, its level of experience, the average size of its PRIs, how frequently it makes PRIs, whether it has an active PRI program, whether it has additional restrictions that apply only to PRI-making, and whether it accepts unsolicited PRI requests.

Once you have developed a list of potential PRI providers using the *Directory,* you should seek current information about each prospect by consulting additional references sources. These sources include foundation annual reports; IRS 990-PF information returns, which are available for all private foundations; and entries in the Center's *The Foundation 1000, Foundation Directory* and *Foundation Directory, Part 2,* as well as local directories and resources. If this is your first venture into foundation research, you may wish to consult *Foundation Fundamentals,* the Center's guidebook to foundations and the funding process, before seeking a PRI. If you are an experienced grantseeker, you should acquaint yourself with the electronic tools available to grantseekers, including *FC Search,* the Foundation Center's comprehensive database on CD-ROM, and the Center's rapidly expanding internet Website at http://www.fdncenter.org which includes the *Foundation Directory Online,* the Foundation Center's online database. These resources and many more are widely available for free public use at the Center's library reference collections nationwide. See the *Resources of the Foundation Center* section for more information.

What are PRIs? Who Makes Them and Who Gets Them?

The following background information about PRIs is drawn from a variety of sources, including the Foundation Center's Program-Related Investments: A Guide to Funders and Trends *(1995),* The PRI Index *(1997) materials produced by the Ford Foundation and the MIT Project on Social Investments, and articles written by Brody & Weiser, a consulting firm.*

A PRI, broadly defined, is an investment by a foundation to support a charitable project or activity involving the potential return of capital within an established time frame. PRIs include financing methods commonly associated with banks or other private investors, such as loans, loan guarantees, linked deposits, and even equity investments in charitable organizations and for-profit businesses. Although reported differently, a PRI is similar to a recoverable grant: the repayment can eventually be recyled for another charitable purpose. For information about the spectrum of financial tools collectively known as program-related investments, see the glossary of terms below.

The term *program-related investment* was created by Congress in the Tax Act of 1969, which also created many of the rules governing private foundations. The IRS defines a PRI as any investment by a foundation that meets the following three tests:

- Its primary purpose is to further the exempt objectives of the foundation;
- The production of income or the appreciation of property is not a significant purpose of the PRI (i.e., it is structured to produce lower-than-market returns on a risk-adjusted basis); and
- It may not be used to support lobbying or political campaign activities.

Responding to efforts by leaders of the philanthropic community, Congress created inducements for the use of PRIs to encourage foundations to use their assets in ways that would further their philanthropic ends. Specifically, PRIs are exempted from classification as jeopardizing investments. In addition, the dollar value of the PRI is counted as a "qualifying distribution" in the year in which it is made, that is, it counts against the IRS requirement that foundations annually pay out the equivalent of 5 percent of the value of their assets. When a PRI is repaid to the foundation by the borrower, the repayment amount is added to the value of the foundation's assets, raising the amount that it is required to pay out in charitable distributions in a subsequent fiscal year.

Who Makes PRIs? Who Gets Them? What Do They Support?

Compared to the universe of active grantmakers, the number of PRI providers remains quite small according to the latest Foundation Center research. Nevertheless, the field is growing: the number of

PRI-makers increased over the last few years. (See "Trends in PRI Financing") Contrary to popular conception, PRI-making is not limited to the largest endowed foundations. In fact, foundations of all sizes and types make PRIs—including family, independent, corporate and community foundations. In addition, many corporations and religious institutions make social investments similar to PRIs.

Most funders, especially those who make relatively small loans, lend money directly to a single agency for a specific capital need or project. Several large experienced PRI funders prefer to work with financial intermediaries (see below), such as the Enterprise Foundation, LISC, and the Nonprofit Facilities Fund. Still other foundations collaborate to make PRIs within the framework of a broad scale national or regional project.

Like PRI providers, recipients or borrowers come in many types and sizes, ranging from small agencies looking for capital for their own projects to special purpose loan funds, banks or other intermediaries which raise capital and relend the money to qualifying nonprofits and projects. Regardless of size, borrowers are active in a broad range of nonprofit fields. While PRIs have been used most extensively to support affordable housing and community development, they have also funded capital projects ranging from preserving historic buildings and repairing churches, to providing emergency loans to social service agencies, to protecting and preserving open space and wildlife habitats. (See "Trends in PRI Financing" for a breakdown of PRIs by geographic distribution, programmatic focus, etc.)

Foundations commonly make PRIs as a supplement to their existing grant programs. In most cases, funders make PRIs to organizations that have an established relationship with the funder as a grantee. When an organization seeks additional funding—possibly for a project with income generating potential or for a project requiring interim financing—the foundation may suggest a PRI in place of a grant. The size of a PRI can range from under $1,000 to several million dollars, and is influenced by the needs of a project or borrower, the ability of a borrower to repay, and varying program strategies among foundations.

Benefits of Using PRIs

For the funder, one obvious benefit of making a PRI is that the repayment or the return of equity can be recycled for another charitable purpose. PRIs may also help a foundation meet IRS pay-out requirements during a time of unexpected asset growth. Other benefits include: allowing a foundation to support a desirable project that requires funding that exceeds a foundation's typical grant size; and helping an organization to attract other lenders to a project and leverage additional funds from banks, corporations, or the government.

For the recipient, the primary benefit is access to capital at lower rates than may otherwise be available. A PRI can also help a recipient to establish a productive, long-term relationship with a funder by creating a partnership with mutual financial and program objectives and can help establish a credit history for an inexperienced nonprofit agency.

PRI-Making: A Growing Field

The increased use of PRIs as alternative financing "tools" reflects three recent trends: first, the growth of the not-for-proft community development/low income housing field, with its large-scale capital needs; second, the increasing emphasis in the nonprofit sector on raising revenue through earned income ventures; and finally, the need to leverage foundation resources to meet increased demands. Despite the wider use of PRI funding, relatively few organizations have experience seeking PRIs compared to grantseeking. Organizations considering seeking funding in this manner should assess the situation carefully to determine whether a PRI is appropriate for their capacity and goals.

Seeking and Securing Alternative Financing: Advice From Experts

The following article, abstracted from the Foundation Center's Program-Related Investments: A Guide to Funders and Trends *(1995), provides advice to nonprofits from experienced funders and recipients on how to decide whether to seek alternative financing and on how to successfully navigate the PRI process from start to finish.*

When to Seek a PRI

Organizations typically seek PRI financing to purchase or construct facilities, develop housing projects, cover predevelopment costs, purchase land or equipment, capitalize a loan fund, start up a business venture, or refinance debt. Nonetheless, PRIs have funded projects ranging from the production of an environmental publication to the purchase of sculpture for a dance company.

You should consider seeking a PRI for your organization:

- after you have explored all other possible sources of support, including grants, public sector financing, commercial financing, intermediaries (e.g., loan funds, credit unions, development banks, venture capital funds), and religious funders. Many foundations consider themselves "lenders of last resort."
- if the funds will be used to leverage other resources. Foundations are often more eager to invest in projects where their resources will be used to attract additional public and/or commercial investment. This is especially true for corporate funders.
- if the project has the potential for returning revenue. Funders may be less inclined to provide PRI support if your projected income will ultimately cover only start up and operating expenses.
- when you believe a foundation can provide more favorable terms of investment. (You should only consider this option after exploring other sources of financing.)
- if the project falls within your funder's guidelines, but the amount of funding needed for your project exceeds the size of the funder's typical grant. (Nevertheless, small loans are made by some funders, particularly as cash flow and bridge loans, which provide short-term capital in cases where another funding source—often government financing—has been committed, but the transfer of funds is delayed. Check to see whether your local community foundation operates such a loan fund.)
- after a foundation declines your grant request by stating that a PRI would be a more appropriate funding vehicle.

If after reviewing these criteria you decide your project or organization would be a good candidate for PRIs, you should consider contacting both funders who have previously made grants to your organization and foundations who have financed similar projects. (Generally, funders will give PRI preference to their grantees.) But remember that, like grants, PRIs must further the charitable purpose of the funder. Foundations that explicitly prohibit loan-making or that do not fund PRIs in your project's program area should not be contacted for support.

For-profit organizations face additional considerations, as many funders limit PRI support to nonprofits. To be eligible for a PRI, your for-profit project or business venture must also be strongly related to the funder's programmatic charitable interests, e.g, creating microenterprise in a poor neighborhood or producing an educational film; have relatively little prospect for making a large profit; and be unable to attract commercial backing.

Developing a PRI Request: Funder Requirements

Because PRIs are of a speculative nature and have a measurable financial return, funders generally seek more comprehensive information than with grant requests, including more detailed financial information. Typically, funders ask for:

- evidence of your organization's financial and managerial health and stability.
- a detailed business plan, including a description of the project, the amount requested, term, proposed interest rate, and your repayment approach.
- financial projections, including cash flow statements.
- names of your other funding sources.
- in some cases, collateral (including future revenues) or the rights to assignment of acquired collateral.
- for intermediaries, a status report on your current loan portfolio.

Negotiating the Terms of a PRI

PRIs require more staff time than grants to prepare the proposal and negotiate the terms and conditions of the agreement. If you do not have an experienced manager on staff who can handle a negotiation, you will need to look for professional assistance—usually a lawyer—to help you negotiate. You can often find such assistance through your board members or through networking in your community. One recipient, who is also an experienced lender, suggested looking for "pockets of volunteerism" for the needed expertise. In communities without resources, the church community may be a source of such expertise.

The terms of a PRI vary widely according to the funder's perspective on returns and the interest rate charged at the time the investment is made. Some funders charge no interest at all; others charge a rate just below market. However, recipients note that the better your track record, the better the terms, since you are perceived as a lower risk.

In general, there is less risk involved in financial arrangements with foundations and the terms are easier to negotiate. As with any negotiation, however, you should be prepared to walk away. If the funder sets terms that are too hard to meet or if the deal is too complex, do not take it. Ultimately, the cost to your organization could be great if you are unable to meet your obligation.

Managing a PRI: Repaying Interest and Principal

The most typical income sources named by recipients for repaying interest and principle include earned income, capital campaigns, foundation grants, government funding, or, in the case of intermediaries, the repayment of loans by secondary borrowers. Regardless of what your principal source of repayment will be, one organization advises borrowers to be sure to have multiple sources of income to repay interest and to plan in advance for repayment of principal.

Advice for Borrowers from Recipients

Recipients offered a number of suggestions to other borrowers for seeking and negotiating PRIs. Specifically:

- do your homework. The funder has a legitimate need for detailed information on your organization, and you must be able to respond accurately to that need.
- have a good business plan and recognize the difference between a plan and a typical grant proposal.
- make sure that you know your field inside and out. The funder will have experts review your proposal and proformas. Unless they are convinced that your have a high likelihood of success, you will not be funded.
- learn about the experience of other borrowers in the field so as not to "reinvent the wheel."
- seek the broadest possible purpose for your PRI; your plans may change in five to seven years.
- use a highly experienced loan manager to negotiate and administer your loans and experienced managers to train your staff in marketing and loan maintenance.
- a PRI is often a long-term commitment. The funder needs to know that your organization's leadership will be there to see the project through repayment.
- be financially prepared for the PRIs to take a long time to close.
- develop a means to measure and quantify the success of your PRI funded project.
- be professional—pay your debts.

Thanks to the Center for Community Self-Help, Nonprofits Insurance Alliance of California, Northeast Ventures Development Fund, Rensselaerville Institute, Structured Employment Economic Development Corporation (SEEDCO), and Self Help Ventures Fund for providing tips and advice included in this essay.

SUMMARY OF THE 26 NATIONAL TAXONOMY OF EXEMPT ENTITIES (NTEE) MAJOR DIVISIONS AND FIELD AREAS

A—Arts, culture, humanities activities
- arts & culture (multipurpose activities)
- media & communications
- visual arts
- museums
- performing arts
- humanities
- historical societies & related historical activities

B—Educational institutions & related activities
- elementary & secondary education (preschool through Grade 12)
- vocational/technical schools
- higher education
- graduate/professional schools
- adult/continuing education
- libraries/archives
- student services & organizations

C—Environmental quality, protection
- pollution abatement & control
- natural resources conservation & protection
- botanic/horticulture activities
- environmental beautification & open spaces
- environmental education & outdoor survival

D—Animal-related activities
- animal protection & welfare
- humane societies
- wildlife preservation & protection
- veterinary services
- zoos & aquariums
- specialty animals & other services

E—Health—general & rehabilitative
- hospitals
- health treatment, primarily outpatient
- reproductive health care
- rehabilitative medical services
- health support services
- emergency medical services
- public health & wellness education
- health care financing/insurance programs
- nursing homes/nursing care

F—Mental health, crisis intervention
- addiction prevention & treatment
- mental health treatment & services
- crisis intervention
- psychiatric/mental health—primary care
- half-way houses (mental health)/transitional care
- counseling/bereavement services
- specific mental health disorders

G—Disease/disorder/medical disciplines (multipurpose)
- birth defects & genetic diseases
- cancer
- diseases of specific organs
- nerve, muscle & bone diseases
- allergy-related diseases
- specific named diseases
- medical disciplines/specialties

H—Medical research
- identical hierarchy to diseases/disorders/medical disciplines in major field "G"
- example: G30 represents American Cancer Society; H30 represents cancer research

I—Public protection: crime/courts/legal services
- police & law enforcement agencies
- correctional facilities & prisoner services
- crime prevention
- rehabilitation of offenders
- administration of justice/courts
- protection against/prevention of neglect, abuse, exploitation
- legal services

J—Employment/jobs
- vocational guidance & training, such as on-the-job programs
- employment procurement assistance
- vocational rehabilitation
- employment assistance for the disabled and aging
- labor unions/organizations
- labor-management relations

K—Food, nutrition, agriculture
- agricultural services aimed at food procurement
- food service/free food distribution
- nutrition promotion
- farmland preservation

L—Housing/shelter
- housing development/construction
- housing search assistance
- low-cost temporary shelters such as youth hostels
- homeless, temporary shelter for
- housing owners/renters organizations
- housing support services

M—Public safety/disaster preparedness & relief
- disaster prevention, such as flood control
- disaster relief (U.S. domestic)
- safety education
- civil defense & preparedness programs

N—Recreation, leisure, sports, athletics
- camps
- physical fitness & community recreation
- sports training
- recreation/pleasure or social clubs
- amateur sports
- Olympics & Special Olympics
- professional athletic leagues

O—Youth development
- youth centers, such as boys clubs
- scouting
- mentoring (including big brothers/sisters)
- agricultural development, such as 4-H
- business development, Junior Achievement
- citizenship programs
- religious leadership development

P—Human service—other/multipurpose
- multipurpose service organizations
- children & youth services
- family services
- personal social services
- emergency assistance (food, clothing)
- residential/custodial care (including hospices)
- centers promoting independence of specific groups, such as senior or women's centers

Q—International
- exchange programs
- international development
- international relief services (foreign disaster relief)
- peace & security (international conflict resolution)
- foreign policy research & analyses
- international human rights

R—Civil rights/civil liberties
- equal opportunity & access
- intergroup/race relations
- voter education/registration
- civil liberties

S—Community improvement/development
- community/neighborhood development
- community coalitions
- economic development, both urban and rural
- business services
- nonprofit management
- community service clubs such as Junior League

T—Philanthropy & voluntarism
- philanthropy associations/societies
- private grantmaking foundations
- public foundations (e.g., women's funds) and community foundations
- voluntarism promotion
- community funds and federated giving

U—Science
- scientific research & promotion
- physical/earth sciences
- engineering/technology
- biological sciences

V—Social sciences
- social science research/studies
- interdisciplinary studies, such as black studies, women's studies, urban studies, etc.

W—Public affairs/society benefit
- public policy research, general
- government & public administration
- transportation systems
- leadership development
- public utilities
- telecommunications (including WWW)
- consumer rights/education
- military/veterans organizations
- financial institutions, services

X—Religion/spiritual development
- Christian churches, missionary societies and related religious bodies
- Jewish synagogues
- other specific religions

Y—Mutual membership benefit organizations
- insurance providers & services (other than health)
- pension/retirement funds
- fraternal beneficiary societies
- cemeteries & burial services

Z99—Unknown, unclassifiable

GLOSSARY

The following list includes important terms used by grantmakers and grantseekers. A number of sources have been consulted in compiling this glossary, including *The Handbook on Private Foundations,* by David F. Freeman and the Council on Foundations (New York: The Foundation Center, 1991); *The Law of Tax-Exempt Organizations,* 7th Edition, by Bruce R. Hopkins (New York: John Wiley & Sons, 1998); and the *NSFRE Fund-Raising Dictionary,* (New York, John Wiley & Sons, 1996).

Annual Report: A *voluntary* report issued by a foundation or corporation that provides financial data and descriptions of grantmaking activities. Annual reports vary in format from simple typewritten documents listing the year's grants to detailed publications that provide substantial information about the grantmaking program.

Assets: The amount of capital or principal—money, stocks, bonds, real estate, or other resources—controlled by the foundation or corporate giving program. Generally, assets are invested and the income is used to make grants.

Beneficiary: In philanthropic terms, the donee or grantee receiving funds from a foundation or corporate giving program is the beneficiary, although society benefits as well. Foundations whose legal terms of establishment restrict their giving to one or more named beneficiaries are not included in this publication.

Bricks and Mortar: An informal term for grants for buildings or construction projects.

Bridge Loan: Short-term loan to provide temporary financing until more permanent financing is available.

Capital Support: Funds provided for endowment purposes, buildings, construction, or equipment, and including, for example, grants for "bricks and mortar."

Cash Flow Financing: Short-term loan providing additional cash to cover cash shortfalls in anticipation of revenue, such as the payment(s) of receivables.

Charitable Use Property: Program-related investments in properties that are used for charitable purposes. In most cases, a property such as a building is held by a foundation, who in turn donates or leases it at below market rates to a nonprofit organization. The property remains an asset of the foundation, and expenses to maintain or improve the property are deducted as charitable disbursements. In other cases, a property consists of either land or buildings that are held for a period of time by a foundation and then either given away as a grant or sold to a nonprofit or to a government agency.

Community Foundation: A 501(c)(3) organization that makes grants for charitable purposes in a specific community or region. Funds are usually derived from many donors and held in an endowment independently administered; income earned by the endowment is then used to make grants. Although a few community foundations may be classified by the IRS as private foundations, most are classified as public charities eligible for maximum income tax-deductible contributions from the general public. (*See also* **501(c)(3); Public Charity**)

Company-Sponsored Foundation (also referred to as Corporate Foundation): A private foundation whose grant funds are derived primarily from the contributions of a profit-making business organization. The company- sponsored foundation may maintain close ties with the donor company, but it is an independent organization with its own endowment and is subject to the same rules and regulations as other private foundations. (*See also* **Private Foundation**)

Cooperative Venture: A joint effort between or among two or more funders (including foundations, corporations, and government agencies). Partners may share in funding responsibilities or contribute information and technical resources.

Corporate Giving Program: A grantmaking program established and administered within a profit-making company. Corporate giving programs do not have a separate endowment and their annual grant totals are generally more directly related to current profits. They are not subject to the same reporting requirements as private foundations. Some companies make charitable contributions through both a corporate giving program and a company-sponsored foundation.

Equity Participation: An ownership position in an organization or venture taken through an investment. Returns on the investment are dependent on the profitability of the organization or venture.

Endowment: Funds intended to be kept permanently and invested to provide income for continued support of an organization.

Expenditure Responsibility: In general, when a private foundation makes a grant to an organization that is not classified by the IRS as a "public charity," the foundation is required by law to provide some assurance that the funds will be used for the intended charitable purposes. Special reports on such grants must be filed with the IRS. Most grantee organizations are public charities and many foundations do not make "expenditure responsibility" grants.

Family Foundation: An independent private foundation whose funds are derived from members of a single family. Family members often serve as officers or board members of the foundation and have a significant role in grantmaking decisions. (*See also* **Operating Foundation; Private Foundation; Public Charity**)

501(c)(3): The section of the Internal Revenue code that defines nonprofit, charitable (as broadly defined), tax-exempt organizations; 501(c)(3) organizations are further defined as public charities, private operating foundations, and private non-operating foundations. (*See also* **Operating Foundation; Private Foundation; Public Charity**)

Form 990-PF: The annual information return that all private foundations must submit to the IRS each year and which is also filed with appropriate state officials. The form requires information on the foundation's assets, income, operating expenses, contributions and grants, paid staff and salaries, program funding areas, grantmaking guidelines and restrictions, and grant application procedures.

General Purpose Foundation: An independent private foundation that awards grants in many different fields of interest. (*See also* **Special Purpose Foundation**)

Guaranteed Loan: A pledge to cover the payment of debt or to perform some obligation if the person liable fails to perform. When a third party guarantees a loan, it promises to pay in the event of a default by the borrower.

Interim Financing: Short-term loan to provide temporary financing until more permanent financing is available.

Independent Foundation: A grantmaking organization usually classified by the IRS as a private foundation. Independent foundations may also be known as family foundations, general purpose foundations, special purpose foundations, or private non-operating foundations. The Foundation Center defines independent foundations and company-sponsored foundations separately; however, federal law normally classifies both as private, non-operating foundations subject to the same rules and requirements. (*See also* **Private Foundation**)

Line of Credit: Agreement by a bank that a company may borrow at any time up to an established limit.

Linked Deposit: A deposit in an account with a financial institution to induce that institution's support for one or more projects. By accruing no interest or low interest on its deposit, a foundation essentially subsidizes the interest rate of the project.

Operating Foundation: A 501(c)(3) organization classified by the IRS as a private foundation whose primary purpose is to conduct research, social welfare, or other programs determined by its governing body or establishment charter. Some grants may be made, but the sum is generally small relative to the funds used for the foundation's own programs. (*See also* **501(c)(3)**)

Payout Requirement: The minimum amount that private foundations are required to expend for charitable purposes (includes grants, program-related investments and other charitable disbursement). In general, a private foundation must meet or exceed an annual payout requirement of five percent of the average market value of the foundation's assets.

Private Foundation: A nongovernmental, nonprofit organization with funds (usually from a single source, such as an individual, family, or corporation) and program managed by its own trustees or directors that was established to maintain or aid social, educational, religious or other charitable activities serving the common welfare, primarily through the making of grants. "Private foundation" also means an organization that is tax-exempt under code section 501(c)(3) and is classified by the IRS as a private foundation as defined in the code. The code definition usually, but not always, identifies a foundation with the characteristics first described. (*See also* **501(c)(3); Public Charity**)

Program Amount: Funds that are expended to support a particular program administered internally by the foundation or corporate giving program.

Program Officer: A staff member of a foundation who reviews proposals and processes applications for the board of trustees. Only a small percentage of foundations have program officers.

Program-Related Investment (PRI): Broad, functional definition: A method of providing support to an organization, consistent with program goals involving the potential return of capital within an established time frame. In the context of this guide, program-related investments include loans, loan guarantees, equity investments, asset purchases or the conversion of asset(s) to charitable use, linked deposits, and recoverable grants.

Proposal: A written application, often with supporting documents, submitted to a foundation or corporate giving program when requesting funding. Preferred procedures and formats vary. Consult published guidelines.

Public Charity: In general, an organization that is tax-exempt under code section 501(c)(3) and is classified by the IRS as a public charity and not a private foundation. Public charities generally derive their funding or support primarily from the general public in carrying out their social, educational, religious, or other charitable activities serving the common welfare. Some public charities engage in grantmaking activities, although most engage in direct service or other tax-exempt activities. Public charities are eligible for maximum income tax-deductible contributions from the public and are not subject to the same rules and restrictions as private foundations. Some are also referred to as "public foundations" or "publicly supported organizations" and may use the term "foundation" in their names. (*See also* **501(c)(3); Private Foundation**)

Qualifying Distributions: Expenditures of private foundations used to satisfy the annual payout requirement. These can include grants, reasonable administrative expenses, set-asides, loans and program-related investments, and amounts paid to acquire assets used directly in carrying out exempt purposes.

Query Letter: A brief letter outlining an organization's activities and its request for funding sent to a foundation or corporation to determine whether it would be appropriate to submit a full proposal. Many grantmakers prefer to be contacted in this way before receiving a full proposal.

Recoverable Grants: Funds provided by a philanthropist to fulfill a role similar to equity. A recoverable grant may include an agreement to treat the investment as a grant if the enterprise is not successful, but to repay the investor if the enterprise meets with success. (These are not included in *The PRI Index* listings; they are included in the Center's grants database.)

RFP: Request For Proposal. When the government issues a new contract or grant program, it sends out RFPs to agencies that might be qualified to participate. The RFP lists project specifications and application procedures. A few foundations occasionally use RFPs in specific fields, but most prefer to consider proposals that are initiated by applicants.

Seed Money: A grant or contribution used to start a new project or organization. Seed grants may cover salaries and other operating expenses of a new project.

Set-Asides: Funds set aside by a foundation for a specific purpose or project that are counted as qualifying distributions toward the foundation's annual payout requirement. Amounts for the project must be paid within five years of the first set-aside.

Special Purpose Foundation: A private foundation that focuses its grantmaking activities in one or a few special areas of interest. For example, a foundation may only award grants in the area of cancer research or child development. (*See also* **General Purpose Foundation**)

Technical Assistance: Operational or management assistance given to nonprofit organizations. It can include fundraising assistance, budgeting and financial planning, program planning, legal advice, marketing, and other aids to management. Assistance may be offered directly by a foundation or corporate staff member, or be offered in the form of a grant to pay for the services of an outside consultant. (*See also* **In-Kind Contributions**)

Trustee: A member of a governing board. A foundation's board of trustees meets to review grant proposals and make decisions. Often also referred to as a "director" or "board member."

ABBREVIATIONS

The following lists contain standard abbreviations frequently used by the Foundation Center's editorial staff. These abbreviations are used most frequently in the addresses of grantmakers and the titles of corporate and grantmaker officers.

TWO LETTER STATE AND TERRITORY ABBREVIATIONS

AK	Alaska	IL	Illinois	ND	North Dakota	SD	South Dakota
AL	Alabama	IN	Indiana	NE	Nebraska	TN	Tennessee
AR	Arkansas	KS	Kansas	NH	New Hampshire	TX	Texas
AZ	Arizona	KY	Kentucky	NJ	New Jersey	UT	Utah
CA	California	LA	Louisiana	NM	New Mexico	VA	Virginia
CO	Colorado	MA	Massachusetts	NV	Nevada	VI	Virgin Islands
CT	Connecticut	MD	Maryland	NY	New York	VT	Vermont
DC	District of Columbia	ME	Maine	OH	Ohio	WA	Washington
DE	Delaware	MI	Michigan	OK	Oklahoma	WI	Wisconsin
FL	Florida	MN	Minnesota	OR	Oregon	WV	West Virginia
GA	Georgia	MO	Missouri	PA	Pennsylvania	WY	Wyoming
HI	Hawaii	MS	Mississippi	PR	Puerto Rico		
IA	Iowa	MT	Montana	RI	Rhode Island		
ID	Idaho	NC	North Carolina	SC	South Carolina		

STREET ABBREVIATIONS

1st	First*	E.	East	N.W.	Northwest	S.W.	Southwest
2nd	Second*	Expwy.	Expressway	No.	Number	Sq.	Square
3rd	Third*	Fl.	Floor	Pkwy.	Parkway	St.	Saint
Apt.	Apartment	Ft.	Fort	Pl.	Place	St.	Street
Ave.	Avenue	Hwy.	Highway	Plz.	Plaza	Sta.	Station
Bldg.	Building	Ln.	Lane	R.R.	Rural Route	Ste.	Suite
Cir.	Circle	M.C.	Mail Code	Rd.	Road	Terr.	Terrace
Ct.	Court	M.S.	Mail Stop	Rm.	Room	Univ.	University
Ctr.	Center	Mt.	Mount	Rte.	Route	W.	West
Dept.	Department	N.	North	S.	South		
Dr.	Drive	N.E.	Northeast	S.E.	Southeast		

*Numerics used always

ABBREVIATIONS USED FOR OFFICER TITLES

Acctg.	Accounting
ADM.	Admiral
Admin.	Administration
Admin.	Administrative
Admin.	Administrator
Adv.	Advertising
Amb.	Ambassador
Assn.	Association
Assoc(s).	Associate(s)
Asst.	Assistant
Bro.	Brother
C.A.O.	Chief Accounting Officer
C.A.O.	Chief Administration Officer
C.E.O.	Chief Executive Officer
C.F.O.	Chief Financial Officer
C.I.O.	Chief Information Officer
C.I.O.	Chief Investment Officer
C.O.O.	Chief Operating Officer
Capt.	Captain
Chair.	Chairperson
Col.	Colonel
Comm.	Committee, Communications
Commo.	Commodore
Compt.	Comptroller
Cont.	Controller
Contrib(s).	Contribution(s)
Coord.	Coordinator
Corp.	Corporate, Corporation
Co(s).	Company(s)
Dep.	Deputy
Devel.	Development
Dir.	Director
Distrib(s).	Distribution(s)
Div.	Division
Exec.	Executive
Ext.	External
Fdn.	Foundation
Fr.	Father
Genl.	General
Gov.	Governor
Govt.	Government
Hon.	Judge
Inf.	Information
Int.	Internal
Intl.	International
Jr.	Junior
Lt.	Lieutenant
Ltd.	Limited
Maj.	Major
Mfg.	Manufacturing
Mgmt.	Management
Mgr.	Manager
Mktg.	Marketing
Msgr.	Monsignor
Mt.	Mount
Natl.	National
Off.	Officer
Opers.	Operations
Org.	Organization
Plan.	Planning
Pres.	President
Prog(s).	Program(s)
RADM.	Rear Admiral
Rels.	Relations
Rep.	Representative
Rev.	Reverend
Rt. Rev.	Right Reverend
Secy.	Secretary
Secy.-Treas.	Secretary-Treasurer
Sen.	Senator
Soc.	Society
Sr.	Senior
Sr.	Sister
Supvr.	Supervisor
Svc(s).	Service(s)
Tech.	Technology
Tr.	Trustee
Treas.	Treasurer
Univ.	University
V.P.	Vice President
VADM.	Vice Admiral
Vice-Chair.	Vice Chairperson

ADDITIONAL ABBREVIATIONS

E-mail	Electronic mail
FAX	Facsimile
SASE	Self-Addressed Stamped Envelope
TDD, TTY	Telecommunication Device for the Deaf
Tel.	Telephone
URL	Uniform Resource Locator (World Wide Web)

Jan.	January
Feb.	February
Mar.	March
Apr.	April
Aug.	August
Sept.	September
Oct.	October
Nov.	November
Dec.	December

BIBLIOGRAPHY

This selected bibliography is compiled from the Foundation Center's bibliographic database. Many of the items are available for free reference use in the Center's New York City, Washington, D.C., Cleveland, San Francisco, and Atlanta libraries and in many of its Cooperating Collections throughout the United States. For further references on such topics as fundraising and proposal development, see *The Literature of the Nonprofit Sector Online: The Foundation Center's Online Catalog with Abstracts,* which can be accessed at http://lnps.fdncenter.org.

Adamson, Rebecca. "Can't Give It Away Fast Enough? Try This." *Foundation News & Commentary,* vol. 39 (January–February 1998): p. 26–7.
Discusses foundations making program-related investments through intermediaries in order to meet their payout and program goals.

Baxter, Christie I. "A Basic Guide to Program-Related Investments." *Grantsmanship Center Magazine* (Fall 1997): p. 22–4.

Baxter, Christie I. *Program-Related Investments: A Technical Manual for Foundations.* New York, NY: John Wiley & Sons. 1997. xix, 475 p. ISBN 0-471-17833-0
Begun in 1968 by the Ford Foundation, program-related investments have grown to become a strategic tool used by a variety of foundations to further their program interests. Among the topics covered in detail are investment processes, policy issues, tax considerations, and documentation matters.

Bowman, Woods. "The Uniqueness of Nonprofit Finance and the Decision to Borrow." *Nonprofit Management & Leadership,* vol. 12 (Spring 2002): p. 293–311.
Explores the relationship between borrowing and endowment using various statistical analyses. Includes bibliographic references.

Cerny, Milton. "Creative Uses of Program-Related Investments." *International Journal of Not-for-Profit Law* vol. 1 (March 1999): p. 7–12.
Discusses typical applications of program-related investments, as well as several emerging international models, such as the PRIs given by the Media Development Loan Fund (MDLF), a private operating foundation established by George Soros in 1995.

Chernoff, David S. "Some Practical Observations About Making, Documenting and Closing Program-Related Investments." *Philanthropy Monthly,* vol. 29 (March 1996): p. 23–31.

Dundjerski, Marina. "Billion-Dollar Growth at Big Funds." *Chronicle of Philanthropy,* vol. 12 (24 February 2000): p. 1, 7–8, 10–16, 19–20.
Discusses the findings of a new Chronicle of Philanthropy survey of U.S. foundations. According to the survey, the assets of 35 of America's wealthiest private foundations grew by $24.9 billion last year to $180.6 billion. Sidebars list the nation's 10 wealthiest foundations, foundation giving projections for 2000, a sampling of large grants made in 1999, and foundation spending on program-related investments. In addition, statistical data regarding grant making at 146 major foundations is provided.

Flamm, Matthew. "Lending Businesswomen a Hand: Venture Fund Provides Start-Ups with Loans, Mentoring Services." *Crain's New York Business,* vol. 13 (15–21 September 1997): p. 32, 37.
Women's Venture Fund, which was founded in 1994 to assist low-income women entrepreneurs, provides mentoring and loans ranging from $400–$7,000.

Greene, Stephen G. "Tiny Loans Power a Global Campaign to Aid the World's Poorest People." *Chronicle of Philanthropy,* vol. 9 (3 April 1997): p. 9–10.
Charities that make microcredit loans to poor people hope that such programs will grow to reach 100 million people by 2005.

Klein, Mary. "Putting the PRI Concept to Work." *Corporate Philanthropy Report,* vol. 10 (April 1995): p. 3–4.
Reports how corporations are being encouraged to make program-related investments to support charitable projects. The Ford Foundation has funded a program at the Massachusetts Institute of Technology to develop a workshop specifically for corporations on PRIs and to create materials for regional

associations of grantmakers to use for their own PRI training sessions.

Knowles, Louis L. "Social Investing Rolls Along." *Foundation News & Commentary,* vol. 36 (March-April 1995): p. 22–5.
Describes how a few foundations are finding ways of using their assets to further their mission, as the world of socially responsible investing continues to evolve. Presents examples of foundations that screen investments from companies whose values conflict with the values of the investor, utilize program-related investments, or engage in shareholder activism.

"Markle Foundation Announces Increased Spending, New Initiatives." *Foundation Giving Watch,* vol. 19 (September 1999): p. 1–2.
The Markle Foundation has announced that it will invest up to $100 million over the next three to five years in an initiative to address the "digital divide" and help to ensure that all people have access to the new communications media and information technologies, regardless of income, education or race. The foundation will focus on four areas: public engagement through interactive technologies, policy development for a networked society, children's interactive media, and health care information technologies. The foundation's recent program-related investment with Oxygen Media, a network of Web sites and a future cable network focusing on women, is highlighted. In addition, recent grants made by the foundation are listed.

Renz, Loren; Massarsky, Cynthia W.; Treiber, Rikard R.; Lawrence, Steven. *Program-Related Investments: A Guide to Funders and Trends.* New York, NY: Foundation Center. 1995. xii, 189 p. ISBN 0-87954-558-5
Part one reports the results of a national survey of funders and recipients of program-related investments. Measures the size and characteristics of the PRI market, assesses the demand for PRIs, examines the motives and disincentives for making and seeking PRIs, and policies and practices in the field. Predicts future directions, and explains why some funders do not make PRIs. Includes commentary by experts in the field on the merits of funding intermediaries, managing the costs, the benefits to the arts community of a revolving loan fund, and the advantages of PRI investing for a small foundation. Part two comprises a directory of PRI providers, with individual records by subject. Includes a section on securing foundation financing, and indexes by subject, recipient name, foundations by fields of interest, and foundation by geographic location. Appendices include the grants and PRI classification system, survey respondents, survey questionnaires, the 100 leading PRI providers, a glossary, and a bibliography.

Stevens, Susan Kenny. "Make Working Capital Work." *Foundation News & Commentary,* vol. 41 (July-August 2000): p. 42–5.
Defines working capital ("unrestricted, flexible cash that, when used strategically, evens out operating cash flow gaps . . . cash left over after bills are paid.") This concept from the business sector is valid for nonprofits, too, and can be encouraged by grantmakers. Some sources of working capital include loans and cash reserve grants (both external) as well as operating surpluses (internal). How funders can help nonprofits to utilize these options for long-term financial management are discussed.

RESOURCES OF THE FOUNDATION CENTER

The Foundation Center is a national service organization founded and supported by foundations to provide a single authoritative source of information on foundation and corporate giving. The Center's programs are designed to help grantseekers select those funders which may be most interested in their projects from the more than 74,000 active U.S. grantmakers. Among its primary activities toward this end are publishing reference books and CD-ROMs, and offering online searchable databases on foundation and corporate philanthropy; disseminating information on grantmaking, grantseeking, and related subjects through its site on the Internet; offering educational courses and workshops; and a nationwide network of library/learning centers and cooperating collections.

Publications and databases of the Foundation Center are the primary working tools of every serious grantseeker. They are also used by grantmakers, scholars, journalists, and legislators—in short, by anyone seeking any type of factual information on philanthropy. All private foundations and a significant number of corporate grantmakers actively engaged in grantmaking, regardless of size or geographic location, are included in one or more of the Center's publications. The publications are of three kinds: directories that describe specific funders, characterizing their program interests and providing fiscal and personnel data; grants indexes that list and classify by subject recent foundation and corporate awards; and guides, monographs, and bibliographies that introduce the reader to funding research, elements of proposal writing, and nonprofit management issues.

For those who wish to access information on grantmakers and their grants electronically, the Center issues *FC Search: The Foundation Center's Database on CD-ROM* containing the full universe of over 72,000 grantmakers and more than 313,000 associated grants. *The Foundation Directory Online Basic* provides access to 10,000 of the nation's largest foundations. *The Foundation Directory Online Plus* contains the top 10,000 foundations plus a searchable database of 250,000 grants. *The Foundation Directory Online Premium* includes 20,000 foundations plus over 250,000 grants. *The Foundation Directory Online Platinum* includes over 74,000 grantmakers plus over 250,000 grants. In addition, the Center's award-winning Web site features a wide array of free information about the philanthropic community.

The Foundation Center's publications and electronic products may be ordered from the Foundation Center, 79 Fifth Avenue, New York, NY 10003-3076, or online at our Web site. For more information about any aspect of the Center's programs or for the name of the Center's library collection nearest you, call 1-800-424-9836, or visit us on the Web at www.fdncenter.org. Please visit our Web site for the most current information available on new products and services of the Foundation Center.

GENERAL RESEARCH DIRECTORIES

THE FOUNDATION DIRECTORY, 2003 Edition

The Foundation Directory has been widely known and respected in the field for more than 40 years. It includes the latest information on the 10,000 largest U.S. foundations based on total giving. The 2003 Edition includes over 1,500 foundations that are new to this edition. *Directory* foundations hold more than $434 billion in assets and award over $24 billion in grants annually.

Each *Directory* entry contains precise information on application procedures, giving limitations, types of support awarded, the publications of each foundation, and foundation staff. In addition, each entry features such vital data as the grantmaker's giving interests, financial data, grant amounts, address, and telephone number. This edition includes over 41,000 selected grants. The Foundation Center works closely with foundations to ensure the accuracy and timeliness of the information provided.

The *Directory* includes indexes by foundation name; subject areas of interest; names of donors, officers, and trustees; geographic location; international interests; types of support awarded; and grantmakers new to the volume. Also included are analyses of the foundation community by geography, asset and grant size, and the different foundation types.

Also available on CD-ROM and Online.
See sections on CD-ROMs and Online Databases.
March 2003
ISBN 1-931923-14-0 / $215
Published annually

THE FOUNDATION DIRECTORY PART 2, 2003 Edition

Following in the tradition of *The Foundation Directory, The Foundation Directory Part 2* brings you the same thorough coverage for the next largest set of 10,000 foundations.

It includes *Directory*-level information on mid-sized foundations, an important group of grantmakers responsible for millions of dollars in funding annually. Essential data on foundations is included along with more than 36,000 recently awarded foundation grants, providing an excellent overview of the foundations' giving interests. Quick access to foundation entries is facilitated by seven indexes, including foundation name; subject areas of interest; names of donors, officers, and trustees; geographic location; international interests; types of support awarded; and grantmakers new to the volume.

March 2003 / ISBN 1-931923-19-1 / $185
Published annually

THE FOUNDATION DIRECTORY SUPPLEMENT

The Foundation Directory Supplement provides the latest-breaking information on *Foundation Directory* and *Foundation Directory Part 2* grantmakers six months after those volumes are published. Each year, thousands of policy and staff changes occur at these foundations. Fundraisers need to know about these crucial changes as rapidly as possible, as they may affect the way fundraisers prepare their grant proposals. The *Supplement* ensures that users of the *Directory* and *Directory Part 2* always have the latest addresses, contact names, policy statements, application guidelines, and financial data for the foundations they're approaching for funding.

September 2003 / ISBN 1-931923-51-5 / $125
Published annually

GUIDE TO U.S. FOUNDATIONS, THEIR TRUSTEES, OFFICERS, AND DONORS

This powerful fundraising reference tool provides fundraisers with current, accurate information on over 64,000 private and community foundations in the U.S. The three-volume set also includes a master list of the names of the people who establish, oversee, and manage those institutions. With access to this information, fundraisers can facilitate their funding research by discovering the philanthropic connections of current donors, board members, volunteers, and prominent families in their geographic area. Because it provides a comprehensive list of U.S. foundations and the people who govern them, the *Guide to U.S. Foundations* also helps fundraisers follow up on any giving leads they may uncover. Each entry includes asset and giving amounts as well as geographic limitations, allowing fundraisers to quickly determine whether or not to pursue a particular grant source.

The *Guide to U.S. Foundations* is the only source of published data on thousands of local foundations. (It includes more than 44,000 grantmakers not covered in other print publications.) Each entry also tells you whether you can find more extensive information on the grantmaker in another Foundation Center reference work.

April 2003/ 1-931923-40-X / $295
Published annually

THE FOUNDATION 1000

Nonprofit fundraisers and other researchers have access to annually published, comprehensive reports on the 1,000 largest foundations in the country. *The Foundation 1000* provides access to extensive and accurate information on this set of powerful funders. *Foundation 1000* grantmakers hold over $290 billion in assets and awarded close to 290,000 grants worth nearly $17 billion to nonprofit organizations nationwide.

The Foundation 1000 provides the most thorough analyses available of the 1,000 largest foundations and their extensive grant programs, including all the data fundraisers need most when applying for grants from these top-level foundations. Each multi-page foundation profile features a full foundation portrait, a detailed breakdown of the foundation's grant programs, and extensive lists of recently awarded foundation grants.

Five indexes give fundraisers the opportunity to target potential funders in a variety of ways: by subject field, type of support, geographic location, international giving, and the names of foundation officers, donors, and trustees.

October 2003 / ISBN 1-931923-60-4 / $295
Published annually

NATIONAL DIRECTORY OF CORPORATE GIVING, 9th Edition

Each year, corporations donate billions of dollars to nonprofit organizations. To help fundraisers tap into this vital source of funding, the *National Directory of Corporate Giving* offers authoritative information on over 3,600 company-sponsored foundations and direct corporate giving programs.

Fundraisers who want access to current, accurate fundraising facts on corporate philanthropies will benefit from the full range of data in this volume. The *National Directory of Corporate Giving* features detailed portraits of over 2,300 company-sponsored foundations plus over 1,300 direct corporate giving programs. Fundraisers will find essential information on these corporate grantmakers, including application information, key personnel, types of support generally awarded, giving limitations, financial data, and purpose and activities statements. Also included in the 9th Edition are over 6,800 selected grants. These grants give you the best indication of a grantmaker's funding priorities by identifying nonprofits it has already funded. The volume also provides data on the companies that sponsor foundations and direct-giving programs—essential background information for corporate grant searches. Each entry gives the company's name and address, a listing of its types of business, its financial data (complete with *Forbes* and *Fortune* ratings), a listing of its subsidiaries, divisions, plants, and offices, and a charitable-giving statement.

The *National Directory of Corporate Giving* also features an extensive bibliography to guide you to further research on corporate funding. Seven essential indexes help you target funding prospects by geographic region; international giving; types of support; subject area; officers, donors, and trustees; types of business; and the names of the corporation, its foundation, and its direct-giving program.

August 2003/ ISBN 1-931923-59-0 / $195
Published annually

CORPORATE FOUNDATION PROFILES, 12th Edition

This updated volume includes comprehensive information on 181 of the largest corporate foundations in the U.S., grantmakers who each give at least $1.25 million annually. Each profile includes foundation giving interests, application guidelines, recently awarded grants, information on the sponsoring company, and many other essential fundraising facts. A section on financial data provides a summary of the size and grantmaking capacity of each foundation and contains a list of assets, gifts or contributions, grants paid, operating programs, expenditures, scholarships, and loans. A quick-scan appendix lists core financial data on over 1,300 corporate foundations, all of which give at least $66,000 in grants every year. Five indexes help grantseekers search for prospective funders by names of donors, officers, trustees, and staff; subject area; types of support; geographic region; and international giving.

February 2002 / ISBN 0-87954-972-6 / $155

DIRECTORY OF MISSOURI GRANTMAKERS, 5th Edition

The *Directory of Missouri Grantmakers* provides a comprehensive guide to grantmakers in the state or that have an interest in Missouri nonprofits—over 2,300 foundations, corporate giving programs, and public charities—from the largest grantmakers to local family foundations. The volume will facilitate your grantseeking with information-filled entries that list giving amounts, fields of interest, purpose statements, selected grants, and much more. Indexes help you target the most appropriate funders by subject interest, types of support, and names of key personnel.

June 2003 / ISBN 1-931923-46-9 / $75
Published biennially

FOUNDATION GRANTS TO INDIVIDUALS, 13th Edition

The only publication devoted entirely to foundation grant opportunities for qualified individual applicants, the 13th Edition of this volume features more than 5,400 entries, all of which profile foundation grants to individuals. Entries include foundation addresses and telephone numbers, financial data, giving limitations, and application guidelines. This volume will save individual grantseekers countless hours of research.

June 2003 / ISBN 1-931923-45-0 / $65
Published biennially

SUBJECT DIRECTORIES

The Foundation Center's National Guide to Funding series is designed to facilitate grantseeking within specific fields of nonprofit activity. Each of the directories described below performs the crucial first step of fundraising research by identifying a set of grantmakers that have already stated or demonstrated an interest in a particular field. Fact-filled entries provide access to foundation addresses, financial data, giving priorities, application procedures, contact names, and key officials. Many entries also feature recently awarded grants, the best indication of a grantmaker's funding priorities. A variety of indexes help fundraisers target potential grant sources by subject area, geographic preferences, types of support, and the names of donors, officers, and trustees.

Subject guides are published biennially.

GUIDE TO FUNDING FOR INTERNATIONAL AND FOREIGN PROGRAMS, 6th Edition

The *Guide to Funding for International and Foreign Programs* covers over 1,300 grantmakers interested in funding projects with an international focus, both within the U.S. and abroad. Program areas covered include international relief, disaster assistance, human rights, civil liberties, community development, education, and much more. The volume also includes descriptions of more than 8,900+ recently awarded grants.

May 2002 / ISBN 0-87954-995-5 / $125

NATIONAL GUIDE TO FUNDING IN AIDS, 3rd Edition

This volume covers more than 560 foundations, corporate giving programs, and public charities that support AIDS- and HIV-related nonprofit organizations involved in direct relief, medical research, legal aid, preventative education, and other programs to empower persons with AIDS and AIDS-related diseases. Over 500 recently awarded grants show the types of projects funded by grantmakers.

June 2003/ ISBN 1-931923-44-2 / $115

NATIONAL GUIDE TO FUNDING IN ARTS AND CULTURE, 7th Edition

This volume covers more than 7,500 grantmakers with an interest in funding dance companies, museums, theaters, and countless other types of arts and culture projects and institutions. The volume also includes more than 16,500 descriptions of recently awarded grants.

May 2002 / ISBN 0-87954-998-X / $155

NATIONAL GUIDE TO FUNDING FOR THE ENVIRONMENT AND ANIMAL WELFARE, 6th Edition

This guide covers over 2,900 grantmakers that fund nonprofits involved in international conservation, ecological research, waste reduction, animal welfare, and much more. The volume includes descriptions of over 7,200 recently awarded grants.

June 2002 / ISBN 1-931923-02-7 / $115

NATIONAL GUIDE TO FUNDING IN HEALTH, 8th Edition

The *National Guide to Funding in Health* contains essential facts on nearly 10,700 grantmakers interested in funding hospitals, universities, research institutes, community-based agencies, national health associations, and a broad range of other health-related programs and services. The volume also includes descriptions of more than 16,000 recently awarded grants.

May 2003 / ISBN 1-931923-42-6 / $155

NATIONAL GUIDE TO FUNDING FOR LIBRARIES AND INFORMATION SERVICES, 7th Edition

This volume provides essential data on more than 800 grantmakers that support a wide range of organizations and initiatives, from the smallest public libraries to major research institutions, academic/research libraries, art, law, and medical libraries, and other specialized information centers. The volume also includes descriptions of over 600 recently awarded grants.

May 2003 / ISBN 1-931923-43-4 / $115

NATIONAL GUIDE TO FUNDING IN RELIGION, 7th Edition

With this volume, fundraisers who work for nonprofits affiliated with religious organizations have access to information on nearly 8,400 grantmakers that have demonstrated or stated an interest in funding churches, missionary societies, religious welfare and education programs, and many other types of projects and institutions. The volume also includes descriptions of more than 10,000 recently awarded grants.

May 2003/ ISBN 1-931923-41-8 / $155

GRANT DIRECTORIES

GRANT GUIDES

Designed for fundraisers who work within defined fields of nonprofit development, this series of guides lists actual foundation grants of $10,000 or more in 12 key areas of grantmaking.

Each title in the series affords immediate access to the names, addresses, and giving limitations of the foundations listed. The grant descriptions provide fundraisers with the grant recipient's name and location; the amount of the grant; the date the grant was authorized; and a description of the grant's intended use.

In addition, each *Grant Guide* includes three indexes, which help fundraisers target possible sources of funding by the type of organization generally funded by the grantmaker, the subject focus of the foundation's grants, and the geographic area in which the foundation has already funded projects.

Each Grant Guide also includes a concise overview of the foundation spending patterns within the specified field. The introduction uses a series of statistical tables to document such important findings as (1) the 25 top funders in your area of interest (by total dollar amount of grants); (2) the 15 largest grants reported; (3) the total dollar amount and number of grants awarded for specific types of support, recipient organization type, and population group; and (4) the total grant dollars received in each U.S. state and many foreign countries.

The *Grant Guide* series gives fundraisers the data they need to target foundations making grants in their field, to network with organizations that share their goals, and to tailor their grant applications to the specific concerns of grantmakers as expressed by the grants they have already made.

Series published annually in December / 2003 / 2004 Editions / $75 each

GUIDEBOOKS, MANUALS, AND REPORTS

AIDS FUNDRAISING

Published in conjunction with Funders Concerned About AIDS, this guide helps nonprofit groups plan a strategy for raising money. *AIDS Fundraising* covers a vast array of money-generating initiatives, from membership drives to special events, direct mail, and grant applications.

July 1991 / ISBN 0-87954-390-6 / $10

ARTS FUNDING IV: An Update on Foundation Trends

This report provides a framework for understanding trends in foundation funding for arts and culture through 2001. Based on a sample of 800+ foundations, it compares growth in arts funding with other sources of public and private support, examines changes in giving for specific arts disciplines, analyzes giving patterns by region, and explores shifts in the types of support funders award. Prepared in cooperation with Grantmakers in the Arts.

July 2003 / ISBN 1-931923-48-5 / $19.95

FAMILY FOUNDATIONS: A Profile of Funders and Trends

Family Foundations is an essential resource for anyone interested in understanding the fastest growing segment of foundation philanthropy. The report provides the most comprehensive measurement to date of the size and scope of the U.S. family foundation community. Through the use of objective and subjective criteria, the report identifies the number of family foundations and their distribution by region and state, size, geographic focus, and decade of establishment; and includes analyses of staffing and public reporting by these funders. *Family Foundations* also examines trends in giving by a sample of larger family foundations between 1993 and 1998 and compares these patterns with independent foundations overall. Prepared in cooperation with the National Center for Family Philanthropy.

August 2000 / ISBN 0-87954-917-3 / $19.95

INTERNATIONAL GRANTMAKING II: An Update on U.S. Foundation Trends, 2nd Edition

An update to 1997's groundbreaking *International Grantmaking* study, this report documents trends in international giving by U.S. foundations in the late 1990s. Based on a sample of over 570 foundations, *International Grantmaking II* identifies shifts in international giving priorities, types of support provided, recipients funded, and countries/regions targeted for support. The report also includes an overview of recent events and factors shaping the international funding environment; and perspectives on the changing funding climate based on a 2000 survey of more than 25 leading international grantmakers. Prepared in cooperation with the Council on Foundations.

November 2000 / ISBN 0-87954-916-5 / $35

THE FOUNDATION CENTER'S GRANTS CLASSIFICATION SYSTEM INDEXING MANUAL WITH THESAURUS, Revised Edition

A complete "how-to" guide, the *Grants Classification Manual* provides an essential resource for any organization that wants to classify foundation grants or their recipients. The *Manual* includes a complete set of all classification codes to facilitate precise tracking of grants and recipients by subject, recipient type, and population categories. It also features a completely revised thesaurus to help identify the "official" terms and codes that represent thousands of subject areas and recipient types in the Center's system of grants classification.

May 1995 / ISBN 0-87954-644-1 / $95

FOUNDATION FUNDAMENTALS: A Guide for Grantseekers, 6th Edition

This comprehensive, easy-to-read guidebook shows you how to use print and electronic funding research directories and databases to develop your prospect list; how to use the World Wide Web to locate information on potential funders; how to target grantmakers by subject interest, types of support, and geographic area; how to shape your proposal to reflect the special concerns of corporate funders; and much more! The 6th Edition is fully revised with up-to-date charts and worksheets to help you manage your fundraising program.

August 1999 / ISBN 0-87954-869-X / $24.95

THE FOUNDATION CENTER'S USER-FRIENDLY GUIDE: A Grantseeker's Guide to Resources, 4th Edition

This helpful book answers the most commonly asked questions about grantseeking in an upbeat, easy-to-read style. Specifically designed for novice grantseekers, the *User Friendly Guide* leads the reader through the maze of unfamiliar jargon and wide range of research guides used successfully by professional fundraisers every day. Whether a grantseeker needs $100 or $100,000 for his or her project or organization, *The Foundation Center's User-Friendly Guide* offers an excellent first step in the fundraising process.

July 1996 / ISBN 0-87954-666-2 / $14.95

FOUNDATIONS TODAY SERIES, 2003 Edition

The successor to the Foundation Center's popular *Foundation Giving* report, the *Foundations Today Series* provides the latest information on foundation growth and trends in foundation giving. A subscription to the 2003 Edition of the *Foundations Today Series* includes copies of all four reports and the estimates update (as they are published) for one low price.

Foundation Giving Trends: Update on Funding Priorities—Examines 2001 grantmaking patterns of a sample of more than 1,000 larger U.S. foundations and compares current giving priorities with trends since 1980. *February 2003*

Foundation Growth and Giving Estimates: 2002 Preview—Provides a first look at estimates of foundation giving for 2002 and final statistics on actual giving and assets for 2001. Presents new top 100 foundation lists. *March 2003*

Foundation Yearbook: Facts and Figures on Private and Community Foundations—Documents the growth in number, giving, and assets of all active U.S. foundations from 1975 through 2001. *June 2003*

Foundation Staffing: Update on Staffing Trends of Private and Community Foundations—Examines changes in the staffing patterns of U.S. foundations through mid-2003, based on an annual survey of nearly 3,000 staffed foundations. *September 2003*

Foundation Reporting: Update on Public Reporting Trends of Private and Community Foundations—Documents changes in voluntary reporting patterns of U.S. foundations through mid-2003, based on an annual survey of more than 3,000 foundations that issued publications. *November 2003*

Annual 2003 / ISBN 1-931923-18-3 / $95

THE FOUNDATION CENTER'S GUIDE TO GRANTSEEKING ON THE WEB, 2003 Edition

Learn how to maximize use of the Web for your funding research. Packed with a wealth of information, the *Guide to Grantseeking on the Web* provides both novice and experienced Web users with a gateway to the numerous online resources available to grantseekers. Foundation Center staff experts have team-authored this guide, contributing their extensive knowledge of Web content as well as their tips and strategies on how to evaluate and use Web-based funding materials. Presented in a concise, "how-to" style, the *Guide* will introduce you to the Web and structure your funding research with a toolkit of resources. These resources include foundation and corporate Web sites, searchable databases for grantseeking, government funding sources, online journals, and interactive services on the Web for grantseekers.

September 2003 / Book / ISBN 1-931923-67-1 / $29.95
CD-ROM / ISBN 1-931923-73-6 / $29.95
Book and CD-ROM / $49.95

THE FOUNDATION CENTER'S GUIDE TO PROPOSAL WRITING, 3rd Edition

The *Guide* is a comprehensive manual on the strategic thinking and mechanics of proposal writing. It covers each step of the process, from pre-proposal planning to the writing itself to the essential post-grant follow-up. The book features many extracts from actual grant proposals and also includes candid advice from grantmakers on the "do's and don't's" of proposal writing. Written by a professional fundraiser who has been creating successful proposals for more than 25 years, *The Foundation Center's Guide to Proposal Writing* offers the kind of valuable tips and in-depth, practical instruction that no other source provides.

February 2001 / ISBN 0-87954-958-0 / $34.95

GUÍA PARA ESCRIBIR PROPUESTAS

The new Spanish language edition of the *Guide to Proposal Writing* (see above) also includes a special appendix listing consultants and technical assistance providers who can help Spanish speakers craft proposals in English, or give advice on fundraising.

March 2003 / ISBN 1-931923-16-7 / $34.95

THE FOUNDATION CENTER'S GUIDE TO WINNING PROPOSALS

The *Guide to Winning Proposals* features twenty grant proposals that have been funded by some of today's most influential grantmakers. Each proposal—reprinted in its entirety—includes a critique by the program officer, executive director, or other funding decision-maker who granted the proposal. The accompanying commentary points to the strengths and weaknesses of each proposal and provides insights into what makes some proposals more successful than others.

To represent the diversity of nonprofits throughout the country, proposals have been selected from large and small, local and national organizations, and for many different support purposes, including basic budgetary support, special projects, construction, staff positions, and more. The *Guide to Winning Proposals* also includes actual letters of inquiry, budgets, cover letters, and vital supplementary documents needed to develop a complete proposal.

September 2003 / ISBN 1-931923-66-3 / $34.95

NEW YORK METROPOLITAN AREA FOUNDATIONS: A Profile of the Grantmaking Community

This study examines the size, scope, and giving patterns of foundations based in the eight-county New York metropolitan area. It documents the New York area's share of all U.S. foundations; details the growth of area foundations through 2000; profiles area foundations by type, size, and geographic focus; compares broad giving trends of New York area and all U.S. foundations between 1992 and 2000; and examines giving by non-New York area grantmakers to recipients in the New York area. Prepared in cooperation with the New York Regional Association of Grantmakers.

December 2002 / ISBN 1-931923-52-3/ $24.95

THE PRI DIRECTORY: Charitable Loans and Other Program-Related Investments by Foundations, 2nd Edition

Certain foundations have developed an alternative financing approach—known as program-related investing—for supplying capital to the nonprofit sector. PRIs have been used to support community revitalization, low-income housing, microenterprise development, historic preservation, human services, and more. This directory lists leading PRI providers and includes tips on how to seek out and manage PRIs. Foundation listings include funder name and state; recipient name, city, and state (or country); and a description of the project funded. There are several helpful indexes to guide PRI-seekers to records by foundation/recipient location, subject/type of support, and recipient name, as well as an index to officers, donors, and trustees.

September 2003/ ISBN 1-931923-49-3 / $75

SOUTHEASTERN FOUNDATIONS II: A Profile of the Region's Grantmaking Community, 2nd Edition

Southeastern Foundations II provides a detailed examination of foundation philanthropy in the booming 12-state Southeast region. The report includes an overview of the Southeast's share of all U.S. foundations, measures the growth of Southeastern foundations since 1992, profiles Southeastern funders by type, size, and geographic focus, compares broad giving trends of Southeastern and all U.S. foundations in 1992 and 1997, and details giving by non-Southeastern grantmakers to recipients in the region. *Produced in cooperation with the Southeastern Council of Foundations*

November 1999 / ISBN 0-87954-775-8 / $19.95

OTHER PUBLICATIONS

AMERICA'S NONPROFIT SECTOR: A Primer, 2nd Edition by Lester M. Salamon

In this revised edition of his classic book, Lester M. Salamon clarifies the basic structure and role of the nonprofit sector in the U.S. Moreover, he places the nonprofit sector into context in relation to the government and business sectors. He also shows how the position of the nonprofit sector has changed over time, both generally and in the major fields in which the sector is active. Illustrated with numerous charts and tables, Salamon's book is an easy-to-understand primer for government officials, journalists, and students—in short, for anyone who wants to comprehend the makeup of America's nonprofit sector.

February 1999 / ISBN 0-87954-801-0 / $14.95

BEST PRACTICES OF EFFECTIVE NONPROFIT ORGANIZATIONS: A Practitioner's Guide

by Philip Bernstein

This volume provides guidance for any nonprofit professional eager to advance your organization's goals. Philip Bernstein has drawn on his own extensive experience as a nonprofit executive, consultant, and volunteer to produce this review of "best practices" adopted by successful nonprofit organizations. The author identifies and explains the procedures which provide the foundation for social achievement in all nonprofit fields. Topics include defining purposes and goals, creating comprehensive financing plans, evaluating services, and effective communication.

February 1997 / ISBN 0-87954-755-3 / $29.95

THE BOARD MEMBER'S BOOK: Making a Difference in Voluntary Organizations, 3rd Edition

by Brian O'Connell

The revised and expanded edition of this popular title by former Independent Sector President, Brian O'Connell, is the perfect guide to the issue, challenges, and possibilities that emerge from the interchange between a nonprofit organization and its board. O'Connell offers practical advice on how to be a more effective board member as well as on how board members can help their organizations make a difference.

March 2003 / ISBN 1-931923-17-5 / $29.95

INVESTING IN CAPACITY BUILDING: A Guide To High-impact Approaches

This new publication by Barbara Blumenthal offers guidance to grantmakers and consultants in designing better approaches to helping nonprofits, while showing nonprofit managers how to obtain more effective assistance. Grantmakers recognize that technical assistance grants and general support have had a modest impact overall in promoting stability, effectiveness, and efficiency in the nonprofits that they support. Based on interviews with over 100 grantmakers, intermediaries, and consultants; 30 evaluations of capacity building programs; and a review of research on capacity building; *Investing in Capacity Building: A Guide to High-Impact Approaches* identifies the most successful strategies for helping nonprofits improve organizational performance.

September 2003 / ISBN 1-931923-65-5 / $34.95

CAREERS FOR DREAMERS AND DOERS: A Guide to Management Careers in the Nonprofit Sector

by Lilly Cohen and Dennis R.Young

A comprehensive guide to management positions in the nonprofit world, *Careers for Dreamers and Doers* offers practical advice for starting a job search and suggests strategies used by successful managers throughout the voluntary sector.

November 1989 / ISBN 0-87954-294-2 / $29.95

ECONOMICS FOR NONPROFIT MANAGERS

by Dennis R. Young and Richard Steinberg

Economics for Nonprofit Managers is a complete course in the economic issues faced by America's nonprofit decision-makers. Young and Steinberg treat micro-economic analysis as an indispensable skill for nonprofit managers. They introduce and explain concepts such as opportunity cost, analysis at the margin, market equilibrium, market failure, and cost-benefit analysis. This volume also focuses on issues of particular concern to nonprofits, such as the economics of fundraising and volunteer recruiting, the regulatory environment, the impact of competition on nonprofit performance, interactions among sources of revenue, and much more.

July 1995 / ISBN 0-87954-610-7 / $34.95

HANDBOOK ON PRIVATE FOUNDATIONS

by David F. Freeman and the Council on Foundations

This publication provides a thorough look at the issues facing the staff and boards of private foundations in the U.S. Author David F. Freeman offers sound advice on establishing, staffing, and governing foundations and provides insights into legal and tax guidelines as well. Each chapter concludes with a useful annotated bibliography. Sponsored by the Council on Foundations.

September 1991
Softbound: ISBN 0-87954-404-X / $29.95
Hardbound: ISBN 0-87954-403-1 / $39.95

THE NONPROFIT ENTREPRENEUR: Creating Ventures to Earn Income

Edited by Edward Skloot

In a well-organized topic-by-topic approach to nonprofit venturing, nonprofit consultant and entrepreneur Edward Skloot demonstrates how nonprofits can launch successful earned-income enterprises without compromising their missions. Skloot has compiled a collection of writings by the nation's top practitioners and advisors in nonprofit enterprise. Topics covered include legal issues, marketing techniques, business planning, avoiding the pitfalls of venturing for smaller nonprofits, and a special section on museums and their retail operations.

September 1988 / ISBN 0-87954-239-X / $19.95

A NONPROFIT ORGANIZATION OPERATING MANUAL: Planning for Survival and Growth

by Arnold J. Olenick and Philip R. Olenick

This straightforward, all-inclusive desk manual for nonprofit executives covers all aspects of starting and managing a nonprofit. The authors discuss legal problems, obtaining tax exemption, organizational planning and development, and board relations; operational, proposal, cash, and capital budgeting; marketing, grant proposals, fundraising, and for-profit ventures; computerization; and tax planning and compliance.

July 1991 / ISBN 0-87954-293-4 / $29.95

PEOPLE POWER: SERVICE, ADVOCACY, EMPOWERMENT
by Brian O'Connell

Throughout his career, Brian O'Connell has broadened the impact of his own nonprofit work with thoughtful essays, speeches, and op-ed articles. *People Power,* a selection of O'Connell's most powerful writings, provides thought-provoking commentary on the nonprofit world. The 25+ essays included in this volume range from keen analyses of the role of voluntarism in American life, to sound advice for nonprofit managers, to suggestions for developing and strengthening the nonprofit sector of the future. Anyone involved in the nonprofit world will appreciate O'Connell's penetrating insights.

October 1994 / ISBN 0-87954-563-1 / $24.95

PHILANTHROPY'S CHALLENGE
Building Nonprofit Capacity Through Venture Grantmaking
by Paul Firstenberg

In this new book, Paul Firstenberg challenges grantors to proactively assist grantee management as the way to maximize the social impact of nonprofit programs, while showing grantseekers how the growing grantor emphasis on organizational capacity building will impact their efforts to win support. The author draws on his years of experience working within both nonprofit and for-profit organizations to explore the roles of grantor and grantee within various models of venture grantmaking. To emphasize the importance that nonprofit boards can play in this process, a full chapter is devoted to governance issues and responsibilities.

January 2003 / ISBN 1-931923-15-9 / $29.95

PROMOTING ISSUES AND IDEAS: A Guide to Public Relations for Nonprofit Organizations, Revised edition
by M Booth & Associates

M Booth & Associates are specialists in promoting the issues and ideas of nonprofit groups. Their book presents proven strategies that will attract the interest of the people you wish to influence and inform. Included are the "nuts-and-bolts" of advertising, publicity, speech-making, lobbying, and special events; how to write and produce informational literature that leaps off the page; public relations on a shoe-string budget; how to plan and evaluate PR efforts; the use of rapidly evolving communication technologies; and a new chapter on crisis management.

December 1995 / ISBN 0-87954-594-1 / $29.95

RAISE MORE MONEY FOR YOUR NONPROFIT ORGANIZATION: A Guide to Evaluating and Improving Your Fundraising
by Anne L. New

In *Raise More Money,* Anne New sets guidelines for a fundraising program that will benefit the incipient as well as the established nonprofit organization. The author divides her text into three sections: "The Basics," which delineates the necessary steps a nonprofit must take before launching a development campaign; "Fundraising Methods," which encourages organizational self-analysis and points the way to an effective program involving many sources of funding; and "Fundraising Resources," a 20-page bibliography that highlights the most useful research and funding directories available.

January 1991 / ISBN 0-87954-388-4 / $14.95

SECURING YOUR ORGANIZATION'S FUTURE: A Complete Guide to Fundraising Strategies
Revised Edition
by Michael Seltzer

In this completely updated edition, Michael Seltzer acts as your personal fundraising consultant. Beginners get bottom-line facts and easy-to-follow worksheets; veteran fundraisers receive a complete review of the basics plus new money-making ideas. Seltzer supplements his text with an extensive bibliography of selected readings and resource organizations. Highly recommended for use as a text in nonprofit management programs at colleges and universities.

February 2001 / ISBN 0-87954-900-9 / $34.95

SUCCEEDING WITH CONSULTANTS: Self-Assessment for the Changing Nonprofit
by Barbara Kibbe and Fred Setterberg

This inspirational book, written by Barbara Kibbe and Fred Setterberg and supported by the David and Lucile Packard Foundation, guides nonprofits through the process of selecting and utilizing consultants to strengthen their organization's operations. The book emphasizes self assessment tools and covers six different areas in which a nonprofit organization might benefit from a consultant's advice: governance, planning, fund development, financial management, public relations and marketing, and quality assurance.

April 1992 / ISBN 0-87954-450-3 / $19.95

THE 21ST CENTURY NONPROFIT
by Paul B. Firstenberg

In *The 21st Century Nonprofit,* Paul B. Firstenberg provides nonprofit managers with the know-how to make their organizations effective agents of change. *The 21st Century Nonprofit* encourages managers to adopt strategies developed by the for-profit sector in recent years. These strategies will help them to expand their revenue base by diversifying grant sources, exploit the possibilities of for-profit enterprises, develop human resources by learning how to attract and retain talented people, and explore the nature of leadership through short profiles of three nonprofit CEOs.

July 1996 / ISBN 0-87954-672-7 / $34.95

MEMBERSHIP PROGRAM

ASSOCIATES PROGRAM
A Special Membership Program

The Associates Program puts important facts and figures on your desk through an e-mail and toll-free telephone reference service, helping you to:

- identify potential sources of foundation funding for your organization; and
- gather important information to use in targeting and presenting your proposals effectively.

Your annual membership in the Associates Program gives you vital information on a timely basis, saving you hundreds of hours of research time.

- Membership in the Associates Program entitles you to important funding information, including information from:
  - —foundation and corporate annual reports, brochures, press releases, grants lists, and other announcements
  - —IRS 990-PF information returns for active grantmaking U.S. foundations—often the only source of information on small foundations
  - —books and periodicals on the grantmaking field, including regulation and nonprofit management
- The annual fee of $995 for the Associates Program entitles you to ten free reference requests per month. Additional reference requests can be made at the rate of $30 per ten questions.
- Membership in the Associates Program allows you to request custom searches of the Foundation Center's computerized databases, which contain information on more than 72,000 U.S. foundations and corporate givers. There is an additional cost for this service.
- Associates Program members may request photocopies of key documents. Important information from 990-PFs, annual reports, application guidelines, and other resources can be copied and either mailed or faxed to your office. Up to 50 pages per month may be requested free of charge.
- All Associates Program members receive the Associates Program quarterly newsletter, which provides news and information about new foundations, changes in boards of directors, new programs, and publications from both the Foundation Center and other publishers in the field.
- Members receive two special e-mail reports each month; one listing a minimum of 75 new or emerging foundations not yet listed in our directories or on our Web site, and a second e-mail report listing updates on current grantmaker profiles.
- Access to program services via Associates Program Online.

Thousands of professional fundraisers find it extremely cost-effective to rely on the Center's Associates Program. Put our staff of experts to work for your fundraising program. For more information call 1-800-424-9836, or visit our World Wide Web site at www.fdncenter.org.

CD-ROMs

FC SEARCH: The Foundation Center's Database on CD-ROM, Version 7.0

The Foundation Center's comprehensive database of grantmakers and their associated grants can be accessed in this fully searchable CD-ROM format. *FC Search* contains the Center's entire universe of 72,000+ grantmaker records, including all known active foundations and corporate giving programs in the United States. It also includes over 313,000 newly reported grants from the largest foundations and the names of more than 324,000 trustees, officers, and donors which can be quickly linked to their foundation affiliations. Users can also link from *FC Search* to the Web sites of 3,000+ grantmakers and close to 1,900 corporations.

Grantseekers and other researchers may select multiple criteria and create customized prospect lists which can be printed or saved. Basic or Advanced search modes and special search options enable users to make searches as broad or as specific as required. Up to 21 different criteria may be selected:

- grantmaker name
- grantmaker type
- grantmaker city
- grantmaker state
- geographic focus
- fields of interest
- types of support
- total assets
- total giving
- trustees, officers, and donors
- establishment date
- corporate name
- corporate location
- recipient name
- recipient city
- recipient state
- recipient type
- subject
- grant amount
- year grant authorized
- text search field

FC Search is a sophisticated fundraising research tool, but it is also user-friendly. It has been developed with both the novice and experienced researcher in mind. Assistance is available through Online Help, a *User Manual* that accompanies *FC Search*, as well as through a free User Hotline.

FC Search, *Version 7.0, March 2003 (prices include fall 2003 Update disk plus one* User Manual).
Standalone (single user) version: $1,195
*Local Area Network (2–8 users in one building) version: $1,895**
Additional copies of User Manual: *$19.95*
New editions of FC Search *are released each spring.*
Larger local area network versions, site licenses, and wide area network versions are also available. For more information, call the* ***Electronic Product Support Line (Mon–Fri., 9 am–5 pm EST) 1-800-478-4661.*

THE FOUNDATION DIRECTORY ON CD-ROM, Version 4.0

Users can search for funding prospects from among the same set of 10,000 *Foundation Directory*-size foundations that appear in our print *Directory,* using the fast-speed search capabilities and high-powered features only available via CD-ROM!

The Foundation Directory on CD-ROM includes over 4,000 foundation records which list approximately 10 sample grants; features a searchable index of 62,000 trustees, officers, and donors; links to over 1,200 foundation Web sites and the Foundation Center's Web site; includes extensive Help file and printed user guide; features Boolean operators between fields; the ability to store search schemes and mark records for use in future sessions; a wide range of printing and saving options; alphabetical or total giving sort; and the ability to affix searchable notes to personalize grantmaker records; and allows users to create customized prospect lists by selecting from 12 search fields:

- grantmaker name
- grantmaker state
- grantmaker city
- fields of interest
- types of support
- trustees, officers, and donors
- geographic focus
- grantmaker type
- total giving
- total assets
- establishment date
- text search

The Foundation Directory on CD-ROM *(includes March 2003 release and Fall 2003 Update disk)*
Standalone (single-user) version: $295
Local Area Network version (2–8 users in one building): $595

THE FOUNDATION DIRECTORY 1 & 2 ON CD-ROM, Version 3.0

We've combined the authoritative data found in our two print classics, *The Foundation Directory* and *The Foundation Directory Part 2,* to bring you 20,000 of the nation's largest and mid-sized foundations in this searchable CD-ROM. Search for funding prospects by choosing from 12 search fields (see *Foundation Directory on CD-ROM* fields listed above). The CD-ROM includes links to close to 1,300 foundation Web sites, a list of sample grants in over 7,000 foundation records, and a searchable index of over 100,000 trustees, officers, and donors.

The Foundation Directory 1 & 2 on CD-ROM (includes March 2003 release and Fall 2003 Update disk)
Standalone (single-user) version: $495
Local Area Network version (2-8 users in one building): $795

THE FOUNDATION GRANTS INDEX ON CD-ROM, Version 4.0

The same data found in our classic print publication, *The Foundation Grants Index,* is available for the first time in a fast-speed CD-ROM format. Search our database of close to 125,000 recently awarded grants by the largest 1,000 funders to help you target foundations by the grants they have already awarded. Choose from twelve search fields:

- Recipient Name
- Recipient State
- Recipient City
- Recipient Type
- Grantmaker Name
- Grantmaker State
- Geographic Focus
- Subject
- Types of Support
- Grant Amount
- Year Authorized
- Text Search

The Foundation Grants Index on CD-ROM
December 2003/ Single User / ISBN 1-931923-74-4 /$165
Call 1-800-478-4661 for network versions.

GUIDE TO GREATER WASHINGTON D.C. GRANTMAKERS ON CD-ROM, Version 2.0

Compiled with the assistance of Washington Grantmakers, an organization with a unique local perspective on the dynamics of D.C. grantmaking, this CD-ROM covers over 1,500 grantmakers located in the D.C. region or that have an interest in D.C.-area nonprofits. It also contains close to 1,800 selected grants and a searchable index of 8,000+ trustees, officers, and donors and their grantmaker affiliations.

Users can generate prospect lists within seconds, using twelve search fields. Grantmaker portraits feature crucial information: address, phone number, contact name, financial data, giving limitations, and names of key officials. For the large foundations—those that give at least $50,000 in grants per year—the volume provides even more data, including application procedures and giving interest statements.

The CD-ROM links to more than 150 grantmaker Web sites; connects to a special Web page with resources of value to D.C. grantseekers; and offers flexible printing and saving options and the ability to mark records.

June 2002 / Single-user: 0-87954-996-3 / $75
Local Area Network: 1-931923-06-X / $125*

**A local area network is defined as 2-8 users within one building.*

GUIDE TO OHIO GRANTMAKERS ON CD-ROM

This new windows-compatible CD-ROM features profiles of over 3,800 foundations in Ohio, plus more than 300 funders outside the state that award grants in Ohio. This comprehensive searchable database provides current information on the foundations, corporate givers and public charities that make grants to Ohio-based nonprofits: crucial contact information, financial data, names of key officials, and in many cases, application procedures, giving interest statements, and a list of recent grants. *Guide to Ohio Grantmakers on CD-ROM* is produced in collaboration with the Ohio Grantmakers Forum and the Ohio Association of Nonprofit Organizations.

November 2003 / ISBN 1-931923-64-7 / $125

SYSTEM CONFIGURATIONS FOR CD-ROM PRODUCTS

- Windows-based PC
- Microsoft Windows™ ME, Windows™ 98, Windows™ 95, Windows™ 2000 or Windows™ NT Windows™ XP
- Pentium microprocessor
- 64MB memory

***Internet access and Netscape's Navigator or Communicator or Microsoft's Internet Explorer browser required to access grantmaker Web sites and Foundation Center Web site.*

ONLINE DATABASES

THE FOUNDATION DIRECTORY ONLINE SUBSCRIPTION SERVICE

The Foundation Directory Online Basic

Search for prospects from among the nation's largest 10,000 foundations and search the index of over 62,000 names of trustees, offices, and donors. Perform searches using up to eight search fields and print results that appear in the browser window.

Monthly subscriptions start at $19.95 per month
Annual subscriptions start at $195 per year

The Foundation Directory Online Plus

Plus service allows users to search the 10,000 largest foundations in the U.S. and the index of over 62,000 names of trustees, offices, and donors—plus over 250,000 grants awarded by the largest 1,200 foundations.

Monthly subscriptions start at $29.95 per month
Annual subscriptions start at $295 per year

The Foundation Directory Online Premium

Research and identify more foundation funding sources online with *The Foundation Directory Online Premium.* In addition to featuring 20,000 of the nation's large and mid-sized foundations and an index of over 100,000 names of trustees, officers, and donors—*Premium* service includes a searchable database of over 250,000 grants awarded by the top 1,200 U.S. foundations.

Monthly subscriptions start at $59.95 per month
Annual subscriptions start at $595 per year

The Foundation Directory Online Platinum

Search our entire universe of U.S. foundations, corporate giving programs, and grantmaking public charities—74,000+ funders in all—in our most comprehensive online subscription service. In addition to more funders, you'll get access to more in-depth data and an index of over 324,000 names of trustees, officers, and donors. Only *The Foundation Directory Online Platinum* offers extensive program details for 1,000+ leading foundations; detailed application guidelines for 6,000+ foundations; and sponsoring company information for corporate givers. This service also includes a searchable file of over 250,000 grants awarded by the top 1,200 funders.

Monthly subscriptions start at $149.95
Annual subscriptions start at $995

Foundation and grants data are updated every two weeks for the above databases. Monthly, annual, and multi-user subscription options are available.
Please visit www.fconline.fdncenter.org to subscribe.

Foundation Grants to Individuals Online

Foundation Grants to Individuals Online features more than 5,600 foundation funding sources for individual grant-seekers in education, research, arts and culture, or for special needs. Updated quarterly, users may choose from up to nine different search fields to discover prospective funders. Foundation records include current, authoritative data on the funder, including the name, address, and contact information; fields of interest; types of support; application information; and descriptions of funding opportunities for individual grantseekers.

One-month subscription: $9.95
Three-month subscription: $26.95
Annual subscription: $99.95

DIALOG

The Center's grantmaker and grants databases are also available online through The Dialog Corporation. For further information, contact The Dialog Corporation at 1-800-334-2564.

DIALOG User Manual and Thesaurus, Revised Edition

The *User Manual and Thesaurus* is a comprehensive guide that will help you retrieve essential fundraising facts quickly and easily. It will greatly facilitate your foundation and corporate giving research through our databases, offered online through Dialog.

November 1995 / ISBN 0-87954-595-X / $50

FOUNDATION CENTER'S WEB SITE www.fdncenter.org

Helping grantseekers succeed, helping grantmakers make a difference

The Foundation Center's Web site (www. fdncenter.org) is the premier online source of fundraising information. Updated and expanded on a daily basis, the Center's site provides grantseekers, grantmakers, researchers, journalists, and the general public with easy access to a range of valuable resources, among them:

- Personalization at the Center's Web site allows registered users to receive content tailored to their fundraising and research interests at key areas of the site, including the home page, *Philanthropy News Digest,* and the Marketplace.

- A Grantmaker Web Sites area provides annotated links to more than 2,000 grantmaker sites that can be searched by subject or geographic key words.
- Foundation Finder, our free foundation look-up tool, includes foundation contact information and brief background data, such as type of foundation, assets, total giving, and EIN, as well as links to 990-PFs (IRS tax filings).
- *Philanthropy News Digest,* features current philanthropy-related articles abstracted from major media outlets, interviews, original content, and the "PND Talk" message board. PND is also available as a weekly listserv.
- *The Literature of the Nonprofit Sector Online,* a searchable bibliographical database, includes 21,300+ entries of works on the field of philanthropy, over 14,000 of which are abstracted.
- Our Online Library features comprehensive answers to FAQs, an online librarian to field questions about grantseeking and the Foundation Center, annotated links to useful nonprofit resources, and an online orientation to the grantseeking process.
- Our popular Virtual Classroom allows visitors to link to a Proposal Writing Short Course (in English and Spanish); Establishing a Nonprofit Organization; Demystifying the 990-PF; and more.
- Information about Center-sponsored orientations, training programs, and seminars can be found on our Library homepage and in the marketplace.
- The locations of our 200+ Cooperating Collections nationwide, and the activities and resources at our five main libraries.
- A new "For Individual Grantseekers" area introduces individuals to the grantseeking process and provides tools and resources to help individuals get started.
- A special section, "For Grantmakers," offers funders the opportunity to help get the word out about their work, answers frequently asked questions, and informs grantmakers on recent developments in the field and how the Center assists grantees and applicants.
- The "For the Media" area provides journalists with current information on key developments in private philanthropy in the U.S.
- Sector Search is a search tool that continuously crawls the Web sites of thousands of private, corporate, community foundations, grantmaking public charities, and nonprofit organizations, and provides relevant, accurate search results. Search by organization type, subject, or individual's name.

All this and more is available at our Web site. The Center's publications and electronic resources can be ordered at the site's marketplace. Visit our Web site often for information on new products and services.

FOUNDATION CENTER COOPERATING COLLECTIONS

FREE FUNDING INFORMATION CENTERS

The Foundation Center is an independent national service organization established by foundations to provide an authoritative source of information on foundation and corporate giving. The New York, Washington D.C., Atlanta, Cleveland, and San Francisco reference collections operated by the Foundation Center offer a wide variety of services and comprehensive resources on foundations and grants. Cooperating Collections are libraries, community foundations, and other nonprofit agencies that make accessible a collection of Foundation Center print and electronic publications, as well as a variety of supplementary materials and education programs in areas useful to grantseekers. The collection includes:

FC SEARCH: THE FOUNDATION CENTER'S DATABASE ON CD-ROM
THE FOUNDATION DIRECTORY 1 AND 2, AND SUPPLEMENT
FOUNDATION FUNDAMENTALS
THE FOUNDATION 1000
FOUNDATIONS TODAY SERIES
FOUNDATION GRANTS TO INDIVIDUALS
THE FOUNDATION CENTER'S GUIDE TO GRANTSEEKING ON THE WEB
THE FOUNDATION CENTER'S GUIDE TO PROPOSAL WRITING
GUIDE TO U.S. FOUNDATIONS, THEIR TRUSTEES, OFFICERS, AND DONORS
NATIONAL DIRECTORY OF CORPORATE GIVING
NATIONAL GUIDE TO FUNDING IN. . . . (SERIES)

All five Foundation Center libraries and most Cooperating Collections have *FC: Search: The Foundation Center's Database on CD-ROM* available for public use and all provide Internet access. Increasingly, those seeking information on fundraising and nonprofit management are referring to our Web site (http://www.fdncenter.org) for a wealth of data and advice on grantseeking, including links to foundation IRS information returns (990-PFs). Because the Cooperating Collections vary in their hours, it is recommended that you call the collection in advance of a visit. To check on new locations or current holdings, call toll-free 1-800-424-9836, or visit our site at http://fdncenter.org/collections/index.html.

REFERENCE COLLECTIONS OPERATED BY THE FOUNDATION CENTER

THE FOUNDATION CENTER
2nd Floor
79 Fifth Ave.
New York, NY 10003
(212) 620-4230

THE FOUNDATION CENTER
312 Sutter St., Suite 606
San Francisco, CA 94108
(415) 397-0902

THE FOUNDATION CENTER
1627 K St., NW, 3rd floor
Washington, DC 20006
(202) 331-1400

THE FOUNDATION CENTER
Kent H. Smith Library
1422 Euclid Ave., Suite 1600
Cleveland, OH 44115
(216) 861-1933

THE FOUNDATION CENTER
Suite 150, Grand Lobby
Hurt Bldg., 50 Hurt Plaza
Atlanta, GA 30303
(404) 880-0094

ALABAMA

BIRMINGHAM PUBLIC LIBRARY
Government Documents
2100 Park Place
Birmingham 35203
(205) 226-3620

HUNTSVILLE PUBLIC LIBRARY
915 Monroe St.
Huntsville 35801
(256) 532-5940

MOBILE PUBLIC LIBRARY
West Regional Library
5555 Grelot Road
Mobile 36609-3643
(251) 340-8555

AUBURN UNIVERSITY AT MONTGOMERY LIBRARY
74-40 East Dr.
Montgomery 36117-3596
(334) 244-3200

ALASKA

CONSORTIUM LIBRARY
3211 Providence Dr.
Anchorage 99508
(907) 786-1848

JUNEAU PUBLIC LIBRARY
292 Marine Way
Juneau 99801
(907) 586-5267

ARIZONA

FLAGSTAFF CITY-COCONINO COUNTY PUBLIC LIBRARY
300 W. Aspen Ave.
Flagstaff 86001
(928) 779-7670

PHOENIX PUBLIC LIBRARY
Information Services Department
1221 N. Central Ave.
Phoenix 85004
(602) 262-4636

TUCSON PIMA PUBLIC LIBRARY
101 N. Stone Ave.
Tucson 87501
(520) 791-4393

ARKANSAS

UNIVERSITY OF ARKANSAS—FT. SMITH BOREHAM LIBRARY
5210 Grand Ave.
P.O. Box 3649
Ft. Smith 72913
(479) 788-7204

CENTRAL ARKANSAS LIBRARY SYSTEM
100 Rock St.
Little Rock 72201
(501) 918-3000

CALIFORNIA

KERN COUNTY LIBRARY
Beale Memorial Library
701 Truxtun Ave.
Bakersfield 93301
(661) 868-0755

HUMBOLDT AREA FOUNDATION
Rooney Resource Center
373 Indianola
Bayside 95524
(707) 442-2993

VENTURA COUNTY COMMUNITY FOUNDATION
Resource Center for Nonprofit Organizations
1317 Del Norte Rd., Suite 150
Camarillo 93010
(805) 988-0196

FRESNO REGIONAL FOUNDATION
Nonprofit Advancement Center
3425 N. First St., Suite 101
Fresno 93726
(559) 226-0216

CENTER FOR NONPROFIT MANAGEMENT IN SOUTHERN CALIFORNIA
Nonprofit Resource Library
606 South Olive St. #2450
Los Angeles 90014
(213) 623-7080

LOS ANGELES PUBLIC LIBRARY
Mid-Valley Regional Branch Library
16244 Nordhoff St.
North Hills 91343
(818) 895-3654

PHILANTHROPY RESOURCE CENTER
Flintridge Foundation
1040 Lincoln Ave, Suite 100
Pasadena 91103
(626) 449-0839

CENTER FOR NONPROFIT RESOURCES
Shasta Regional Community Foundation's Center
Bldg. C, Suite A
2280 Benton Dr.
Redding 96003
(530) 244-1219

RICHMOND PUBLIC LIBRARY
325 Civic Center Plaza
Richmond 94804
(510) 620-6561

RIVERSIDE CITY PUBLIC LIBRARY
3581 Mission Inn Ave.
Riverside 92501
(909) 826-5201

NONPROFIT RESOURCE CENTER
Sacramento Public Library
328 I St., 2nd Floor
Sacramento 95814
(916) 264-2772

SAN DIEGO FOUNDATION
Funding Information Center
1420 Kettner Blvd., Suite 500
San Diego 92101
(619) 235-2300

COMPASSPOINT NONPROFIT SERVICES
Nonprofit Development Library
1922 The Alameda, Suite 212
San Jose 95126
(408) 248-9505

PENINSULA COMMUNITY FOUNDATION
Peninsula Nonprofit Center
1700 S. El Camino Real, #R201
San Mateo 94402-3049
(650) 358-9392

LOS ANGELES PUBLIC LIBRARY
San Pedro Regional Branch
931 S. Gaffey St.
San Pedro 90731
(310) 548-7779

VOLUNTEER CENTER OF GREATER ORANGE COUNTY
Nonprofit Resource Center
1901 E. 4th St., Suite 100
Santa Ana 92705
(714) 953-5757

SANTA BARBARA PUBLIC LIBRARY
40 E. Anapamu St.
Santa Barbara 93101-1019
(805) 962-7653

SANTA MONICA PUBLIC LIBRARY
1324 Fifth St.
Santa Monica 90401
(310) 458-8600

SONOMA COUNTY LIBRARY
3rd & E Sts.
Santa Rosa 95404
(707) 545-0831

SEASIDE BRANCH LIBRARY
550 Harcourt Ave.
Seaside 93955
(831) 899-8131

SIERRA NONPROFIT SUPPORT CENTER
39 No. Washington St. #F
Sonora 95370
(209) 533-1093

COLORADO

PENROSE LIBRARY
20 N. Cascade Ave.
Colorado Springs 80903
(719) 531-6333

DENVER PUBLIC LIBRARY
10 W. 14th Ave. Pkwy.
Denver 80204
(720) 865-1111

CONNECTICUT

DANBURY PUBLIC LIBRARY
170 Main St.
Danbury 06810
(203) 797-4527

GREENWICH LIBRARY
101 W. Putnam Ave.
Greenwich 06830
(203) 622-7900

HARTFORD PUBLIC LIBRARY
500 Main St.
Hartford 06103
(860) 695-6295

NEW HAVEN FREE PUBLIC LIBRARY
133 Elm St.
New Haven 06510-2057
(203) 946-7431

DELAWARE

UNIVERSITY OF DELAWARE
Hugh Morris Library
181 South College Ave.
Newark 19717-5267
(302) 831-2432

FLORIDA

VOLUSIA COUNTY LIBRARY CENTER
City Island
105 E. Magnolia Ave.
Daytona Beach 32114-4484
(386) 257-6036

NOVA SOUTHEASTERN UNIVERSITY
Einstein Library
3301 College Ave.
Fort Lauderdale 33313
(954) 262-4513

INDIAN RIVER COMMUNITY COLLEGE
Learning Resources Center
3209 Virginia Ave.
Fort Pierce 34981-5596
(561) 462-4757

JACKSONVILLE PUBLIC LIBRARIES
Grants Resource Center
122 N. Ocean St.
Jacksonville 32202
(904) 630-2665

MIAMI-DADE PUBLIC LIBRARY
Humanities/Social Science
101 W. Flagler St.
Miami 33130
(305) 375-5575

ORANGE COUNTY LIBRARY SYSTEM
Social Sciences Department
101 E. Central Blvd.
Orlando 32801
(407) 425-4694

SELBY PUBLIC LIBRARY
Reference
1331 1st St.
Sarasota 34236
(941) 861-1100

STATE LIBRARY OF FLORIDA
R.A. Gray Building
Tallahassee 32399-0250
(850) 245-6600

HILLSBOROUGH COUNTY PUBLIC LIBRARY COOPERATIVE
John F. Germany Public Library
900 N. Ashley Dr.
Tampa 33602
(813) 273-3652

COMMUNITY FOUNDATION OF PALM BEACH & MARTIN COUNTIES
324 Datura St., Suite 340
West Palm Beach 33401
(561) 659-6800

GEORGIA

HALL COUNTY LIBRARY SYSTEM
127 Main Street NW
Gainesville 30501
(770) 532-3311

UNITED WAY OF CENTRAL GEORGIA
Community Resource Center
277 Martin Luther King Jr. Blvd., Suite 301
Macon 31201-0513
(478) 745-4732

THOMAS COUNTY PUBLIC LIBRARY
201 N. Madison St.
Thomasville 31792
(912) 225-5252

HAWAII

UNIVERSITY OF HAWAII
Hamilton Library
2550 The Mall
Honolulu 96822
(808) 956-7214

IDAHO

BOISE PUBLIC LIBRARY
Funding Information Center
715 S. Capitol Blvd.
Boise 83702
(208) 384-4024

CALDWELL PUBLIC LIBRARY
1010 Dearborn St.
Caldwell 83605
(208) 459-3242

ILLINOIS

DONORS FORUM OF CHICAGO
208 S. LaSalle, Suite 735
Chicago 60604
(312) 578-0175

EVANSTON PUBLIC LIBRARY
1703 Orrington Ave.
Evanston 60201
(847) 866-0300

ROCK ISLAND PUBLIC LIBRARY
401 19th St.
Rock Island 61201-8143
(309) 732-7323

UNIVERSITY OF ILLINOIS AT SPRINGFIELD, LIB 236
Brookens Library
Springfield 62794-9243
(217) 206-6633

INDIANA

EVANSVILLE-VANDERBURGH PUBLIC LIBRARY
22 SE 5th St.
Evansville 47708
(812) 428-8200

ALLEN COUNTY PUBLIC LIBRARY
900 Webster St.
Ft. Wayne 36802
(260) 421-1238

INDIANAPOLIS-MARION COUNTY PUBLIC LIBRARY
202 North Alabama
Indianapolis 46206
(317) 269-1700

VIGO COUNTY PUBLIC LIBRARY
1 Library Square
Terre Haute 47807
(812) 232-1113

IOWA

CEDAR RAPIDS PUBLIC LIBRARY
500 1st St., SE
Cedar Rapids 52401
(319) 398-5123

SOUTHWESTERN COMMUNITY COLLEGE
Learning Resource Center
1501 W. Townline Rd.
Creston 50801
(515) 782-7081

PUBLIC LIBRARY OF DES MOINES
100 Locust
Des Moines 50309-1791
(515) 283-4152

SIOUX CITY PUBLIC LIBRARY
Siouxland Funding Research Center
529 Pierce St.
Sioux City 51101-1203
(712) 255-2933

KANSAS

PIONEER MEMORIAL LIBRARY
375 West 4th St.
Colby 67701
(785) 462-4470

DODGE CITY PUBLIC LIBRARY
1001 2nd Ave.
Dodge City 67801
(316) 225-0248

KEARNY COUNTY LIBRARY
101 East Prairie
Lakin 67860
(620) 355-6674

SALINA PUBLIC LIBRARY
301 West Elm
Salina 67401
(785) 825-4624

TOPEKA AND SHAWNEE COUNTY PUBLIC LIBRARY
1515 SW 10th Ave.
Topeka 66604
(785) 580-4400

WICHITA PUBLIC LIBRARY
223 S. Main St.
Wichita 67202
(316) 261-8500

KENTUCKY

WESTERN KENTUCKY UNIVERSITY
Helm-Cravens Library
110 Helm Library
Bowling Green 42101-3576
(270) 745-6163

LEXINGTON PUBLIC LIBRARY
140 E. Main St.
Lexington 40507-1376
(859) 231-5520

LOUISVILLE FREE PUBLIC LIBRARY
301 York St.
Louisville 40203
(502) 574-1617

LOUISIANA

EAST BATON ROUGE PARISH LIBRARY
Centroplex Branch Grants Collection
120 St. Louis St.
Baton Rouge 70802
(225) 389-4967

BEAUREGARD PARISH LIBRARY
205 S. Washington Ave.
De Ridder 70634
(337) 463-6217

OUACHITA PARISH PUBLIC LIBRARY
1800 Stubbs Ave.
Monroe 71201
(318) 327-1490

NEW ORLEANS PUBLIC LIBRARY
Business & Science Division
219 Loyola Ave.
New Orleans 70112
(504) 596-2580

SHREVE MEMORIAL LIBRARY
424 Texas St.
Shreveport 71120-1523
(318) 226-5894

MAINE

UNIVERSITY OF SOUTHERN MAINE LIBRARY
Maine Philanthropy Center
314 Forrest Ave.
Portland 04104-9301
(207) 780-5029

MARYLAND

ENOCH PRATT FREE LIBRARY
Social Science & History Dept.
400 Cathedral St.
Baltimore 21201
(410) 396-5320

MASSACHUSETTS

ASSOCIATED GRANT MAKERS OF MASSACHUSETTS
55 Court St.
Room 520
Boston 02108
(617) 426-2606

BOSTON PUBLIC LIBRARY
Soc. Sci. Reference
700 Boylston St.
Boston 02116
(617) 536-5400

WESTERN MASSACHUSETTS FUNDING RESOURCE CENTER
65 Elliot St.
Springfield 01101-1730
(413) 452-0697

WORCESTER PUBLIC LIBRARY
Grants Resource Center
3 Salem Sq.
Worcester 01608
(508) 799-1654

MICHIGAN

ALPENA COUNTY LIBRARY
211 N. 1st St.
Alpena 49707
(989) 356-6188

UNIVERSITY OF MICHIGAN-ANN ARBOR
Graduate Library
Reference & Research Services Department
Ann Arbor 48109-1205
(734) 763-1539

WILLARD PUBLIC LIBRARY
Nonprofit & Funding Resource Collections
7 W. Van Buren St.
Battle Creek 49017
(616) 968-8166

HENRY FORD CENTENNIAL LIBRARY
16301 Michigan Ave.
Dearborn 48126
(313) 943-2330

WAYNE STATE UNIVERSITY
134 Purdy/Kresge Library
Detroit 48202
(313) 577-6424

MICHIGAN STATE UNIVERSITY LIBRARIES
Main Library
Funding Center
100 Library
East Lansing 48824-1049
(517) 353-8700

FARMINGTON COMMUNITY LIBRARY
32737 W. 12 Mile Rd.
Farmington Hills 48334
(248) 553-0300

UNIVERSITY OF MICHIGAN—FLINT
Frances Willson Thompson Library
Flint 48502-1950
(810) 762-3413

GRAND RAPIDS PUBLIC LIBRARY
1100 Hynes Ave.
Grand Rapids 49507
(616) 988-5400

MICHIGAN TECHNOLOGICAL UNIVERSITY
Van Pelt Library
1400 Townsend Dr.
Houghton 49931-1295
(906) 487-2507

NORTHWESTERN MICHIGAN COLLEGE
Mark & Helen Osterlin Library
1701 E. Front St.
Traverse City 49686
(231) 995-1060

MINNESOTA

BRAINERD PUBLIC LIBRARY
416 South Fifth St.
Brainerd 56401
(218) 829-5574

DULUTH PUBLIC LIBRARY
520 W. Superior St.
Duluth 55802
(218) 723-3802

SOUTHWEST STATE UNIVERSITY
University Library
N. Hwy. 23
Marshall 56253
(507) 537-6108

MINNEAPOLIS PUBLIC LIBRARY
250 Marquette Ave.
Minneapolis 55401
(612) 630-6000

ROCHESTER PUBLIC LIBRARY
101 2nd St. SE
Rochester 55904-3777
(507) 285-8002

ST. PAUL PUBLIC LIBRARY
90 W. Fourth St.
St. Paul 55102
(651) 266-7000

MISSISSIPPI

LIBRARY OF HATTIESBURG, PETAL AND FORREST COUNTY
329 Hardy St.
Hattiesburg 39401-3824
(601) 582-4461

JACKSON/HINDS LIBRARY SYSTEM
300 N. State St.
Jackson 39201
(601) 968-5803

MISSOURI

COUNCIL ON PHILANTHROPY
University of Missouri—Kansas City
Center for Business Innovation
4747 Troost, #207
Kansas City 64171-0813
(816) 235-1176

KANSAS CITY PUBLIC LIBRARY
311 E. 12th St.
Kansas City 64106
(816) 701-3541

ST. LOUIS PUBLIC LIBRARY
1301 Olive St.
St. Louis 63103
(314) 241-2288

SPRINGFIELD-GREENE COUNTY LIBRARY
The Library Center
4653 S. Campbell
Springfield 65810
(417) 874-8110

MONTANA

MONTANA STATE UNIVERSITY—BILLINGS
Library—Special Collections
1500 N. 30th St.
Billings 59101-0245
(406) 657-1687

BOZEMAN PUBLIC LIBRARY
220 E. Lamme
Bozeman 59715
(406) 582-2402

MONTANA STATE LIBRARY
Library Services
1515 E. 6th Ave.
Helena 59620-1800
(406) 444-3115

LINCOLN COUNTY PUBLIC LIBRARIES
Libby Public Library
220 West 6th St.
Libby 59923
(406) 293-2778

UNIVERSITY OF MONTANA
Mansfield Library
32 Campus Dr. #9936
Missoula 59812-9936
(406) 243-6800

NEBRASKA

UNIVERSITY OF NEBRASKA—LINCOLN
225C Love Library
14th & R Sts.
Lincoln 68588-2848
(402) 472-2848

OMAHA PUBLIC LIBRARY
W. Dale Clark Library
Social Sciences Dept.
215 S. 15th St.
Omaha 68102
(402) 444-4826

NEVADA

GREAT BASIN COLLEGE LIBRARY
1500 College Parkway
Elko 89801
(775) 753-2222

CLARK COUNTY LIBRARY
1401 E. Flamingo
Las Vegas 89119
(702) 507-3400

WASHOE COUNTY LIBRARY
301 S. Center St.
Reno 89501
(775) 327-8300

NEW HAMPSHIRE

CONCORD PUBLIC LIBRARY
45 Green St.
Concord 03301
(603) 225-8670

PLYMOUTH STATE COLLEGE
Herbert H. Lamson Library
Plymouth 03264
(603) 535-2258

NEW JERSEY

CUMBERLAND COUNTY LIBRARY
800 E. Commerce St.
Bridgeton 08302
(856) 453-2210

FREE PUBLIC LIBRARY OF ELIZABETH
11 S. Broad St.
Elizabeth 07202
(908) 354-6060

NEWARK ENTERPRISE COMMUNITY RESOURCE DEVELOPMENT CENTER
303-309 Washington St., 5th floor
Newark 07102
(973) 624-8300

COUNTY COLLEGE OF MORRIS
Learning Resource Center
214 Center Grove Rd.
Randolph 07869
(973) 328-5296

NEW JERSEY STATE LIBRARY
185 W. State St.
Trenton 08625-0520
(609) 292-6220

NEW MEXICO

ALBUQUERQUE/BERNALILLO COUNTY LIBRARY SYSTEM
501 Copper Avenue NW
Albuquerque 87102
(505) 768-5141

JEMEZ PUEBLO COMMUNITY LIBRARY
020 Mission Road
Jemez Pueblo 87024
(505) 834-9171

NEW MEXICO STATE LIBRARY
Information Services
1209 Camino Carlos Rey
Santa Fe 87507
(505) 476-9702

NEW YORK

NEW YORK STATE LIBRARY
Humanities Reference
Cultural Education Center, 6th Fl.
Empire State Plaza
Albany 12230
(518) 474-5355

BROOKLYN PUBLIC LIBRARY
Society, Science and Technology Division
Grand Army Plaza
Brooklyn 11238
(718) 230-2122

BUFFALO & ERIE COUNTY PUBLIC LIBRARY
Business, Science & Technology Dept.
1 Lafayette Square
Buffalo 14203-1887
(716) 858-7097

HUNTINGTON PUBLIC LIBRARY
338 Main St.
Huntington 11743
(631) 427-5165

QUEENS BOROUGH PUBLIC LIBRARY
Social Sciences Division
89-11 Merrick Blvd.
Jamaica 11432
(718) 990-0700

LEVITTOWN PUBLIC LIBRARY
1 Bluegrass Ln.
Levittown 11756
(516) 731-5728

ADRIANCE MEMORIAL LIBRARY
Special Services Department
93 Market St.
Poughkeepsie 12601
(914) 485-3445

THE RIVERHEAD FREE LIBRARY
330 Court St.
Riverhead 11901
(631) 727-3228

ROCHESTER PUBLIC LIBRARY
Social Sciences
115 South Ave.
Rochester 14604
(585) 428-8120

ONONDAGA COUNTY PUBLIC LIBRARY
447 S. Salina St.
Syracuse 13202-2494
(315) 435-1900

UTICA PUBLIC LIBRARY
303 Genesee St.
Utica 13501
(315) 735-2279

WHITE PLAINS PUBLIC LIBRARY
100 Martine Ave.
White Plains 10601
(914) 422-1480

YONKERS PUBLIC LIBRARY
Riverfront Library
One Larkin Center
Yonkers 10701
(914) 337-1500

NORTH CAROLINA

PACK MEMORIAL LIBRARY
Community Foundation of Western North Carolina
67 Haywood St.
Asheville 28801
(828) 254-4960

THE DUKE ENDOWMENT
100 N. Tryon St., Suite 3500
Charlotte 28202-4012
(704) 376-0291

DURHAM COUNTY PUBLIC LIBRARY
300 N. Roxboro St.
Durham 27702
(919) 560-0100

FORSYTH COUNTY PUBLIC LIBRARY
660 W. 5th St.
Winston-Salem 27408
(336) 727-2264

NORTH DAKOTA

BISMARCK PUBLIC LIBRARY
515 N. 5th St.
Bismarck 58501-4081
(701) 222-6410

FARGO PUBLIC LIBRARY
102 N. 3rd St.
Fargo 58102
(701) 241-1491

MINOT PUBLIC LIBRARY
516 Second Avenue SW
Minot 58701-3792
(701) 852-1045

OHIO

STARK COUNTY DISTRICT LIBRARY
715 Market Ave. N.
Canton 44702
(330) 452-0665

PUBLIC LIBRARY OF CINCINNATI & HAMILTON COUNTY
Grants Resource Center
800 Vine St.—Library Square
Cincinnati 45202-2071
(513) 369-6000

COLUMBUS METROPOLITAN LIBRARY
Business and Technology
96 S. Grant Ave.
Columbus 43215
(614) 645-2590

DAYTON METRO LIBRARY
Grants Information Center
215 E. Third St.
Dayton 45402
(937) 227-9500

MANSFIELD/RICHLAND COUNTY PUBLIC LIBRARY
43 W. 3rd St.
Mansfield 44902
(419) 521-3100

PORTSMOUTH PUBLIC LIBRARY
1220 Gallia St.
Portsmouth 45662
(740) 354-5688

TOLEDO–LUCAS COUNTY PUBLIC LIBRARY
325 Michigan St.
Toledo 43612
(419) 259-5209

PUBLIC LIBRARY OF YOUNGSTOWN & MAHONING COUNTY
305 Wick Ave.
Youngstown 44503
(330) 744-8636

OKLAHOMA

OKLAHOMA CITY UNIVERSITY
Dulaney Browne Library
2501 N. Blackwelder
Oklahoma City 73106
(405) 521-5822

TULSA CITY–COUNTY LIBRARY
400 Civic Center
Tulsa 74103
(918) 596-7977

OREGON

OREGON INSTITUTE OF TECHNOLOGY
Library
3201 Campus Dr.
Klamath Falls 97601-8801
(541) 885-1770

PACIFIC NON-PROFIT NETWORK
Southern Oregon University
1600 N. Riverside #1001
Medford 97501
(541) 552-8207

MULTNOMAH COUNTY LIBRARY
801 SW 10th Ave.
Portland 97205
(503) 988-5123

OREGON STATE LIBRARY
State Library Bldg.
250 Winter St. NE
Salem 97301-3950
(503) 378-4277

PENNSYLVANIA

NORTHAMPTON COMMUNITY COLLEGE
The Paul and Harriet Mack Library
3835 Green Pond Rd.
Bethlehem 18017
(610) 861-5360

ERIE COUNTY LIBRARY SYSTEM
160 E. Front St.
Erie 16507
(814) 451-6927

DAUPHIN COUNTY LIBRARY SYSTEM
East Shore Area Library
4501 Ethel St.
Harrisburg 17109
(717) 652-9380

LANCASTER COUNTY LIBRARY
125 N. Duke St.
Lancaster 17602
(717) 394-2651

FREE LIBRARY OF PHILADELPHIA
Regional Foundation Center
1901 Vine St.
Philadelphia 19103-1189
(215) 686-5423

CARNEGIE LIBRARY OF PITTSBURGH
Foundation Collection
414 Wood St.
Pittsburgh 15222
(412) 281-7143

POCONO NORTHEAST DEVELOPMENT FUND
James Pettinger Memorial Library
1151 Oak St.
Pittston 18640
(570) 655-5581

READING PUBLIC LIBRARY
100 S. 5th St.
Reading 19602
(610) 655-6355

JAMES V. BROWN LIBRARY
19 East Fourth Street
Williamsport 17701
(570) 326-0536

MARTIN LIBRARY
159 E. Market St.
York 17401
(717) 846-5300

RHODE ISLAND

PROVIDENCE PUBLIC LIBRARY
225 Washington St.
Providence 02906
(401) 455-8088

SOUTH CAROLINA

ANDERSON COUNTY LIBRARY
300 N. McDuffie St.
Anderson 29622
(864) 260-4500

CHARLESTON COUNTY LIBRARY
68 Calhoun St.
Charleston 29401
(843) 805-6930

SOUTH CAROLINA STATE LIBRARY
1500 Senate St.
Columbia 29211-1469
(803) 734-8666

COMMUNITY FOUNDATION OF GREATER GREENVILLE
27 Cleveland St., Suite 101
Greenville 29601
(864) 233-5925

SOUTH DAKOTA

SINTE GLESKA UNIVERSITY LIBRARY
Rosebud Sioux Reservation
Mission 57555-0107
(605) 856-2355

SOUTH DAKOTA STATE LIBRARY
800 Governors Dr.
Pierre 57501-2294
(605) 773-3131
(800) 592-1841 (SD residents)

DAKOTA STATE LIBRARY
Nonprofit Grants Assistance
2505 Career Ave.
Sioux Falls 57107
(605) 782-3089

SIOUXLAND LIBRARIES
201 N. Main Ave.
Sioux Falls 57104
(605) 367-8720

TENNESSEE

UNITED WAY OF GREATER CHATTANOOGA
Center for Nonprofits
406 Frazier Ave.
Chattanooga 37405
(423) 265-0514

KNOX COUNTY PUBLIC LIBRARY
500 W. Church Ave.
Knoxville 37902
(865) 215-8751

MEMPHIS & SHELBY COUNTY PUBLIC LIBRARY
3030 Poplar Ave.
Memphis 38111
(901) 415-2734

NASHVILLE PUBLIC LIBRARY
615 Church St.
Nashville 37219
(615) 862-5800

TEXAS

NONPROFIT RESOURCE CENTER
Funding Information Library
500 S. Chestnut, Suite 1634
Abilene 79604
(915) 677-8166

AMARILLO AREA FOUNDATION
Grants Center
801 S. Filmore, Suite 700
Amarillo 79101
(806) 376-4521

HOGG FOUNDATION FOR MENTAL HEALTH
Regional Foundation Library
3001 Lake Austin Blvd., Suite 400
Austin 78703
(512) 471-5041

BEAUMONT PUBLIC LIBRARY
801 Pearl St.
Beaumont 77704-3827
(409) 838-6606

CORPUS CHRISTI PUBLIC LIBRARY
Funding Information Center
805 Comanche St.
Reference Dept.
Corpus Christi 78401
(361) 880-7000

DALLAS PUBLIC LIBRARY
Urban Information
1515 Young St.
Dallas 75201
(214) 670-1487

SOUTHWEST BORDER NONPROFIT RESOURCE CENTER
1201 W. University Dr.
Edinburgh 78539-2999
(956) 384-5920

UNIVERSITY OF TEXAS AT EL PASO
Institute for Community-Based Teaching and Learning Community Non-profit Grant Library
500 W. University, Benedict Hall, Rm. 103
El Paso 79968-0547
(915) 747-7969

FUNDING INFORMATION CENTER OF FORT WORTH
329 S. Henderson St.
Ft. Worth 76104
(817) 334-0228

HOUSTON PUBLIC LIBRARY
Bibliographic Information Center
500 McKinney
Houston 77002
(832) 393-1313

NONPROFIT MANAGEMENT AND VOLUNTEER CENTER
Laredo Public Library
1120 E. Calton Rd.
Laredo 78041
(956) 795-2400

LONGVIEW PUBLIC LIBRARY
222 W. Cotton St.
Longview 75601
(903) 237-1350

LUBBOCK AREA FOUNDATION, INC.
1655 Main St., Suite 209
Lubbock 79401
(806) 762-8061

NONPROFIT RESOURCE CENTER OF TEXAS
7404 Hwy. 90 W.
San Antonio 78212-8270
(210) 227-4333

WACO-MCLENNAN COUNTY LIBRARY
1717 Austin Ave.
Waco 76701
(254) 750-5941

NONPROFIT MANAGEMENT CENTER OF WICHITA FALLS
2301 Kell Blvd., Suite 218
Wichita Falls 76308
(940) 322-4961

UTAH

SALT LAKE CITY PUBLIC LIBRARY
210 E. 400 S.
Salt Lake City 84111
(801) 524-8200

VERMONT

ILSLEY PUBLIC LIBRARY
75 Main St.
Middlebury 05753
(802) 388-4095

VERMONT DEPT. OF LIBRARIES
Reference & Law Info. Services
109 State St.
Montpelier 05609
(802) 828-3261

VIRGINIA

WASHINGTON COUNTY PUBLIC LIBRARY
205 Oak Hill St.
Abingdon 24210
(276) 676-6222

HAMPTON PUBLIC LIBRARY
4207 Victoria Blvd.
Hampton 23669
(757) 727-1314

RICHMOND PUBLIC LIBRARY
Business, Science & Technology Dept.
101 E. Franklin St.
Richmond 23219
(804) 646-7223

ROANOKE CITY PUBLIC LIBRARY SYSTEM
Main Library
706 S. Jefferson
Roanoke 24016
(540) 853-2471

WASHINGTON

MID-COLUMBIA LIBRARY
1620 South Union St.
Kennewick 99338
(509) 783-7878

KING COUNTY LIBRARY SYSTEM
Redmond Regional Library
15990 NE 85th
Redmond 98052
(425) 885-1861

SEATTLE PUBLIC LIBRARY
Fundraising Resource Center
800 Pike St.
Seattle 98101-3922
(206) 386-4645

SPOKANE PUBLIC LIBRARY
Funding Information Center
906 W. Main Ave.
Spokane 99201
(509) 444-5300

UNIVERSITY OF WASHINGTON TACOMA LIBRARY
1900 Commerce St.
Tacoma 98403-3100
(253) 692-4440

WENATCHEE VALLEY COLLEGE
John A. Brown Library
1300 Fifth St.
Wenatchee 98807
(509) 664-2520

WEST VIRGINIA

KANAWHA COUNTY PUBLIC LIBRARY
123 Capitol St.
Charleston 25301
(304) 343-4646

WISCONSIN

UNIVERSITY OF WISCONSIN–MADISON
Memorial Library, Grants Information Center
728 State St.
Madison 53706
(608) 262-3242

MARQUETTE UNIVERSITY MEMORIAL LIBRARY
Funding Information Center
1415 W. Wisconsin Ave.
Milwaukee 53201-3141
(414) 288-1515

UNIVERSITY OF WISCONSIN—STEVENS POINT
Library—Foundation Collection
900 Reserve St.
Stevens Point 54481-3897
(715) 346-2540

WYOMING

CASPER COLLEGE
Goodstein Foundation Library
125 College Dr.
Casper 82601
(307) 268-2269

LARAMIE COUNTY COMMUNITY COLLEGE
Instructional Resource Center
1400 E. College Dr.
Cheyenne 82007-3299
(307) 778-1206

CAMPBELL COUNTY PUBLIC LIBRARY
2101 4-J Rd.
Gillette 82718
(307) 687-0115

TETON COUNTY LIBRARY
125 Virginian Ln.
Jackson 83001
(307) 733-2164

SHERIDAN COUNTY FULMER PUBLIC LIBRARY
335 West Alger St.
Sheridan 82801
(307) 674-8585

PUERTO RICO

UNIVERSIDAD DEL SAGRADO CORAZON
M.M.T. Guevara Library
Santurce 00914
(787) 728-1515

Participants in the Foundation Center's Cooperating Collections network are libraries or nonprofit information centers that provide fundraising information and other funding-related technical assistance in their communities. Cooperating Collections agree to provide free public access to a basic collection of Foundation Center publications during a regular schedule of hours, offering free funding research guidance to all visitors. Many also provide a variety of services for local nonprofit organizations, using staff or volunteers to prepare special materials, organize workshops, or conduct orientations.

A key initiative of the Foundation Center is to reach under-resourced and underserved populations throughout the United States, who are in need of useful information and training to become successful grantseekers. One of the ways we intend to accomplish this goal is by designating new Cooperating Collection libraries in regions that have the ability to serve the nonprofit communities most in need of Foundation Center resources. We are seeking proposals from qualified institutions (i.e. public, academic or special libraries) that can help us carry out this important initiative. If you are interested in establishing a funding information library in your area, or would like to learn more about the program, please contact the Coordinator of Cooperating Collections: Erika Wittlieb, The Foundation Center, 79 Fifth Avenue, New York, NY 10003 (E-mail: eaw@fdncenter.org).

DESCRIPTIVE DIRECTORY

1

The Abell Foundation, Inc.
111 S. Calvert St., Ste. 2300
Baltimore, MD 21202-6174 (410) 547-1300
Contact: Robert C. Embry, Jr., Pres.
PRI Contact: Eileen M. O'Rourke, Treas.
FAX: (410) 539-6579; E-mail: abell@abell.org;
URL: http://www.abell.org

Incorporated in 1953 in MD. PRI-related activities began in 1991.
Donor(s): A.S. Abell Co., Harry C. Black,‡ Gary Black, Sr.‡
Grantmaker type: Independent foundation
General financial activity (yr. ended 12/31/01): Assets, $237,925,990 (M); expenditures, $15,654,395; qualifying distributions, $14,868,290; giving activities include $10,677,418 for 274 grants (high: $623,030; low: $109; average: $5,000–$50,000), $229,745 for employee matching gifts, $385,970 for 4 foundation-administered programs and $1,110,003 for 7 PRIs.
Cumulative PRI activity (through 12/31/01): The currently outstanding PRI portfolio includes 17 PRIs totaling $2,647,332 (high: $400,000; low: $63,300; average: $150,000). The typical outstanding PRI has a 6 month to 40 year term with an average term of 9 years and earns 0 to 9 percent interest with an average of 2.91 percent.
General purpose and activities: Supports education with emphasis on public education, including early childhood and elementary education, educational research, and minority education; community development, including workforce development; human services, including programs for child welfare and development and health and family services; the arts and culture; conservation; and the homeless, including hunger issues.
General fields of interest: Arts/cultural programs; education, research; early childhood education; child development, education; elementary school/education; natural resources conservation & protection; environment; health care; substance abuse, services; employment, services; food services; youth development, services; children & youth, services; family services; community development; leadership development; minorities; economically disadvantaged; homeless.
Program-related investment (PRI) activity: The foundation has made PRIs in the areas of the arts, housing, human services, health, education, environment, media, community development, recreation, and employment. PRIs have provided interim financing, supported facility acquisition and improvement, and funded equipment acquisition. The foundation has occasionally provided PRIs to intermediaries (e.g., loan funds and venture capital funds).
Limitations: Giving limited to MD, with emphasis on Baltimore. Generally no support for medical facilities. No grants to individuals, or for operating budgets, sponsorships, memberships, sustaining funds, or deficit financing. PRIs are limited to organizations in the state of MD. The foundation accepts applications for PRIs.
Publications: Annual report (including application guidelines), application guidelines, newsletter, occasional report, program policy statement.
PRI program information: Application form required. The foundation maintains a formal PRI program. The foundation makes PRIs on a frequent but not annual basis.
Officers and Trustees:* Gary Black, Jr.,* Chair.; Robert C. Embry, Jr.,* Pres.; Anne LaFarge Culman, V.P.; Frances Murray Keenan, V.P., Finance; Esthel M. Summerfield, Secy.; Eileen M. O'Rourke, Treas.; W. Shepherdson Abell, George L. Bunting, Jr., Robert Garrett, Sally J. Michel, Walter Sondheim, Jr.
Number of staff: 8 full-time professional; 6 part-time professional; 3 full-time support; 1 part-time support.
EIN: 526036106
PRI recipients:
1-1. Baltimore Childrens Museum, Baltimore, MD, $22,976. Program-related investment. 2001.
1-2. Baltimore Development Corporation, Baltimore, MD, $100,000. Program-related investment for expenses related to relocation of national headquarters of Phi Alpha Delta, law fraternity, to Baltimore City. 1999.
1-3. Baltimore School for the Arts Foundation, Baltimore, MD, $340,000. Program-related investment for purchase of building for expansion of School for the Arts, Baltimore City School. 2001.
1-4. Community Law Center, Baltimore, MD, $63,300. Program-related investment. 2001.
1-5. Comprehensive Housing Assistance, Baltimore, MD, $43,987. Program-related investment. 2001.
1-6. Comprehensive Housing Assistance, Baltimore, MD, $43,332. Program-related investment to promote acquisition and renovation of housing in targeted area of Baltimore. 2000.
1-7. Comprehensive Housing Assistance, Baltimore, MD, $30,000. Loan to promote acquisitions and renovations of housing in targeted area of Baltimore City. 1999.

1-8. Constellation Foundation, Baltimore, MD, $550,000. Loan for restoration efforts for Frigate, U.S.S. Constellation. 1999.

1-9. Downtown Partnership of Baltimore Foundation, Baltimore, MD, $100,000. Loan to support city-wide art exhibit. 2000.

1-10. Harford Land Trust, Churchville, MD, $365,000. Program-related investment for purchase of 30 plus acres as interim measure before resale and title transfer to Harford County for public recreational use. 2001.

1-11. Living Classrooms Foundation, Baltimore, MD, $448,614. Program-related investment toward establishment of Frederick Douglass-Isaac Myers Maritime Park, to provide education and job training for at-risk youth and create historic attraction for tourism in the inner harbor. 2000.

1-12. Maryland Center for Arts and Technology, Baltimore, MD, $131,005. Bridge loan to establish commercial credit company training program for welfare recipients. 2000.

1-13. Maryland Center for Arts and Technology, Baltimore, MD, $250,818. Bridge loan for establishment of commercial credit company training program for welfare recipients. 1999.

1-14. Neighborhood Revitalization Fund, Baltimore, MD, $24,740. Program-related investment. 2001.

1-15. Patterson Park Community Development Corporation, Baltimore, MD, $250,000. Program-related investment. 2001.

1-16. Patterson Park Community Development Corporation, Baltimore, MD, $296,200. Program-related investment to purchase and renovate houses in Patterson Park community. 2000.

1-17. Patterson Park Community Development Corporation, Baltimore, MD, $245,000. Loan for purchase and renovation of housing in Patterson Park community. 1999.

2
Alavi Foundation

500 5th Ave., 39th Fl.
New York, NY 10110-0397

Incorporated in 1973 in NY.
Grantmaker type: Independent foundation
General financial activity (yr. ended 03/31/02): Assets, $85,045,636 (M); gifts received, $12,981; expenditures, $2,984,752; qualifying distributions, $3,249,287; giving activities include $1,765,799 for 53 grants (high: $192,000; low: $100), $1,091,435 for 3 foundation-administered programs and $633,500 for 7 PRIs.
Cumulative PRI activity (through 03/31/02): Since beginning PRI activity, the foundation has made 13 PRIs totaling $1,475,720.
General purpose and activities: To help and assist (1) individuals and organizations that conduct academic research on Islam and (2) Muslim organizations that operate public houses of worship; also distributes educational, cultural and religious books, assists educational and religious centers and Sunday schools for teaching Middle Eastern languages, Islamic religion and culture.
General fields of interest: Arts/cultural programs; education; Islam.
Program-related investment (PRI) activity: The foundation makes PRIs, in the form of interest-free loans, to Islamic organizations and to Islamic schools.
Limitations: Applications not accepted. Giving on a national basis.
Officers and Directors:* Mohammad Geramian, Pres.; Alireza Ebrahimi,* Secy.; Abbas Mirakhor,* Treas.; Hoshang Ahmadi, Mehdi Hodjat, Mohammad Pirayandeh.
Number of staff: 3 full-time professional; 2 full-time support.
EIN: 237345978
PRI recipients:

2-1. Al Zahra Islamic Center, Antioch, TN, $25,000. Loan for purchase of property for Center. 2000.

2-2. Alrasool Center, Salt Lake City, UT, $50,000. Loan for repayment of mortgage on Religious Center. 2001.

2-3. American Moslem Foundation, Kent, WA, $100,000. Loan for construction of Center. 2000.

2-4. Aramgah Memorial Garden Foundation, Wynnewood, PA, $100,000. Loan for purchase of property for religious affairs. 2002.

2-5. Islamic Ahlulbait Annotation, Havertown, PA, $38,000. Loan for purchase of property for Center. 2000.

2-6. Islamic Center of Portland, Beaverton, OR, $70,000. Loan for repayment of mortgage on Religious Center. 2002.

2-7. Islamic Education Center of Tampa, Tampa, FL, $300,000. Loan for purchase and improvement of property for Center. 2000.

2-8. Islamic House of Wisdom, Dearborn Heights, MI, $150,000. Loan for construction of school. 2001.

2-9. Islamic House of Wisdom, Dearborn Heights, MI, $150,000. Loan for construction of school. 2000.

2-10. Islamic Institute of Ahl Albait, Manchester, CT, $51,500. Loan for purchase of property for Center. 2002.

2-11. Islamic Institute of New York, Woodside, NY, $207,360. Loan for purchase of property for religious affairs. 2001.

2-12. Islamic Shia Ithna Asheri Jamaat of Albany, Albany, NY, $25,000. Loan for construction of Center. 2000.

2-13. Jafaria Association of Connecticut, West Hartford, CT, $192,000. Loan for purchase of property for Center. 2002.

2-14. Masjid Al-Islam, DC, $30,000. Loan for construction of Center and School. 2002.

2-15. Pars Academy, Arlington, TX, $18,000. Loan for renovation of Islamic Center. 2001.

2-16. Shia Ithna Asheri Jamaat of Pennsylvania, Allentown, PA, $100,000. Loan for construction of Center. 2002.

2-17. Zainabia Nonprofit, Dunwoody, GA, $90,000. Loan for construstruciton of Center and School. 2002.

3

Judd S. Alexander Foundation, Inc.

500 3rd St., Ste. 320
P.O. Box 2137
Wausau, WI 54402-2137 (715) 845-4556
Contact: Gary W. Freels, Pres.
FAX: (715) 848-9336

Incorporated in 1973 in WI. PRI-related activities began in 1980.
Donor(s): Anne M. Alexander.‡
Grantmaker type: Independent foundation
General financial activity (yr. ended 06/30/02): Assets, $59,483,424 (M); expenditures, $3,277,839; qualifying distributions, $3,261,205; giving activities include $2,872,680 for 104 grants (high: $1,000,000; low: $150; average: $1,000–$50,000); no PRIs paid.
Cumulative PRI activity (through 06/30/02): The currently outstanding PRI portfolio includes 11 PRI totaling $1,210,810 (high: $250,000; low: $9,000; average: $100,000). The typical outstanding PRI has a 3- to 5-year term and earns 0 to 5 percent interest with an average of 4 percent.
General purpose and activities: Giving for the direct benefit of residents of Marathon County, WI; primary areas of interest include community development, social services, youth, educational programs, and economic development.
General fields of interest: Arts/cultural programs; early childhood education; elementary school/education; higher education; adult/continuing education; education; health care; crime/law enforcement; human services; children & youth, services; community development; economic development.
Program-related investment (PRI) activity: The foundation has made PRIs in the areas of education, the environment, economic development, human services, and the arts. PRIs have occasionally provided interim financing, capitalized loan funds, and supported facility improvement.
Types of PRI Support: Loans/promissory notes, interim financing, loan guarantees, capitalizing loan funds/other intermediaries.
Limitations: Giving limited to Marathon County, WI, or to organizations directly benefiting the residents of Marathon County. No grants to individuals, or for endowment funds, fellowships, research, publications, travel, or conferences, or private businesses. PRI applications not accepted.
PRI program information: The foundation does not maintain a formal PRI program. The foundation makes PRIs on a frequent but not annual basis.
Officers and Directors:* Stanley F. Staples, Jr.,* Chair.; Gary W. Freels,* Pres.; Richard D. Dudley,* V.P.; John F. Michler,* Secy.-Treas.; Dwight D. Davis, Harry N. Heinmann, Jr., Dir. Emeritus.
Number of staff: None.
EIN: 237323721
PRI recipients:

3-1. DAV Fixed Asset Account, Wausau, WI, $33,400. Program-related investment. 2000.
3-2. Marathon County Development Corporation (MCDEVCO), Wausau, WI, $450,000. Program-related investment. 2001.
3-3. Marathon County Development Corporation (MCDEVCO), Wausau, WI, $280,000. Program-related investment. 2000.
3-4. Marathon County Development Corporation (MCDEVCO), Wausau, WI, $200,000. Program-related investment. 1999.
3-5. Northland Lutheran Good News, Wausau, WI, $150,000. Program-related investment. 1999.
3-6. Northland Lutheran Good News, Wausau, WI, $40,000. Program-related investment. 1999.
3-7. Wausau and Marathon County Parks Foundation, Wausau, WI, $30,000. Program-related investment. 1999.

4

Consuelo Zobel Alger Foundation

110 N. Hotel St.
Honolulu, HI 96817
Contact: San Vuong, C.F.O.
FAx: (808) 532-3930; E-mail: info@consuelo.org; URL: http://www.consuelo.org

Established in 1988 in HI. PRI-related activities began in 1997.
Donor(s): Consuelo Zobel Alger.‡
Grantmaker type: Operating foundation
General financial activity (yr. ended 12/31/01): Assets, $130,135,323 (M); gifts received, $20,000; expenditures, $6,342,151; qualifying distributions, $4,309,293; giving activities include $129,400 for 5 grants (high: $84,400; low: $5,000; average: $5,000–$20,000), $2,259,855 for 4 foundation-administered programs and $45,205 for 2 PRIs.
Cumulative PRI activity (through 12/31/01): Since 1997, the foundation has made 2 PRIs totaling $511,924. The currently outstanding PRI portfolio includes 2 PRIs totaling $301,397 (high: $11,000; average: $2,000). The typical outstanding PRI has a 10- to 15-year term with an average term of 10 years and earns 0 to 5.5 percent interest with an average of 2 percent.
General purpose and activities: Giving to operate and support programs in Hawaii and the Philippines that improve the quality of life of disadvantages children, women and families.
General fields of interest: Youth, services; family services; women.
Program-related investment (PRI) activity: The foundation made PRIs in the form of non-interest bearing loans to Dumaguete City government for construction of low-income housing.
Types of PRI Support: Loans/promissory notes.
Limitations: Applications not accepted. Giving on an international basis, with emphasis on the Philippines; some giving also in HI. No grants to individuals. PRI applications not accepted.

Publications: Annual report.
PRI program information: The foundation does not maintain a formal PRI program. The foundation makes PRIs occasionally.
Officers: Jeffrey N. Watanabe, Chair.; Patti J. Lyons, C.E.O. and Pres.; Constance H. Lau, Secy.-Treas.
Directors: Rosemary B. Clarkin, Donald W. Layden, Jr., Alejandro Z. Padilla, Robert S. Tsushima.
Number of staff: 20 full-time professional; 15 full-time support.
EIN: 990266163

5
The Paul G. Allen Forest Protection Foundation
505 Fifth Ave. S., Ste. 900
Seattle, WA 98104
Contact: Jo Allen Patton, Exec. Dir.
E-mail: info@pgafoundations.com; URL: http://www.pgafoundations.com

Established in 1997 in WA.
Donor(s): Paul G. Allen.
Grantmaker type: Independent foundation
General financial activity (yr. ended 12/31/01): Assets, $5,116,004 (M); gifts received, $6,715,000; expenditures, $2,371,743; qualifying distributions, $2,596,101; giving activities include $2,371,101 for 7 grants (high: $1,500,000; low: $40,000; average: $40,000–$250,000) and $225,000 for 1 PRI.
Cumulative PRI activity (through 12/31/01): The currently outstanding PRI portfolio includes 1 PRI totaling $225,000.
General purpose and activities: To protect old growth forests and other special forest lands for the preservation of wildlife habitat and, where possible, for the provision of recreational use. Through its grantmaking the Paul G. Allen Forest Protection Foundation seeks to safeguard the beauty, natural resources, and recreational opportunities distinctive to the Pacific Northwest for present and future generations.
General fields of interest: Natural resources conservation & protection; environment.
Program-related investment (PRI) activity: The foundation has made PRIs for land conservation projects.
Types of PRI Support: Loans/promissory notes.
Limitations: Giving limited to the Pacific Northwest. No support for religious organizations for religious purposes. No grants to individuals or for annual fund drives or federated campaigns.
Publications: Biennial report (including application guidelines).
PRI program information: The foundation makes PRIs occasionally.
Officers and Directors:* Paul G. Allen,* Chair.; Bert E. Kolde, Pres.; Richard E. Leigh, Jr., V.P. and Secy.; Jo Allen Patton,* V.P. and Exec. Dir.; Nathaniel T. Brown, V.P.
Number of staff: 2 full-time professional; 1 full-time support.
EIN: 911764177
PRI recipients:
5-1. Cascade Land Conservancy, Seattle, WA, $225,000. Loan as additional draw to fund regional projects designed to maintain ecological integrity and land use protection. 2001.
5-2. Cascade Land Conservancy, Seattle, WA, $545,000. Loan for land purchases to fund Middle Fork Snoqualmie Valley Reservation Project involving maintaining ecological integrity and to protect low-impact recreational opportunities for citizens of the region. 2000.

6
Alpha & Omega Family Foundation
c/o Adler Management, L.L.C.
101 S. Phillips Ave., Ste. 102
Sioux Falls, SD 57104 (605) 357-8694

Established in 1994 in SD.
Grantmaker type: Independent foundation
General financial activity (yr. ended 12/31/01): Assets, $28,394,033 (M); expenditures, $1,594,340; qualifying distributions, $1,371,710; giving activities include $1,422,010 for 15 grants (high: $506,730; low: $5,000; average: $10,000–$100,000) and $5,408 for PRIs.
Cumulative PRI activity (through 12/31/01): The currently outstanding PRI portfolio includes 3 PRIs totaling $185,687.
General purpose and activities: Giving primarily for scholarships, athletic facilities, and for the building of a new chapel.
General fields of interest: Scholarships/financial aid; Alzheimer's disease research; religion.
Program-related investment (PRI) activity: The foundation has made PRIs to a private foundation.
Types of PRI Support: Loans/promissory notes.
Limitations: Applications not accepted. Giving primarily in MN. No grants to individuals.
Officers and Directors:* J.R. Mahoney,* Pres. and Treas.; John Agee,* V.P.; A.R. Goldman,* Secy.; John H. Harris.
EIN: 460434399
PRI recipients:
6-1. Calvert Social Investment Foundation, Bethesda, MD, $175,000. Loan for Project Enterprise, initiative to assist low-income entrpreneurs. 1999.

7
Alpha Research Foundation, Inc.
3 Newbold Ct.
Bethesda, MD 20817-2221
Contact: Carl R. Alving, Pres.
Application address: c/o B.R. Fierst, 200-A Monroe St., Ste. 100, Rockville, MD 20850, tel.: (301) 762-8872

Established in 1997 in MD.
Grantmaker type: Independent foundation

General financial activity (yr. ended 12/31/01): Assets, $1,251,918 (M); expenditures, $384,313; qualifying distributions, $371,779; giving activities include $368,517 for 2 grants (high: $349,000; low: $19,517); no PRIs paid.
General purpose and activities: Giving for biomedical research.
General fields of interest: Medical research.
Program-related investment (PRI) activity: The foundation made an interest free loan to a medical research laboratory to cover rent, cleaning, telephone, FAX and waste disposal expenses.
Types of PRI Support: Loans/promissory notes.
Limitations: Giving primarily in MD. No grants to individuals.
Officers: Carl R. Alving, M.D., Pres.; Barbara M. Alving, M.D., Secy.-Treas.
Director: Amy E. Alving, Ph.D.
EIN: 522035198
PRI recipients:
7-1. Blood Research Foundation, San Francisco, CA, $32,500. Interest-free loan to cover rent, cleaning, telephone, fax, mail and waste. 1999.

8
Alphawood Foundation

(Formerly WPWR-TV Channel 50 Foundation)
2451 N. Lincoln Ave., Ste. 205
Chicago, IL 60614 (773) 477-8984
Contact: Agnes Meneses, Grants Mgr.
E-mail: info@alphawoodfoundation.org

Established in 1991 in IL.
Donor(s): Fred Eychaner, Newsweb Corp.
Grantmaker type: Independent foundation
General financial activity (yr. ended 02/28/02): Assets, $95,978,425 (M); gifts received, $2,160,250; expenditures, $4,688,247; qualifying distributions, $3,974,829; giving activities include $3,948,723 for 265 grants (high: $300,000; low: $2,500; average: $5,000–$50,000); no PRIs paid.
General purpose and activities: Primary areas of interest include the arts, including arts education for children, and institutional advocacy, domestic violence intervention programs, and architecture and preservation.
General fields of interest: Arts education; historic preservation/historical societies; arts/cultural programs; domestic violence prevention.
Program-related investment (PRI) activity: The foundation has made loans to arts organizations.
Limitations: Giving primarily in the metropolitan Chicago, IL, area and northwestern IN. No support for religious or fraternal purposes, or for political campaigns. No grants to individuals, or for scholarships, underwriting or tables for events, or special projects or productions.
Publications: Application guidelines.
Officers and Directors:* Fred Eychaner,* Pres. and Treas.; Don Hilliker,* Secy.; Barbara Eychaner.
Number of staff: 2 full-time professional.
EIN: 363805338
PRI recipients:
8-1. Joffrey Ballet of Chicago, Chicago, IL, $385,000. Loan at 7 percent interest. 1999.

9
American Savings Foundation

(Formerly American Savings Charitable Foundation, Inc.)
P.O. Box 10
New Britain, CT 06050
URL: http://www.americansavingsfoundation.org/home.cfm

Established in 1995 in CT. PRI-related activities began in 2000.
Donor(s): American Financial Holdings, Inc., American Savings Bank.
Grantmaker type: Company-sponsored foundation
General financial activity (yr. ended 12/31/01): Assets, $65,329,071 (M); expenditures, $2,057,687; qualifying distributions, $1,862,421; giving activities include $1,012,785 for 186 grants (high: $74,555; low: $50; average: $500–$25,000), $321,848 for 234 grants to individuals (high: $3,500; low: $500) and $130,000 for 1 PRI.
Cumulative PRI activity (through 12/31/01): Since 2000, the foundation has made 1 PRI totaling $130,000. The currently outstanding PRI portfolio includes 1 PRI totaling $130,000.
General purpose and activities: Giving primarily for programs that support children, youth, and families in the areas of education, human services, and arts and culture; support also for college scholarships.
General fields of interest: Arts/cultural programs; youth development; human services; family services.
Program-related investment (PRI) activity: The foundation has made a PRI to a human service agency to establish a loan fund program.
Limitations: Giving primarily in 47 towns in central CT, and WA. PRI applications not accepted.
Publications: Application guidelines, informational brochure (including application guidelines).
PRI program information: The foundation does not maintain a formal PRI program. The foundation makes PRIs occasionally.
Officers and Directors:* Robert T. Kenney,* Chair. and C.E.O.; Sheri C. Pasqualoni,* V.P.; Richard J. Moore,* Secy.; Charles J. Boulier III,* Treas.; Charles S. Beach, Donald Davidson, Norman E.W. Erickson, Marie Gustin, Joseph T. Hughes, Harry N. Mazadoorian, Geddes Parsons, Stanley W. Shepard, William Solberg.
Number of staff: 3 full-time professional; 1 full-time support.
EIN: 061563163

10
The Anonymous Fund

c/o Joseph M. Bryan, Jr.
P.O. Box 9908
Greensboro, NC 27429

Established in 1995 in NC.
Grantmaker type: Independent foundation
General financial activity (yr. ended 12/31/01): Assets, $22,398,659 (M); expenditures, $2,099,490; qualifying distributions, $2,053,395; giving activities include $1,952,500 for 22 grants (high: $250,000; low: $12,500); no PRIs paid.
General purpose and activities: Giving primarily for the arts and human services.
General fields of interest: Arts/cultural programs; natural resources conservation & protection; human services; children, services; hospices; Roman Catholic agencies & churches.
Program-related investment (PRI) activity: The foundation has made a PRI, in the form of an interest-free loan, to a college for the purpose of improving school facilities and for a capital improvement program.
Limitations: Applications not accepted. Giving on a national basis, with emphasis on NC. No grants to individuals.
Officers: Joseph M. Bryan, Jr., Pres.; Ronald P. Johnson, Secy.
Trustee: William P. Massey.
EIN: 562152734
PRI recipients:
10-1. Guilford College, Greensboro, NC, $1,750,000. Interest-free loan to improve school facilities and for capital improvement program. 2000.

11
ArtPace, A Foundation for Contemporary Art/San Antonio

445 N. Main Ave.
San Antonio, TX 78205 (210) 212-4900
Contact: Marketing Assoc.
FAX: (210) 212-4990; E-mail: info@artpace.org;
URL: http://www.artpace.org

Established in 1993 in TX.
Donor(s): Linda M. Pace.
Grantmaker type: Operating foundation
General financial activity (yr. ended 12/31/01): Assets, $1,927,596 (M); gifts received, $725,354; expenditures, $1,695,250; qualifying distributions, $1,559,132; giving activities include $25,575 for 19 grants (high: $5,000; low: $40), $1,386,979 for 2 foundation-administered programs and $80,464 for PRIs.
Cumulative PRI activity (through 12/31/01): Since beginning PRI activity, the foundation has made PRIs totaling $95,663.
General purpose and activities: Giving for the arts and higher education.
General fields of interest: Visual arts; arts, artist's services; arts/cultural programs; international exchange, arts.
Program-related investment (PRI) activity: The foundation maintains two programs for resident artists to produce and display works of art. The foundation allows their premises and equipment to be used for this program and treats related expenses as PRIs.
Types of PRI Support: Charitable use assets.
Limitations: Applications not accepted. Giving primarily in San Antonio, TX.
Trustee: Linda M. Pace.
Number of staff: 10 full-time professional; 3 full-time support; 2 part-time support.
EIN: 742664002

12
The Atlantic Foundation of New York

125 Park Ave., 21st Fl.
New York, NY 10017-5581 (212) 922-0350
Contact: Cynthia R. Richards, V.P.
FAX: (212) 922-0360; URL: http://www.atlanticphilanthropies.org

Established in 1989 in NY.
Donor(s): Atlan Management Corp., Interpacific Holdings, Inc., General Atlantic Corp.
Grantmaker type: Independent foundation
General financial activity (yr. ended 12/31/01): Assets, $69,299,233 (M); expenditures, $36,269,148; qualifying distributions, $36,640,397; giving activities include $36,036,295 for 210 grants (high: $1,960,500; low: $5,000; average: $75,000–$200,000) and $500,000 for 1 PRI.
Cumulative PRI activity (through 12/31/01): The currently outstanding PRI portfolio includes 3 PRIs totaling $1,815,000.
General purpose and activities: Support primarily for education and international goodwill; support also for community improvement, and the aging.
General fields of interest: Education; children, services; aging, centers & services; international affairs, goodwill promotion; community development; aging.
Program-related investment (PRI) activity: The foundation has made interest-free loans to assist nonprofits and help them improve technology and communication abilities.
Types of PRI Support: Loans/promissory notes.
Limitations: Applications not accepted. Giving on a national basis. No grants to individuals. PRI support primarily to national and international organizations in New York, NY, and Washington, DC. PRI applications not accepted.
PRI program information: The foundation does not maintain a formal PRI program. The foundation makes PRIs occasionally.
Officers and Directors:* John R. Healy,* Chair. and Pres.; Cynthia R. Richards, V.P.; Alan Ruby,* Secy.-Treas.; Harvey

P. Dale, Elizabeth McCormack, Frederick A.O. Schwarz, Jr., Michael Sovern.
EIN: 133562971
PRI recipients:
12-1. JSTOR, NYC, NY, $500,000. Non-recourse loan to help JSTOR (Journal Storage) assist libraries and other not-for-profits digitize scholarly literature. 2001.
12-2. Public Radio International (PRI), Minneapolis, MN, $1,000,000. Interest-free loan to support efforts to enable member stations and listeners to communicate via the Internet. 2000.

13
Charles J. & Burton S. August Family Foundation
c/o Monro Muffler Brake Inc.
200 Holleder Pkwy.
Rochester, NY 14615-3808
Contact: Charles J. August, Tr.; or Burton S. August, Tr.
Tel.: (585) 647-6400, ext. 315 or 302

Established in 1989 in NY.
Donor(s): Burton S. August, Charles J. August.
Grantmaker type: Independent foundation
General financial activity (yr. ended 06/30/02): Assets, $3,290,973 (M); gifts received, $35,813; expenditures, $190,575; qualifying distributions, $173,632; giving activities include $174,710 for 34 grants (high: $30,000; low: $200; average: $1,000–$5,000) and $225,600 for PRIs.
General purpose and activities: Giving primarily for health and human services and education.
General fields of interest: Higher education; health care; domestic violence prevention; human services; children & youth, services; federated giving programs; disabled; aging; homeless; general charitable giving.
Program-related investment (PRI) activity: The foundation has made a mortgage loan to a crisis center
Types of PRI Support: Loans/promissory notes.
Limitations: Giving limited to Rochester and Monroe County, NY. No grants to individuals, or for continuing support.
Officers and Trustees:* Charles J. August,* Chair.; Burton S. August,* Vice-Chair.; Elizabeth August,* Secy.; Andrew August, Burton Stuart August, Jan August, Jean B. August, John August, Robert August, Susan Eastwood, David C. Mitchell, Hon. Michael Telesea.
Number of staff: None.
EIN: 161355601

14
The AVI CHAI Foundation
(Formerly AVI CHAI - A Philanthropic Foundation)
1015 Park Ave.
New York, NY 10028 (212) 396-8850
Contact: Yossi Prager, Exec. Dir., North America

Established in 1984 in NY. PRI-related activities began in 1998.
Donor(s): Zalman Chaim Bernstein.‡
Grantmaker type: Independent foundation
General financial activity (yr. ended 12/31/01): Assets, $475,050,185 (M); gifts received, $45,649,712; expenditures, $28,667,365; qualifying distributions, $37,516,173; giving activities include $23,644,963 for 130 grants (high: $17,100,602; low: $450; average: $10,000–$100,000), $1,711,758 for 4 foundation-administered programs and $10,075,000 for 12 PRIs.
Cumulative PRI activity (through 12/31/01): Since 1998, the foundation has made 14 PRIs totaling $11,100,000. The currently outstanding PRI portfolio includes 29 PRIs totaling $15,203,227 (high: $1,000,000; low: $250,000; average: $1,000,000). The typical outstanding PRI has a 2- to 5-year term with an average term of 5 years.
General purpose and activities: To encourage those of the Jewish faith towards greater commitment to Jewish observance and lifestyle by increasing their understanding, appreciation, and practice of Jewish traditions, customs, and laws; and to encourage mutual understanding and sensitivity among Jews of different religious backgrounds and commitments to observance.
General fields of interest: Education; human services; youth, services; Jewish federated giving programs.
General international interests: Israel.
Program-related investment (PRI) activity: The foundation makes loans only for the construction and renovation of Jewish day schools.
Types of PRI Support: Loans/promissory notes, capitalizing loan funds/other intermediaries.
Limitations: Applications not accepted. Giving primarily in North America and Israel. No grants for deficits. The foundation accepts applications for PRIs.
Publications: Multi-year report.
PRI program information: The foundation maintains a formal PRI program. The foundation makes PRIs on an annual basis.
Officers and Trustees:* Arthur W. Fried,* Chair., Pres., and Treas.; Marlene Wasserman, Secy.; Yossi Prager, Exec. Dir.; Mem Bernstein, Meir Buzaglo, Avital Darmon, Alan R. Feld, Lauren K. Merkin, George Rohr, Lief Rosenblatt, David Tadmor, Henry Taub, Ruth Wisse.
Number of staff: 7 full-time professional; 4 full-time support.
EIN: 133252800
PRI recipients:
14-1. Cincinnati Hebrew Upper School, Cincinnati, OH, $250,000. Loan. 1999.
14-2. Hebrew Academy of Long Beach, Long Beach, NY, $1,000,000. Loan. 2001.
14-3. Hyman Brand Hebrew Academy, Overland Park, KS, $300,000. Loan. 1999.
14-4. Jewish Day School Association, Shaker Heights, OH, $1,000,000. Loan. 2001.
14-5. Jewish Educational Center, Elizabeth, NJ, $1,000,000. Loan. 2001.

14-6. Jewish Heritage Day School of Buffalo, Getzville, NY, $475,000. Loan. 2001.
14-7. Melvin J. Berman Hebrew Academy, Rockville, MD, $1,000,000. Loan. 1999.
14-8. New Jewish High School, Burlington, MA, $250,000. Loan. 1999.
14-9. Rabbinical Seminary of America, Forest Hills, NY, $1,000,000. Loan. 2000.
14-10. Ramaz School, NYC, NY, $300,000. Loan. 2000.
14-11. Raymond and Ruth Perelman Jewish Day School, Wynnewood, PA, $250,000. Loan. 2001.
14-12. Robert Beren Academy, Houston, TX, $1,000,000. Loan. 2000.
14-13. Shalhevet High School, Beverly Hills, CA, $1,000,000. Loan. 2000.
14-14. Solomon Schechter Day School, Saint Louis, MO, $1,000,000. Loan. 2001.
14-15. Solomon Schechter Day School of Boston, Boston, MA, $1,000,000. Loan. 2001.
14-16. Solomon Schechter Day School of Greater Hartford, West Hartford, CT, $1,000,000. Loan. 2000.
14-17. Solomon Schechter School of Westchester, White Plains, NY, $1,000,000. Loan. 2001.
14-18. Talmudic College of Florida, Miami Beach, FL, $1,000,000. Loan. 2001.
14-19. Yavneh Academy, Paramus, NJ, $1,000,000. Loan. 2000.
14-20. Yavneh Day School, Los Gatos, CA, $1,000,000. Loan. 2000.
14-21. Yeshiva and Mesivta Toras Chaim of Greater New York, Brooklyn, NY, $1,000,000. Loan. 1999.
14-22. Yeshiva Elementary School, Milwaukee, WI, $500,000. Loan. 2001.
14-23. Yeshiva of Far Rockaway, Far Rockaway, NY, $850,000. Loan. 2001.
14-24. Yeshiva of Greater Washington School, Silver Spring, MD, $1,000,000. Loan. 2000.
14-25. Yeshiva of North Jersey, River Edge, NJ, $1,000,000. Loan. 2001.
14-26. Yeshiva Shaare Torah, Brooklyn, NY, $1,000,000. Loan. 2000.
14-27. Yeshiva Shaare Torah, Brooklyn, NY, $300,000. Loan. 2000.
14-28. Yeshiva Tiferes Yisroel, Brooklyn, NY, $1,000,000. Loan. 1999.

15

Mary Reynolds Babcock Foundation, Inc.

2920 Reynolda Rd.
Winston-Salem, NC 27106-3016 (336) 748-9222
Contact: Gayle Williams, Exec. Dir.
FAX: (336) 777-0095; E-mail: info@mrbf.org;
URL: http://www.mrbf.org

Incorporated in 1953 in NC.
Donor(s): Mary Reynolds Babcock,‡ Charles H. Babcock.‡
Grantmaker type: Independent foundation
General financial activity (yr. ended 12/31/02): Assets, $108,875,105 (M); gifts received, $154,786; expenditures, $6,853,163; qualifying distributions, $5,717,501; giving activities include $5,717,501 for 158 grants (high: $583,334; low: $1,000; average: $10,000–$75,000) and $30,773 for foundation-administered programs; no PRIs paid.
General purpose and activities: The foundation supports people in the southeast to build just and caring communities that nurture people, spur enterprise, bridge differences, foster fairness, and promote civility. The foundation is committed to assisting organizations that are having a demonstrable impact on racism and poverty. The foundation carries out this commitment through three funding areas: enterprise and asset development, community problem solving, and grassroots leadership development.
General fields of interest: Human services; race/intergroup relations; community development; leadership development; economically disadvantaged.
Program-related investment (PRI) activity: The foundation has made a PRI in the form of a low-interest loan to a community development organization.
Types of PRI Support: Loans/promissory notes.
Limitations: Giving in the southeastern U.S., with emphasis on eastern AL, AR, GA, LA, MS, NC, SC, TN, north and central FL, and the Appalachian regions of KY and WV. No support for medical or health programs and international activities. No grants for endowment funds, building funds, renovation projects, film or video production, scholarships, fellowships, or research; no student loans.
Publications: Annual report (including application guidelines).
Officers and Directors:* Nathaniel Irvin III,* Pres.; Barbara B. Millhouse,* V.P.; David Dodson,* Secy.; Akosva Barthwell Evans,* Treas.; Gayle Williams, Exec. Dir.; Bruce M. Babcock, Victoria Creed, Wayne Flynt, Sybil J. Hampton, Wendy Johnson, Katharine B. Mountcastle, Katherine R. Mountcastle, Kenneth F. Mountcastle III, Laura L. Mountcastle, Mary Mountcastle, Carol P. Zippert.
Number of staff: 5 full-time professional; 3 full-time support; 1 part-time support.
EIN: 560690140
PRI recipients:
15-1. Southern Rural Development Initiative, Raleigh, NC, $500,000. Loan at 2 percent to assist in making deposits with Community Development Financial Institutes (CDFI). 1999.

16

Helen Bader Foundation, Inc.

233 N. Water St., 4th Fl.
Milwaukee, WI 53202 (414) 224-6464
Contact: Daniel J. Bader, Pres.
PRI Contact: Kathryn Dunn, Community Investment Off.
FAX: (414) 224-1441; E-mail: info@hbf.org;
URL: http://www.hbf.org

Established in 1991 in WI. PRI-related activities began in 2000.
Grantmaker type: Independent foundation
General financial activity (yr. ended 08/31/01): Assets, $2,402,968 (M); gifts received, $12,500,000; expenditures, $13,538,620; qualifying distributions, $13,445,204; giving activities include $11,762,550 for 289 grants (high: $1,504,000; low: $500; average: $10,000–$100,000); no PRIs paid.
Cumulative PRI activity (through 08/31/01): The currently outstanding PRI portfolio includes a high PRI value of $200,000 and a low PRI value of $50,000. The typical outstanding PRI has a 3- to 5-year term.
General purpose and activities: The foundation's mission is to support innovative projects and programs which advance the well-being of people and promote successful relationships with their families and communities. The foundation currently concentrates grantmaking in six program areas: Alzheimer's disease and dementia; education; economic development; early childhood development in Israel; Jewish life and learning; and Sankofa-neighborhood renewal. The foundation prefers funding programs that demonstrate results, are coordinated with other community programs, and can be replicated.
General fields of interest: Elementary/secondary education; Alzheimer's disease; medical research; human services; children & youth, services; economic development; community development; Jewish federated giving programs; Jewish agencies & temples; religion.
General international interests: Israel.
Program-related investment (PRI) activity: The foundation actively seeks opportunities to make PRIs to strengthen and expand the impact of five of the foundation's program areas working in Milwaukee and throughout Wisconsin: Alzheimer's Disease and Dementia; Economic Development; Education; Jewish Life and Learning; and Sankofa-Neighborhood Renewal.
Types of PRI Support: Loans/promissory notes, loan guarantees, equity investments, capitalizing loan funds/other intermediaries.
Limitations: Giving primarily in the greater Milwaukee, WI, area for education and economic development; giving locally and nationally for Alzheimer's disease and dementia; giving in Israel for early childhood development. No grants to individuals. Funds from PRIs cannot support lobbying or the influencing of pending legislation. The foundation accepts applications for PRIs.
Publications: Annual report (including application guidelines), grants list, application guidelines.
PRI program information: The criteria for evaluating proposals for PRIs include the project's potential impact, its financial feasibility, and the extent to which it is related to the foundation's program areas. The foundation maintains a formal PRI program. The foundation makes PRIs on an annual basis.
Officers and Directors:* Jere D. McGaffey,* Chair. and Secy.-Treas.; Daniel J. Bader,* Pres.; David M. Bader,* V.P.; Lisa Hiller, V.P., Admin.; Robin Bieger Mayrl, V.P., Prog. Devel.; Linda C. Bader, Michelle Henkin Bader, Deirdre H. Britt, Frances Wolff.
Number of staff: 7 full-time professional; 2 part-time professional; 3 full-time support; 1 part-time support.
EIN: 391710914
PRI recipients:

16-1. La Causa, Day Care Center, Milwaukee, WI, $50,000. Program-related investment for Child and Family Center. 2002.

16-2. Legacy Redevelopment Corporation, Milwaukee, WI, $198,000. Program-related investment for Legacy Home Development Revolving Loan Fund. 2002.

16-3. Menomonee Valley Partners, Milwaukee, WI, $100,000. Program-related investment for brownfields pre-development in Menomonee Valley. 2002.

16-4. YWCA of Greater Milwaukee, Milwaukee, WI, $150,000. Program-related investment for JEMZS client tracking and outcomes measurement and reporting software services. 2002.

17

Bank of America Foundation, Inc.

100 N. Tryon St., NC1-007-18-01
Charlotte, NC 28255-0001
Contact: Mike Sweeney, Dir.
URL: http://www.bankofamerica.com/foundation

Established under current name in 1998 following the merger of NationsBank Corporation and BankAmerica Corporation.
Donor(s): Bank of America Corp., and subsidiaries.
Grantmaker type: Company-sponsored foundation
General financial activity (yr. ended 12/31/00): Assets, $2,212,307 (M); gifts received, $82,431,561; expenditures, $85,737,445; qualifying distributions, $85,755,841; giving activities include $77,996,221 for 5,801 grants (high: $10,000,000; low: $40; average: $1,000–$100,000) and $7,759,620 for employee matching gifts; no PRIs paid.
Cumulative PRI activity (through 12/31/00): The currently outstanding PRI portfolio includes PRIs totaling $80,000.
General purpose and activities: The foundation directs charitable giving on behalf of Bank of America. The foundation contributes financial assistance to nonprofit institutions and organizations that enhance the quality of life and promote public interest in the areas where the company conducts business. The foundation's primary

areas of focus are early childhood, professional development for teachers, and consumer education.
General fields of interest: Arts/cultural programs; education; health care; human services; community development.
Types of PRI Support: Loans/promissory notes.
Limitations: Giving limited to areas of major company operations, including 21 states and Washington, DC, and other select areas where there is a company presence. No support for organizations lacking 501(c)(3) status, religious organizations for sectarian purposes, athletic events and programs, agencies receiving support from the United Way or arts councils, public or private K-12 schools, or disease advocacy organizations. No grants to individuals, or for book, film, or video development or production.
EIN: 582429625

18
BANK ONE Foundation

(Formerly First National Bank of Chicago Foundation)
1 BANK ONE Plz., Ste. 0308
Chicago, IL 60670 (312) 407-8052
Contact: James E. Donovan, Treas.

Incorporated in 1961 in IL.
Donor(s): The First National Bank of Chicago, First Chicago Equity Corp., Bank One, N.A.
Grantmaker type: Company-sponsored foundation
General financial activity (yr. ended 12/31/01): Assets, $55,693,035 (M); gifts received, $57,988,173; expenditures, $30,184,895; qualifying distributions, $30,371,395; giving activities include $29,811,532 for 1,064 grants (high: $500,000; low: $500; average: $5,000–$100,000), $358,573 for 594 employee matching gifts and $207,000 for 3 PRIs.
General purpose and activities: Giving primarily for human services, including housing programs and race relations; community development, civic affairs, and crime and law enforcement; education, especially business and other higher education, libraries, and education building funds; and the arts and culture, including museums, music, dance, and the theater.
General fields of interest: Visual arts; museums; performing arts; dance; theater; music; arts/cultural programs; education, fund raising; higher education; business school/education; libraries/library science; education; natural resources conservation & protection; environment; crime/law enforcement; housing/shelter, development; human services; youth, services; minorities/immigrants, centers & services; race/intergroup relations; civil rights; urban/community development; business & industry; community development; federated giving programs; government/public administration; minorities.
Program-related investment (PRI) activity: The foundation makes PRIs for community and economic development, housing, and employment.
Types of PRI Support: Loans/promissory notes, capitalizing loan funds/other intermediaries.
Limitations: Giving primarily in areas of company operations in AZ, DE, IL, MI, OH, and WI, with emphasis on the metropolitan Chicago, IL, area. No support for fraternal or religious organizations, preschool, elementary, or secondary education, public agencies, or United Way/Crusade of Mercy-supported agencies. No grants to individuals, or for emergency funds, deficit financing, land acquisition, research, publications, conferences, or multi-year operating pledges; no loans (except for program-related investments).
Publications: Informational brochure (including application guidelines).
Officers and Directors:* Melinda McMullen,* Pres.; Michael J. Cavanagh,* V.P.; David E. Donovan,* V.P.; Christine Edwards,* V.P.; Margaret E. O'Hara,* V.P.; Norma J. Lauder,* V.P.; Lesley D. Slavitt,* V.P.; Marie I. Jordan, Secy.; James E. Donovan, Treas.
Number of staff: 2 full-time professional; 1 full-time support.
EIN: 366033828
PRI recipients:

18-1. ACCION Chicago, Chicago, IL, $72,000. Loan to provide capital for ACCION Chicago Loan Fund. 2001.
18-2. ACCION Chicago, Chicago, IL, $175,000. Program-related investment to provide capital for ACCION Chicago Loan Fund. 1999.
18-3. Ahkenaton Community Development Corporation, Chicago, IL, $37,500. Program-related investment for operating support for community redevelopment initiatives. 1999.
18-4. Chicago Association of Neighborhood Development Organizations (CANDO), Chicago, IL, $80,000. Program-related investment to provide capital for new Self-Employment Loan Fund. 1999.
18-5. Chicago Community Loan Fund, Chicago, IL, $35,000. Loan to provide capital for pre-development loans for housing and community development. 2001.
18-6. Chicago Community Loan Fund, Chicago, IL, $130,000. Program-related investment to provide loans for housing and community development. 1999.
18-7. Lake County Economic Development Fund, Merrillville, IN, $25,000. Program-related investment to provide capital for new micro-loan fund. 1999.
18-8. North Side Community Federal Credit Union, Chicago, IL, $100,000. Program-related investment. 2001.
18-9. United Neighborhood Organization of Chicago, Chicago, IL, $30,000. Program-related investment for predevelopment expenses of housing development project. 1999.
18-10. West Cook Community Development Corporation, Westchester, IL, $50,000. Program-related investment to provide operating support for community redevelopment initiatives. 1999.
18-11. Womens Business Development Center, Chicago, IL, $10,000. Program-related investment to provide capital for new micro-loan fund. 1999.

19

Barberton Community Foundation
460 W. Paige St.
Barberton, OH 44203 (330) 745-5995
Contact: Thomas L. Harnden, Exec. Dir.
FAX: (330) 745-3990; URL: http://www.bcfcharity.org

Established in 1996 in OH; converted from the sale of Barberton Citizens Hospital to Quorum Health Group, Inc. PRI-related activities began in 1998.
Grantmaker type: Community foundation
General financial activity (yr. ended 12/31/02): Assets, $78,989,847 (M); gifts received, $75,743; expenditures, $3,890,083; giving activities include $3,086,325 for 56 grants (high: $2,297,123; low: $100; average: $100–$2,297,123) and $5,412,471 for 7 foundation-administered programs; no PRIs paid.
Cumulative PRI activity (through 12/31/02): Since 1998, the foundation has made 13 PRIs totaling $11,627,783. The currently outstanding PRI portfolio includes 11 PRI totaling $9,589,762 (high: $3,034,472; low: $5,000). The typical outstanding PRI has a 2- to 5-year term, and earns 2 to 6 percent interest.
General purpose and activities: The foundation supports projects that benefit the citizens of Barberton, Ohio. The foundation administers donor-advised funds.
General fields of interest: Urban/community development.
Program-related investment (PRI) activity: The Barberton Community Foundation is committed to its mission of improving the lives of the citizens of Barberton by investing in Barberton businesses and helping local residents improve their homes through low interest loans. In order to provide these loans in an effective and cost efficient manner, the Foundation has partnered with the Barberton Community Development Corporation, Neighborhood Conservation Services and local Barberton banks. Loan information is available on the foundation's website: http://www.bcfcharity.org/bcf/loans/.
Types of PRI Support: Loans/promissory notes, linked deposits.
Limitations: Giving limited to Barberton, OH. No grants to individuals. PRI applications not accepted.
Publications: Annual report, informational brochure (including application guidelines), application guidelines, newsletter.
PRI program information: The foundation maintains a formal PRI program. The foundation makes PRIs on an annual basis.
Officers and Trustees:* Jerry Pecko,* Chair.; Helen F. Scott,* Vice-Chair.; Esther Sarb,* Secy.; Thomas D. Doak,* Treas.; Thomas L. Harnden, Exec. Dir.; Kenneth R. Cox, Paul DeWitt, Beth Gagnon, Robert J. Genet, Milan Pavkov, Randy Hart, Daniel C. Knoor, Kathryn Maybin, Diane A. McConnell, Leon T. Ricks, Walter S. Ritzman.
Number of staff: 4 full-time professional; 1 part-time professional.
EIN: 341846432

20

Bass Foundation
309 Main St.
Fort Worth, TX 76102 (817) 336-0494
Contact: Valleau Wilkie, Jr., Exec. Dir.
PRI Contact: Cindy Alexander

Established in 1945 in TX.
Donor(s): Perry R. Bass, Lee M. Bass, Edward P. Bass, Sid Richardson Carbon and Gasoline Co., Perry R. Bass, Inc.
Grantmaker type: Independent foundation
General financial activity (yr. ended 12/31/02): Assets, $5,222,234 (M); expenditures, $1,637,885; qualifying distributions, $1,604,984; giving activities include $1,569,001 for 13 grants (high: $550,000; low: $2,500; average: $2,500–$250,000); no PRIs paid.
General purpose and activities: Giving primarily for the arts and cultural institutions; some support for conservation.
General fields of interest: Arts/cultural programs; natural resources conservation & protection.
Program-related investment (PRI) activity: The foundation has made PRIs supporting educational and arts organizations. PRIs have provided support for programs and debt reduction.
Types of PRI Support: Loans/promissory notes.
Limitations: Applications not accepted. Giving primarily in Fort Worth, TX. PRI applications not accepted.
PRI program information: The foundation does not maintain a formal PRI program. The foundation makes PRIs occasionally.
Officers and Directors:* Perry R. Bass,* Pres.; Edward P. Bass,* V.P.; Lee M. Bass,* V.P.; Nancy Lee Bass,* V.P.; Cynthia K. Alexander, Secy.-Treas.; Valleau Wilkie, Jr., Exec. Dir.
Number of staff: 3 part-time professional.
EIN: 756033983

21

Robert T. Bates Foundation
c/o First Iowa State Bank
19 Benton Ave. E.
Albia, IA 52531 (641) 932-2144
Contact: Raymond H. Davis, Pres.

Established in 1992 in IA.
Donor(s): Robert T. Bates, Robert L. Kaldenberg.
Grantmaker type: Independent foundation
General financial activity (yr. ended 12/31/01): Assets, $2,744,142 (M); gifts received, $30,000; expenditures, $150,968; qualifying distributions, $82,292; giving activities include $17,871 for 5 grants (high: $4,879; low: $3,000) and $64,421 for 3 grants to individuals (high: $57,881; low: $540); no PRIs paid.
General purpose and activities: Giving primarily for historical preservation and Christian organizations.

General fields of interest: Historic preservation/historical societies.
Program-related investment (PRI) activity: The foundation makes PRIs for real estate purchases.
Limitations: Giving primarily in Albia, IA.
Officers: Raymond Davis, Pres. and Tres.; Carroll Rhine, V.P.; David Johnson, Secy.
EIN: 421392613

22

Baton Rouge Area Foundation

406 N. 4th St.
Baton Rouge, LA 70802 (225) 387-6126
Contact: John G. Davies, C.E.O. and Pres.
FAX: (225) 387-6153; E-mail: jdavies@braf.org;
URL: http://www.braf.org

Incorporated in 1964 in LA.
Grantmaker type: Community foundation
General financial activity (yr. ended 12/31/01): Assets, $200,132,000 (M); gifts received, $34,366,000; expenditures, $71,150,000; giving activities include $52,387,000 for 1,000 grants (high: $402,000; low: $100); no PRIs paid.
Cumulative PRI activity (through 12/31/01): The currently outstanding PRI portfolio includes 6 PRIs totaling $1,090,125.
General purpose and activities: The foundation funds programs in the areas of the arts and humanities, community development, education, the environment, human services, health and medical issues, and religion. Primary areas of interest include elementary and secondary education and health. Preference given to those projects which promise to affect a broad segment of the population or which tend to help a segment of the citizenry who are not being adequately served by the community's resources.
General fields of interest: Arts/cultural programs; child development, education; elementary school/education; secondary school/education; medical school/education; nursing school/education; education; environment; health care; health associations; human services; children & youth, services; child development, services; aging, centers & services; women, centers & services; community development; religion; disabled; aging; women; economically disadvantaged.
Program-related investment (PRI) activity: The foundation has made PRIs in the areas of the arts and humanities, community development, philanthropy, and education.
Types of PRI Support: Loans/promissory notes.
Limitations: Giving limited to the Baton Rouge, LA, area, including East Baton Rouge, West Baton Rouge, Livingston, Ascension, Iberville, Pointe Coupee, East Feliciana, and West Feliciana parishes. No grants for continuing support, annual campaigns, deficit financing, fellowships, or operating budgets. PRI applications not accepted.
Publications: Annual report (including application guidelines), application guidelines, newsletter, informational brochure.
PRI program information: The foundation does not maintain a formal PRI program. The foundation makes PRIs occasionally.
Officers and Directors:* Virginia B. Noland,* Chair.; John G. Davies,* C.E.O. and Pres.; Hans Dekker, Exec. V.P.; Kevin R. Lyle, V.P.; L. Lane Grigsby, Secy.; Ralph J. Stephens, Treas.; and 17 additional directors.
Trustee Bank: Bank One, N.A.
Number of staff: 16 full-time professional.
EIN: 726030391
PRI recipients:

22-1. Arts Council of Greater Baton Rouge, Baton Rouge, LA, $100,000. Loan for fundraising-related expenses. 2000.
22-2. Baton Rouge Community College Foundation, Baton Rouge, LA, $75,000. Loan toward expenses for search and recruitment of new Chancellor. 2000.
22-3. Community Foundations of America, Louisville, KY, $200,000. Loan toward development of donor services platform. 2000.
22-4. Scotlandville Community Development Corporation, Baton Rouge, LA, $15,460. Loan toward development of donor services platform. 2001.
22-5. West Baton Rouge Foundation for Academic Excellence, Port Allen, LA, $100,000. Loan for fundraising-related expenses. 2000.

23

Battle Creek Community Foundation

(Formerly Greater Battle Creek Foundation)
1 Riverwalk Ctr.
34 W. Jackson St.
Battle Creek, MI 49017-3505 (269) 962-2181
Contact: Angela Graham, V.P.
PRI Contact: Kelly Boles Chapman, Prog. Dir.
FAX: (269) 962-2182; E-mail: bccf@bccfoundation.org; URL: http://www.bccfoundation.org

Established in 1974 in MI. PRI-related activities began in 2000.
Grantmaker type: Community foundation
General financial activity (yr. ended 03/31/02): Assets, $59,424,044 (M); gifts received, $7,708,361; expenditures, $6,957,288; giving activities include $5,314,565 for grants; no PRIs paid.
Cumulative PRI activity (through 03/31/02): Since 2000, the foundation has made 1 PRI totaling $17,500. The currently outstanding PRI portfolio includes 1 PRI totaling $11,139. The typical outstanding PRI has an average term of 2 years.
General purpose and activities: Grantmaking for programming in the Battle Creek, Michigan, area that serves the citizens of the community through education, health,

human services, arts, public affairs, and community development; scholarships are also available to students residing in the greater Battle Creek area.
General fields of interest: Arts/cultural programs; child development, education; adult education—literacy, basic skills & GED; reading; education; animal welfare; hospitals (general); health care; health associations; children & youth, services; child development, services; minorities/immigrants, centers & services; community development; public affairs; minorities.
Program-related investment (PRI) activity: The foundation's first PRI was a loan to a nonprofit organization.
Types of PRI Support: Loans/promissory notes.
Limitations: Giving limited to the greater Battle Creek, MI, area. No grants for operating budgets, deficit financing, endowments, or research; no loans (except for program-related investments).
Publications: Annual report, grants list, newsletter, application guidelines, financial statement, informational brochure, program policy statement, biennial report (including application guidelines).
PRI program information: Apply through normal grant application process. Initial approach by letter or telphone. The foundation does not maintain a formal PRI program. The foundation makes PRIs occasionally.
Officers and Trustees:* Velma Laws-Clay,* Chair.; James P. Baldwin,* Vice-Chair.; Brenda L. Hunt, C.E.O.; Angela Graham, V.P.; Susan S. Day, Secy.; David E. Kinnisten, Treas.; Charles Cooper, Jr., Roberta H. Cribbs, Stephanie M. Demarest, Annie Dunsky, David H. Eddy, James R.C. Hazel, Jr., James F. Hettinger, Peter M. Kelley, Samir Kulkarni, David P. Lucas, Fred F. Meyer, Kathleen D. Rizor, David L. Schweitzer, Clara J. Stewart.
Number of staff: 9 full-time professional; 1 part-time professional; 3 full-time support; 1 part-time support.
EIN: 382045459
PRI recipients:
23-1. Guardian, Inc. of Calhoun County, Battle Creek, MI, $17,500. Program-related investment. 2000.

24
Eula Mae and John Baugh Foundation
1390 Enclave Pkwy.
Houston, TX 77077

Established in 1995 in TX.
Donor(s): Eula Mae Baugh, John F. Baugh.
Grantmaker type: Independent foundation
General financial activity (yr. ended 12/31/01): Assets, $15,813,083 (M); expenditures, $313,720; qualifying distributions, $3,267,698; giving activities include $268,240 for 11 grants (high: $50,000; low: $1,000), $48,000 for 1 loan to an individual and $3,000,000 for 1 PRI.
General fields of interest: Higher education; education; Christian agencies & churches.
Program-related investment (PRI) activity: The foundation made a low-interest loan to Baylor University in 2001.
Types of PRI Support: Loans/promissory notes.
Limitations: Applications not accepted. Giving primarily in TX. No grants to individuals. PRI giving limited to TX.
Trustees: Eula Mae Baugh, John F. Baugh, E. James Lowrey, Jaqueline Morrison Moore, Barbara Baugh Morrison, Julia Morrison Ortiz.
EIN: 760457820
PRI recipients:
24-1. Baylor University, Waco, TX, $3,000,000. Program-related investment. 2001.

25
Norwin S. and Elizabeth N. Bean Foundation
c/o New Hampshire Charitable Foundation
37 Pleasant St.
Concord, NH 03301-4005 (603) 225-6641
Contact: Nike F. Speltz, Sr. Prog. Off.
FAX: (603) 225-1700

Trust established in 1957 in NH; later became an affiliated trust of the New Hampshire Charitable Foundation.
Donor(s): Norwin S. Bean,‡ Elizabeth N. Bean.‡
Grantmaker type: Independent foundation
General financial activity (yr. ended 12/31/01): Assets, $15,833,435 (M); expenditures, $626,421; qualifying distributions, $595,320; giving activities include $562,209 for 44 grants (high: $50,000; low: $1,000); no PRIs paid.
Cumulative PRI activity (through 12/31/01): The typical outstanding PRI has a 2- to 5-year term, and earns 3 to 6 percent interest.
General purpose and activities: Giving primarily for human services, including low-income housing programs and youth; support also for education, including secondary education, health associations, the arts, and environment.
General fields of interest: Arts/cultural programs; secondary school/education; education; health care; health associations; housing/shelter, development; human services; youth, services.
Program-related investment (PRI) activity: The foundation funds housing-related activities through PRI support for a revolving loan fund administered by the New Hampshire Charitable Foundation. PRIs from the New Hampshire Community Loan Fund are made at below market rates to provide for a variety of needs, including cash flow management, acquisition of property and equipment, and repairs or improvements to facilities, particularly when these improvements make facilities more energy efficient.
Types of PRI Support: Capitalizing loan funds/other intermediaries.
Limitations: Giving limited to Amherst and Manchester, NH. No grants to individuals, or for scholarships, fellowships, operating budgets, deficit financing, or endowment funds. PRI applications not accepted.

Publications: Annual report (including application guidelines), informational brochure (including application guidelines), application guidelines.
PRI program information: The foundation makes PRIs occasionally.
Trustees: William Donoghue, Thomas J. Donovan, Keith A. Lammers, Claira P. Morier, Toni Pappas, Paul D. Spiess, William G. Steele.
Number of staff: 2 shared staff.
EIN: 026013381

26
Claude Worthington Benedum Foundation
1400 Benedum-Trees Bldg.
223 4th Ave.
Pittsburgh, PA 15222 (412) 288-0360
Contact: William P. Getty, Pres.
URL: http://www.fdncenter.org/grantmaker/benedum

Incorporated in 1944 in PA.
Donor(s): Michael Late Benedum,‡ Sarah N. Benedum.‡
Grantmaker type: Independent foundation
General financial activity (yr. ended 12/31/01): Assets, $324,645,569 (M); expenditures, $18,142,651; qualifying distributions, $16,062,679; giving activities include $14,183,564 for 195 grants (high: $500,000; low: $3,000; average: $25,000–$75,000) and $250,000 for 1 PRI.
Cumulative PRI activity (through 12/31/01): Since beginning PRI activity, the foundation has made 5 PRIs totaling $3,300,000. The currently outstanding PRI portfolio includes 2 PRIs totaling $2,200,000.
General purpose and activities: Grants to WV organizations are in the areas of education, health and human services, community and economic development, and the arts. Local initiatives and partnerships are encouraged. In southwestern PA, grants are made primarily to projects for regional economic development, including business development and workforce education. In selected rural counties, grants are made to advance the quality of life for rural populations through a broad range of approaches.
General fields of interest: Arts/cultural programs; higher education; education; health care; human services; children & youth, services; economic development; community development.
Program-related investment (PRI) activity: The foundation has made PRIs to organizations that help create low and moderate-income housing and foster the rehabilitation of existing housing units, as well as to generate economic development activity.
Types of PRI Support: Loans/promissory notes.
Limitations: Giving limited to southwestern PA and WV. No support for national health and welfare campaigns, medical research, religious activities, national organizations, or individual elementary or secondary schools. No grants to individuals, or for student aid, fellowships, travel, ongoing operating expenses, annual appeals, membership drives, conferences, films, books, or audio-visual productions, unless an integral part of a foundation supported program.
Publications: Annual report, application guidelines, informational brochure (including application guidelines).
PRI program information: The foundation does not maintain a formal PRI program. The foundation makes PRIs occasionally.
Officers and Trustees:* Paul G. Benedum, Jr.,* Chair.; William P. Getty,* Pres.; Dwight M. Keating, V.P. and C.I.O.; Beverly Railey Walter, V.P., Progs.; Rose A. McKee, Secy. and Dir., Admin.; Marcie G. Berry, Treas.; Esther L. Barazzone, Ralph J. Bean, Jr., G. Nicholas Beckwith, Gaston Caperton, G. Randolph Worls.
Number of staff: 7 full-time professional; 4 full-time support.
EIN: 251086799
PRI recipients:
26-1. ALMONO, LLP, Pittsburgh, PA, $1,200,000. Program-related investment to purchase brownfield site and for operating support. 2001.
26-2. Ohio Valley Foundation, Wheeling, WV, $321,000. Program-related investment for Victorian Village, economic development project in Wheeling. 2001.
26-3. Strategic Investment Fund, Pittsburgh, PA, $1,250,000. Program-related investment to provide real estate investments in depressed areas of Southwestern Pennsylvania. 2001.

27
Benmen Fund
48 Concord Dr.
Monsey, NY 10952

Established in 1991 in NY.
Donor(s): Harvey Brecher, Miriam Brecher.
Grantmaker type: Independent foundation
General financial activity (yr. ended 11/30/02): Assets, $3,317 (M); gifts received, $31,223; expenditures, $152,460; qualifying distributions, $150,572; giving activities include $150,377 for 460 grants (high: $50,000; low: $18); no PRIs paid.
General purpose and activities: Giving primarily for Jewish organizations.
General fields of interest: Elementary/secondary education; Jewish agencies & temples.
Program-related investment (PRI) activity: The foundation makes PRIs, in the form of loans, to Jewish organizations.
Limitations: Applications not accepted. Giving primarily in Monsey, NY. No grants to individuals.
Officers and Directors:* Harvey Brecher,* Pres. and Treas.; Miriam Brecher,* V.P. and Secy.; Yossie Brecher,* V.P.; Malkie Kahn,* V.P.; Eli S. Garber.
EIN: 133620970
PRI recipients:
27-1. Congregation Zichron Schneur, Brooklyn, NY, $10,000. Loan. 2001.
27-2. Keren Hachesed, Monsey, NY, $50,000. Loan. 2001.

28

Benwood Foundation, Inc.

SunTrust Bank Bldg.
736 Market St., Ste. 1600
Chattanooga, TN 37402 (423) 267-4311
Contact: Corinne Allen, Exec. Dir.
FAX: (423) 267-9049; E-mail:
Benwoodfnd@Benwood.org

Incorporated in 1944 in DE, and 1945 in TN.
Donor(s): George Thomas Hunter.‡
Grantmaker type: Independent foundation
General financial activity (yr. ended 12/31/02): Assets, $93,894,413 (M); expenditures, $5,242,814; qualifying distributions, $4,514,893; giving activities include $4,209,591 for 124 grants (high: $210,000; low: $250; average: $1,000–$50,000); no PRIs paid.
Cumulative PRI activity (through 12/31/02): The currently outstanding PRI portfolio includes 1 PRI totaling $25,354.
General purpose and activities: Support for secondary and early childhood education, social welfare, health agencies, cultural programs, arts and humanities, including the performing arts, and the environment, including beautification programs.
General fields of interest: Performing arts; humanities; arts/cultural programs; early childhood education; secondary school/education; environment; health associations; human services; economic development; urban/community development.
Limitations: Giving primarily in the Chattanooga, TN, area. No support for political organizations or causes. No grants to individuals, or for general operating expenses, financial deficits, fundraising, endowments, or multi-year grants; no loans (except for program related investments).
Publications: Application guidelines.
PRI program information: The foundation makes PRIs occasionally.
Officers and Trustees:* E.Y. Chapin III,* Chair.; Robert J. Sudderth, Jr.,* Pres.; Sebert Brewer, Jr.,* Secy.-Treas.; Corinne Allen, Exec. Dir.
Number of staff: 3 full-time professional; 1 part-time professional.
EIN: 620476283

29

H. N. & Frances C. Berger Foundation

P.O. Box 13390
Palm Desert, CA 92255-3390 (760) 341-5293
Contact: Christopher M. McGuire, V.P.
URL: http://www.hnberger.org

Established in 1993 in CA, AZ, and TX.
Grantmaker type: Independent foundation
General financial activity (yr. ended 12/31/01): Assets, $461,647,578 (M); expenditures, $35,016,304; qualifying distributions, $18,035,159; giving activities include $13,435,001 for 113 grants (high: $2,500,000; low: $250; average: $10,000–$150,000) and $1,033,267 for 2 foundation-administered programs; no PRIs paid.
General purpose and activities: Emphasis on higher education, cultural programs, public health organizations, and hospitals. Committed to long-term support of present donees.
General fields of interest: Arts/cultural programs; higher education; hospitals (general); health care; health associations.
Program-related investment (PRI) activity: The foundation has made loans benefiting the arts, housing, children and youth, and education. The foundation also owns an office building and leases its space to nonprofits at below-market rates.
Types of PRI Support: Loans/promissory notes, charitable use assets.
Limitations: Giving primarily in CA. No grants to individuals.
Officers and Directors:* Ronald M. Auen,* Pres.; John N. Berger,* V.P.; Darrell Burrage,* V.P.; Christopher M. McGuire,* V.P.; Douglass Vance,* V.P.; Joan C. Auen,* Secy.-Treas.; Lewis Webb, Jr.
EIN: 521757452

30

The Blandin Foundation

(Formerly Charles K. Blandin Foundation)
100 N. Pokegama Ave.
Grand Rapids, MN 55744 (218) 326-0523
Contact: Paul M. Olson, C.E.O.
Additional tel.: (877) 882-2257; FAX: (218) 327-1949; E-mail: bfinfo@blandinfoundation.org; URL: http://www.blandinfoundation.org

Incorporated in 1941 in MN.
Donor(s): Charles K. Blandin.‡
Grantmaker type: Independent foundation
General financial activity (yr. ended 12/31/02): Assets, $333,701,300 (M); gifts received, $14,914,140; expenditures, $31,855,389; qualifying distributions, $29,970,494; giving activities include $25,924,161 for grants, $684,475 for grants to individuals, $3,361,858 for foundation-administered programs and $1,000,000 for 1 PRI.
Cumulative PRI activity (through 12/31/02): Since beginning PRI activity, the foundation has made 23 PRIs totaling $9,671,000. The currently outstanding PRI portfolio includes 4 PRIs totaling $5,604,000.
General purpose and activities: Giving primarily in four areas for rural MN: 1) community leadership; 2) economic opportunity; 3) life-long learning; and 4) diversity.
General fields of interest: Higher education; education; economic development; rural development; community development; leadership development.
Program-related investment (PRI) activity: The foundation has made PRIs in support of rural economic development,

the environment, public policy, and employment programs for people with disabilities. PRIs have provided support for land and equipment acquisition, facility construction and improvement, and operating support.
Types of PRI Support: Loans/promissory notes.
Limitations: Giving limited to rural areas of MN; scholarships limited to graduates of an Itasca County, Hill City, or Remer, Blackduck, or Northome, MN, high school. No support for religious activities or camping programs. No grants to individuals (except for Blandin Educational Awards), for operating budgets, annual campaigns, deficit financing, government services, capital funds (outside home community), endowments, publications, travel, medical research, films or videos, conferences, or seminars (outside of those sponsored by the foundation and related to its grantmaking). PRI applications not accepted.
Publications: Informational brochure (including application guidelines).
PRI program information: The foundation does not maintain a formal PRI program. The foundation makes PRIs occasionally.
Officers and Trustees:* Kenneth Lundgren,* Chair.; Kathleen R. Annette, M.D.,* Vice-Chair.; Paul M. Olson, C.E.O. and Pres.; Kathryn Jensen, Sr. V.P.; Eugene Radecki,* Secy.; James Bensen, John Hawkinson, James Hoolihan, Helen Klassen, Sandy Layman, Marcie McLaughlin, Bruce Stender, George Thompson.
Number of staff: 12 full-time professional; 13 full-time support.
EIN: 416038619
PRI recipients:
30-1. Minnesota Diversified Industries, Saint Paul, MN, $1,300,000. Program-related investment for capital support to provide career opportunities for developmentally disabled individuals in Grand Rapids and Hibbing. 1999.
30-2. SOTA TEC Fund, Saint Paul, MN, $500,000. Program-related investment. 2000.
30-3. Trust for Public Land, Midwest Regional Office, Minneapolis, MN, $126,000. Program-related investment for Harbor Park project in Grand Marais area. 2000.

31
The Jacob and Hilda Blaustein Foundation, Inc.
10 E. Baltimore St., Ste.1111
Baltimore, MD 21202 (410) 347-7201
Contact: Betsy F. Ringel, Exec. Dir.
E-mail: info@blaufund.org

Incorporated in 1957 in MD.
Donor(s): Jacob Blaustein.‡
Grantmaker type: Independent foundation
General financial activity (yr. ended 12/31/01): Assets, $92,869,876 (M); gifts received, $2,433,333; expenditures, $8,309,102; qualifying distributions, $5,552,441; giving activities include $7,229,855 for 146 grants (high: $2,000,000; low: $50; average: $10,000–$100,000); no PRIs paid.
General purpose and activities: Giving in five broad program areas: arts and culture, intergroup relations, advancement of individual human rights, health and mental health, and Jewish identity and continuity.
General fields of interest: Humanities; arts/cultural programs; health care; race/intergroup relations; international human rights; Jewish agencies & temples.
General international interests: Israel.
Program-related investment (PRI) activity: The foundation made a one time PRI to community development fund.
Limitations: Giving primarily in MD; no local projects outside Baltimore, MD. No support for unaffiliated schools or synagogues. No grants to individuals, or for fundraising events, or direct mail solicitations; no loans (except for program-related investments).
Publications: Grants list.
PRI program information: Applications not accepted. The foundation does not maintain a formal PRI program.
Officers and Trustees:* Michael J. Hirschhorn,* Pres.; David Hirschhorn,* Pres. Emeritus; Barbara B. Hirschhorn,* V.P.; Arthur E. Roswell,* V.P.; Elizabeth B. Roswell,* V.P.; Lynn Wintriss,* Secy.; Maureen L. Stewart, Treas.; Betsy F. Ringel, Exec. Dir.; Gina B. Hirschhorn, Barbara S. Roswell, Sarah H. Shapiro, Judith R. Weinstein.
Number of staff: 2 full-time professional; 2 full-time support.
EIN: 526038382
PRI recipients:
31-1. Shefa Fund, Philadelphia, PA, $200,000. Program-related investment. 1999.

32
The Blowitz-Ridgeway Foundation
1 Northfield Plz.
570 Frontage Rd., Ste. 528
Northfield, IL 60093-1213 (847) 446-1010
Contact: Tina Erickson, Admin.
FAX: (847) 446-6318; E-mail: TMEBRF@aol.com;
URL: http://fdncenter.org/grantmaker/blowitz

Status changed from public charity to private foundation in 1984; converted from Ridgeway Hospital. PRI-related activities began in 1994.
Grantmaker type: Independent foundation
General financial activity (yr. ended 09/30/02): Assets, $20,086,852 (M); expenditures, $1,886,046; qualifying distributions, $1,388,526; giving activities include $1,388,526 for grants and $100,000 for 1 PRI.
Cumulative PRI activity (through 09/30/02): Since 1994, the foundation has made 9 PRIs totaling $1,850,000. The currently outstanding PRI portfolio includes PRIs totaling $825,000 (high: $250,000; low: $100,000; average: $125,000). The typical outstanding PRI has a maximum term of 7 years, and earns an average of 3 percent interest.
General purpose and activities: Giving through program, general operating capital, and research grants primarily in

the areas of health, mental and physical disability, and social services, with emphasis on children and youth.
General fields of interest: Health care; mental health/crisis services; medical research; human services; children & youth, services; disabled.
Program-related investment (PRI) activity: The foundation makes PRIs to an intermediary, the Illinois Facilities Fund, (e.g., loan fund) in support of Illinois health and social service agencies.
Types of PRI Support: Loans/promissory notes, capitalizing loan funds/other intermediaries.
Limitations: Giving generally limited to IL, except for medical research grants. No support for government agencies, religious purposes, or organizations that subsist mainly on third-party funding. No grants to individuals, or for production or writing of audio-visual materials. PRI applications not accepted.
Publications: Annual report (including application guidelines), grants list, informational brochure (including application guidelines).
PRI program information: The foundation maintains a formal PRI program. The foundation makes PRIs on an annual basis.
Officers and Trustees:* Max Pastin,* Pres.; Daniel L. Kline,* V.P.; Rev. James W. Jackson,* Secy.; Anthony M. Dean,* Treas.; Arthur R. Collison, Pierre LeBreton, Ph.D., Patricia A. MacAlister, Marvin J. Pitluk, Ph.D., Sandra Swantek, M.D., Samuel G. Winston.
Number of staff: 1 full-time professional; 1 full-time support.
EIN: 362488355
PRI recipients:
32-1. Illinois Facilities Fund, Chicago, IL, $100,000. Loan to allow Fund to be able to provide loans to Chicago health and social services agencies. 2002.
32-2. Illinois Facilities Fund, Chicago, IL, $250,000. Loan to allow Fund to be able to provide loans to Chicago health and social services agencies. 2001.
32-3. Illinois Facilities Fund, Chicago, IL, $250,000. Loan to allow Fund to be able to provide loans to Chicago health and social services agencies. 2000.
32-4. Illinois Facilities Fund, Chicago, IL, $250,000. Loan to allow Fund to be able to provide loans to Chicago health and social services agencies. 1999.

33
The Lynde and Harry Bradley Foundation, Inc.
P.O. Box 510860
Milwaukee, WI 53203-0153 (414) 291-9915
Contact: Daniel P. Schmidt, Exec. V.P. and C.O.O.
PRI Contact: Robert Berkopec, Treas. and C.F.O.
FAX: (414) 291-9991; URL: http://www.bradleyfdn.org

Incorporated in 1942 in WI as the Allen-Bradley Foundation, Inc.; adopted present name in 1985.
Donor(s): Harry L. Bradley,‡ Caroline D. Bradley,‡ Margaret B. Bradley,‡ Margaret Loock Trust, Allen-Bradley Co.
Grantmaker type: Independent foundation
General financial activity (yr. ended 12/31/01): Assets, $584,752,379 (M); expenditures, $46,515,594; qualifying distributions, $41,749,713; giving activities include $35,097,061 for 646 grants (high: $1,000,000; low: $102; average: $25,000–$250,000); no PRIs paid.
General purpose and activities: Support for projects that cultivate a renewed, healthier, and more vigorous sense of citizenship, at home and abroad. Projects will reflect the assumption that free men and women are genuinely self-governing, personally responsible citizens, able to run their daily affairs without the intrusive therapies of the bureaucratic, social service state. Consequently, they will seek to reinvigorate and revive the authority of the traditional institutions of civil society - families, schools, churches, neighborhoods, and entrepreneurial enterprises - that cultivate and provide room for the exercise of citizenship, individual responsibility, and strong moral character. Projects reflecting this view of citizenship and civil society may be demonstrations with national significance; public policy research in economics, politics, culture, or foreign affairs; or media and public education undertakings. Local support is directed toward cultural programs, education, social services, medical and health programs, and public policy research.
General fields of interest: Humanities; history & archaeology; arts/cultural programs; education, research; higher education; education; youth development, citizenship; foreign policy; international affairs; economics; political science; public policy, research; public affairs, citizen participation; public affairs.
Program-related investment (PRI) activity: The foundation has made PRIs on a limited basis and supports the areas of community improvement and public/society benefit.
Types of PRI Support: Loans/promissory notes.
Limitations: Giving primarily in Milwaukee, WI; giving also on a national and international basis. No support for strictly denominational projects. No grants to individuals, or for endowment funds.
Publications: Application guidelines, occasional report (including application guidelines), annual report.
PRI program information: Inquiry letter including a brief history of the organization and description of its mission; if within policy guidelines, applicant will receive further application information. The foundation makes PRIs occasionally.
Officers and Directors:* Thomas L. "Dusty" Rhodes,* Chair.; Michael W. Grebe,* Pres. and C.E.O.; Daniel P. Schmidt, Exec. V.P. and C.O.O.; Thomas L. Smallwood, Secy.; Robert N. Berkopec, Treas. and C.F.O.; Cynthia Friauf, Cont.; William Armstrong, Reed Coleman, Terry Considine, Pierre S. duPont IV, Br. Bob Smith, David V. Uihlein, Jr.
Number of staff: 9 full-time professional; 8 full-time support; 3 part-time support.
EIN: 396037928
PRI recipients:
33-1. Southeast Wisconsin Professional Baseball District, Milwaukee, WI, $16,000,000. Program-related

investment for construction of new public baseball stadium complex in Milwaukee. 1999.

34

Otto Bremer Foundation

445 Minnesota St., Ste. 2000
St. Paul, MN 55101-2107 (651) 227-8036
Contact: John Kostishack, Exec. Dir.
Additional tel.: (888) 291-1123; FAX: (651) 312-3665; E-mail: obf@bremer.com; URL: http://fdncenter.org/grantmaker/bremer

Trust established in 1944 in MN. PRI-related activities began in 1983.
Donor(s): Otto Bremer.‡
Grantmaker type: Independent foundation
General financial activity (yr. ended 12/31/02): Assets, $411,000,000 (M); expenditures, $19,146,018; qualifying distributions, $23,969,832; giving activities include $17,523,111 for 697 grants (high: $250,000; low: $840; average: $10,000–$50,000) and $4,530,000 for 14 PRIs.
Cumulative PRI activity (through 12/31/02): Since 1983, the foundation has made 176 PRIs totaling $30,742,540. The currently outstanding PRI portfolio includes 80 PRIs totaling $15,661,797 (high: $850,000; low: $8,500; average: $222,050). The typical outstanding PRI has a 1- to 5-year term with an average term of 5 years, and earns an average of 5 percent interest.
General purpose and activities: Emphasis on human rights and equality. Support also for post-secondary education in MN, human services, health, religion, community affairs, and flood relief and recovery.
General fields of interest: Early childhood education; child development, education; higher education; libraries (public); education; family planning; health care; mental health/crisis services; health associations; crime/violence prevention, youth; domestic violence prevention; legal services; nutrition; housing/shelter, development; youth development, citizenship; human services; children & youth, services; child development, services; hospices; women, centers & services; minorities/immigrants, centers & services; homeless, human services; international peace/security; international human rights; civil rights, immigrants; civil rights, minorities; civil rights, disabled; civil rights, women; civil rights, aging; civil rights, gays/lesbians; race/intergroup relations; civil rights; rural development; community development; voluntarism promotion; public affairs, citizen participation; minorities; Asians/Pacific Islanders; African Americans/Blacks; Hispanics/Latinos; Native Americans/American Indians; disabled; aging; women; people with AIDS (PWAs); gays/lesbians; immigrants/refugees; economically disadvantaged; homeless.
Program-related investment (PRI) activity: The foundation maintains a PRI program and makes PRIs annually to nonprofit organizations engaged in projects of community benefit. Recent PRIs have provided support for the construction and renovation of child care centers, the development of affordable housing for young people and adults, and support for human service agencies serving specific ethnic populations.
Types of PRI Support: Loans/promissory notes, interim financing.
Limitations: Giving limited to organizations whose beneficiaries are residents of MN, MT, ND and WI. No support for national health organizations, sporting activities, or K-12 education. No grants to individuals, or for endowment funds, medical research, professorships, annual fund drives, benefit events, camps, or artistic or media projects. No PRI support to venture capital funds. The foundation accepts applications for PRIs.
Publications: Annual report (including application guidelines), grants list.
PRI program information: The foundation maintains a formal PRI program. The foundation makes PRIs on an annual basis.
Officer: John Kostishack, Exec. Dir.
Trustees: Charlotte S. Johnson, William H. Lipschultz, Daniel C. Reardon.
Number of staff: 7 full-time professional; 1 part-time professional.
EIN: 416019050
PRI recipients:

34-1. Acorn Dual Language Community Academy, Saint Paul, MN, $200,000. Program-related investment to purchase building. 1999.

34-2. Advocating Change Together (ACT), Saint Paul, MN, $75,000. Program-related investment for development of video-related training materials. 2000.

34-3. Aitkin County Advocates Against Domestic Abuse, Aitkin, MN, $65,000. Program-realted investment to purchase home which will be used as transitional housing for women and children leaving abusive environments. 2000.

34-4. Aitkin County Daytime Activity Center, McGregor, MN, $30,000. Program-related investment to expand worksite and services of organization that provides training and employment services to persons who have developmental disabilities. 2002.

34-5. American Indian Housing Corporation, Minneapolis, MN, $100,000. Program-related investment to develop Many Rivers, apartment and small business complex. 2001.

34-6. American Red Cross, Minn-Kota Chapter, Moorhead, MN, $400,000. Program-related investment for capital campaign for new building. 2001.

34-7. American Red Cross, Minn-Kota Chapter, Moorhead, MN, $600,000. Program-related investment to construct multi-purpose campus for disaster response and other service activities. 2000.

34-8. Center for Victims of Torture, Minneapolis, MN, $400,000. Program-related investment to purchase and renovate new treatment center for survivors of politically-motivated torture. 2001.

34-9. Central Community Housing Trust, Minneapolis, MN, $300,000. Program-related investment to provide affordable housing and related services. 2002.

34-10. Centro Cultural Chicano, Minneapolis, MN, $187,500. Program-related investment to purchase building and make space modifications for mental health program. 1999.

34-11. Chicanos Latinos Unidos En Servicios (CLUES), Saint Paul, MN, $150,000. Program-related investment to remodel office building. 2001.

34-12. Childrens Safety Center Network, Saint Paul, MN, $100,000. Program-related investment for new facility for organization that provides opportunities for safe parental visits. 2000.

34-13. Chrysalis, A Center for Women, Minneapolis, MN, $500,000. Program-related investment to secure new building to expand services to women and their families. 1999.

34-14. Churches United for the Homeless, Moorhead, MN, $600,000. Program-related investment to relocate and expand shelter for homeless. 2002.

34-15. Community Homes and Resources in Service to Many, Fargo, ND, $60,000. Program-related investment to purchase and renovate CHARISM Youth Center. 2001.

34-16. Community Reinvestment Fund, Minneapolis, MN, $500,000. Program-related investment to expand secondary market for affordable housing development loans. 2001.

34-17. Community Solutions Fund, Saint Paul, MN, $115,000. Program-related investment to purchase software that will help to design on-line workplace giving system. 2001.

34-18. Crookston Firefighters Association, Crookston, MN, $95,000. Program-related investment for purchase of tanker truck. 2000.

34-19. Dakota Science Center, Grand Forks, ND, $110,000. Program-related investment to complete renovation and acquire adjacent building. 2000.

34-20. Disabled and Elderly Transportation, Menomonie, WI, $135,000. Program-related investment to purchase new operations facility. 1999.

34-21. Dunn County Interfaith Volunteer Caregivers, Menomonie, WI, $100,000. Program-related investment to purchase building for food pantry. 2002.

34-22. East Side Neighborhood Service, Minneapolis, MN, $750,000. Program-related investment to acquire new building. 2000.

34-23. Exodus Community Development Company, Minneapolis, MN, $200,000. Program-related investment to purchase property that iwll be converted into child care center. 2000.

34-24. Face to Face Health and Counseling Service, Saint Paul, MN, $136,000. Program-related investment for building renovations. 2001.

34-25. Family Health Care Center, Fargo, ND, $125,000. Program-related investment to strengthen delivery of health care to special populations in Cass and Clay counties. 1999.

34-26. Family Tree, Saint Paul, MN, $32,000. Program-related investment to purchase euipment. 2001.

34-27. Friends School of Minnesota, Saint Paul, MN, $250,000. Program-related investment to construct health education facility. 2000.

34-28. Girl Scouts of the U.S.A., Peacepipe Council, Redwood Falls, MN, $25,000. Program-related investment to purchase and renovate new building. 2001.

34-29. Greater Menomonie Area Community Foundation, Menomonie, WI, $275,000. Program-related investment to develop Community Partnership Center, building that will house nonprofit agencies that provide multiple services for distressed families. 2002.

34-30. Greater Minnesota Family Services, Willmar, MN, $100,000. Program-related investment to create extended care home for chemically dependent youth. 1999.

34-31. Greater Minnesota Housing Fund, Saint Paul, MN, $500,000. Program-related investment to capitalize affordable housing interim loan fund. 2002.

34-32. Higher Ground Academy, Saint Paul, MN, $400,000. Program-related investment for development of alternative school which will feature experiential and community service learning opportunities. 1999.

34-33. Hope Adoption and Family Services International, Oak Park Heights, MN, $500,000. Program-related investment for purchase and renovation of new facility. 2002.

34-34. Hope Community, Minneapolis, MN, $300,000. Program-related investment for planning and pre-closing costs on housing development projects. 2002.

34-35. Impact Seven, Almena, WI, $525,000. Program-related investment to capitalize Greater Wisconsin Fund, revolving loan program serving distressed communities. 2002.

34-36. Lake Agassiz Regional Development Corporation, Fargo, ND, $200,000. Program-related investment to develop senior congregate apartments in Wahpeton. 2001.

34-37. Larimore, City of, Larimore, ND, $40,000. Program-related investment to purchase new ambulance. 2000.

34-38. Migizi Communications, Minneapolis, MN, $150,000. Program-related investment for development of technology resource center to assist nonprofit organizations increase digital communication capacity. 2000.

34-39. Minnesota Indian Primary Residential Treatment Center, Sawyer, MN, $100,000. Program-related investment to construct adolescent treatment center for chemical dependency. 2001.

34-40. Minot Area Youth Skating Association, Minot, ND, $500,000. Program-related investment for construction of ice arena. 2000.

34-41. Minot Public Library, Minot, ND, $100,000. Program-related investment to remodel and expand library. 2001.

34-42. Minot Vocational Adjustment Workshop, Minot, ND, $400,000. Program-related investment to purchase building for employment program serving people with disabilities. 2000.

34-43. Model Cities Health Center, Saint Paul, MN, $350,000. Program-related investment to purchase and renovate new building. 2001.

34-44. Model Cities of Saint Paul, Saint Paul, MN, $625,000. Program-related investment to develop Model Cities Brownstone to provide economic opportunities for low-income residents. 1999.

34-45. Northwood Deaconness Health Center, Northwood, ND, $50,000. Program-related investment to purchase ambulance. 1999.

34-46. Opportunities Industrialization Center, American Indian, Minneapolis, MN, $400,000. Program-related investment to renovate job training center. 2001.

34-47. Otter Tail-Wadena Community Action Council, New York Mills, MN, $300,000. Program-related investment to build houses for families of low- to moderate-income in rural communities. 2002.

34-48. Partners in Progress, Portland, ND, $200,000. Program-related investment to support farmers who are in financial and emotional distress due to downturn in agricultural economy. 2001.

34-49. PEAKS Charter School, Pillager, MN, $30,000. Program-related investment to establish alternative school that will emphasize experiential learning and physical training. 1999.

34-50. Plymouth Christian Youth Center, Minneapolis, MN, $500,000. Program-related investment to purchase and renovate expanded facility for youth center. 2000.

34-51. Prairieland Home Health Agency, Fargo, ND, $114,445. Program-related investment for automated data system used in managing home health care. 2000.

34-52. Red River Community Housing Development Organization, Grafton, ND, $73,000. Program-related investment for lease purchase pilot program that will provide homes for low-income single parent families. 2001.

34-53. Resources for Child Caring, Saint Paul, MN, $500,000. Program-related investment to relocate to another building. 2002.

34-54. Ronald McDonald House Charities, Upper Midwest, Minneapolis, MN, $500,000. Program-related investment to expand guest facilities for families of children who are being treated at area hospitals. 2001.

34-55. Second Harvest North Central Food Bank, Grand Rapids, MN, $100,000. Program-related investment to construct building. 2002.

34-56. Union Gospel Mission Association of Saint Paul, Saint Paul, MN, $500,000. Program-related investment for interim financing for Snail Lake capital project. 2000.

34-57. Wayside House, Saint Louis Park, MN, $443,000. Program-related investment to renovate home for women recovering from chemical dependency. 1999.

34-58. West Central Wisconsin Community Action Agency, Glenwood City, WI, $20,000. Program-related investment for general operating support for Jump Start Transportation Program that helps low-income working families buy automobiles. 2000.

34-59. West Central Wisconsin Community Action Agency, Glenwood City, WI, $243,000. Program-related investment to purchase and renovate building to be used for community food center. 1999.

34-60. West Side Community Health Center, Saint Paul, MN, $500,000. Program-related investment for capital campaign to construct projects designed to increase access to health care and social services for West Side and South Minneapolis communities. 2001.

34-61. Wilderness Inquiry, Minneapolis, MN, $500,000. Program-related investment to purchase and renovate new facility that provides equal access to American Wilderness areas for people with and without physical disabilities. 1999.

34-62. Wisconsin Womens Business Initiative Corporation, Milwaukee, WI, $100,000. Program-related investment to support Wisconsin Rural Childcare Initiative Partnership, pilot program that will increase quality of childcare services. 2002.

34-63. YMCA, Kandiyohi County Area Family, Willmar, MN, $400,000. Program-related investment for construction of community center. 2002.

34-64. YMCA, Minot Family, Minot, ND, $300,000. Program-related investment to construct and equip new multiple service community center. 2000.

35
Brookmore Apartment Corporation

2320 S. Fremont Ave.
Alhambra, CA 91803

Grantmaker type: Independent foundation
General financial activity (yr. ended 12/31/01): Assets, $3,928,497 (M); gifts received, $499,303; expenditures, $12,222; qualifying distributions, $328,063; giving activities include $12,222 for foundation-administered programs and $328,063 for 3 PRIs.
General purpose and activities: Invests in partnerships to provide affordable housing to low income families and elderly persons.
Program-related investment (PRI) activity: The foundation has made PRIs, in the form of investments in partnerships that provide affordable housing to elderly persons and to families with low income.
Limitations: Applications not accepted. No grants to individuals.
Officers: Morgan Sly, Pres.; Guy Paultre, Treas.; Roy Haugen, Secy.
EIN: 954245088

36
Joe W. & Dorothy Dorsett Brown Foundation
1 Galleria Plz., Ste. 2105
Metairie, LA 70001-7509 (504) 834-3433
Contact: D.P. Spencer, Pres.

Established in 1959 in LA.
Donor(s): Joe W. Brown,‡ Dorothy Dorsett Brown.‡
Grantmaker type: Independent foundation
General financial activity (yr. ended 12/31/01): Assets, $116,886,570 (M); expenditures, $3,750,222; qualifying distributions, $6,167,182; giving activities include $2,546,209 for 116 grants (high: $285,190; low: $500; average: $5,000–$25,000) and $1,931,920 for 10 PRIs.
Cumulative PRI activity (through 12/31/01): The currently outstanding PRI portfolio includes 60 PRIs totaling $3,950,724.
General purpose and activities: Giving primarily to natural resources conservation and protection, hospitals, food services, human services with special emphasis on services for the homeless.
General fields of interest: Natural resources conservation & protection; hospitals (general); food services; human services; homeless, human services; homeless.
Program-related investment (PRI) activity: The foundation has an active PRI program providing loans for low-income and temporary housing and for medical research.
Types of PRI Support: Loans/promissory notes.
Limitations: Giving primarily in southern LA and the Gulf Coast of MS. No grants to individuals.
PRI program information: The foundation makes PRIs on a frequent but not annual basis.
Officers: D.P. Spencer, Pres.; V.C. Rodriguez, V.P.; B.G. Spencer, V.P.; D.B. Spencer, V.P.; E.K. Hunter, Secy.; B.M. Estopinal, Treas.
Number of staff: 2 full-time professional; 2 part-time professional.
EIN: 726027232
PRI recipients:
36-1. Alliance of Cardiovascular Researchers, Metairie, LA, $284,000. Program-related investment to support medical research on MRI compatible stents. 2001.
36-2. Alliance of Cardiovascular Researchers, Metairie, LA, $138,700. Program-related investment to support research on stent coatings. 2001.
36-3. Ascension Orthopedics, Austin, TX, $409,233. Program-related investment to support research on silicone joint MCP. 2001.
36-4. Education and Treatment Council, Lake Charles, LA, $450,174. Loan of working capital for construction. 1999.
36-5. Fellowship of Orthaopeadic Researchers, New Orleans, LA, $250,000. Program-related investment to sponsor research on disc replacement prostheses. 2001.
36-6. Louisiana State University and A & M College, Baton Rouge, LA, $348,893. Program-related investment to support research on heart repair and heart regeneration. 2001.
36-7. Louisiana State University and A & M College, Baton Rouge, LA, $170,638. Program-related investment to support research on fluoride releasing dental resin. 2001.
36-8. Methodist Home for Children, New Orleans, LA, $109,000. Loan for playground equipment. 2001.
36-9. My House, New Orleans, LA, $30,000. Loan for operations. 2001.
36-10. Neighborhood Housing Services of New Orleans, New Orleans, LA, $80,000. Low-interest bearing loan to provide low-cost housing to new home owners. 2001.
36-11. Neighborhood Housing Services of New Orleans, New Orleans, LA, $45,000. Low-interest loan to provide low-cost housing to new home owners. 1999.
36-12. New Orleans Mission, New Orleans, LA, $100,000. Loan to construct homeless shelter. 1999.
36-13. Tulane University, New Orleans, LA, $111,456. Program-related investment to support research on diagnostic test for volume expansion as treatment for mediated essential hypertension. 2001.
36-14. Tulane University, New Orleans, LA, $58,750. Program-related investment to support polymer research as it relates to heart disease. 1999.
36-15. Tulane University, New Orleans, LA, $52,568. Program-related investment to support research on graft fluorelastomer copolymer for production of piezoelectric angioplasty balloons. 1999.
36-16. Volunteers of America, Metairie, LA, $300,000. Low-interest loan to construct homeless shelters. 1999.

37
The Buhl Foundation
650 Smithfield St., Ste. 2300
Pittsburgh, PA 15222 (412) 566-2711
Contact: Dr. Doreen E. Boyce, Pres.

Established as a trust in 1927 in PA; reincorporated in 1992. PRI-related activities began in 1995.
Donor(s): Henry Buhl, Jr.,‡ Henry C. Frick.‡
Grantmaker type: Independent foundation
General financial activity (yr. ended 06/30/02): Assets, $72,319,732 (M); expenditures, $3,347,380; qualifying distributions, $3,019,168; giving activities include $2,572,609 for 85 grants (high: $501,300; low: $750; average: $1,000–$150,000), $25,498 for employee matching gifts and $50,000 for 1 PRI.
Cumulative PRI activity (through 06/30/02): The currently outstanding PRI portfolio includes 4 PRIs totaling $787,320 (high: $1,000,000; low: $100,000). The typical outstanding PRI has a 5- to 10-year term, and earns 2.50 to 3 percent interest.
General purpose and activities: Emphasis on developmental or innovative grants to regional institutions, with special interest in education at all levels and in regional concerns, particularly those related to problems of children and youth.

General fields of interest: Early childhood education; child development, education; elementary school/education; secondary school/education; higher education; adult/continuing education; libraries/library science; education; children & youth, services; child development, services; engineering & technology; science; minorities.
Program-related investment (PRI) activity: Since 1995, the foundation has made PRIs in Pittsburgh for economic and program development. The foundation also makes PRIs to educational and community development organizations.
Types of PRI Support: Loans/promissory notes, capitalizing loan funds/other intermediaries.
Limitations: Giving primarily in southwestern PA, with emphasis on the Pittsburgh area. No support for religious or political activities, or nationally funded organizations. No grants to individuals, or for building funds, overhead costs, accumulated deficits, operating budgets, scholarships, fellowships, fundraising campaigns; no loans (except for program-related investments). The foundation accepts applications for PRIs.
Publications: Annual report, informational brochure (including application guidelines).
PRI program information: The foundation does not maintain a formal PRI program. The foundation makes PRIs occasionally.
Officers and Directors:* Francis B. Nimick, Jr.,* Chair.; Helen S. Faison,* Vice-Chair.; William H. Rea,* Vice-Chair.; Jean A. Robinson,* Vice-Chair.; Albert C. Van Dusen,* Vice-Chair.; Doreen E. Boyce, Pres.; Marsha Zahumensky, Secy.-Treas.
Number of staff: 2 full-time professional; 1 part-time professional; 2 full-time support.
EIN: 250378910
PRI recipients:
37-1. Strategic Investment Fund, Pittsburgh, PA, $250,000. Limited partnership for private capital investment fund to fill gaps in key development-driven projects in Pittsburgh. 2002.

38
The Bullitt Foundation
1212 Minor Ave.
Seattle, WA 98101-2825 (206) 343-0807
Contact: Denis Hayes, Pres.
FAX: (206) 343-0822; E-mail: info@bullitt.org;
URL: http://www.bullitt.org

Incorporated in 1952 in WA. PRI-related activities began in 1992.
Donor(s): Members of the Bullitt family.
Grantmaker type: Independent foundation
General financial activity (yr. ended 12/31/01): Assets, $102,977,986 (M); expenditures, $6,423,743; qualifying distributions, $6,214,990; giving activities include $4,802,240 for 166 grants (high: $160,000; low: $5,000; average: $10,000–$50,000), $248,405 for 148 employee matching gifts and $420,000 for 3 PRIs.
Cumulative PRI activity (through 12/31/01): The currently outstanding PRI portfolio includes 6 PRIs totaling $3,600,000 (high: $1,620,000; low: $40,000). The typical outstanding PRI has a 1- to 2-year term with an average term of 1 years and earns 3.34 to 6.33 percent interest with an average of 5 percent.
General purpose and activities: Giving for the protection and restoration of the environment in the Pacific Northwest, including mountains, forests, rivers, wetlands, coastal areas, soils, fish, and wildlife.
General fields of interest: Natural resources conservation & protection; energy; environmental education; environment; animals/wildlife; transportation.
Program-related investment (PRI) activity: The foundation makes PRIs for environmental purposes in the Pacific Northwest.
Types of PRI Support: Loans/promissory notes, interim financing, equity investments.
Limitations: Giving exclusively in the Pacific Northwest. No support for political organizations. No grants to individuals, or for capital campaigns. The foundation accepts applications for PRIs.
Publications: Annual report, application guidelines.
PRI program information: The foundation does not maintain a formal PRI program. The foundation makes PRIs on a frequent but not annual basis.
Officers and Trustees:* B. Gerald Johnson,* Chair.; Katherine M. Bullitt,* Vice-Chair.; Denis Hayes,* Pres.; David Buck, Secy.; Tomoko Moriguchi-Matsuno,* Treas.; Jennifer Belcher, Harriet Bullitt, Estella Leopold, Hubert G. Locke, Ph.D., James Youngren.
Number of staff: 5 full-time professional; 1 part-time professional.
EIN: 916027795
PRI recipients:
38-1. Archimedes Institute, Seattle, WA, $100,000. Loan. 2001.
38-2. Cascade Land Conservancy, Seattle, WA, $60,000. Loan. 2000.
38-3. Evergreen Forest Trust, Seattle, WA, $40,000. Loan. 2001.
38-4. Northwest Ecosystem Alliance, Bellingham, WA, $500,000. Loan. 1999.
38-5. River Network, Portland, OR, $280,000. Loan. 2001.
38-6. Trust for Public Land, Seattle, WA, $1,500,000. Loan for Arrowleaf Project. 2000.
38-7. World Stewardship Institute, Santa Rosa, CA, $1,620,000. Loan. 2000.

39
Fritz B. Burns Foundation
4001 W. Alameda Ave., Ste. 203
Burbank, CA 91505-4338 (818) 840-8802
Contact: Joseph E. Rawlinson, Pres.

Incorporated in 1955 in CA.
Donor(s): Fritz B. Burns.‡

Grantmaker type: Independent foundation
General financial activity (yr. ended 09/30/02): Assets, $139,010,711 (M); gifts received, $2,479,868; expenditures, $8,849,574; qualifying distributions, $7,257,715; giving activities include $7,162,180 for 97 grants (high: $1,000,000; low: $1,250; average: $10,000–$250,000); no PRIs paid.
General purpose and activities: Grants primarily for education, hospitals and medical research organizations; support also for Roman Catholic religious associations and schools, social welfare agencies, and church support.
General fields of interest: Higher education; education; hospitals (general); medical research; human services; Roman Catholic federated giving programs; Roman Catholic agencies & churches.
Program-related investment (PRI) activity: The foundation has made PRIs in the form of interest-free loans to human service and educational organizations.
Types of PRI Support: Loans/promissory notes.
Limitations: Giving primarily in the Los Angeles, CA, area. No support for private foundations. No grants to individuals.
Officers and Directors:* Joseph E. Rawlinson,* Pres.; W.K. Skinner,* Exec. V.P. and Secy.-Treas.; Lorraine Perry, Cont.; Don Freeberg, Rex J. Rawlinson, Edward F. Slattery.
Number of staff: None.
EIN: 943218106
PRI recipients:
39-1. Alexandria House, Los Angeles, CA, $100,000. Interest-free loan. 1999.
39-2. Immaculate Heart High School, Los Angeles, CA, $272,000. Interest-free loan. 1999.

40

Edyth Bush Charitable Foundation, Inc.

199 E. Welbourne Ave.
P.O. Box 1967
Winter Park, FL 32790-1967 (407) 647-4322
Contact: Deborah J. Hessler, Prog. Off.
PRI Contact: David A. Odahowski, Pres.
Additional tel.: (888) 647-4322; FAX: (407) 647-7716; E-mail: dhessler@edythbush.org; URL: http://www.edythbush.org

Originally incorporated in 1966 in MN; reincorporated in 1973 in FL.
Donor(s): Edyth Bassler Bush.‡
Grantmaker type: Independent foundation
General financial activity (yr. ended 08/31/02): Assets, $64,797,956 (M); expenditures, $4,143,212; qualifying distributions, $3,654,766; giving activities include $2,671,678 for 57 grants (high: $223,233; low: $100; average: $1,000–$10,000), $29,469 for 54 employee matching gifts and $77,701 for 4 foundation-administered programs; no PRIs paid.
Cumulative PRI activity (through 08/31/02): The typical outstanding PRI has an average term of 3 years.
General purpose and activities: Support for charitable, educational, and health service organizations, with emphasis on human services, the elderly, youth services, the handicapped, and nationally recognized quality arts or cultural programs. Provides limited number of program-related investment loans for construction, land purchase, emergency or similar purposes to organizations otherwise qualified to receive grants. Active programs directly managed and/or financed for management/volunteer development of nonprofits.
General fields of interest: Arts/cultural programs; education; health care; domestic violence prevention; human services; children & youth, services; aging, centers & services; nonprofit management; philanthropy/voluntarism, association; disabled; aging; women; economically disadvantaged; homeless.
Program-related investment (PRI) activity: The foundation makes loans to safety organizations for emergencies, construction, renovation, and interim financing.
Types of PRI Support: Loans/promissory notes, interim financing, charitable use assets.
Limitations: Giving primarily within Orange, Seminole, Osceola and Lake counties, FL. No support for alcohol or drug abuse prevention/treatment projects or organizations, religious facilities or functions, primarily (50 percent or more) tax-supported institutions, advocacy organizations, foreign organizations, or, generally, for cultural programs. No grants to individuals, or for scholarships or individual research projects, endowments, fellowships, travel, routine operating expenses, annual campaigns, or deficit financing.
Publications: Program policy statement, application guidelines, financial statement, grants list, informational brochure (including application guidelines).
PRI program information: Loan requests require a complete grant request and must comply with all of the foundation's grant policies. Requests may be filed at any time during the year. Contact the foundation before filing a loan request. The foundation makes PRIs occasionally.
Officers and Directors:* H. Clifford Lee,* Chair.; Mary Gretchen Belloff,* Vice-Chair.; David A. Odahowski,* Pres. and C.E.O.; Michael R. Cross, V.P., Finance, and Treas.; Deborah J. Hessler, Corp. Secy. and Prog. Off.; Frederick M. Belloff, Gerald F. Hilbrich, Herbert W. Holm, John S. Lord, Joan Ruffier.
Number of staff: 3 full-time professional; 3 full-time support.
EIN: 237318041

41

The Butler Family Fund

One Dupont Cir., N.W., Ste. 700
Washington, DC 20036 (202) 463-8288
Contact: Martha A. Toll, Exec. Dir.
FAX: (202) 467-0790; E-mail: butlerfmfd@sysnet.net; URL: http://fdncenter.org/grantmaker/butler

Established in 1992 in DC.
Donor(s): J.E. and Z.B. Butler Foundation.

Grantmaker type: Independent foundation
General financial activity (yr. ended 12/31/01): Assets, $14,701,960 (M); expenditures, $1,603,948; qualifying distributions, $1,494,168; giving activities include $1,349,000 for 103 grants (high: $80,000; low: $1,000; average: $1,000–$50,000); no PRIs paid.
Cumulative PRI activity (through 12/31/01): Since beginning PRI activity, the foundation has made 4 PRIs totaling $300,000. The currently outstanding PRI portfolio includes PRIs totaling $300,000.
General purpose and activities: Support for homeless families and criminal justice reform (death penalty, juvenile justice, and drug policy); also global warming.
General fields of interest: Crime/law enforcement, reform; housing/shelter; civil liberties, death penalty issues; homeless.
Program-related investment (PRI) activity: The foundation has made low-interest loans for low-income housing and community development. Loans have included support for an intermediary (i.e., venture capital fund).
Types of PRI Support: Loans/promissory notes, capitalizing loan funds/other intermediaries.
Limitations: Applications not accepted. Giving on a national basis, with emphasis on Los Angeles, San Diego and the San Francisco Bay Area, CA, Washington, DC, Chicago, IL, NY, Philadelphia, PA, and WI. No grants to individuals. PRI applications not accepted.
Publications: Grants list, program policy statement.
PRI program information: Supports only pre-selected organizations. The foundation does not maintain a formal PRI program. The foundation makes PRIs occasionally.
Officers and Directors:* Alan B. Morrison,* Pres.; John B. Hirsch,* V.P. and Treas.; Anne S. Morrison,* Secy.; Suzanne H. Binswanger, Lowell A. Blankfort, Laurence A. Gravin, Colette Hirsch, Steven B. Hirsch, Lucia Horan, Peggy A. Horan, Nina Morrison.
Number of staff: 1 part-time professional; 1 part-time support.
EIN: 521786778

42
C.I.O.S.
P.O. Box 20815
Waco, TX 76702
Contact: Paul P. Piper, Jr., Tr.

Incorporated about 1952 in TN; corporation liquidated into a charitable trust in 1987.
Donor(s): Paul P. Piper, Sr., Mrs. Paul P. Piper, Paul P. Piper, Jr., Piper Industries, Inc.
Grantmaker type: Independent foundation
General financial activity (yr. ended 06/30/02): Assets, $131,374,966 (M); gifts received, $2,052,200; expenditures, $5,330,980; qualifying distributions, $6,967,345; giving activities include $5,153,745 for 29 grants (high: $4,330,644; low: $300) and $1,779,066 for 27 PRIs.
Cumulative PRI activity (through 06/30/02): Since beginning PRI activity, the foundation has made PRIs totaling $21,475,978. The currently outstanding PRI portfolio includes a high PRI value of $100,000 and a low PRI value of $10,000. The typical outstanding PRI has a 6- to 10-year term.
General purpose and activities: Grants for Protestant church support and religious programs, including Christian education, evangelism, welfare, and support for foreign missions.
General fields of interest: Theological school/education; human services; Christian agencies & churches; Protestant agencies & churches.
Program-related investment (PRI) activity: The foundation maintains a formal PRI program targeting the areas of church support, education, and human services. PRIs have also included no-interest loans to churches and denominational agencies to develop single-unit housing for low-income families.
Types of PRI Support: Loans/promissory notes.
Limitations: Applications not accepted. Giving on a national basis. No grants to individuals.
Trustees: Mary J. Piper, Paul P. Piper, Sr., Paul P. Piper, Jr., Polly Piper Rickard.
Number of staff: None.
EIN: 742472778
PRI recipients:
42-1. Alabama Baptist Convention, Mobile, AL, $100,000. Low-interest church loans. 2002.
42-2. American Thai Foundation for Education, Waco, TX, $25,000. No-interest student loans for students at Yonok College in Thailand. 2002.
42-3. Asbury Theological Seminary, Wilmore, KY, $40,000. No-interest student loans. 2002.
42-4. Baptist General Convention of Texas, Dallas, TX, $249,066. Low-interest church loans. 2002.
42-5. Baptist General Convention of Texas, Dallas, TX, $129,000. Low-interest housing loans. 2002.
42-6. Baylor University, Truett Seminary, Waco, TX, $500,000. No-interest endowment loan. 2002.
42-7. Brownsville Housing Finance Corporation, Brownsville, TX, $76,000. Low-interest housing loans. 2002.
42-8. Bryan College, Dayton, TN, $25,500. No-interest student loans. 2002.
42-9. Buckner Adoption and Maternity Services, Dallas, TX, $50,000. Low-interest loans to allow for adoptions. 2002.
42-10. Columbia International University, Columbia, SC, $70,000. No-interest student loans. 2002.
42-11. Greenville College, Greenville, IL, $28,500. No-interest student loans. 2002.
42-12. Hardin-Simmons University, Abilene, TX, $12,000. No-interest student loans. 2002.
42-13. King College, Bristol, TN, $26,000. No-interest student loans. 2002.
42-14. Lee University, Cleveland, TN, $95,000. No-interest student loans. 2002.

42-15. Mars Hill College, Mars Hill, NC, $15,000. No-interest student loans. 2002.
42-16. Millsaps College, Jackson, MS, $26,500. No-interest student loans. 2002.
42-17. Mississippi College, Clinton, MS, $97,500. No-interest student loans. 2002.
42-18. Ouachita Baptist University, Arkadelphia, AR, $95,000. No-interest student loans. 2002.
42-19. Trinity University, San Antonio, TX, $15,000. No-interest student loans. 2002.
42-20. Wheaton College, Wheaton, IL, $50,000. No-interest student loans. 2002.

43
The Cafesjian Family Foundation, Inc.

4001 Tamiami Trail, Ste. 425
Naples, FL 34103
Contact: Lou Ann Matossian, Prog. Off.
Application address: 15 S. 5th St., Ste. 900, Minneapolis, MN 55402; URL: http://www.cafesjianfoundation.org

Established in 1996 in FL. PRI-related activities began in 1999.
Donor(s): Gerard L. Cafesjian.
Grantmaker type: Independent foundation
General financial activity (yr. ended 12/31/01): Assets, $42,201,082 (M); expenditures, $3,978,184; qualifying distributions, $3,047,888; giving activities include $1,166,634 for 14 grants (high: $285,700; low: $1,000), $79,886 for 2 foundation-administered programs and $1,535,634 for 3 PRIs.
Cumulative PRI activity (through 12/31/01): Since 1999, the foundation has made 5 PRIs totaling $2,203,273.
General purpose and activities: Giving primarily for Armenian organizations and churches; funding also for children's services.
General fields of interest: Arts/cultural programs; education; health care; human services; children, services; community development; Orthodox Catholic agencies & churches.
Program-related investment (PRI) activity: In 1999, 2000, and 2001 the foundation made a PRI to a company dedicated to the research and development of alternative energy sources to benefit and improve the infrastructure of Armenia for its citizens. In 2001, it also made a PRI to an Armenian company working to improve the delivery of media in Armenia, and it made a PRI to an Armenian company working to improve the delivery of television media in Armenia.
Types of PRI Support: Equity investments.
Limitations: Applications not accepted. Giving primarily in Washington, DC, and New York, NY. No grants to individuals. PRI applications not accepted.
PRI program information: The foundation does not maintain a formal PRI program. The foundation makes PRIs on an annual basis.
Officers and Directors:* Gerard L. Cafesjian,* Pres.; Cleo T. Cafesjian,* V.P.; John Waters,* Secy.-Treas.; Lou Ann Matossian, Prog. Off.
EIN: 593417473
PRI recipients:
43-1. A-Up, Yerevan, Armenia, $185,710. Equity investment in company working to improve delivery of television within Armenia. 2001.
43-2. Armenia TV, Yerevan, Armenia, $683,559. Equity investment for company working to improve delivery of media within Armenia. 2001.
43-3. Solar En, Naples, FL, $666,365. Equity investment in company dedictated to research and development of alternative energy sources to benefit and improve infrastructure for citizens of Armenia. 2001.
43-4. Solar En, Naples, FL, $450,000. Program-related investment for research to develop alternative energy sources to benefit and improve infrastructure for citizens of Armenia. 2000.
43-5. Solar En, Naples, FL, $217,639. Program-related investment for research and development of alternative energy sources to benefit and improve infrastructure of Armenia. 1999.

44
California Community Foundation

445 S. Figueroa St., Ste. 3400
Los Angeles, CA 90071 (213) 413-4130
Contact: Judith Spiegel, Sr. V.P., Progs. and Catherine Stringer, Dir., Comm.
PRI Contact: Ken Gregorio, Prog. Off.
FAX: (213) 383-2046; E-mail: info@ccf-la.org; URL: http://www.calfund.org

Established in 1915 in CA by bank resolution. PRI-related activities began in 1991.
Grantmaker type: Community foundation
General financial activity (yr. ended 06/30/02): Assets, $535,945,270 (M); gifts received, $74,849,995; expenditures, $70,401,109; giving activities include $56,551,166 for grants and $5,350,000 for 8 PRIs.
General purpose and activities: Giving in the areas of arts and culture, civic affairs, community education, health and medicine, human services, children and youth, community development, animal welfare, and the environment. Funding through four main strategies: 1) Building Healthy Communities- To ensure the physical and mental strength for individuals to be self-supporting; 2) Improve Early Academic Achievement-To provide children from preschool through eighth grade with a solid educational base; 3) Revitalize Neighborhoods- To establish communities where every individual feels they have a stake in the community's well being; and 4) Strengthen and Expand Economic Opportunities-To place adults into jobs that provide livable wages and ease their entry into the work force.
General fields of interest: Arts/cultural programs; education; environment; animal welfare; health care; AIDS;

AIDS research; domestic violence prevention; housing/shelter, development; human services; children & youth, services; aging, centers & services; race/intergroup relations; community development; public affairs; Asians/Pacific Islanders; African Americans/Blacks; Hispanics/Latinos; Native Americans/American Indians; disabled; aging; women; people with AIDS (PWAs); gays/lesbians; immigrants/refugees; economically disadvantaged; homeless.
Program-related investment (PRI) activity: Since 1991, the foundation made PRIs annually through the Affordable Housing Loan Fund. This $1 million revolving loan fund assisted California's community-based developers of affordable housing with predevelopment costs. In 2002, the foundation expanded the program. Now called the Program-Related Investment Loan Fund, this $10 million fund, in addition to housing, makes loans for commercial/retail enterprises, charter schools, community centers, and health clinics.
Types of PRI Support: Loans/promissory notes, interim financing, loan guarantees, capitalizing loan funds/other intermediaries.
Limitations: Giving limited to the greater Los Angeles County, CA, area. No support for sectarian purposes. No grants to individuals (except through the Brody and Getty arts funds), or for building funds, annual campaigns, equipment, endowment funds, debt reduction, operating budgets, scholarships, fellowships, films, conferences, dinners, or special events.
Publications: Annual report (including application guidelines), application guidelines, informational brochure, newsletter, financial statement, informational brochure (including application guidelines).
PRI program information: The foundation maintains a formal PRI program.
Officers: Jack Shakely, Pres.; Joe Lumarda, Exec. V.P., Ext. Affairs; Steve Cobb, V.P. and C.F.O.; Judith A. Spiegel, Sr. V.P., Progs.
Board of Governors: Jane G. Pisano, Chair.; Virgil Patrick Roberts, Chair. Emeritus; Vilma S. Martinez, Vice-Chair.; Bruce C. Corwin, Dorothy Avila Courtney, Jane B. Eisner, Richard M. Ferry, Ronald Gother, Paul C. Hudson, Kenneth Lombard, Olivia E. Mitchell, Luis G. Nogales, Ki Suh Park, Virgil Roberts, Albert R. Rodriguez, Robert Segal, John C. Siciliano, Andrea L. Van de Kamp.
Number of staff: 24 full-time professional; 18 full-time support.
EIN: 953510055

45
The California Endowment

21650 Oxnard St., Ste. 1200
Woodland Hills, CA 91367 (800) 449-4149
Contact: Rebecca Martin, Grants Mgr.
Additional tel.: (818) 703-3311, ext. 234; FAX: (818) 703-4193; E-mail: bmartin@calendow.org; URL: http://www.calendow.org

Established in 1996 in CA; converted from Blue Cross of California.
Grantmaker type: Independent foundation
General financial activity (yr. ended 02/28/02): Assets, $3,366,256,063 (M); gifts received, $87,987,174; expenditures, $202,905,536; qualifying distributions, $186,030,172; giving activities include $150,646,157 for 885 grants (high: $15,000,000; low: $1,089; average: $25,000–$250,000), $334,044 for employee matching gifts and $5,752,173 for foundation-administered programs; no PRIs paid.
Cumulative PRI activity (through 02/28/02): Since beginning PRI activity, the foundation has made 1 PRI totaling $20,000,000. The currently outstanding PRI portfolio includes 1 PRI totaling $20,000,000.
General purpose and activities: To expand access to affordable, quality health care for underserved individuals and communities and to promote fundamental improvements in the health status of all Californians.
General fields of interest: Medicine/medical care, equal rights; health care; minorities; economically disadvantaged.
Program-related investment (PRI) activity: The foundation has made PRIs for community and rural development and health care.
Types of PRI Support: Loans/promissory notes.
Limitations: Giving limited to CA. No grants to individuals.
Publications: Annual report, application guidelines, occasional report.
PRI program information: The foundation does not maintain a formal PRI program. The foundation makes PRIs occasionally.
Officers and Directors:* Laura S. Wiltz, Ph.D.,* Chair.; Cynthia Ann Telles,* Vice-Chair.; Robert K. Ross, M.D.,* Pres. and C.E.O.; Julie Tugend, V.P. and C.O.O.; Rakesh Varma, V.P. and C.F.O.; Dennis Hunt, V.P., Comm. and Public Affairs; Alicia Lara, V.P., of Progs.; Alex Hsiao, C.I.O. and Treas.; Leroy T. Barnes, Jr., Tessie Guillermo, Beverly L. Hamilton, Marilyn Hamilton, Sherry M. Hirota, Sr. Ruth Marie Nickerson, Peter Pennecamp, E. Lewis Reid, Rita Scardacci, Fermando M. Torres, Ph.D., Maria Tripp, Winnie Wilis, Sc.D.
Number of staff: 168 full-time professional; 11 full-time support; 2 part-time support.
EIN: 954523232
PRI recipients:
45-1. Rural Community Assistance Corporation, West Sacramento, CA, $20,000,000. Loan, non-interest bearing, to improve health care conditions of agricultural workers. 1999.

46

The CARLISLE Foundation

P.O. Box 2464
Framingham, MA 01703 (508) 872-6377
Contact: Richard A. Goldblatt, Exec. Dir.
FAX: (508) 872-6377; E-mail:
rag@carlislefoundation.org; URL: http://
www.carlislefoundation.org

Established in 1991 in MA.
Donor(s): Helene T. Wilson, Grant M. Wilson.
Grantmaker type: Operating foundation
General financial activity (yr. ended 11/30/02): Assets, $4,164,423 (M); gifts received, $60,093; expenditures, $1,907,103; qualifying distributions, $1,898,669; giving activities include $1,639,909 for 139 grants (high: $500,000); no PRIs paid.
General purpose and activities: The foundation is dedicated to work in partnership with community coalitions to promote the health and well-being of children and families.
General fields of interest: Substance abuse, services; mental health/crisis services; housing/shelter, development; children & youth, services; family services; homeless, human services; economic development.
Program-related investment (PRI) activity: The foundation has made PRIs to fund an extended day care program and a youth and family services program.
Limitations: Giving limited to New England, with emphasis on MA, including the greater Boston area. No grants to individuals.
Publications: Grants list, informational brochure (including application guidelines), multi-year report.
Officers and Trustees:* Helene T. Wilson,* Pres.; Grant M. Wilson,* Secy.-Treas.; Richard A. Goldblatt, Exec. Dir.; George B. Foote, Jr., Edward S. Heald, Kristen Wilson.
Number of staff: 1 full-time professional; 1 part-time professional.
EIN: 046689264
PRI recipients:

46-1. Boston University Residential Charter School, Boston, MA, $190,000. Program-related investment. 1999.
46-2. Carlisle Extended Day Care Program, Carlisle, MA, $587,500. Program-related investment. 2001.
46-3. Carlisle Extended Day Care Program, Carlisle, MA, $614,500. Program-related investment. 2000.
46-4. Carlisle Extended Day Care Program, Carlisle, MA, $601,500. Program-related investment. 1999.
46-5. Concord Youth and Family Services of Acton, Acton, MA, $160,000. Program-related investment. 2001.

47

Eugene B. Casey Foundation

800 S. Frederick Ave., Ste. 100
Gaithersburg, MD 20877-4102 (301) 948-4595
Contact: Betty Brown Casey, Chair.

Established in 1981 in MD.
Grantmaker type: Independent foundation
General financial activity (yr. ended 08/31/02): Assets, $171,703,050 (M); expenditures, $54,387,084; qualifying distributions, $52,210,956; giving activities include $52,470,000 for 26 grants (high: $45,853,750; low: $5,000; average: $10,000–$100,000); no PRIs paid.
Cumulative PRI activity (through 08/31/02): The currently outstanding PRI portfolio includes PRIs totaling $140,649.
General purpose and activities: Support primarily for higher education and medical research; support also for the fine arts and community development.
General fields of interest: Visual arts; performing arts; higher education; medical research; community development.
Program-related investment (PRI) activity: The foundation has made mortgage loans.
Limitations: Giving primarily in the greater Washington, DC, area, and MD.
Officers and Trustees:* Betty Brown Casey,* Chair., Pres., and Treas.; Stephen N. James,* V.P. and Secy.; Douglas R. Casey, W. James Price.
EIN: 526220316

48

Chester County Community Foundation

The Lincoln Bldg.
28 W. Market St.
West Chester, PA 19382 (610) 696-8211
Contact: H. McPherson, V.P.
FAX: (610) 696-8213; E-mail: Miker@chescosf.org;
URL: http://www.chescocf.org

Established in 1994 in PA.
Grantmaker type: Community foundation
General financial activity (yr. ended 06/30/02): Assets, $13,587,610 (L); gifts received, $6,504,922; expenditures, $2,542,891; giving activities include $1,157,853 for grants; no PRIs paid.
General purpose and activities: To maintain and enhance the quality of life in Chester County, PA. The foundation administers donor-advised funds_.
General fields of interest: Arts/cultural programs; libraries/library science; scholarships/financial aid; education; health care; community development, neighborhood development; women; youth development.
Program-related investment (PRI) activity: The foundation operates the Fund for Coatesville, which awards interest-free one-year loans to organizations to provide help in restoring the Coatesville community.

Types of PRI Support: Loans/promissory notes.
Limitations: Giving primarily in Chester County, PA. PRI support is limited to the Coatesville, PA area. The foundation accepts applications for PRIs.
Publications: Annual report, financial statement, newsletter, informational brochure, application guidelines.
PRI program information: The foundation maintains a formal PRI program.
Officers and Directors:* John A. Featherman III,* Chair.; Michael J. Rawl,* Pres.; and 14 additional directors.
Number of staff: 3 full-time professional; 2 part-time professional; 1 full-time support.
EIN: 232773822

49
Christian Mission Concerns
P.O. Box 20815
Waco, TX 76702

Established in 1984 in TX.
Donor(s): Paul Piper, Sr., Paul Piper, Jr.
Grantmaker type: Independent foundation
General financial activity (yr. ended 12/31/02): Assets, $18,208,940 (M); gifts received, $4,687; expenditures, $856,986; qualifying distributions, $580,622; giving activities include $426,923 for 47 grants (high: $108,000; low: $500) and $60,000 for 2 PRIs.
General purpose and activities: Giving primarily to Baptist churches and organizations.
General fields of interest: Human services; Protestant agencies & churches.
Program-related investment (PRI) activity: Historically, the foundation has made a low-interest loan to an organization for the purchase of psychiatric facilites for children. The foundation has also made a PRI, in the form of a loan, to a senior ministry, for cash flow needs, and a PRI, in the form of a loan to a Baptist laity institute, to be used for scholarships. The foundation has made a PRI, in the form of a no-interest loan, to an educational institution, to be used for no-interest loans to students. The foundation has also made a PRI, in the form of a no-interest loan, to a church, to complete building.
Types of PRI Support: Loans/promissory notes.
Limitations: Applications not accepted. Giving primarily in Waco, TX. No grants to individuals.
Officers and Directors:* Kent Reynolds,* Pres.; Paul Piper, Jr.,* V.P.; H.H. Reynolds,* Secy.; J.D. Hudson,* Treas.
EIN: 742317938
PRI recipients:
49-1. Cedar Crest Foundation, Belton, TX, $750,000. Low-interest loan to purchase facility for psychiatric services for children. 1999.
49-2. Central Texas Senior Ministry, Waco, TX, $60,000. Program-related investment for cash flow needs. 2000.
49-3. Texas Baptist Laity Institute, Dallas, TX, $25,000. No-interest loan for scholarships. 2000.

50
The Clark Foundation
1 Rockefeller Plz., 31st Fl.
New York, NY 10020 (212) 977-6900
Contact: Charles H. Hamilton, Exec. Dir.

Incorporated in 1931 in NY; merged with Scriven Foundation, Inc. in 1973.
Donor(s): Members of the Clark family.
Grantmaker type: Independent foundation
General financial activity (yr. ended 06/30/02): Assets, $469,042,395 (M); gifts received, $400; expenditures, $23,757,434; qualifying distributions, $20,705,141; giving activities include $17,939,478 for grants; no PRIs paid.
General purpose and activities: Support for a hospital and museums in Cooperstown, NY; grants also for charitable and educational purposes, including undergraduate scholarships to students residing in the Cooperstown area. Support also for health, educational, youth, cultural, environmental, and community organizations and institutions. The foundation owns and supports the Clark Sports Center, which is located in Cooperstown, NY.
General fields of interest: Museums; education; environment; health care; health associations; AIDS; health organizations; AIDS research; employment; human services; children & youth, services; economically disadvantaged; general charitable giving.
Program-related investment (PRI) activity: The foundation has made PRIs for environmental conservation.
Types of PRI Support: Loans/promissory notes.
Limitations: Giving primarily in upstate NY and New York City; scholarships restricted to students residing in the Cooperstown, NY, area. No grants to individuals (except as specified in restricted funds), or for deficit financing or matching gifts.
Publications: Program policy statement, application guidelines.
Officers and Directors:* Jane Forbes Clark,* Pres.; Edward W. Stack,* V.P.; Alexander F. Treadwell,* V.P.; Charles H. Hamilton, Secy. and Exec. Dir.; Kevin S. Moore,* Treas.; Kent L. Barwick, Felicia H. Blum, William M. Evarts, Gates Helms Hawn, Archie F. MacAllaster, Mrs. Edward B. McMenamin, Kevin S. Moore, Thomas Q. Morris, M.D., Anne L. Peretz, Edward W. Stack, John Hoyt Stookey, Clifton R. Wharton, Jr.
Number of staff: 4 full-time professional; 3 part-time professional; 43 full-time support; 20 part-time support.
EIN: 135616528
PRI recipients:
50-1. Trust for Public Land, NYC, NY, $1,000,000. Loan. 1999.

51
Clay Foundation, Inc.
1426 Kanawha Blvd. E.
Charleston, WV 25301 (304) 344-8656
Contact: Charles M. Avampato, Pres.
FAX: (304) 344-3805

Incorporated in 1986 in WV.
Donor(s): Charles M. Avampato, George Diab.
Grantmaker type: Independent foundation
General financial activity (yr. ended 10/31/02): Assets, $54,962,179 (M); expenditures, $2,159,631; qualifying distributions, $1,781,685; giving activities include $1,364,338 for 19 grants (high: $596,450; low: $5,000; average: $5,000–$75,000); no PRIs paid.
General purpose and activities: Giving primarily for secondary and higher education, social service organizations, and the arts.
General fields of interest: Arts/cultural programs; elementary/secondary education; higher education; human services; federated giving programs.
Program-related investment (PRI) activity: The foundation has made PRIs to provide financing for construction of low and moderate income housing developments.
Types of PRI Support: Loans/promissory notes.
Limitations: Giving limited to WV, with emphasis on the greater Kanawha Valley area. No support for religious purposes or private functions. No grants to individuals, or for operating expenses, deficit financing, or annual campaigns.
Officers and Directors:* Buckner W. Clay,* Co-Chair.; Lyell B. Clay,* Co-Chair.; Charles M. Avampato,* Pres.; Hamilton G. Clay,* V.P.; James K. Brown,* Secy.; Whitney Clay Diller,* Treas.
Number of staff: 1.
EIN: 550670193
PRI recipients:
51-1. McCabe-Henley Properties Limited Partnership, West Virginia Housing Development Fund, Charleston, WV, $675,000. Loan at 4.5 percent interest to develop housing for low-income people. 1999.

52
The Cleveland Foundation
1422 Euclid Ave., Ste. 1300
Cleveland, OH 44115-2001 (216) 861-3810
Contact: Steven A. Minter, Pres.
FAX: (216) 589-9039; TTY: (216) 861-3806; E-mail: ldunford@clevefdn.org; URL: http://www.clevelandfoundation.org

Established in 1914 in OH by bank resolution and declaration of trust.
Grantmaker type: Community foundation
General financial activity (yr. ended 12/31/02): Assets, $1,312,166,868 (M); gifts received, $34,962,985; expenditures, $73,443,672; giving activities include $63,144,990 for 1,756 grants; no PRIs paid.
Cumulative PRI activity (through 12/31/02): The currently outstanding PRI portfolio includes 3 PRIs totaling $3,750,000 (high: $2,000,000; low: $250,000). The typical outstanding PRI earns an average of 3 percent interest.
General purpose and activities: The Cleveland Foundation is the nation's first community foundation and model for community foundations nationwide and around the world. Its purpose is to enhance the quality of life for all the citizens of greater Cleveland by building community endowment, addressing needs through grantmaking, and providing leadership on key community issues. The foundation awards grants in seven program areas: arts and culture, civic affairs, economic development, education, the environment, health and social services. Special cross-functional grantmaking initiatives include neighborhoods and housing, strengthening the arts and cultural community, downtown redevelopment and other projects of scale, public school improvement, strengthening the quality of life in early childhood, combating persistent poverty.
General fields of interest: Visual arts; performing arts; arts/cultural programs; elementary school/education; secondary school/education; higher education; medical school/education; environment; health care; health associations; AIDS; medical research; AIDS research; housing/shelter, development; human services; youth, services; aging, centers & services; urban/community development; community development; economics; government/public administration; aging.
Program-related investment (PRI) activity: Historically, the foundation makes PRIs in special circumstances to nonprofit and for-profit organizations for projects that address its highest program priorities; those in the areas of economic development, community development, and housing. PRIs have provided interim financing and supported housing development projects, construction, facility improvement, and earned income ventures. The foundation has also made PRIs to a local arts organization and a vocational center serving the aging disabled.
Types of PRI Support: Loans/promissory notes, interim financing, loan guarantees, equity investments, capitalizing loan funds/other intermediaries.
Limitations: Giving limited to the greater Cleveland, OH, area, with primary emphasis on Cleveland, Cuyahoga, Lake, and Geauga counties, unless specified by donor. No support for sectarian or religious activities, community services such as fire and police protection, and library and welfare services. No grants to individuals, or for endowment funds, operating costs, debt reduction, fundraising campaigns, publications, films and audiovisual materials (unless they are an integral part of a program already being supported), memberships, travel for bands, sports teams, classes and similar groups; no capital support for planning, construction, renovation, or purchase of buildings, equipment and materials, land acquisition, or renovation of public space unless there is strong evidence

that the program is of priority to the foundation. The foundation accepts applications for PRIs.
Publications: Annual report (including application guidelines), newsletter, occasional report, application guidelines, financial statement, informational brochure.
PRI program information: The foundation maintains a formal PRI program. The foundation makes PRIs on a frequent but not annual basis.
Officers: Steven A. Minter, Pres.; J.T. Mullen, Sr. V.P., Treas. and C.F.O.; Richard Batyko, V.P., Comm.; Marlene Casini, V.P., Gift Planning and Donor Rels.; Robert E. Eckardt, V.P., Prog.; Lynn M. Sargi, V.P. Admin. and Human Resources; Leslie A. Dunford, Corp. Secy., and C.O.S.
Directors: John Sherwin, Jr., Chair.; Jerry Sue Thorton, Vice-Chair.; James E. Bennett III, Terri Hamilton Brown, Tana N. Carney, David Goldberg, Ric Harris, Joseph P. Keithley, Benson Lee, Catherine Monroe Lewis, Alex Machaskee, Rev. Otis Moss, Jr., Maria Jose Pujana, M.D., Alayne L. Reitman, Jacqueline F. Woods.
Trustees: Bank One, N.A., FirstMerit Bank, N.A., The Huntington National Bank, KeyBank, N.A., National City Bank.
Number of staff: 41 full-time professional; 18 full-time support; 1 part-time support.
EIN: 340714588
PRI recipients:

52-1. BioEnterprise Corporation, Cleveland, OH, $2,000,000. Program-related Investment. 2002.

52-2. Cleveland Advanced Manufacturing Program (CAMP), Cleveland, OH, $1,000,000. Program-related investment. 1999.

52-3. Cleveland Foundation (Inc.), Cleveland, OH, $500,000. Program-related investment for second phase of The Cleveland Foundation, Inc. technology project. 2001.

52-4. Cleveland Foundation (Inc.), Cleveland, OH, $750,000. Loan for restoration of historic elements of The Arcade. 1999.

52-5. Cleveland Tomorrow, Cleveland, OH, $1,000,000. Program-related investment. 1999.

52-6. Goodrich-Gannett Neighborhood Center, Cleveland, OH, $100,000. Program-related investment for purchase of former Hofbrau Haus property. 2002.

52-7. Historic Gateway Neighborhood Corporation, Cleveland, OH, $750,000. Program-related investment. 1999.

52-8. Neighborhood Progress, Cleveland, OH, $2,000,000. Program-related investment. 2001.

52-9. West Side Ecumenical Ministry, Cleveland, OH, $600,000. Loan toward reducing existing bank line of credit for renovation of administrative facility. 1999.

52-10. West Side Ecumenical Ministry, Cleveland, OH, $600,000. Program-related investment. 1999.

52-11. YMCA of Cleveland, Cleveland, OH, $1,500,000. Program-related investment for construction of new Geauga YMCA building. 2002.

53
The Coca-Cola Foundation, Inc.

1 Coca-Cola Plz., N.W.
Atlanta, GA 30301 (404) 676-2568
Contact: Ingrid Saunders Jones, Chair.
Application address: P.O. Drawer 1734, Atlanta, GA 30301; FAX: (404) 676-8804; URL: http://www2.coca-cola.com/citizenship/foundation_coke.html

Incorporated in 1984 in GA.
Donor(s): The Coca-Cola Co.
Grantmaker type: Company-sponsored foundation
General financial activity (yr. ended 12/31/01): Assets, $59,075,032 (M); expenditures, $12,214,710; qualifying distributions, $12,591,774; giving activities include $12,091,774 for 174 grants (high: $1,250,000; low: $2,000; average: $25,000–$200,000) and $500,000 for 1 PRI.
Cumulative PRI activity (through 12/31/01): The currently outstanding PRI portfolio includes 2 PRIs totaling $1,000,000.
General purpose and activities: The mission of the Coca-Cola Foundation is to improve the quality of life in the community and enhance individual opportunity through education. The foundation supports educational programs primarily within three main areas: higher education, classroom teaching and learning, and international education. Programs support scholarships for aspiring students; encourage and motivate young people to stay in school; and foster cultural understanding.
General fields of interest: Education, association; elementary school/education; secondary school/education; higher education; education, services; international exchange, students; international economic development; business & industry; minorities.
Program-related investment (PRI) activity: The foundation has made a PRI to a business consortium fund.
Limitations: No support for religious organizations or religious endeavors, political, fraternal or veterans' organizations, hospitals, or local chapters of national organizations. No grants to individuals, or for workshops, travel costs, conferences or seminars, and related advertising publications, equipment, or land acquisition; generally, no loans (except for program-related investments).
Publications: Annual report, application guidelines.
PRI program information: The foundation makes PRIs occasionally.
Officers and Directors:* Ingrid Saunders Jones,* Chair.; R. Michelle Beale,* Secy.; Gary P. Fayard,* Treas.; Helen Smith Price, Exec. Dir.; Carol Hayes, Genl. Counsel; Carlton L. Curtis, Randal W. Donaldson, John H. Downs, Jr., Joseph W. Jones, Melody Justice.
Number of staff: 6 full-time professional; 5 full-time support.
EIN: 581574705
PRI recipients:

53-1. Business Consortium Fund, $500,000. Program-related investment. 2001.

54

Naomi and Nehemiah Cohen Foundation

(Formerly Cohen-Solomon Family Foundation, Inc.)
P.O. Box 73708
Washington, DC 20056 (202) 234-5454
Contact: Alison McWilliams, Assoc. Dir.
FAX: (202) 234-8797; E-mail: NNCF@erols.com

Incorporated in 1959 in DC. PRI-related activities began in 1995.
Donor(s): Emanuel Cohen,‡ N.M. Cohen,‡ Naomi Cohen,‡ Israel Cohen,‡ Daniel Solomon, Lillian Cohen Solomon,‡ David Solomon, Stuart Brown, Diane Brown.
Grantmaker type: Independent foundation
General financial activity (yr. ended 12/31/01): Assets, $87,419,263 (M); gifts received, $10,208,399; expenditures, $3,771,737; qualifying distributions, $3,537,751; giving activities include $3,379,200 for 116 grants (high: $140,000; low: $1,000; average: $1,000–$50,000) and $50,000 for 1 PRI.
Cumulative PRI activity (through 12/31/01): Since 1995, the foundation has made 3 PRIs totaling $460,000. The currently outstanding PRI portfolio includes 2 PRIs totaling $410,000 (high: $360,000; low: $50,000). The typical outstanding PRI has a 5- to 10-year term, and earns 1 to 2 percent interest.
General purpose and activities: The focus of the foundation is on human services, civic affairs and Jewish causes in Washington, DC and Israel.
General fields of interest: Environment; youth development, adult and child programs; human services; international human rights; civil rights; community development; Jewish agencies & temples.
General international interests: Israel.
Program-related investment (PRI) activity: The foundation gave PRIs in the form of low-interest loans to support a community development loan fund and to a youth center for puschase of a business franchise to be used as a job training center.
Types of PRI Support: Loans/promissory notes.
Limitations: Giving primarily in Washington, DC and Israel. No grants to individuals. PRI applications not accepted.
Publications: Grants list, application guidelines.
PRI program information: The foundation does not maintain a formal PRI program. The foundation makes PRIs occasionally.
Officers and Directors:* David Solomon,* Pres.; Diane Solomon Brown,* Secy.; Daniel Solomon,* Treas.
Number of staff: 1 full-time professional.
EIN: 526054166
PRI recipients:

54-1. Latin American Youth Center, DC, $50,000. Loan to purchase business franchise to be used as low-income job training center. 2001.

54-2. Shefa Fund, Philadelphia, PA, $360,000. Loan to support community development loan fund established to assist poor and blighted communities. 1999.

55

The Coleman Foundation, Inc.

575 W. Madison, Ste. 4605-2
Chicago, IL 60661 (312) 902-7120
Contact: Michael W. Hennessy, Pres.
E-mail: coleman@colemanfoundation.org; URL: http://www.colemanfoundation.org

Trust established in 1951 in IL. PRI-related activities began in 1998.
Donor(s): J.D. Stetson Coleman,‡ Dorothy W. Coleman.‡
Grantmaker type: Independent foundation
General financial activity (yr. ended 12/31/02): Assets, $132,674,459 (M); expenditures, $9,212,227; qualifying distributions, $8,723,269; giving activities include $7,948,017 for 223 grants (high: $300,000; low: $1,000; average: $10,000–$100,000); no PRIs paid.
Cumulative PRI activity (through 12/31/02): Since 1998, the foundation has made 5 PRIs totaling $900,000. The currently outstanding PRI portfolio includes PRIs totaling $500,000 (high: $500,000). The typical outstanding PRI has a 1- to 3-year term, and earns 0 to 2 percent interest.
General purpose and activities: Giving for post-secondary, community, secondary and elementary education programs which focus on developing awareness of self-employment, and other selected post-secondary, secondary, and elementary education projects. Support also for cancer research and care as well as programs to aid the developmentally disabled.
General fields of interest: Elementary school/education; secondary school/education; higher education; business school/education; adult/continuing education; education; medical care, rehabilitation; cancer; cancer research; human services, special populations; community development, small businesses; community development; minorities; disabled; economically disadvantaged.
Program-related investment (PRI) activity: The foundation gives low-interest rate loans to nonprofit organizations.
Types of PRI Support: Loans/promissory notes.
Limitations: Giving primarily in the Midwest, with emphasis on the metropolitan Chicago, IL, area; support also outside the Midwest for selected programs. No grants to individuals, or for deficit financing, or ticket purchases. PRI applications not accepted.
Publications: Annual report, financial statement, application guidelines.
PRI program information: The foundation does not maintain a formal PRI program. The foundation makes PRIs occasionally.
Officers and Directors:* John E. Hughes,* Chair.; Michael W. Hennessy,* C.E.O. and Pres.; James H. Jones,* Secy.; Trevor C. Davies,* Treas.; C. Hugh Albers, R. Michael Furlong.

Number of staff: 4 full-time professional.
EIN: 363025967
PRI recipients:
55-1. ACCION Chicago, Chicago, IL, $400,000. Low-interest rate loan. 2001.
55-2. ACCION Chicago, Chicago, IL, $100,000. Low-interest loans. 2000.
55-3. ACCION Chicago, Chicago, IL, $100,000. Low-interest loan. 1999.

56
The Colorado Trust
The Colorado Trust Bldg.
1600 Sherman St.
Denver, CO 80203-1604 (303) 837-1200
Contact: Jean D. Merrick, Sr. V.P., Prog. and Admin.
PRI Contact: John L. Samuelson
Additional tel.: (888) 847-9140; FAX: (303) 839-9034; E-mail: Rachel@coloradotrust.org; URL: http://www.coloradotrust.org

Established in 1985 in CO; converted from the proceeds of the sale of Presbyterian/St. Luke's Healthcare Corp. to AM1.
Donor(s): Presbyterian/St. Lukes Healthcare Corp.
Grantmaker type: Independent foundation
General financial activity (yr. ended 12/31/01): Assets, $388,507,836 (M); expenditures, $19,820,422; qualifying distributions, $18,220,803; giving activities include $15,273,980 for 105 grants (high: $1,224,217; low: $9,110; average: $10,000–$100,000) and $137,915 for employee matching gifts; no PRIs paid.
General purpose and activities: To advance the health and well-being of the people of Colorado.
General fields of interest: Health care; health associations; family services.
Program-related investment (PRI) activity: The foundation has made a loan for public safety.
Types of PRI Support: Loans/promissory notes.
Limitations: Giving limited to CO. No support for religious organizations for religious purposes, private foundations, or direct subsidization of care to the medically indigent. No grants to individuals, or for endowments, deficit financing or debt retirement, building funds, real estate acquisition, medical research, fundraising drives and events, testimonial dinners, or advertising. PRI applications not accepted.
Publications: Annual report, application guidelines, newsletter, occasional report.
PRI program information: The foundation does not maintain a formal PRI program. The foundation makes PRIs occasionally.
Officers and Trustees:* Jean C. Jones,* Chair.; Sr. Lillian Murphy,* Vice-Chair.; John R. Moran, Jr., C.E.O. and Pres.; Jean D. Merrick, Sr. V.P., Prog. and Admin.; John L. Samuelson, V.P. and C.F.O.; Jerome M. Buckley, M.D.,* Secy.; Judith B. Wagner,* Treas.; Sarah Moore, Comm. Assoc.; Patricia Baca, Stephen B. Clark, William N. Maniatis, M.D., Kathryn A. Paul, A. Gordon Rippey, Reginald Washington.
Number of staff: 11 full-time professional; 8 full-time support.
EIN: 840994055

57
The Columbia Foundation
10221 Wincopin Cir.
Columbia, MD 21044-2624 (410) 730-7840
Contact: Barbara K. Lawson, Exec. Dir.
FAX: (410) 715-3043; E-mail: info@columbiafoundation.org; URL: http://www.columbiafoundation.org

Incorporated in 1969 in MD.
Grantmaker type: Community foundation
General financial activity (yr. ended 12/31/00): Assets, $7,958,314 (M); gifts received, $902,193; expenditures, $691,433; giving activities include $514,350 for grants (average: $500–$30,000); no PRIs paid.
Cumulative PRI activity (through 12/31/00): The currently outstanding PRI portfolio includes PRIs totaling $51,313 (high: $35,000; low: $10,000). The typical outstanding PRI has a maximum term of 5 years, and earns 1.50 to 4 percent interest.
General purpose and activities: Grants for health and human services, including programs for youth, the aged, and the disabled; arts and culture, including music, the performing arts, and historic preservation; educational programs; and housing. The foundation administers donor-advised funds_.
General fields of interest: Performing arts; music; historic preservation/historical societies; arts/cultural programs; education; environment; animals/wildlife; health care; housing/shelter, development; human services; children & youth, services; family services; aging, centers & services; disabled; aging.
Program-related investment (PRI) activity: The foundation currently makes PRIs to an assisted living facility for expansion, and to a therapeutic riding facility for the construction of a barn.
Types of PRI Support: Loans/promissory notes.
Limitations: Giving limited to Howard County, MD. No support for projects of a sectarian religious nature. No grants to individuals, or for annual campaigns, deficit financing, land acquisition, medical research, or general or special endowments. PRI applications not accepted.
Publications: Financial statement, application guidelines, grants list, newsletter, informational brochure (including application guidelines), annual report.
PRI program information: The foundation does not maintain a formal PRI program. The foundation makes PRIs occasionally.
Officers and Trustees:* James R. Moxley, Jr.,* Pres.; Bruce I. Rothschild,* V.P.; Carole Parnes,* Secy.; H. Elizabeth

Horowitz,* Treas.; Barbara K. Lawson, Exec. Dir.; and 26 additional trustees.
Number of staff: 1 full-time professional; 2 part-time professional; 1 full-time support.
EIN: 520937644

58
Community Foundation for Muskegon County
(Formerly Muskegon County Community Foundation, Inc.)
425 W. Western Ave., Ste. 200
Muskegon, MI 49440 (231) 722-4538
Contact: Chris Ann McGuigan, Pres.
FAX: (231) 722-4616;E-mail: info@cffmc.org;
URL: http://www.cffmc.org

Incorporated in 1961 in MI. PRI-related activities began in 1997.
Donor(s): Alta Daetz,‡ Harold Frauenthal,‡ Charles Goodnow,‡ George Hilt, Jack Hilt, John Hilt, Paul C. Johnson,‡ Henry Klooster,‡ Ernest Settle.‡
Grantmaker type: Community foundation
General financial activity (yr. ended 12/31/01): Assets, $76,190,540 (M); gifts received, $6,483,278; expenditures, $7,139,899; giving activities include $4,405,371 for grants (average: $250–$50,000); no PRIs paid.
Cumulative PRI activity (through 12/31/01): Since 1997, the foundation has made 3 PRIs totaling $385,000. The currently outstanding PRI portfolio includes an average PRI value of $25,000. The typical outstanding PRI has a 1- to 3-year term with an average term of 1 years, and earns an average of 4 percent interest.
General purpose and activities: To assist worthwhile projects, with emphasis on health and human services, arts and culture, education, community development, and youth. Of particular interest are pilot programs and collaborative projects. The foundation administers donor-advised funds_.
General fields of interest: Theater; arts/cultural programs; education; health care; health associations; human services; urban/community development; community development.
Program-related investment (PRI) activity: The foundation has made PRIs in the areas of the arts, conservation, and community development. PRIs have financed low-income housing, including housing for the elderly.
Types of PRI Support: Loans/promissory notes.
Limitations: Giving limited to Muskegon County, MI. No support for sectarian religious programs, or individual schools. No grants to individuals (except for scholarships), or for deficit financing, routine operating expenses, capital equipment, endowment campaigns, special fundraising events, or for advertising. PRI applications not accepted.
Publications: Annual report (including application guidelines), program policy statement, newsletter, financial statement, grants list, informational brochure (including application guidelines), application guidelines.
PRI program information: The foundation does not maintain a formal PRI program. The foundation makes PRIs occasionally.
Officers and Trustees:* James M. Sheridan, Chair.; Michael Bozym, Vice-Chair.; Patricia B. Johnson, Vice-Chair.; Chris Ann McGuigan,* Pres. and Secy.; Scott Musselman,* Treas.; Tim Achtherhoft, Dennis Albrechtsen, David Bliss, Lowell Dana, Barb DeBruyn, William C. Eyke, Jr., Holly Hughes, Donald Huizenga, Michael K. Olthoff, Hon. Greg Pittman, Rev. Charles Poole, Bruce Rice, William Schroeder, B.C. Thompson, Peter Turner, Sue Wierengo, Judith Wilcox, John Workman.
Trustee Banks: Comerica Bank, Fifth Third Bank, National City Bank, The Huntington National Bank.
Number of staff: 7 full-time professional; 5 full-time support.
EIN: 386114135

59
The Community Foundation for the National Capital Region
(Formerly The Foundation for the National Capital Region)
1112 16th St. N.W., Ste. 340
Washington, DC 20036 (202) 955-5890
Contact: Terri Lee Freeman, Pres.
FAX: (202) 955-8084; E-mail: cfncr@aol.com;
URL: http://www.cfncr.org

Incorporated in 1973 in DC.
Grantmaker type: Community foundation
General financial activity (yr. ended 03/31/01): Assets, $153,896,592 (M); gifts received, $80,905,289; expenditures, $28,436,828; giving activities include $26,729,312 for 1,758 grants (high: $4,000,000; low: $70; average: $10,000–$100,000); no PRIs paid.
Cumulative PRI activity (through 03/31/01): The currently outstanding PRI portfolio includes 1 PRI totaling $30,000.
General purpose and activities: The foundation exists to foster a culture of giving in the diverse and dynamic community comprising Washington, DC, and nearby MD and VA. Through its programs and discretionary grants, the foundation works to build philanthropic capital dedicated to improving the region's quality of life, to strengthen the region's nonprofit organizations and improve their financial stability, and to fund projects and experiments offering new solutions to community needs.
General fields of interest: Arts/cultural programs; education; natural resources conservation & protection; health care; substance abuse, services; human services; children & youth, services; community development; economically disadvantaged; homeless.
Program-related investment (PRI) activity: The foundation makes PRIs through two loan funds. The Emergency Loan Fund, established in 1983, provides short-term, low-interest loans to nonprofit organizations facing fiscal emergencies. The Housing Development Revolving Loan Fund, established in 1993, provides low-interest-rate loans to

organizations affiliated with Jubilee Enterprises, Inc., for the purpose of financing the acquisition and development costs of low-income housing projects.
Types of PRI Support: Loans/promissory notes, interim financing.
Limitations: Giving limited to the metropolitan Washington, DC, area. No grants to individuals (except for scholarships and fellowships), or from discretionary funds for annual campaigns, endowment funds, equipment, land acquisition, renovation projects, operating budgets, or matching gifts.
Publications: Annual report, financial statement, program policy statement, application guidelines.
Officers and Trustees:* Lawrence Hough,* Chair.; Terri Lee Freeman,* Pres.; Kenny Emson, V.P. and C.F.O.; Thomas Troyer,* Secy. and Genl. Counsel; John Schwieters, Treas.; Diane Benstein, Charito Kruvant, Victoria P. Sant, Kenneth R. Thornton, Ladislaus von Hoffmann, and 16 additional directors.
Number of staff: 9 full-time professional; 2 part-time professional; 2 full-time support; 1 part-time support.
EIN: 237343119

60

Community Foundation of Greater Greensboro, Inc.

(Formerly The Foundation of Greater Greensboro, Inc.)
100 S. Elm St., Ste. 307
Greensboro, NC 27401-2638 (336) 379-9100
Contact: H. Walker Sanders, Pres.
FAX: (336) 378-0725; E-mail: info@cfgg.org, or wsanders@cfgg.org; URL: http://www.cfgg.org

Established in 1983.
Grantmaker type: Community foundation
General financial activity (yr. ended 06/30/02): Assets, $60,681,312 (M); gifts received, $10,192,211; expenditures, $10,602,209; giving activities include $9,885,458 for grants; no PRIs paid.
Cumulative PRI activity (through 06/30/02): The currently outstanding PRI portfolio includes PRIs totaling $253,600.
General purpose and activities: The foundation is dedicated to strengthening the community for both present and future generations by promoting philanthropy, building a collection of endowment funds, and serving as a leader in shaping effective responses to community issues and opportunities in the greater Greensboro, NC, area.
General fields of interest: Arts/cultural programs; education; health care; health associations; AIDS; housing/shelter, development; human services; children & youth, services; community development, neighborhood development; community development; government/public administration.
Program-related investment (PRI) activity: The foundation makes loans for low-income housing.
Types of PRI Support: Loans/promissory notes.
Limitations: Giving primarily in the greater Greensboro, NC, area. No support for political or partisan purposes or for programs in which religious teachings are an integral part. No grants to individuals, (except for scholarships), or for capital campaigns, multi-year commitments, building funds, operating budgets or endowments. PRI applications not accepted.
Publications: Annual report, application guidelines, program policy statement, newsletter, financial statement, grants list, informational brochure.
PRI program information: The foundation does not maintain a formal PRI program. The foundation makes PRIs occasionally.
Officers and Directors:* Van King,* Chair.; R. David Sprinkle,* Chair. Elect; H. Walker Sanders, Pres.; Tara M. Sandercock, V.P., Progs.; Marie W. Schettino, V.P., Finance and Admin.; Melissa M. Staples, V.P., Marketing and Comm.; Patrick A. Weiner, V.P., Donor Svcs. and Devel.; Martha T. Stukes,* Secy.; Michael Cashwell,* Treas.; Albert Lineberry, Jr., and 25 additional directors.
Number of staff: 12 full-time professional; 1 part-time professional.
EIN: 561380249

61

The Community Foundation of Herkimer & Oneida Counties, Inc.

(Formerly Utica Foundation, Inc.)
270 Genesee St.
Utica, NY 13502 (315) 735-8212
Contact: Susan D. Smith, Sr. Prog. Off. or Margaret Anne O'Shea
FAX: (315) 735-9363; E-mail: commfdn@borg.com

Incorporated in 1952 in NY.
Grantmaker type: Community foundation
General financial activity (yr. ended 12/31/01): Assets, $50,147,196 (L); gifts received, $2,621,630; expenditures, $2,443,194; giving activities include $1,781,108 for grants (high: $107,000); no PRIs paid.
Cumulative PRI activity (through 12/31/01): The currently outstanding PRI portfolio includes a high PRI value of $254,000 and a low PRI value of $60,000. The typical outstanding PRI has an average term of 5 years.
General purpose and activities: Giving to programs and projects that: offer the greatest opportunity for positive and significant change in the community; identify and enhance local strengths to address and provide creative solutions for important existing or emerging community issues; develop organizational and/or individual self-sufficiency; focus on identifiable outcomes that will make a difference; leverage investment of other community resources; and improve the quality or scope of charitable works in the community. The foundation administers a donor-advised fund.
General fields of interest: Arts/cultural programs; higher education; libraries/library science; education; environment; hospitals (general); health care; human services; children & youth, services; family services; aging, centers & services; public affairs; disabled.

Program-related investment (PRI) activity: The foundation has made a PRI to a revolving loan fund that underwrites home rehabilitation in the Utica, NY, area.
Types of PRI Support: Loans/promissory notes, loan guarantees.
Limitations: Giving limited to Oneida and Herkimer counties, NY. No support for religious purposes or government agencies and organizations. No grants to individuals, or for ongoing operating support. PRIs are awarded only in Oneida and Herkimer Counties, NY. PRI applications not accepted.
Publications: Annual report, application guidelines, newsletter.
PRI program information: The foundation does not maintain a formal PRI program.
Officers and Directors:* Milton Bloch,* Pres.; Jane A. Halbritter,* V.P.; Richard Hanna,* V.P.; Camille T. Kahler,* Secy.; Lauren E. Bull,* Treas.; Gordon M. Hayes, Exec. Dir.; Harold T. Clark, Jr., Timothy Foley, Judith B. Gorman, Mary K. Griffith, Joseph H. Hobika, Sr., John Livingston, Grace McLaughlin, Mary Morse, Earle C. Reed, Faye Short, Sheila Smith, William Stevens.
Trustee Banks: Fleet National Bank, HSBC Bank USA.
Number of staff: 5 full-time professional; 1 full-time support.
EIN: 156016932

62
Community Foundation of New Jersey

35 Knox Hill Rd.
P.O. Box 317
Morristown, NJ 07963-0317 (973) 267-5533
Contact: James C. Kellogg, Pres.
FAX: (973) 267-2903; E-mail: cfnj@bellatlantic.net

Incorporated in 1979 in NJ.
Grantmaker type: Community foundation
General financial activity (yr. ended 04/30/02): Assets, $90,151,898 (M); gifts received, $39,975,588; expenditures, $9,923,010; giving activities include $8,330,297 for 3,173 grants (high: $1,000,000; low: $100; average: $100–$1,000,000) and $18,500 for 1 PRI.
Cumulative PRI activity (through 04/30/02): The currently outstanding PRI portfolio includes 3 PRIs totaling $28,520 (high: $18,500). The typical outstanding PRI has an average term of 5 years and earns 6.50 to 8 percent interest with an average of 7.25 percent.
General purpose and activities: Support for innovative programs which can exert a multiplier effect or through which research may contribute to the solution or easing of important community problems.
General fields of interest: Arts/cultural programs; education; environment; health care; health associations; AIDS; AIDS research; youth development, services; human services; family services; urban/community development; community development; leadership development; public affairs; economically disadvantaged.
Program-related investment (PRI) activity: The foundation provides PRI support to the New Jersey State Opera.
Types of PRI Support: Loans/promissory notes.
Limitations: Giving on a national basis for the benefit of NJ. No grants to individuals, or for continuing support, emergency funds, or deficit financing. PRI applications not accepted.
Publications: Annual report (including application guidelines), newsletter, informational brochure.
PRI program information: The foundation makes PRIs occasionally.
Officers and Trustees:* Stuart D. Sendell,* Chair.; James C. Kellogg,* Pres. and C.E.O.; Marilyn M. Pfaltz,* Secy.; Susan I. Soldivieri, C.F.O.; Scot R. Guempel,* Treas.; Faith A. Krueger, C.A.O.; Thomas W. Berry, Geoffrey M. Conner, Christine G. Cox, John P. Duffy, Kenneth L. Estabrook, Dan Gaby, Lynn S. Glasser, Michael M. Horn, Robert B. Jones, Ph.D., Russell J. Lucas, James H. Lynch, Jr., John J. Oros, Ingrid W. Reed, Mark J. Sandler, Stephen A. Tyler, Florence P. Williams, Virginia H. Worden.
Number of staff: 6 full-time professional; 1 part-time professional; 2 full-time support.
EIN: 222281783
PRI recipients:
62-1. New Jersey State Opera, Newark, NJ, $18,500. Loan. 2002.
62-2. New Jersey State Opera, Newark, NJ, $10,000. Loan. 2001.

63
Community Foundation of North Central Washington

(Formerly Greater Wenatchee Community Foundation)
7 N. Wenatchee Ave., Ste. 201
P.O. Box 3332
Wenatchee, WA 98807-3332 (509) 663-7716
Contact: G. Raymond Taylor, C.E.O. and Pres.
FAX: (509) 667-2208; E-mail: foundation@cfncw.org

Incorporated in 1986 in WA. PRI-related activities began in 2001.
Grantmaker type: Community foundation
General financial activity (yr. ended 06/30/02): Assets, $12,955,000 (M); gifts received, $742,000; expenditures, $1,190,000; giving activities include $883,769 for 387 grants (high: $10,000; low: $500; average: $1,000–$5,000), $100,645 for 120 grants to individuals (high: $4,000; low: $154; average: $250–$1,000) and $192,000 for 3 foundation-administered programs; no PRIs paid.
Cumulative PRI activity (through 06/30/02): Since 2001, the foundation has made 4 PRIs totaling $23,000. The currently outstanding PRI portfolio includes 1 PRI totaling $1,550 (high: $8,200; low: $1,550). The typical outstanding PRI has a 6-month to 1-year term with an average term of 6 months, and earns 0 to 4 percent interest.
General purpose and activities: Primary areas of interest include the arts, education, the environment, and the

disadvantaged, with emphasis on child welfare and the elderly. The foundation administers a donor-advised fund.
General fields of interest: Media/communications; visual arts; museums; performing arts; theater; music; humanities; history & archaeology; historic preservation/historical societies; arts/cultural programs; early childhood education; child development, education; elementary school/education; higher education; adult/continuing education; adult education—literacy, basic skills & GED; libraries/library science; reading; education; natural resources conservation & protection; environment; animal welfare; wildlife preservation & protection; hospitals (general); family planning; medical care, rehabilitation; health care; substance abuse, services; mental health/crisis services; AIDS; alcoholism; food services; housing/shelter, development; safety/disasters; recreation; human services; children & youth, services; child development, services; family services; hospices; aging, centers & services; women, centers & services; minorities/immigrants, centers & services; homeless, human services; community development; voluntarism promotion; minorities; disabled; aging; women; economically disadvantaged; homeless.
Program-related investment (PRI) activity: The foundation makes PRIs for the purposes of financing theater productions, financing capital improvement, and for interim financing for an Arbor Day event.
Types of PRI Support: Loans/promissory notes, interim financing, lines of credit.
Limitations: Giving limited to north central WA, especially Chelan, Douglas, Grant, and Okanogan counties. No support for religious sectarian purposes. No grants to individuals (except for designated scholarships), or for continuing support, annual campaigns, general operating budgets, or conferences. The foundation accepts applications for PRIs.
Publications: Annual report, application guidelines, informational brochure, occasional report, grants list.
PRI program information: The foundation maintains a formal PRI program. The foundation makes PRIs on an annual basis.
Officers and Trustees:* Terry Sorom,* Chair.; John J. "Jack" Snyder, Jr.,* Vice-Chair.; G. Raymond Taylor,* C.E.O. and Pres.; Mall Boyd,* Secy.-Treas.; Lloyd L. Berry, Roger Bumps, Gerald E. Gibbons, M.D., Courtney Guderian, Dennis S. Johnson, Grant Johnson, Frank Konz, Judith Lurie, Kenneth Martin, Brian Nelson, Christine Scull, Christopher Stahler, Wayne Wright.
Number of staff: 1 full-time professional; 1 part-time professional; 1 part-time support.
EIN: 911349486

64
Community Foundation of Northern Illinois

(Formerly Rockford Community Foundation)
946 N. 2nd St.
Rockford, IL 61107 (815) 962-2110
Contact: Gloria Lundin, Pres.
FAX: (815) 962-2116; E-mail: info@cfnil.org;
URL: http://www.cfnil.org

Established in 1953 in IL. PRI-related activities began in 1995.
Grantmaker type: Community foundation
General financial activity (yr. ended 06/30/01): Assets, $39,683,677 (M); gifts received, $2,452,119; expenditures, $5,535,383; giving activities include $4,927,649 for grants (average: $50–$235,000); no PRIs paid.
Cumulative PRI activity (through 12/31/01): The currently outstanding PRI portfolio includes 3 PRIs totaling $986,937. The typical outstanding PRI has a 2-month to 2-year term with an average term of 2 months.
General purpose and activities: Giving primarily for human and social services; support also for arts and culture, education, health services, and housing, neighborhoods, economic and community development, youth children, and families. In Youth We Trust group of the foundation supports programs initiated by and operated for people under 21. The foundation administers a donor-advised fund.
General fields of interest: Arts/cultural programs; education; health care; housing/shelter; human services; youth, services; child development, services.
Program-related investment (PRI) activity: The foundation makes PRIs to: provide investment capital for project and revenue-making ventures; to encourage the economic independence and stability of nonprofit organizations; to provide alternatives or to augment traditional funding sources; and, to meet emergency situations.
Limitations: Giving primarily in the metropolitan Rockford, IL, area, including Winnebago, Boone, Ogle, and Stephenson. No grants to individuals, except scholarships. PRI giving limited to non-profit organizations that have been in business for a minimum of one year, and have the skills, financial resources, and capability to meet the agreed upon payment schedule. The foundation accepts applications for PRIs.
Publications: Annual report, application guidelines, program policy statement, newsletter, informational brochure (including application guidelines).
PRI program information: PRI application form available on the foundation's Web site. The foundation maintains a formal PRI program. The foundation makes PRIs on a frequent but not annual basis.
Officers and Trustees:* Estelle Black,* Chair.; Sue Grans,* Vice-Chair; Gloria Lundin,* Pres.; Mike Gann,* Treas.; Jennifer Kruchten, C.F.O.
Trustee Banks: AMCORE Bank, N.A., Bank One, N.A.
Number of staff: 4 full-time professional; 2 part-time professional; 1 full-time support; 1 part-time support.
EIN: 366076171

65

The Community Foundation of Santa Cruz County

(Formerly Greater Santa Cruz County Community Foundation)
2425 Porter St., Ste. 17
Soquel, CA 95073-2425 (831) 477-0800
Contact: Lance Linares, Exec. Dir.
FAX: (831) 477-0991; E-mail: info@cfscc.org, or lance@cfscc.org; URL: http://www.cfscc.org

Incorporated in 1982 in CA.
Grantmaker type: Community foundation
General financial activity (yr. ended 12/31/01): Assets, $24,012,375 (M); gifts received, $8,433,316; expenditures, $3,121,107; giving activities include $1,414,771 for 360 grants (high: $190,000; low: $100; average: $2,000–$50,000); no PRIs paid.
Cumulative PRI activity (through 12/31/01): Since beginning PRI activity, the foundation has made 2 PRIs totaling $15,000.
General purpose and activities: The purpose of the foundation is to strengthen the community, and to inspire philanthropy and community involvement in Santa Cruz County, CA. The foundation administers a donor-advised fund.
General fields of interest: Humanities; historic preservation/historical societies; arts/cultural programs; education; environment; health care; human services; community development.
Program-related investment (PRI) activity: The foundation maintains a bridge loan fund available to nonprofit agencies for short-term needs, such as delays in confirmed funding from other sources.
Limitations: Giving limited to Santa Cruz County, CA. No support for religious purposes. No grants to individuals (except for scholarships from designated funds), or for annual campaigns, deficit financing, capital campaigns, building or renovation funds, land acquisition, fellowships, or research; no student loans.
Publications: Annual report, application guidelines, informational brochure.
Officers and Directors:* Norman Schwartz,* Pres.; Jill Wilson,* Secy.; James Thompson,* Treas.; Lance Linares, Exec. Dir.
Number of staff: 7 full-time professional; 1 part-time professional; 2 full-time support; 1 part-time support.
EIN: 942808039

66

Community Foundation Sonoma County

(Formerly The Sonoma County Community Foundation)
250 D St., Ste. 205
Santa Rosa, CA 95404 (707) 579-4073
Contact: Kay M. Marquet, C.E.O. and Pres.
FAX: (707) 579-4801; URL: http://www.sonomacf.org

Incorporated in 1983 in CA.
Grantmaker type: Community foundation
General financial activity (yr. ended 12/31/01): Assets, $71,144,549 (M); gifts received, $5,637,936; expenditures, $16,861,305; giving activities include $14,323,125 for 475 grants (high: $4,000,000; low: $25; average: $1,000–$25,000); no PRIs paid.
General purpose and activities: Giving primarily to arts and humanities, education, the environment, and health and human services.
General fields of interest: Humanities; arts/cultural programs; education; environment; health care; human services.
Limitations: Giving limited to Sonoma County, CA. No support for religious purposes or advocacy activities. No grants for special fundraising events, annual fund campaigns, or debt retirement.
Publications: Annual report, financial statement, newsletter, application guidelines, informational brochure.
PRI program information: The foundation makes PRIs occasionally.
Officers and Directors:* Henry Wendt,* Chair.; Herb Dwight, Chair. Elect; Kay M. Marquet, C.E.O. and Pres.; Paul Demarco, V.P., Finance and Admin.; Dan Condron, Secy.; Reuben Weinzveg, Treas.; Jeannette Anglin, Mary T. Colhoun, Christopher Dobson, Barbara Graves, Judith L. Jordan, Jean Schulz, Ernest Shelton, Paula Thomas, Neva Turer, Francisco Vazquez, Ph.D., Glenn Yamamoto.
Number of staff: 9 full-time professional; 3 full-time support; 1 part-time support.
EIN: 680003212

67

Community Memorial Foundation

15 Spinning Wheel Rd., Ste. 326
Hinsdale, IL 60521 (630) 654-4729
Contact: James Durkan, C.E.O and Pres.
FAX: (630) 654-3402; E-mail: info@cmfdn.org; URL: http://cmfdn.org

Established in 1995 in IL; converted from sale of La Grange Memorial Hospital to Columbia/HCA.
Donor(s): Helen Prempas Trust, LaGrange Memorial Health System, Marion O. Crion Trust, Harris Associates.
Grantmaker type: Independent foundation
General financial activity (yr. ended 12/31/01): Assets, $88,105,852 (M); gifts received, $22,475; expenditures,

$4,590,897; qualifying distributions, $4,201,028; giving activities include $3,371,757 for 85 grants (high: $250,000; low: $1,000; average: $2,000–$100,000); no PRIs paid.
Cumulative PRI activity (through 12/31/01): The currently outstanding PRI portfolio includes PRIs totaling $750,000.
General purpose and activities: Giving primarily to improve health.
General fields of interest: Health care; youth development; family services; community development; aging.
Program-related investment (PRI) activity: The foundation supports a loan program with The Illinois Facilities Fund, which provides equipment and real estate loans.
Types of PRI Support: Loans/promissory notes.
Limitations: Giving limited to the 27 communities in western Cook and southeastern DuPage counties, IL. No support for organizations which limit services to any one religious group or members of a specific sectarian perspective. No grants to individuals, or for endowments, capital projects, sponsoring dinners, or advertising space.
Publications: Annual report (including application guidelines), grants list.
Officers and Directors:* Donald J. Gralen,* Chair.; Timothy R. Hansen, Ph.D.,* Vice-Chair.; James Durkan,* C.E.O and Pres.; William B. Frymark, Sr., M.D.,* Secy.; C. Roger Brown,* Treas.; Ruth Ann Althaus, Ph.D., Richard J. Carroll, M.D., Linda M. Eastman, Jeffrey J. Frommelt, Paul Naffah, M.D., Timothy H. Ricordati, Ed.D.
Number of staff: 4 full-time professional; 1 full-time support.
EIN: 364012380
PRI recipients:
67-1. Illinois Facilities Fund, Chicago, IL, $250,000. Program-related investment for Community Health Care Capital Fund that provides equipment and real estate loans. 1999.

68
Crail-Johnson Foundation

222 W. 6th St., Ste. 1010
San Pedro, CA 90731 (310) 519-7413
Contact: Eric C. Johnson, Chair.
FAX: (310) 519-7221; E-mail: Eric-Johnson@crail-johnson.org; URL: http://www.crail-johnson.org

Established in 1987 in CA.
Donor(s): Jerry L. Johnson,‡ Robert Johnson.‡
Grantmaker type: Independent foundation
General financial activity (yr. ended 12/31/00): Assets, $14,204,354 (M); gifts received, $2,425,000; expenditures, $2,860,255; qualifying distributions, $3,030,255; giving activities include $2,589,144 for 136 grants (high: $501,320; low: $50; average: $5,000–$50,000), $50,996 for 92 employee matching gifts and $170,000 for 1 PRI.
General purpose and activities: The foundation promotes the well-being of children in need through the effective application of human and financial resources.
General fields of interest: Early childhood education; child development, education; elementary school/education; reading; health care; children & youth, services; child development, services; family services; science; mathematics.
Program-related investment (PRI) activity: The foundation made a PRI to a charter school for the purchase of land for a new campus.
Types of PRI Support: Loans/promissory notes.
Limitations: Giving primarily in Los Angeles County and the greater Los Angeles, CA, area. Generally no support for athletic events, religious programs or causes, political causes, or post-graduate education. No grants to individuals, or for research.
Publications: Annual report (including application guidelines), financial statement, grants list.
Officers and Directors:* Eric C. Johnson,* Chair.; Carolyn E. Johnson,* Pres.; Alan C. Johnson,* V.P.; Ann L. Johnson,* V.P.; Craig C. Johnson,* V.P.; Jack S. Peterson,* Secy.; S.L. Hutchison,* C.F.O.; John Berwald, Mary A. Castagna.
Number of staff: 1 full-time professional.
EIN: 330247161
PRI recipients:
68-1. Accelerated School, Los Angeles, CA, $170,000. Loan to purchase property for new campus for charter school. 2000.

69
Joe and Jessie Crump Fund

c/o Bank One Trust Co., N.A.
P.O. Box 1308
Milwaukee, WI 53201-1308

Trust established in 1965 in TX.
Grantmaker type: Independent foundation
General financial activity (yr. ended 09/30/02): Assets, $18,342,398 (M); expenditures, $1,028,606; qualifying distributions, $1,338,694; giving activities include $741,667 for 16 grants (high: $332,667; low: $1,000) and $600,000 for 3 PRIs.
Cumulative PRI activity (through 09/30/02): Since beginning PRI activity, the foundation has made 4 PRIs totaling $800,000.
General purpose and activities: Giving primarily for an Episcopal theological seminary; support also for cancer research, aid to handicapped children, and the Episcopal church.
General fields of interest: Theological school/education; medical care, rehabilitation; cancer; medical research; cancer research; Protestant agencies & churches; disabled.
Program-related investment (PRI) activity: The foundation has made low-interest loans to Episcopal churches for their building programs, often through local dioceses.
Types of PRI Support: Loans/promissory notes.
Limitations: Applications not accepted. Giving primarily in TX. No grants to individuals, or for building or endowment funds, matching gifts, or general purposes.

Trustee: Bank One, Texas, N.A.
Number of staff: 1 shared staff.
EIN: 756045044
PRI recipients:

69-1. Calvary Episcopal Church, Bastrop, TX, $200,000. Loan at below-market interest rate for religious purposes. 1999.

69-2. Church of the Holy Apostles, Fort Worth, TX, $200,000. Below-market interest loan for church building. 2001.

69-3. Church of the Holy Cross, Dallas, TX, $200,000. Below-market interest loan for church building. 2001.

69-4. Emmanuel Episcopal Church, Houston, TX, $200,000. Below-market interest loan for religious purposes. 2002.

69-5. Episcopal Church of the Holy Spirit, Houston, TX, $200,000. Below-market interest loan for religious purposes. 2002.

69-6. Saint Francis by the Lake Episcopal Church, Canyon Lake, TX, $200,000. Below-market interest loan for church building. 2001.

69-7. Saint Johns Episcopal Church, Odessa, TX, $200,000. Loan at below-market interest rate for religious purposes. 1999.

69-8. Saint Laurence Episcopal Church, Southlake, TX, $200,000. Loan at below-market interest rate for religious purposes. 1999.

69-9. Saint Nicholas Episcopal Church, Midland, TX, $200,000. Below-market interest loan for religious purposes. 2002.

69-10. Saint Stephens Episcopal Church, Houston, TX, $200,000. Below-market interest loan for church building. 2001.

69-11. Trinity Episcopal Church, The Woodlands, TX, $200,000. Loan at below-market interest rate for religious purposes. 1999.

70

Dade Community Foundation, Inc.

(Formerly Dade Foundation)
200 S. Biscayne Blvd., Ste. 505
Miami, FL 33131-2343 (305) 371-2711
Contact: Ruth Shack, Pres.
FAX: (305) 371-5342; E-mail: rshack01@bellsouth.net; URL: http://www.dadecommunityfoundation.org

Established in 1967 in FL.
Grantmaker type: Community foundation
General financial activity (yr. ended 12/31/01): Assets, $68,401,730 (M); gifts received, $6,001,826; expenditures, $9,138,514; giving activities include $6,983,399 for grants (high: $543,239; low: $5; average: $1,000–$10,000) and $110,300 for grants to individuals (high: $2,500; low: $500; average: $500–$2,500); no PRIs paid.
Cumulative PRI activity (through 12/31/01): The currently outstanding PRI portfolio includes PRIs totaling $15,900 (average: $5,000). The typical outstanding PRI earns an average of 2 percent interest.
General purpose and activities: Giving primarily to reduce cultural alienation and lack of community cohesion, and considers all grant proposals in the context of this commitment. Grants are made in broad program areas including education, health, human services, arts and culture, environment, community and economic development, social justice, and religion. In addition, field of interest and special funding initiatives have enabled significant grantmaking addressing the issues of abused and neglected children, immigrants and refugees, AIDS, homelessness, and community and affordable housing. The foundation also provides technical assistance through grant support and one-on-one consultations to build the capacity of nonprofits.
General fields of interest: Arts, multipurpose centers/programs; visual arts; arts/cultural programs; animal welfare; health associations; heart & circulatory diseases; AIDS; child abuse prevention; housing/shelter; disasters, 9/11/01; children & youth, services; homeless, human services; civil rights, minorities; civil rights, gays/lesbians; civil rights; community development, neighborhood development; religion; African Americans/Blacks; aging; people with AIDS (PWAs); gays/lesbians; homeless.
Program-related investment (PRI) activity: The foundation makes bridge loans to performing arts organizations.
Types of PRI Support: Loans/promissory notes.
Limitations: Giving limited to Dade County, FL. No grants to individuals (except through scholarship funds), or for memberships, fundraising, memorials, deficit financing, or conferences.
Publications: Annual report, application guidelines, newsletter, occasional report.
PRI program information: The foundation makes PRIs on a frequent but not annual basis.
Officers and Governors:* Hugh A. Westbrook,* Chair.; Thomas R. McGuigan,* Vice-Chair.; Ruth Shack, Pres.; Sergio M. Ganzalez, Secy.; Cynthia W. Curry, Treas.; Anthony Brunson, and 16 additional governors.
Investment Managers: American Century, Barr Rosenberg, First Union National Bank of Florida, Fox Asset Management, Mellon Bank, N.A., Morgan Stanley, Bank of America, Neuberger and Berman Trust Co., Northern Trust Bank of Florida, N.A., PIMCO, State Street Global Advisors, SunTrust Banks, Inc., TIFF, World Asset Management.
Number of staff: 5 full-time professional; 4 full-time support; 1 part-time support.
EIN: 650350357

71
Dakota Foundation

c/o Janet L. Holaday
P.O. Box 1535
Jamestown, ND 58402-1535
Application address: c/o Lynn B. Villella, Exec. Dir., 46 Camino Barranca, Placitas, NM 87043-9314

Established in 1997 in IL and NM. PRI-related activities began in 1998.
Donor(s): A. Bart Holaday.
Grantmaker type: Independent foundation
General financial activity (yr. ended 12/31/01): Assets, $6,128,684 (M); expenditures, $53,596; qualifying distributions, $250,067; giving activities include $225,000 for 3 PRIs.
Cumulative PRI activity (through 12/31/01): Since 1998, the foundation has made 6 PRIs totaling $205,000. The currently outstanding PRI portfolio includes 6 PRIs totaling $204,039 (high: $50,000; low: $10,000; average: $35,000). The typical outstanding PRI has a 5- to 7-year term with an average term of 6 years and earns 4 to 7 percent interest with an average of 5 percent.
General purpose and activities: Giving to entrepreneurial enterprises, and socially and ecologically responsible enterprises.
General fields of interest: Human services.
Program-related investment (PRI) activity: The foundation makes PRIs, in the form of low-interest loans, to organizations that generate jobs in low-income communities, and to organizations that provide and operate job development and training enterprises.
Types of PRI Support: Loans/promissory notes, equity investments.
Limitations: Giving primarily in ND and NM. No grants to individuals. PRIs are only awarded to non-profit or non-profit related organizations. The foundation accepts applications for PRIs.
PRI program information: The foundation maintains a formal PRI program. The foundation makes PRIs on an annual basis.
Officers: A. Bart Holaday, Chair.; Janet L. Holaday, Treas.; Lynn B. Villella, Exec. Dir.
Advisory Committee: Alberta B. Holaday, Brett C. Holaday, Jerry Villella, Patrick B. Holaday, Paul S. Villella, Peter B. Villella.
Number of staff: 1 part-time professional.
EIN: 367213554
PRI recipients:

71-1. Lewis and Clark CommunityWorks, Bismarck, ND, $50,000. Loan to create revolving loan fund to assist low-income families in obtaining affordable housing. 2001.

71-2. Partners in Progress, Portland, ND, $50,000. Short-term line of credit to assist in restructuring of specific farmer's financial conditions. 2000.

71-3. Pioneer Human Services, Seattle, WA, $50,000. Loan to provide working capital for acquisition and operation of job development and training enterprises. 1999.

71-4. Pride, Inc., Bismarck, ND, $100,000. Loan for construction of building for organization which provides services to individuals with disabilities. 2001.

71-5. Sustainable Jobs Development Corporation, Durham, NC, $12,500. Program-related investment to provide capital for recycling and environmental businesses that generate jobs in low-income communities. 1999.

71-6. University of North Dakota, Center for Innovation Fund, Grand Forks, ND, $75,000. Loan to establish seed fund to improve program for young entrepreneurs and local economic development. 2001.

71-7. Urban Enterprise Fund, Bismarck, ND, $50,000. Program-related investment for fund which promotes self-sufficiency by focusing job creation on those who are otherwise likely to be unemployable. 2000.

71-8. Womens Economic Self-Sufficiency Team (WESST), Albuquerque, NM, $10,000. Program-related investment. 2000.

72
Development Credit Fund, Inc.

2530 N. Charles St., Ste. 200
Baltimore, MD 21218 (410) 467-7500
Contact: Angela M. Moore, Loan Admin.

Established around 1993.
Donor(s): Community Development Financing Institution, Enterprise Foundation.
Grantmaker type: Independent foundation
General financial activity (yr. ended 12/31/01): Assets, $6,139,907 (M); gifts received, $240,000; expenditures, $1,108,367; qualifying distributions, $1,969,500; giving activities include $1,969,500 for 31 PRI.
Cumulative PRI activity (through 12/31/01): Since beginning PRI activity, the foundation has made 73 PRIs totaling $4,157,051.
General purpose and activities: Loans made to qualified members of economically, historically and socially disadvantaged groups doing business within MD.
Program-related investment (PRI) activity: The foundation makes low-interest loans to qualified small businesses to facilitate their development.
Types of PRI Support: Loans/promissory notes.
Limitations: Giving limited to MD.
Officers and Directors:* David K. Elam, Sr.,* Chair.; Acknell M. Muldrow, C.E.O., Pres., and Treas.; Kenneth N. Oliver, Sr. V.P.; Stacey Harvey-Reid, V.P.; Erik Johnson, V.P.; Omar S. Muhammad, V.P.; Alagra D. McClendon, Cont. and C.F.O.; Angela M. Cook, Loan Admin.; Luis Borunda, Earle Bradford, Timothy D.A. Chriss, David K. Elam, Sr., Tracie Evans-Gross, Alice Ann Finnerty, T. Randy F. Jones, F. Lee Lawson, Michael McIntyre, Kimberly Morton, Osbourne A. Payne, E. John Pipitone, Sueh Ying Tsai.
EIN: 521281837
PRI recipients:

72-1. A Dab of Muscle LLC, Rockville, MD, $75,000. Loan. 2001.

72-2. **Auto Intentions**, Fallston, MD, $30,000. Loan. 2001.
72-3. **Barnes-Powell Enterprises, Inc.**, Cumberland, MD, $97,870. Loan. 2000.
72-4. **Beths Bridal Boutique and Formalwear**, Bel Air, MD, $54,733. Loan. 2000.
72-5. **Bird 33**, Baltimore, MD, $73,526. Loan. 1999.
72-6. **Blue Cow Cafe**, Columbia, MD, $35,000. Loan. 2001.
72-7. **BOLM Micro Speedway**, Westminster, MD, $10,000. Loan. 2001.
72-8. **Butlers Varsity Sports**, Marlow Heights, MD, $119,614. Loan. 1999.
72-9. **Byron Desbordes, Inc.**, Baltimore, MD, $31,353. Loan. 2000.
72-10. **Cherry Tomato Boutique**, Baltimore, MD, $35,000. Loan. 2001.
72-11. **Chesapeake, Inc.**, Tyaskin, MD, $50,000. Loan. 2000.
72-12. **Cosmos Cleaners**, Baltimore, MD, $15,000. Loan. 1999.
72-13. **Cypnana, Inc.**, Baltimore, MD, $325,000. Loan. 2001.
72-14. **Danie Dollar LC**, Falls Church, VA, $115,266. Loan. 2000.
72-15. **Dogwood Video**, Baltimore, MD, $20,000. Loan. 2001.
72-16. **Donrit Corporation**, Baltimore, MD, $100,000. Loan. 2000.
72-17. **Easy Trucking Company, Inc.**, Woolford, MD, $75,000. Loan. 2000.
72-18. **Eccentrics Hair Studio**, Hanover, MD, $12,000. Loan. 2001.
72-19. **ES Holding Company**, Baltimore, MD, $15,000. Loan. 2001.
72-20. **Everlast Tub and Tile Refinishing**, Queenstown, MD, $15,000. Loan. 2001.
72-21. **Fabara, Inc.**, Baltimore, MD, $140,809. Loan to open One World Cafe. 1999.
72-22. **Garrison Company**, Baltimore, MD, $20,000. Loan. 2001.
72-23. **Hamid Taxi**, Pikesville, MD, $20,000. Loan. 1999.
72-24. **Hazport Solutions**, DC, $50,000. Loan. 2001.
72-25. **Hazport Solutions**, DC, $25,000. Loan. 2001.
72-26. **HealthCare Resolutions**, Laurel, MD, $75,000. Loan. 2001.
72-27. **HealthCare Resolutions**, Laurel, MD, $50,000. Loan. 2001.
72-28. **Hong Phat-Saigon Remembered**, Baltimore, MD, $65,000. Loan. 2001.
72-29. **H2O Tommy**, Pasadena, MD, $25,000. Loan. 2001.
72-30. **Jack in the Box Toy Company**, Glen Burnie, MD, $100,000. Loan. 2001.
72-31. **Jamon Foods**, Monkton, MD, $30,000. Loan to open Jimmie's Place. 1999.
72-32. **JH Transportation**, Frostburg, MD, $33,191. Loan. 2000.
72-33. **JH Transportation**, Frostburg, MD, $45,492. Loan. 1999.
72-34. **JRH Educational Services**, Sylvan Learning Center, Chestertown, MD, $135,000. Loan. 2001.
72-35. **Lisa Carter Insurance, Inc.**, Catonsville, MD, $23,048. Loan. 2000.
72-36. **Lordrone Athletic Club**, Baltimore, MD, $48,000. Loan. 1999.
72-37. **Lynch Manor Subway**, Baltimore, MD, $95,000. Loan. 2001.
72-38. **Michelle L. Kirkner, Inc.**, Baltimore, MD, $19,331. Loan. 2000.
72-39. **Miracles-N-More Unisex Salon, Inc.**, Baltimore, MD, $15,827. Loan. 2000.
72-40. **P&R Sales**, Baltimore, MD, $16,999. Loan. 1999.
72-41. **Patriot Construction Management**, Baltimore, MD, $100,000. Loan. 2001.
72-42. **Pepes, Inc.**, Owings Mills, MD, $82,834. Loan. 1999.
72-43. **Petit Louis**, Baltimore, MD, $112,561. Loan. 2000.
72-44. **Prism Auto Glass**, Cheltenham, MD, $99,838. Loan. 1999.
72-45. **Rabbit Transportation**, Joppa, MD, $11,105. Loan. 2000.
72-46. **Ransoms Boutique**, Towson, MD, $50,000. Loan. 2000.
72-47. **Repertory Theater of America**, Baltimore, MD, $10,000. Loan. 2001.
72-48. **Shoe Biz**, Baltimore, MD, $61,185. Loan. 1999.
72-49. **Simmones Balloon Gallery**, Baltimore, MD, $15,000. Loan. 2001.
72-50. **TMG Services**, Baltimore, MD, $200,000. Loan. 2001.
72-51. **TMG Services**, Baltimore, MD, $50,000. Loan. 1999.
72-52. **Triple M Welding Service**, Dunkirk, MD, $20,000. Loan. 2001.
72-53. **Ultimate Driving Academy**, Baltimore, MD, $51,000. Loan. 2001.
72-54. **Varsity Sports**, Marlow Heights, MD, $56,000. Loan. 2000.
72-55. **WW Contractors**, Randallstown, MD, $300,000. Loan. 2001.
72-56. **WW Contractors**, Randallstown, MD, $50,000. Loan. 2001.
72-57. **WW Contractors**, Randallstown, MD, $310,000. Loan. 1999.

73

Geraldine R. Dodge Foundation, Inc.

163 Madison Ave., 6th Fl.
P.O. Box 1239
Morristown, NJ 07962-1239 (973) 540-8442
Contact: David Grant, Exec. Dir.
FAX: (973) 540-1211; E-mail: info@grdodge.org;
URL: http://www.grdodge.org

Incorporated in 1974 in NJ.
Donor(s): Geraldine R. Dodge.‡
Grantmaker type: Independent foundation

General financial activity (yr. ended 12/31/01): Assets, $306,376,880 (M); expenditures, $24,719,277; qualifying distributions, $23,578,175; giving activities include $19,852,079 for 605 grants (high: $600,000; low: $200; average: $30,000–$50,000), $152,667 for grants to individuals, $28,779 for 133 employee matching gifts and $656,291 for 7 foundation-administered programs; no PRIs paid.
Cumulative PRI activity (through 12/31/01): The currently outstanding PRI portfolio includes 1 PRI totaling $1,000,000.
General purpose and activities: The mission of the foundation is to support and encourage those educational, cultural, social and environmental values that contribute to making our society more human and our world more livable.
General fields of interest: Media/communications; visual arts; museums; performing arts; dance; theater; music; humanities; language & linguistics; literature; arts/cultural programs; education, research; elementary school/education; secondary school/education; education; natural resources conservation & protection; energy; environment; animal welfare; wildlife preservation & protection; family planning; population studies; leadership development.
Program-related investment (PRI) activity: The foundation has made PRIs to establish a loan fund for arts organizations and for an environmental agency.
Types of PRI Support: Loans/promissory notes.
Limitations: Giving primarily in NJ, with support for the arts and local humane groups limited to NJ, and support for other local projects limited to the Morristown-Madison area; some giving in the other Middle Atlantic states and New England, and to national organizations. No support for religious, higher education, health, or conduit organizations. No grants for capital projects, equipment purchases, indirect costs, endowment funds, deficit financing, or scholarships.
Publications: Annual report (including application guidelines), application guidelines.
PRI program information: The foundation makes PRIs occasionally.
Officers and Trustees:* Robert LeBuhn,* Chair.; Christopher J. Elliman,* Pres.; James W. Stevens,* Treas.; John E. Yingling, Jr., C.F.O. and C.A.O.; David N.W. Grant III, Exec. Dir.; Robert H.B. Baldwin, Barbara Knowles Debs, John Lloyd Huck, Betsy S. Michel, Paul J. O'Donnell.
Number of staff: 10 full-time professional; 3 part-time professional; 8 full-time support; 1 part-time support.
EIN: 237406010
PRI recipients:
73-1. Nonprofit Finance Fund, NYC, NY, $1,000,000. Program-related investment to establish loan program for arts and cultural organizations in New Jersey. 1999.
73-2. Open Space Institute, NYC, NY, $2,500,000. Program-related investment for project support. 2001.
73-3. Open Space Institute, NYC, NY, $100,000. Program-related investment for project support. 2001.

74
Doran Family Foundation, Inc.
3090 Mayberry Ave.
Huntingtown, MD 20639-3913
Application address: P.O. Box 238, Barstow, MD 20610, tel.: (410) 414-9300

Established in 1999 in MD.
Donor(s): John T. Doran.
Grantmaker type: Operating foundation
General financial activity (yr. ended 12/31/01): Assets, $22,272,938 (M); gifts received, $16,418,479; expenditures, $2,393,077; qualifying distributions, $1,824,566; giving activities include $1,978,141 for 6 grants (high: $1,600,000; low: $5,234) and $500,000 for 1 PRI.
General purpose and activities: Giving for family life and youth centers.
General fields of interest: Youth development, centers & clubs; family services.
Limitations: Giving primarily in Calvert, St. Charles, St. Mary's, and Prince George's counties, MD.
Officers: John T. Doran, Pres.; Jean L. Doran, V.P.; Catherine J. Doran-Neal, Secy.-Treas.
EIN: 522136560
PRI recipients:
74-1. Archdiocese of Washington, DC, $500,000. Short-term loan to assist cash flow for Victory Center to complete construction of youth center. 2001.

75
Jessie Ball duPont Fund
(Formerly Jessie Ball duPont Religious, Charitable and Educational Fund)
1 Independent Dr., Ste. 1400
Jacksonville, FL 32202-5011 (904) 353-0890
Contact: Dr. Sherry P. Magill, Pres.
PRI Contact: Edward King, Jr., Sr. Prog. Off., Religion
Additional tel.: (800) 252-3452; FAX: (904) 353-3870; E-mail: smagill@dupontfund.org (for Sherry Magill), jbennett@dupontfund.org (for Jo Ann Bennett), sdouglass@dupontfund.org (for Sally Douglass), ekingjr.@dupontfund.org (for Edward King), and sgreene@dupontfund.org (for Sharon Greene); URL: http://www.dupontfund.org

Trust established in 1976 in FL. PRI-related activities began in 1987.
Donor(s): Jessie Ball duPont.‡
Grantmaker type: Independent foundation
General financial activity (yr. ended 10/31/02): Assets, $268,804,043 (M); gifts received, $70,000; expenditures, $14,877,741; qualifying distributions, $12,067,999; giving activities include $11,759,005 for 436 grants (high: $1,000,000; low: $1,814; average: $5,000–$100,000) and

$338,135 for 7 foundation-administered programs; no PRIs paid.

Cumulative PRI activity (through 10/31/02): Since 1987, the foundation has made 46 PRIs totaling $1,150,000. The currently outstanding PRI portfolio includes 12 PRIs totaling $124,000 (high: $70,000; low: $5,000; average: $20,000). The typical outstanding PRI has a 2- to 5-year term with an average term of 5 years.

General purpose and activities: Grants limited to those institutions to which the donor contributed personally during the five-year period ending December 31, 1964. Among the 331 institutions eligible to receive funds are higher and secondary education institutions, cultural and historic preservation programs, social service organizations, hospitals, health agencies, churches and church-related organizations, and youth agencies.

General fields of interest: Historic preservation/historical societies; arts/cultural programs; secondary school/education; higher education; education; health care; crime/violence prevention; human services; children, day care; youth, services; economic development; community development; religion; people with AIDS (PWAs); economically disadvantaged; homeless.

Program-related investment (PRI) activity: In 1987, the foundation established its Repair and Restoration of Churches Program primarily to help small, rural parishes with senior congregations maintain their buildings.

Types of PRI Support: Loans/promissory notes.

Limitations: Giving primarily in the South, especially DE, FL, and VA. No support for organizations other than those awarded gifts by the donor from 1960-1964. No grants to individuals, or generally for capital campaigns or endowments. First-time applicant must submit proof with initial application that a contribution was received from the donor between 1960 and 1964.

Publications: Annual report (including application guidelines), application guidelines, informational brochure, grants list, occasional report, financial statement.

PRI program information: The foundation maintains a formal PRI program. The foundation makes PRIs on an annual basis.

Officers and Trustees:* Rev. Frank S. Cerveny,* Chair.; Jean W. Ludlow,* Vice-Chair.; Sherry P. Magill, Ph.D., Pres.; Jo Ann P. Bennett, Exec. Secy. and Dir., Admin.; Mary K. Phillips.

Corporate Trustees: Stephen A. Lynch III, Northern Trust Bank of Florida, N.A.

Number of staff: 4 full-time professional; 4 full-time support.

EIN: 596368632

PRI recipients:

75-1. Christ Church Christiana Hundred, Greenville, DE, $20,000. Loan for repair and restoration. 1999.

75-2. Church of God in Christ, Port Saint Joe, FL, $20,000. Loan for repair and restoration. 1999.

75-3. Epiphany Episcopal Church, Rector's Discretionary Fund, Timonium, MD, $20,000. Loan for Repair and Restoration Fund. 2000.

75-4. Episcopal Diocese of Florida, Jacksonville, FL, $20,000. Promissory note. 2000.

75-5. First Baptist Church, Wewahitchka, FL, $70,000. Loan for repair and restoration fund for remodeling project to education building. 1999.

75-6. First Baptist Church Of White City, Wewahitchka, FL, $20,000. Promissory note. 2000.

75-7. White Marsh United Methodist Church, Irvington, VA, $74,000. Loan for repair and restoration projects for roof and furnace. 1999.

75-8. White Marsh United Methodist Church, Irvington, VA, $50,000. Loan. 1999.

75-9. Wicomico United Methodist Church, Kilmarnock, VA, $20,000. Promissory note. 2001.

76
Dyson Foundation

25 Halcyon Rd.
Millbrook, NY 12545-9611 (845) 677-0644
Contact: Diana M. Gurieva, Exec. Dir.
FAX: (845) 677-0650; E-mail: info@dyson.org;
URL: http://www.dysonfoundation.org

Trust established in 1949 in NY; incorporated in 1957 in DE.

Donor(s): Charles H. Dyson,‡ Margaret M. Dyson.‡

Grantmaker type: Independent foundation

General financial activity (yr. ended 12/31/02): Assets, $254,790,487 (M); expenditures, $14,622,839; qualifying distributions, $13,434,889; giving activities include $12,183,484 for 183 grants (high: $1,000,000; low: $500; average: $5,000–$50,000) and $81,460 for 2 PRIs.

Cumulative PRI activity (through 12/31/02): The currently outstanding PRI portfolio includes 1 PRI totaling $200,000 (average: $100,000). The typical outstanding PRI has a 4- to 10-year term.

General purpose and activities: The foundation supports grant programs in the Mid-Hudson Valley of NY; national programs in community pediatrics; and grants that are linked to longtime interests of the Dyson family.

General fields of interest: Arts/cultural programs; medical school/education; education; health care; medical research; human services; children & youth, services; economically disadvantaged.

Program-related investment (PRI) activity: The foundation makes PRIs on a case-by-case basis.

Types of PRI Support: Loans/promissory notes, interim financing, loan guarantees.

Limitations: Giving primarily in Dutchess County, NY, and organizations providing services in Dutchess County; limited grants to other Mid-Hudson Valley counties. National and other grants on a solicited basis. No support for international organizations. No grants to individuals, or for debt reduction, direct mail campaign or fundraising events. The foundation accepts applications for PRIs.

Publications: Annual report (including application guidelines).

PRI program information: The foundation maintains a formal PRI program. The foundation makes PRIs on an annual basis.

Officers and Directors:* Robert R. Dyson,* Pres.; Diana M. Gurieva, Exec. V.P.; John S. FitzSimmons, Secy.; Marc Feldman, Treas.; Raymond A. Lamontagne, Timmian C. Massie, Michael P. Murphy, David G. Nathan.
Number of staff: 2 full-time professional; 1 part-time professional; 4 full-time support; 1 part-time support.
EIN: 136084888
PRI recipients:
76-1. Family Services of the Mid-Hudson and Harlem Valleys, Poughkeepsie, NY, $400,000. Loan for capital support. 1999.
76-2. YMCA of Dutchess County, Poughkeepsie, NY, $100,000. Program-related investment. 1999.

77
East Tennessee Foundation
550 W. Main St., Ste. 550
Knoxville, TN 37902 (865) 524-1223
Contact: Jerry W. Asken, Exec. Dir.
FAX: (865) 637-6039; E-mail: etf@etf.org; URL: http://www.easttennesseefoundation.org

Incorporated in 1958 in TN.
Grantmaker type: Community foundation
General financial activity (yr. ended 12/31/01): Assets, $49,163,230 (M); gifts received, $8,788,162; expenditures, $15,883,949; giving activities include $14,955,595 for 721 grants (high: $2,000,000; low: $100); no PRIs paid.
Cumulative PRI activity (through 12/31/01): Since beginning PRI activity, the foundation has made 9 PRIs totaling $750,000. The typical outstanding PRI earns an average of 5 percent interest.
General purpose and activities: Giving to organizations which strengthen the capacity of existing institutions to reach a broader segment of the community, encourage cooperation, decrease duplication of services, and develop partnerships that can have a synergistic effect; address diversity and positive change; encourage citizen participation in meeting community challenges; demonstrate vision, action, effectiveness, good management and quality; focus on prevention and education; and provides models for replication. The foundation administers donor-advised funds.
General fields of interest: Arts/cultural programs; education; children & youth, services; community development.
Program-related investment (PRI) activity: The foundation makes PRIs to local organizations for affordable housing and for community development via its Affordable Housing Trust Fund. The foundation also acquired housing that it is rehabilitating for low-income individuals.
Types of PRI Support: Loans/promissory notes, charitable use assets.
Limitations: Giving limited to Knoxville, TN, and its 20 surrounding counties. No grants for annual campaigns, capital fund drives, research projects, or general operating budgets. The foundation accepts applications for PRIs.
Publications: Annual report, newsletter, application guidelines, informational brochure (including application guidelines).
PRI program information: The foundation maintains a formal PRI program.
Officers and Directors:* Lloyd Montgomery III,* Chair.; Rabbi Howard A. Simon,* Vice-Chair.; J. Daniel Pressley, Secy.-Treas.; and 38 additional directors.
Number of staff: 7 full-time professional; 1 part-time professional; 4 full-time support.
EIN: 620807696

78
Eddy Foundation
123 Lake Shore Rd.
Essex, NY 12936 (518) 962-2795
Contact: James Phillips, Treas.

Established in 1996 in CA.
Donor(s): Elizabeth Eddy.
Grantmaker type: Independent foundation
General financial activity (yr. ended 12/31/01): Assets, $3,455,585 (M); gifts received, $402,642; expenditures, $274,119; qualifying distributions, $1,062,434; giving activities include $28,547 for grants (high: $5,000) and $829,433 for 3 PRIs.
Program-related investment (PRI) activity: The foundation purchases property that it uses to help spur the growth of small and medium sized companies that promote sustainable development in the fields of agriculture, forestry, and ecotourism.
Types of PRI Support: Charitable use assets.
Limitations: Giving primarily in CA and NY.
Officers: Elizabeth A. Eddy, Pres.; James S. Phillips, Treas.
EIN: 330721979
PRI recipients:
78-1. Black Kettle Farm, Essex, NY, $241,030. Program-related investment for restoration of 18th Century farmstead into working farm using sustainable methods. 2001.
78-2. Black Kettle Farm, Essex, NY, $340,960. Program-related investment for restoration of 18th Century farmstead into working farm using sustainable methods. 2000.
78-3. Boquet Mountain, Essex, NY, $167,386. Program-related investment to purchase real property to preserve wildlife habitats. 1999.
78-4. Boquet River Association, Elizabethtown, NY, $37,910. Program-related investment to purchase land to preserve wildlife habitats. 2000.
78-5. Coyuchi, Inc., Point Reyes Station, CA, $12,500. Program-related investment. 2000.
78-6. Coyuchi, Inc., Point Reyes Station, CA, $25,000. Program-related investment. 1999.
78-7. EcoEnterprises Fund, Arlington, VA, $50,000. Program-related investment for work to spur development of small- and medium-sized companies

that promote sustainable development in fields such as agriculture, non-timber forest products, sustainable forestry and ecotourism. 1999.

78-8. Fallbrook Land Conservancy, Fallbrook, CA, $121,325. Loan to purchase Rock Mountain property to preserve land and wildlife habitats. 2000.

78-9. Larch Pond, $57,661. Program-related investment to purchase land to preserve wildlife habitats. 1999.

78-10. Wildlife Works, Kenya, $25,000. Program-related investment for work to teach former wildlife poachers in Kenya alternate livelihoods such as clothing manufacturing. 2001.

78-11. Wildlife Works, Kenya, $25,000. Program-related investment for work to teach former wildlife poachers in Kenya alternate livelihoods such as clothing manufacturing. 2000.

79

O. P. and W. E. Edwards Foundation, Inc.

P.O. Box 2445
Red Lodge, MT 59068 (406) 446-1077
Contact: Jo Ann Eder, Pres.
FAX: (406) 446-1363; E-mail: joeder@mac.com;
URL: http://fdncenter.org/grantmaker/edwards

Incorporated in 1962 in NY.
Donor(s): William E. Edwards,‡ J.N. Edwards,‡ Harriet E. Gamper.
Grantmaker type: Independent foundation
General financial activity (yr. ended 08/31/02): Assets, $6,150,501 (M); gifts received, $250,000; expenditures, $3,909,036; qualifying distributions, $3,375,474; giving activities include $3,379,400 for 67 grants (high: $150,000; low: $500; average: $10,000–$25,000); no PRIs paid.
Cumulative PRI activity (through 08/31/02): The currently outstanding PRI portfolio includes a high PRI value of $100,000 and a low PRI value of $10,000. The typical outstanding PRI earns 2 to 6 percent interest, and earns an average of 3 percent.
General purpose and activities: Major interest in programs helping economically disadvantaged young people become able to survive and thrive on their own, with preference to smaller, comprehensive programs that are integral parts of their communities' networks of services.
General fields of interest: Visual arts; performing arts; human services; children & youth, services; family services; community development; astronomy; economically disadvantaged.
General international interests: Developing countries.
Program-related investment (PRI) activity: The foundation makes PRIs to for-profit and nonprofit institutions involved in economic development in poor neighborhoods. PRIs have included: deposits in community development banks and Federal community development credit unions; loans for low-income housing and other real estate primarily through intermediaries, such as community loan funds; and investments in the Cooperative Assistance Fund, which makes investments in small, minority-owned businesses.
Types of PRI Support: Loans/promissory notes, equity investments, capitalizing loan funds/other intermediaries, linked deposits.
Limitations: Applications not accepted. Giving on a national basis; some interest also in Third World countries. No grants to individuals. PRI applications not accepted.
Officers and Trustees:* Jo Ann Eder,* Pres. and Treas.; Harriet E. Gamper,* V.P.; David E. Gamper,* Secy.
Number of staff: None.
EIN: 136100965
PRI recipients:

79-1. Louisville Community Development Bank, Louisville, KY, $50,000. Program-related investment for organization formed to make community-based low-income loans. 2000.

80

El Paso Community Foundation

310 N. Mesa, 10th Fl.
El Paso, TX 79901 (915) 533-4020
Contact: Janice W. Windle, Pres.
Mailing address: P.O. Box 272, El Paso, TX, 79943-0272; FAX: (915) 532-0716; E-mail: info@epcf.org; URL: http://www.epcf.org

Incorporated in 1977 in TX.
Grantmaker type: Community foundation
General financial activity (yr. ended 12/31/00): Assets, $99,399,763 (M); gifts received, $4,516,975; expenditures, $5,907,466; giving activities include $2,828,028 for 692 grants (high: $106,700; low: $1,000; average: $5,000–$10,000); no PRIs paid.
General purpose and activities: Giving for education, social services, health and disabilities, arts and humanities, the environment, and community benefit and development. The foundation administers donor-advised funds.
General fields of interest: Arts/cultural programs; education; environment; health care; human services; community development.
Program-related investment (PRI) activity: The foundation makes occasional PRIs for all of its program areas, including education, social services, health and disabilities, arts and humanities, the environment, and community benefit and development. PRIs have provided interim financing and supported the establishment of a revolving loan fund.
Types of PRI Support: Loans/promissory notes, interim financing, capitalizing loan funds/other intermediaries.
Limitations: Giving limited to the El Paso, TX, area. No support for medical research, religious projects or political organizations. No grants to individuals (except for scholarships), or for deficit financing, annual campaigns, travel, capital campaigns, fundraising events, or ongoing support.
Publications: Annual report, application guidelines, newsletter, informational brochure.

PRI program information: The foundation makes PRIs on a frequent but not annual basis.
Officers and Directors:* Joe Alcantar, Jr.,* Chair.; Frances R. Axelson,* Vice-Chair.; Tommye Duncan,* Vice-Chair.; Janice W. Windle, Pres.; Virginia Kemendo, Exec. V.P.; Nestor Valencia, V.P., Plan.; Cathy Hill, V.P.; Carl E. Ryan, Secy.; Marylee Warwick,* Treas.; Margaret Varner Bloss, Yvonne Carrillo, Lillian Crouch, Mabel Fayant, Richard H. Feuille, Tom Hussmann, Jose Manuel Mascarenas, Don Melendez, Guillermo Ochoa, Rebeca Ramos, Mary Carmen Saucedo, Dorothy White.
Number of staff: 13 full-time professional; 2 full-time support; 1 part-time support.
EIN: 741839536

81
El Pomar Foundation
10 Lake Cir.
Colorado Springs, CO 80906 (719) 633-7733
Contact: William J. Hybl, Chair.
Additional tel.: (800) 554-7711; FAX: (719) 471-6185; URL: http://www.elpomar.org

Incorporated in 1937 in CO.
Donor(s): Spencer Penrose,‡ Mrs. Spencer Penrose.‡
Grantmaker type: Independent foundation
General financial activity (yr. ended 12/31/01): Assets, $464,243,436 (M); gifts received, $45,590; expenditures, $23,093,980; qualifying distributions, $20,976,039; giving activities include $15,488,953 for 569 grants (high: $2,000,000; average: $5,000–$100,000), $3,191,848 for 4 foundation-administered programs and $266,634 for 1 in-kind gift; no PRIs paid.
General purpose and activities: Grants only to nonprofit organizations for public, educational, arts and humanities, health, and welfare purposes, including child welfare, the disadvantaged, and housing; municipalities may request funds for specific projects.
General fields of interest: Media/communications; visual arts; museums; performing arts; theater; music; humanities; historic preservation/historical societies; arts/cultural programs; child development, education; elementary school/education; secondary school/education; vocational education; higher education; adult/continuing education; adult education—literacy, basic skills & GED; libraries/library science; reading; education; natural resources conservation & protection; environment; hospitals (general); pharmacy/prescriptions; health care; substance abuse, services; health associations; employment; food services; nutrition; housing/shelter, development; recreation; human services; children & youth, services; child development, services; family services; hospices; aging, centers & services; homeless, human services; community development; voluntarism promotion; transportation; minorities; disabled; aging; economically disadvantaged; homeless.
Program-related investment (PRI) activity: In 1991, the foundation acquired and renovated the former Colorado Springs, CO, estate of its founders to help promote excellence within the third sector. The Center develops education programs in nonprofit management, provides meeting space, and maintains a library of resources on the third sector. The ongoing development, renovation, and operating costs of the Center are considered operating programs of the foundation and are funded as PRIs. Recent PRIs have also provided support for the operation and maintenance of a foundation-owned historical landmark and an office building providing facilities for nonprofit organizations.
Types of PRI Support: Charitable use assets.
Limitations: Giving limited to CO. No support for organizations that distribute funds to other grantees, religious or political organizations, primary or secondary education, or for camps or seasonal facilities. No grants to individuals, or for annual campaigns, travel, film or other media projects, conferences, deficit financing, endowment funds, research, matching gifts, seed money, or publications. PRI applications not accepted.
Publications: Annual report (including application guidelines), application guidelines, grants list, informational brochure.
PRI program information: The foundation does not maintain a formal PRI program.
Officers and Trustees:* William J. Hybl,* Chair. and C.E.O.; R. Thayer Tutt, Jr.,* Pres. and C.I.O.; Robert J. Hilbert,* Sr. V.P., Admin. and Secy.-Treas.; David J. Palenchar,* Sr. V.P., Opers.; Henry L.T. Koren, Jr., V.P., Progs.; Kristen H. Donovan, Assoc. V.P.; Susan S. Woodward, Assoc. V.P.; Judith M. Bell, Cortlandt S. Dietler, Kent O. Olin, Brenda J. Smith, William R. Ward.
Number of staff: 35 full-time professional; 17 full-time support; 3 part-time support.
EIN: 846002373

82
The Emmerich Foundation Charitable Trust
7302 Claredon Dr.
Edina, MN 55439

Established in 1992 in MN.
Donor(s): Karol D. Emmerich, Richard J. Emmerich.
Grantmaker type: Independent foundation
General financial activity (yr. ended 12/31/01): Assets, $5,180,297 (M); gifts received, $2,000,000; expenditures, $302,004; qualifying distributions, $299,950; giving activities include $299,950 for 25 grants (high: $75,000; low: $200); no PRIs paid.
Cumulative PRI activity (through 12/31/01): Since beginning PRI activity, the foundation has made 1 PRI totaling $25,000.
General purpose and activities: Support primarily for evangelical Christian organizations.
General fields of interest: Christian agencies & churches.

Program-related investment (PRI) activity: Historically, the foundation has made a PRI, in the form of a loan, to a right-to-life organization.
Types of PRI Support: Loans/promissory notes.
Limitations: Applications not accepted. Giving on a national basis. No grants to individuals. PRI applications not accepted.
PRI program information: The foundation does not maintain a formal PRI program. The foundation makes PRIs occasionally.
Trustees: Karol D. Emmerich, Richard J. Emmerich.
EIN: 411712553
PRI recipients:
82-1. Americans United for Life, Chicago, IL, $25,000. Loan. 1999.

83
The Lois & Richard England Family Foundation, Inc.
(Formerly The Lois & Richard England Foundation, Inc.)
P.O. Box 11582
Washington, DC 20008 (202) 244-4636
Contact: Margaret Siegel, Prog. Dir.
FAX: (202) 244-9566; E-mail: Engfmfdn@mail.clark.net; URL: http://fdncenter.org/grantmaker/england

Established in 1990 in MD. PRI-related activities began in 1998.
Donor(s): Richard England, Lois H. England.
Grantmaker type: Independent foundation
General financial activity (yr. ended 12/31/01): Assets, $9,239,988 (M); expenditures, $622,752; qualifying distributions, $571,407; giving activities include $487,654 for 82 grants (high: $20,000; low: $1,000); no PRIs paid.
Cumulative PRI activity (through 12/31/01): Since 1998, the foundation has made 1 PRI totaling $20,000. The currently outstanding PRI portfolio includes 1 PRI totaling $20,000. The typical outstanding PRI has an average term of 10 years.
General purpose and activities: The foundation is committed to improving the lives of those in need. The foundation focuses on human services, education, arts and programs that strengthen Jewish life and culture. Under the new guidelines, it will only accept proposals from organizations working on out-of-school time programs in the District of Columbia and from Jewish organizations.
General fields of interest: Arts/cultural programs; education; human services; community development, neighborhood development; Jewish agencies & temples.
General international interests: Israel.
Program-related investment (PRI) activity: The foundation has made a low interest loan to a religious organization.
Types of PRI Support: Loans/promissory notes.
Limitations: Applications not accepted. Giving primarily in the Washington, DC, area. No grants to individuals. PRI applications not accepted.
PRI program information: The foundation does not maintain a formal PRI program. The foundation makes PRIs occasionally.
Officers and Board Members:* Catherine S. England,* Chair.; Richard England,* Pres.; Lois H. England,* V.P.; Richard England, Jr.,* Treas.; Larry Akman, Nonie Akman, Diana England.
Number of staff: 1 part-time support.
EIN: 521691418
PRI recipients:
83-1. Shefa Fund, Philadelphia, PA, $20,000. Loan at below market rate. 1999.

84
W. C. English Foundation
c/o English Construction Co.
P.O. Box P7000
Lynchburg, VA 24505
Contact: Mrs. L.T. English, Tr.

Established in 1954 in VA.
Donor(s): Members of the English family.
Grantmaker type: Independent foundation
General financial activity (yr. ended 05/31/02): Assets, $25,595,846 (M); expenditures, $1,475,135; qualifying distributions, $1,338,189; giving activities include $1,344,888 for 40 grants (high: $175,000; low: $1,000) and $67,211 for PRIs.
General purpose and activities: Giving primarily for social services and Christian causes.
General fields of interest: Education; human services; children & youth, services; Christian agencies & churches; Protestant agencies & churches.
Program-related investment (PRI) activity: The foundation owns the facilities used by a religious academy and treats the upkeep and additions as PRIs.
Types of PRI Support: Charitable use assets.
Limitations: Giving primarily in VA. No grants to individuals.
Trustees: Joan E. Allen, Beverly E. Dalton, Louise T. English, Margaret E. Lester, Suzanne E. Morse.
EIN: 546061817
PRI recipients:
84-1. Faith Christian Academy, Hurt, VA, $67,212. Loan to provide physical facilities for school. 1999.

85
Environment Now Foundation
450 Newport Ctr. Dr., Ste. 450
Newport Beach, CA 92660 (949) 644-1850
Contact: Paul C. Heeschen, Secy.-Treas.

Established in 1989 in CA.
Donor(s): Frank G. Wells,‡ Luanne C. Wells.
Grantmaker type: Independent foundation

General financial activity (yr. ended 12/31/01): Assets, $34,720,695 (M); gifts received, $40,000; expenditures, $2,964,486; qualifying distributions, $1,928,516; giving activities include $932,511 for grants (high: $170,000) and $965,293 for 4 foundation-administered programs; no PRIs paid.
General purpose and activities: Support for environmental conservation.
General fields of interest: Natural resources conservation & protection.
Program-related investment (PRI) activity: The foundation has made PRIs to environmental organizations in the form of low or no-interest loans. In addition, the foundation has also provided a line of credit to a Santa Monica based organization.
Limitations: Applications not accepted. Giving on a national basis. No grants to individuals. PRI support primarily in CA.
Officers: Kevin Wells, Pres.; Paul C. Heeschen, Secy.-Treas.; Terry Tamminen, Exec. Dir.
Directors: Dan Emmett, Mary Nichols, Briant Wells, Luanne C. Wells.
EIN: 954247242
PRI recipients:
85-1. Santa Monica BayKeeper, Newport Beach, CA, $14,535. Credit line. 1999.

86
Everlasting Private Foundation
c/o Annie M.H. Chan
19770 Stevens Creek Blvd.
Cupertino, CA 95014 (408) 343-1088
Contact: Michelle Woo

Established in 1996 in CA.
Donor(s): Annie M.H. Chan.
Grantmaker type: Operating foundation
General financial activity (yr. ended 12/31/01): Assets, $40,098,045 (M); expenditures, $791,873; qualifying distributions, $454,659; giving activities include $111,475 for 4 grants (high: $55,000; low: $475); no PRIs paid.
Cumulative PRI activity (through 12/31/01): The currently outstanding PRI portfolio includes PRIs totaling $7,803,405.
General purpose and activities: To foster Christian beliefs through operation of the Lakeview Conference Center, a religious/Bible camp and Christian community center.
General fields of interest: Christian agencies & churches.
Program-related investment (PRI) activity: The foundation made a loan, to a private foundation in order to fund its operations to provide multi-media edudational material to K-12th grade students for home and school use.
Types of PRI Support: Loans/promissory notes.
Limitations: Applications not accepted. Giving on a national basis. No grants to individuals. PRIs primarily awarded in CA.
Officers: Annie M.H. Chan, Pres.; Myong Shin Woo, Secy. and C.F.O.
Number of staff: 3 full-time professional; 2 part-time professional.
EIN: 770425562
PRI recipients:
86-1. Ohana Foundation for Technical Development, Ohana Learning, Honolulu, HI, $6,873,405. Loan for operations to provide multimedia educational material to K-12th grade children for home and school use. 2000.

87
The Faith Foundation, Inc.
2746 Front St., N.E.
Salem, OR 97303
Contact: Daniel L. Kerr, Secy.-Treas.

Established in 1993 in OR.
Grantmaker type: Independent foundation
General financial activity (yr. ended 12/31/01): Assets, $16,594,885 (M); gifts received, $2,200,250; expenditures, $834,736; qualifying distributions, $1,805,855; giving activities include $813,500 for 5 grants (high: $775,000; low: $7,500; average: $10,000–$15,000) and $984,685 for 3 PRIs.
Cumulative PRI activity (through 12/31/01): Since beginning PRI activity, the foundation has made 10 PRIs totaling $3,076,181. The currently outstanding PRI portfolio includes 9 PRIs totaling $2,738,000 (high: $1,100,000; low: $65,000; average: $350,000). The typical outstanding PRI has a 2- to 10-year term with an average term of 5 years and earns 0 to 5 percent interest with an average of 5 percent.
General purpose and activities: The primary focus of the foundation is to provide low-interest loans for capital improvements, or to refinance real estate loans at a lower rate. The foundation also focuses on youth programs.
General fields of interest: Youth development, adult and child programs; Christian agencies & churches.
General international interests: Canada.
Program-related investment (PRI) activity: The foundation makes loans to organizations for real estate acquisitions and capital improvements.
Limitations: Giving primarily in OR. No grants to individuals. The foundation accepts applications for PRIs.
PRI program information: Letter including property's market value, property's cost to requesting party, year it was purchased, amount of loan needed and list of sources of repayment. Loans are not to exceed more than 70 percent of property value. The foundation does not maintain a formal PRI program. The foundation makes PRIs on a frequent but not annual basis.
Officers and Directors:* Richard G. Faith,* Pres.; Jodie Ross, V.P.; Jennifer Rowland,* V.P.; Daniel L. Kerr,* Secy.-Treas.
Number of staff: None.
EIN: 931115227
PRI recipients:

87-1. Canby Grove Conference Center, Canby, OR, $1,100,000. Loan refinancing for building. 1999.
87-2. Catholic Community Services, Salem, OR, $496,502. Loan to purchase and remodel building. 2001.
87-3. Catholic Community Services, Salem, OR, $140,000. Loan for construction and and to refinance debt on Wardell's Foster Home. 2001.
87-4. Habitat for Humanity, Salem, OR, $41,003. Program-related investment for purchase of land. 2000.
87-5. Holy Family Church, Portland, OR, $65,000. Loan to purchase school building. 1999.
87-6. Salem Theater-Auditorium Group Enterprise (STAGE), Salem, OR, $348,183. Loan for construction and working capital. 2001.

88

Fannie Mae Foundation

N. Tower, Ste. 1
4000 Wisconsin Ave., N.W.
Washington, DC 20016-2800 (202) 274-8057
PRI Contact: Michelle Greanias, Dir., Grants Admin.
FAX: (202) 274-8123; E-mail: grants@fanniemaefoundation.org; URL: http://www.fanniemaefoundation.org

Established in 1979 in DC.
Donor(s): Fannie Mae.
Grantmaker type: Company-sponsored foundation
General financial activity (yr. ended 12/31/01): Assets, $468,969,010 (M); gifts received, $300,000,000; expenditures, $107,264,375; qualifying distributions, $110,331,602; giving activities include $32,186,547 for 1,293 grants (high: $2,317,906; low: $100; average: $10,000–$20,000), $717,988 for 25 grants to individuals (high: $46,299; low: $831; average: $10,000–$40,000), $1,969,816 for 562 employee matching gifts, $69,427,479 for 3 foundation-administered programs and $6,596,551 for 19 PRIs.
Cumulative PRI activity (through 12/31/01): The currently outstanding PRI portfolio includes PRIs totaling $12,778,789.
General purpose and activities: The foundation creates affordable homeownership and housing opportunities through innovative partnerships and initiatives that build healthy, vibrant communities across the United States. The foundation supports local activities and programs that fit its philanthropic priority areas, as well as organizations engaged in issues and activities of national scope and concern. The foundation is especially committed to improving the quality of life for the people of its hometown, Washington, DC, and to enhancing the livability of the city's neighborhoods.
General fields of interest: Housing/shelter.
Program-related investment (PRI) activity: Through its Community and Neighborhood Development Fund, the foundation makes low-interest loans to nonprofits to expand affordable housing for low-income and underserved families throughout the U.S. PRIs sometimes support intermediaries (e.g., loan funds) and provide for predevelopment, construction, or gap financing for specific projects.
Types of PRI Support: Loans/promissory notes, interim financing, capitalizing loan funds/other intermediaries.
Limitations: Giving within the United States only. No support for sectarian organizations. No grants to individuals (except for housing-related research grants and fellowships), or for endowments, capital campaigns, or for general or scholarship support of institutions of higher learning or secondary education.
Publications: Annual report, application guidelines, newsletter.
PRI program information: Apply to Community Outreach Grant Program at DC office, for national organizations, or to regional Fannie Mae offices.
Officers and Directors:* Franklin D. Raines,* Chair.; Jamie S. Gorelick, Vice-Chair.; Stacey Davis Stewart,* C.E.O. and Pres.; Glen S. Howard, Sr. V.P., Genl. Counsel, and Secy.; Beverly L. Barnes, Sr. V.P., Communications; Peter Beard, Sr. V.P., Knowledge Access and Technology Strategy; James H. Carr,* Sr. V.P., Innovation, Research and Technology; Andrew Plepler, Sr. V.P., Housing and Community Initiatives; Kevin Smith, Sr. V.P., Finance and Admin.; Kenneth J. Bacon, Rev. Floyd Flake, Stephen Goldsmith, Charles V. Greener, Colleen Hernandez, Louis W. Hoyes, Stewart Kwoh, Robert J. Levin, William R. Maloni, Dan Mudd, John Sasso, Rebecca Senhauser, Karen Hastie Williams, Barry Zigas.
Number of staff: 77 full-time professional; 20 full-time support; 5 part-time support.
EIN: 521172718
PRI recipients:
88-1. Alliance for Building Communities, Allentown, PA, $250,000. Loan. 2001.
88-2. Asian Inc., San Francisco, CA, $300,000. Loan. 2001.
88-3. BRIDGE Housing Corporation, San Francisco, CA, $300,000. Loan. 2000.
88-4. Charlotte-Mecklenburg Housing Partnership, Charlotte, NC, $300,000. Loan. 2000.
88-5. Chattanooga Neighborhood Enterprise, Chattanooga, TN, $300,000. Loan. 2001.
88-6. Chicago Community Loan Fund, Chicago, IL, $250,000. Loan. 2001.
88-7. Cleveland Housing Network, Cleveland, OH, $500,000. Loan. 2001.
88-8. CommonBond Communities, Saint Paul, MN, $100,000. Loan. 2001.
88-9. CommonBond Communities, Saint Paul, MN, $200,000. Program-related investment for community and neighborhood development loan funds. 1999.
88-10. Community Financing Consortium, West Palm Beach, FL, $200,000. Loan. 2000.
88-11. Cornerstone, DC, $300,000. Loan. 2000.
88-12. Corporation for Supportive Housing, NYC, NY, $500,000. Loan. 2001.

88-13. Delaware Valley Community Reinvestment Fund, Philadelphia, PA, $500,000. Loan. 2001.
88-14. East of the River Community Development Corporation, DC, $400,000. Loan. 2001.
88-15. East of the River Community Development Corporation, DC, $450,000. Loan. 2000.
88-16. El Paso Collaborative for Community and Economic Development, El Paso, TX, $125,000. Loan. 2000.
88-17. Enterprise Foundation, Columbia, MD, $1,000,000. Loan. 2000.
88-18. Fifth Avenue Committee, Brooklyn, NY, $120,000. Loan. 2000.
88-19. Homes in Partnership, Apopka, FL, $250,000. Program-related investment for community and neighborhood development loan funds. 1999.
88-20. Jubilee Community Development Corporation, Miami, FL, $250,000. Loan. 2000.
88-21. McAllen Affordable Homes, McAllen, TX, $200,000. Loan. 2001.
88-22. Mid America Housing Partnership, Cedar Rapids, IA, $300,000. Loan. 2001.
88-23. Mobile Historic Development Commission, Mobile, AL, $300,000. Loan. 2001.
88-24. National Council of La Raza, DC, $500,000. Program-related investment for community and neighborhood development loan funds. 1999.
88-25. National Housing Trust Enterprise Preservation Corporation, DC, $500,000. Loan. 2001.
88-26. Neighborhood Housing Services of Phoenix, Phoenix, AZ, $175,000. Loan. 2000.
88-27. New Economics for Women, Los Angeles, CA, $250,000. Loan. 2000.
88-28. NHP Foundation, DC, $500,000. Loan. 2001.
88-29. Northwestern Housing Enterprises, Boone, NC, $500,000. Loan. 2001.
88-30. Reynoldstown Revitalization Corporation, Atlanta, GA, $300,000. Loan. 2001.
88-31. Rural Housing Institute, Wilton, IA, $400,000. Loan. 2001.
88-32. San Antonio Alternative Housing Corporation, San Antonio, TX, $246,551. Loan. 2001.
88-33. Vermont Community Loan Fund, Montpelier, VT, $250,000. Loan. 2001.
88-34. Virginia Foundation for Housing Preservation, Richmond, VA, $250,000. Loan. 2000.

89

The Farber Foundation

100 S. Wood St.
Neosho, MO 64850
Contact: Rudolph E. Farber, Mgr.

Established in 1997 in MO.
Donor(s): Rudolph E. Farber.
Grantmaker type: Independent foundation
General financial activity (yr. ended 12/31/02): Assets, $2,250,158 (M); gifts received, $543,309; expenditures, $113,125; qualifying distributions, $140,170; giving activities include $109,000 for 12 grants (high: $50,000; low: $100) and $32,000 for 1 PRI.
General purpose and activities: Giving primarily for education and human services, with emphasis on economic programs that benefit Newton County, MO.
General fields of interest: Higher education; health care, patient services; human services.
Program-related investment (PRI) activity: The foundation has made a PRI, in the form of an interest-free loan, to a school district charitable trust, to help with the purchase of land for a new school.
Limitations: Giving limited to Jasper, Newton, and McDonald counties, MO.
Officer: Rudolph E. Farber, Mgr.
EIN: 431763102
PRI recipients:
89-1. Neosho R-5 School District Charitable Foundation, Neosho, MO, $32,000. Interest-bearing loan to help with purchase of land for new school. 2002.
89-2. Neosho R-5 School District Charitable Foundation, Neosho, MO, $177,047. Interest-free loan toward purchase of land for new school. 2001.

90

Richard and Deborah Felder Foundation, Inc.

c/o R. Stepakof
9416 Holbrook Ln.
Potomac, MD 20854

Established in 1997 in MD.
Donor(s): Deborah S. Felder, Richard B. Felder.
Grantmaker type: Independent foundation
General financial activity (yr. ended 12/31/01): Assets, $871,403 (M); gifts received, $270,630; expenditures, $133,220; qualifying distributions, $119,762; giving activities include $119,000 for 10 grants (high: $30,000; low: $2,000) and $795 for PRIs.
Cumulative PRI activity (through 12/31/01): Since beginning PRI activity, the foundation has made PRIs totaling $19,700.
General fields of interest: Radio; opera; performing arts, education; ballet; music; orchestra (symphony); arts/cultural programs; higher education.
Program-related investment (PRI) activity: The foundation makes PRIs, in the form of the acquisition of unique musical works of art, and the subsequent donation of these items to an organization capable of displaying them to the public as a means of enhancing public enjoyment and appreciation of such artistic endeavors.
Types of PRI Support: Charitable use assets.
Limitations: Applications not accepted. Giving primarily in AZ and CO. No grants to individuals.

Officers: Richard B. Felder, Pres.; Deborah S. Felder, Secy.-Treas.
Director: Jonathan E. Felder.
EIN: 522052154

91
First Union Regional Community Development Corporation, Inc.

(Formerly CoreStates Community Development Corporation, Inc.)
1339 Chestnut St., 13th Fl., PA 4360
Philadelphia, PA 19107 (267) 321-7661
Contact: Kimberly Allen
FAX: (267) 321-7656

Established in 1993 in PA.
Donor(s): CoreStates Financial Corp.
Grantmaker type: Company-sponsored foundation
General financial activity (yr. ended 12/31/01): Assets, $6,487,272 (M); expenditures, $116,317; qualifying distributions, $75,000; giving activities include $50,000 for 4 grants of $12,500 each and $25,000 for 1 PRI.
Cumulative PRI activity (through 12/31/01): Since beginning PRI activity, the foundation has made 3 PRIs totaling $122,500.
General purpose and activities: Giving primarily for community and economic development in low-income communities.
Program-related investment (PRI) activity: The foundation has made a PRI in the form of a purchase in a limited partnership interest in an early stage venture capital partnership, for the purpose of stimulating business development and significant job creation. It also has made a PRI in the form of a partnership in a community loan fund, for the purpose of increasing the supply of pre-development loan funds available to non-profit housing developers.
Limitations: Giving primarily in DE, NJ, and the eastern half of PA.
PRI program information: The foundation makes PRIs on a frequent but not annual basis.
Officers and Board Members:* Stephanie W. Naidoff,* Chair.; Robert L. Reid,* Pres.; Denise McGregor Armbrister,* Secy.-Treas. and Exec. Dir.; Robert S. Appleby, Reginald Davis, Lillian Escobar Haskins, Eleanor Horne, Ernest Jones, George Lynett, Patricia McFate, Shannon McFayden, Marlin Miller, Jr., Malcolm Pryor, Peter S. Strawbridge, John D. Wallace.
Number of staff: 4 shared staff.
EIN: 232735410
PRI recipients:

91-1. Early Stage Enterprises, Skillman, NJ, $25,000. Program-related investment to purchase interest in limited partnership designed to invest in start-up companies with goal of stimulating business development and supporting significant job creation. 2001.

91-2. Early Stage Enterprises, Skillman, NJ, $42,500. Program-related investment to purchase interest in limited partnership designed to invest in start-up companies with goal of stimulating business development and supporting significant job creation. 2000.

91-3. Early Stage Enterprises, Skillman, NJ, $42,500. Program-related investment to purchase interest in limited partnership designed to invest in start-up companies with goal of stimulating business development and supporting significant job creation. 1999.

92
Firstfruits Foundation

P.O. Box 239
Elverson, PA 19520-0239

Established in 1995 in PA.
Donor(s): Robert L. Cone, Dawn M. Cone.
Grantmaker type: Independent foundation
General financial activity (yr. ended 12/31/01): Assets, $13,840,073 (M); expenditures, $917,778; qualifying distributions, $1,000,012; giving activities include $805,000 for 16 grants (high: $285,000; low: $7,500); no PRIs paid.
Cumulative PRI activity (through 12/31/01): Since beginning PRI activity, the foundation has made 4 PRIs totaling $226,738.
General purpose and activities: Giving primarily to Baptist churches, schools, and ministries.
General fields of interest: Higher education; theological school/education; education; Protestant agencies & churches.
Program-related investment (PRI) activity: The foundation has made a PRI, in the form of a mortgage loan, to a Baptist church. Historically, the foundation has made a PRI, in the form of a mortgage loan, to a ministry.
Limitations: Applications not accepted. Giving on a national basis. No grants to individuals.
Officers: Robert L. Cone, Pres. and Treas.; Edward H. Cone, V.P. and Secy.
Director: Derial H. Sanders.
EIN: 232808624
PRI recipients:

92-1. Tri-City Baptist Church, $200,000. Mortgage loan. 2000.

93
The Ford Foundation

320 E. 43rd St.
New York, NY 10017 (212) 573-5000
Contact: Secy.
FAX: (212) 351-3677; E-mail: office-secretary@fordfound.org; URL: http://www.fordfound.org

Incorporated in 1936 in MI. PRI-related activities began in 1968.
Donor(s): Henry Ford,‡ Edsel Ford.‡
Grantmaker type: Independent foundation
General financial activity (yr. ended 09/30/02): Assets, $9,300,140,000 (M); expenditures, $659,557,506; qualifying distributions, $620,392,481; giving activities include $505,738,032 for 2,904 grants (high: $8,000,000; low: $2,000), $1,212,508 for 41 grants to individuals (high: $75,000; low: $1,000), $1,381,093 for 883 employee matching gifts and $14,300,000 for 8 PRIs.
Cumulative PRI activity (through 09/30/02): Since 1968, the foundation has made 327 PRIs totaling $. The currently outstanding PRI portfolio includes 122 PRIs totaling $162,756,122 (high: $3,000,000; low: $500,000; average: $1,750,000). The typical outstanding PRI has a 5- to 15-year term with an average term of 10 years and earns 0 to 3 percent interest with an average of 1 percent.
General purpose and activities: The foundation's mission is to serve as a resource for innovative people and institutions worldwide. Its goals are to: strengthen democratic values, reduce poverty and injustice, promote international cooperation, and advance human achievement. Grants are made primarily within three broad categories: (1) asset building and community development; (2) knowledge, creativity, and freedom; and (3) peace and social justice. Local needs and priorities, within these subject areas, determine program activities in individual countries.
General fields of interest: Media/communications; film/video; museums; performing arts; dance; theater; music; arts/cultural programs; education, research; early childhood education; elementary school/education; secondary school/education; higher education; education; natural resources conservation & protection; environment; health care, reproductive health; health education, sexuality; public health, STDs; AIDS; abuse prevention; legal services; employment; agriculture; housing/shelter, development; youth development; human services; women, centers & services; minorities/immigrants, centers & services; international economic development; arms control; foreign policy; international human rights; international affairs; race/intergroup relations; civil rights; urban/community development; rural development; community development; philanthropy/voluntarism; social sciences; economics; law/international law; international studies; public policy, research; government/public administration; public affairs, citizen participation; leadership development; religion, interfaith issues; minorities; women; immigrants/refugees; economically disadvantaged.
General international interests: Caribbean; Eastern Europe; Russia; Africa; Latin America; Asia; Middle East; Southeast Asia.
Program-related investment (PRI) activity: The foundation established a Program-Related Investments office in 1968. In recent years, the foundation has made PRIs in the U.S. and overseas totaling approximately $16 million per year, mostly to intermediaries (e.g., loan funds and venture capital funds). PRIs primarily serve to meet the credit needs of economic development organizations in low-income communities. Recent PRIs have also supported the establishment and capitalization of loan funds benefiting housing organizations, cultural institutions, educational programs, enterprise and employment development, and farmers.
Types of PRI Support: Loans/promissory notes, interim financing, loan guarantees, equity investments, capitalizing loan funds/other intermediaries.
Limitations: Giving on an international basis, including the U.S., Eastern Europe, Africa and the Middle East, Asia, Russia, Latin America and the Caribbean. No support for programs for which substantial support from government or other sources is readily available, or for religious sectarian activities as such. No grants for routine operating costs, construction or maintenance of buildings, or undergraduate scholarships; graduate fellowships generally channeled through grants to universities or other organizations; no grants for purely personal or local needs. PRIs must fit within the foundation's program goals and demonstrate a strong likelihood of repayment. Funding occurs primarily through intermediaries (e.g., loan funds) that specialize in financing and development work. Many organizations receiving PRIs are either current or past foundation grant recipients. Borrowers have been located throughout the U.S. and, to a lesser extent, in developing countries. The foundation accepts applications for PRIs.
Publications: Annual report (including application guidelines), occasional report, informational brochure (including application guidelines), newsletter.
PRI program information: The foundation maintains a formal PRI program. The foundation makes PRIs on an annual basis.
Officers and Trustees:* Paul A. Allaire,* Chair.; Susan V. Berresford,* Pres.; Barron M. Tenny, Exec. V.P., Genl. Counsel, and Secy.; Barry D. Gaberman, Sr. V.P.; Linda B. Strumpf, V.P. and C.I.O.; Alison R. Bernstein, V.P., Knowledge, Creativity, and Freedom; Melvin L. Oliver, V.P., Asset Bldg. and Community Devel.; Bradford K. Smith, V.P., Peace and Social Justice; Alexander Wilde, V.P., Comm.; Nicholas M. Gabriel, Treas. and Dir., Financial Svcs.; Nancy P. Feller, Assoc. Genl. Counsel; Alain J.P. Belda, Afsaneh M. Beschloss, Anke A. Ehrhardt, Kathryn S. Fuller, Juliet V. Garcia, Wilmot G. James, Yolanda Kakabadse, Wilma P. Mankiller, Richard Moe, Yolanda T. Moses, Luis G. Nogales, Deval L. Patrick, Ratan N. Tata, Carl B. Weisbrod, W. Richard West.
Number of staff: 317 full-time professional; 1 part-time professional; 295 full-time support; 2 part-time support.
EIN: 131684331
PRI recipients:
93-1. Alliance for Community Development of the San Francisco Bay Area, Bay Area Community Equity Fund I, LP, San Francisco, CA, $2,000,000. Loan for partial capitalization of community development fund to create employment opportunities and wealth for low-income people. 2002.

93-2. Bhartiya Samruddhi Investments and Consulting Services, Hyderabad, India, $1,000,000. Program-related investment for group of financial service companies that are providing financing for sustainable rural livelihoods in India. 1999.

93-3. Chattanooga Neighborhood Enterprise, Chattanooga, TN, $1,000,000. Loan for partial capitalization of revolving loan fund to finance home renovations for low-income homeowners. 2002.

93-4. Coastal Enterprises, Wiscasset, ME, $3,000,000. Program-related investment to provide capitalization of two enterprise development funds for creating and retaining employment opportunities for disadvantageded people. 2001.

93-5. Community Development Venture Capital Alliance, NYC, NY, $2,000,000. Program-related investment for investment fund that provides subordinated debt and equity to small enterprisess. 1999.

93-6. Community Loan Technologies, Minneapolis, MN, $2,000,000. Working capital for Round Two of Working Capital Fund, a program to strengthen leading mid-size minority cultural organizations. 2000.

93-7. Community Loan Technologies, Minneapolis, MN, $1,000,000. Program-related investment to expand loan fund that will strengthen minority arts organizations. 1999.

93-8. Corporation for Public Broadcasting, DC, $2,000,000. Loan for working capital to Public Interactive, which provides public broadcasters with products and services designed to enable them to compete more efficiently with larger, national media outlets. 2002.

93-9. Council for Adult and Experiential Learning, Chicago, IL, $2,000,000. Working capital for the expansion of employer-based tuition-assistance programs and transitional services for workers at risk of job loss. 2000.

93-10. Desarrolladora de Emprendedores, Mexico City, Mexico, $1,000,000. Program-related investment for credit and savings program for low-income, self-employed micro-entrepreneurs in Mexico. 1999.

93-11. Ecotrust, Portland, OR, $2,000,000. Loan to purchase building to serve as its headquarters and as center for preservation of the conservation economy that integrates the three Es, Environment, Equity and Economy. 2000.

93-12. Eda Rural Systems Private Limited, Gurgaon, India, $1,000,000. Program-related investment to establish guaranty fund that will provide credit enhancements for loans made to microfinance institutions in India. 1999.

93-13. Enterprise Corporation of the Delta, Jackson, MS, $1,500,000. Loan to capitalize loan fund that will serve as secondary market conduit for mortgages that do not conform to current sectionary market criteria. 2002.

93-14. Enterprise Corporation of the Delta, Jackson, MS, $1,500,000. Program-related investment to help capitalize expansion of small business lending in lower Mississippi Delta region through credit enhancement of private sector debt. 2001.

93-15. Enterprise Corporation of the Delta, Jackson, MS, $1,500,000. Loan for investment fund that provides subordinated debt and equity to small enterprises. 1999.

93-16. Enterprise Corporation of the Delta, Jackson, MS, $1,500,000. Equity investment for investment fund that provides subordinated debt and equity to small enterprises. 1999.

93-17. Enterprise Foundation, Columbia, MD, $3,000,000. Loan for partial capitalization of a revolving loan fund for homeownership projects. 2000.

93-18. Focus: Hope, Detroit, MI, $3,000,000. Program-related investment to capitalize student loan fund for use in financing tuition costs of participants in educational programs. 2001.

93-19. Kentucky Highlands Investment Corporation, London, KY, $2,000,000. Program-related investment for investment fund that provides debt and equity to small enterprises. 1999.

93-20. Kenya Women Finance Trust Limited, Nairobi, Kenya, $1,000,000. Loan for partial financing of microfinance program serving low-income women entrepreneurs. 2002.

93-21. Kenya Women Finance Trust Limited, Nairobi, Kenya, $2,000,000. Program-related investment for microfinance program serving low-income entrepreneurs. 1999.

93-22. Low Income Housing Fund, Oakland, CA, $3,000,000. Program-related investment to provide additional capital for revolving loan fund to increase homeownership opportunities for disadvantaged people. 2001.

93-23. Manchester Bidwell Corporation, Pittsburgh, PA, $1,000,000. Loan for working capital for Manchester Craftsmen's Guild's various jazz programs. 2002.

93-24. National Federation of Community Development Credit Unions, NYC, NY, $3,000,000. Program-related investment to expand capitalization program to assist community development credit unions to meet new regulatory standards and to provide predatory relief loans. 2001.

93-25. Neighborhood Housing Services of America, Oakland, CA, $1,500,000. Capitalization of loan fund that would provide home safety improvement loans to low-income homeowners participating in a demonstration program to make affordable property insurance more available. 2000.

93-26. Neighborhood Housing Services of Chicago, Chicago, IL, $2,000,000. Loan for partial capitalization of loan fund to assist low-income homeowners to retain ownership of their homes. 2002.

93-27. Origin, NYC, NY, $1,000,000. Loan for partial capitalization of new, nonprofit social venture designed to prepare and place low-income individuals in technology-intensive jobs. 2002.

93-28. Puerto Rican Legal Defense and Education Fund, NYC, NY, $1,500,000. Loan to finance acquisition and renovation of office space adjacent to current offices. 2002.

93-29. Shorebank Enterprise Group Cleveland, Cleveland, OH, $2,000,000. Capitalization for business development and financing strategy within selected industry clusters to create jobs for low-income residents of Cleveland. 2000.

93-30. Shorecap International LLC, Chicago, IL, $3,000,000. Loan for partial capitalization of investment company that will invest in development finance institutions providing financing to low-income microentrepreneurs and small businesses that will create employment opportunities for disadvantaged people in developing and transitional economies. 2002.

93-31. Southern Development Bancshares, Arkadelphia, AR, $3,000,000. Loan to partially capitalize expansion to the Mississippi Delta region of Mississippi. 2000.

93-32. Success for All Foundation, Baltimore, MD, $2,000,000. Program-related investment for start-up support. 1999.

93-33. TRF Urban Growth Partners, Philadelphia, PA, $3,000,000. Program-related investment to provide capitalization of enterprise development fund to create small businesses and create quality jobs for low-income people. 2001.

93-34. Working Today, Brooklyn, NY, $1,000,000. Loan to capitalize Portable Benefits Fund, which will provide insurance for independent workers and low-income households. 2000.

94

Foundation for Global Awakening

(Formerly Van Camp Foundation)
P.O. Box 366
Point Reyes Station, CA 94956-0366
Contact: Tish Van Camp, Pres.
FAX: (415) 663-0855; E-mail: fga@ffga.org;
URL: http://www.ffga.org

Trust established in 1962 in CA. PRI-related activities began in 1999.
Donor(s): Gilbert C. Van Camp, Sr., Family Trust.
Grantmaker type: Independent foundation
General financial activity (yr. ended 12/31/01): Assets, $6,066,905 (M); expenditures, $416,488; qualifying distributions, $378,381; giving activities include $139,180 for grants (average: $250–$75,000); no PRIs paid.
Cumulative PRI activity (through 12/31/01): Since 1999, the foundation has made 3 PRIs totaling $3,000,000.
General purpose and activities: Support for heart-centered consciousness change at local and global levels.
General fields of interest: Media/communications; philosophy/ethics; international affairs; public affairs, research; leadership development.
Program-related investment (PRI) activity: Historically, the foundation has made a PRI in the form of paying the interest on a line of credit for a conservation organization, and treating it as a charitable interest-free loan. The foundation no longer makes PRIs.
Types of PRI Support: Loans/promissory notes.
Limitations: No grants to individuals. PRI applications not accepted.
Publications: Newsletter, occasional report, informational brochure.
PRI program information: The foundation does not maintain a formal PRI program.
Officers and Trustees:* Tish Van Camp,* Pres.; Alexander S. Kochkin,* Exec. V.P.
Number of staff: 2 full-time professional; 1 part-time professional; 1 part-time support.
EIN: 956039680
PRI recipients:

94-1. Fund for Global Awakening, Point Reyes Station, CA, $187,202. Line of credit treated as non-interest bearing loan. 2000.

94-2. Fund for Global Awakening, Point Reyes Station, CA, $46,038. Interest paid on line of credit which is being treated as a non-interest bearing loan. 1999.

95

Friedman Family Foundation

PMB 719
204 E. 2nd Ave.
San Mateo, CA 94401 (650) 342-8750
Contact: Lisa Kawahara
FAX: (650) 342-8750; E-mail: fffdn@aol.com;
URL: http://www.friedmanfamilyfoundation.org

Established in 1964 in CA.
Donor(s): Phyllis K. Friedman, Howard Friedman.‡
Grantmaker type: Independent foundation
General financial activity (yr. ended 02/28/02): Assets, $18,158,681 (M); expenditures, $1,927,448; qualifying distributions, $1,786,616; giving activities include $1,751,000 for 159 grants (high: $120,000; low: $1,000; average: $1,000–$25,000); no PRIs paid.
Cumulative PRI activity (through 02/28/02): Since beginning PRI activity, the foundation has made 5 PRIs totaling $500,000. The currently outstanding PRI portfolio includes 5 PRIs totaling $500,000 (high: $100,000). The typical outstanding PRI has a 1- to 12-year term with an average term of 3 years, and earns 1 to 2 percent interest.
General purpose and activities: Support for programs which attempt to end the cycle of poverty, especially programs that provide tools, support, asset building, and opportunity to people in need in order to overcome the root causes of their poverty, and in which the people to be helped are part of the design and decision making of the organization or project. Preference is given to new and creative programs, and programs working for systemic change.
General fields of interest: Economic development; community development; economically disadvantaged; homeless.

Program-related investment (PRI) activity: Currently, the foundation makes PRIs to a community loan fund and a women's organization.
Types of PRI Support: Loans/promissory notes, charitable use assets.
Limitations: Giving primarily in the San Francisco Bay Area, CA. No grants to individuals, or for films, videos, conferences, seminars, capital campaigns, scholarships, research, or special or fundraising events. The foundation accepts applications for PRIs.
Publications: Multi-year report (including application guidelines).
PRI program information: The foundation does not maintain a formal PRI program. The foundation makes PRIs on a frequent but not annual basis.
Officers and Directors:* Phyllis K. Friedman,* Pres.; Eleanor Friedman,* V.P.; David A. Friedman,* Secy.; Robert E. Friedman,* Treas.
Number of staff: 1 part-time professional.
EIN: 946109692
PRI recipients:
95-1. Calvert Social Investment Foundation, Bethesda, MD, $100,000. Program-related investment. 1999.
95-2. Count Me In for Womens Economic Independence, DC, $100,000. Program-related investment. 2000.
95-3. EcoTimber Industrial, $100,000. Program-related investment. 1999.
95-4. Northern California Community Loan Fund, San Francisco, CA, $100,000. Program-related investment. 2000.
95-5. Shefa Fund, Philadelphia, PA, $100,000. Program-related investment. 1999.

96
The Frist Foundation
(Formerly The HCA Foundation)
3319 West End Ave., Ste. 900
Nashville, TN 37203-1076 (615) 292-3868
Contact: Peter F. Bird, Jr., C.E.O. and Exec. Dir.
FAX: (615) 292-5843; E-mail: askfrist@fristfoundation.org; URL: http://www.fristfoundation.org

Established in 1982 in TN.
Donor(s): Hospital Corp. of America.
Grantmaker type: Independent foundation
General financial activity (yr. ended 12/31/02): Assets, $151,733,000 (M); expenditures, $11,414,931; qualifying distributions, $11,401,743; giving activities include $10,636,363 for 417 grants (high: $200,000; low: $450; average: $500–$200,000); no PRIs paid.
Cumulative PRI activity (through 12/31/02): The currently outstanding PRI portfolio includes 2 PRIs totaling $4,900,000.
General purpose and activities: Giving primarily to strengthen the capacity of Nashville-based nonprofit agencies to serve the community.
General fields of interest: Visual arts; performing arts; arts/cultural programs; education; health associations; human services; community development; federated giving programs.
Program-related investment (PRI) activity: The foundation has made low-interest term loans to a visual arts center.
Types of PRI Support: Loans/promissory notes.
Limitations: Giving primarily in Nashville, TN. No support for political activities, start-up expenses, disease-specific organizations seeking support for national projects, private foundations, religious organizations for religious purposes, hospitals, nursing homes, or retirement homes. No grants to individuals, or for endowment funds, biomedical or clinical research, social events or similar fundraising events, promotional materials including goodwill advertising, telethons, sponsorships, publications, trips, tours, or organizations whose principal work is outside of middle Tennessee.
Publications: Annual report (including application guidelines), informational brochure (including application guidelines).
Officers and Directors:* Thomas F. Frist, Jr.,* Chair.; Peter F. Bird, Jr.,* C.E.O. and Exec. Dir.; Kenneth L. Roberts,* Pres.; Lani Wilkeson, Secy. and Sr. Prog. Off.; Colette R. Easter, Treas.; Jack O. Bovender, Jr., Robert C. Crosby, Helen K. Cummings, Frank F. Drowota III, Patricia C. Frist, Fred Russell, Dir., Emeritus.
Number of staff: 3 full-time professional; 1 part-time professional; 2 full-time support; 1 part-time support.
EIN: 621134070
PRI recipients:
96-1. Frist Center for the Visual Arts Foundation, Nashville, TN, $600,000. Term loan with below-market interest rate. 2001.
96-2. Frist Center for the Visual Arts Foundation, Nashville, TN, $4,300,000. Term loan with below-market interest rate. 2000.

97
The Garber Fund
508 Hemlock Dr.
Cedarhurst, NY 11516

Established in 1987 in NY.
Donor(s): Harvey Brecher, Eli S. Garber, Harriette Garber.
Grantmaker type: Independent foundation
General financial activity (yr. ended 09/30/01): Assets, $704,883 (M); expenditures, $151,900; qualifying distributions, $270,293; giving activities include $120,193 for 57 grants (high: $26,800; low: $10) and $200,000 for 1 PRI.
Cumulative PRI activity (through 09/30/01): The currently outstanding PRI portfolio includes PRIs totaling $102,500.
General purpose and activities: Giving primarily to Jewish agencies, temples, and schools; some support also for health associations.

General fields of interest: Education; health associations; human services; children & youth, services; Jewish federated giving programs; Jewish agencies & temples.
Program-related investment (PRI) activity: The foundation makes PRIs in the areas of Jewish culture, education, and youth services.
Types of PRI Support: Loans/promissory notes.
Limitations: Applications not accepted. Giving primarily in NY. No grants to individuals. PRI support limited to NY. PRI applications not accepted.
Officers and Directors:* Eli S. Garber,* Pres.; Harriette Garber,* V.P.; Harvey Brecher.
EIN: 112910964
PRI recipients:
97-1. Keren Hachesed, Monsey, NY, $200,000. Loan. 2001.
97-2. Keren Hachesed, Monsey, NY, $75,000. Loan. 2000.
97-3. Keren Hachesed, Monsey, NY, $75,000. Loan. 1999.

98
Gebbie Foundation, Inc.

Hotel Jamestown Bldg., Rm. 308
110 W. 3rd St.
Jamestown, NY 14701 (716) 487-1062
Contact: Dr. Thomas M. Cardman, Exec. Dir.
FAX: (716) 484-6401

Incorporated in 1963 in NY.
Donor(s): Marion B. Gebbie,‡ Geraldine G. Bellinger.‡
Grantmaker type: Independent foundation
General financial activity (yr. ended 09/30/02): Assets, $64,842,249 (M); expenditures, $4,702,855; qualifying distributions, $4,196,396; giving activities include $4,018,226 for 67 grants (high: $500,000; low: $100; average: $5,000–$75,000); no PRIs paid.
Cumulative PRI activity (through 09/30/02): The currently outstanding PRI portfolio includes 2 PRIs totaling $351,284.
General purpose and activities: Grants primarily for the arts, children and youth services, community development, education, and human services.
General fields of interest: Arts/cultural programs; education; human services; children & youth, services; community development.
Program-related investment (PRI) activity: The foundation has made PRIs to a community development organization and a YMCA.
Types of PRI Support: Loans/promissory notes.
Limitations: Giving primarily in Chautauqua County in western NY, especially the Jamestown, NY, area. No support for sectarian or religious organizations. No grants to individuals.
Publications: Application guidelines.
Officers and Directors:* Rhoe B. Henderson III,* Pres.; Lillian V. Ney, M.D.,* V.P.; Daniel Kathman,* Secy.; Linda V. Swanson,* Treas.; Thomas M. Cardman, Ph.D., Exec. Dir.; Martin Coyle, George A. Campbell, Charles T. Hall, John Lloyd, Bertram Parker, Kristy Zabrodsky.
Number of staff: 1 full-time professional; 3 full-time support.
EIN: 166050287
PRI recipients:
98-1. Jamestown Center City Development Corporation, Jamestown, NY, $1,300,000. No-interest loan. 2000.

99
John F. and Mary A. Geisse Foundation

(Formerly The Geisse Foundation)
38050 Jackson Rd.
Chagrin Falls, OH 44022-2025 (216) 595-1700
Contact: Tim Geisse, Tr.
FAX: (216) 595-1707; E-mail: timgeisse@aol.com

Established in 1969. PRI-related activities began in 1997.
Donor(s): John F. Geisse,‡ Mary A. Geisse.‡
Grantmaker type: Independent foundation
General financial activity (yr. ended 12/31/02): Assets, $11,416,207 (M); expenditures, $1,231,607; qualifying distributions, $1,082,378; giving activities include $1,082,378 for 64 grants (high: $200,000; low: $50; average: $50–$200,000), $300,000 for 2 foundation-administered programs and $300,000 for 2 PRIs.
Cumulative PRI activity (through 12/31/02): Since 1997, the foundation has made 6 PRIs totaling $950,000. The currently outstanding PRI portfolio includes 4 PRIs totaling $750,000 (high: $250,000; low: $100,000; average: $162,500). The typical outstanding PRI has a 1- to 2-year term with an average term of 1.5 years and earns 0 to 4 percent interest with an average of 2 percent.
General purpose and activities: Support for programs that help the very poor of the developing world reach a higher standard of living.
General fields of interest: International development.
General international interests: Developing countries.
Program-related investment (PRI) activity: The foundation has made PRIs to encourage lending in underprivileged or underserved areas, to create a loan fund for Latin American micolending programs, and to capitalize a microcredit bank.
Types of PRI Support: Loans/promissory notes, equity investments, capitalizing loan funds/other intermediaries, linked deposits.
Limitations: Giving primarily on an international basis. No grants to individuals. The foundation accepts applications for PRIs.
Publications: Occasional report, informational brochure (including application guidelines).
PRI program information: The foundation does not maintain a formal PRI program. The foundation makes PRIs on a frequent but not annual basis.
Trustees: Lawrence J. Geisse, M.D., Timothy F. Geisse.
Number of staff: 1 full-time professional.
EIN: 237049780
PRI recipients:
99-1. Opportunity International, Oak Brook, IL, $250,000. Interest-free loan. 2001.

100
The Gentine Foundation, Inc.
P.O. Box 386
Plymouth, WI 53073
Contact: Ann M. Sturzl, Pres.
Application address: N6604 Riverview Rd., Plymouth, WI 53073; E-mail: esturzl@excel.net

Established in 1989 in WI.
Donor(s): Leonard A. Gentine, Sr.,‡ Dolores A. Gentine.
Grantmaker type: Independent foundation
General financial activity (yr. ended 06/30/02): Assets, $3,667,333 (M); gifts received, $3,000; expenditures, $247,039; qualifying distributions, $233,680; giving activities include $228,680 for grants (high: $50,000; low: $680; average: $20,000–$50,000) and $5,000 for 1 PRI.
Cumulative PRI activity (through 06/30/02): Since beginning PRI activity, the foundation has made PRIs totaling $191,600.
General purpose and activities: Giving primarily for higher education, human services, community projects, and Christian churches and agencies.
General fields of interest: Higher education; human services; community development, neighborhood development; Christian agencies & churches.
Program-related investment (PRI) activity: The foundation makes PRIs to an organization that manages real estate for rental to nonprofit organizations.
Limitations: Giving primarily in the Midwest.
Officers: Ann Sturzl, Pres.; Lee M. Gentine, V.P. and Treas.; Kristin Gentine, Secy.
Number of staff: None.
EIN: 391654230
PRI recipients:
100-1. Plymouth Coalition, Plymouth, WI, $179,600. Loan. 1999.

101
George Family Foundation
1818 Oliver Ave. S.
Minneapolis, MN 55405 (612) 377-8400
Contact: Diane B. Neimann, Exec. Dir.
FAX: (612) 377-8407; URL: http://www.fpadvisors.com/george.htm

Established in 1992 in MN.
Donor(s): Penny Pilgram George, William W. George.
Grantmaker type: Independent foundation
General financial activity (yr. ended 12/31/01): Assets, $26,674,465 (M); gifts received, $759,503; expenditures, $1,717,908; qualifying distributions, $1,801,876; giving activities include $1,186,790 for 60 grants (high: $100,000; low: $500), $272,737 for 2 foundation-administered programs and $100,000 for 1 PRI.
General purpose and activities: The mission of the foundation is to foster human development - spiritual, intellectual, physical and psychological - and to enhance the work of people and organizations devoted to exemplary service in the community. Giving primarily for integrated healing, education, youth development, overcoming barriers, and spirituality.
General fields of interest: Education; health associations; youth development; human services; religion.
Program-related investment (PRI) activity: The foundation has made a PRI, in the form of a loan, to a neighborhood foundation, for the purpose of acquiring real property.
Types of PRI Support: Loans/promissory notes.
Limitations: Giving primarily in the Twin Cities area, MN. No grants to individuals, or for endowments, capital campaigns, memberships, debt reduction, fundraisers, special events, or for operating expenses.
Publications: Annual report (including application guidelines), application guidelines, informational brochure.
Officers: Penny Pilgram George, Pres.; William W. George, V.P.
Directors: Jeffrey Pilgram George, Jonathan Roulette George.
EIN: 411730855
PRI recipients:
101-1. Plymouth Church Neighborhood Foundation, Minneapolis, MN, $100,000. No interest loan for purpose of acquiring real property. 2001.

102
Wallace Alexander Gerbode Foundation
470 Columbus Ave., Ste. 209
San Francisco, CA 94133-3930 (415) 391-0911
Contact: Thomas C. Layton, Pres.
FAX: (415) 391-4587; E-mail: maildesk@gerbode.org; URL: http://www.fdncenter.org/grantmaker/gerbode

Incorporated in 1953 in CA.
Donor(s): Members of the Gerbode family.
Grantmaker type: Independent foundation
General financial activity (yr. ended 12/31/01): Assets, $71,199,657 (M); expenditures, $5,127,251; qualifying distributions, $3,541,068; giving activities include $3,024,159 for 134 grants (high: $300,000; low: $500; average: $5,000–$25,000); no PRIs paid.
Cumulative PRI activity (through 12/31/01): Since beginning PRI activity, the foundation has made 19 PRIs totaling $3,660,000. The currently outstanding PRI portfolio includes 5 PRIs totaling $1,000,000 (high: $250,000; low: $100,000; average: $250,000). The typical outstanding PRI has an average term of 12 years, and earns an average of 2 percent interest.
General purpose and activities: Support for programs and projects offering potential for significant impact in the areas of arts and culture, the environment, population, reproductive rights, citizen participation/building communities/inclusiveness, the strength of the philanthropic process and the nonprofit sector, and foundation-initiated special projects.

General fields of interest: Arts/cultural programs; environment; reproductive rights; civil rights; community development; philanthropy/voluntarism; public policy, research; public affairs.
Program-related investment (PRI) activity: The foundation makes PRIs for the arts, health, environmental conservation, housing, and small business development. PRIs have provided interim financing and capitalized earned income ventures, occasionally through intermediaries (e.g., loan funds and venture capital funds).
Limitations: Giving primarily to programs directly affecting residents of Alameda, Contra Costa, Marin, San Francisco, and San Mateo counties in CA, and HI. No support for religious purposes or private schools. No grants to individuals, or for direct services, deficit budgets, general operating funds, building or equipment funds, general fundraising campaigns, publications, or scholarships. PRI applications not accepted.
Publications: Grants list, annual report (including application guidelines), application guidelines.
PRI program information: The foundation maintains a formal PRI program. The foundation makes PRIs occasionally.
Officers and Trustees:* Maryanna G. Stockholm,* Chair.; Charles M. Stockholm,* Vice-Chair. and Treas.; Frank A. Gerbode, M.D.,* Vice-Chair. and Secy.; Thomas C. Layton,* Pres.
Number of staff: 2 full-time professional; 2 full-time support; 1 part-time support.
EIN: 946065226
PRI recipients:
102-1. Hawaii Community Loan Fund, Honolulu, HI, $150,000. Program-related investment for organizational development. 2000.
102-2. Northern California Community Loan Fund, San Francisco, CA, $250,000. Program-related investment for organizational development. 2000.

103
Gerry Foundation, Inc.
P.O. Box 311
Liberty, NY 12754 (845) 295-2400
Contact: Darrell Supak

Established in 1997 in NY.
Donor(s): Alan Gerry.
Grantmaker type: Operating foundation
General financial activity (yr. ended 10/31/01): Assets, $140,129,286 (M); expenditures, $4,662,940; qualifying distributions, $8,809,315; giving activities include $1,665,100 for 9 grants (high: $500,000; low: $100; average: $150,000–$300,000), $433,764 for 4 foundation-administered programs and $4,409,525 for PRIs.
Cumulative PRI activity (through 10/31/01): Since beginning PRI activity, the foundation has made PRIs totaling $6,161,346.
General purpose and activities: Emphasis on higher education, medical institutes, and community development.
General fields of interest: Museums; education; hospitals (general); community development.
Program-related investment (PRI) activity: The foundation provides PRIs for the purchase of land and buildings.
Limitations: Giving primarily in Sullivan County, NY.
Officers and Directors:* Alan Gerry,* Pres.; Louis J. Boyd, Secy.-Treas.; Adam Gerry, Annelise Gerry, Robyn Gerry, Sandra Gerry.
EIN: 141798234

104
Global Environment Project Institute, Inc.
P.O. Box 158
Pacific Palisades, CA 90272
Contact: Rampa R. Hormel, Pres. and Treas.

Established in 1986 in ID.
Donor(s): Thomas D. Hormel.
Grantmaker type: Independent foundation
General financial activity (yr. ended 12/31/01): Assets, $1,458,861 (M); gifts received, $926,420; expenditures, $691,807; qualifying distributions, $642,760; giving activities include $604,200 for 11 grants (high: $105,000; low: $5,000; average: $500–$200,000); no PRIs paid.
General purpose and activities: The institute promotes the conservation of biodiversity and the sustainability of life on earth.
General fields of interest: Environment.
Program-related investment (PRI) activity: The foundation has agreed to assist and support the development and construction of a community garden project by leasing land to the project and paying for improvements. These costs are accounted for as PRIs.
Types of PRI Support: Charitable use assets.
Limitations: Applications not accepted. Giving on a national basis.
Publications: Grants list.
Officers and Directors:* Rampa R. Hormel,* Pres. and Treas.; Diane Ives,* Secy.; Drummond Pike.
Number of staff: None.
EIN: 820421067

105
Golden Family Foundation
500 Fifth Ave., 50th Fl.
New York, NY 10110 (212) 391-8960
Contact: William T. Golden, Pres.

Incorporated in 1952 in NY.
Donor(s): William T. Golden, Sibyl L. Golden.‡
Grantmaker type: Independent foundation
General financial activity (yr. ended 12/31/02): Assets, $50,345,794 (M); expenditures, $3,133,912; qualifying distributions, $2,974,376; giving activities include

$2,675,049 for 179 grants (high: $800,000; low: $100; average: $500–$75,000); no PRIs paid.
Cumulative PRI activity (through 12/31/02): Since beginning PRI activity, the foundation has made 12 PRIs totaling $4,790,000. The currently outstanding PRI portfolio includes 2 PRIs totaling $262,600.
General purpose and activities: Support for a broad range of programs in higher education, science, public affairs, and cultural areas.
General fields of interest: Arts/cultural programs; higher education; engineering & technology; science; public policy, research.
Program-related investment (PRI) activity: The foundation makes PRIs in the form of loans to educational, environmental, and housing organizations.
Types of PRI Support: Loans/promissory notes.
Limitations: Applications not accepted. Giving primarily in NY. No grants to individuals. PRI applications not accepted.
PRI program information: The foundation does not maintain a formal PRI program. The foundation makes PRIs occasionally.
Officers and Directors:* William T. Golden,* Pres.; Sibyl R. Golden,* V.P.; Helene L. Kaplan,* Secy.; Ralph E. Hansmann,* Treas.; Pamela P. Golden, M.D.
Number of staff: None.
EIN: 237423802
PRI recipients:
105-1. Black Rock Forest Preserve, NYC, NY, $150,000. Loan for construction of Science and Education Center. 1999.
105-2. Columbia University, NYC, NY, $200,000. Loan for construction of CCD imager for MDM Observatory which is located in Arizona and owned and operated by a consortium of four universities, the University of Michigan, Dartmouth College, Ohio State University and Columbia University. 1999.
105-3. Hebrew Free Loan Society, NYC, NY, $500,000. Note recievable for general support. 2000.
105-4. Tongore Pines Housing Development Fund, Phoenicia, NY, $25,000. Loan for construction of residential housing for low-income elderly. 1999.

106
Gordon Lovejoy Foundation
P.O. Box 12317
Seattle, WA 98111

Established in 1998 in WA.
Donor(s): Nicholas Lovejoy, Barbara Gordon.
Grantmaker type: Independent foundation
General financial activity (yr. ended 12/31/01): Assets, $2,637,727 (M); gifts received, $33,101; expenditures, $132,681; qualifying distributions, $115,610; giving activities include $42,500 for 3 grants (high: $20,000; low: $2,500); no PRIs paid.
General purpose and activities: Giving primarily for environmental conservation.
General fields of interest: Environment.
Program-related investment (PRI) activity: Historically, the foundation has made 1 PRI, in the form of a loan, for environmental conservation.
Limitations: Applications not accepted. Giving primarily in CA. No grants to individuals.
Officers: Barbara Gordon, Pres.; Nicholas Lovejoy, Secy.-Treas.
EIN: 911941495
PRI recipients:
106-1. Trust for Public Land, San Francisco, CA, $1,000,000. Program-related investment for Arrowleaf Project. 2000.

107
Philip L. Graham Fund
c/o The Washington Post Co.
1150 15th St., N.W.
Washington, DC 20071 (202) 334-6640
Contact: Candice C. Bryant, Pres.
FAX: (202) 334-4498; E-mail: plgfund@washpost.com

Trust established in 1963 in DC.
Donor(s): Katharine Graham,‡ Frederick S. Beebe,‡ The Washington Post Co., Newsweek, Inc., Post-Newsweek Stations.
Grantmaker type: Independent foundation
General financial activity (yr. ended 12/31/02): Assets, $107,235 (M); expenditures, $5,357,514; qualifying distributions, $5,148,955; giving activities include $5,112,500 for 201 grants (high: $300,000; low: $2,500; average: $5,000–$100,000); no PRIs paid.
General purpose and activities: Support for arts and culture, education, health and human services, with an emphasis on youth agencies, and community affairs. Grants also for journalism and communications.
General fields of interest: Media/communications; journalism & publishing; arts/cultural programs; early childhood education; education; human services; youth, services.
Program-related investment (PRI) activity: The foundation makes loans to organizations related to religious institutions and activities.
Types of PRI Support: Loans/promissory notes.
Limitations: Giving primarily in the metropolitan Washington, DC, area. No support for national or international organizations, religious organizations for religious purposes, or for political activities. No grants to individuals, or for medical services, research, annual campaigns, fundraising events, conferences, publications, tickets, films, travel expenses, courtesy advertising, advocacy, or litigation.
Publications: Program policy statement, grants list.
Officers and Trustees:* Candice C. Bryant, Pres.; Mary M. Bellor,* Secy.; Martin Cohen,* Treas.; Donald E. Graham, Theodore M. Lutz, Lionel W. Neptune, Vincent E. Reed, Emeritus.

Number of staff: 1 full-time professional; 1 full-time support.
EIN: 526051781
PRI recipients:
107-1. Wellspring Ministries, DC, $20,000. Loan, non-interest bearing. 1999.

108

The George Gund Foundation

1845 Guildhall Bldg.
45 Prospect Ave., W.
Cleveland, OH 44115-1018 (216) 241-3114
Contact: David Abbott, Exec. Dir.
PRI Contact: Robert B. Jaquay, Assoc. Dir.
FAX: (216) 241-6560; URL: http://www.gundfdn.org

Incorporated in 1952 in OH. PRI-related activities began in 1982.
Donor(s): George Gund.‡
Grantmaker type: Independent foundation
General financial activity (yr. ended 12/31/01): Assets, $424,502,237 (M); expenditures, $24,125,437; qualifying distributions, $21,121,817; giving activities include $20,345,592 for 518 grants (high: $1,000,000; low: $1,000; average: $10,000–$50,000) and $19,683 for 1 PRI.
Cumulative PRI activity (through 12/31/01): The currently outstanding PRI portfolio includes 11 PRI totaling $7,733,241 (high: $3,650,000; low: $100,000; average: $703,022). The typical outstanding PRI has a 6- to 20-year term, and earns 1 to 2 percent interest.
General purpose and activities: Priority to education projects, with emphasis on new concepts and methods of teaching and learning, and on increasing educational opportunities for the disadvantaged; programs advancing economic revitalization and job creation; projects promoting neighborhood development; projects for improving human services, employment opportunities, housing for minority and low-income groups; support also for ecology, civic affairs, and the arts. Preference is given to pilot projects and innovative programs which present prospects for broad replication.
General fields of interest: Arts/cultural programs; education, research; early childhood education; elementary school/education; secondary school/education; higher education; education; natural resources conservation & protection; environment; AIDS; AIDS research; crime/law enforcement; employment; housing/shelter, development; human services; children & youth, services; women, centers & services; minorities/immigrants, centers & services; race/intergroup relations; urban/community development; community development; government/public administration; public affairs; minorities; women; economically disadvantaged.
Program-related investment (PRI) activity: Traditionally, the foundation has made PRIs to support housing, economic development, and community revitalization. PRIs have generally funded nonprofit intermediaries (e.g., loan funds and venture capital funds) but have also provided for the direct capitalization of housing developments. In recent years, the foundation has made efforts to alert program staff from all areas to use of PRIs.
Types of PRI Support: Loans/promissory notes, equity investments, linked deposits.
Limitations: Giving primarily in northeastern OH and the greater Cleveland, OH, area. No support for political groups, services for the physically, mentally or developmentally disabled, or the elderly. Generally, no grants to individuals, or for building or endowment funds, political campaigns, debt reduction, equipment, renovation projects, or to fund benefit events. The foundation accepts applications for PRIs.
Publications: Annual report (including application guidelines), application guidelines.
PRI program information: The foundation does not maintain a formal PRI program. The foundation makes PRIs on a frequent but not annual basis.
Officers and Trustees:* Geoffrey Gund,* Pres. and Treas.; Llura A. Gund,* V.P.; Ann L. Gund,* Secy.; David Abbott, Exec. Dir.; Marjorie M. Carlson, Catherine Gund, George Gund III, Zachary Gund, Robert D. Storey.
Number of staff: 5 full-time professional; 5 full-time support.
EIN: 346519769
PRI recipients:
108-1. Historic Gateway Neighborhood Corporation, Cleveland, OH, $750,000. Loan to finance acquisition and renovation of Old Arcade Historic Building on Lower Euclid Avene in downtown Cleveland. 1999.
108-2. Ohio City Near West Development Corporation, Cleveland, OH, $250,000. Low-interest loan to convert former bank building into Cleveland Environmental Center, green office building housing businesses and nonprofits. 2001.
108-3. Playhouse Square Foundation, Cleveland, OH, $500,000. Loan to finance acquisition of Buckley and Hanna buildings to influence development of Euclid Avenue Theater Area of downtown Cleveland. 1999.
108-4. Shorebank Enterprise Group Cleveland, Cleveland, OH, $19,683. Deposit agreement increase which allows Shorebank to provide loans at affordable rates to further commercial development in disadvantaged neighborhoods in Cleveland. 2001.
108-5. Shorebank Enterprise Group Cleveland, Cleveland, OH, $12,425. Deposit agreement increase which allows Shorebank to provide loans at affordable rates to further commercial development in disadvantaged neighborhoods in Cleveland. 2000.
108-6. Shorebank Enterprise Group Cleveland, Cleveland, OH, $614,888. Program-related investment in the form of a deposit agreement to provide loans at affordable rates to futher commerical development in disadvantaged neighborhoods of Cleveland. 1999.

109
Hall Family Foundation

c/o Charitable & Crown Investment-323
P.O. Box 419580
Kansas City, MO 64141-6580 (816) 274-8516
Contact: Jeanne Bates, V.P., John Laney, V.P., or Sally Groves, Prog. Off.
PRI Contact: William A. Hall

Hallmark Educational Foundation incorporated in 1943 in MO; Hallmark Educational Foundation of KS incorporated in 1954 in KS; combined funds formerly known as Hallmark Educational Foundations; current name adopted due to absorption of Hall Family Foundation of Kansas in 1993. PRI-related activities began in 1981.
Donor(s): Hallmark Cards, Inc., Joyce C. Hall,‡ E.A. Hall,‡ R.B. Hall.‡
Grantmaker type: Independent foundation
General financial activity (yr. ended 12/31/01): Assets, $741,132,396 (M); expenditures, $41,907,991; qualifying distributions, $38,065,014; giving activities include $36,693,490 for 105 grants (high: $12,375,000; low: $8,000), $265,500 for 178 grants to individuals (high: $3,000; low: $750) and $250,000 for 1 PRI.
Cumulative PRI activity (through 12/31/01): The currently outstanding PRI portfolio includes 6 PRIs totaling $3,328,576 (high: $6,000,000; low: $50,000). The typical outstanding PRI has a 2- to 15-year term, and earns 5 to 10 percent interest.
General purpose and activities: Giving within four main areas of interest: 1) the performing and visual arts; 2) education - all levels; 3) children, youth and families; and 4) community development.
General fields of interest: Performing arts; arts/cultural programs; early childhood education; child development, education; elementary school/education; secondary school/education; higher education; education; housing/shelter, development; human services; youth, services; child development, services; family services; minorities/immigrants, centers & services; homeless, human services; urban/community development; community development; minorities; homeless.
Program-related investment (PRI) activity: The foundation has made PRIs for construction of low-income housing and to a minority owned bank and a sports foundation.
Types of PRI Support: Loans/promissory notes, capitalizing loan funds/other intermediaries.
Limitations: Giving limited to Kansas City, MO. No support for international or religious organizations or for political purposes. No grants to individuals (except for employee-related scholarships), or for travel, operating deficits, conferences, scholarly or medical research, or fundraising campaigns such as telethons. PRI applications not accepted.
Publications: Annual report, informational brochure (including application guidelines).
PRI program information: The foundation does not maintain a formal PRI program. The foundation makes PRIs occasionally.
Officers: William A. Hall, Pres.; John A. MacDonald, V.P. and Treas.; Jeanne Bates, V.P.; John Laney, V.P.; Danita M.H. Robinson, Secy.
Directors: Donald J. Hall, Chair.; Irvine O. Hockaday, Jr., David H. Hughes, Robert A. Kipp, Sandra Lawrence, John P. Mascotte, Margaret Hall Pence, Morton I. Sosland.
Number of staff: 2 full-time professional; 1 part-time professional; 1 full-time support.
EIN: 446006291
PRI recipients:
109-1. National Association of Basketball Coaches, Overland Park, KS, $250,000. Program-related investment. 2001.

110
Hallmark Corporate Foundation

P.O. Box 419580, M.D. 323
Kansas City, MO 64141-6580 (816) 545-6906
Contact: Karen Bartz, V.P.
PRI Contact: William A. Hall, Pres.

Established in 1983 in MO. PRI-related activities began in 1991.
Donor(s): Hallmark Cards, Inc.
Grantmaker type: Company-sponsored foundation
General financial activity (yr. ended 12/31/01): Assets, $5,438,710 (M); expenditures, $5,609,432; qualifying distributions, $5,591,851; giving activities include $4,793,616 for 2,016 grants (high: $500,000; low: $50; average: $1,000–$25,000) and $526,082 for 442 employee matching gifts; no PRIs paid.
Cumulative PRI activity (through 12/31/01): The currently outstanding PRI portfolio includes 1 PRI totaling $1,300,000. The typical outstanding PRI has a maximum term of 15 years, and earns 9 to 10 percent interest.
General purpose and activities: Support for a broad range of programs in areas of health and human services, arts and culture, education, and civic affairs.
General fields of interest: Museums; performing arts; theater; humanities; arts/cultural programs; early childhood education; child development, education; elementary school/education; secondary school/education; higher education; adult education—literacy, basic skills & GED; reading; education; mental health/crisis services; AIDS; domestic violence prevention; employment; housing/shelter, development; youth development, services; human services; children & youth, services; child development, services; family services; hospices; minorities/immigrants, centers & services; homeless, human services; urban/community development; business & industry; community development; voluntarism promotion; leadership development; public affairs; minorities; disabled; economically disadvantaged.

Program-related investment (PRI) activity: Historically, the foundation has made PRIs in the areas of housing, community development, and the arts. PRIs are handled through Hallmark's Social Investments Program.
Types of PRI Support: Loans/promissory notes.
Limitations: Giving limited to the Kansas City, MO, area, and communities where major Hallmark facilities are located, including Enfield, CT, Columbus, GA, Metamora, IL, Lawrence, Leavenworth, and Topeka, KS, Liberty, MO, and Center, TX. No support for religious, fraternal, political, international or veterans' organizations, athletic or labor groups, social clubs, non-tax-exempt organizations, or disease-specific organizations. No grants to individuals, or for scholarships, endowment funds, past operating deficits, travel, conferences, sponsorships, scholarly or health-related research, charitable advertisements, or mass media campaigns such as walk-a-thons or telethons. PRI applications not accepted.
Publications: Corporate giving report, informational brochure (including application guidelines).
PRI program information: The foundation does not maintain a formal PRI program. The foundation makes PRIs occasionally.
Officers and Directors:* Donald J. Hall,* Chair.; William A. Hall, Pres.; Karen Bartz, V.P.; Danita M. Robinson,* Secy.; John A. MacDonald, Treas.; Donald J. Hall, Jr., Irvine O. Hockaday, Jr., Robert Kipp.
Number of staff: 4 full-time professional; 1 full-time support.
EIN: 431303258

111
Hammer International Foundation
2425 Olympic Blvd., Ste. 140E
Santa Monica, CA 90404
Contact: Michael A. Hammer, Pres.

Established in 1998 in CA.
Grantmaker type: Independent foundation
General financial activity (yr. ended 12/31/00): Assets, $20,944,517 (M); expenditures, $11,522,432; qualifying distributions, $4,504,292; giving activities include $10,092,509 for 47 grants (high: $8,415,540; low: $100) and $3,389,749 for 2 PRIs.
General purpose and activities: Giving primarily for Christian agencies and churches in the U.S. and the Cayman Islands in the British West Indies.
General fields of interest: Christian agencies & churches.
Program-related investment (PRI) activity: The foundation has made a PRI, in the form of an investment to promote cinematic arts and to produce film/media to spread positive family and Christian values. It has also made a PRI, in the form of an interest-free loan to a not-for-profit school to enable it to purchase additional facility space and to increase programming.
Limitations: Giving on a national and international basis, with emphasis on CA, and on the Cayman Islands in the British West Indies. No grants to individuals.
Officers and Directors:* Michael A. Hammer,* C.E.O. and Pres.; Scott Deitrick, V.P.; Dru Hammer,* Secy.
EIN: 980153886

112
Hansen Foundation
(Formerly William Stucki Hansen Foundation)
2600 Neville Rd.
Pittsburgh, PA 15225
Contact: William S. Hansen, Pres.

Established in 1984 in PA.
Donor(s): Hansen, Inc.
Grantmaker type: Independent foundation
General financial activity (yr. ended 11/30/01): Assets, $3,684,095 (M); expenditures, $398,989; qualifying distributions, $1,673,300; giving activities include $373,300 for 15 grants (high: $112,000; low: $2,500) and $1,300,000 for 1 PRI.
General purpose and activities: Giving to public services, higher education, federated giving programs and religion.
General fields of interest: Higher education; federated giving programs; religion.
Program-related investment (PRI) activity: The foundation made a low-interest loan to a New York-based organization in 2001 to fund the establishment of a historical and heritage experience center for the general public of New York City.
Limitations: Applications not accepted. Giving primarily in western PA. No grants to individuals. PRI support primarily in New York City, NY.
Officers and Directors:* William S. Hansen,* Pres.; William Gregg Hansen,* V.P.; Nancy K. Hansen,* Secy.-Treas.
Number of staff: None.
EIN: 251483674
PRI recipients:
112-1. New York Initiative, NYC, NY, $1,300,000. Loan to establish historical and heritage experience for general public with respect to New York City and it's history. 2001.

113
Phil Hardin Foundation
1921 24th Ave.
Meridian, MS 39301 (601) 483-4282
Contact: C. Thompson Wacaster, V.P.
FAX: (601) 483-5665; E-mail: info@philhardin.org; URL: http://www.philhardin.org

Incorporated in 1964 in MS.
Donor(s): Philip Bernard Hardin,‡ Hardin's Bakeries Corp.
Grantmaker type: Independent foundation
General financial activity (yr. ended 12/31/02): Assets, $34,625,245 (M); expenditures, $2,156,460; qualifying distributions, $2,098,243; giving activities include $1,746,523 for grants; no PRIs paid.

Cumulative PRI activity (through 12/31/02): The currently outstanding PRI portfolio includes PRIs totaling $1,500,000 (high: $1,500,000; low: $2,000; average: $10,000). The typical outstanding PRI has an average term of 5 years.
General purpose and activities: Grants to museums, educational institutions and programs.
General fields of interest: Education, association; education, research; early childhood education; higher education; education; minorities.
Program-related investment (PRI) activity: The foundation has made PRIs to educational institutions. Purposes of PRI support have included equipment acquisition and the development of endowed funds.
Types of PRI Support: Loans/promissory notes.
Limitations: Giving primarily in MS; support also to out-of-state organizations for programs and projects benefiting the education of Mississippians. No grants to individuals, or for deficit financing or land acquisition. The foundation accepts applications for PRIs.
Publications: Application guidelines, program policy statement, grants list, informational brochure (including application guidelines).
PRI program information: The foundation maintains a formal PRI program. The foundation makes PRIs on a frequent but not annual basis.
Officers and Directors:* Robert F. Ward,* Pres.; Stephen O. Moore,* V.P.; C. Thompson Wacaster, V.P., Educational Progs. and Research; R.B. Deen, Jr.,* Secy.; Archie R. McDonnell,* Treas.; Joe S. Covington, M.D., Edwin E. Downer, Lynn Taleff, Sarah W. Wile.
Number of staff: 1 full-time professional; 1 full-time support.
EIN: 646024940

114

Pearl M. and Julia J. Harmon Foundation

P.O. Box 52568
Tulsa, OK 74152-0568 (918) 743-6191
Contact: George L. Hangs, Jr., Exec. Dir.
URL: http://www.harmonfoundation.com

Established in 1962 in OK. PRI-related activities began in 1981.
Donor(s): Claude C. Harmon,‡ Julia J. Harmon.‡
Grantmaker type: Independent foundation
General financial activity (yr. ended 05/31/02): Assets, $35,687,781 (M); expenditures, $726,559; qualifying distributions, $2,049,582; giving activities include $266,598 for 56 grants (high: $104,989; low: $15), $232,874 for foundation-administered programs and $1,549,585 for 3 PRIs.
Cumulative PRI activity (through 05/31/02): Since 1981, the foundation has made 3 PRIs totaling $921,135. The currently outstanding PRI portfolio includes a high PRI value of $3,500,000 and a low PRI value of $10,000. The typical outstanding PRI has a 6-month to 15-year term.
General purpose and activities: Giving for low interest loans to charitable organizations.
General fields of interest: Arts/cultural programs; elementary/secondary education; human services; community development.
Program-related investment (PRI) activity: The foundation's principal PRI activity has been making loans for projects that, either through revenue production or cost savings, can repay the loan and any interest charged. Purposes of PRI support have included financing for facility acquisition and renovation and for equipment acquisition.
Types of PRI Support: Loans/promissory notes, interim financing, charitable use assets.
Limitations: Giving limited to AR, KS, NM, OK, and TX, with preference given to northeastern OK. No support for medical research or evangelism organizations. No grants to individuals, or loans to individuals. No loans made to organizations to re-lend. The foundation accepts applications for PRIs.
Publications: Application guidelines.
PRI program information: Write a one-page letter outlining your need and describing your charity. The foundation maintains a formal PRI program. The foundation makes PRIs on an annual basis.
Officer and Trustees:* George L. Hangs, Jr.,* Exec. Dir.; C.H. Frederick, Jean M. Kuntz, B.L. Lee, C.K. Owens.
EIN: 736095893
PRI recipients:

114-1. A New Leaf, Broken Arrow, OK, $10,000. Program-related investment to purchase van. 2001.

114-2. Association for Retarded Citizens of Washington County, Bartlesville, OK, $200,000. Loan to finance construction of group home. 1999.

114-3. Bishop Kelley High School, Tulsa, OK, $1,250,000. Program-related investment to renovate Brother David Poos Science and Technology Center. 2001.

114-4. Community Action Project of Tulsa County, Tulsa Children's Coalition, Tulsa, OK, $1,000,000. Program-related investment to build new Headstart facility. 2002.

114-5. Diocese of Tulsa, Tulsa, OK, $500,000. Program-related investment to purchase and renovate classroom property in Bishop Kelley High School for Harmon Science Center. 2000.

114-6. Grand Lake Mental Health Center, Nowata, OK, $292,835. Program-related investment to purchase and renovarte mental health clinic in Pryor, Oklahoma. 2000.

114-7. Grand Lake Mental Health Center, Nowata, OK, $128,300. Program-related investment to renovate Ottawa County Oklahoma Mental Health Clinic. 2000.

114-8. Planned Parenthood of Eastern Oklahoma and Western Arkansas, Tulsa, OK, $475,000. Program-related investment to build new headquarters and purchase computer systems. 2002.

114-9. Youth and Family Services of Washington County, Bartlesville, OK, $74,585. Program-related investment to renovate offices and counseling center. 2002.

114-10. Youth and Family Services of Washington County, Bartlesville, OK, $240,415. Program-related investment to acquire and renovate new office building. 2001.

114-11. Youth and Family Services of Washington County, Bartlesville, OK, $90,332. Loan to finance construction of Administrative/Counseling office. 1999.

115
Harris Bank Foundation

P.O. Box 755
Chicago, IL 60690-0755 (312) 461-5834
Contact: Donna Streibich, Secy.-Treas.

Incorporated in 1953 in IL. PRI-related activities began in 1996.
Donor(s): Harris Bankcorp, Inc., Harris Trust and Savings Bank.
Grantmaker type: Company-sponsored foundation
General financial activity (yr. ended 12/31/02): Assets, $3,747,092 (M); gifts received, $1,856,905; expenditures, $1,538,046; qualifying distributions, $949,346; giving activities include $692,058 for 52 grants (high: $190,000; low: $800; average: $5,000–$20,000) and $257,288 for employee matching gifts; no PRIs paid.
Cumulative PRI activity (through 12/31/02): The currently outstanding PRI portfolio includes PRIs totaling $50,000 (average: $15,000). The typical outstanding PRI has a 1- to 2.5-year term, and earns an average of 2 percent interest.
General purpose and activities: Emphasis on community reinvestment and education reform efforts, including an employee matching gift program; support also for cultural activities, neighborhood development, and social services.
General fields of interest: Education; employment; human services; community development.
Program-related investment (PRI) activity: The foundation provides low-interest PRIs to a community loan fund.
Types of PRI Support: Loans/promissory notes, capitalizing loan funds/other intermediaries.
Limitations: Giving limited to the greater metropolitan Chicago, IL, area, with emphasis on North Lawndale, except for matching gift program. No support for sectarian or religious organizations, fraternal organizations, political activities, hospitals, national health organizations, or private elementary and secondary schools. No grants to individuals (except for employee-related scholarships for dependents of Harris Bank employees), or for research, publications, conferences, testimonials, or advertisements. The foundation accepts applications for PRIs.
Publications: Program policy statement, application guidelines.
PRI program information: The foundation does not maintain a formal PRI program. The foundation makes PRIs occasionally.
Officers and Directors:* Edward J. Williams,* Pres.; Robin S. Coffey,* V.P.; Donna Streibich,* Secy.-Treas.; Anne Coon,* Recording Secy.; Michael Chin, Angela Smith, Joleen S. Spencer, Joseph Teller.
Number of staff: 2 full-time professional; 1 part-time professional; 1 full-time support.
EIN: 366033888
PRI recipients:

115-1. Chicago Community Loan Fund, Chicago, IL, $30,000. Loan at two percent interest. 1999.

115-2. Chicago Community Loan Fund, Chicago, IL, $20,000. Loan at two percent interest. 1999.

116
Hartford Foundation for Public Giving

85 Gillett St.
Hartford, CT 06105 (860) 548-1888
Contact: Christopher H. Hall, Dir., Progs. and Special Projects
FAX: (860) 524-8346; E-mail: chall@hfpg.org;
URL: http://www.hfpg.org

Established in 1925 in CT by resolution and declaration of trust.
Grantmaker type: Community foundation
General financial activity (yr. ended 12/31/02): Assets, $497,392,716 (M); gifts received, $8,548,578; expenditures, $31,729,556; giving activities include $22,730,797 for 1,148 grants (high: $1,150,000; low: $250; average: $25,000–$150,000); no PRIs paid.
General purpose and activities: Giving for demonstration programs and capital purposes, with emphasis on community advancement, educational institutions, youth groups, hospitals, social services, including the aged, and cultural and civic endeavors.
General fields of interest: Arts/cultural programs; education; hospitals (general); health care; health associations; AIDS; AIDS research; human services; children & youth, services; aging, centers & services; community development; government/public administration; aging.
Program-related investment (PRI) activity: The foundation's PRIs are granted by the Greater Hartford Nonprofit Loan Fund and provide area agencies with cash-flow and working-capital financing. The fund may also be used for leasehold improvements and capital equipment purchases. The fund is administered by the Greater Hartford Business Development Center (GHBDC).
Types of PRI Support: Loans/promissory notes, interim financing.
Limitations: Giving limited to the greater Hartford, CT, area. No support for sectarian purposes or tax-supported agencies. No grants to individuals (except for scholarships), or for operating budgets, continuing support, annual campaigns, deficit financing, endowment funds, research, publications, or conferences. Loan Fund applicants must have a clear source of repayment. Maximum amount for PRI is $75,000.
Publications: Annual report, application guidelines, program policy statement, newsletter, informational brochure.

PRI program information: Loan applicants should contact GHBDC directly by calling (860) 527-1301.
Officers and Directors:* Blanche Goldenberg,* Chair.; Rosaida Morales Rosario,* Vice-Chair.; Edward J. Forand, Jr.,* Treas.; Michael R. Bangser,* Exec. Dir.; Francisco L. Borges, Nancy T. Grover, Mark F. Korber, Thomas Malloy, Stephen B. Middlebrook, Nancy T. Rankin.
Trustee Banks: Fleet National Bank, State Street Corp., Trust Co. of Connecticut.
Number of staff: 29 full-time professional; 4 part-time professional; 13 full-time support.
EIN: 060699252

117

The F. B. Heron Foundation

100 Broadway, 17th Fl.
New York, NY 10005 (212) 404-1800
Contact: Mary Jo Mullan, V.P., Progs.
PRI Contact: Luther M.Ragin, Jr., V.P., Social Investing
FAX: (212) 404-1805; URL: http://www.fdncenter.org/grantmaker/fbheron

Established in 1992 in DE. PRI-related activities began in 1997.
Grantmaker type: Independent foundation
General financial activity (yr. ended 12/31/01): Assets, $255,959,796 (M); expenditures, $14,553,495; qualifying distributions, $16,457,073; giving activities include $12,021,045 for 195 grants (high: $150,000; average: $25,000–$100,000), $13,815 for employee matching gifts and $2,652,500 for 9 PRIs.
Cumulative PRI activity (through 12/31/01): Since 1997, the foundation has made 33 PRIs totaling $11,002,000. The currently outstanding PRI portfolio includes 32 PRIs totaling $10,437,500 (high: $750,000; low: $100,000; average: $350,000). The typical outstanding PRI has a 3- to 10-year term with an average term of 6 years and earns 1 to 6 percent interest with an average of 3 percent.
General purpose and activities: The foundation focuses its grantmaking and mission-related investing on five wealth-creation strategies for low-income families and communities. These five areas are: 1) access to capital; 2) quality and affordable child care; 3) comprehensive community development; 4) enterprise development; and 5) home ownership.
General fields of interest: Housing/shelter, home owners; children, services; community development, neighborhood development; economic development; economically disadvantaged.
Program-related investment (PRI) activity: The foundation makes PRIs to organizations whose work closely corresponds with the foundation's programmatic interests in wealth creation for low-income families and communities.
Limitations: Giving on a national basis in both urban and rural clusters. No grants to individuals, or for endowments or for capital campaigns. Preference is given to organization's with whom the foundation has or has had a grant relationship. PRIs are only made where the proceeds will be used to support an organization's direct charitable activities. Amounts may not exceed $1 million and term may not exceed 10 years. PRIs will not be made to support endowments. The foundation accepts applications for PRIs.
Publications: Annual report (including application guidelines), application guidelines.
PRI program information: Foundation staff or consultants conduct a comprehensive review of a prospective investee's program achievements, governance, management and program competencies, financial health, and future plans so as to assess its ability to meet terms of investment. The foundation maintains a formal PRI program. The foundation makes PRIs on an annual basis.
Officers and Directors:* William M. Dietel,* Chair.; Sharon B. King, Pres.; Mary Jo Mullan, V.P. Progs. and Secy.-Treas.; Wallace Cook, James Sligar.
Number of staff: 9 full-time professional; 1 part-time professional; 4 full-time support.
EIN: 133647019
PRI recipients:

117-1. Adena Ventures, Athens, OH, $52,500. Limited partnership interest in New Markets Venture Company to promote economic development in twenty-nine counties of southeastern Ohio, state of West Virginia, portion of western Maryland that falls within boundaries of Appalachian region and several counties in northeast Kentucky. 2001.

117-2. Boston Community Loan Fund, Boston, MA, $150,000. Equity investment to act as permanent capital for borrower's financing of affordable housing, community facilities, and other projects of benefit to low-income communities. 2001.

117-3. Boston Community Loan Fund, Boston, MA, $350,000. Senior loan to finance affordable housing, community facilities, and other projects beneficial to low-income communities. 2000.

117-4. Calvert Social Investment Foundation, Bethesda, MD, $500,000. Senior loan to provide loans to rural and inner-city community development corporations and emerging community development financial institutions through Calvert Community Investment Notes Program. 2000.

117-5. Chicago Community Loan Fund, Chicago, IL, $250,000. Senior loan for real estate development, equipment purchase and working capital. 2001.

117-6. Coastal Enterprises, Wiscasset, ME, $500,000. Loan to expand capacity of Lease-Purchase Homeownership Program. 1999.

117-7. Community Reinvestment Fund, Minneapolis, MN, $500,000. Senior loan, with conversion option, to facilitate creating of secondary market by purchasing and securitizing community development loans. 2001.

117-8. East Bay Asian Local Development Corporation, Oakland, CA, $300,000. Senior loan to finance development of commercial real estate projects to create and preserve jobs for low-income people in Oakland. 2001.

117-9. East Bay Asian Local Development Corporation, Oakland, CA, $100,000. Senior loan to finance development of commercial real estate projects to create and preserve jobs for low-income people in Oakland. 2001.

117-10. Federation of Appalachian Housing Enterprises, Berea, KY, $350,000. Loan for working capital for rural home ownership development in Central Appalachia. 1999.

117-11. Greenpoint Manufacturing and Design Center Local Development Corporation, Brooklyn, NY, $500,000. Loan for real estate acquisition and development for small businesses in low-income neighborhoods in Brooklyn. 2000.

117-12. Greyston Foundation, Yonkers, NY, $250,000. Senior loan to establish debt service reserve for construction of new bakery employing homeless men and women. 2000.

117-13. Housing Assistance Council, DC, $500,000. Loan for working capital for rural home ownership programs. 1999.

117-14. Illinois Facilities Fund, Chicago, IL, $500,000. Loan to support variety of financial products to assist nonprofits in facility-related matters. 1999.

117-15. Low Income Housing Fund, Oakland, CA, $500,000. Senior loan to finance development of center-based and family child care. 2001.

117-16. Manna, DC, $400,000. Loan for working capital for home ownership projects. 1999.

117-17. McAuley Institute, Silver Spring, MD, $400,000. Senior loan to finance development of homeownership units. 2000.

117-18. National Federation of Community Development Credit Unions, NYC, NY, $500,000. Deposits for rural community development credit unions. 2001.

117-19. New Community Corporation, Newark, NJ, $500,000. Senior loan for working capital for modular housing factory and business assistance center. 2000.

117-20. New Mexico Community Development Loan Fund, Albuquerque, NM, $300,000. Senior loan to make capital available for enterprise development, home ownership, community facilities, or other projects beneficial to low-income communities. 2001.

117-21. North Carolina Minority Support Center, Durham, NC, $500,000. Loan to assist credit unions serving low-income communities to increase home and business lending. 1999.

117-22. Pioneer Human Services, Seattle, WA, $500,000. Loan for acquisition and operation of job development and training enterprises. 1999.

117-23. Quitman County Federal Credit Union, Marks, MS, $100,000. Insured deposit to match deposit from Community Development Revolving Loan Program. 2000.

118
The Herrick Theatre Foundation, Inc.

c/o Rhoda R. Herrick
605 Park Ave., No. 7A
New York, NY 10021

Established around 1983; classified as a private operating foundation in 1985.
Donor(s): David Rosenthal,‡ Rhoda R. Herrick.
Grantmaker type: Operating foundation
General financial activity (yr. ended 05/31/02): Assets, $1,083,143 (M); gifts received, $25,000; expenditures, $226,669; qualifying distributions, $229,094; giving activities include $204,514 for grants (high: $27,800) and $6,000 for 1 PRI.
Cumulative PRI activity (through 05/31/02): Since beginning PRI activity, the foundation has made 3 PRIs totaling $87,500.
General fields of interest: Museums; theater; arts/cultural programs; medical school/education; Jewish agencies & temples; women.
Program-related investment (PRI) activity: The foundation makes PRIs to fund the production of plays. In 2001, the foundation funded a play titled "When They Speak of Rita". The loan paid for production costs and various expenses.
Limitations: Applications not accepted. Giving primarily in New York, NY. No grants to individuals.
Officers and Directors:* Rhoda R. Herrick,* Pres.; Thomas E. Gough,* Secy.; Robert M. Rosenthal.
EIN: 133171936

119
The William and Flora Hewlett Foundation

2121 Sand Hill Rd.
Menlo Park, CA 94025 (650) 234-4500
Contact: Paul Brest, Pres.
FAX: (650) 234-4501; E-mail: info@hewlett.org; URL: http://www.hewlett.org

Incorporated in 1966 in CA.
Donor(s): Flora Lamson Hewlett,‡ William R. Hewlett.‡
Grantmaker type: Independent foundation
General financial activity (yr. ended 12/31/01): Assets, $6,080,721,309 (M); gifts received, $3,092,854,201; expenditures, $133,720,398; qualifying distributions, $144,706,531; giving activities include $119,955,933 for 773 grants (high: $5,000,000; low: $5,000; average: $50,000–$200,000) and $1,171,637 for foundation-administered programs; no PRIs paid.
General purpose and activities: Emphasis on conflict resolution, the environment, performing arts, education at both the K-12 and the college/university level, population studies, family and community development, and U.S.-Latin American relations.
General fields of interest: Performing arts; dance; theater; music; arts/cultural programs; elementary/secondary

education; higher education; libraries (academic/research); natural resources conservation & protection; environment; family planning; youth development, services; family services; urban/community development; community development; population studies; international studies; public policy, research; minorities.
General international interests: Latin America.
Program-related investment (PRI) activity: The foundation has made a PRI for product development.
Types of PRI Support: Loans/promissory notes.
Limitations: Giving limited to the San Francisco Bay Area, CA, for family and community development program; performing arts primarily limited to the Bay Area; environment programs limited to North American West. No support for medicine and health-related projects, law, criminal justice, and related fields, juvenile, delinquency or drug and alcohol addiction, prevention or treatment programs, problems of the elderly and the handicapped, or television or radio projects. No grants to individuals, or for building funds or capital construction funds, basic research, equipment, seminars, conferences, festivals, touring costs, fundraising drives, scholarships, or fellowships; no loans.
Publications: Annual report (including application guidelines), program policy statement, application guidelines, informational brochure, grants list.
Officers and Directors:* Walter B. Hewlett,* Chair.; Paul Brest, Pres.; Laurance Hoagland, V.P. and C.I.O.; Nancy Strausser, Corp. Secy.; Susan Ketcham, Treas.; Robert F. Erburu, James C. Gaither, Eleanor H. Gimon, H. Irving Grousbeck, Mary H. Jaffe, Herant Katchadourian, M.D., Richard Levin, Jean Stromberg.
Number of staff: 20 full-time professional; 11 full-time support; 4 part-time support.
EIN: 941655673
PRI recipients:
119-1. HyperCar, Basalt, CO, $2,000,000. Equity investment to support next phase of HyperCar product development as lightweight, efficient solution to producing energy efficient, sustainable automotive vehicles. 2002.

120
The Highland Street Connection
P.O. Box 5209
Framingham, MA 01701
E-mail: tobydouthwright@highlandstreet.org;
URL: http://www.highlandstreet.org

Established in 1994 in MA.
Donor(s): David J. McGrath, Jr.
Grantmaker type: Independent foundation
General financial activity (yr. ended 12/31/01): Assets, $174,287,765 (M); gifts received, $332,297; expenditures, $8,934,760; qualifying distributions, $7,946,067; giving activities include $7,103,623 for 188 grants (high: $500,000; low: $250; average: $1,000–$100,000) and $434,631 for 2 PRIs.
General purpose and activities: Giving primarily for education and children's mentoring programs.
General fields of interest: Arts/cultural programs; education.
Program-related investment (PRI) activity: The foundation purchased real estate for use by a private school.
Types of PRI Support: Charitable use assets.
Limitations: Applications not accepted. Giving primarily in MA. No grants to individuals.
Trustees: Christopher R. McGrath, David J. McGrath III, Holly L. McGrath, Joann McGrath, Scott J. McGrath, Sean P. McGrath.
EIN: 043048298
PRI recipients:
120-1. Nativity Prep of New Bedford, New Bedford, MA, $134,631. Purchase of real estate by Foundation so School can be opened in New Bedford. School will use property for classrooms and faculty housing. 2001.
120-2. Nativity Prep of New Bedford, New Bedford, MA, $1,014,992. Purchase of real estate by Foundation so School can be opened in New Bedford. School will use property for classrooms and faculty housing. 2000.

121
Conrad N. Hilton Foundation
100 W. Liberty St., Ste. 840
Reno, NV 89501 (775) 323-4221
Contact: Steven M. Hilton, Pres.
FAX: (775) 323-4150; E-mail: foundation@hiltonfoundation.org; URL: http://www.hiltonfoundation.org

Established in 1944; incorporated in 1950 in CA; incorporated in 1989 in NV. PRI-related activities began in 1994.
Donor(s): Conrad N. Hilton.‡
Grantmaker type: Independent foundation
General financial activity (yr. ended 02/28/03): Assets, $591,884,963 (M); gifts received, $14,285,878; expenditures, $30,970,528; qualifying distributions, $26,394,781; giving activities include $26,367,977 for 184 grants (high: $2,867,500; low: $1,000; average: $1,000–$300,000) and $26,804 for 40 employee matching gifts; no PRIs paid.
Cumulative PRI activity (through 02/28/03): Since 1994, the foundation has made 5 PRIs totaling $18,000,000. The currently outstanding PRI portfolio includes 5 PRIs totaling $17,300,000 (high: $10,000,000; low: $300,000). The typical outstanding PRI has a 5- to 20-year term with an average term of 12 years and earns 0 to 3 percent interest with an average of 2 percent.
General purpose and activities: The greater part of the foundation's giving is devoted to several major long-term projects; funding for smaller scale miscellaneous grants is very limited. Special areas of interest are: 1) Works of Catholic Sisters funded through Conrad N. Hilton Fund for Sisters; 2) Substance abuse prevention education funded through the BEST Foundation for a Drug-Free Tomorrow; 3)

Multi-handicapped blind services funded through Perkins School for the Blind; and 4) Water development in West Africa, funded through World Vision and multiple entities.
General fields of interest: Environment, water resources; substance abuse, prevention; eye diseases; children & youth, services.
General international interests: Africa.
Program-related investment (PRI) activity: The foundation has made PRIs to finance endowment, renovations, and construction at educational, healthcare, and religious institutions, and to finance expenses incurred by a health organization as a result of the 9/11 terrorist attack.
Types of PRI Support: Loans/promissory notes.
Limitations: No support for political organizations. No grants to individuals. PRI applications not accepted.
Publications: Informational brochure.
PRI program information: The foundation does not maintain a formal PRI program. The foundation makes PRIs occasionally.
Officers and Directors:* Donald H. Hubbs,* Chair. and C.E.O.; Steven M. Hilton,* Pres.; Patrick Modugno, V.P., Admin. and C.F.O.; Dyanne M. Hayes, V.P., Prog.; Conrad N. Hilton III,* V.P., Information Technology & Special Projects; Judy Miller, V.P. and Dir., Humanitarian Prize; Deborah Kerr, Secy.-Treas.; Robert Buckley, M.D., Gregory R. Dillon, James R. Galbraith, Barron Hilton, Eric M. Hilton, William B. Hilton, Jr.
Number of staff: 10 full-time professional; 1 part-time professional; 6 full-time support.
EIN: 943100217
PRI recipients:
121-1. Archdiocese of Los Angeles, Los Angeles, CA, $1,000,000. Loan as promissory note at 3 percent interest. 1999.
121-2. Archdiocese of Los Angeles, Los Angeles, CA, $1,000,000. Loan as promissory note at 3 percent interest. 1999.
121-3. Archdiocese of Los Angeles, Los Angeles, CA, $1,000,000. Loan as promissory note at 3 percent interest. 1999.
121-4. Archdiocese of Los Angeles, Los Angeles, CA, $1,000,000. Loan as promissory note at 3 percent interest. 1999.
121-5. Archdiocese of Los Angeles, Los Angeles, CA, $1,000,000. Loan as promissory note at 3 percent interest. 1999.
121-6. Helen Keller International, NYC, NY, $500,000. Program-related investment. 2002.
121-7. Perkins School for the Blind, Watertown, MA, $5,000,000. Promissory notes. 2000.
121-8. Saint Johns Hospital and Health Center, Santa Monica, CA, $2,000,000. Loan to support redevelopment of facility after earthquake damaged building. 2001.

122
The Hitachi Foundation

1509 22nd St., N.W.
Washington, DC 20037-1073 (202) 457-0588
Contact: Barbara Dyer, Pres. and C.E.O.; or Renata Hron, Prog. Off.
PRI Contact: Scott Lippmann, Dir., Finance and Admin.
URL: http://www.hitachifoundation.org

Established in 1985 in DC. PRI-related activities began in 1989.
Donor(s): Hitachi America, Ltd.
Grantmaker type: Company-sponsored foundation
General financial activity (yr. ended 12/31/01): Assets, $22,842,973 (M); gifts received, $1,180,668; expenditures, $5,503,006; qualifying distributions, $4,348,066; giving activities include $3,047,825 for 44 grants (high: $500,000; average: $10,000–$50,000); no PRIs paid.
Cumulative PRI activity (through 12/31/01): The currently outstanding PRI portfolio includes PRIs totaling $405,675 (average: $100,000). The typical outstanding PRI has an average term of 3 years, and earns 3 to 5.5 percent interest.
General purpose and activities: Giving is directed to organizations dealing with community and economic development, education, workforce development, and corporate citizenship. The foundation also has an annual award recognizing young people for exemplary service to the community.
General fields of interest: Elementary school/education; education; youth development, services; community development.
Program-related investment (PRI) activity: PRIs support nonprofit and for-profit organizations in the areas of education, community development, and global citizenship.
Types of PRI Support: Loans/promissory notes, loan guarantees.
Limitations: Applications not accepted. Giving primarily in the U.S. No support for sectarian or denominational religious organizations, health programs, or social organizations. No grants to individuals (except for Yoshiyama Awards for community service), or for fundraising events, building funds, publications, conferences and seminars, endowments, advertising, or capital campaigns. The foundation only considers PRI applications in response to a specific request for proposals (RFP) issued by the foundation.
Publications: Annual report, informational brochure, occasional report.
PRI program information: The foundation maintains a formal PRI program.
Officers and Directors:* Joseph E. Kasputys, Chair.; Barbara Dyer,* Pres. and C.E.O.; James J. Gillespie, C.F.O.; Clara R. Apodaca, Sherry Salway Black, Hon. Charles Bowsher, David Dodson, Patricia Albjerg Graham.
Number of staff: 4 full-time professional; 3 full-time support.
EIN: 521429292

123
HKH Foundation

521 5th Ave., Ste. 1612
New York, NY 10175-1699
Contact: Harriet Barlow
E-mail: hkh@hkhfdn.org; URL: http://www.hkhfdn.org

Foundation established in 1980 in NY. PRI-related activities began in 1994.
Grantmaker type: Independent foundation
General financial activity (yr. ended 12/31/01): Assets, $35,798,575 (M); expenditures, $2,500,998; qualifying distributions, $1,991,032; giving activities include $1,991,032 for 48 grants (high: $433,341; low: $1,500; average: $5,000–$25,000) and $125,000 for 2 PRIs.
Cumulative PRI activity (through 12/31/01): Since 1994, the foundation has made 6 PRIs totaling $700,000. The currently outstanding PRI portfolio includes 6 PRIs totaling $700,000 (high: $250,000; low: $25,000; average: $100,000). The typical outstanding PRI has a 3- to 5-year term with an average term of 4 years and earns 2 to 4 percent interest with an average of 3 percent.
General purpose and activities: Funding considered only in the following areas: 1) disarmament and the prevention of war; 2) civil liberties; and 3) environmental protection.
General fields of interest: Natural resources conservation & protection; environment; international peace/security; arms control; civil liberties, advocacy; civil rights.
Program-related investment (PRI) activity: Historically, the foundation has made PRIs to economic and environmental organizations.
Types of PRI Support: Loans/promissory notes.
Limitations: Applications not accepted. Giving limited to the U.S. No grants to individuals. PRI applications not accepted.
PRI program information: The foundation does not maintain a formal PRI program. The foundation makes PRIs occasionally.
Number of staff: 2 part-time professional; 1 part-time support.
EIN: 136784950
PRI recipients:
123-1. Institute for Agriculture and Trade Policy, Minneapolis, MN, $25,000. Program-related investment. 1999.
123-2. Northern Forest Center, Concord, NH, $25,000. Program-related investment. 2001.
123-3. Sustainable Forest Futures, Concord, NH, $100,000. Program-related investment. 2001.
123-4. Sustainable Woods Cooperative, Spring Green, WI, $25,000. Program-related investment. 2000.
123-5. Trust for Public Land, San Francisco, CA, $250,000. Program-related investment. 1999.

124
Hoblitzelle Foundation

5956 Sherry Ln., Ste. 901
Dallas, TX 75225-6522 (214) 373-0462
Contact: Paul W. Harris, Exec. V.P.
URL: http://home.att.net/~hoblitzelle

Trust established in 1942 in TX; incorporated in 1953.
Donor(s): Karl St. John Hoblitzelle,‡ Esther T. Hoblitzelle.‡
Grantmaker type: Independent foundation
General financial activity (yr. ended 04/30/02): Assets, $116,998,699 (M); gifts received, $30,689; expenditures, $6,856,181; qualifying distributions, $6,366,594; giving activities include $5,833,111 for 65 grants (high: $1,000,000; low: $1,000; average: $10,000–$100,000) and $1,500,000 for PRIs.
Cumulative PRI activity (through 04/30/02): The currently outstanding PRI portfolio includes 1 PRI totaling $1,500,000.
General purpose and activities: Grants for higher, secondary, vocational, scientific and medical education, hospitals and health services, youth agencies, cultural programs, social services, and community development.
General fields of interest: Visual arts; performing arts; historic preservation/historical societies; arts/cultural programs; secondary school/education; vocational education; higher education; medical school/education; adult/continuing education; adult education—literacy, basic skills & GED; reading; education; hospitals (general); medical care, rehabilitation; health care; AIDS; alcoholism; housing/shelter, development; human services; children & youth, services; aging, centers & services; community development; science; minorities; aging; economically disadvantaged.
Program-related investment (PRI) activity: The foundation made a low-interest loan to the United Way for facility construction.
Limitations: Giving limited to TX, primarily Dallas. No support for religious organizations for sectarian purposes. No grants to individuals; only occasional board-initiated support for operating budgets, debt reduction, research, scholarships media productions, publications, or endowments; no loans (except for program-related investments).
Publications: Annual report (including application guidelines), program policy statement, newsletter.
Officers and Directors:* Gerald W. Fronterhouse,* Chair.; George A. Shafer,* C.E.O. and Pres.; Paul W. Harris, Exec. V.P.; Donna C. Berry,* Secy.; Caren H. Prothro,* Treas.; Lillian M. Bradshaw, Dorothy R. Cullum, Linda P. Custard, Jerry Farrington, James W. Keay, William T. Solomon, Charles C. Sprague, M.D., Kern Wildenthal, M.D., Ph.D., J. McDonald Williams.
Number of staff: 1 full-time professional; 1 full-time support.
EIN: 756003984
PRI recipients:
124-1. United Way of Metropolitan Dallas, Dallas, TX, $1,500,000. Low-interest loan for completion of new facility construction. 2002.

125
Ervin G. Houchens Foundation, Inc.

(Formerly Houchens Foundation, Inc.)
P.O. Box 109
Bowling Green, KY 42102-0109
Contact: Suel Houchens, Dir.
Application address: P.O. Box 90009 Bowling Green, KY 42102-9009

Incorporated in 1954 in KY.
Donor(s): Houchens Markets, Inc., B.G. Wholesale, Inc.
Grantmaker type: Independent foundation
General financial activity (yr. ended 12/31/01): Assets, $3,369,196 (M); gifts received, $16,236; expenditures, $425,262; qualifying distributions, $1,065,377; giving activities include $326,994 for 54 grants (high: $151,000; low: $60), $38,999 for 2 foundation-administered programs and $678,000 for 14 PRIs.
Cumulative PRI activity (through 12/31/01): Since beginning PRI activity, the foundation has made 39 PRIs totaling $1,299,075. The currently outstanding PRI portfolio includes PRIs totaling $2,386,155.
General purpose and activities: Support mainly in the form of loans to Baptist and Methodist churches; smaller cash contributions to youth agencies and education.
General fields of interest: Arts/cultural programs; education; children & youth, services; federated giving programs; Protestant agencies & churches.
Program-related investment (PRI) activity: The foundation makes interest-free and low-interest loans to Methodist and Baptist churches as well as to public charities.
Types of PRI Support: Loans/promissory notes.
Limitations: Giving limited to southwestern KY.
Officers: Covella H. Biggers, Pres.; C. Cecil Martin, V.P.; Lynn B. Martin, Secy.-Treas.
Directors: George Suel Houchens, Tara Biggers Parker.
EIN: 610623087
PRI recipients:
125-1. Bethel Fellowship, Leitchfield, KY, $15,000. Low- or no-interest loan. 2000.
125-2. Bowling Green Seventh Day Adventists Church, Bowling Green, KY, $50,000. Low- or no-interest loan. 2000.
125-3. Cave Springs Missionary Baptist Church, Smiths Grove, KY, $50,000. Loan. 2001.
125-4. Cedar Grove Baptist Church, Rocky Mount, NC, $30,000. Low- or no-interest loan. 2000.
125-5. Christian County Rescue Team, Hopkinsville, KY, $12,000. Low- or no-interest loan. 2000.
125-6. East Barren Volunteer Fire Department, Glasgow, KY, $20,000. Low- or no-interest loan. 2000.
125-7. Fairview United Methodist Church, NC, $65,000. Loan. 2001.
125-8. Faith Missionary Baptist Church, $68,000. Loan. 2001.
125-9. Family Enrichment Center, $46,000. Loan. 2001.
125-10. First Apostolic Church, $40,000. Loan. 2001.
125-11. First Baptist Church of Woodburn, $60,000. Loan. 2001.
125-12. Grace Baptist Church, $20,000. Low- or no-interest loan. 2000.
125-13. Greenmeadows United Baptist Church, $28,000. Low- or no-interest loan. 2000.
125-14. Lebanon United Methoidst Church, Clarendon, NC, $50,000. Loan. 2001.
125-15. Little Barren Baptist Church, $40,000. Loan. 2001.
125-16. Little Clifty Baptist Church, $65,000. Loan. 2001.
125-17. Morning Star Baptist Church, $30,000. Low- or no-interest loan. 2000.
125-18. Mount Roberts Baptist Church, Campbellsville, KY, $27,000. Low- or no-interest loan. 2000.
125-19. Mount Vernon Baptist Church, $13,000. Loan. 2001.
125-20. Munfordville Church of God, Munfordville, KY, $15,000. Low- or no-interest loan. 2000.
125-21. New Bethel United Methodist Church, Salyersville, KY, $46,000. Loan. 2001.
125-22. Old Blue Springs Baptist Church, Hiseville, KY, $20,000. Low- or no-interest loan. 2000.
125-23. Rough Creek Missionary Baptist Church, $30,000. Loan. 2001.
125-24. Servant Valley United Baptist Church, $15,000. Low- or no-interest loan. 2000.
125-25. Shiloh General Baptist Church, KY, $20,000. Loan. 2001.
125-26. Smith Grove Presbyterian Church, $85,000. Loan. 2001.
125-27. Taylors Chapel United Methodist Church, Crossville, TN, $27,000. Low- or no-interest loan. 2000.
125-28. Vincent Church, $10,000. Low- or no-interest loan. 2000.
125-29. White Stone Quarry Baptist Church, Bowling Green, KY, $55,000. Low- or no-interest loan. 2000.

126
Hubert Foundation

7929 Okeana-Drewersburg Rd.
Okeana, OH 45053-9500

Established in 1984 in OH.
Donor(s): Edward Hubert, Hubert Enterprises, Hubert Holding Company, Inc.
Grantmaker type: Independent foundation
General financial activity (yr. ended 06/30/02): Assets, $18,096,219 (M); gifts received, $8,003,750; expenditures, $428,856; qualifying distributions, $1,100,314; giving activities include $388,647 for 54 grants (high: $86,000; low: $1,000) and $704,580 for PRIs.
General purpose and activities: Giving primarily to Roman Catholic churches and programs; support also for secondary education and grants and loans for low income housing programs; minor support for civic and community projects.
General fields of interest: Education; human services; Roman Catholic agencies & churches.

Program-related investment (PRI) activity: The foundation makes PRIs to support low-income housing projects and civic projects.
Types of PRI Support: Loans/promissory notes.
Limitations: Applications not accepted. Giving primarily in Cincinnati, OH. No grants to individuals. PRI applications not accepted.
Trustees: Edward Hubert, George Hubert, Jr., Sharon Hubert, Howard Thomas.
EIN: 311129121

127
John Russell Hunt Memorial Fund

1324 Friar Ln.
Columbus, OH 43221 (614) 457-8095
Contact: Denham Pride, Tr.

Established in 1967 in OH. PRI-related activities began in 1970.
Grantmaker type: Independent foundation
General financial activity (yr. ended 12/31/01): Assets, $1,819,110 (M); expenditures, $20,861; qualifying distributions, $318,991; giving activities include $315,300 for 3 PRIs.
Cumulative PRI activity (through 12/31/01): Since 1970, the foundation has made 40 PRIs totaling $4,551,444. The currently outstanding PRI portfolio includes 16 PRIs totaling $1,355,315 (high: $150,000; low: $65,000; average: $100,000). The typical outstanding PRI has a 10- to 15-year term with an average term of 10 years and earns 6 to 7 percent interest with an average of 6 percent.
General purpose and activities: Providing low interest loans to churches of Christ in OH to build meeting houses.
General fields of interest: Christian agencies & churches.
Program-related investment (PRI) activity: The foundation makes mortgage loans to churches for building improvements.
Types of PRI Support: Loans/promissory notes.
Limitations: Giving limited to OH. No grants to individuals. The foundation accepts applications for PRIs.
Publications: Financial statement, informational brochure (including application guidelines).
PRI program information: Contact fund. The foundation maintains a formal PRI program. The foundation makes PRIs on a frequent but not annual basis.
Trustees: Gary D. Mann, Denham Pride, Randall J. Richardson.
EIN: 316059048
PRI recipients:
127-1. Bradford Church of Christ, Pomeroy, OH, $13,735. Mortgage loan to build church building. 2001.
127-2. Bradford Church of Christ, Pomeroy, OH, $50,265. Mortgage loan to build church building. 2000.
127-3. Buckeye Christian Church, Grove City, OH, $150,000. Mortgage loan to build church building. 2000.
127-4. Dublin Christian Church, Dublin, OH, $151,565. Mortgage loan to build church building. 2001.
127-5. McComb Church of Christ, Ontario, OH, $104,000. Mortgage loan to build church building. 2000.
127-6. McComb Church of Christ, Ontario, OH, $46,000. Loan for mortgage to build church. 1999.
127-7. Ontario Christian Church, Ontario, OH, $100,000. Loan for mortgage to build church. 1999.
127-8. Pleasant Run Church of Christ, Cincinnati, OH, $150,000. Mortgage loan to build church building. 2001.
127-9. Springfield Church of Christ, Springfield, OH, $150,000. Mortgage loan to build church building. 2000.

128
The Jon and Karen Huntsman Foundation

c/o Huntsman, Inc.
500 Huntsman Way
Salt Lake City, UT 84108-1235

Established in 1988 in UT.
Donor(s): Jon M. Huntsman.
Grantmaker type: Independent foundation
General financial activity (yr. ended 12/31/01): Assets, $44,139,910 (M); expenditures, $10,299,221; qualifying distributions, $10,418,629; giving activities include $9,935,817 for 24 grants (high: $5,500,000; low: $1,000; average: $10,000–$50,000) and $467,422 for PRIs.
Cumulative PRI activity (through 12/31/01): The currently outstanding PRI portfolio includes 3 PRIs totaling $1,840,777.
General purpose and activities: Giving primarily for music, education, health care, science, and Christian agencies and churches.
General fields of interest: Music; education; health care; science; Christian agencies & churches.
Program-related investment (PRI) activity: The foundation made PRIs for the construction of a school and housing for earthquake victims and other low-income families of Armenia.
Types of PRI Support: Loans/promissory notes.
Limitations: Applications not accepted. Giving on a national basis. No grants to individuals.
Officers and Trustees:* Jon M. Huntsman,* Pres.; Kimo J. Esplin, V.P. and Treas.; Christena Durham,* V.P.; David Gardner,* V.P.; Kathleen H. Huffman,* V.P.; David H. Huntsman,* V.P.; James H. Hunstman,* V.P.; Karen H. Huntsman,* V.P.; Paul C. Huntsman,* V.P.; Jennifer H. Parkin,* V.P.; Robert B. Lence,* Secy.
EIN: 742521914
PRI recipients:
128-1. Armenia, Government of, Yerevan, Armenia, $467,422. Loan to construct school and approximately 400 apartment units. School and apartment units will be used for earthquake victims and other low-income families in Armenia. 2001.

128-2. Armenia, Government of, Yerevan, Armenia, $980,159. Loan to construct school and approximately 400 apartment units. School and apartment units will be used for earthquake victims and other low-income families in Armenia. 2000.

128-3. Armenia, Government of, Yerevan, Armenia, $393,196. Loan to construct school and approximately 400 apartment units. School and apartment units will be used for earthquake victims and other low-income families in Armenia. 1999.

129
Hutton Foundation

101 W. Anapamu St., 4th Fl.
Santa Barbara, CA 93101 (805) 957-4740
Contact: Pam Hamlin, Asst. Dir.
FAX: (805) 957-4743; E-mail: 1hutton@west.net; URL: http://www.huttonfoundation.org

Established in 1980. PRI-related activities began in 1995.
Donor(s): Betty L. Hutton Trust.
Grantmaker type: Independent foundation
General financial activity (yr. ended 12/31/01): Assets, $52,338,143 (M); expenditures, $1,541,017; qualifying distributions, $1,891,768; giving activities include $993,950 for 122 grants (high: $67,552; low: $100; average: $1,000–$10,000) and $600,000 for 2 PRIs.
Cumulative PRI activity (through 12/31/01): Since 1995, the foundation has made 16 PRIs totaling $4,815,489. The currently outstanding PRI portfolio includes a high PRI value of $500,000, a low PRI value of $160,000, and an average PRI value of $300,000. The typical outstanding PRI has a 1.5- to 7-year term with an average term of 5 years, and earns an average of 6 percent interest.
General purpose and activities: To provide funding to local and regional non-profit organizations and their programs.
General fields of interest: Education; medical care, in-patient care; human services; children & youth, services; family services; community development.
Program-related investment (PRI) activity: The foundation has made PRI, in the form of a loan to combine and refinance 2 existing loans to a resource center for develomentally disabled individuals and their families. The foundation has also made a PRI, in the form of a loan, to an alzheimer's association, to refinance assumed mortgage on a recently acquired building. The foundation also made a PRI, in the form of a loan, to a resource center that provides residential living, independent living skills training, work services, and supported employment opportunities to developmentally disabled adults, to refinance an existing mortgage.
Types of PRI Support: Loans/promissory notes.
Limitations: Giving primarily in Orange and Santa Barbara counties, CA. No grants to individuals. PRI support limited to Southern CA. The foundation accepts applications for PRIs.
PRI program information: Deadlines for PRI applications are May 15th and Nov. 15th. Application form required. The foundation maintains a formal PRI program. The foundation makes PRIs on an annual basis.
Officers: Thomas C. Parker, Pres.; Arlene R. Craig, V.P. and Treas.; Susan Parker, V.P.; Sylvia Law, Secy.
EIN: 330779894
PRI recipients:

129-1. Alpha Resource Center of Santa Barbara, Santa Barbara, CA, $223,442. Loan to combine and refinance two existing loans. 1999.

129-2. Alzheimers Disease and Related Disorders Association, Santa Barbara, CA, $160,000. Loan to refinance assumed mortage on recently acquired building. 1999.

129-3. Community Environmental Council, Santa Barbara, CA, $200,000. Loan to complete renovations to South Coast Watershed Resource Center. 2001.

129-4. Direct Relief International, Santa Barbara, CA, $500,000. Loan to refinance mortgage on existing office and warehouse spaces. 2000.

129-5. Girls Inc. of Carpinteria, Carpinteria, CA, $384,665. Loan to refinance mortgage on current club property. 2000.

129-6. Jewish Federation of Santa Barbara, Santa Barbara, CA, $232,000. Loan to refinance mortgage on recently purchased property. 2000.

129-7. Life Options Vocational and Resource Center, Lompoc, CA, $65,000. Loan to refinance exisiting mortgage. 1999.

129-8. Mental Health Association of Santa Barbara, Santa Barbara, CA, $400,000. Loan to purchase property to relocate Drop-In Center and administrative offices. 2001.

129-9. Santa Barbara Rescue Mission, Santa Barbara, CA, $200,000. Loan to refinance existing construction loan at lower interest rate. Initial loan is to construct Bethel House, center for homeless women and children. 2000.

130
The Hyams Foundation, Inc.

(Formerly Sarah A. Hyams Fund)
175 Federal St., 14th Fl.
Boston, MA 02110 (617) 426-5600
Contact: Elizabeth B. Smith, Exec. Dir.
FAX: (617) 426-5696; E-mail: info@hyamsfoundation.org; URL: http://www.hyamsfoundation.org

Established in 1929 in MA as the Sarah A. Hyams Fund; in 1991 merged with the Godfrey Hyams Trust and adapted current name.
Donor(s): Godfrey M. Hyams,‡ Sarah A. Hyams.‡
Grantmaker type: Independent foundation
General financial activity (yr. ended 12/31/01): Assets, $120,285,437 (M); expenditures, $6,535,939; qualifying distributions, $4,890,130; giving activities include

$4,890,130 for 200 grants (high: $100,000; low: $1,000; average: $20,000–$25,000); no PRIs paid.
Cumulative PRI activity (through 12/31/01): The currently outstanding PRI portfolio includes PRIs totaling $426,139.
General purpose and activities: The mission of the foundation is to increase economic and social justice and power within low-income communities. The foundation believes that investing in strategies that enable low-income people to increase their communities will have the greatest social return in these times. The foundation will carry out its mission by: supporting civic participation by low-income communities; promoting economic development that benefits low-income neighborhoods and their residents; and developing the talents and skills of low-income youth.
General fields of interest: Adult/continuing education; family planning; AIDS; housing/shelter, development; human services; youth, services; family services; homeless, human services; race/intergroup relations; urban/community development; community development; Asians/Pacific Islanders; African Americans/Blacks; Hispanics/Latinos; Native Americans/American Indians; disabled; aging; people with AIDS (PWAs); gays/lesbians; immigrants/refugees; economically disadvantaged.
Program-related investment (PRI) activity: The foundation has made PRIs to a social venture fund that provides equity financing for businesses in inner-city neighborhoods that lack access to traditional sources of capital.
Types of PRI Support: Loans/promissory notes, equity investments.
Limitations: Giving primarily in Boston and Chelsea, MA. No support for municipal, state, or federal agencies; institutions of higher learning for standard educational programs; religious organizations for sectarian religious purposes; or national or regional health organizations; support for medical research is being phased out. No grants to individuals, or for endowment funds, hospitals and health centers, capital campaigns, fellowships, publications, conferences, films or videos or curriculum development.
Publications: Annual report, grants list, informational brochure (including application guidelines).
Officers and Trustees:* John H. Clymer,* Chair.; Elizabeth B. Smith, Exec. Dir.; Pierre August, Marie Estela Carrion, Barbara E. Casey, Meizhu Lui, Lewis H. Spence, Edward M. Swan, Jr., Roslyn M. Watson.
Number of staff: 6 full-time professional; 2 full-time support; 1 part-time support.
EIN: 046013680
PRI recipients:
130-1. Boston Community Capital, Boston, MA, $249,680. Equity investment. 2000.
130-2. Boston Community Loan Fund, Boston, MA, $125,000. Program-related investment in form of direct membership interest. 1999.

131
Immanuel Bible Foundation

1301 S. Fell Ave.
Normal, IL 61761-3642
Contact: Michael J. Krippel, Exec. Dir.
FAX: (309) 862-4121

Incorporated in 1944 in IL.
Donor(s): Keiser-Van Leer Assn. Trust.
Grantmaker type: Independent foundation
General financial activity (yr. ended 12/31/01): Assets, $2,840,000 (M); expenditures, $141,000; qualifying distributions, $181,425; giving activities include $1,700 for 3 grants (high: $1,000; low: $200), $184,073 for 4 foundation-administered programs and $5,703 for 2 PRIs.
General fields of interest: Children & youth, services; Christian agencies & churches.
Program-related investment (PRI) activity: The foundation makes PRIs for capital improvements and for acquisitions for related facilities.
Types of PRI Support: Charitable use assets.
Limitations: Giving limited to McLean County, IL. No grants to individuals.
Publications: Informational brochure, program policy statement.
Officer and Directors:* Michael J. Krippel,* Exec. Dir.; Paul Brown, Mark Hughey, Debbie Rawlins, Cindy Weaver, W. Charles Witte.
Number of staff: 3 full-time professional.
EIN: 370688539

132
Independence Community Foundation

182 Atlantic Ave.
Brooklyn, NY 11201 (718) 722-2300
Contact: Marilyn Gelber, Exec. Dir.
FAX: (718) 722-5757; E-mail: inquiries@icfny.org; URL: http://www.icfny.org

Established in 1998 in NY.
Donor(s): Independence Community Bank Corp.
Grantmaker type: Company-sponsored foundation
General financial activity (yr. ended 12/31/01): Assets, $70,718,884 (M); gifts received, $214,450; expenditures, $4,976,663; qualifying distributions, $4,871,242; giving activities include $4,241,127 for 490 grants (high: $135,000; low: $35; average: $1,000–$55,000) and $284,813 for 2 PRIs.
Cumulative PRI activity (through 12/31/01): The currently outstanding PRI portfolio includes 3 PRIs totaling $784,813.
General purpose and activities: Giving primarily for community development, social services, and quality of life improvement in New York, NY, neighborhoods.
General fields of interest: Arts/cultural programs; education; housing/shelter, development; human services; community development.

Program-related investment (PRI) activity: The foundation has made PRIs for the arts, housing, and community development.
Types of PRI Support: Loans/promissory notes.
Limitations: Giving primarily in New York, NY.
Officers and Directors:* Charles J. Hamm,* Chair.; Alan H. Fishman,* Pres.; Marilyn G. Gelber, Exec. Dir.; Steven Adubato, Willard N. Archie, Fred W. Beaufait, Robert B. Catell, Donald H. Elliott, David R. Jones, Donald M. Karp, Donald E. Kolowsky, Malcolm MacKay, Joseph S. Morgano, Maria Fiorini Ramirez, Wesley D. Ratcliff, Victor M. Richel, Mikki Shepaid.
EIN: 113422729
PRI recipients:
132-1. Brooklyn Youth Chorus, Brooklyn, NY, $269,813. Interest-free loan. 2001.
132-2. Habitat for Humanity - New York City, Brooklyn, NY, $500,000. Interest-free loan. 2000.
132-3. Jackson Heights Community Development Corporation, Jackson Heights, NY, $15,000. Interest-free loan. 2001.

133
The Inverso-Baglivo Foundation

824 Hood Rd.
Swarthmore, PA 19081-2814 (610) 544-5960
Contact: Anthony W. Inverso, V.P. and Secy.

Established in 1994 in DE and PA.
Donor(s): Rina A. Sukartawidjaja.
Grantmaker type: Independent foundation
General financial activity (yr. ended 12/31/01): Assets, $210,863 (M); gifts received, $894,916; expenditures, $852,830; qualifying distributions, $230,497; giving activities include $280,139 for 25 grants (high: $56,355; low: $664); no PRIs paid.
General fields of interest: Higher education; cancer; human services.
General international interests: Indonesia.
Program-related investment (PRI) activity: The foundation generally does not provide PRIs except to organizations with which they are very familiar. Recently, the foundation made very short-term PRIs to a healthcare foundation in order to keep it in operation.
Types of PRI Support: Loans/promissory notes.
Limitations: Giving on a national and international basis. No grants to individuals. Only organizations with which the foundation is familiar will be considered for PRIs. PRIs are only granted on an infrequent basis when the foundation has adequate resources in its asset base to support them. PRI applications not accepted.
PRI program information: The foundation does not maintain a formal PRI program. The foundation makes PRIs occasionally.
Officers and Directors:* Daniel A. Inverso,* Chair. and Pres.; Anthony W. Inverso,* V.P. and Secy.-Treas.; Carmella Adams, Daniel Baglivo, Angelo J. Inverso, Gloria C. Melloni, Antoinette Sgro.
EIN: 232775468

134
The James Irvine Foundation

1 Market St.
Steuart Tower, Ste. 2500
San Francisco, CA 94105 (415) 777-2244
Contact: Ann Clarke, Dir., Grants Admin.
FAX: (415) 777-0869; Southern CA office: 725 S. Figueroa St., Ste. 3075, Los Angeles, CA 90017-5430; tel.: (213) 236-0552; FAX: (213) 236-0537;
URL: http://www.irvine.org

Incorporated in 1937 in CA. PRI-related activities began in 1989.
Donor(s): James Irvine.‡
Grantmaker type: Independent foundation
General financial activity (yr. ended 12/31/01): Assets, $1,378,433,649 (M); gifts received, $34,000; expenditures, $77,583,845; qualifying distributions, $70,161,993; giving activities include $59,017,797 for 222 grants (high: $2,250,000; low: $500; average: $20,000–$250,000) and $1,936,460 for 4 foundation-administered programs; no PRIs paid.
Cumulative PRI activity (through 12/31/01): Since 1989, the foundation has made 14 PRIs totaling $8,100,000. The currently outstanding PRI portfolio includes PRIs totaling $779,127 (high: $1,000,000; low: $150,000; average: $500,000). The typical outstanding PRI has an average term of 5 years, and earns an average of 5 percent interest.
General purpose and activities: Giving primarily for the arts, higher education, workforce development, civic culture, sustainable communities, and children, youth, and families.
General fields of interest: Arts, multipurpose centers/programs; arts, cultural/ethnic awareness; folk arts; arts councils; performing arts; performing arts centers; dance; ballet; theater; orchestra (symphony); opera; higher education; college; university; higher education reform; natural resources conservation & protection; employment, services; employment, job counseling; employment, training; employment, retraining; youth development, centers & clubs; youth development, services; race/intergroup relations; community development, management/technical aid; community development, volunteer services; community development, neighborhood development; economic development; rural development; nonprofit management; philanthropy/voluntarism, association; philanthropy/voluntarism, administration/regulation; philanthropy/voluntarism, information services; foundations (public); foundations (community); voluntarism promotion; philanthropy/voluntarism; public policy, research.
Program-related investment (PRI) activity: The foundation established a Program Related Investment Fund (PRIF) to

provide PRIs in support of its program interests. PRIs have provided interim financing and financing for pre-development expenses, land acquisition, construction, rehabilitation, and equipment purchases. PRIs have also provided working capital for business ventures sponsored by nonprofit organizations.
Types of PRI Support: Loans/promissory notes, interim financing, loan guarantees.
Limitations: Giving limited to CA. No support for agencies receiving substantial government support. No grants to individuals. PRIs made only in cases where deemed more appropriate than grants, and when conventional financing is either unavailable or prohibitively expensive. PRIs to a single borrower may not exceed $1 million. PRI applications not accepted.
Publications: Annual report, newsletter.
PRI program information: The foundation does not maintain a formal PRI program. The foundation makes PRIs occasionally.
Officers and Directors:* James C. Gaither,* Chair.; James E. Canales,* C.E.O. and Pres.; John R. Jenks, C.I.O. and Treas.; James E. Canales, V.P. and Corp. Secy.; Samuel H. Armacost, Frank H. Cruz, Cheryl White Mason, David Mas Masumoto, Molly Munger, Patricia Pineda, Gary B. Pruitt, Toby Rosenblatt, Peter W. Stanley, Ph.D., Peter J. Taylor, Kathryn L. Wheeler, Hon. Dir.
Number of staff: 25 full-time professional; 1 part-time professional; 18 full-time support.
EIN: 941236937

135
Island Foundation, Inc.

589 Mill St.
Marion, MA 02738-1553 (508) 748-2809
Contact: Julie A. Early, Exec. Dir.
FAX: (508) 748-0991; E-mail: islandfdn@earthlink.net

Incorporated in 1979 in MA as Ram Island, Inc.; current entity formed in 1986 by merger with Green Island, Inc.
Donor(s): W. Van Alan Clark, Jr.‡
Grantmaker type: Independent foundation
General financial activity (yr. ended 12/31/01): Assets, $36,186,988 (M); expenditures, $1,901,849; qualifying distributions, $1,688,825; giving activities include $1,590,069 for 58 grants (high: $300,000; low: $1,500); no PRIs paid.
Cumulative PRI activity (through 12/31/01): The currently outstanding PRI portfolio includes a high PRI value of $100,000 and a low PRI value of $10,000. The typical outstanding PRI has an average term of 1 years, and earns 1 to 2 percent interest.
General purpose and activities: Giving primarily for: 1) coastal water protection in New England environmental projects: right whale research, impact of toxins on wildlife-research, land use conservation in southeast MA, and 2) building the capacity of individuals and neighborhoods in the city of New Bedford, MA; and 3) alternative education programs.
General fields of interest: Education; natural resources conservation & protection; environment; wildlife preservation & protection; economic development; community development; marine science; biological sciences; public policy, research.
Program-related investment (PRI) activity: The foundation occasionally makes PRIs to support education, the environment, and community development. PRIs have provided interim financing, supported facilities renovation, and capitalized housing development projects.
Types of PRI Support: Loans/promissory notes, interim financing.
Limitations: Giving primarily in New Bedford, MA, for economic and community development, MA, ME, and RI for environmental programs. No support for religious organizations for sectarian purposes or political organizations. No grants to individuals. PRI applications not accepted.
Publications: Annual report (including application guidelines).
PRI program information: The foundation does not maintain a formal PRI program. The foundation makes PRIs occasionally.
Officers: Jo-Ann Watson, Pres.; Michael Moore, V.P.; Peter Nesbeda, Treas.; Julie A. Early, Exec. Dir.
Directors: K. Clark, Stephen Clark, Hannah Moore, Christopher Tupper, Douglas Watson.
Number of staff: 1 full-time professional.
EIN: 042670567

136
The Jeniam Foundation

(also known as The Jeniam Clarkson Foundation)
270 Bremington Pl.
Memphis, TN 38111 (901) 454-7080
Contact: Charlotte G. King, Exec. Dir.

Established in 1992 in TN. PRI-related activities began in 1994.
Donor(s): Andrew M. Clarkson, Carole G. Clarkson.
Grantmaker type: Independent foundation
General financial activity (yr. ended 12/31/01): Assets, $13,134,059 (M); gifts received, $549,850; expenditures, $361,176; qualifying distributions, $352,440; giving activities include $281,150 for 13 grants (high: $76,400; low: $1,000; average: $2,500–$35,000) and $17,650 for 1 PRI.
Cumulative PRI activity (through 12/31/01): Since 1994, the foundation has made 3 PRIs totaling $40,650. The currently outstanding PRI portfolio includes 4 PRIs totaling $43,000 (high: $20,000; low: $5,000; average: $10,750). The typical outstanding PRI has a 1- to 3-year term with an average term of 2 years and earns 1 to 5 percent interest with an average of 3 percent.

General fields of interest: Museums (children's); education; natural resources conservation & protection; nursing home/convalescent facility; youth development, services; aging.
Program-related investment (PRI) activity: The foundation recently made a PRI, in the form of a loan to a museum. Historically, the foundation made PRIs in the form of loans, for youth development and the arts.
Types of PRI Support: Loans/promissory notes.
Limitations: Giving on a national basis for conservation; in New Canaan, CT, for education and aging; and in Memphis, TN, for the arts. No grants to individuals, or for ongoing operating support. PRI support primarily in CT and TN. The foundation accepts applications for PRIs.
Publications: Informational brochure (including application guidelines).
PRI program information: The foundation does not maintain a formal PRI program. The foundation makes PRIs occasionally.
Officer: Charlotte G. King, Exec. Dir.
Trustees: Andrew M. Clarkson, Carole G. Clarkson, Jennifer M. Clarkson.
Number of staff: 1 full-time professional.
EIN: 621516244
PRI recipients:
136-1. Brooks Museum of Art, Memphis, TN, $17,650. Loan. 2001.
136-2. Circuit Playhouse, Memphis, TN, $13,000. Loan. 2000.
136-3. Circuit Playhouse, Memphis, TN, $10,000. Loan. 1999.

137

Jerome Foundation

125 Park Square Ct.
400 Sibley St.
St. Paul, MN 55101-1928 (651) 224-9431
Contact: Cynthia A. Gehrig, Pres.
Additional tel.: (800) 995-3766 (MN and NY only); FAX: (651) 224-3439; E-mail: info@jeromefdn.org; URL: http://www.jeromefdn.org

Incorporated in 1964 in MN. PRI-related activities began in 1989.
Donor(s): J. Jerome Hill.‡
Grantmaker type: Independent foundation
General financial activity (yr. ended 04/30/02): Assets, $84,136,278 (M); gifts received, $40,000; expenditures, $4,464,604; qualifying distributions, $4,090,859; giving activities include $2,670,502 for 127 grants (high: $120,000; low: $5,000; average: $10,000–$100,000), $642,169 for grants to individuals and $73,507 for foundation-administered programs; no PRIs paid.
Cumulative PRI activity (through 04/30/02): Since 1989, the foundation has made 3 PRIs totaling $203,441. The currently outstanding PRI portfolio includes 1 PRI totaling $100,000. The typical outstanding PRI earns 0 to 3 percent interest, and earns an average of 3 percent.
General purpose and activities: Support for arts programs only, including dance, media arts, literature, music, theater, performance art, visual arts and arts criticism. The foundation is concerned primarily with providing financial assistance to emerging creative artists of promise, including choreographers, media artists, composers, literary and visual artists, playwrights, and multidisciplinary creators.
General fields of interest: Media/communications; visual arts; performing arts; dance; theater; music; literature; arts/cultural programs.
Program-related investment (PRI) activity: The foundation provides a revolving loan fund for artists in artspace buildings.
Types of PRI Support: Loans/promissory notes, capitalizing loan funds/other intermediaries.
Limitations: Giving limited to MN and New York, NY. No support for educational programs in the arts and humanities. No grants to individuals (except for Media Arts Program, Minnesota Travel and Study Grant Program and Building Admin. Capacity Program), or for undergraduate or graduate student research projects, capital or endowment funds, equipment, scholarships, or matching gifts. The purpose of any PRI has to be consistent with Jerome Foundation's focus: to directly assist emerging creative artists. PRI applications not accepted.
Publications: Informational brochure (including application guidelines), application guidelines, financial statement, grants list.
PRI program information: The foundation does not maintain a formal PRI program. The foundation makes PRIs occasionally.
Officers and Directors:* Janice Plimpton,* Chair.; Seitu Jones,* Vice-Chair.; Cynthia A. Gehrig,* Pres.; Vickie Benson, V.P.; Marcia Tucker, Secy.; Rodney Boren,* Treas.; Karen F. Fjorden, Cont.; Tom Borrup, Laurie Carlos, Jessica Hagedorn, Libby Larson.
Number of staff: 2 full-time professional; 1 part-time professional; 1 full-time support; 2 part-time support.
EIN: 416035163

138

The Jewish Healthcare Foundation of Pittsburgh

Centre City Tower, Ste. 2330
650 Smithfield St.
Pittsburgh, PA 15222 (412) 594-2550
Contact: Karen Wolk Feinstein, Ph.D., Pres.
FAX: (412) 232-6240; E-mail: info@jhf.org; URL: http://www.jhf.org

Established in 1990 in PA; converted as a result of Montefiore Hospital's merger with Presbyterian University Hospital.
Donor(s): Presbyterian University Health Systems, Inc.
Grantmaker type: Independent foundation
General financial activity (yr. ended 12/31/01): Assets, $119,803,018 (M); gifts received, $2,881,883; expenditures, $9,509,194; qualifying distributions, $7,056,169; giving

activities include $5,888,997 for 52 grants (high: $900,000; low: $2,223; average: $20,000–$250,000); no PRIs paid.
General purpose and activities: To support and foster the provision of health care services, health care education, and to respond to the health-related needs of the elderly, underprivileged, indigent, and underserved populations in western PA. The foundation will assist in the treatment and care of those who are elderly, sick, infirm, or in any way afflicted with physical or mental disease, in both the Jewish and general community. Current foundation priorities include: 1) Perfecting patient care; 2) Building health workforce; and 3) Applying medical knowledge.
General fields of interest: Hospitals (general); health care; mental health/crisis services; health associations; AIDS; AIDS research; nutrition; human services; children & youth, services; family services, single parents; aging, centers & services; women, centers & services; Jewish federated giving programs; aging; women.
Program-related investment (PRI) activity: The foundation has made PRIs for medical research.
Limitations: Giving limited to western PA. No support for political campaigns, and any other programs without a health care component. No grants to individuals (including scholarships or fellowships), or for research or travel, general operations, endowment programs, capital needs, operating deficits, or retirement of debt.
Publications: Annual report, application guidelines, newsletter, occasional report, program policy statement.
Officers and Trustees:* Charles Cohen,* Chair.; Patricia Siger, Vice-Chair.; Karen Wolk Feinstein, Ph.D.,* Pres.; Robert Nelkin, Secy.; Stephen Halpern, Treas.; and 44 additional trustees.
Number of staff: 15 full-time professional; 2 part-time professional; 7 full-time support; 1 part-time support.
EIN: 251624347
PRI recipients:
138-1. Demegen Corporation, Pittsburgh, PA, $155,000. Program-related investment. 1999.
138-2. University of Pittsburgh, Pittsburgh, PA, $105,000. Program-related investment for international research on traditional Chinese medicine. 1999.

139
James Hervey Johnson Charitable Educational Trust

P.O. Box 16160
San Diego, CA 92176
Contact: Kevin Munnelly, Tr.
Additional address: c/o Paul A. Gonseth, Withers & Goulding, 2251 San Diego Ave., Ste. B-251, San Diego, CA 92110; FAX: (619) 297-9036

Established in 1989 in CA.
Grantmaker type: Independent foundation
General financial activity (yr. ended 07/31/01): Assets, $11,783,739 (M); expenditures, $366,902; qualifying distributions, $112,214; giving activities include $30,000 for 2 grants of $15,000 each; no PRIs paid.
Cumulative PRI activity (through 07/31/01): Since beginning PRI activity, the foundation has made 2 PRIs totaling $423,000.
General purpose and activities: Giving primarily to organizations involved in free thinking, humanism, the separation of church and state, and freedom from religion; support also for natural hygiene and promotion and advocacy of vegetarianism.
General fields of interest: Agriculture/food.
Program-related investment (PRI) activity: The foundation has made loans to two organizations to allow them to produce and disseminate their materials on religion and health.
Types of PRI Support: Loans/promissory notes.
Limitations: No grants to individuals.
Trustee: Kevin V. Munnelly.
EIN: 336081439
PRI recipients:
139-1. James Hervey Johnson Truth Seeker Trust, San Diego, CA, $200,000. Loan to provide capital and funding to facilitate organization's ability to publish, produce and disseminate materials espousing views of James Hervey Johnson on religion and health. 1999.
139-2. Truth Seeker Company, San Diego, CA, $223,000. Loan to provide capital and funding to facilitate organization's ability to publish, produce and disseminate materials espousing views of James Hervey Johnson on religion and health. 1999.

140
Christian A. Johnson Endeavor Foundation

1060 Park Ave.
New York, NY 10128-1033 (212) 534-6620
Contact: Julie J. Kidd, Pres.
FAX: (212) 410-5909

Incorporated in 1952 in NY.
Donor(s): Christian A. Johnson.‡
Grantmaker type: Independent foundation
General financial activity (yr. ended 12/31/01): Assets, $217,301,844 (M); gifts received, $535,161; expenditures, $13,250,117; qualifying distributions, $13,189,704; giving activities include $11,413,993 for 132 grants (high: $887,060; low: $500; average: $10,000–$250,000), $266,270 for foundation-administered programs and $200,000 for 1 PRI.
Cumulative PRI activity (through 12/31/01): The currently outstanding PRI portfolio includes 1 PRI totaling $200,000.
General purpose and activities: Giving concentrated on private institutions of higher learning at the baccalaureate level and on educational outreach programs of visual and performing arts organizations in New York City; occasional support for perceived needs in other areas of education and the arts.
General fields of interest: Arts/cultural programs; higher education; education.
General international interests: Europe.

Program-related investment (PRI) activity: The foundation has made a PRI to a performing arts group.
Types of PRI Support: Loans/promissory notes.
Limitations: Giving limited to the eastern U.S. No support for government agencies, or for community or neighborhood projects, religious institutions, or for health care. No grants to individuals, or for continuing support, annual campaigns, emergency funds, deficit financing, land acquisitions, building projects, medical research, demonstration projects, publications, or conferences; no loans (except for program-related investments).
Publications: Financial statement, program policy statement, application guidelines.
PRI program information: The foundation makes PRIs occasionally.
Officers and Trustees:* Julie J. Kidd,* Pres. and Treas.; Christin Kidd, Secy.; Donald W. Harwood, Ann B. Spence.
Number of staff: 2 full-time professional; 1 full-time support.
EIN: 136147952
PRI recipients:
140-1. Orpheon, The Little Orchestra Society, NYC, NY, $200,000. Program-related investment. 2001.

141
The Robert Wood Johnson Foundation

Rte. 1 and College Rd. E.
P.O. Box 2316
Princeton, NJ 08543-2316 (609) 452-8701
Contact: Richard J. Toth, Dir., Office of Proposal Mgmt.
E-mail: mail@rwjf.org; URL: http://www.rwjf.org

Incorporated in 1936 in NJ; became a national philanthropy in 1972. PRI-related activities began in 1982.
Donor(s): Robert Wood Johnson.‡
Grantmaker type: Independent foundation
General financial activity (yr. ended 12/31/02): Assets, $8,012,367,000 (M); gifts received, $1,410,342; expenditures, $455,687,191; qualifying distributions, $460,054,133; giving activities include $357,306,381 for grants and $3,041,085 for employee matching gifts; no PRIs paid.
Cumulative PRI activity (through 12/31/02): The currently outstanding PRI portfolio includes 6 PRIs totaling $11,467,718 (high: $5,500,000; low: $500,000; average: $500,000). The typical outstanding PRI has a 6- to 10-year term with an average term of 10 years and earns 2 to 4 percent interest with an average of 3 percent.
General purpose and activities: The foundation is devoted exclusively to health and health care and concentrates its grantmaking in four areas: assuring access to quality health services for all Americans at reasonable cost; improving quality of care and support for people with chronic health conditions; promoting healthy communities and lifestyles; and reducing the harm caused by substance abuse - tobacco, alcohol, and illicit drugs.
General fields of interest: Child development, education; medical school/education; hospitals (general); health care, cost containment; nursing care; health care; substance abuse, services; smoking; mental health/crisis services; health associations; children & youth, services; child development, services; family services; hospices; aging, centers & services; homeless, human services; voluntarism promotion; minorities; Native Americans/American Indians; disabled; aging; homeless.
Program-related investment (PRI) activity: The foundation made its first PRI to provide a reserve for a loan fund serving women and minorities in medicine. In the following years, PRI support has included funding for organizations focused on the aging, the housing needs of the chronic mentally ill, and increasing the effectiveness of rural hospitals. Specifically, PRIs have supported facilities improvement and equipment acquisition, and capitalized earned income ventures and housing development projects.
Types of PRI Support: Loans/promissory notes, interim financing, lines of credit.
Limitations: Giving limited to the U.S. No support for political organizations, international activities, programs or institutions concerned solely with a specific disease or basic biomedical research. No grants to individuals, or for ongoing general operating expenses, endowment funds, capital costs, including construction, renovation, or equipment, or research on unapproved drug therapies or devices.
Publications: Annual report (including application guidelines), informational brochure, application guidelines, occasional report, newsletter, grants list.
PRI program information: The foundation makes PRIs occasionally.
Officers and Trustees:* Robert E. Campbell,* Chair.; Risa Lavizzo-Mourey, M.D., MBA,* C.E.O. and Pres.; Calvin Bland, Chief of Staff; John R. Lumpkin, M.D., Sr. V.P. and Dir., Health Care; J. Michael McGinnis, M.D., Sr. V.P. and Dir., Health Group; J. Warren Wood III, V.P., Secy., and Genl. Counsel; Peter Goodwin, V.P. and Treas.; James Knickman, V.P., Research and Evaluation; David J. Morse, V.P., Comm.; Albert O. Shar, Ph.D., V.P., Info. Tech.; David L. Waldman, V.P., H.R.; Brian O'Neill, C.I.O.; G. Russell Henshaw, Jr., Cont.; Nancy-Ann DeParle, George S. Frazza, James R. Gavin III, M.D., Linda Griego, Wendy Hagen, Edward J. Hartnett, Robert Wood Johnson IV, Hon. Thomas H. Kean, Ralph Larsen, Edward E. Matthews, William L. Roper, M.D., Marla E. Salmon, Sc.D., R.N., Gail L. Warden, Richard B. Worley.
Number of staff: 130 full-time professional; 6 part-time professional; 99 full-time support; 5 part-time support.
EIN: 226029397
PRI recipients:
141-1. New Brunswick Affiliated Hospitals, New Brunswick, NJ, $250,000. Non-interest bearing loan for Cancer Institute of New Jersey to complete financing required to construct permanent facility. 1999.

142

Joukowsky Family Foundation

410 Park Ave., Ste. 1610
New York, NY 10022
Contact: Ms. Nina J. Koprulu, Pres. and Dir.
E-mail: info@joukowsky.org; URL: http://www.joukowsky.org

Established in 1981 in NY.
Grantmaker type: Independent foundation
General financial activity (yr. ended 10/31/02): Assets, $72,419,120 (M); expenditures, $10,966,631; qualifying distributions, $10,613,493; giving activities include $9,787,518 for grants (average: $1,000–$50,000); no PRIs paid.
General purpose and activities: Giving primarily for higher and secondary education.
General fields of interest: Education.
Program-related investment (PRI) activity: Loan to school to purchase land for construction of larger school.
Types of PRI Support: Loans/promissory notes.
Limitations: Applications not accepted. Giving primarily in the northeastern U.S.
Officers and Directors:* Nina J. Koprulu,* Pres.; Emily R. Kessler, Exec. Dir.; Randall G. Drain, Artemis A.W. Joukowsky, Martha S. Joukowsky.
Number of staff: 2 full-time professional; 1 part-time professional.
EIN: 133242753
PRI recipients:
142-1. Eliot Montessori School, South Natick, MA, $940,000. Loan to purchase land to construct larger school. 2001.

143

Kalamazoo Community Foundation

(Formerly Kalamazoo Foundation)

151 S. Rose St., Ste. 332
Kalamazoo, MI 49007 (269) 381-4416
Contact: David D. Gardiner, V.P., Progs.
FAX: (269) 381-3146; E-mail: info@kalfound.org; URL: http://www.kalfound.org

Established in 1925; incorporated in 1930 in MI.
PRI-related activities began in 1990.
Grantmaker type: Community foundation
General financial activity (yr. ended 12/31/02): Assets, $209,537,807 (M); gifts received, $8,948,954; expenditures, $17,051,237; giving activities include $11,690,154 for 1,877 grants (high: $1,253,167; low: $25), $1,585,145 for 451 grants to individuals (high: $11,600; low: $250; average: $250–$11,600) and $1,672,886 for 9 PRIs.
Cumulative PRI activity (through 12/31/02): Since 1990, the foundation has made 17 PRIs totaling $6,220,616. The currently outstanding PRI portfolio includes 16 PRIs totaling $5,966,503 (high: $1,520,000; low: $20,000; average: $369,056). The typical outstanding PRI has a 2- to 7-year term with an average term of 5 years and earns 1 to 2 percent interest with an average of 1.5 percent.
General purpose and activities: Primary areas of giving include 1) economic development, 2) education and learning, 3) community engagement and youth development and 4) individuals and families. Grants largely for capital purposes and innovative programs.
General fields of interest: Elementary/secondary education; environment; health care; housing/shelter, development; economic development.
Program-related investment (PRI) activity: In 1990, the foundation established the Community Development Loan Fund to provide low-interest loans to nonprofit agencies in the areas of housing and economic development. PRIs have provided cash flow financing, supported facility improvement, and capitalized housing development projects. In 2001, the foundation adopted a new PRI policy which provides for an expanded program of PRIs in an amount up to 10 percent of unrestricted assets.
Types of PRI Support: Loans/promissory notes, loan guarantees, equity investments.
Limitations: Giving limited to Kalamazoo County, MI. No grants to individuals (except for scholarships), or for endowment funds. The foundation accepts applications for PRIs.
Publications: Annual report (including application guidelines), informational brochure (including application guidelines), newsletter, application guidelines, financial statement, grants list.
PRI program information: The foundation maintains a formal PRI program. The foundation makes PRIs on an annual basis.
Officers, Trustees and Distribution Committee:* Jeffrey L. DeNooyer,* Chair.; Marilyn J. Schlack,* Vice-Chair.; John E. "Jack" Hopkins, C.E.O., Pres. and Secy.-Treas.; Wesley Freeland, V.P., Donor Svcs.; David D. Gardiner, V.P., Progs.; Gloria Z. Royal, V.P., Mktg. Comm.; Susan Springgate, V.P., Finance and Admin.; Karen Racette, Cont.; J. Louis Felton, David L. Hatfield, Judith Maze, Ronda E. Stryker, Donald J. Vander Kooy.
Custodian Bank: National City Bank.
Number of staff: 15 full-time professional; 3 part-time professional; 8 full-time support; 1 part-time support.
EIN: 383333262
PRI recipients:
143-1. Downtown Tomorrow, Kalamazoo, MI, $625,000. Bridge loan for Festival Site. 2002.
143-2. Kalamazoo Area Housing Corporation, Kalamazoo, MI, $250,000. For program-related investment loan to purchase property upon which to build affordable housing for low-income individuals and families. 2001.
143-3. Kalamazoo Aviation History Museum, Air Zoo, Kalamazoo, MI, $1,000,000. Loan for construction. 2002.
143-4. Kalamazoo Aviation History Museum, Kalamazoo, MI, $4,000,000. Low-interest loan for Air Zoo Legacy of Flight project, contingent upon project's progress. 2000.

143-5. Local Initiatives Support Corporation (LISC), Kalamazoo, MI, $1,000,000. Loan for loan fund to provide low-interest loans and technical assistance to promote community and economic development in low-income neighborhoods. 2001.

143-6. Southwest Michigan First Corporation, Kalamazoo, MI, $2,000,000. Loan for construction of Innovation Center, new Business Technology and Research Park, state-of-the-art facility designed to nurture and develop start-up firms in both early and later stages. 2002.

144
The J. M. Kaplan Fund, Inc.

261 Madison Ave., 19th Fl.
New York, NY 10016 (212) 767-0630
Contact: William P. Falahee, Cont.
FAX: (212) 767-0639; Application address for publication program: Furthermore, P.O. Box 667, Hudson, NY 12534; tel.: (518) 828-8900; URL: http://www.jmkfund.org

Incorporated in 1948 in NY as Faigel Leah Foundation, Inc.; The J.M. Kaplan Fund, Inc., a DE corporation, merged with it in 1975 and was renamed The J.M. Kaplan Fund, Inc. PRI-related activities began in 1989.
Donor(s): Members of the J.M. Kaplan family.
Grantmaker type: Independent foundation
General financial activity (yr. ended 12/31/01): Assets, $146,189,671 (M); expenditures, $13,265,251; qualifying distributions, $9,915,085; giving activities include $8,854,895 for 351 grants (high: $500,000; low: $150; average: $5,000–$150,000); no PRIs paid.
Cumulative PRI activity (through 12/31/01): The currently outstanding PRI portfolio includes PRIs totaling $825,000.
General purpose and activities: Giving primarily in five areas: City Life (the arts, reading and knowledge acquisition, urban greening, and human services programs); Environment and Sustainable Business (partnerships between environmental groups and business); Exploration and New Technologies (the application of new technologies in archeology, geology, and geography); Human Rights; and Research and Public Policy. The fund offers program-related investments to encourage ventures of particular interest. The fund also has a trustee-initiated grants program that considers grant requests invited by the trustees.
General fields of interest: History & archaeology; arts/cultural programs; libraries/library science; natural resources conservation & protection; environment; human services; community development; public policy, research.
Program-related investment (PRI) activity: The foundation began making PRIs in 1989 in the areas of the arts, housing, wilderness preservation, and human services. PRIs have provided financing to nonprofit organizations for land acquisition, facilities acquisition and renovation, and to capitalize community financial institutions.
Limitations: Giving primarily in NY, with emphasis on New York City. No grants to individuals, including scholarships and fellowships, or for construction or building programs, endowment funds, operating budgets of educational or medical institutions, film or video, or sponsorship of books, dances, plays, or other works of art.
Publications: Annual report (including application guidelines).
PRI program information: The foundation makes PRIs occasionally.
Officers and Trustees:* Peter W. Davidson,* Chair.; William P. Falahee, Cont.; Conn Nugent, Exec. Dir.; Betsy Davidson, G. Bradford Davidson, J. Matthew Davidson, Joan K. Davidson, Caio Fonseca, Elizabeth K. Fonseca, Isabel Fonseca, Quina Fonseca, Richard D. Kaplan, Mary E. Kaplan.
Number of staff: 3 full-time professional; 1 full-time support.
EIN: 136090286
PRI recipients:

144-1. Open Space Institute, NYC, NY, $250,000. Program-related investment to preserve open space in New York area. 2000.

144-2. Trust for Public Land, NYC, NY, $250,000. Program-related investment to preserve open land in New York area. 2000.

145
Ewing Marion Kauffman Foundation

4801 Rockhill Rd.
Kansas City, MO 64110-2046 (816) 932-1000
Contact: Kate Pope Hodel, Dir., Comm.
PRI Contact: Paul J. Schofer, Treas.
FAX: (816) 932-1100; E-mail: info@emkf.org; URL: http://www.emkf.org

Established in 1966 in MO. PRI-related activities began in 1995.
Donor(s): Ewing M. Kauffman.‡
Grantmaker type: Independent foundation
General financial activity (yr. ended 06/30/02): Assets, $1,687,454,656 (M); expenditures, $118,711,637; qualifying distributions, $77,808,297; giving activities include $47,295,893 for grants (high: $3,800,000; low: $100), $44,381 for 21 grants to individuals (high: $7,562; low: $23), $935,788 for 529 employee matching gifts and $500,000 for 1 PRI.
Cumulative PRI activity (through 06/30/02): Since 1995, the foundation has made 5 PRIs totaling $3,850,000. The currently outstanding PRI portfolio includes 1 PRI totaling $500,000 (high: $2,400,000; low: $200,000; average: $838,000). The typical outstanding PRI has a 1- to 10-year term with an average term of 4.25 years and earns 0 to 2.3 percent interest with an average of 1 percent.
General purpose and activities: The foundation works toward the vision of self-sufficient people in healthy communities. The mission is to research and identify unfulfilled needs of society and to develop, implement, and/or fund breakthrough solutions that have a lasting impact and offer people a choice and hope for the future.

The foundation's work is focused on two areas: Youth Development and Entrepreneurial Leadership. Youth Development investments focus on families, neighborhoods and education, primarily in Kansas City, MO and Kansas City, KS. The Kauffman Center for Entrepreneurial Leadership promotes the growth of entrepreneurship in America through educational programs for children and adults nationwide.
General fields of interest: Elementary/secondary education; early childhood education; economic development; community development, small businesses; social sciences.
Program-related investment (PRI) activity: The foundation has made PRIs on occasion for community development.
Types of PRI Support: Loans/promissory notes.
Limitations: Giving limited to the U.S., with emphasis on the bi-state metropolitan Kansas City area (KS/MO) for youth development. No support for political, social, fraternal, or arts organizations, and capital campaigns or construction projects. No grants to individuals, or for fund endowments, special events or international programs. PRI applications not accepted.
Publications: Annual report (including application guidelines), informational brochure (including application guidelines), grants list.
PRI program information: The foundation does not maintain a formal PRI program. The foundation makes PRIs occasionally.
Officers and Directors:* Michael F. Morrissey,* Chair.; Carl J. Schramm,* Pres. and C.E.O.; David C. Lady, Sr. V.P. and Chief Admin. Off.; John E. Tyler III, Sr. V.P. and Legal Counsel; Kurt H. Mueller, Sr. V.P., Kansas City's New Economy; Eugene R. Wilson, Sr. V.P., Devel.; Sharon Cohen, V.P. and Chief Comm. Off.; Paul Schofer, V.P. and Treas.; Rhonda Holman, V.P., Entrepreneurial Devel.; Lisa Klein, Ph.D., V.P., Early Education; Janine Lee, V.P., Mentoring; Susan Wally, V.P., K-12 Education; Judith A. Cone, V.P., Transition Planning; Gene A. Budig, Patricia M. Cloherty, Robert A. Compton, Richard C. Green, Jr., John A. Mayer, Jr., Anne Hodges Morgan, Ph.D., Brian O'Connell, Michie P. Slaughter.
Number of staff: 88 full-time professional; 3 part-time professional; 71 full-time support; 11 part-time support.
EIN: 436064859
PRI recipients:
145-1. Community Builders of Kansas City, Kansas City, MO, $2,400,000. Program-related investment to support Call Center in Mount Cleveland neighborhood of Kansas City in effort to combat community deterioration, lessen neighborhood tension, eliminate prejudices, lessen burdens of government, promote social welfare and support economic development in this area. Call Center is expected to result in significant job creation and is expected to serve as a magnet in attracting other for-profit entities to Brush Creek Corridor. 2000.
145-2. Habitat for Humanity of Kaw Valley, Kansas City, KS, $500,000. Program-related investment toward strengthening organization's internal financial stability and supporting program expansion. 2002.
145-3. Jazz District Redevelopment Corporation, Kansas City, MO, $500,000. Program-related investment to support redevelopment in historic Jazz District which will help combat community deterioration and promote social welfare within the Jazz District. 1999.

146
W. K. Kellogg Foundation

1 Michigan Ave. E.
Battle Creek, MI 49017-4058 (269) 968-1611
Contact: Debbie Rey, Supervisor of Proposal Processing
FAX: (269) 968-0413; URL: http://www.wkkf.org

Incorporated in 1930 in MI. PRI-related activities began in 1997.
Donor(s): W.K. Kellogg,‡ W.K. Kellogg Foundation Trust.
Grantmaker type: Independent foundation
General financial activity (yr. ended 08/31/02): Assets, $5,530,494,099 (M); gifts received, $786,224; expenditures, $259,669,905; qualifying distributions, $200,745,771; giving activities include $200,745,771 for grants; no PRIs paid.
Cumulative PRI activity (through 08/31/02): Since 1997, the foundation has made 2 PRIs totaling $3,000,000. The currently outstanding PRI portfolio includes 2 PRIs totaling $3,000,000 (high: $2,000,000; low: $1,000,000). The typical outstanding PRI has an average term of 10 years, and earns an average of 1 percent interest.
General purpose and activities: The W.K. Kellogg Foundation was established in 1930 to help people help themselves through the practical application of knowledge and resources to improve their quality of life and that of future generations. The foundation targets its grants toward specific focal points or areas. These include: health; food systems and rural development; youth and education; and philanthropy and voluntarism. Learn from the knowledge, experiences, and lessons learned by all of its projects as they apply to leadership, information and communication technology, capitalizing on diversity, and social and economic community development. Grants are concentrated in the United States, Latin America and the Caribbean, and in the countries of Botswana, Lesotho, Mozambique, South Africa, Swaziland, and Zimbabwe.
General fields of interest: Early childhood education; elementary school/education; secondary school/education; health sciences school/education; adult/continuing education; education; health care, support services; health care; health associations; agriculture; agriculture/food; youth development, services; youth, services; aging, centers & services; minorities/immigrants, centers & services; community development, neighborhood development; rural development; community development; voluntarism promotion; computer science; international studies;

leadership development; minorities; African Americans/Blacks; aging.
General international interests: Caribbean; Botswana; Lesotho; Mozambique; South Africa; Swaziland; Zimbabwe; Latin America.
Program-related investment (PRI) activity: The foundation makes loans to economic development agencies and organizations serving small business entrepreneurs.
Types of PRI Support: Loans/promissory notes.
Limitations: Giving primarily in the U.S., Latin America and the Caribbean, and the south African countries of Botswana, Lesotho, South Africa, Swaziland, Zimbabwe and Mozambique. No support for religious purposes or for capital facilities. No grants to individuals (except through fellowship programs), or for endowment funds, development campaigns, films, equipment, publications, conferences, or radio and television programs unless they are an integral part of a project already being funded; no grants for operating budgets, or capital facilities. The foundation accepts applications for PRIs.
Publications: Annual report (including application guidelines), informational brochure (including application guidelines), newsletter, occasional report, financial statement, application guidelines, program policy statement.
PRI program information: Applications should include proposal including cash flows and payback ability. The foundation maintains a formal PRI program. The foundation makes PRIs occasionally.
Officers and Trustees:* William C. Richardson, Ph.D.,* Pres. and C.E.O.; Gregory A. Lyman, Sr. V.P. and Corp. Secy.; Anne C. Petersen, Sr. V.P., Progs.; La June J. Montgomery-Talley, V.P., Finance and Treas.; Richard M. Foster, V.P., Progs.; Marguerite Johnson, V.P., Progs.; Paul J. Lawler, V.P. and C.I.O.; Robert F. Long, V.P., Progs.; Gail D. McClure, V.P., Progs.; Shirley D. Bowser, Dorothy A. Johnson, Fred P. Keller, Hanmin Liu, Russell G. Mawby, Cynthia H. Milligan, Wenda Weekes Moore, Howard F. Sims, Jonathan T. Walton, Joseph M. Stewart.
Number of staff: 119 full-time professional; 1 part-time professional; 77 full-time support.
EIN: 381359264
PRI recipients:

146-1. Coastal Enterprises, Wiscasset, ME, $2,000,000. Loan to strengthen rural community organizations by increasing their access to investment capital and technical assistance activities. 1999.

146-2. Coastal Enterprises, Wiscasset, ME, $800,000. Program-related investment to provide technical assistance and permanent loan fund capital to strengthen rural community organizations by increasing their access to investment capital and technical assistance activities. 1999.

146-3. Northern Economic Initiatives Corporation, Marquette, MI, $1,050,000. Loan to provide technical assistance and permanent loan fund capital as part of effort to strengthen capacity of rural loan fund to increase employment and business development in Upper Peninsula of Michigan. 1999.

146-4. Northern Economic Initiatives Corporation, Marquette, MI, $1,000,000. Loan to strengthen capacity of rural loan fund to increase employment and business development in Upper Peninsula of Michigan. 1999.

147

Harris and Eliza Kempner Fund, Inc.

2201 Market St., Ste. 601
Galveston, TX 77550-1529 (409) 762-1603
Contact: Elaine R. Perachio, Exec. Dir.
FAX: (409) 762-5435; E-mail: information@kempnerfund.org; URL: http://www.kempnerfund.org

Established in 1946 in TX; incorporated in 2001.
PRI-related activities began in 1992.
Donor(s): Various interests and members of the Kempner family.
Grantmaker type: Independent foundation
General financial activity (yr. ended 12/31/01): Assets, $41,263,559 (M); gifts received, $6,128; expenditures, $1,903,883; qualifying distributions, $2,175,222; giving activities include $1,373,627 for 146 grants (high: $180,000; low: $1,000; average: $1,000–$25,000), $255,877 for 502 employee matching gifts and $271,339 for 49 loans to individuals; no PRIs paid.
Cumulative PRI activity (through 12/31/01): Since 1992, the foundation has made 8 PRIs totaling $360,000. The currently outstanding PRI portfolio includes 2 PRIs totaling $64,689 (high: $100,000; low: $25,000; average: $45,000). The typical outstanding PRI has a 10- to 15-year term and earns 2 to 5 percent interest with an average of 3.12 percent.
General purpose and activities: Support primarily for human services, arts and humanities, education, community development, and Jewish issues in the Galveston, TX area, and a small allocation for international issues.
General fields of interest: Visual arts; museums; performing arts; dance; theater; humanities; history & archaeology; historic preservation/historical societies; arts/cultural programs; early childhood education; child development, education; elementary school/education; secondary school/education; higher education; medical school/education; adult education—literacy, basic skills & GED; reading; education; natural resources conservation & protection; environment; family planning; health care; substance abuse, services; mental health/crisis services; health associations; cancer; heart & circulatory diseases; biomedicine; medical research; cancer research; heart & circulatory research; crime/law enforcement; food services; housing/shelter, development; youth development, services; human services; youth, services; child development, services; hospices; minorities/immigrants, centers & services; homeless, human services; international economic development; international relief; international affairs; race/intergroup relations; community development; federated giving programs; economics; population studies;

leadership development; Jewish agencies & temples; minorities; Native Americans/American Indians; disabled; economically disadvantaged; homeless.
General international interests: Africa; Mexico.
Program-related investment (PRI) activity: Historically, the foundation has made PRIs in arts and cultural programs.
Types of PRI Support: Loans/promissory notes.
Limitations: Giving primarily in Galveston County, TX. No grants to individuals (except for student loans), non-U.S. based organizations, fundraising benefits, or for direct mail solicitations. PRIs are trustee originated. PRI applications not accepted.
Publications: Annual report (including application guidelines).
PRI program information: The foundation maintains a formal PRI program. The foundation makes PRIs on a frequent but not annual basis.
Officers and Trustees:* Robert L.K. Lynch,* Chair.; John Thornton Currie,* Vice-Chair.; Barbara Weston Sasser,* Secy.; Peter Kempner Thompson, M.D.,* Treas.; Elaine R. Perachio, Exec. Dir.; Hetta Towler Kempner, Isaac Herbert Kempner III, James Lee Kempner, Lyda Ann Quinn Thomas, Daniel Kempner Thorne.
Number of staff: 2 part-time professional; 1 full-time support; 1 part-time support.
EIN: 760680130

148
The Robert S. and Grayce B. Kerr Foundation, Inc.
P.O. Box, 20000, PMB 25106
Jackson, WY 83001-7000
Contact: William G. Kerr, Pres., or Sarah J. Lacy, Admin. Asst.

Chartered in 1986 in OK.
Donor(s): Grayce B. Kerr Flynn.‡
Grantmaker type: Independent foundation
General financial activity (yr. ended 12/31/00): Assets, $36,748,229 (M); expenditures, $1,650,864; qualifying distributions, $1,758,938; giving activities include $1,240,458 for grants (average: $5,000–$10,000) and $330,169 for 5 PRIs.
Cumulative PRI activity (through 12/31/00): Since beginning PRI activity, the foundation has made PRIs totaling $1,411,013.
General purpose and activities: Giving limited to organizations that benefit the specified fields of interest and geographic affiliations of the foundation.
General fields of interest: Arts education; natural resources conservation & protection; wildlife preservation & protection.
Program-related investment (PRI) activity: The foundation makes PRIs in the form of artwork leased to a museum at nominal cost.
Types of PRI Support: Charitable use assets.
Limitations: Applications not accepted. Giving primarily in OK and WY; some giving also in OH. No grants to individuals, or for endowments, annual campaigns, memberships, or medical or scientific research. PRI applications not accepted.
PRI program information: The foundation does not maintain a formal PRI program. The foundation makes PRIs occasionally.
Officers and Trustees:* William G. Kerr,* Chair. and Pres.; Joffa Kerr, Sr.,* V.P.; Mara Kerr,* Secy.; James G. Anderson,* Treas.
Number of staff: 1 part-time professional.
EIN: 731256123
PRI recipients:
148-1. National Museum of Wildlife Art, Jackson, WY, $104,689. Program-related investment in the form of artwork, loaned to museum. 2000.
148-2. National Museum of Wildlife Art, Jackson, WY, $100,000. Program-related investment in the form of artwork, loaned to museum. 2000.
148-3. National Museum of Wildlife Art, Jackson, WY, $100,000. Program-related investment in the form of artwork, loaned to museum. 2000.
148-4. National Museum of Wildlife Art, Jackson, WY, $25,000. Program-related investment in the form of artwork, loaned to museum. 2000.
148-5. National Museum of Wildlife Art, Jackson, WY, $85,000. Program-related investment in the form of artwork, loaned to museum. 1999.

149
Khesed Foundation
c/o The Northern Trust Co.
50 S. La Salle St., Ste. L-5
Chicago, IL 60675

Established in 2001 in IL.
Donor(s): Janet Willis, Scott Willis.
Grantmaker type: Independent foundation
General financial activity (yr. ended 01/31/02): Assets, $7,455,420 (M); gifts received, $9,398,996; expenditures, $522,584; qualifying distributions, $1,520,000; giving activities include $520,000 for 2 grants (high: $400,000; low: $120,000) and $1,000,000 for 1 PRI.
General purpose and activities: Giving primarily to Christian ministries.
General fields of interest: Christian agencies & churches.
Program-related investment (PRI) activity: The foundation has made a PRI, in the form of a promissory note, to a Bible league.
Types of PRI Support: Loans/promissory notes.
Limitations: Applications not accepted. Giving primarily in IL. No grants to individuals.
Directors: Amy Willis Moody, Daniel Willis, Janet Willis, Scott Willis, Toby Willis.
EIN: 260036863
PRI recipients:
149-1. Bible League, South Holland, IL, $1,000,000. Promissory note. 2002.

150

The Knapp Foundation, Inc.
P.O. Box O
St. Michaels, MD 21663 (410) 745-5660
Contact: Ruth M. Capranica, V.P. and Secy.

Incorporated in 1929 in NC.
Donor(s): Joseph Palmer Knapp.‡
Grantmaker type: Independent foundation
General financial activity (yr. ended 12/31/01): Assets, $25,694,413 (M); expenditures, $713,140; qualifying distributions, $597,950; giving activities include $490,923 for 31 grants (high: $99,530; low: $500); no PRIs paid.
Cumulative PRI activity (through 12/31/01): Since beginning PRI activity, the foundation has made 1 PRI totaling $18,016.
General purpose and activities: Grants primarily for conservation and preservation of wildlife and wildfowl, and for assistance to college and university libraries in the purchasing of reading materials and equipment to improve education.
General fields of interest: Higher education; libraries/library science; wildlife preservation & protection.
Program-related investment (PRI) activity: The foundation holds MD property as a habitat for waterfowl and wildlife. Improvements on the property are handled as PRIs.
Types of PRI Support: Charitable use assets.
Limitations: Giving limited to the U.S., primarily in the eastern region, including CT, FL, GA, MA, MD, ME, NC, NH, NJ, NY, PA, RI, SC, VA, and VT. No support for foreign projects. No grants to individuals, or for endowment or building funds, operating budgets, or research. PRI support limited to MD. PRI applications not accepted.
Publications: Application guidelines.
PRI program information: The foundation does not maintain a formal PRI program. The foundation makes PRIs occasionally.
Officers and Trustees:* Antoinette P. Vojvoda,* Pres.; Ruth M. Capranica,* V.P. and Secy.; Steven F. Capranica,* Treas.; Krista L. Hodgkin, Margaret P. Newcombe, Sylvia V. Penny.
Number of staff: 1 part-time professional.
EIN: 136001167

151

John S. and James L. Knight Foundation
(Formerly Knight Foundation)
Wachovia Financial Ctr., Ste. 3300
200 S. Biscayne Blvd.
Miami, FL 33131-2349 (305) 908-2600
Contact: Attn: Grant Request
Additional tel. for publication requests: (305) 908-2629; E-mail: publications@knightfdn.org, web@knightfdn.org; URL: http://www.knightfdn.org

Incorporated in 1950 in OH. PRI-related activities began in 1988.
Donor(s): John S. Knight,‡ James L. Knight,‡ and their families.
Grantmaker type: Independent foundation
General financial activity (yr. ended 12/31/02): Assets, $1,718,236,238 (M); expenditures, $96,222,793; qualifying distributions, $85,617,981; giving activities include $85,617,981 for grants; no PRIs paid.
Cumulative PRI activity (through 12/31/02): Since 1988, the foundation has made 9 PRIs totaling $7,325,000. The currently outstanding PRI portfolio includes 2 PRIs totaling $2,629,854 (high: $500,000; low: $250,000; average: $500,000). The typical outstanding PRI has a 1- to 3-year term with an average term of 3 years and earns 7.50 to 11 percent interest with an average of 9 percent.
General purpose and activities: The foundation promotes excellence in journalism worldwide and invests in the vitality of 26 U.S. communities. Focus is on two signature programs, Journalism and Knight Community Partners, which includes education, well-being of children and families, housing and community development, economic development, civic engagement/positive human relations, and vitality of cultural life, each area with its own eligibility requirements. A third program, The National Venture Fund, supports innovative opportunities and initiatives at the national level that relate directly or indirectly to Knight's work in its 26 communities.
General fields of interest: Journalism & publishing; arts/cultural programs; education; housing/shelter, development; housing/shelter; children, services; family services; race/intergroup relations; community development, neighborhood development; economic development; public affairs, citizen participation.
Program-related investment (PRI) activity: The foundation began making PRIs in 1988 on a limited basis to fund the development of low-cost housing. PRIs have provided support for nonprofit intermediaries (e.g., loan funds) participating in the National Community Development Initiative (NCDI). PRIs currently support community development and low-income housing.
Types of PRI Support: Loans/promissory notes, interim financing.
Limitations: Giving limited to projects serving the 26 communities where the Knight brothers published newspapers for Community Initiatives Program and local grants: Long Beach and San Jose, CA, Boulder, CO, Boca Raton, Bradenton, Miami, and Tallahassee, FL, Columbus, Macon, and Milledgeville, GA, Fort Wayne and Gary, IN, Wichita, KS, Lexington, KY, Detroit, MI, Duluth and St. Paul, MN, Biloxi, MS, Charlotte, NC, Grand Forks, ND, Akron, OH, Philadelphia and State College, PA, Columbia and Myrtle Beach, SC, and Aberdeen, SD;international for Journalism. No support for organizations whose mission is to prevent, eradicate and/or alleviate the effects of a specific disease; hospitals, unless for community-wide capital campaigns; activities to propagate a religious faith or restricted to one religion or denomination; political candidates; international programs, except U.S.-based organizations supporting free press around the world;

charities operated by service clubs; or activities that are the responsibility of government (the foundation will in selective cases, join with units of government in supporting special projects). No grants to individuals, or generally for fundraising events; second requests for previously funded capital campaigns; operating deficits; films, videos, or television programs; honoraria for distinguished guests-except in initiatives of the foundation in all three cases; a second proposal from any institution or organization that has applied for support in the last 12 months, whether the result of the previous application was positive or negative; group travel; memorials; medical research; or conferences. PRI applications not accepted.
Publications: Annual report (including application guidelines), newsletter, occasional report, informational brochure.
PRI program information: The foundation does not maintain a formal PRI program. The foundation makes PRIs occasionally.
Officers and Trustees:* W. Gerald Austen, M.D.,* Chair.; Jill Ker Conway,* Vice-Chair.; Hodding Carter III,* C.E.O. and Pres.; Penelope McPhee, V.P., Secy., and Chief Prog. Off.; Beatriz G. Clossick, V.P., Acctg. and Treas.; Belinda Turner Lawrence, V.P. and C.A.O.; Timothy J. Crowe, V.P. and C.I.O.; Larry Meyer, V.P., Comm.; Juan J. Martinez, Cont.; Cesar L. Alvarez, Creed C. Black, Robert Briggs,* Marjorie Knight Crane, Paul S. Grogan, Gordon E. Heffern, Michael Maidenberg, Rolfe Neill, Mariam C. Noland, Beverly Knight Olson, John W. Rogers, Jr.
Number of staff: 19 full-time professional; 13 full-time support; 2 part-time support.
EIN: 650464177
PRI recipients:

151-1. California Neuropsychology Services, San Rafael, CA, $325,000. Program-related investment for Talking Fingers, Inc. to publish and market support materials to enhance Read, Write and Type instructional software. 1999.

152
Lannan Foundation

313 Read St.
Santa Fe, NM 87501 (505) 986-8160
Contact: Linda Hughes, Admin.
FAX: (505) 986-8195; FAX: (505) 954-5143;
URL: http://www.lannan.org

Established in 1960 in IL.
Donor(s): J. Patrick Lannan.‡
Grantmaker type: Independent foundation
General financial activity (yr. ended 12/31/01): Assets, $223,109,486 (M); expenditures, $16,817,340; qualifying distributions, $20,017,961; giving activities include $8,790,289 for 149 grants (high: $1,000,000; low: $1,000), $910,382 for 30 grants to individuals (high: $200,000; low: $5,312; average: $25,000–$50,000), $17,030 for 16 employee matching gifts, $1,106,129 for 3 foundation-administered programs and $3,293 for 1 PRI.
Cumulative PRI activity (through 12/31/01): The currently outstanding PRI portfolio includes 2 PRIs totaling $525,000.
General purpose and activities: The foundation is a family foundation dedicated to cultural freedom, diversity and creativity through projects which support exceptional contemporary artists and writers, as well as inspired Native activists in rural indigenous communities. The foundation recognizes the profound and often unquantifiable value of the creative process and is willing to take risks and make substantial investments in ambitious and experimental thinking. Understanding that globalization threatens all cultures and ecosystems, the foundation is particularly interested in projects that encourage freedom of inquiry, imagination, and expression. The foundation supports this mission with long-term special projects requiring multi-year commitments of funding and technical assistance in the areas of contemporary visual art, literature, indigenous communities, and issues of cultural freedom.
General fields of interest: Visual arts; museums; literature; historic preservation/historical societies; arts/cultural programs; Native Americans/American Indians.
Program-related investment (PRI) activity: The foundation gives loans to educational and cultural programs.
Types of PRI Support: Loans/promissory notes, interim financing.
Limitations: Applications not accepted. No grants to individuals (except for Lannan Literary Awards), or for documentary film or video projects, performing arts or theater, or crafts or decorative arts. PRI applications not accepted.
PRI program information: The foundation does not maintain a formal PRI program. The foundation makes PRIs occasionally.
Officers and Directors:* J. Patrick Lannan, Jr.,* Pres.; Frank C. Lawler,* V.P. and Dir., Opers.; Ruth Simms, Cont.; Jaune Evans, Exec. Dir., Projs.; Marian P. Day, Meghan Ferrill, Sharon Ferrill, William Johnston, Sharron Lannan Korybut, John J. Lannan, John R. Lannan, Lawrence P. Lannan, Jr., Mary M. Plauche.
Number of staff: 8 full-time professional; 5 full-time support; 2 part-time support.
EIN: 366062451
PRI recipients:

152-1. Indian Law Resource Center, DC, $70,000. Loan for salary to hire Development Director. 1999.

152-2. Museum of Jurassic Technology, Culver City, CA, $650,000. Loan to assist museum in acquiring new facility. 1999.

152-3. Skystone Foundation, Skystone House, Flagstaff, AZ, $18,705. Mortgage payments on home of artist coordinating major art project. 2000.

152-4. Skystone Foundation, Flagstaff, AZ, $18,520. Loan for renovations at Coburn House. 1999.

152-5. Skystone Foundation, Flagstaff, AZ, $18,457. Mortgage payments on home occupied by artist coordinating major art project. 1999.

152-6. Washiw Itlu Gawgayay, Gardnerville, NV, $25,000. Loan for operating support for Immersion Language School. 1999.

153
Layne Foundation

29214 Whites Point Dr.
Rancho Palos Verdes, CA 90275-4644
(310) 544-4700
Contact: Wesley M. Mason, Pres.

Incorporated in 1927 in CA.
Grantmaker type: Independent foundation
General financial activity (yr. ended 12/31/01): Assets, $20,827,025 (M); expenditures, $257,594; qualifying distributions, $2,610,517; giving activities include $2,610,516 for 15 PRIs.
Cumulative PRI activity (through 12/31/01): The currently outstanding PRI portfolio includes a high PRI value of $1,600,000 and a low PRI value of $200,000. The typical outstanding PRI has an average term of 10 years, and earns an average of 10 percent interest.
General purpose and activities: Assistance limited to program-related investments in Christian churches and religious organizations in CA, principally for churches ineligible for loans from other sources.
General fields of interest: Christian agencies & churches.
Program-related investment (PRI) activity: The foundation provides PRI support to Christian churches and religious organizations and for Christian education, principally for churches ineligible for loans from other sources.
Limitations: Giving strictly limited to CA. Support strictly limited to CA.
PRI program information: The foundation makes PRIs on an annual basis.
Officers: Wesley M. Mason, Pres.; Lowell L. Semans, V.P.; Paul R. Nelson, Secy.-Treas.
Number of staff: 1 full-time professional.
EIN: 951765157
PRI recipients:

153-1. Apostolic Assembly of the Faith in Christ Jesus, Rancho Cucamonga, CA, $900,000. Program-related investment. 2000.
153-2. Apostolic Assembly of the Faith in Christ Jesus, Rancho Cucamonga, CA, $300,000. Program-related investment. 2000.
153-3. Apostolic Assembly of the Faith in Christ Jesus, Rancho Cucamonga, CA, $252,000. Loan. 1999.
153-4. Calvary Apostolic Church, Concord, CA, $1,150,000. Program-related investment. 2000.
153-5. Calvary Apostolic Church, Concord, CA, $58,000. Program-related investment. 2000.
153-6. Calvary Apostolic Tabernacle, Ontario, CA, $1,000,000. Program-related investment. 2000.
153-7. Charisma in Mission, East Los Angeles, CA, $417,000. Loan. 1999.
153-8. Church of Jesus Christ, San Diego, CA, $380,000. Loan. 1999.
153-9. First United Pentecostal Church, San Jose, CA, $2,400,000. Program-related investment. 2000.
153-10. Fountain of Truth Church, Fontana, CA, $430,000. Program-related investment. 2000.
153-11. Light of the World Christian Community Church, San Diego, CA, $41,605. Program-related investment. 2000.
153-12. Light of the World Christian Community Church, San Diego, CA, $23,862. Program-related investment. 2000.
153-13. North Park Apostolic Church, San Diego, CA, $844,851. Loan. 1999.
153-14. Regency Christian Center, Whittier, CA, $1,300,000. Program-related investment. 2000.
153-15. Revival Pentecostal Tabernacle, San Diego, CA, $600,000. Program-related investment. 2000.
153-16. Saint Stephens Church of God in Christ, San Diego, CA, $1,600,000. Loan. 1999.
153-17. South Bay Pentecostal Church, Chula Vista, CA, $702,588. Loan. 1999.
153-18. Visions of God Christian Fellowship, Spring Valley, CA, $24,704. Program-related investment. 2000.
153-19. Visions of God Christian Fellowship, Spring Valley, CA, $640,000. Loan. 1999.
153-20. Young Eun Korean Presbyterian Church, Whittier, CA, $36,025. Program-related investment. 2000.

154
Robert & Dee Leggett Foundation

P.O. Box 240
Great Falls, VA 22066
Contact: Robert N. Leggett, Jr., Pres.
FAX: (703) 430-9608; E-mail: rnleggett@aol.com

Established in 1999 in VA.
Donor(s): Robert Leggett, Dee C. Leggett.
Grantmaker type: Operating foundation
General financial activity (yr. ended 12/31/01): Assets, $3,857,648 (M); gifts received, $993,910; expenditures, $952,258; qualifying distributions, $1,055,858; giving activities include $385,478 for 35 grants (high: $21,117; low: $1,000) and $115,100 for 1 PRI.
General fields of interest: Education; environment; Christian agencies & churches; religion; economically disadvantaged.
Program-related investment (PRI) activity: The foundation has made a PRI in the form of preliminary construction costs and architectural fees for a non-profit conference and research center, with most of the land being placed under conservation easement.
Limitations: Applications not accepted. Giving primarily in the Blue Ridge region, VA. No grants to individuals.
Publications: Financial statement, informational brochure.
Officers: Robert "Bob" N. Leggett, Jr., Pres.; Dee C. Leggett, V.P.; Donna I. Measell, Secy.-Treas.

Directors: W. James Athearn, David James Chadwick, Laura L. Leggett, David Lillard, Charles W. Sloan.
Number of staff: 3 full-time professional; 1 part-time professional.
EIN: 541921311

155
Naftali Zvi Leshkowitz Memorial Foundation

270 Madison Ave., 17th Fl.
New York, NY 10016
Contact: C.H. Leshkowitz, Tr.

Established in 1986 in NY.
Donor(s): C.H. Leshkowitz, Joseph Leshkowitz.
Grantmaker type: Independent foundation
General financial activity (yr. ended 11/30/01): Assets, $1,415,509 (M); gifts received, $325,035; expenditures, $272,211; qualifying distributions, $260,655; giving activities include $260,655 for grants; no PRIs paid.
General purpose and activities: Giving primarily for education, human services, Jewish organizations and educational institutions.
General fields of interest: Education; human services; Jewish federated giving programs; Jewish agencies & temples.
Program-related investment (PRI) activity: The foundation makes loans to Jewish organizations and yeshivas.
Types of PRI Support: Loans/promissory notes.
Limitations: Applications not accepted. Giving primarily in NY. No grants to individuals. PRI support primarily in New York City, NY.
PRI program information: The foundation makes PRIs on a frequent but not annual basis.
Trustees: C.H. Leshkowitz, Joseph Leshkowitz.
EIN: 133394520

156
Libra Foundation

3 Canal Plz.
P.O. Box 17516
Portland, ME 04112-8516 (207) 879-6280
Contact: Owen W. Wells, Pres. and Secy.
FAX: (207) 879-6281; URL: http://www.librafoundation.org

Established in 1989 in ME.
Donor(s): Elizabeth B. Noyce.‡
Grantmaker type: Independent foundation
General financial activity (yr. ended 12/31/01): Assets, $278,929,244 (M); gifts received, $137,714,238; expenditures, $12,559,843; qualifying distributions, $24,168,571; giving activities include $10,396,470 for 123 grants (high: $2,435,000; low: $1,000; average: $5,000–$500,000) and $12,911,453 for 1 PRI.
General purpose and activities: Giving primarily for arts and culture, science, recreation and sports, human services, education, environment, and public/society benefit.
General fields of interest: Arts/cultural programs; education; recreation; human services; science; general charitable giving.
Program-related investment (PRI) activity: The foundation has made capital contributions to organizations to encourage community growth and create jobs in the local economy.
Types of PRI Support: Equity investments.
Limitations: Giving limited to ME. No grants to individuals.
Publications: Annual report, application guidelines, informational brochure (including application guidelines), grants list.
Officers and Trustees:* Owen W. Wells,* Pres. and Secy.; Craig N. Denekas, V.P.; Jere G. Michelson, C.F.O.; Henry G. Brooks,* Treas.; Pendred E. Noyce, William J. Ryan.
Number of staff: 1 full-time professional; 2 full-time support.
EIN: 046626994
PRI recipients:

156-1. Freshway, Inc., Presque Isle, ME, $12,911,453. Capital contribution to encourage community growth and create jobs in the local economy. 2001.
156-2. Freshway, Inc., Presque Isle, ME, $1,300,000. Capital contribution to encourage community growth and create jobs in the local economy. 2000.
156-3. Kent, Inc., Fort Kent, ME, $1,500,000. Capital contribution to encourage community growth and create jobs in the local economy. 2000.

157
The Lincy Foundation

150 S. Rodeo Dr., Ste. 250
Beverly Hills, CA 90212
Contact: James D. Aljian, Pres.

Established in 1989 in CA.
Grantmaker type: Independent foundation
General financial activity (yr. ended 09/30/02): Assets, $47,864,380 (M); gifts received, $52,149,542; expenditures, $49,532,454; qualifying distributions, $49,919,165; giving activities include $47,597,671 for 41 grants (high: $39,010,658; low: $2,000; average: $20,000–$100,000) and $528,838 for 1 PRI.
Cumulative PRI activity (through 09/30/02): The currently outstanding PRI portfolio includes 4 PRIs totaling $18,128,934.
General purpose and activities: Support primarily for Armenian charities, education, and human services.
General fields of interest: Arts/cultural programs; education; medical research; human services; aging, centers & services; international relief; religion; aging.
Program-related investment (PRI) activity: The foundation has made PRIs to the government of Armenia.
Types of PRI Support: Loans/promissory notes.

Limitations: Giving primarily in CA. No grants to individuals.
Officers and Directors:* James D. Aljian,* Chair. and Pres.; Harut Sassounian,* Vice-Chair.; Walter C. Hoffer, V.P.; Alex Yemenidjian,* V.P.; Anthony Mandekic,* Secy.-Treas. and C.F.O.; Kirk Kerkorian, Walter M. Sharp.
EIN: 954238697
PRI recipients:
157-1. Armenia, Government of, Yerevan, Armenia, $528,838. Loan. 2002.
157-2. Armenia, Government of, Yerevan, Armenia, $8,437,780. Loan. 2001.
157-3. Armenia, Government of, Yerevan, Armenia, $7,433,500. Loan receivable. 2000.
157-4. Armenia, Government of, Yerevan, Armenia, $3,032,825. Loan receivable. 1999.

158
John D. and Catherine T. MacArthur Foundation
140 S. Dearborn St., Ste. 1100
Chicago, IL 60603-5285 (312) 726-8000
Contact: Richard Kaplan, Asst. V.P., Institutional Research and Grants Mgmt.
FAX: (312) 920-6258; TDD: (312) 920-6285; E-mail: 4answers@macfound.org; URL: http://www.macfound.org

Incorporated in 1970 in IL. PRI-related activities began in 1983.
Donor(s): John D. MacArthur,‡ Catherine T. MacArthur.‡
Grantmaker type: Independent foundation
General financial activity (yr. ended 12/31/01): Assets, $4,215,930,831 (M); expenditures, $234,950,492; qualifying distributions, $203,974,660; giving activities include $148,029,162 for 1,094 grants (high: $5,212,000; low: $2,500), $17,455,833 for 134 grants to individuals, $2,460,331 for 134 employee matching gifts and $10,000,000 for 8 PRIs.
Cumulative PRI activity (through 12/31/01): The currently outstanding PRI portfolio includes 122 PRIs totaling $109,800,000 (high: $5,000,000; average: $1,000,000). The typical outstanding PRI has a 5- to 15-year term with an average term of 10 years and earns 0 to 5 percent interest with an average of 3 percent.
General purpose and activities: The foundation is a private, independent grantmaking institution dedicated to helping groups and individuals foster lasting improvement in the human condition. The foundation seeks the development of healthy individuals and effective communities; peace within and among nations; responsible choices about human reproduction; and a global ecosystem capable of supporting healthy human societies. The foundation pursues this mission by supporting research, policy development, dissemination, education and training, and practice.
General fields of interest: Media/communications; film/video; education, public education; early childhood education; higher education; natural resources conservation & protection; health care, reproductive health; health care; mental health/crisis services, public policy; crime/violence prevention, youth; gun control; international economic development; international peace/security; foreign policy; international affairs; community development, neighborhood development; public policy, research.
General international interests: Russia; Africa; Nigeria; Mexico; India.
Program-related investment (PRI) activity: The foundation actively seeks opportunities to make PRIs in order to expand the range and impact of its programs. The purposes for which the foundation makes PRIs are essentially the purposes of its grantmaking programs. The foundation usually invests in intermediary organizations that subsequently make loans to individual projects. It also considers direct investment in projects closely related to the foundation's grantmaking goals and not served by intermediary organizations. In the field of community and economic development, the foundation has used PRIs to help capitalize organizations that finance business development, community facilities, and affordable housing. Two current priority areas for PRI activity are: Affordable Housing Preservation and Community development Venture Capital.
Types of PRI Support: Loans/promissory notes, equity investments, capitalizing loan funds/other intermediaries, linked deposits, charitable use assets.
Limitations: Giving on a national and international basis, with emphasis on Chicago, IL. No support for churches or religious programs, political activities or campaigns. No grants for capital or endowment funds, equipment purchases, plant construction, conferences, publications, media productions, debt retirement, development campaigns, fundraising appeals, scholarships, or fellowships (other than those sponsored by the foundation). PRIs support U.S. and overseas organizations. Both nonprofit and for-profit organizations are eligible. However, the foundation rarely invests directly in individual community development projects located outside of Chicago or Palm Beach County, FL. The foundation does not make PRIs for the purchase or construction of buildings, except as part of a community development program. The foundation accepts applications for PRIs.
Publications: Annual report, informational brochure (including application guidelines), newsletter.
PRI program information: To apply for a program-related investment, organizations should submit a two- to five-page letter of inquiry along with a recent financial statement. The foundation maintains a formal PRI program. The foundation makes PRIs on an annual basis.
Officers and Directors:* Sara Lawrence-Lightfoot,* Chair.; Jonathan F. Fanton,* Pres.; Arthur Sussman, V.P. and Secy.; Lyn Hutton, V.P. and C.F.O; William E. Lowry, V.P., Human Resources; Joshua J. Mintz, V.P. and Genl. Counsel; Julia M. Stasch, V.P. Progs., Human and Community Devel.; Mitchel B. Wallerstein, V.P. Progs., Global Security and Sustainability; Marc P. Yanchura, Treas.; Sharon R. Burns,

C.I.O.; Lloyd Axworthy, John Seeley Brown, Drew Saunders Days III, Robert E. Denham, William H. Foege, M.D., Jamie S. Gorelick, Mary Graham, John P. Holdren, Mario J. Molina, George A. Ranney, Jr., Thomas C. Theobold.
Number of staff: 99 full-time professional; 88 full-time support.
EIN: 237093598
PRI recipients:

158-1. Boston Community Capital, Boston, MA, $2,000,000. Equity investment in BCLF Ventures, community development venture capital fund serving low-income people and communitie in metropolitan Boston and the northeastern U.S. 2002.

158-2. Calvert Social Investment Foundation, Bethesda, MD, $100,000. Program-related investment to support research on nonprofit capital markets and strategic planning. 2002.

158-3. Calvert Social Investment Foundation, Bethesda, MD, $50,000. Program-related investment for strategic planning. 2001.

158-4. Chicago Community Loan Fund, Chicago, IL, $500,000. Program-related investment for community development lending in low-income communities. 1999.

158-5. ChicagoLand Real Estate Development Institution, Chicago, IL, $1,000,000. Program-related investment to establish institution as financial intermediary so it may facilitate redevelopment of brownfield sites in Chicago's lower-income communities. Grant made through The Delta Institute. 1999.

158-6. Coalition of Community Development Financial Institutions, Philadelphia, PA, $200,000. Program-related investment to support policy analysis, communications, and other activities to strengthen U.S. community development finance field. 2002.

158-7. Coastal Enterprises, Wiscasset, ME, $1,000,000. Equity investment in CEI Community Ventures Fund, LLC, New Markets Venture Capital Company targeting low-income areas of Maine and neighboring states. 2002.

158-8. Coastal Enterprises, Wiscasset, ME, $1,000,000. Equity investment in Coastal Ventures II LLC, community development venture capital fund focusing on quality employment opportunities for low-income people and sustainable enterprises throughout New England. 2002.

158-9. Community Development Venture Capital Alliance, NYC, NY, $400,000. Program-related investment for general operations in support of training, research, and other activities that promote the use of venture capital tools to advance the livelihood of low-income people and revitalize economically distressed communities. 2002.

158-10. Community Reinvestment Fund, Minneapolis, MN, $5,000,000. Loan to increase availability of private investment capital for community economic development and affordable housing nationwide through expansion of secondary-market loan purchases and other financial innovations. 2002.

158-11. Corporation for Enterprise Development (CFED), DC, $800,000. Program-related investment to provide continued support for Community Development Financial Institutions Data Project. 2002.

158-12. Corporation for Enterprise Development (CFED), DC, $250,000. Program-related investment to support product development and innovation among leading community development financial institutions in the U.S. 2002.

158-13. Corporation for Enterprise Development (CFED), DC, $1,000,000. Program-related investment for Community Development Financial Institutions Data Project. 2001.

158-14. Delaware Valley Community Reinvestment Fund, Philadelphia, PA, $3,000,000. Equity investment in community development venture capital fund targeting high-growth companies with potential to generate significant financial returns and job opportunities in urban centers of the Mid-Atlantic region. 2002.

158-15. Enterprise Corporation of the Delta, Jackson, MS, $2,000,000. Program-related investment for economic development in the Mississippi Delta region. 1999.

158-16. Enterprise Foundation, Columbia, MD, $750,000. Program-related investment for National Community Development Initiative. 2001.

158-17. Environmental Enterprises Assistance Fund, Arlington, VA, $1,000,000. Program-related investment to promote use of photovoltaic energy in developing countries. 2001.

158-18. Florida Community Loan Fund, Orlando, FL, $1,000,000. Program-related investment to support lending to community-based organizations in southern Florida. 1999.

158-19. Housing Partnership Network, Boston, MA, $2,500,000. Program-related investment to provide capital for affordable housing preservation and development efforts. 2001.

158-20. Illinois Facilities Fund, Chicago, IL, $1,000,000. Program-related investment in support of bridge loans to Chicago nonprofit organizations that are developing facilities. 1999.

158-21. Kentucky Highlands Investment Corporation, London, KY, $2,000,000. Program-related investment for work to create employment opportunities in rural Kentucky through use of venture capital or equity investments in growing regional businesses. 1999.

158-22. Local Initiatives Support Corporation (LISC), NYC, NY, $2,250,000. Program-related investment for community development in 23 cities. 2001.

158-23. Local Initiatives Support Corporation (LISC), West Palm Beach, FL, $1,000,000. Program-related investment to finance projects to yield homeownership units for low- to moderate-income buyers, a range of rental housing and community amenities such as parks and child care facilities in Florida. 1999.

158-24. Low Income Housing Fund, Oakland, CA, $1,000,000. Program-related investment to finance projects serving low-income and special needs populations. 1999.

158-25. Media Development Loan Fund, NYC, NY, $1,000,000. Program-related investment to provide new investment capital to expand impact in emerging democracies. 2000.

158-26. Mercy Housing, Denver, CO, $3,000,000. Program-related investment for development and preservation of affordable rental housing. 2001.

158-27. National Community Capital Association, Philadelphia, PA, $500,000. Program-related investment for general operations in support of training, research, policy analysis, product development and other activities that increase capital resources and other opportunities for economically disadvantaged people and communities. 2002.

158-28. National Community Investment Fund, Chicago, IL, $200,000. Program-related investment to increase financial resources and effectiveness of depository community development financial institutions in the U.S. 2002.

158-29. National Housing Trust, Enterprise Preservation Corporation, DC, $1,500,000. Program-related investment for efforts to preserve affordable housing for low-income households. 2000.

158-30. National Housing Trust Enterprise Preservation Corporation, DC, $4,000,000. Program-related investment to preserve affordable rental housing. 2001.

158-31. Neighborhood Capital Corporation, Cleveland, OH, $2,000,000. To provide capital for affordable housing and development efforts. 2001.

158-32. Neighborhood Housing Services of Chicago, Chicago, IL, $450,000. Program-related investment for management information systems to improve organizational performance and support expanded financial services for low-income and minority Chicago residents. 2002.

158-33. Northeast Ventures Development Fund, Duluth, MN, $2,000,000. Loan to community development venture capital fund catalyzing economic development and entrepreneurial culture in Northeast Minnesota. 2002.

158-34. Organic Commodity Project, Cambridge, MA, $2,000,000. Program-related investment to promote environmentally sustainable production of cacao in developing countries. 2001.

158-35. Organic Commodity Project, Cambridge, MA, $1,000,000. Program-related investment for work to increase number and capacity of organic chocolate producers and to expand organic chocolate market. 1999.

158-36. Preservation of Affordable Housing (POAH), Boston, MA, $3,000,000. Loan to national organization dedicated to preserving rental housing properties affordable to low-income families and seniors. 2002.

158-37. Rocky Mountain Mutual Housing Association, Denver, CO, $2,500,000. Program-related investment for efforts to develop and preserve affordable rental housing. 2001.

158-38. Southern Appalachian Fund, Oak Ridge, TN, $1,000,000. Equity investment in New Markets Venture Capital Company affiliated with Kentucky Highlands Investment Corporation, fostering business development in designated low-income communities across Southern Appalachia. 2002.

158-39. Sustainable Jobs Development Corporation, Durham, NC, $1,000,000. Program-related investment for start-up support for recycling and environmental businesses that generate jobs in low-income communities. 1999.

158-40. Terra Capital Investors, Sao Paulo, Brazil, $1,000,000. Program-related investment for Terra Capital Fund which will make investments in Latin American businesses that involve sustainable use of natural resources and foster preservation of biological diversity. 1999.

158-41. Union de Credito Estatal de Productores, Oaxaca, Mexico, $1,000,000. Program-related investment to finance commercial coffee activity during harvest season and for member needs, commercial pepper production and subsistence corn production during non-harvest season. Grant made through Shorebank Corporation. 1999.

159

The Maclellan Foundation, Inc.

Provident Bldg., Ste. 501
Chattanooga, TN 37402 (423) 755-1366
Contact: Hugh O. Maclellan, Jr., Pres.
FAX: (423) 755-1640; E-mail: info@maclellan.net;
URL: http://www.maclellanfdn.org

Incorporated in 1945 in DE; reincorporated in TN in 1992.
Donor(s): Robert J. Maclellan,‡ and members of the Maclellan family.
Grantmaker type: Independent foundation
General financial activity (yr. ended 12/31/01): Assets, $403,953,114 (M); expenditures, $20,299,571; qualifying distributions, $18,705,860; giving activities include $17,796,860 for 23 grants (high: $2,200,950; low: $55; average: $1,000–$100,000); no PRIs paid.
General purpose and activities: Grants largely for Christian higher education, Protestant missions support, religious associations, and youth agencies.
General fields of interest: Higher education; children & youth, services; Protestant agencies & churches.
General international interests: Eastern Europe; Africa; Latin America; Asia; Middle East.
Program-related investment (PRI) activity: The foundation makes interest free loans to Christian organizations.
Types of PRI Support: Loans/promissory notes.

Limitations: Giving nationally, with emphasis on the Chattanooga, TN, area; giving internationally in Eastern Europe, Asia, Africa, Latin America, and the Middle East. No grants to individuals, or for emergency funds, deficit financing, land acquisition, endowment funds, research, demonstration projects, publications, or conferences; generally no grants for renovations.
Officers and Trustees:* Hugh O. Maclellan, Jr.,* Pres.; Charlotte M. Heffner,* V.P.; Thomas H. McCallie III, Secy. and Exec. Dir.; Robert H. Maclellan,* Treas.; Ron Blue, Frank A. Brock, G. Richard Hostetter, Pat MacMillan.
Number of staff: 3 full-time professional; 6 full-time support.
EIN: 626041468
PRI recipients:
159-1. Progressive Vision, San Clemente, CA, $650,000. Interest-free loan. 1999.

160
J. F Maddox Foundation

P.O. Box 2588
Hobbs, NM 88241-2588 (505) 393-6338
Contact: Robert J. Reid, Exec. Dir.
FAX: (505) 397-7266; URL: http://www.jfmaddox.org

Established in 1963 in NM. PRI-related activities began in 1994.
Donor(s): J.F Maddox,‡ Mabel S. Maddox.‡
Grantmaker type: Independent foundation
General financial activity (yr. ended 12/31/01): Assets, $157,524,045 (M); gifts received, $1,929; expenditures, $10,390,751; qualifying distributions, $7,351,532; giving activities include $6,279,836 for 166 grants (high: $1,548,267; low: $1,250; average: $2,500–$1,548,267), $153,323 for 23 grants to individuals (high: $36,252; low: $1,250; average: $2,500–$15,000), $10,000 for 1 in-kind gift and $14,750 for 17 loans to individuals; no PRIs paid.
Cumulative PRI activity (through 12/31/01): Since 1994, the foundation has made 8 PRIs totaling $1,457,185. The currently outstanding PRI portfolio includes 5 PRIs totaling $869,790 (high: $372,911; low: $45,000; average: $174,000). The typical outstanding PRI has a 5- to 10-year term with an average term of 8 years.
General purpose and activities: The mission of the J.F Maddox Foundation is to significantly improve the quality of life in southeastern New Mexico by investing in education, community development, and other social programs. The foundation particularly supports initiatives driven by innovative leadership, designed for substantial impact, and committed to lasting value.
General fields of interest: Elementary/secondary school reform; higher education; education; substance abuse, services; human services; children & youth, services; aging, centers & services; aging.
Program-related investment (PRI) activity: The foundation has made loans where, in it's judgement, doing so was more appropriate than making grants. The foundation does not have a loan program, instead utilizes loans as part of its overall grant strategy.
Types of PRI Support: Loans/promissory notes.
Limitations: Giving primarily in southeast NM; scholarships limited to Lea County, NM, residents. No support for private foundations. No grants for operating budgets, endowment funds, or grants to individuals, other than scholarships. PRI support limited to southeast NM. The foundation accepts applications for PRIs.
Publications: Annual report (including application guidelines), biennial report.
PRI program information: The foundation does not maintain a formal PRI program. The foundation makes PRIs occasionally.
Officers and Directors:* James M. Maddox,* Pres.; Don Maddox,* V.P.; Robert J. Reid, Secy.-Treas. and Exec. Dir.; Patty A. Robbins, Cont.; Harry H. Lynch, Benjamin W. Maddox, John L. Maddox, Thomas M. Maddox, Ann M. Utterback.
Number of staff: 3 full-time professional; 2 part-time professional; 4 full-time support; 2 part-time support.
EIN: 756023767
PRI recipients:
160-1. Habitat for Humanity, Hobbs, Hobbs, NM, $70,500. Loan for program support. 2000.
160-2. Opportunity House, Hobbs, NM, $99,900. Loan, interest-free, to purchase property which includes residential facility. 1999.
160-3. Reins for Life, Dexter, NM, $127,000. Loan to purchase real property and make improvements to house program activities. 1999.

161
The Maine Community Foundation, Inc.

245 Main St.
Ellsworth, ME 04605 (207) 667-9735
PRI Contact: James E. Geary, C.F.O./V.P, Fin. Svcs.
Portland mailing address: 1 Monument Way, Ste. 200, P.O. Box 7380, Portland, ME 04112; Additional tels.: (207) 761-2440, (877) 700-6800; FAX: (207) 667-0447; E-mail: info@mainecf.org; grants@mainecf.org; URL: http://www.mainecf.org

Incorporated in 1983 in ME.
Grantmaker type: Community foundation
General financial activity (yr. ended 12/31/00): Assets, $95,872,327 (M); gifts received, $25,561,777; expenditures, $8,280,072; giving activities include $6,003,975 for 1,750 grants (high: $100,000; low: $25), $778,033 for 777 grants to individuals (high: $10,000; low: $33), $6,500 for 3 employee matching gifts and $987,000 for 2 foundation-administered programs; no PRIs paid.
Cumulative PRI activity (through 12/31/00): Since beginning PRI activity, the foundation has made 1 PRI totaling $10,000.
General purpose and activities: Primary areas of interest include the arts, child welfare and youth, the

disadvantaged, education, health, community development, and sustainable development. The foundation administers donor-advised funds.
General fields of interest: Arts/cultural programs; education; natural resources conservation & protection; environment; health care; health associations; youth development, services; human services; children & youth, services; aging, centers & services; urban/community development; community development; leadership development; economically disadvantaged.
Program-related investment (PRI) activity: The foundation has made occasional PRIs for low-income housing, ecologically-sensitive economic development, sports, and the arts. PRIs have provided interim financing and financing for an intermediary (e.g., loan fund).
Types of PRI Support: Loans/promissory notes, interim financing, capitalizing loan funds/other intermediaries.
Limitations: Giving limited to ME. No support for religious organizations for religious purposes. No grants to individuals (except for scholarship funds), or for endowment funds, equipment, or annual campaigns for regular operations or for capital campaigns. PRI applications not accepted.
Publications: Annual report, informational brochure, newsletter, application guidelines, grants list.
PRI program information: The foundation does not maintain a formal PRI program. The foundation makes PRIs occasionally.
Officers and Directors:* Charles Roscoe,* Chair.; Henry Schmelzer, Pres.; James E. Geary, V.P., Fin Svcs. and C.F.O.; Ellen Pope, V.P. Dev.; Meredith Jones, V.P. for Philanthropic Services; Sarah Luck, V.P., Southern ME; Sidney St. F. Thaxter, Clerk; and 23 additional directors.
Number of staff: 15 full-time professional; 3 full-time support; 1 part-time support.
EIN: 010391479

162
Marin Community Foundation

5 Hamilton Landing, Ste. 200
Novato, CA 94949 (415) 464-2500
Contact: Fred Silverman, Dir. of Comm.
FAX: (415) 464-2502; E-mail: mcf@marincf.org;
URL: http://www.marincf.org

Incorporated in 1986 in CA; the Leonard and Beryl Buck Foundation, its original donor, was established in 1973 and administered by the San Francisco Foundation through 1986. PRI-related activities began in 1986.
Grantmaker type: Community foundation
General financial activity (yr. ended 06/30/01): Assets, $1,150,556,205 (M); gifts received, $26,377,249; expenditures, $70,171,204; giving activities include $48,939,475 for grants (high: $3,100,000; low: $100), $1,415,163 for grants to individuals (high: $3,000; low: $1,000; average: $1,000–$3,000), $170,075 for 172 employee matching gifts and $2,100,000 for 3 PRIs.
Cumulative PRI activity (through 06/30/01): Since 1986, the foundation has made 45 PRIs totaling $13,700,000. The currently outstanding PRI portfolio includes 11 PRI totaling $3,770,239 (high: $2,000,000; low: $85,000; average: $488,000). The typical outstanding PRI has a 1- to 15-year term with an average term of 7 years and earns 1 to 5.5 percent interest with an average of 4 percent.
General purpose and activities: The Marin Community Foundation is a tax-exempt charity that administers private funds for public purposes. It was established in 1986 to help improve the human condition and enhance the quality of life for all residents of the community. The foundation supports a broad array of programs, projects, and services, including fund development and management for individuals and organizations who place their philanthropic funds in its care. The foundation accepts applications for funding in seven program areas: Human Needs, Community Development, Community Recognition Awards, Education and Training, Religion, Environment, and Arts.
General fields of interest: Arts/cultural programs; adult education—literacy, basic skills & GED; education; environment; AIDS; legal services; employment; housing/shelter, development; human services; community development; religion; disabled; aging; homeless.
Program-related investment (PRI) activity: The foundation makes PRIs through its Community Investment Loan Fund (CILF) to provide investment in capital projects and revenue-producing ventures; to encourage the economic independence and stability of nonprofit organizations; to offer alternatives to, or augment, traditional funding sources; and to meet emergency situations. PRIs are also used to increase nonprofit organizations' access to other funding sources. Areas of PRI interest include the arts, education, the environment, health, housing, human services, and community development. PRIs have been provided for interim financing, facility acquisition, capitalizing earned income ventures, financing intermediaries, capitalizing housing development projects, and refinancing existing debt.
Types of PRI Support: Loans/promissory notes, interim financing, loan guarantees, capitalizing loan funds/other intermediaries.
Limitations: Giving from Buck Trust limited to Marin County, CA; other giving on a national and international basis with emphasis on the San Francisco Bay Area. No grants for planning initiatives, research, or generally for capital projects (except those meeting criteria specified in the funding guidelines). Other limitations specific to each program area are outlined in the funding guidelines. PRI support limited to nonprofit organizations located in and/or serving the residents of Marin County, CA. Loan applications must meet appropriate grantmaking program guidelines. The foundation accepts applications for PRIs.
Publications: Annual report, application guidelines, newsletter, informational brochure (including application guidelines).

PRI program information: The foundation maintains a formal PRI program. The foundation makes PRIs occasionally.
Officers: Thomas Peters, Ph.D., C.E.O. and Pres.; Sid Hartman, V.P., and Treas.; Marsha E. Bonner, V.P., Progs.; Michael Groza, V.P., Community Outreach; Fred Silverman, V.P., Comm.; Patrick Woods, V.P., Fund Devel.; Susan Clay, Corp. Secy.; Aileen Sweeney, Cont.
Trustees: Larry E. Rosenberger, Chair.; Faye D'Opal, Vice-Chair.; Sara Barnes, Charles "Chuck" H. Curley, Cassandra Flipper, Nancy Kamei, Lois Merriweather Moore, Carlos Porrata, Karin Urquhart.
Number of staff: 26 full-time professional; 6 part-time professional; 6 full-time support; 1 part-time support.
EIN: 943007979

163
Mathile Family Foundation

P.O. Box 13615
Dayton, OH 45413-0615 (937) 264-4600
Contact: Brenda Carnal, Asst. to the Exec. Dir.
FAX: (937) 264-4805; E-mail: brenda.carnal@cymi.com

Established in 1987 in OH. PRI-related activities began in 1997.
Donor(s): Clayton Lee Mathile, MaryAnn Mathile.
Grantmaker type: Independent foundation
General financial activity (yr. ended 11/30/02): Assets, $247,377,842 (M); gifts received, $1,675,100; expenditures, $22,770,830; qualifying distributions, $19,975,624; giving activities include $19,975,624 for grants; no PRIs paid.
Cumulative PRI activity (through 11/30/02): Since 1997, the foundation has made 3 PRIs totaling $740,000.
General purpose and activities: To reach out and implement through others, ways to help men, women, and children reach their full potential. Focus placed on three main areas: children, education, and meeting basic human needs.
General fields of interest: Education; food services; children & youth, services; homeless, human services.
Program-related investment (PRI) activity: The foundation has made PRIs for free enterprise education and and to a children's treatment center.
Types of PRI Support: Loans/promissory notes, loan guarantees, equity investments.
Limitations: Giving primarily in the Dayton, OH, area, with emphasis on Montgomery County. No grants to individuals, or for endowment funds.
Publications: Annual report (including application guidelines).
PRI program information: The foundation makes PRIs occasionally.
Officers and Trustees:* MaryAnn Mathile,* Chair and C.E.O.; Clayton Lee Mathile,* Pres.; Leslie S. Banwart,* Vice-Pres.; Richard J. Chernesky,* Secy.; C. Jeanine Hufford, Exec. Dir.
Number of staff: 3 full-time professional; 3 part-time professional; 1 full-time support.
EIN: 311257219
PRI recipients:
163-1. Saint Joseph Childrens Treatment Center, Cincinnati, OH, $500,000. Loan for operating support. 2001.

164
Robert R. McCormick Tribune Foundation

(Formerly Robert R. McCormick Charitable Trust)
435 N. Michigan Ave., Ste. 770
Chicago, IL 60611 (312) 222-3512
Contact: Prog. Dirs.
FAX: (312) 222-3523; E-mail: rrmtf@tribune.com; URL: http://www.rrmtf.org

Trust established in 1955 in IL; became a foundation in 1990.
Donor(s): Robert R. McCormick,‡ The National Football League, Uni-Mart.
Grantmaker type: Independent foundation
General financial activity (yr. ended 12/31/02): Assets, $1,855,000,000 (M); gifts received, $60,016,665; expenditures, $105,235,246; qualifying distributions, $98,635,246; giving activities include $98,635,246 for grants; no PRIs paid.
Cumulative PRI activity (through 12/31/02): The currently outstanding PRI portfolio includes 4 PRIs totaling $789,548 (average: $200,000). The typical outstanding PRI has a 2- to 5-year term, and earns 3 to 4 percent interest.
General purpose and activities: Giving primarily to improve the social and economic environment; to encourage a free and responsible discussion of issues affecting the nation; to enhance the effectiveness of American education; and to stimulate responsible citizenship.
General fields of interest: Journalism & publishing; early childhood education; child development, education; vocational education; employment; housing/shelter, development; youth development, citizenship; human services; children & youth, services; child development, services; homeless, human services; civil liberties, first amendment; community development; voluntarism promotion; government/public administration; public affairs, citizen participation; minorities; economically disadvantaged; homeless.
General international interests: Latin America.
Program-related investment (PRI) activity: Through the PRI program, the foundation purchased a building and has financed loans in targeted low-income neighborhoods.
Limitations: Giving primarily in the metropolitan Chicago, IL, area; except for Journalism Program which gives on a national basis and in Latin America; and communities program which operates in: Phoenix, AZ, Anaheim,

Escondido, Los Angeles, Sacramento and San Diego, CA, Denver, CO, Fort Lauderdale and Orlando, FL, Atlanta, GA, Chicago, IL, Indianapolis, IN, Manhattan, KS, New Orleans, LA, Boston and Lowell, MA, New York, NY, Cleveland, OH, Philadelphia and York, PA, Dallas, Houston, and El Paso, TX, and Newport News, VA. No grants to individuals, or for endowment funds, scholarships, or single events. PRI applications not accepted.
Publications: Annual report (including application guidelines), application guidelines, informational brochure (including application guidelines).
Officers and Directors:* John W. Madigan,* Chair.; Richard A. Behrenhausen, C.E.O. and Pres.; David L. Grange, Exec. V.P. and C.O.O.; Nicholas Goodban, Sr. V.P., Philanthropy; Louis J. Marsico, Jr., V.P., Finance and Admin.; Charles T. Brumback, James C. Dowdle, Dennis J. FitzSimons, Jack Fuller.
Number of staff: 16 full-time professional; 6 full-time support.
EIN: 363689171
PRI recipients:

164-1. Inter American Press Association (IAPA), Press Institute, Miami, FL, $500,000. Program-related investment for purchase of new headquarters building. 1999.

164-2. South Shore Bank of Chicago, Chicago, IL, $100,000. Program-related investment to finance rehabilitation loans in targeted low-income neighborhoods. 2001.

164-3. South Shore Bank of Chicago, Chicago, IL, $100,000. Program-related investment to finance rehabilitation loans in targeted low-income neighborhoods. 2000.

164-4. South Shore Bank of Chicago, Chicago, IL, $100,000. Program-related investment for financing rehab loans in targeted low-income neighborhoods. 1999.

165
McCune Charitable Foundation

(Formerly Marshall L. & Perrine D. McCune Charitable Foundation)
345 E. Alameda St.
Santa Fe, NM 87501-2229 (505) 983-8300
Contact: Frances R. Sowers, Assoc. Dir.
FAX: (505) 983-7887; E-mail: fsowers@trail.com;
URL: http://www.nmmccune.org

Established in 1992 in NM.
Donor(s): Perrine Dixon McCune,‡ Marshall L. McCune.‡
Grantmaker type: Independent foundation
General financial activity (yr. ended 12/31/01): Assets, $132,635,861 (M); expenditures, $9,654,385; qualifying distributions, $8,935,811; giving activities include $7,686,800 for 455 grants (high: $150,000; low: $900; average: $5,000–$50,000) and $370,566 for 2 PRIs.
Cumulative PRI activity (through 12/31/01): The currently outstanding PRI portfolio includes PRIs totaling $2,864,963.
General purpose and activities: Primary areas of interest include the arts, education, youth, health, social services and environment.
General fields of interest: Visual arts; museums; performing arts; dance; theater; music; history & archaeology; historic preservation/historical societies; arts/cultural programs; early childhood education; child development, education; elementary school/education; secondary school/education; vocational education; higher education; adult/continuing education; adult education—literacy, basic skills & GED; libraries/library science; reading; education; natural resources conservation & protection; environment; animal welfare; wildlife preservation & protection; hospitals (general); family planning; medical care, rehabilitation; health care; substance abuse, services; mental health/crisis services; health associations; cancer; heart & circulatory diseases; AIDS; alcoholism; crime/violence prevention, youth; crime/law enforcement; employment; agriculture; food services; nutrition; housing/shelter, development; youth development, services; youth development, citizenship; human services; children & youth, services; child development, services; family services; hospices; aging, centers & services; women, centers & services; minorities/immigrants, centers & services; homeless, human services; rural development; community development; federated giving programs; public affairs, citizen participation; leadership development; public affairs; minorities; Native Americans/American Indians; disabled; aging; women; gays/lesbians; economically disadvantaged; homeless.
Program-related investment (PRI) activity: The foundation has made PRIs for the rehabilitation and revitalization of downtown Albuquerque.
Limitations: Giving limited to NM. No grants to individuals, or for endowments, research, voter registration drives, or to cover deficits.
Publications: Biennial report, application guidelines.
Officers and Directors:* Sarah McCune Losinger,* Chair.; Owen M. Lopez, Exec. Dir.; Frances Sowers, Assoc. Dir.; James M. Edwards, John R. McCune VI.
Number of staff: 1 full-time professional; 1 full-time support.
EIN: 850429439
PRI recipients:

165-1. Historic District Improvement Company, Albuquerque, NM, $150,566. Program-related investment for revitalization of downtown Albuquerque. 2001.

165-2. Historic District Improvement Company, Albuquerque, NM, $3,594,720. Program-related investment for revitalization of downtown Albuquerque. 2000.

165-3. Historic District Improvement Company, Albuquerque, NM, $2,285,213. Program-related investment for revitalzation of downtown Albuquerque. 1999.

165-4. Magnifico Arts Incorporated, Albuquerque, NM, $220,000. Program-related investment in Magnifico Building. 2001.

166
McCune Foundation
750 6 PPG Pl.
Pittsburgh, PA 15222 (412) 644-8779
Contact: Henry S. Beukema, Exec. Dir.
PRI Contact: Robert Lukitsch, Business Mgr.
FAX: (412) 644-8059; E-mail: info@mccune.org;
URL: http://www.mccune.org

Established in 1979 in PA. PRI-related activities began in 1995.
Donor(s): Charles L. McCune.‡
Grantmaker type: Independent foundation
General financial activity (yr. ended 09/30/02): Assets, $497,804,987 (M); expenditures, $25,588,279; qualifying distributions, $25,375,494; giving activities include $23,986,227 for 189 grants (high: $2,000,000; low: $500; average: $50,000–$500,000) and $1,389,267 for 3 PRIs.
Cumulative PRI activity (through 09/30/02): Since 1995, the foundation has made 8 PRIs totaling $5,189,267. The currently outstanding PRI portfolio includes 7 PRIs totaling $4,574,773 (average: $55,000). The typical outstanding PRI has an average term of 6 years.
General purpose and activities: Following the donor's granting interests, the foundation emphasizes two major program areas: independent higher education and human services. The foundation also recognizes the importance of civic, cultural, and community-based organizations that are working to remedy the effects of economic dislocation, while addressing future issues. The foundation is particularly interested in collaborative approaches among groups addressing strategic regional issues and bringing innovative approaches to traditional challenges.
General fields of interest: Museums; performing arts; historic preservation/historical societies; arts/cultural programs; higher education; adult education—literacy, basic skills & GED; libraries/library science; health care; medical research; employment; housing/shelter, development; youth development, services; human services; economic development; urban/community development.
Program-related investment (PRI) activity: The foundation has made PRIs in support of artists' housing and economic development in southwestern Pennsylvania.
Limitations: Giving primarily in southwestern PA, with emphasis on the Pittsburgh area. No grants to individuals, or for general operating purposes. PRI applications not accepted.
Publications: Annual report (including application guidelines), application guidelines.
PRI program information: The foundation maintains a formal PRI program. The foundation makes PRIs on a frequent but not annual basis.
Officers: Henry S. Beukema, Exec. Dir.; Martha J. Perry, Assoc. Exec. Dir.
Distribution Committee: James M. Edwards, Chair.; Richard D. Edwards, Chair. Emeritus; Michael M. Edwards, John R. McCune VI.
Trustee: National City Bank of Pennsylvania.
Number of staff: 4 full-time professional; 2 full-time support.
EIN: 256210269
PRI recipients:
166-1. Pittsburgh Gateways Corporation, Pittsburgh, PA, $350,000. Program-related investment for economic development projects. 1999.
166-2. Strategic Regional Development, Pittsburgh, PA, $2,000,000. Program-related investment as limited partnership for development of former LTV Coke Works in Hazelwood. 2001.

167
The McIntosh Foundation
1730 M St. N.W., Ste. 204
Washington, DC 20036-4534 (202) 338-8055

Incorporated in 1949 in NY. PRI-related activities began in 1972.
Donor(s): Josephine H. McIntosh,‡ Karen McIntosh,‡ Peter McIntosh.‡
Grantmaker type: Independent foundation
General financial activity (yr. ended 12/31/02): Assets, $34,877,977 (M); expenditures, $2,959,636; qualifying distributions, $2,925,390; giving activities include $2,476,390 for 56 grants (high: $1,820,000; low: $1,000) and $7,487,398 for 1 PRI.
Cumulative PRI activity (through 12/31/02): The currently outstanding PRI portfolio includes 1 PRI totaling $7,487,398.
General purpose and activities: Giving primarily for environmental conservation.
General fields of interest: Natural resources conservation & protection.
Program-related investment (PRI) activity: The foundation has made loans to purchase boats used on trips in Tongass National Forest, AK.
Types of PRI Support: Charitable use assets.
Limitations: Applications not accepted. Giving limited to southeastern AK. PRI applications not accepted.
PRI program information: The foundation does not maintain a formal PRI program. The foundation makes PRIs occasionally.
Officers and Directors:* Michael A. McIntosh,* Pres. and C.I.O.; Joan H. McIntosh,* V.P.; Winsome D. McIntosh,* V.P.; Frederick A. Terry, Jr.,* Secy.; Hunter H. McIntosh, Michael A. McIntosh, Jr.
Number of staff: 1 full-time professional; 1 part-time professional; 1 full-time support.
EIN: 136096459

168
The McNeely Foundation

444 Pine St.
St. Paul, MN 55101 (651) 228-4503
Contact: Karen M. Reynolds

Established in 1981 in MN.
Donor(s): Lee and Rose Warner Foundation.
Grantmaker type: Independent foundation
General financial activity (yr. ended 12/31/01): Assets, $18,156,157 (M); expenditures, $671,391; qualifying distributions, $1,353,567; giving activities include $1,333,946 for 186 grants (high: $450,000; low: $50; average: $1,000–$50,000) and $125,000 for PRIs.
Cumulative PRI activity (through 12/31/01): The typical outstanding PRI has a 3-month to 2-year term.
General purpose and activities: Support for economics and business education; grants also for selected community projects, environmental programs and for arts education. Specific interest in funding projects that benefit the St. Paul area, especially the East Side neighborhoods.
General fields of interest: Business school/education; education; environment; health care; children & youth, services; community development; economics.
Limitations: Giving primarily in the Minneapolis-St. Paul Metro area, especially in East Side St. Paul neighborhoods. No grants to individuals. PRI applications not accepted.
Publications: Application guidelines.
PRI program information: The foundation does not maintain a formal PRI program.
Trustees: Armar A. Archbold, W.E. Barness, Gregory McNeely, Harry G. McNeely III, Shannon McNeely Whitaker.
Number of staff: 1 part-time professional.
EIN: 411392221

169
The Meadows Foundation, Inc.

Wilson Historic District
3003 Swiss Ave.
Dallas, TX 75204-6090 (214) 826-9431
Contact: Bruce H. Esterline, V.P., Grants
Additional Tel.: (800) 826-9431; FAX: (214) 827-7042; E-mail: grants@mfi.org; URL: http://www.mfi.org

Incorporated in 1948 in TX. PRI-related activities began in 1981.
Donor(s): Algur Hurtle Meadows,‡ Virginia Meadows.‡
Grantmaker type: Independent foundation
General financial activity (yr. ended 12/31/01): Assets, $796,146,859 (M); expenditures, $37,134,590; qualifying distributions, $43,562,423; giving activities include $35,141,061 for 324 grants (high: $4,000,000; low: $2,000; average: $25,000–$250,000), $55,435 for employee matching gifts, $102,000 for foundation-administered programs and $367,751 for 2 PRIs.
Cumulative PRI activity (through 12/31/01): The currently outstanding PRI portfolio includes PRIs totaling $38,110,533. The typical outstanding PRI has a 2- to 7-year term with an average term of 6 years and earns 0 to 3 percent interest with an average of 3 percent.
General purpose and activities: Support for the arts, social services, community and rural development, health including mental health, education, and civic and cultural programs. Operates a historic preservation investment-related program using a cluster of Victorian homes as offices for nonprofit agencies.
General fields of interest: Media/communications; architecture; museums; humanities; history & archaeology; historic preservation/historical societies; arts/cultural programs; education, public education; early childhood education; child development, education; medical school/education; adult/continuing education; adult education—literacy, basic skills & GED; libraries/library science; reading; education; natural resources conservation & protection; environment; wildlife preservation & protection; dental care; medical care, rehabilitation; nursing care; health care; substance abuse, services; mental health/crisis services; AIDS; alcoholism; AIDS research; crime/law enforcement; employment; agriculture; nutrition; housing/shelter, development; safety/disasters; recreation; youth development, services; human services; children & youth, services; child development, services; family services; hospices; aging, centers & services; homeless, human services; race/intergroup relations; urban/community development; rural development; community development; voluntarism promotion; government/public administration; transportation; leadership development; public affairs; Christian agencies & churches; aging; economically disadvantaged; homeless.
Program-related investment (PRI) activity: In 1981, the foundation authorized its first program-related investment effort, known as the Wilson Historic Block District Project. The project involved the acquisition and restoration of 16 distressed Victorian homes located in downtown Dallas and conversion of those properties into office space for the foundation and for the nonprofit community. A second phase involved revitalizing the surrounding neighborhood by purchasing, renovating, and constructing 12 additional buildings. Capital investments for this project total over $50 million. PRIs have also been used to finance loan funds for affordable housing and microenterprise development, to support a food bank, to revitalize properties in other parts of Texas, and to provide interim financing.
Limitations: Giving limited to TX. No grants to individuals; generally, no grants for annual campaigns, fundraising events, professional conferences and symposia, travel expenses for groups to perform or compete outside of TX, or construction of churches and seminaries. The foundation accepts applications for PRIs.
Publications: Annual report (including application guidelines), application guidelines.

PRI program information: The foundation does not maintain a formal PRI program. The foundation makes PRIs on a frequent but not annual basis.
Officers and Directors:* Robert A. Meadows,* Chair.; Linda P. Evans,* C.E.O. and Pres.; Martha L. Benson, V.P., Treas. and C.F.O.; Michael E. Patrick, V.P. and C.I.O.; Bruce H. Esterline, V.P., Grants; Robert E. Weiss, V.P., Admin.; Emily J. Jones, Corp. Secy.; Evelyn Meadows Acton, Dir. Emeritus; John W. Broadfoot, J.W. Bullion, Dir. Emeritus; True Miller Campbell, Daniel H. Chapman, Judy B. Culbertson, John A. Hammack, Sally R. Lancaster, Dir. Emeritus; P. Mike McCullough, Curtis W. Meadows, Jr., Dir. Emeritus; Eric Richard Meadows, Mark A. Meadows, Michael L. Meadows, Sally C. Miller, Dir. Emeritus; William A. Nesbitt, G. Tomas Rhodus, Evy Kay Ritzen, Eloise Meadows Rouse, Dir. Emeritus; Dorothy C. Wilson, Dir. Emeritus; Stephen Wheeler Wilson.
Number of staff: 23 full-time professional; 1 part-time professional; 21 full-time support; 2 part-time support.
EIN: 756015322
PRI recipients:
169-1. Guadalupe Economic Services Corporation, Lubbock, TX, $300,000. Loan to revolving construction loan fund to be used in constructing affordable single-family homes for economically disadvantaged families. 2000.
169-2. Trust for Public Land, Austin, TX, $350,000. Loan toward effort to establish North Texas field office and statewide revolving loan fun for acquiring parkland and green space for public use in areas affected by urban sprawl. 2001.
169-3. Wilson Historic Block District Project, Dallas, TX, $17,751. Program-related investment for renovation of Wilson District historic building to serve needs of a nonprofit organization tenant. 2001.
169-4. Wilson Historic Block District Project, Dallas, TX, $145,552. Program-related investment for renovation of Wilson District Building to serve needs of a nonprofit tenant organization including updating building througout as well as transforming warehouse space into office and programmatic space. 2000.
169-5. Wilson Historic Block District Project, Dallas, TX, $5,743,680. Program-related investment for restoration of historic Saint James AME Temple which now serves as corporate offices for two nonprofit agencies and for demolition, site preparation and construction (including installation of ADA-approved sidewalks, etc.) of new office building to provide space for three nonprofit arts organizations, gallery space and a sculpture garden. 1999.

170
Media Development Loan Fund

(Formerly Fund for Independent Media)
45 W. 21st St., 4th Fl.
New York, NY 10010 (212) 807-1304
FAX: (212) 807-0540; URL: http://www.mdlf.org

Established in 1993 in NY.
Donor(s): Open Society Institute, Swedish International Development Fund, Eurasia Foundation, Swiss Department of Foreign Affairs, Department of State, U.S. Government.
Grantmaker type: Independent foundation
General financial activity (yr. ended 12/31/01): Assets, $15,943,803 (M); gifts received, $2,808,642; expenditures, $4,142,004; qualifying distributions, $7,576,073; giving activities include $952,987 for 27 grants (high: $160,000; low: $2,000) and $5,126,174 for 19 PRIs.
General purpose and activities: Provides loans and grants to outlets in Russia and Eastern Europe for media and communications.
General fields of interest: Media/communications.
General international interests: Eastern Europe; Russia.
Program-related investment (PRI) activity: The foundation makes low-interest loans to media outlets in Russia and Eastern Europe for media and communications development. It also leases and distributes equipment to these outlets and handles related costs as PRIs.
Types of PRI Support: Loans/promissory notes, charitable use assets.
Limitations: Applications not accepted. Giving on an international basis. No grants to individuals. PRIs made primarily in Russia and Eastern Europe.
Trustees: Kenneth Anderson, Stuart Auerbach, Roberto Eisenmann, Annette Laborey, Aryeh Neier, Bernard Poulet, John Ryle, Sasa Vucinic.
EIN: 137024057
PRI recipients:
170-1. Aldea Global, Guatemala City, Guatemala, $750,000. Loan for working capital. 2001.
170-2. Aldea Global, Guatemala City, Guatemala, $499,827. Loan for purchase of equipment. 2001.
170-3. Aldea Global, Guatemala City, Guatemala, $750,173. Loan for working capital. 2000.
170-4. AltaPress, Barnaul, Russia, $50,000. Loan to refurbish printing facility and for additional financing. 2001.
170-5. AltaPress, Barnaul, Russia, $1,189,961. Leasing of equipment by foundation for use by recipient. 2000.
170-6. AltaPress, Barnaul, Russia, $100,000. Loan for refurbishment of printing facility, and additional financing. 2000.
170-7. AltaPress, Barnaul, Russia, $70,000. Loan for refurbishment of printing facility, and additional financing. 2000.
170-8. AltaPress, Barnaul, Russia, $50,000. Loan for refurbishment of printing facility. 2000.

170-9. AltaPress, Barnaul, Russia, $30,000. Loan for preparatory work for construction of printing facility. 1999.

170-10. Beta Bojnice, Bojnice, Slovakia, $30,000. Loan for working capital. 1999.

170-11. Commercial Broadcasting Studio Network (ATVs), Stavropol, Russia, $76,011. Leasing of equipment by foundation for use by recipient. 2000.

170-12. CR Manager, Chelyabinsk, Russia, $196,609. Loan for purchase of securities. 2000.

170-13. CR Manager, Chelyabinsk, Russia, $182,043. Equity investment. 1999.

170-14. Dani Civitas, Sarajevo, Bosnia-Herzegovina, $30,000. Loan toward financing of purchase of office premises. 1999.

170-15. Drina Press, Srebrenica, Bosnia-Herzegovina, $18,900. Loan for establishment of Central Studio. 1999.

170-16. Eisk TV, Krasnodar, Russia, $22,450. Leasing of equipment by foundation for use by recipient. 2000.

170-17. Express, Kiev, Ukraine, $1,189,340. Loan for acquisition of equipment. 2001.

170-18. Express, Kiev, Ukraine, $731,020. Loan for acquisition of equipment. 2001.

170-19. Express, Kiev, Ukraine, $29,600. Loan for purchase of newsprint. 1999.

170-20. Express, Kiev, Ukraine, $21,700. Leasing of equipment by foundation for use by recipient. 1999.

170-21. Magyar Narancs-Magazine, Budapest, Hungary, $180,000. Equity investment. 2001.

170-22. Magyar Narancs-Magazine, Budapest, Hungary, $60,000. Loan for marketing campaign and printing services. 2000.

170-23. Magyar Narancs-Magazine, Budapest, Hungary, $60,000. Loan for marketing campaign and working capital. 2000.

170-24. Magyar Narancs-Magazine, Budapest, Hungary, $60,000. Loan for marketing campaign and for working capital. 1999.

170-25. Magyar Narancs-Magazine, Budapest, Hungary, $20,000. Loan for working capital. 1999.

170-26. Malasyakini, Inc., Kuala Lumpur, Malaysia, $50,000. Equity investment. 2001.

170-27. Media Works, Belgrade, Yugoslavia, $13,000. Loan as deposit for purchase of equipment. 2001.

170-28. Novi List, Kijeka, Croatia, $265,000. Loan for working capital. 2000.

170-29. Novi List, Kijeka, Croatia, $939,045. Equity investment. 1999.

170-30. Onogost, Niksic, Yugoslavia, $16,000. Loan for purchase of printing/binding pre-press and small equipment. 2001.

170-31. Paritet, Moscow, Russia, $185,000. Loan for construction of warm storage room and for purchase of spare parts. 2000.

170-32. Paritet, Moscow, Russia, $25,000. Loan for purchase of small printing press. 2000.

170-33. Paritet, Moscow, Russia, $1,084,000. Leasing of equipment by foundation for use by recipient. 1999.

170-34. Paritet, Moscow, Russia, $531,171. Loan for refurbishment of printing facility and working capital. 1999.

170-35. Paritet, Moscow, Russia, $60,820. Loan for construction of warm storage room and for working capital. 1999.

170-36. Paritet, Moscow, Russia, $30,000. Loan for construction of storage room for finished print works. 1999.

170-37. Paritet, Moscow, Russia, $28,224. Leasing of equipment by foundation for use by recipient. 1999.

170-38. Premier Publishing Group, Vologda, Russia, $421,000. Loan for acquisition of equipment. 2001.

170-39. Premier Publishing Group, Vologda, Russia, $129,000. Loan for acquisition of equipment. 2001.

170-40. PT Media Lintas inti Nusantara, Jakarta, Indonesia, $20,000. Loan for purchase of small computer equipment. 2000.

170-41. Radio Television B92, Belgrade, Yugoslavia, $750,000. Loan for working capital. 2001.

170-42. Reporter, Banja Luka, Bosnia-Herzegovina, $50,000. Loan for printing services. 2001.

170-43. Rijecki List, Rijeka, Croatia, $939,590. Loan for ownership restructuring through purchase of shares of stock. 1999.

170-44. Roto-Slog, Podgorica, Yugoslavia, $220,000. Loan for purchase of land, construction of printing house, and moving of printing presses. 2001.

170-45. Roto-Slog, Podgorica, Yugoslavia, $50,000. Loan for construction of printing facility. 2001.

170-46. Roto-Slog, Podgorica, Yugoslavia, $135,000. Loan for purchase of equipment. 1999.

170-47. Roto-Slog, Podgorica, Yugoslavia, $63,600. Loan for purchase of newsprint. 1999.

170-48. Roto-Slog, Podgorica, Yugoslavia, $12,295. Loan for purchase of newsprint. 1999.

170-49. Tiskara Maslina, Zagreb, Croatia, $40,000. Loan for purchase of print-finishing equipment. 1999.

170-50. Tiskara Maslina, Zagreb, Croatia, $20,000. Loan for purchase of print-binding equipment. 1999.

170-51. Tiskara Maslina, Zagreb, Croatia, $15,000. Loan for working capital. 1999.

170-52. TV 2, Tomsk, Russia, $15,496. Loan for aquisition of equipment. 2001.

170-53. TV 2, Tomsk, Russia, $98,767. Leasing of equipment by foundation for use by recipient. 2000.

171
Richard King Mellon Foundation

1 Mellon Bank Ctr.
500 Grant St., 41st Fl., Ste. 4106
Pittsburgh, PA 15219-2502 (412) 392-2800
Contact: Michael Watson, V.P.
FAX: (412) 392-2837; URL: http://fdncenter.org/grantmaker/rkmellon

Trust established in 1947 in PA; incorporated in 1971 in PA.

Donor(s): Richard K. Mellon.‡
Grantmaker type: Independent foundation
General financial activity (yr. ended 12/31/02): Assets, $1,393,565,202 (M); expenditures, $76,423,092; qualifying distributions, $69,322,864; giving activities include $61,843,303 for grants and $4,577,889 for PRIs.
General purpose and activities: Local grant programs emphasize conservation, education, families and youth, regional economic development, system reform; support also for conservation of natural areas and wildlife preservation elsewhere in the United States.
General fields of interest: Early childhood education; education; natural resources conservation & protection; environment; youth development, services; human services; children & youth, services; family services; urban/community development; community development.
Program-related investment (PRI) activity: In 1988, the foundation initiated the American Land Conservation Program to acquire land, threatened by development, that has lasting historical or environmental value to the nation. Working with the Conservation Fund and state and federal conservation agencies, the foundation augments the work of public agencies and nonprofit organizations with direct acquisitions and gifts of high-priority conservation properties. PRIs paid through this program in 1999, 2000, and 2001 totaled $32.03 million, $3.78 million, and $11.78 million respectively.
Types of PRI Support: Charitable use assets.
Limitations: Giving primarily in Pittsburgh and southwestern PA, except for nationwide conservation programs. No grants outside the U.S. No grants to individuals, or for fellowships or scholarships, or conduit organizations. PRI applications not accepted.
Publications: Annual report (including application guidelines), informational brochure.
PRI program information:
Officers and Trustees:* Richard P. Mellon,* Chair.; Seward Prosser Mellon,* Pres.; Arthur D. Miltenberger, V.P.; Michael Watson,* V.P. and Dir.; Scott Izzo, Secy. and Assoc. Dir.; Robert B. Burr, Jr.,* Treas.; John J. Turcik, Cont.; Lawrence S. Busch.
Number of staff: 3 full-time professional; 7 part-time professional; 1 full-time support; 14 part-time support.
EIN: 251127705
PRI recipients:

171-1. Strategic Investment Fund, Pittsburgh, PA, $3,000,000. For program-related investment to enable gap financing for economic development projects in southwestern Pennsylvania. 2002.

172
The Melville Charitable Trust

P.O. Box 6767
Providence, RI 02940-6767

Established in 1987 in NY.
Donor(s): Dorothy Melville.‡
Grantmaker type: Independent foundation
General financial activity (yr. ended 12/31/01): Assets, $143,496,533 (M); gifts received, $81,671,358; expenditures, $6,808,377; qualifying distributions, $7,183,475; giving activities include $5,852,512 for 57 grants (high: $625,000; low: $5,000; average: $50,000–$250,000) and $560,000 for 6 PRIs.
General purpose and activities: Giving primarily for housing and human services.
General fields of interest: Housing/shelter, services; housing/shelter; human services; homeless, human services.
Program-related investment (PRI) activity: The foundation has made PRIs to community service, housing, and religious organizations. PRIs have included support for land acquisition.
Types of PRI Support: Loans/promissory notes.
Limitations: Applications not accepted. Giving primarily in CT. No grants to individuals. PRI support only to pre-selected organizations. PRI applications not accepted.
Trustee: Fleet National Bank.
Distribution Committee: John R. Gibb, Alan Melville, Frank Melville, Stephen Melville.
EIN: 133415258
PRI recipients:

172-1. Columbus House, New Haven, CT, $129,900. Program-related investment. 1999.

172-2. Connecticut Coalition to End Homelessness, Wethersfield, CT, $10,000. Loan to help with emergency short-term cash flow. 2001.

172-3. Greater New Haven Community Loan Fund, New Haven, CT, $50,000. Program-related investment for Community Loan Pool that finances below-market interest rate loans to nonprofit developers creating or rehabilitating affordable housing in New Haven area. 2001.

172-4. Mutual Housing Association of South Central Connecticut, New Haven, CT, $50,000. Program-related investment for pre-development loan fund to spur affordable housing initiatives in Naugatuck Valley. 2001.

172-5. Mutual Housing Association of Southwestern Connecticut, Stamford, CT, $100,000. Program-related investment. 1999.

172-6. New Haven Homeless Resource Center, New Haven, CT, $175,000. Program-related investment. 1999.

172-7. Philanthropic Initiative, Boston, MA, $50,000. Program-related investment. 1999.

173
Mertz Gilmore Foundation

(Formerly Joyce Mertz-Gilmore Foundation)
218 E. 18th St.
New York, NY 10003-3694 (212) 475-1137
Contact: Jay Beckner, Exec. Dir.
FAX: (212) 777-5226; E-mail: info@mertzgilmore.org; URL: http://www.mertzgilmore.org

Incorporated in 1959 in NY. PRI-related activities began in 1990.
Donor(s): Robert Gilmore,‡ Joyce Mertz.‡
Grantmaker type: Independent foundation
General financial activity (yr. ended 12/31/01): Assets, $104,952,751 (M); expenditures, $8,755,140; qualifying distributions, $7,760,479; giving activities include $6,124,212 for 162 grants (high: $1,700,000; low: $500; average: $20,000–$75,000); no PRIs paid.
Cumulative PRI activity (through 12/31/01): Since 1990, the foundation has made 8 PRIs totaling $2,837,331. The currently outstanding PRI portfolio includes 3 PRIs totaling $625,000 (high: $300,000; low: $100,000; average: $200,000). The typical outstanding PRI has a 5- to 10-year term with an average term of 8 years, and earns an average of 5 percent interest.
General purpose and activities: Current concerns include human rights, the environment, peace and security issues in the Middle East, and New York City cultural, social, and civic concerns.
General fields of interest: Dance; energy; international peace/security; international human rights; civil rights, immigrants; civil rights, gays/lesbians; community development, equal rights; community development, citizen coalitions; community development.
General international interests: Israel; West Bank/Gaza.
Program-related investment (PRI) activity: In 1990, the foundation began making PRIs in the areas of economic development and the environment. PRIs are made only on an occasional basis and in response to specific needs. PRI support has also provided interim financing, supported facility acquisition and debt restructuring, and capitalized an earned income venture. Some PRI support has been provided through a financial intermediary.
Types of PRI Support: Loans/promissory notes, interim financing, equity investments, linked deposits.
Limitations: Giving on a national and international basis, with the exception of the New York City Program. No support for sectarian religious concerns. No grants to individuals, or for endowments, annual fund appeals, fundraising events, conferences, workshops, publications, film or media projects, scholarships, research, fellowships, or travel; no loans (except for program-related investments).
Publications: Biennial report (including application guidelines), application guidelines, informational brochure.
Officers and Directors:* Larry E. Condon,* Chair.; Elizabeth Burke Gilmore,* Vice-Chair. and Secy.; Denise Nix Thompson,* Treas.; Jay Beckner, Exec. Dir.; Harlan Cleveland, Robert Crane, Hal Harvey, Patricia Ramsay, Peggy Saika, Mikki Shepard, Franklin W. Wallin.
Number of staff: 5 full-time professional; 1 part-time professional; 5 full-time support; 2 part-time support.
EIN: 132872722
PRI recipients:
173-1. E and Co, Bloomfield, NJ, $100,000. Loan, at 5 percent interest. 1999.

174
MetLife Foundation

(Formerly Metropolitan Life Foundation)
1 Madison Ave.
New York, NY 10010-3690 (212) 578-6272
Contact: Sibyl C. Jacobson, C.E.O. and Pres.
PRI Contact: Dennis White, V.P.
FAX: (212) 685-1435; URL: http://www.metlife.org

Incorporated in 1976 in NY. PRI-related activities began in 1984.
Donor(s): Metropolitan Life Insurance Co.
Grantmaker type: Company-sponsored foundation
General financial activity (yr. ended 12/31/01): Assets, $181,570,141 (M); expenditures, $18,743,176; qualifying distributions, $18,725,320; giving activities include $16,863,094 for 247 grants (high: $1,000,000; average: $5,000–$100,000), $675,000 for grants to individuals, $933,509 for employee matching gifts, $188,250 for 1 foundation-administered program and $133,333 for PRIs.
Cumulative PRI activity (through 12/31/01): Since 1984, the foundation has made PRIs totaling $. The currently outstanding PRI portfolio includes 17 PRIs totaling $13,896,197 (high: $8,000,000; low: $250,000; average: $2,000,000). The typical outstanding PRI has a 1- to 15-year term with an average term of 7 years and earns 4.50 to 8 percent interest with an average of 6 percent.
General purpose and activities: To make donations for higher education, health, including substance abuse programs, civic purposes, social services, and United Way chapters; grants also for cultural programs, including public broadcasting, music, dance, and theater, and urban development, including housing and public policy; also makes program-related investments.
General fields of interest: Museums; dance; theater; music; arts/cultural programs; education, association; higher education; medical school/education; adult education—literacy, basic skills & GED; reading; education; nursing care; health care; substance abuse, services; health associations; AIDS; alcoholism; AIDS research; crime/law enforcement; employment; housing/shelter, development; safety/disasters; human services; children & youth, services; family services; women, centers & services; minorities/immigrants, centers & services; homeless, human services; urban/community development; community development; public policy, research; government/public administration; minorities; disabled; women; homeless.
Program-related investment (PRI) activity: The foundation established its Social Investment Program in 1984 to expand its philanthropic activities. PRIs serve to underwrite projects in affordable housing, commercial revitalization, land preservation, health and rehabilitative treatment centers, business development, and the arts. PRIs are usually structured as loans and made primarily to nonprofit organizations and their subsidiaries. Occasionally, the foundation may take an equity position, guarantee a loan, or target a special bank deposit to achieve financial or program objectives. Specific purposes of PRIs have

included interim financing, land acquisition and facility improvement, and capitalizing housing development projects and earned income ventures. In 1994, the foundation's activities were supplemented with a Social Investment Program using MetLife company funds. Since 1997, nearly all social investments were funded directly through the company.

Types of PRI Support: Loans/promissory notes, loan guarantees, equity investments, linked deposits.

Limitations: No support for private foundations, religious, fraternal, athletic, political, social, or veterans' organizations, organizations already receiving support through United Way campaigns, local chapters of national organizations, disease-specific organizations, labor groups, organizations whose activities are mainly international, organizations primarily engaged in patient care or direct treatment, drug treatment centers and community health clinics, or elementary or secondary schools. No grants to individuals (except for medical research awards), or for endowment funds, hospital capital fund campaigns, courtesy advertising, or festival participation. The foundation gives preference to investments in areas where Met Life has a major presence, and to organizations that are regional or national in scope. PRI applications not accepted.

Publications: Corporate giving report, application guidelines, annual report (including application guidelines).

PRI program information: The foundation does not maintain a formal PRI program. The foundation makes PRIs on a frequent but not annual basis.

Officers and Directors:* Catherine A. Rein,* Chair.; Sibyl C. Jacobson,* C.E.O. and Pres.; A. Dennis White, V.P.; Joseph A. Reali, Secy. and Counsel; Timothy Schmidt,* Treas.; Robert C. Tarnok, Cont.; James M. Benson, C. Robert Henrikson, Vincent P. Reusing, William J. Toppeta, Lisa M. Weber.

Number of staff: None.

EIN: 132878224

PRI recipients:

174-1. College of Insurance, NYC, NY, $127,551. Loan. 2000.

174-2. College of Insurance, NYC, NY, $120,332. Program-related investment. 1999.

174-3. Retail Initiative, NYC, NY, $133,333. Investment in partnership which invests in inner-city supermarkets throughout the country. 2001.

174-4. Retail Initiative, NYC, NY, $532,917. Program-related investment in limited partnership that will invest in retail centers anchored by large supermarkets in low-income areas. 1999.

174-5. The Recovery Center, $1,400,000. Loan. 2000.

174-6. Whitelaw Housing Development, DC, $27,473. Program-related investment. 1999.

175

Eugene and Agnes E. Meyer Foundation

1400 16th St., N.W., Ste. 360
Washington, DC 20036 (202) 483-8294
Contact: Julie L. Rogers, Pres.
PRI Contact: G. Albert Ruesga, V.P., Progs. and Comm.
FAX: (202) 328-6850; E-mail: meyer@meyerfdn.org;
URL: http://www.meyerfoundation.org

Incorporated in 1944 in NY. PRI-related activities began in 1995.

Donor(s): Eugene Meyer,‡ Agnes E. Meyer.‡

Grantmaker type: Independent foundation

General financial activity (yr. ended 12/31/02): Assets, $143,257,373 (M); gifts received, $3,100; expenditures, $8,745,252; qualifying distributions, $9,110,252; giving activities include $6,577,055 for 283 grants (high: $450,000; low: $1,000; average: $1,000–$450,000) and $365,000 for 6 PRIs.

Cumulative PRI activity (through 12/31/02): Since 1995, the foundation has made 119 PRIs totaling $4,502,636. The currently outstanding PRI portfolio includes 5 PRIs totaling $224,500 (high: $75,000; low: $15,000; average: $47,222). The typical outstanding PRI has an average term of 6 months and earns an average of 2 percent interest.

General purpose and activities: Grants principally for neighborhood development/housing, education, health and mental health, the arts and humanities, law and justice, community service, nonprofit sector strengthening and management assistance.

General fields of interest: Theater; humanities; arts/cultural programs; early childhood education; child development, education; elementary school/education; secondary school/education; vocational education; adult education—literacy, basic skills & GED; reading; education; family planning; medical care, rehabilitation; health care; substance abuse, services; mental health/crisis services; health organizations; legal services; crime/law enforcement; employment; housing/shelter, development; youth development, services; human services; children & youth, services; child development, services; women, centers & services; minorities/immigrants, centers & services; homeless, human services; race/intergroup relations; civil rights; urban/community development; community development; voluntarism promotion; leadership development; minorities; women; immigrants/refugees; economically disadvantaged; homeless; general charitable giving.

Program-related investment (PRI) activity: Through its Cash Flow Loan Program, the foundation makes short-term loans of up to $75,000 against delayed receivables from approved government, foundation or corporate grants and contracts.The loans are made on a first-come, first-served basis from a $1,000,000 revolving fund. Recent PRIs have supported education, health and mental health, the arts and humanities, community services, human services, and neighborhood development and housing organizations.

Types of PRI Support: Loans/promissory notes, interim financing.
Limitations: Giving limited to the metropolitan Washington, DC, area, including Montgomery, Prince George's, Calvert, Charles, and St. Mary's counties in suburban MD and Arlington, Fairfax, Loudoun, Prince William and Stafford counties, and the cities of Alexandria, Falls Church, Manassas, and Manassas Park in northern VA. No support for sectarian purposes, or for programs that are national or international in scope. No grants to individuals, or for annual campaigns, deficit financing, endowment funds, equipment, scholarships, fellowships, scientific or medical research, publications, special events or conferences. Only organizations that have received foundation grants since 1990 are eligible for PRI support. PRI applications not accepted.
Publications: Application guidelines, annual report (including application guidelines), grants list.
PRI program information: The foundation maintains a formal PRI program. The foundation makes PRIs on an annual basis.
Officers and Directors:* James W. Jones,* Chair.; Edward H. Bersoff, Ph.D.,* Vice-Chair.; Julie L. Rogers, Pres.; Kristen Conte, V.P., Finance and Admin.; G. Albert Ruesga, V.P., Progs. and Comm.; Thomas W. Chapman,* Secy.-Treas.; Joshua B. Bernstein, Maria S. Gomez, Eric H. Holder, Jr., Boisfeuillet Jones, Jr., Barbara J. Krumsiek, Patricia A. McGuire, Francey Lim Youngberg.
Number of staff: 9 full-time professional; 1 part-time professional; 5 full-time support; 1 part-time support.
EIN: 530241716
PRI recipients:

175-1. Advocates for Justice and Education, DC, $30,000. Cash flow loan. 2001.
175-2. African Continuum Theater Company, DC, $10,000. Cash flow loan. 2002.
175-3. Andrew Cacho African Drummers and Dancers, DC, $10,000. Program-related investment for general operating support. 2000.
175-4. Byte Back, DC, $50,000. Cash flow loan. 2000.
175-5. Byte Back, DC, $40,000. Cash flow loan. 1999.
175-6. Calvary Bilingual Multicultural Learning Center, DC, $75,000. Cash flow loan. 2002.
175-7. Capital Childrens Museum, DC, $75,000. Cash flow loan. 1999.
175-8. Center for Multicultural Human Services, Falls Church, VA, $50,000. Cash flow loan. 2000.
175-9. Center for Multicultural Human Services, Falls Church, VA, $40,000. Cash flow loan. 2000.
175-10. Center for Multicultural Human Services, Falls Church, VA, $50,000. Cash flow loan. 1999.
175-11. Center for Multicultural Human Services, Falls Church, VA, $49,000. Cash flow loan. 1999.
175-12. Clean and Pure Kids, DC, $10,000. Cash flow loan. 1999.
175-13. Council for Court Excellence, DC, $75,000. Cash flow loan. 1999.
175-14. Dance Exchange, Takoma Park, MD, $75,000. Cash flow loan. 2000.
175-15. Dance Exchange, Takoma Park, MD, $75,000. Cash flow loan. 2000.
175-16. Dance Exchange, Takoma Park, MD, $75,000. Cash flow loan. 2000.
175-17. DC Central Kitchen, DC, $75,000. Cash flow loan. 1999.
175-18. DC Coalition Against Domestic Violence, DC, $50,000. Cash flow loan. 2000.
175-19. DC Coalition Against Domestic Violence, DC, $50,000. Cash flow loan. 2000.
175-20. DC SCORES, DC, $20,000. Cash flow loan. 1999.
175-21. District of Columbia Developing Families Center, DC, $75,000. Cash flow loan. 2000.
175-22. East River Family Strengthening Collaborative, DC, $30,000. Cash flow loan. 2001.
175-23. Excel Institute, DC, $50,000. Cash flow loan. 2000.
175-24. Housing and Community Services of Northern Virginia, Springfield, VA, $55,000. Cash flow loan. 2002.
175-25. Housing and Community Services of Northern Virginia, Springfield, VA, $45,000. Cash flow loan. 2001.
175-26. Housing and Community Services of Northern Virginia, Springfield, VA, $45,000. Cash flow loan. 2000.
175-27. Housing and Community Services of Northern Virginia, Springfield, VA, $25,000. Cash flow loan. 2000.
175-28. Housing and Community Services of Northern Virginia, Springfield, VA, $10,000. Cash flow loan. 1999.
175-29. Housing Initiative Partnership, Hyattsville, MD, $50,000. Cash flow loan. 2000.
175-30. Jobs Have Priority (JHP), DC, $30,000. Cash flow loan. 2001.
175-31. Jobs Have Priority (JHP), DC, $40,000. Cash flow loan. 2000.
175-32. Latino Economic Development Corporation of Washington, DC, DC, $75,000. Cash flow loan. 2002.
175-33. Life Skills Center, DC, $15,300. Cash flow loan. 2000.
175-34. Metropolitan-Delta Adult Literacy Council, DC, $25,000. Cash flow loan. 1999.
175-35. National Child Day Care Association, DC, $68,498. Cash flow loan. 2000.
175-36. National Child Day Care Association, DC, $75,000. Cash flow loan. 1999.
175-37. North Capitol Neighborhood Development, DC, $75,000. Cash flow loan. 2002.
175-38. North Capitol Neighborhood Development, DC, $75,000. Cash flow loan. 2001.
175-39. Sexual Minority Youth Assistance League, DC, $50,000. Cash flow loan. 2001.
175-40. Suitland Family Life and Development Corporation, Suitland, MD, $75,000. Cash flow loan. 2001.

175-41. Suitland Family Life and Development Corporation, Suitland, MD, $25,000. Cash flow loan. 2000.

175-42. Support Center of Washington, DC, $75,000. Cash flow loan. 2001.

175-43. Support Center of Washington, DC, $40,000. Cash flow loan. 2000.

175-44. Support Center of Washington, DC, $45,000. Cash flow loan. 1999.

175-45. Time Dollar Institute, DC, $50,000. Cash flow loan. 2000.

175-46. Tony Powell Music and Movement, Silver Spring, MD, $16,000. Cash flow loan. 2000.

175-47. Top Banana Home Delivered Groceries, Brandywine, MD, $28,000. Cash flow loan. 2000.

175-48. U Street Theater Foundation, DC, $75,000. Cash flow loan. 2000.

175-49. University Legal Services, DC, $75,000. Cash flow loan. 1999.

175-50. Washington Chamber Symphony, DC, $75,000. Cash flow loan. 2002.

175-51. Washington Parks and People, DC, $50,000. Cash flow loan. 2000.

175-52. World Arts Focus, Mount Rainier, MD, $15,000. Cash flow loan. 2001.

176
Meyer Memorial Trust

(Formerly Fred Meyer Charitable Trust)
425 N.W. 10th Ave., Ste. 400
Portland, OR 97209 (503) 228-5512
Contact: Doug Stamm, Exec. Dir.
FAX: (503) 228-5840; E-mail: mmt@mmt.org;
URL: http://www.mmt.org

Trust established by will in 1978; obtained IRS status in 1982 in OR. PRI-related activities began in 1989.
Donor(s): Fred G. Meyer.‡
Grantmaker type: Independent foundation
General financial activity (yr. ended 03/31/02): Assets, $475,766,000 (M); expenditures, $26,970,827; qualifying distributions, $21,718,146; giving activities include $22,130,646 for grants (high: $1,000,000; low: $754; average: $10,000–$250,000) and $1,176,000 for 1 PRI.
Cumulative PRI activity (through 03/31/02): Since 1989, the foundation has made 8 PRIs totaling $2,951,000. The currently outstanding PRI portfolio includes 1 PRI totaling $1,176,000 (high: $1,176,000; low: $50,000; average: $147,000). The typical outstanding PRI has a 5- to 8-year term with an average term of 6 years, and earns 0 to 3 percent interest.
General purpose and activities: The trust provides general purpose grants, primarily in Oregon and Clark County, WA, for education, the arts and humanities, health, and social welfare. Under general purpose, the trust operates the Small Grants Program, which provides awards of $500 to $12,000 for small projects in Oregon. The Support for Teacher Initiatives Program provides awards of up to $7,000 to teachers in Oregon and Clark County, WA.
General fields of interest: Museums; performing arts; humanities; historic preservation/historical societies; arts/cultural programs; child development, education; higher education; education; natural resources conservation & protection; environment; health care; health associations; crime/violence prevention, youth; housing/shelter, development; human services; children & youth, services; child development, services; family services; aging, centers & services; community development; aging.
Program-related investment (PRI) activity: The trust has made PRIs to support projects including low-income housing development, adolescent mentoring, and recreation. PRIs have been used to finance construction and equipment acquisition, earned income ventures, and to provide program support.
Types of PRI Support: Loans/promissory notes.
Limitations: Giving primarily in OR and Clark County, WA. No support for sectarian or religious organizations for religious purposes. No grants to individuals or for endowment funds, annual campaigns, deficit financing, scholarships, fellowships, or indirect or overhead costs, except as specifically and essentially related to the grant project; occasional program-related loans only. The foundation accepts applications for PRIs.
Publications: Annual report, application guidelines.
PRI program information: The foundation does not maintain a formal PRI program. The foundation makes PRIs occasionally.
Officers and Trustees:* Debbie F. Craig,* Chair.; Wayne G. Pierson, C.F.O. and Treas.; Doug Stamm, Exec. Dir.; John Emrick, Orcilla Z. Forbes, Warne Nunn, Gerry Pratt.
Number of staff: 4 full-time professional; 3 part-time professional; 5 full-time support; 1 part-time support.
EIN: 930806316
PRI recipients:

176-1. Court Appointed Special Advocates (CASA) of Multnomah County, Portland, OR, $11,000. Program-related investment. 2000.

176-2. Habitat for Humanity of Portland, Portland, OR, $200,000. Loan to build homes for low-income residents in north Portland. 1999.

176-3. HOST Development, Portland, OR, $200,000. Program-related investment to provide financing for land costs of new affordable housing complex in Saint John's neighborhood of north Portland. 2001.

176-4. YWCA of Portland, Portland, ME, $1,176,000. No-interest loan to provide interim financing for renovation of downtown headquarters, community space, and transitional housing. 2002.

177
Michigan Capital Fund for Housing Non-Profit Housing Corporation
530 W. Iona St., Ste. F
Lansing, MI 48933-1062

Grantmaker type: Operating foundation
General financial activity (yr. ended 12/31/01): Assets, $29,921,374 (M); expenditures, $3,612,925; qualifying distributions, $6,594,555; giving activities include $551,963 for 78 grants (high: $100,000; low: $25), $361,473 for foundation-administered programs and $6,043,248 for PRIs.
General purpose and activities: Giving primarily to the delivery of quality, affordable housing to the poor and underprivileged, the promotion of efforts to facilitate self-sufficiency and upward mobility of very-low and low-income households, and the preservation of social welfare through efforts to facilitate the construction and development of housing for very low-, low- and moderate-income households in a manner directed to eliminate prejudice and discrimination, lessen neighborhood tensions, and combat the deterioration of communities throughout MI.
General fields of interest: Housing/shelter; economically disadvantaged.
Program-related investment (PRI) activity: The foundation makes PRIs, in the form of below market rate loans to non-profit organizations to allow them to develop affordable housing for low income tenants.
Types of PRI Support: Loans/promissory notes.
Limitations: Applications not accepted. Giving primarily in MI. No grants to individuals.
Officers: Mark McDaniel, Pres.; Christopher Cox, V.P.
EIN: 383126310
PRI recipients:
177-1. Autumn Grove Housing, Newaygo, MI, $10,018. Loan to develop low-income housing. 2001.
177-2. Central Detroit Christian Community Development Corporation, Detroit, MI, $33,000. Loan to develop low-income housing. 2000.
177-3. College Park Commons, Detroit, MI, $147,227. Loan to develop low-income housing. 1999.
177-4. Genesis Community Development Corporation, Detroit, MI, $25,244. Loan to develop low-income housing. 1999.
177-5. Golden Oaks, Detroit, MI, $346,694. Loan to develop low-income housing. 2001.
177-6. Golden Oaks, Detroit, MI, $158,466. Loan to develop low-income housing. 2000.
177-7. Golden Oaks, Detroit, MI, $153,517. Loan to develop low-income housing. 1999.
177-8. Hollander Development Corporation, Kalamazoo, MI, $11,020. Loan to develop low-income housing. 2000.
177-9. Kercheval Townhouses, Detroit, MI, $50,585. Loan to develop low-income housing. 2000.
177-10. Michigan Capital Fund for Housing, Lansing, MI, $2,685,009. Bridge loan to develop low-income housing. 2000.
177-11. Northern Homes Community Development, Boyne City, MI, $100,181. Loan to develop low-income housing. 2001.
177-12. Northstar Community Development Corporation, Detroit, MI, $52,663. Loan to develop low-income housing. 1999.
177-13. Paddock Nonprofit Housing Corporation, Lansing, MI, $50,585. Loan to develop low-income housing. 2000.
177-14. Riverside Estates, MI, $50,585. Loan to develop low-income housing. 2000.
177-15. Simon House, Detroit, MI, $30,411. Loan to develop low-income housing for women and children with HIV/AIDS. 2000.
177-16. Southwest Nonprofit Housing Corporation, Detroit, MI, $51,119. Loan to develop low-income housing. 1999.
177-17. Trinity Village Nonprofit Housing Corporation, Muskegon, MI, $33,914. Loan to develop low-income housing. 2001.
177-18. U-SNAP-BAC Nonprofit Housing Corporation, Detroit, MI, $45,983. Loan to develop low-income housing. 2001.

178
The Miller Foundation
(Formerly Albert L. and Louise B. Miller Foundation, Inc.)
310 WahWahTaySee Way
Battle Creek, MI 49015 (269) 964-3542
Contact: Fred Woodruff, Pres. and C.E.O.
FAX: (269) 964-8455; URL: http://www.willard.lib.mi.us/npa/miller

Incorporated in 1963 in MI.
Donor(s): Louise B. Miller,‡ Robert B. Miller.‡
Grantmaker type: Independent foundation
General financial activity (yr. ended 12/31/01): Assets, $33,246,004 (M); expenditures, $1,639,910; qualifying distributions, $1,647,552; giving activities include $976,875 for 61 grants (high: $200,000; low: $100) and $225,000 for 1 PRI.
Cumulative PRI activity (through 12/31/01): Since beginning PRI activity, the foundation has made PRIs totaling $225,000.
General purpose and activities: Local support for higher education, public schools, local municipal improvements, and cultural programs.
General fields of interest: Adult/continuing education; human services; children & youth, services; community development, neighborhood development; economic development.
Program-related investment (PRI) activity: The foundation has made a PRI to a school development corporation.

Limitations: Giving limited to the greater Battle Creek, MI, area. No grants to individuals, or for endowments.
Publications: Annual report.
Officers and Trustees:* Arthur W. Angood,* Chair.; Fred M. Woodruff, Jr.,* Pres. and C.E.O.; Barbara L. Comai,* V.P.; Rance L. Leaders,* Secy.-Treas.; Allen L. Miller, Robert B. Miller, Jr., Paul R. Ohm, Gloria J. Robertson.
Number of staff: 2 full-time professional.
EIN: 386064925
PRI recipients:
178-1. Private School Development Corporation, Battle Creek, MI, $225,000. Program-related investment. 2001.

179
The Claude Moore Charitable Foundation
P.O. Box 208
Oakton, VA 22124
Contact: Jesse B. Wilson III, Tr.

Established in 1987.
Donor(s): Claude Moore.‡
Grantmaker type: Independent foundation
General financial activity (yr. ended 12/31/01): Assets, $100,376,475 (M); expenditures, $2,714,106; qualifying distributions, $2,913,391; giving activities include $2,403,636 for 6 grants (high: $1,895,387; low: $374); no PRIs paid.
General purpose and activities: Giving primarily for the enhancement of educational opportunities for young people.
General fields of interest: Museums; adult education—literacy, basic skills & GED; reading; Boy Scouts.
Program-related investment (PRI) activity: The foundation leases land to the National Capital Council of the Boy Scouts of America for camping and other scouting activities. The set-aside of this land was approved in 1992 as a charitable grant. Additional land, valued at $13.1 million, was designated for use by the Boy Scouts in 1997. In 2001, a portion of the property under lease was sold
Types of PRI Support: Charitable use assets.
Limitations: Giving primarily in Washington, DC, and VA. No grants to individuals. PRI applications not accepted.
Officer: J. Hamilton Lambert, Exec. Dir.
Trustees: Peter A. Arnston, Leigh B. Middleditch, Jr., Verlin W. Smith, Jesse B. Wilson III.
Number of staff: None.
EIN: 521558571

180
Gordon and Betty Moore Foundation
The Presidio
P.O. Box 29910
San Francisco, CA 94129-0910 (415) 561-7700
PRI Contact: Genny Biggs
E-mail: info@moore.org; URL: http://www.moore.org

Established in 2000 in CA. PRI-related activities began in 2002.
Donor(s): Gordon E. Moore, Betty I. Moore.
Grantmaker type: Independent foundation
General financial activity (yr. ended 12/31/01): Assets, $163,342,305 (M); gifts received, $155,781,250; expenditures, $56,333,293; qualifying distributions, $46,873,357; giving activities include $42,504,796 for 37 grants (high: $25,000,000; low: $1,000); no PRIs paid.
Cumulative PRI activity (through 12/31/01): Since 2002, the foundation has made 1 PRI totaling $10,000,000. The currently outstanding PRI portfolio includes an average PRI value of $10,000,000. The typical outstanding PRI has an average term of 4 years.
General purpose and activities: The foundation supports four major programs areas: education, scientific research, the environment, and select San Francisco Bay Area projects. The foundation strives to fund projects that will further it's mission— projects chosen through careful research, projects promising significant measurable results.
General fields of interest: Higher education; environment; science.
Program-related investment (PRI) activity: The foundation has made a PRI to a conservation organization to help with purchase and upkeep of a new facility.
Types of PRI Support: Loans/promissory notes.
Limitations: Applications not accepted. Giving on a worldwide basis, with some focus on the San Francisco, CA, area for selected projects. No grants to individuals. PRI applications not accepted.
PRI program information: The foundation does not maintain a formal PRI program. The foundation makes PRIs occasionally.
Officers and Trustees:* Gordon E. Moore,* Chair, Secy., and C.F.O.; Lewis W. Coleman,* Pres.; Betty I. Moore, Kenneth G. Moore, Steven E. Moore, Kenneth F. Siebel.
EIN: 943397785
PRI recipients:
180-1. Nature Conservancy, Arlington, VA, $10,000,000. Program-related investment for Palmyra Island (Pacific Island ecosystem) acquisition. 2002.

181
The Morey Foundation
P.O. Box 1000
Winn, MI 48896
Contact: Lon Morey, Pres.

Established in 1990 in MI.
Donor(s): Norval Morey.
Grantmaker type: Independent foundation
General financial activity (yr. ended 12/31/01): Assets, $33,788,675 (M); gifts received, $22,897,474; expenditures, $470,187; qualifying distributions, $225,233; giving activities include $69,169 for 6 grants (high: $50,000; low: $500) and $156,064 for PRIs.

Cumulative PRI activity (through 12/31/01): Since beginning PRI activity, the foundation has made PRIs totaling $5,567,415.
General purpose and activities: Scholarships for students enrolled at Central Michigan University.
General fields of interest: Elementary/secondary education; human services.
Program-related investment (PRI) activity: The foundation made program-related investments that were used by a public school academy for educational purposes, including the building of a school, and the purchase of equipment and furniture.
Types of PRI Support: Charitable use assets.
Limitations: Applications not accepted. Giving primarily in MI.
Officers and Trustee:* Lon Morey,* Pres.; Jeffery Power, Secy.; Larry H. Hoch, Treas.
EIN: 382965346

182
Moriah Fund

1 Farragut Sq. S.
1634 I St., N.W., Ste. 1000
Washington, DC 20006 (202) 783-8488
Contact: Mary Ann Stein, Pres.
PRI Contact: Rubie Coles, Assoc. Dir.
FAX: (202) 783-8499; Request in Israel: Susan Feit, P.O.Box 2788, Neve Monosson, Israel 60190; E-mail: info@moriahfund.org; URL: http://www.moriahfund.org/index.htm

Established in 1985 in IN.
Donor(s): Clarence W. Efroymson,‡ Robert A. Efroymson,‡ Ben-Ephraim Gershon Fund, Gustave Aaron Efroymson Fund.
Grantmaker type: Independent foundation
General financial activity (yr. ended 12/31/02): Assets, $131,295,982 (M); gifts received, $165,592; expenditures, $12,239,388; qualifying distributions, $11,073,402; giving activities include $9,757,500 for 237 grants (high: $1,538,000; low: $1,000; average: $20,000–$50,000) and $75,000 for 1 PRI.
Cumulative PRI activity (through 12/31/02): Since beginning PRI activity, the foundation has made 2 PRIs totaling $200,000. The currently outstanding PRI portfolio includes 1 PRI totaling $100,000 (average: $100,000). The typical outstanding PRI has an average term of 5 years, and earns an average of 2 percent interest.
General purpose and activities: Support primarily for pluralism, democracy, and community development in Israel; human rights, civic participation and leadership of indigenous people, rural development, and social justice in Guatemala for reproductive health and conservation of biodiversity domestically and internationally; and community-based development and programs to help families overcome poverty and gain self-sufficiency in Washington, DC, only.
General fields of interest: Natural resources conservation & protection; environment; health care, reproductive health; family planning; family services, single parents; international human rights; civil rights; rural development; community development; leadership development.
General international interests: Russia; Ukraine; Latin America; Guatemala; Israel.
Program-related investment (PRI) activity: The foundation has made PRIs to an organization that rehabilitates housing for low-income people for facility aquisition, and to an organization in support of its efforts to capitalize eco-enterprises rooted in poor communities in rural Guatemala.
Types of PRI Support: Loans/promissory notes.
Limitations: Giving nationally and internationally, including Israel and Latin America; giving primarily in Washington, DC for poverty program. No support for lobbying or political campaigns, private foundations, or arts organizations. No grants to individuals, or for medical research. PRI applications not accepted.
Publications: Annual report (including application guidelines), application guidelines.
PRI program information: The fund resumed PRI actiuvity in 2001. All inquiries should be directed to the Washington, DC, office. The foundation maintains a formal PRI program. The foundation makes PRIs occasionally.
Officers and Program Board:* Mary Ann Stein,* Pres.; Judith Lichtman,* 1st V.P. and Treas.; Shira Saperstein, 2nd V.P. and Prog. Dir., Women's Rights and Reprod; Karl Mathiasen,* Secy.; Geeta Rao Gupta, Noah Stein, Dorothy Stein Swamy.
Number of staff: 8 full-time professional; 6 full-time support; 1 part-time support.
EIN: 311129589
PRI recipients:
182-1. EcoLogic Enterprise Ventures, Cambridge, MA, $100,000. Loan to support financing community-based enterprises engaged in production or processing of activities that foster environemtnal, conservation and socially equitable development in Guatemala. 2001.

183
The Mosaic Foundation of R. & P. Heydon

2394 Winewood St.
P.O. Box 7801
Ann Arbor, MI 48107-7801
Contact: Peter N. Heydon, Dir.

Established in 1990 in MI.
Donor(s): Kenneth F. Montgomery, Peter N. Heydon, Henrietta M. Heydon.
Grantmaker type: Independent foundation
General financial activity (yr. ended 12/31/00): Assets, $3,094,563 (M); gifts received, $5,226; expenditures, $333,906; qualifying distributions, $354,744; giving activities include $293,238 for grants and $61,506 for 1 PRI.

General purpose and activities: Giving primarily for the arts and education.
General fields of interest: Radio; museums; arts/cultural programs; elementary/secondary education; higher education; environment; animals/wildlife; human services.
Program-related investment (PRI) activity: The foundation makes PRIs, in the form of building and improvements to be used by a feline refuge. The feline refuge does not pay for building expenses or rent.
Types of PRI Support: Charitable use assets.
Limitations: Applications not accepted. Giving in the U.S., with emphasis on MI. No grants to individuals.
Directors: James R. Beuche, Henrietta M. Heydon, Peter N. Heydon.
EIN: 382910797
PRI recipients:
183-1. Mosaic Feline Refuge, Ann Arbor, MI, $61,506. Program-related investment for building and improvements. 2000.
183-2. Mosaic Feline Refuge, Ann Arbor, MI, $119,507. Program-related investment for building improvements. Refuge does not pay for building expenses or rent. 1999.

184
The New Hampshire Charitable Foundation

37 Pleasant St.
Concord, NH 03301-4005 (603) 225-6641
Contact: Racheal Stuart, V.P., Progs.
PRI Contact: Stuart Comstock-Gay, V.P., Prog.
FAX: (603) 225-1700; E-mail: info@nhcf.org, or rs@nhcf.org; URL: http://www.nhcf.org

Incorporated in 1962 in NH.
Grantmaker type: Community foundation
General financial activity (yr. ended 12/31/01): Assets, $230,219,273 (M); gifts received, $17,469,155; expenditures, $16,397,597; giving activities include $8,688,340 for 2,019 grants (high: $500,000; low: $100; average: $5,000–$15,000), $1,799,102 for 1,358 grants to individuals (average: $500–$3,000), $474,464 for loans to individuals and $113,646 for 2 PRIs.
Cumulative PRI activity (through 12/31/01): Since beginning PRI activity, the foundation has made 36 PRIs totaling $2,078,225. The currently outstanding PRI portfolio includes 7 PRIs totaling $294,807 (high: $100,000; low: $10,000). The typical outstanding PRI has a 2- to 5-year term, and earns 5.10 to 9 percent interest.
General purpose and activities: Giving for charitable and educational purposes including the arts, humanities, the environment and conservation, health, and social and community services; grants primarily to inaugurate new programs and strengthen existing charitable organizations, with emphasis on programs rather than capital needs; support also for college scholarships.
General fields of interest: Humanities; arts/cultural programs; education; natural resources conservation & protection; environment; health care; health associations; human services.
Program-related investment (PRI) activity: Since the early 1970s, the foundation has served as a lender of last resort to nonprofit organizations in New Hampshire. The majority of loans are made through permanent revolving loan funds established in specific areas, including health, human services, the environment, historic preservation, and the arts. The foundation also maintains several general purpose revolving loan funds. In addition, the foundation has made loans from undistributed income and, occasionally, from permanent foundation assets. Loans have provided interim financing, supported facility improvements and land and equipment acquisition, and capitalized earned income ventures and housing development projects.
Types of PRI Support: Loans/promissory notes, loan guarantees.
Limitations: Giving limited to NH. No support for sectarian or religious purposes. No grants to individuals (except for student aid and special awards); generally no grants for building funds, endowments, operating support, deficit financing, capital campaigns for acquisition of land or renovations to facilities, purchase of major equipment, academic research, out-of-state travel, or to replace public funding or for purposes which are a public responsibility. The foundation accepts applications for PRIs.
Publications: Annual report, program policy statement, informational brochure (including application guidelines), financial statement, grants list, newsletter, application guidelines, informational brochure.
PRI program information: The foundation does not maintain a formal PRI program. The foundation makes PRIs on a frequent but not annual basis.
Officers and Directors:* Mary Susan Leahy,* Chair.; Lewis M. Feldstein,* Pres.; Stuart Comstock-Gay, C.O.O.; Racheal Stuart, V.P., Progs.; Harold W. Janeway,* Treas.; Stephen P. Barba, Barry L. Brensinger, John D. Crosier, Ann Mclane Kuster, Joan R. Leitzel, Stuart V. Smith, Jr., Elizabeth Story Wright.
Number of staff: 23 full-time professional; 6 part-time professional; 6 full-time support; 2 part-time support.
EIN: 026005625
PRI recipients:
184-1. Granite State Ballet, Nashua, NH, $10,000. Loan. 1999.
184-2. Merrimack Valley AIDS Project, Concord, NH, $50,000. Loan. 1999.
184-3. Neighborhood Housing Services of Manchester, Manchester, NH, $18,230. Loan. 2000.
184-4. Neighborhood Housing Services of Manchester, Manchester, NH, $11,917. Loan. 1999.
184-5. New Hampshire Public Radio, Concord, NH, $95,679. Loan. 2001.
184-6. New Hampshire Symphony, Manchester, NH, $85,000. Loan. 2000.

185

The Samuel Roberts Noble Foundation, Inc.
2510 Sam Noble Pkwy.
P.O. Box 2180
Ardmore, OK 73402 (580) 223-5810
Contact: Michael A. Cawley, C.E.O. and Pres.
PRI Contact: Donna K. Windel, Prog. Off.
URL: http://www.noble.org

Trust established in 1945 in OK; incorporated in 1952. PRI-related activities began in 1999.
Donor(s): Lloyd Noble.‡
Grantmaker type: Independent foundation
General financial activity (yr. ended 10/31/01): Assets, $863,492,527 (M); expenditures, $53,056,818; qualifying distributions, $49,046,914; giving activities include $7,595,699 for 109 grants (high: $770,000; low: $2,500; average: $5,000–$500,000), $296,750 for 86 grants to individuals (high: $5,000; low: $1,500; average: $1,500–$5,000), $104,051 for 51 employee matching gifts, $37,653,241 for 3 foundation-administered programs and $644,000 for 1 PRI.
Cumulative PRI activity (through 10/31/01): Since 1999, the foundation has made 3 PRIs totaling $1,057,867. The currently outstanding PRI portfolio includes 3 PRIs totaling $1,057,867 (high: $644,000; low: $63,867). The typical outstanding PRI has an average term of 2 years.
General purpose and activities: Support through three operating programs for: 1) enabling individual farmers and ranchers to better understand resource management and achieve their goals through consultation, education, research and demonstration; 2) enhancing plant productivity through fundamental research and applied biotechnology; and 3) assisting community service, health research and delivery systems, educational and other selected nonprofit organizations through grants and employee involvement. The foundation also administers a matching gift program for Noble Co. employees.
General fields of interest: Higher education; health care; medical research; human services.
Program-related investment (PRI) activity: The foundation has made loans to a neighborhood revitalization group and a life sciences research firm.
Types of PRI Support: Loans/promissory notes, equity investments.
Limitations: Giving primarily in the Southwest, with emphasis on OK. No grants to individuals (except through the scholarship program for children of employees of Noble organizations); no loans (except for program-related investments). No new PRI proposals are being reviewed at present. PRI applications not accepted.
Publications: Annual report, application guidelines, informational brochure.
PRI program information: The foundation does not maintain a formal PRI program. The foundation makes PRIs occasionally.
Officers and Trustees:* Michael A. Cawley,* C.E.O. and Pres.; Larry Pulliam, Exec. V.P.; Elizabeth A. Aldridge, Secy.; Ann Noble Brown, D. Randolph Brown, Susan Brown, James C. Day, Vivian N. Dubose, William R. Goddard, Jr., Shelley Dru Mullins, Edward E. Noble, Maria Noble, Nick Noble, Rusty Noble, Marianne Rooney, William G. Thurman.
Number of staff: 120 full-time professional; 160 full-time support.
EIN: 730606209
PRI recipients:
185-1. Eastside Renaissance, Ardmore, OK, $63,867. Program-related investment. 2000.
185-2. Oklahoma Life Sciences Fund, Ardmore, OK, $644,000. Program-related investment. 2001.
185-3. Oklahoma Life Sciences Fund, Ardmore, OK, $350,000. Program-related investment. 2000.

186

Norcross Wildlife Foundation, Inc.
Caller Box No. 611
250 W. 88th St., Ste. 806
New York, NY 10024 (212) 362-4831
Contact: Richard S. Reagan, Pres., or John McMurray, Prog. Off.
Additional tel.: (718) 791-2094; Application address: Grants Admin., P.O. Box 269, Wales, MA 01081; URL: http://www.norcrossws.org

Established in 1964 in NY.
Donor(s): Arthur D. Norcross,‡ June Norcross Webster.‡
Grantmaker type: Independent foundation
General financial activity (yr. ended 12/31/01): Assets, $67,553,653 (M); gifts received, $102,000; expenditures, $4,419,058; qualifying distributions, $5,892,376; giving activities include $1,869,461 for 272 grants (high: $55,000; low: $750; average: $5,000–$10,000) and $699,000 for 4 PRIs.
General purpose and activities: Support primarily for conservation, including environmental and wildlife organizations, and historical preservation; extremely limited support also for health organizations, assistance for the handicapped, drug abuse programs, and education.
General fields of interest: Natural resources conservation & protection; environment; wildlife preservation & protection.
Program-related investment (PRI) activity: The foundation made PRIs in the form of non-interest bearing loans to nonprofit organizations. The foundation has also invested in a company for land purchases.
Types of PRI Support: Loans/promissory notes.
Limitations: Giving primarily in North America. No grants to individuals, or for operating support, overhead expenses, research endowments, conferences, matching gifts, or multi-year grants.
Publications: Annual report (including application guidelines), application guidelines, multi-year report.
Officers and Directors:* Richard S. Reagan,* Pres.; Joseph A. Catalano,* V.P. and Secy.; Karen Outlaw, Treas.; Warren Balgooyen, Albia Dugger, Edward Gallagher, Arthur D.

Norcross, Jr., Michael D. Patrick, Denise Schlener, Christof von Strasser, Ted Williams.
Number of staff: 3 full-time professional; 1 full-time support.
EIN: 132041622

187
Northern Michigan Foundation
P.O. Box 932
Elk Rapids, MI 49629 (800) 652-4326
Contact: Charles S. McDowell, Exec. V.P.

Established in 1996 in MI.
Donor(s): Stephen L. Ranzini.
Grantmaker type: Operating foundation
General financial activity (yr. ended 12/31/01): Assets, $1,585,263 (M); gifts received, $11,795; expenditures, $133,763; qualifying distributions, $126,935; giving activities include $16,705 for grants (high: $5,005) and $115,303 for 15 PRIs.
General purpose and activities: The foundation makes loans to businesses in economically distressed counties in the eastern upper and northern lower peninsula of Michigan. Applicants to be considered for loan purposes must be denied credit by traditional lending institutions such as commercial banks and credit unions.
General fields of interest: Community development, business promotion; community development, small businesses.
Program-related investment (PRI) activity: The foundation provides loans to local businesses in economically distressed areas of northern Michigan that cannot secure credit from traditional institutions.
Types of PRI Support: Loans/promissory notes.
Limitations: Giving limited to MI. PRI giving primarily in northern MI.
PRI program information: The foundation makes PRIs on a frequent but not annual basis.
Officers: Joseph L. Ranzini, Pres.; Charles S. McDowell, Exec. V.P.; Stephen Lange Ranzini, Treas.
Directors: Andrew Johnson, Stuart Merillat, Sharon Teeple, Mary L. Trucks, James Trumbull.
EIN: 383136089

188
Northwest Minnesota Foundation (NWMF)
4225 Technology Dr. N.W.
Bemidji, MN 56601 (218) 759-2057
Contact: Tim Wang, Fin. Dir.
Additional tel.: (800) 659-7859; FAX: (218) 759-2328; E-mail: nwmf@nwmf.org; URL: http://www.nwmf.org

Established in 1986 in MN.
Donor(s): McKnight Foundation.
Grantmaker type: Community foundation
General financial activity (yr. ended 06/30/02): Assets, $30,133,937 (M); gifts received, $2,443,159; expenditures, $2,705,883; giving activities include $778,924 for 101 grants (high: $58,400; low: $150; average: $150–$58,400), $44,050 for 53 grants to individuals, $245,245 for 8 foundation-administered programs, $412,409 for 1 in-kind gift and $1,036,775 for 16 loans to individuals; no PRIs paid.
General purpose and activities: Invests resources, creates opportunities and promotes philanthropy to make the region a better place to live and work.
General fields of interest: Youth development; community development, business promotion; leadership development; economically disadvantaged.
Program-related investment (PRI) activity: The foundation has made PRIs in the form of loans for business start-ups and expansions that create jobs leading to long-term community impact, diversification of the economy, and that leverage other sources of funds to increase total capital investment in the region. The foundation has also made PRIs, in the form of loans, to help develop small business and self-employment opportunities.
Limitations: Giving limited to Beltrami, Clearwater, Hubbard, Kittson, Lake of the Woods, Mahnomen, Marshall, Norman, Pennington, Polk, Red Lake, and Roseau counties, MN. No support for religious or political activities. No grants for capital campaigns, equipment, annual campaigns, endowments, building, or general/operating expenses. PRI giving limited to MN.
Publications: Application guidelines, annual report, informational brochure, newsletter.
PRI program information: The foundation maintains multiple loan economic development loan funds.
Officers and Directors:* Kip Fontaine,* Chair.; John Ostrem, Pres.; Bruce Meade,* V.P.; Carolyn Eeg,* Secy.; Ranae Womack, Ph.D.,* Treas.; Linda Bentson, Diane Blair, Dean Johnson, Kelly Myers, Victor Olson, Gary Purata, Terry Anderson Rothschadl, Mary Beth Sargent.
Number of staff: 13 full-time professional; 3 full-time support.
EIN: 411556013

189
Oberkotter Foundation
1600 Market St., Ste. 3600
Philadelphia, PA 19103-7286 (215) 751-2601
Contact: George H. Nofer, J.D., Exec. Dir.
FAX: (215) 751-2678; E-mail: RSTRAUS@Schnader.com

Established in 1985 in PA.
Donor(s): Paul Oberkotter.‡
Grantmaker type: Independent foundation
General financial activity (yr. ended 11/30/01): Assets, $152,736,260; gifts received, $3,354,537; expenditures, $32,683,633; qualifying distributions, $27,556,235; giving activities include $27,181,235 for 143 grants (high: $1,600,000; low: $1,000; average: $10,000–$200,000),

$2,778,873 for 4 foundation-administered programs and $375,000 for 1 PRI.
Cumulative PRI activity (through 11/30/01): The currently outstanding PRI portfolio includes PRIs totaling $3,520,000.
General purpose and activities: The foundation limits its grants to educational institutions and centers for the deaf that use the auditory/oral or auditory/verbal method exclusively; research in the area of hearing-impairment where interdisciplinary resources are used; outreach programs for the treatment of diabetes; and research in the area of diabetes.
General fields of interest: Education, special; speech & hearing centers; diabetes; ear & throat research; diabetes research.
Program-related investment (PRI) activity: The foundation made a PRI to purchase school building.
Types of PRI Support: Loans/promissory notes.
Officer and Trustees:* George H. Nofer, J.D.,* Exec. Dir.; Bruce A. Rosenfield, Assoc. Exec. Dir.; Mildred Oberkotter.
Number of staff: 1 full-time professional; 1 part-time support.
EIN: 232686151
PRI recipients:
189-1. Alexander Graham Bell Association for the Deaf, DC, $375,000. Loan for building project at Volta Place. 2001.
189-2. River School, Charleston, WV, $3,520,000. Short-term loan to enable school to purchase building. 1999.

190
Open Society Institute
400 W. 59th St., 4th Fl.
New York, NY 10019 (212) 548-0600
Contact: Inquiry Mgr.
FAX: (212) 548-4605; URL: http://www.soros.org

Established in 1993 in NY.
Donor(s): George Soros.
Grantmaker type: Operating foundation
General financial activity (yr. ended 12/31/01): Assets, $176,900,034 (M); gifts received, $220,378,692; expenditures, $165,767,095; qualifying distributions, $166,731,723; giving activities include $91,485,757 for 807 grants (high: $10,000,000; low: $75; average: $10,000–$500,000), $16,970,534 for 1,346 grants to individuals (high: $116,600; low: $16; average: $1,500–$40,000), $626,650 for 234 employee matching gifts, $22,847,579 for foundation-administered programs and $1,500,000 for 1 PRI.
Cumulative PRI activity (through 12/31/01): The currently outstanding PRI portfolio includes PRIs totaling $1,975,000.
General purpose and activities: The Open Society Institute (OSI) promotes the development and maintenance of open societies around the world by supporting an array of activities dealing with educational, social, legal, and health care reform, and by encouraging alternative approaches to complex and controversial issues. Based in New York City, OSI is a private operating and grantmaking foundation. OSI offices in New York and Budapest develop programs that are administered in over 50 countries by a network of regional Soros foundations. OSI has three broad categories of programs: international network programs, other international initiatives, and U.S. programs. The Open Society Institute also has offices in Brussels, Paris, and Washington, DC, which work to establish relationships with governments, government aid programs, and international donor organizations.
General fields of interest: Media/communications; arts/cultural programs; education; health care; international economic development; international human rights; science; law/international law.
Program-related investment (PRI) activity: The foundation has made loans to organizations for the alleviation of community deterioration and poverty in devastated areas and to distribute a drug for use as an emergency contraceptive.
Types of PRI Support: Loans/promissory notes.
Limitations: Giving on a national and international basis.
Publications: Annual report.
Officers and Trustees:* George Soros,* Chair.; Aryeh Neier,* C.E.O. and Pres.; Stewart Paperin, Exec. V.P.; Gara LaMarche, V.P.; Morton Abramowitz, Leon Botstein, Geoffrey Canada, Joan B. Dunlop, Lani Guinier, Bill D. Moyers, David J. Rothman, Thomas M. Scanlan, Jr., John G. Simon, Herbert Sturz.
EIN: 137029285
PRI recipients:
190-1. Construction Management Alliance (Europe), Oxford, England, $1,750,000. Loan for alleviation of community deterioration and poverty in devasted areas, and advancement of education, science and culture. 2000.
190-2. Construction Management Alliance (Europe), Oxford, England, $750,000. Loan for alleviation of community deterioration and poverty in devasted areas, and advancement of education, science and culture. 2000.
190-3. Womens Capital Corporation, DC, $1,500,000. Program-related investment to develop, procure, package, market, and distribute Levonoregestrel in the U.S. and certain other countries for use as emergency contraceptive. 2001.

191
Gerald Oppenheimer Family Foundation
(Formerly Gerald and Virginia Oppenheimer Family Foundation)
P.O. Box 30
Beverly Hills, CA 90213-0030 (310) 276-2101
Contact: Tracey Boldemann, V.P. and Secy.

Established in 1987 in CA.
Donor(s): Gerald H. Oppenheimer.

Grantmaker type: Independent foundation
General financial activity (yr. ended 11/30/01): Assets, $20,947,146 (M); gifts received, $985,317; expenditures, $1,260,267; qualifying distributions, $1,243,294; giving activities include $1,181,047 for grants (average: $500–$1,000); no PRIs paid.
Cumulative PRI activity (through 11/30/01): Since beginning PRI activity, the foundation has made 2 PRIs totaling $311,000. The currently outstanding PRI portfolio includes 3 PRIs totaling $300,000.
General purpose and activities: Giving primarily for health care and the arts.
General fields of interest: Arts/cultural programs; higher education; health care; human services.
Program-related investment (PRI) activity: The foundation has made low-interest loans to provide medical information for the blind and visually impaired and to landscape and preserve a veterans' cemetery.
Types of PRI Support: Loans/promissory notes.
Limitations: Applications not accepted. Giving primarily in Los Angeles, CA. No grants to individuals. PRI applications not accepted.
PRI program information: The foundation does not maintain a formal PRI program. The foundation makes PRIs occasionally.
Officers and Directors:* Gerald H. Oppenheimer,* Pres.; Tracey Boldemann,* V.P. and Secy.; Bill Oppenheimer,* V.P.; Mark Oppenheimer,* V.P.; Linda Valliant,* V.P.; Stephen Petty,* Treas.
Number of staff: None.
EIN: 953957582
PRI recipients:

191-1. E-Access Foundation, Van Nuys, CA, $300,000. Program-related investment to provide medical information via the Internet to the blind and visually impaired at no charge. 1999.

191-2. Veterans Park Preserve, Los Angeles, CA, $11,000. Program-related investment to landscape and preserve Veterans National Cemetery. 1999.

192
Pacific Northwest Foundation

(Formerly Cook Family Trust, Inc.)
7619 S.W. 26th Ave.
Portland, OR 97219-2538 (503) 977-3226
Contact: Anna M. Salanti, Pres.
FAX: (503) 244-9946; E-mail: asalanti@attbi.com or frank-cook@attbi.com; URL: http://www.pnf.org

Established in 1988 in OR as partial successor to the Cook Brothers Educational Fund.
Donor(s): Howard F. Cook.‡
Grantmaker type: Independent foundation
General financial activity (yr. ended 12/31/01): Assets, $3,314,133 (M); expenditures, $227,323; qualifying distributions, $213,509; giving activities include $94,625 for grants (average: $250–$47,732); no PRIs paid.
General fields of interest: General charitable giving.
Program-related investment (PRI) activity: The foundation generally does not make PRIs. However, the foundation will award infrequent PRIs to local area charities under certain circumstances.
Limitations: Applications not accepted. Giving on a national basis. No grants to individuals. PRIs limited to the Portland, OR area. PRI applications not accepted.
Publications: Annual report, financial statement.
PRI program information: The foundation does not maintain a formal PRI program. The foundation makes PRIs occasionally.
Officers: Anna M. Salanti, Pres.; Franklin C. Cook, V.P. and Secy.-Treas.; Kathleen M. Cook, V.P.
Board Members: Adria Dodici, Tim Mulvihill.
Number of staff: 2 part-time professional.
EIN: 770177829

193
The David and Lucile Packard Foundation

300 2nd St., Ste. 200
Los Altos, CA 94022 (650) 948-7658
Contact: Prog. Off. of area of interest
PRI Contact: Edward Diener
URL: http://www.packard.org

Incorporated in 1964 in CA. PRI-related activities began in 1987.
Donor(s): David Packard,‡ Lucile Packard.‡
Grantmaker type: Independent foundation
General financial activity (yr. ended 12/31/01): Assets, $6,196,520,868 (M); expenditures, $650,603,713; qualifying distributions, $512,033,075; giving activities include $427,596,659 for 2,197 grants (high: $30,000,000; low: $2,500; average: $2,500–$30,000,000), $226,258 for 344 employee matching gifts, $17,308,000 for 3 foundation-administered programs and $35,640,934 for 14 PRIs.
Cumulative PRI activity (through 12/31/01): The currently outstanding PRI portfolio includes 18 PRIs totaling $84,903,061 (high: $14,200,000; low: $212,500; average: $3,800,000). The typical outstanding PRI has a 1- to 20-year term with an average term of 3 years and earns 1 to 3 percent interest with an average of 3 percent.
General purpose and activities: The foundation provides grants to nonprofit organizations in the following program areas: Children, Families, and Communities; Population; and Science and Conservation; National and international grants are provided, with a special focus on the local northern California counties of San Mateo, Santa Clara, Santa Cruz, and Monterey.
General fields of interest: Performing arts; dance; theater; music; arts/cultural programs; early childhood education; natural resources conservation & protection; energy; environment; wildlife, fisheries; family planning; health care, insurance; youth development, services; human services; children & youth, services; children, day care;

child development, services; reproductive rights; urban/community development; community development; philanthropy/voluntarism; marine science; engineering & technology; science; population studies; economically disadvantaged.

Program-related investment (PRI) activity: The foundation makes PRIs within its program areas when organizations can demonstrate that repayment will be forthcoming. Recent PRIs have supported the acquisition of land for environmental conservation purposes, construction of a childcare and family services center, and development and distribution of an emergency contraceptive product.

Types of PRI Support: Loans/promissory notes, interim financing, loan guarantees, linked deposits.

Limitations: Giving for the arts and community development primarily in Santa Clara, San Mateo, Santa Cruz, and Monterey counties, CA; Pueblo, CO, Los Altos and national giving for child health and development; national and international giving for population and the environment. No support for religious purposes. No grants to individuals. The foundation accepts applications for PRIs.

PRI program information: The foundation maintains a formal PRI program. The foundation makes PRIs on an annual basis.

Officers and Trustees:* Susan Packard Orr,* Chair.; Nancy Packard Burnett,* Vice-Chair.; Julie E. Packard,* Vice-Chair.; Richard T. Schlosberg III,* Pres. and C.E.O.; Carol S. Larson, V.P. and Dir., Fdn. Progs.; Barbara P. Wright, Secy.; George Vera, C.F.O. and Dir., Finance and Admin.; Dean O. Morton,* Treas.; Jane Lubchenco, Franklin M. Orr, Lew E. Platt, William K. Reilly, Allan Rosenfield, Robert Stephens, Colburn S. Wilbur.

Number of staff: 93 full-time professional; 5 part-time professional; 62 full-time support; 4 part-time support.

EIN: 942278431

PRI recipients:

193-1. Audubon Society, National, NYC, NY, $5,000,000. Loan for acquisitions associated with San Francisco Baylands program. 2001.

193-2. Bank of America Community Development Bank, Walnut Creek, CA, $14,434. Guaranty of 90 days of interest of child care financing loan to Educational Enrichment Systems. 2001.

193-3. Bank of America Community Development Bank, Walnut Creek, CA, $310,888. Program-related investment to provide guarantee support and interest subsidies in a loan program providing affordable financing for nonprofit child care facilities. 1999.

193-4. Big Sur Land Trust, Carmel, CA, $3,038,000. Loan for acquisition of Grant Rock Dunes just north of Monterey Peninsula for coastal habitat protection. 2000.

193-5. Big Sur Land Trust, Carmel, CA, $3,000,000. Loan to pay off seller's note on Point Lobos Ranch property to protect against development. 2000.

193-6. Boys and Girls Club of the Peninsula, Menlo Park, CA, $750,000. Loan for construction and renovation of three local youth facilities. 2000.

193-7. BRIDGE Housing Corporation, San Francisco, CA, $7,000,000. Program-related investment to provide multi-family affordable housing in Phase III of Gateway 101 Project in East Palo Alto. 1999.

193-8. Danco Laboratories, NYC, NY, $4,200,000. Loan to support contraceptive technology development. 2001.

193-9. Danco Laboratories, NYC, NY, $9,500,000. Program-related investment to help support contraceptive technology development. 1999.

193-10. East Palo Alto Community Alliance and Neighborhood Development Organization (EPA CAN DO), East Palo Alto, CA, $212,500. Loan for acquisition of land for Nugent Square affordable housing project. 2001.

193-11. Independent Press Association, San Francisco, CA, $500,000. Loan for revolving loan program that supports independent periodicals published by nonprofit publishers in the public interest. 2000.

193-12. Napa County Land Trust, Napa, CA, $2,200,000. Loan for acquisition and protection of Calistoga Palisades property which connects Calistoga with Robert Louis Stevenson State Park. 2000.

193-13. Nature Conservancy, Arlington, VA, $5,000,000. Loan for acquisition of conservation easements on dairy land along lower Consumnes River in California. 2001.

193-14. Nature Conservancy, Arlington, VA, $12,000,000. Loan to acquire Palmyra atoll in the U.S. tropics for marine wilderness protection. 2000.

193-15. Nature Conservancy, Arlington, VA, $10,000,000. Program-related investment for Sacramento River Project for conservation and habitat preservation for endagered species. 1999.

193-16. Nature Conservancy, Arlington, VA, $2,000,000. Program-related investment for acquisition of Lakeview Meadows Ranch and habitat preservation for endangered species. 1999.

193-17. Resource Area for Teachers (RAFT), Sunnyvale, CA, $3,000,000. Program-related investment to allow RAFT to purchase its own facility in San Jose. 1999.

193-18. River Network, Portland, OR, $1,975,000. Loan for acquisition of Schmidt Bar and Weinandt properties on Hoh River in Washington. 2001.

193-19. Samaritan House, San Mateo, CA, $1,440,000. Loan for acquisition of permanent clinic site in San Mateo. 2001.

193-20. Santa Cruz Montessori School, Aptos, CA, $1,239,000. Loan for construction of building that will house new toddler care center offering expanded services. 2001.

193-21. Santa Cruz Montessori School, Aptos, CA, $652,000. Loan for acquisition and renovation of building that will house new toddler care center offering expanded services. 2000.

193-22. Save Mount Diablo, Walnut Creek, CA, $625,000. Program-related investment for acquisition of Silva property for conservation and habitat preservation for endangered species. 1999.

193-23. Shelter Network of San Mateo County, Burlingame, CA, $2,250,000. Loan to Network and Women's Recovery Association of San Mateo County for joint acquisition of office building in San Mateo County to help advance organizations' complementary missions of emergency shelter and substance abuse treatment. 2000.

193-24. Trust for Public Land, San Francisco, CA, $8,000,000. Loan for acquisition of Bixby Ocean Ranch in Big Sur, California to protect against development. 2001.

193-25. Trust for Public Land, San Francisco, CA, $3,905,000. Loan for acquisition of Khlae village site for addition to Puuhonua O Honaunau National Historical Park on the island of Hawaii. 2001.

193-26. Trust for Public Land, San Francisco, CA, $2,127,630. Loan for Phase II of acquisition of Shallenberger Ridge property for expansion of Donner Memorial State Park in California. 2001.

193-27. Trust for Public Land, San Francisco, CA, $1,027,370. Loan for Phase I of acquisition of Shallenberger Ridge property for expansion of Donner Memorial State Park in California. 2001.

193-28. Womens Capital Corporation, DC, $1,000,000. Loan for affordable distribution and marketing of FDA-approved emergency contraceptive product. 2001.

193-29. Womens Capital Corporation, DC, $500,000. Loan for affordable distribution and marketing of FDA-approved emergency contraceptive product. 2001.

193-30. Womens Capital Corporation, DC, $3,000,000. Loan for affordable distribution and marketing of FDA-approved emergency contraceptive product. 2000.

193-31. Womens Capital Corporation, DC, $500,000. Program-related investment to help support contraceptive technology development. 1999.

194
Parnell Family Foundation

P.O. Box 1390
Eastsound, WA 98245-1390

Established in 1990 in CA.
Donor(s): Melissa D. Parnell, Mike D. Parnell.
Grantmaker type: Independent foundation
General financial activity (yr. ended 12/31/01): Assets, $7,791,428 (M); gifts received, $543; expenditures, $287,822; qualifying distributions, $153,781; giving activities include $129,305 for 12 grants (high: $114,274; low: $25) and $21,023 for foundation-administered programs; no PRIs paid.
General purpose and activities: Giving primarily for education, particularly a Christian school, as well as for social services, Christian organizations, and to a Seventh-Day Adventist church.
General fields of interest: Education; human services; Christian agencies & churches; Protestant agencies & churches.
Program-related investment (PRI) activity: The foundation builds and leases buildings to a religious organization for their use and handles those costs as PRIs.
Types of PRI Support: Charitable use assets.
Limitations: Applications not accepted. Giving primarily in Orcas Island, WA. No grants to individuals.
Officers: Mike D. Parnell, Pres.; Melissa D. Parnell, Secy.; Mike Taylor, C.F.O.
EIN: 330433123
PRI recipients:

194-1. Seventh-Day Adventist Church, Eastsound, WA, $174,564. Program-related investment for purchase of land on Orcas Island by foundation to construct church and parochial school. Land and buildings will be leased to Church. 2000.

194-2. Seventh-Day Adventist Church, Eastsound, WA, $2,556,529. Program-related investment for construction of buildings for lease to Church. Foundation is leasing land and buildings to the Church and operating and managing the leasing arrangement as a direct charitable activity. Lease agreement provides for nominal rent. 1999.

195
The William Penn Foundation

2 Logan Sq., 11th Fl.
100 N. 18th St.
Philadelphia, PA 19103-2757 (215) 988-1830
Contact: Kathryn Engebretson, Pres.
FAX: (215) 988-1823; E-mail: moreinfo@williampennfoundation.org; URL: http://www.williampennfoundation.org

Incorporated in 1945 in DE.
Donor(s): Otto Haas,‡ Phoebe W. Haas,‡ Otto Haas & Phoebe W. Haas Charitable Trusts.
Grantmaker type: Independent foundation
General financial activity (yr. ended 12/31/02): Assets, $904,488,083 (M); gifts received, $15,543,570; expenditures, $72,927,193; qualifying distributions, $64,676,176; giving activities include $63,726,388 for grants and $949,788 for employee matching gifts; no PRIs paid.
General purpose and activities: The foundation strives to improve the quality of life in the Philadelphia region through efforts that foster rich cultural expression, strengthen children's futures, and deepen connections to nature and community.
General fields of interest: Arts, multipurpose centers/programs; performing arts; historic preservation/historical societies; arts/cultural programs; child development, education; elementary school/education; secondary school/education; elementary/secondary school reform; natural resources conservation & protection; environment, beautification programs; environment; youth development; human services; children & youth, services; child development,

services; family services; community development, neighborhood development; community development, neighborhood associations; urban/community development; economically disadvantaged.
Program-related investment (PRI) activity: The foundation made a PRI for community development and landbanking in Philadelphia, PA and Camdon, NJ.
Limitations: Giving limited to the six-county greater Philadelphia region: Camden County, NJ and Philadelphia, Bucks, Chester, Delaware, and Montgomery counties, PA; environmental giving in expanded region including portions of the Delaware, Schuykill, and Chesapeake Bay watersheds in DE, MD, NJ, and PA. No support for sectarian religious activities, recreational programs, political lobbying or legislative activities, nonpublic schools, pass-through organizations, mental health or retardation treatment programs, or programs focusing on a particular disease, disability, or treatment for addiction, or profit-making enterprises; no support for private foundations. No grants to individuals, or for debt reduction, hospital capital projects, medical research, programs that replace lost government support, housing construction or rehabilitation, scholarships, or fellowships; no loans (except for program-related investments).
Publications: Annual report.
Officers and Directors:* David W. Haas,* Chair.; Frederick R. Haas,* Vice-Chair. and Secy.; Kathryn J. Engebretson, Ph.D.,* Pres.; Louis J. Mayer, V.P., Finance and Investments; Louise M. Foster, Cont.; Carol R. Collier, Joseph A. Dworetzky, Nancy B. Haas, Robert E. Hanrahan, Jr., Ernest E. Jones, Thomas M. McKenna, John P. Mulroney, Hon. Anthony Scirica, Lise Yasui.
Number of staff: 17 full-time professional; 1 part-time professional; 7 full-time support.
EIN: 231503488
PRI recipients:
195-1. Delaware Valley Community Reinvestment Fund, Philadelphia, PA, $5,000,000. Program-related investment for loans and other finance products for development activities in targeted communities and for landbanking in Philadelphia and Camden. 2002.

196
The Pew Charitable Trusts

1 Commerce Sq.
2005 Market St., Ste. 1700
Philadelphia, PA 19103-7077 (215) 575-9050
Contact: Rebecca W. Rimel, C.E.O. and Pres.
PRI Contact: Henry B. Bernstein, Dir., Finance
FAX: (215) 575-4939; E-mail: info@pewtrusts.com;
URL: http://www.pewtrusts.com

Pew Memorial Trust, J.N. Pew, Jr. Charitable Trust, J. Howard Pew Freedom Trust, Mabel Pew Myrin Trust, Medical Trust, Knollbrook Trust, and Mary Anderson Trust established in 1948, 1956, 1957, 1957, 1979, 1965, and 1957 respectively. PRI-related activities began in 1990.

Donor(s): Mary Ethel Pew,‡ Mabel Pew Myrin,‡ J. Howard Pew,‡ Joseph N. Pew, Jr.‡
Grantmaker type: Independent foundation
General financial activity (yr. ended 12/31/02): Assets, $3,753,638,080 (M); expenditures, $264,362,973; qualifying distributions, $264,362,973; giving activities include $238,151,626 for grants and $383,196 for 649 employee matching gifts; no PRIs paid.
Cumulative PRI activity (through 12/31/02): Since 1990, the foundation has made 15 PRIs totaling $76,975,000. The currently outstanding PRI portfolio includes 8 PRIs totaling $43,900,000 (high: $10,000,000; low: $750,000; average: $6,000,000). The typical outstanding PRI has a 5- to 12-year term with an average term of 8 years and earns 0 to 4 percent interest with an average of 2 percent.
General purpose and activities: The Pew Charitable Trusts support nonprofit activities in the areas of culture, education, the environment, health and human services, public policy and religion. Based in Philadelphia, the trusts make strategic investments to help organizations and citizens develop practical solutions to difficult problems.
General fields of interest: Journalism & publishing; visual arts; museums; performing arts; dance; theater; music; humanities; historic preservation/historical societies; arts/cultural programs; education, research; child development, education; education; natural resources conservation & protection; energy; environment; wildlife preservation & protection; public health; health care; biomedicine; employment; housing/shelter, development; safety/disasters; youth development, services; youth development, citizenship; human services; children & youth, services; child development, services; family services; aging, centers & services; minorities/immigrants, centers & services; homeless, human services; civil rights; urban/community development; rural development; community development; voluntarism promotion; biological sciences; science; social sciences; government/public administration; public affairs, election regulation; public affairs, citizen participation; leadership development; public affairs; religion, research; Christian agencies & churches; Protestant agencies & churches; religion; minorities; immigrants/refugees; economically disadvantaged; homeless.
Program-related investment (PRI) activity: The foundation began making PRIs in 1990. They are provided on a very limited basis and are often administered by intermediaries (e.g., loan funds). PRIs are considered in all of the foundation's program areas, although projects must first meet the specific criteria for grant support.
Types of PRI Support: Loans/promissory notes, interim financing, capitalizing loan funds/other intermediaries.
Limitations: Giving on a national basis, with a special commitment to the Philadelphia, PA, region. No support for political organizations. No grants to individuals, or for endowment funds, capital campaigns, construction, equipment, deficit financing, scholarships, or fellowships (except those identified or initiated by the trusts). PRI applications not accepted.

Publications: Grants list, occasional report, application guidelines.
PRI program information: The foundation does not maintain a formal PRI program. The foundation makes PRIs occasionally.
Officer and Board Members:* Rebecca W. Rimel,* C.E.O. and Pres.; Susan W. Catherwood, Robert H. Campbell, Thomas W. Langfitt, M.D., Arthur E. Pew III, J. Howard Pew II, J.N. Pew III, Joseph N. Pew IV, M.D., Mary Catherine Pew, M.D., R. Anderson Pew, Richard F. Pew, Robert G. Williams.
Trustee: The Glenmede Trust Co.
Number of staff: 80 full-time professional; 3 part-time professional; 58 full-time support; 3 part-time support.
PRI recipients:
196-1. Bryn Mawr College, Bryn Mawr, PA, $8,500,000. Program-related investment to implement Plan for the New Century by making faculty appointments in key academic programs, increasing opportunities for student internships and renovating facilities. 1999.
196-2. Cornell University, Office of Foundation Relations, Ithaca, NY, $8,500,000. Program-related investment to develop undergraduate courses and programs in ethical reasoning and information science. 1999.
196-3. Grove City College, Grove City, PA, $8,500,000. Program-related investment for construction of new academic building. 1999.
196-4. Philadelphia Museum of Art, Philadelphia, PA, $8,500,000. Program-related investment for acquisition and renovation of Reliance Standard Life Insurance Company building and renovation of original museum building. 1999.
196-5. University of Pennsylvania, Department of Development and Alumni Relations, Philadelphia, PA, $8,500,000. Program-related investment to expand cognitive science and genomics programs, provide fellowships to minority students who aspire to become faculty and increase community outreach. 1999.

197
The Dr. P. Phillips Foundation
60 W. Robinson St.
P.O. Box 3753
Orlando, FL 32802 (407) 422-6105
Contact: J.A. Hinson, Pres. or Ann F. Manley, Ed.D., Exec. Dir.
FAX: (407) 422-4952

Incorporated in 1953 in FL.
Donor(s): Della Phillips,‡ Howard Phillips,‡ Dr. Phillips, Inc.
Grantmaker type: Independent foundation
General financial activity (yr. ended 05/31/02): Assets, $37,419,758 (M); expenditures, $2,140,963; qualifying distributions, $2,051,088; giving activities include $1,694,761 for 86 grants (high: $500,000; low: $225; average: $1,000–$25,000) and $60,024 for 1 foundation-administered program; no PRIs paid.
Cumulative PRI activity (through 05/31/02): The currently outstanding PRI portfolio includes 2 PRIs totaling $401,381.
General purpose and activities: Emphasis on education, child development and welfare, youth, the elderly, and community development, including arts and culture, museums, recreation, and social and family services.
General fields of interest: Arts/cultural programs; child development, education; education; human services; children & youth, services; child development, services; family services; aging, centers & services; community development; aging.
Program-related investment (PRI) activity: On an infrequent basis, the foundation has made PRIs in lieu of a grant. Support has been for facility improvement and equipment acquisition.
Types of PRI Support: Loans/promissory notes, interim financing.
Limitations: Giving generally limited to Orange and Osceola counties, FL. No grants to individuals, or for endowment funds. The foundation accepts applications for PRIs.
Publications: Application guidelines.
PRI program information: The foundation does not maintain a formal PRI program. The foundation makes PRIs occasionally.
Officers and Directors:* J.A. Hinson,* Chair. and Pres.; E.F. Furey,* Secy.-Treas.; Ann F. Manley, Exec. Dir.; H.L. Burnett, Richard L. Fletcher, Jr., L. Evans Hubbard, Thomas T. Ross.
Number of staff: 1 full-time professional; 1 full-time support.
EIN: 596135403
PRI recipients:
197-1. YMCA, Central Florida, Orlando, FL, $484,940. Loan to enable completion of Youth Center serving Dr. Phillips community in Orange County, Florida. 2000.

198
The Pittsburgh Foundation
1 PPG Pl., 30th Fl.
Pittsburgh, PA 15222-5401 (412) 391-5122
Contact: Dr. William E. Trueheart, C.E.O. and Pres.
FAX: (421) 391-7259; E-mail: email@pghfdn.org; URL: http://www.pittsburghfoundation.org

Established in 1945 in PA by bank resolution and declaration of trust. PRI-related activities began in 1996.
Donor(s): 440 historical donors,‡ 440 current donors.
Grantmaker type: Community foundation
General financial activity (yr. ended 12/31/02): Assets, $467,377,868 (M); gifts received, $30,709,366; expenditures, $33,459,890; giving activities include $25,916,244 for 2,048 grants (high: $882,996; low: $49; average: $500–$75,000); no PRIs paid.
Cumulative PRI activity (through 12/31/02): Since 1996, the foundation has made 2 PRIs totaling $560,000. The currently outstanding PRI portfolio includes 2 PRIs totaling $644,211.

General purpose and activities: The foundation promotes and champions the betterment of the greater Pittsburgh, PA, community and the quality of life for all its citizens by helping a wide variety of donors fulfill their philanthropic interests through providing leadership in identifying and addressing significant community needs. The foundation provides a vehicle to make giving easy, personally satisfying and effective. The foundation is organized for the permanent administration of funds placed in trust for public charitable and educational purposes. Funds are used for programs of regularly established agencies for organizational capacity building, systemic change, improved service delivery, planning and program development, capital and equipment, operating support and community building. Grants are made primarily in the areas of achieving educational excellence and equity; supporting families; fostering economic development; reducing health disparities; and advancing the arts. Unless specified by the donor, grants are generally nonrecurring.
General fields of interest: Arts, cultural/ethnic awareness; arts/cultural programs; education; health care; youth development; family services; community development, public/private ventures; economic development; community development.
Program-related investment (PRI) activity: The foundation makes PRIs to local entities for the development of their programs. PRIs have been made in the areas of human services and small business development and have included financing for facility construction and renovation, building expansion, and equipment acquisition.
Types of PRI Support: Loans/promissory notes, equity investments.
Limitations: Giving from unrestricted funds limited to Pittsburgh and Allegheny County, PA. No support for churches, private and parochial schools, or hospitals (from unrestricted funds). No grants to individuals (from unrestricted funds except for the Isabel P. Kennedy Award) or for annual campaigns, endowment funds, travel, operating budgets, scholarships, fellowships, internships, awards, special events or research of a highly technical or specialized nature; no loans to individuals. PRI applications not accepted.
Publications: Annual report, application guidelines, newsletter, informational brochure (including application guidelines).
PRI program information: The foundation does not maintain a formal PRI program. The foundation makes PRIs occasionally.
Officers and Directors:* James S. Broadhurst,* Chair; Frieda G. Shapira,* Vice-Chair. Emerita; Dr. William E. Trueheart, C.E.O. and Pres.; Carol Carter, V.P., Devel.; Kimberly J. Hammer, V.P., Donor Services; Thomas S. Hay, V.P., Finance and Admin.; Gerri Kay, V.P., Prog. and Policy; Jane Shorall, V.P., Comm.; Aaron A. Walton,* Treas.; Robert P. Bozzone, Joanne E. Burley, Joseph L. Calihan, Estelle F. Comay, William J. Copeland, Dir. Emeritus; George A. Davidson, Jr., Linda A. Dickerson, Robert Dickey III, Dir. Emeritus; Arthur J. Edmunds, John c. Harmon, Mary Lou McLaughlin, Alvin Rogal, Nancy D. Washington, Gregory R. Spencer, Samuel Y. Stroh, Dorothy R. Williams, Dir. Emerita.
Trustee Banks: Mellon Bank, N.A., National City Bank of Pennsylvania, PNC Bank, N.A.
Number of staff: 15 full-time professional; 1 part-time professional; 18 full-time support; 1 part-time support.
EIN: 250965466
PRI recipients:
198-1. Lemington Home for the Aged, Pittsburgh, PA, $500,000. Loan guarantee extension. 1999.

199
The PNC Foundation

(Formerly PNC Bank Foundation)
c/o PNC Advisors
620 Liberty Ave., 25th Fl., 2 PNC Plz.
Pittsburgh, PA 15222 (412) 762-7076
Contact: Mia Hallett Bernard, Mgr.

Established in 1970 in PA. PRI-related activities began in 1998.
Donor(s): PNC Bank, N.A.
Grantmaker type: Company-sponsored foundation
General financial activity (yr. ended 12/31/01): Assets, $745,925 (M); expenditures, $11,968,545; qualifying distributions, $11,738,337; giving activities include $11,028,683 for 837 grants (high: $340,362; low: $100; average: $5,000–$114,000) and $550,372 for 827 employee matching gifts; no PRIs paid.
General purpose and activities: Giving primarily for cultural programs, education, human services, youth agencies, and economic and community development. Also giving for the United Way.
General fields of interest: Arts/cultural programs; education; human services; children & youth, services; community development; federated giving programs.
Program-related investment (PRI) activity: The foundation has made PRIs to organizations for community development and family services.
Types of PRI Support: Loans/promissory notes.
Limitations: Giving primarily in headquarters and company locations: DE, IN, KY, NJ, OH, and PA. No support for churches or for religious purposes. No grants to individuals, or for endowment funds; no loans (except for program-related investments).
Publications: Annual report (including application guidelines).
PRI program information: The foundation maintains a formal PRI program.
Trustee: PNC Bank, N.A.
EIN: 251202255
PRI recipients:
199-1. Family Service of Morris County, Morristown, NJ, $25,000. Program-related investment. 1999.
199-2. Jireh Development Corporation, Cincinnati, OH, $75,000. Program-related investment. 1999.

200

Presbyterian Health Foundation

655 Research Pkwy., Ste. 500
Oklahoma City, OK 73104-5023
Contact: Jean G. Gumerson, C.E.O. and Pres.
FAX: (405) 271-2911

Established in 1985 in OK; converted from the proceeds of the sale of Presbyterian Hospital to HCA.
Grantmaker type: Independent foundation
General financial activity (yr. ended 09/30/02): Assets, $154,249,984 (M); gifts received, $80,379; expenditures, $14,612,622; qualifying distributions, $20,374,933; giving activities include $10,630,122 for 62 grants (high: $2,000,000; low: $44; average: $25,000–$250,000) and $9,027,716 for 4 PRIs.
General purpose and activities: Support primarily for health, including medical research and medical education, clinical pastoral education, resource development through medical technology transfer, community health-related programs and to Oklahoma Health Center Institutions.
General fields of interest: Medical school/education; theological school/education; medicine/medical care, community health systems; medical research; engineering & technology.
Program-related investment (PRI) activity: The foundation is involved in the construction of three buildings for a medical research park. The facilities are held as PRIs, and project costs also are accounted for as PRIs. The foundation has also provided PRI support for housing and human services organizations.
Types of PRI Support: Charitable use assets.
Limitations: Giving primarily in OK.
Publications: Annual report, informational brochure (including application guidelines).
Officers and Trustees:* Stanton L. Young,* Chair.; Dr. Michael D. Anderson,* Vice-Chair.; Jean G. Gumerson,* C.E.O. and Pres.; Dennis McGrath,* V.P.; Fred H. Zahn,* Secy.; William M. Beard,* Treas.; William F. Barnes, M.D., R.B. Carl, M.D., Richard G. Dotter, M.D., Carl Edwards, Nancy Payne Ellis, Robert S. Ellis, M.D., Christy Everest, Clyde Ingle, David Parke, M.D., J.V. Smith, Harry B. Tate, M.D., Jerry B. Vannatta, M.D.
Number of staff: 2 full-time professional; 2 full-time support.
EIN: 730709836
PRI recipients:

200-1. Research Park Project, Oklahoma City, OK, $4,611,466. Program-related investment for construction on Building No. 4. 2002.
200-2. Research Park Project, Oklahoma City, OK, $3,177,263. Program-related investment for construction on Building No. 3. 2002.
200-3. Research Park Project, Oklahoma City, OK, $1,090,092. Program-related investment for construction on Building No. 2. 2002.
200-4. Research Park Project, Oklahoma City, OK, $148,895. Program-related investment for construction on Building No. 1. 2002.
200-5. Research Park Project, Oklahoma City, OK, $19,810,807. Program-related investment for construction on Building No. 3. 2001.
200-6. Research Park Project, Oklahoma City, OK, $202,920. Program-related investment for construction on Building No. 1. 2001.
200-7. Research Park Project, Oklahoma City, OK, $87,993. Program-related investment for construction on Building No. 2. 2000.
200-8. Research Park Project, Oklahoma City, OK, $29,420. Program-related investment for construction on Building No. 1. 2000.
200-9. Research Park Project, Oklahoma City, OK, $5,383,349. Program-related investment for construction on Building No. 2. 1999.
200-10. Research Park Project, Oklahoma City, OK, $1,205,017. Program-related investment for construction on Building No. 1. 1999.
200-11. Research Park Project, Oklahoma City, OK, $803,668. Program-related investment for construction on Building No. 3. 1999.

201

The Presser Foundation

385 Lancaster Ave., No. 205
Haverford, PA 19041 (610) 658-9030
Contact: Edith A. Reinhardt, Pres.

Founded in 1916; incorporated in 1939 in PA.
Donor(s): Theodore Presser.‡
Grantmaker type: Independent foundation
General financial activity (yr. ended 06/30/02): Assets, $53,188,629 (M); gifts received, $958,709; expenditures, $3,065,822; qualifying distributions, $2,836,728; giving activities include $1,466,924 for 80 grants (high: $250,000; low: $1,000; average: $5,000–$100,000) and $1,177,573 for grants to individuals; no PRIs paid.
Cumulative PRI activity (through 06/30/02): The currently outstanding PRI portfolio includes PRIs totaling $762,609.
General purpose and activities: To provide scholarship aid grants to accredited colleges and universities in the field of music; to increase music education in institutions of learning and to popularize the teaching of music as a profession. Grants to individuals limited to providing emergency aid to worthy music teachers in need.
General fields of interest: Arts education; music; higher education.
Program-related investment (PRI) activity: The foundation has made PRIs to a music publishing company.
Officers and Trustees:* Edith A. Reinhardt,* Pres.; Thomas M. Hyndman, Jr.,* V.P.; Bruce Montgomery,* Secy.; William M. Davison IV,* Treas.; Leon Bates, David Boe, Robert Capanna, Anthony P. Checchia, Robert W. Denious, Herbert P. Evert, Martin A. Hechscher, Helen Laird, Wendell Pritchett, Michael Stairs, Henderson Supplee III, Radclyffe F. Thompson, Vera Wilson.
Number of staff: 1 full-time professional.

EIN: 232164013
PRI recipients:
201-1. Theodore Presser Company, King of Prussia, PA, $122,158. Program-related investment in music company to facilitate relocation and other upgrades. 2001.

202
The Prudential Foundation

Prudential Plz.
751 Broad St., 15th Fl.
Newark, NJ 07102-3777 (973) 802-4791
Contact: Lata N. Reddy, Secy.
PRI Contact: John Kinghorn, V.P., Social Investments
E-mail: community.resources@prudential.com;
URL: http://www.prudential.com

Incorporated in 1977 in NJ. PRI-related activities began in 1993.
Donor(s): The Prudential Insurance Co. of America.
Grantmaker type: Company-sponsored foundation
General financial activity (yr. ended 12/31/01): Assets, $101,178,198 (M); expenditures, $38,482,303; qualifying distributions, $40,424,523; giving activities include $26,228,739 for 1,311 grants (high: $3,000,000; low: $250; average: $250–$100,000), $11,289,640 for 20,426 employee matching gifts and $2,625,000 for PRIs.
Cumulative PRI activity (through 12/31/01): Since 1993, the foundation has made 80 PRIs totaling $39,123,921. The currently outstanding PRI portfolio includes 17 PRIs totaling $17,105,000 (high: $5,000,000; low: $175,000; average: $2,000,000). The typical outstanding PRI has a 1- to 15-year term with an average term of 1 years and earns 3 to 5.25 percent interest with an average of 5 percent.
General purpose and activities: The foundation provides support to innovative direct service programs that address the needs of society in three areas: Ready to Learn, Ready to Live, and Ready to Work.
Program-related investment (PRI) activity: Since 1993, the foundation has made low-interest loans in conjunction with the Prudential Insurance Company of America's Social Investment Program, which makes low-interest loans to socially valuable projects. Investments focus on the areas of affordable housing, economic development, minority entrepreneurship, community services, and education. PRIs are made to both nonprofit and for-profit organizations and can total up to $10 million per year.
Limitations: Giving primarily in areas of company operations, with emphasis on Phoenix, AZ, Los Angeles, CA, Jacksonville, FL, Atlanta, GA, Minneapolis, MN, Newark, NJ, Philadelphia, PA, and Houston, TX. No support for veterans', labor, religious, fraternal, or athletic groups, or general operating funds for single-disease health organizations. No grants to individuals, or for endowment funds, goodwill advertising, or fundraising events. PRI support focuses on five urban communities where Prudential has its most significant business presence: Los Angeles, CA, Jacksonville, FL, Minneapolis, MN, Newark, NJ, and Philadelphia, PA, with some support also in Phoenix, AZ, Atlanta, GA, Chicago, IL, Boston, MA, Houston, TX, and Washington, DC. Strategic funding initiatives with a national scope will also be considered, especially where a significant portion of the funds will be directed to a target city. No support is provided for construction loans, letters of credit, or guarantees. The foundation accepts applications for PRIs.
Publications: Annual report (including application guidelines).
PRI program information: The foundation maintains a formal PRI program. The foundation makes PRIs on an annual basis.
Officers and Trustees:* Sharon C. Taylor,* Chair.; Gabriella Morris, Pres.; Lata N. Reddy, Secy.; E. Charles Chaplin, Treas.; Anthony Piszel, Cont.; Robert C. Golden, Jon F. Hanson, Constance J. Horner, Arthur F. Ryan, Ida F.S. Schmertz, Stanley C. Van Ness.
Number of staff: 6 full-time professional; 4 full-time support.
EIN: 222175290
PRI recipients:
202-1. Academy Charter School, South Belmar, NJ, $100,000. Program-related investment. 2000.
202-2. Academy Charter School, South Belmar, NJ, $100,000. Loan for start-up working capital. 1999.
202-3. CALLA Charter School, Plainfield, NJ, $175,000. Program-related investment. 2000.
202-4. CALLA Charter School, Plainfield, NJ, $175,000. Loan for start-up working capital. 1999.
202-5. Camino Nuevo Charter Academy, Los Angeles, CA, $650,000. Program-related investment. 2001.
202-6. College Preparatory Academy Charter School, Dover, NJ, $150,000. Program-related investment. 2000.
202-7. East Orange Community Charter School, East Orange, NJ, $385,000. Program-related investment. 2002.
202-8. East Orange Community Charter School, East Orange, NJ, $425,000. Program-related investment. 2001.
202-9. East Orange Community Charter School, East Orange, NJ, $365,000. Program-related investment. 2000.
202-10. East Orange Community Charter School, East Orange, NJ, $340,000. Loan for start-up working capital. 1999.
202-11. Elysian Charter School, Hoboken, NJ, $250,000. Program-related investment. 2001.
202-12. Elysian Charter School, Hoboken, NJ, $250,000. Loan for start-up working capital. 1999.
202-13. Emily Fisher Charter School of Advanced Studies, Trenton, NJ, $50,000. Program-related investment. 2001.
202-14. Emily Fisher Charter School of Advanced Studies, Trenton, NJ, $100,000. Program-related investment. 2000.
202-15. Family Alliance Charter School, Willingboro, NJ, $71,500. Loan for start-up working capital. 1999.

202-16. Financial Foundation for Texas Charter Schools, Houston, TX, $500,000. Loan for short-term working capital for charter schools. 1999.
202-17. Galloway Kindergarten Charter School, Smithville, NJ, $100,000. Program-related investment. 2000.
202-18. Granville Charter School, Trenton, NJ, $725,000. Program-related investment. 2002.
202-19. Gray Charter School, Newark, NJ, $120,000. Program-related investment. 2000.
202-20. Greater Brunswick Charter School, New Brunswick, NJ, $120,000. Program-related investment. 2002.
202-21. Greenville/ACORN Charter School, Jersey City, NJ, $200,000. Loan for start-up working capital. 1999.
202-22. Hoboken Charter School, Hoboken, NJ, $200,000. Loan for start-up working capital. 1999.
202-23. Hope Charter School, Clifton, NJ, $100,000. Program-related investment. 2001.
202-24. LEAP Academy Charter School, Camden, NJ, $500,000. Program-related investment. 2002.
202-25. LEAP Academy Charter School, Camden, NJ, $500,000. Program-related investment. 2001.
202-26. LEAP Academy Charter School, Camden, NJ, $700,000. Loan. 1999.
202-27. Learning Community Charter School, Jersey City, NJ, $175,000. Program-related investment. 2002.
202-28. Learning Community Charter School, Jersey City, NJ, $350,000. Program-related investment. 2001.
202-29. Learning Community Charter School, Jersey City, NJ, $350,000. Program-related investment. 2000.
202-30. Learning Community Charter School, Jersey City, NJ, $350,000. Loan. 1999.
202-31. Multicultural Community Services, Edison, NJ, $350,000. Program-related investment. 2002.
202-32. New Jersey Performing Arts Center Corporation, Newark, NJ, $900,000. Loan for revolving line of credit to cover operating cash flow shortfalls. 1999.
202-33. Ocean City Charter School, Charter Tech, Linwood, NJ, $275,000. Loan for start-up working capital. 1999.
202-34. Oceanside Charter School, Atlantic City, NJ, $350,000. Program-related investment. 2002.
202-35. Oceanside Charter School, Atlantic City, NJ, $350,000. Program-related investment. 2001.
202-36. Oceanside Charter School, Atlantic City, NJ, $200,000. Program-related investment. 2000.
202-37. Oceanside Charter School, Atlantic City, NJ, $150,000. Program-related investment. 2000.
202-38. Oceanside Charter School, Atlantic City, NJ, $400,000. Loan for start-up working captial. 1999.
202-39. Paterson Charter School for Science and Technology, Paterson, NJ, $145,000. Program-related investment. 2002.
202-40. Paterson Charter School for Urban Leadership, Paterson, NJ, $150,000. Program-related investment. 2000.
202-41. Pleasantville Charter School for Academic Excellence, Pleasantville, NJ, $650,000. Program-related investment. 2001.
202-42. REACH Charter School, Egg Harbor City, NJ, $600,000. Loan for start-up working capital. 1999.
202-43. REACH Charter School, Egg Harbor City, NJ, $200,000. Loan for start-up working capital. 1999.
202-44. Russell Byers Charter School, Philadelphia, PA, $150,000. Program-related investment. 2000.
202-45. Samuel Proctor DeWitt Academy Charter School, Trenton, NJ, $300,000. Program-related investment. 2000.
202-46. Samuel Proctor DeWitt Academy Charter School, Ewing, NJ, $200,000. Loan. 1999.
202-47. Simon Bolivar Charter School, Newark, NJ, $200,000. Loan for start-up working capital. 1999.
202-48. University Academy Charter High School, Jersey City, NJ, $200,000. Program-related investment. 2002.

203
Nelson Puett Foundation

P.O. Box 9038
Austin, TX 78766 (512) 453-6611
Contact: Nelson Puett, Pres.

Established in 1955 in TX.
Donor(s): Nelson Puett, Nelson Puett Mortgage Co.
Grantmaker type: Independent foundation
General financial activity (yr. ended 02/28/02): Assets, $13,642,680 (M); gifts received, $457,000; expenditures, $143,877; qualifying distributions, $56,428; giving activities include $56,428 for 53 grants (high: $9,600; low: $25); no PRIs paid.
Cumulative PRI activity (through 02/28/02): Since beginning PRI activity, the foundation has made PRIs totaling $1,132,349. The currently outstanding PRI portfolio includes PRIs totaling $2,229,740.
General purpose and activities: Giving for education, religion, and social services; also provides homeowner loans to individuals residing in the Austin, TX, area.
General fields of interest: Education; housing/shelter; human services; religion.
Program-related investment (PRI) activity: The foundation has made loans for the development of affordable housing.
Types of PRI Support: Loans/promissory notes.
Limitations: Giving primarily in TX. No grants to individuals.
Publications: Financial statement.
Officers: Nelson Puett, Pres.; Ruth B. Puett, V.P.; Janis Schultz, Secy.-Treas.
Number of staff: None.
EIN: 746062365
PRI recipients:
203-1. Project Home, Austin, TX, $1,283,549. Loans to build low-income housing. 2001.
203-2. Project Home, Austin, TX, $1,132,349. Loan to develop affordable housing. 2000.

204
John Nesbit Rees and Sarah Henne Rees Charitable Foundation

314 S. Franklin St., Ste. B
P.O. Box 325
Titusville, PA 16354-0325 (814) 827-1844
Contact: Richard W. Roeder, Tr.
FAX: (814) 827-6620; E-mail: jnrshrees@stargate.net

Established in 1989 in PA.
Donor(s): John Nesbit Rees,‡ Sarah Henne Rees.‡
Grantmaker type: Independent foundation
General financial activity (yr. ended 12/31/01): Assets, $13,476,966 (M); expenditures, $760,928; qualifying distributions, $699,463; giving activities include $676,813 for 36 grants (high: $100,000; low: $100); no PRIs paid.
Cumulative PRI activity (through 12/31/01): Since beginning PRI activity, the foundation has made 2 PRIs totaling $220,000. The currently outstanding PRI portfolio includes 2 PRIs totaling $160,744 (high: $150,000; low: $70,000).
General purpose and activities: Giving primarily for local civic causes, the performing arts, and education in the sciences.
General fields of interest: Performing arts; dance; arts/cultural programs; higher education; medicine/medical care, formal/general education; health care; health associations; youth, services; science, formal/general education.
Program-related investment (PRI) activity: The foundation holds mortgage loans for 2 cultural organizations, and forgives the annual interest on those loans.
Types of PRI Support: Loans/promissory notes.
Limitations: Giving primarily in the Titusville, PA, area, including parts of Forest, Crawford, Venango, and Warren counties. The foundation accepts applications for PRIs.
Publications: Annual report, application guidelines.
PRI program information: The foundation does not maintain a formal PRI program. The foundation makes PRIs occasionally.
Trustees: Richard W. Roeder, Barbara L. Smith.
Number of staff: 2 part-time professional.
EIN: 256264847
PRI recipients:

204-1. Academy Theater Foundation, Meadville, PA, $150,000. Program-related investment for mortgage on Theater. Annual interest is forgiven and over a period of years, the principal sum will be forgiven. 1999.

204-2. Oil Creek Railroad Historical Society, Titusville, PA, $70,000. Security agreement on rolling stock applied toward cost of locomotive to decrease Society's reliance on commercial operation. Interest is annually forgiven. 1999.

205
The Retirement Research Foundation

8765 W. Higgins Rd., Ste. 430
Chicago, IL 60631-4170 (773) 714-8080
Contact: Marilyn Hennessy, Pres.
FAX: (773) 714-8089; E-mail: info@rrf.org, hennessy@rrf.org; URL: http://www.rrf.org

Incorporated in 1950 in MI. PRI-related activities began in 1989.
Donor(s): John D. MacArthur.‡
Grantmaker type: Independent foundation
General financial activity (yr. ended 12/31/01): Assets, $171,567,885 (M); expenditures, $14,422,205; qualifying distributions, $13,344,848; giving activities include $11,700,550 for 340 grants (high: $165,663; low: $1,000; average: $12,000–$40,000) and $183,420 for 121 employee matching gifts; no PRIs paid.
Cumulative PRI activity (through 12/31/01): Since 1989, the foundation has made 7 PRIs totaling $2,680,946. The currently outstanding PRI portfolio includes PRIs totaling $1,287,147 (high: $500,000; low: $250,000; average: $383,000). The typical outstanding PRI has a 7- to 9-year term, and earns 3 to 4 percent interest.
General purpose and activities: Support principally to improve the quality of life of older persons in the U.S. Priority interests are innovative model projects and research designed to: 1) improve the availability and quality of community-based long-term care by: increasing the availability and effectiveness of community programs designed to maintain older persons in their own homes, as well as those in residential settings; improving the quality of nursing home care; and integrating the provision of acute and long-term care for older persons with chronic conditions by supporting efforts that provide continuity of care, prevention, early intervention, and client education; 2) provide new and expanded opportunities for older adults to engage in meaningful roles in society such as employment and voluntarism, that will strengthen the community through activities including, but not limited to, advocacy, community leadership, community services, and intergenerational programs; 3) seek causes and solutions to significant problems of older adults through support of selected basic, applied, and policy research for which federal funding is not available; and 4) increase the number of professionals and paraprofessionals adequately prepared to serve the elderly population through support of selected education and training initiatives that enhance knowledge and skills of participants.
General fields of interest: Health care; mental health/crisis services; health associations; geriatrics; medical research; employment; human services; aging, centers & services; homeless, human services; social sciences; public policy, research; aging; homeless.
Program-related investment (PRI) activity: The foundation makes PRIs to nonprofit and for-profit organizations in support of housing renovation and development for low-income senior citizens.

Types of PRI Support: Loans/promissory notes, interim financing.
Limitations: Giving limited to the Midwest (IA, IL, IN, KY, MI, MO, WI) and FL for direct service projects not having the potential of national impact. No grants to individuals, or for computers, construction, general operating expenses of established organizations, endowment or developmental campaigns, emergency funds, deficit financing, land acquisition, publications, conferences, scholarships, media productions, dissertation research, annual campaigns, or renovation projects. The foundation accepts applications for PRIs.
Publications: Biennial report (including application guidelines), occasional report, grants list, informational brochure, application guidelines.
PRI program information: The foundation does not maintain a formal PRI program. The foundation makes PRIs on a frequent but not annual basis.
Officers and Trustees:* Edward J. Kelly,* Chair.; Marilyn Hennessy, Pres.; Sharon F. Markham, Assoc. V.P.; Ruth Ann Watkins,* Secy.; William J. Gentle,* Treas.; Webster H. Hurley, Nathaniel McParland, M.D., Marvin Meyerson, Bart T. Murphy, John F. Santos, Ph.D., Sr. Stella Louise Slomka, C.S.F.N.
Number of staff: 4 full-time professional; 1 part-time professional; 4 full-time support.
EIN: 362429540

206
Sid W. Richardson Foundation

309 Main St.
Fort Worth, TX 76102 (817) 336-0494
Contact: Valleau Wilkie, Jr., Exec. Dir.
URL: http://www.sidrichardson.org

Established in 1947 in TX.
Donor(s): Sid W. Richardson,‡ and associated companies.
Grantmaker type: Independent foundation
General financial activity (yr. ended 12/31/02): Assets, $230,343,000 (M); expenditures, $14,577,445; qualifying distributions, $12,880,635; giving activities include $11,031,450 for 141 grants (high: $1,000,000; low: $1,000; average: $2,500–$150,000), $662,141 for 1 foundation-administered program and $500,000 for 1 PRI.
Cumulative PRI activity (through 12/31/02): The currently outstanding PRI portfolio includes a high PRI value of $500,000. The typical outstanding PRI has a maximum term of 4 years.
General purpose and activities: Giving primarily for education, health, the arts, and social service programs.
General fields of interest: Performing arts; arts/cultural programs; higher education; education; health care; health associations; human services.
Program-related investment (PRI) activity: The foundation has made PRIs in the areas of health and the arts. PRIs have provided operating and program support.
Types of PRI Support: Loans/promissory notes.
Limitations: Giving limited to TX, with emphasis on Fort Worth for the arts and human services, and statewide for health and education. No support for religious organizations. No grants to individuals, or for scholarships or fellowships; no loans (except for program-related investments). PRIs made only in special case situations. PRI applications not accepted.
Publications: Annual report (including application guidelines).
PRI program information: The foundation does not maintain a formal PRI program. The foundation makes PRIs occasionally.
Officers and Directors:* Perry R. Bass,* Chair.; Edward P. Bass,* Pres.; Valleau Wilkie, Jr., Exec. V.P. and Exec. Dir.; Lee M. Bass,* V.P.; Nancy Lee Bass,* V.P.; Sid R. Bass,* V.P.; Jo Helen Rosacker, Secy.; M.E. Chappell,* Treas.
Number of staff: 6 full-time professional.
EIN: 756015828
PRI recipients:
206-1. Fort Worth Art Association, Fort Worth, TX, $500,000. Loan for operating support at Modern Art Museum of Fort Worth. 2002.

207
Righteous Persons Foundation

2800 28th St., Ste. 105
Santa Monica, CA 90405 (310) 314-8393
Contact: Rachel Levin, Prog. Off.
FAX: (310) 314-8396

Established in 1994 in CA.
Donor(s): Steven Spielberg.
Grantmaker type: Independent foundation
General financial activity (yr. ended 12/31/01): Assets, $2,223,905 (M); gifts received, $4,590,493; expenditures, $4,695,223; qualifying distributions, $4,705,154; giving activities include $20,988,887 for 58 grants (high: $16,750,387; low: $2,500; average: $10,000–$150,000) and $20,000 for 1 PRI.
General purpose and activities: Giving primarily for Jewish arts and culture, Jewish youth, synagogue revitalization, intergroup relations and social justice.
General fields of interest: Arts/cultural programs; education; children & youth, services; civil rights, advocacy; Jewish agencies & temples.
Program-related investment (PRI) activity: Historically, the foundation has made loans to cultural organizations.
Types of PRI Support: Loans/promissory notes.
Limitations: Giving on a national basis. No support for individual schools or synagogues. No grants to individuals or for research, publications, or projects related to the Middle East.
Publications: Application guidelines.
Officers and Directors:* Steven Spielberg,* Chair.; Gerald Breslauer,* Pres.; Michael Rutman,* Secy. and C.F.O.; Margery Tabankin, Exec. Dir.; Bruce Ramer.

Number of staff: 1 full-time professional; 1 part-time professional; 1 full-time support; 1 part-time support.
EIN: 954497916
PRI recipients:
207-1. Survivors of the Shoah Visual History Foundation, Los Angeles, CA, $20,000. Loan. 2001.
207-2. Survivors of the Shoah Visual History Foundation, Los Angeles, CA, $4,950,387. Loan. 2000.
207-3. Survivors of the Shoah Visual History Foundation, Los Angeles, CA, $3,880,000. Loan. 1999.

208
Gilroy & Lillian P. Roberts Charitable Foundation
10 Presidential Blvd., Ste. 250
Bala Cynwyd, PA 19004 (610) 668-1998
Contact: Stanley Merves, Mgr.

Established in 1982 in PA. PRI-related activities began in 1997.
Donor(s): Gilroy Roberts,‡ Lillian Roberts.‡
Grantmaker type: Independent foundation
General financial activity (yr. ended 06/30/02): Assets, $9,102,346 (M); expenditures, $534,137; qualifying distributions, $505,663; giving activities include $468,835 for 87 grants (high: $152,000; low: $5) and $100,000 for 1 PRI.
Cumulative PRI activity (through 06/30/02): Since 1997, the foundation has made 1 PRI totaling $100,000. The currently outstanding PRI portfolio includes 1 PRI totaling $100,000. The typical outstanding PRI has an average term of 5 years, and earns an average of 6 percent interest.
General purpose and activities: Giving primarily for higher education, health, and the arts.
General fields of interest: Arts/cultural programs; higher education; hospitals (general); human services; Jewish federated giving programs; Jewish agencies & temples.
Program-related investment (PRI) activity: Historically, the foundation made a mortgage loan in 1997 to a nonprofit organization to enable the organization to purchase land next to a historic house to facilitate educational tours and workshops about the historic house. The foundation renewed the loan in 2003.
Types of PRI Support: Loans/promissory notes.
Limitations: Giving primarily in Montgomery and Delaware counties, PA. No grants to individuals. PRI support primarily in the Philadelphia, PA area. PRI applications not accepted.
PRI program information: The foundation does not maintain a formal PRI program. The foundation makes PRIs occasionally.
Officer and Trustees:* Stanley Merves,* Mgr.; Walter G. Arader, Audrey Merves, Jenifer Merves, John T. Roberts.
EIN: 232219044

209
The Rockefeller Foundation
420 5th Ave.
New York, NY 10018-2702 (212) 869-8500
Contact: Lynda Mullen, Corp. Secy.
PRI Contact: Laura Callanan, Assoc. Dir., Investments or Jacqueline L. Khor, Asst. Dir., ProVenEx
URL: http://www.rockfound.org

Incorporated in 1913 in NY. PRI-related activities began in 1991.
Donor(s): John D. Rockefeller, Sr.‡
Grantmaker type: Independent foundation
General financial activity (yr. ended 12/31/02): Assets, $2,679,064,000 (M); expenditures, $198,992,836; qualifying distributions, $184,429,000; giving activities include $125,406,598 for grants, $3,210,085 for grants to individuals, $225,070 for employee matching gifts, $15,099,847 for foundation-administered programs and $1,250,000 for 2 PRIs.
Cumulative PRI activity (through 12/31/02): Since 1991, the foundation has made 15 PRIs totaling $27,450,000. The currently outstanding PRI portfolio includes 7 PRIs totaling $5,426,190 (high: $2,232,143; low: $744,047). The typical outstanding PRI has a 6- to 10-year term and earns 3 to 10 percent interest with an average of 5.1 percent.
General purpose and activities: The foundation is a knowledge-based, global foundation with a commitment to enrich and sustain the lives and livelihoods of poor and excluded people throughout the world. This will be done through integrated programs in food, health, work, and creative expression to employ tools of science, research, analysis, and local knowledge to address daily challenges of globe's poorest; and renewed effort to catalyze positive change through partnerships. Funding will be focused among four themes: creativity and culture, food security, health equity, working communities; and the cross theme: global inclusion.
General fields of interest: Health care; employment; agriculture/food; disasters, 9/11/01.
General international interests: Africa; Developing countries; Asia.
Program-related investment (PRI) activity: The foundation's PRI activity is managed by its Program Venture Investments Program (ProVenEx). ProVenEx makes PRIs and investments related to program in businesses that will directly further the goals of one of the foundation's four thematic areas: Working Communities, Health Equity, Food Security, and Creativity and Culture.
Limitations: Giving on a national and international basis. No support for the establishment of local hospitals, churches, schools, libraries, or welfare agencies. No grants for capital or endowment funds or scholarships; building or operating funds; no loans, except program-related investments. All PRIs must directly further the work of one of the foundation's four thematic areas. The foundation accepts applications for PRIs.

Publications: Annual report (including application guidelines), program policy statement, application guidelines, financial statement.
PRI program information: E-mail an executive summary of not more than three pages to pkohn@rockfound.org. The foundation maintains a formal PRI program. The foundation makes PRIs on a frequent but not annual basis.
Officers and Trustees:* James F. Orr III,* Chair.; Gordon Conway,* Pres.; Denise A. Gray-Felder, V.P., Admin. and Comm.; Robert W. Herdt, V.P., Prog. Admin.; Julia I. Lopez, V.P., Prog. Admin.; Lynda Mullen, Corp. Secy.; Donna Dean, Treas. and C.I.O.; Charles J. Lang, Compt.; Fernando Henrique Cardoso, David de Ferranti, William H. Foege, Thomas J. Healey, Antonia Hernandez, Linda Hill, David M. Lawrence, Jessica Tuchman Mathews, Mamphela Ramphele, Rev. Cannon Frederick Boyd Williams, D. Min., D.C.L., Vo-Tong Xuan.
Number of staff: 67 full-time professional; 82 full-time support.
EIN: 131659629
PRI recipients:
209-1. Boston Community Capital, Boston, MA, $750,000. Program-related investment for investments in businesses in Massachusetts and northeastern U.S. that can generate financial and social returns through creation and retention of high-quality entry- and mid-level jobs for low-income and other disadvantaged groups. 2002.
209-2. Origin, NYC, NY, $750,000. Program-related investment to support efforts to connect welfare recipients and other low-income people who are unemployed or working at low-wage jobs to information technology-related jobs with large corporations. 2002.
209-3. Pioneer Social Ventures, LLC, Seattle, WA, $50,000. Program-related investment. 1999.
209-4. Silicon Valley Community Ventures, San Francisco, CA, $500,000. Program-related investment to support efforts that will provide economic opportunity in low-income and disadvantaged communities in the San Francisco Bay area. 2001.
209-5. Smithsonian Institution, DC, $500,000. Program-related investment for Global Sound Network Project. 2001.

210
The Winthrop Rockefeller Foundation

308 E. 8th St.
Little Rock, AR 72202-3999 (501) 376-6854
Contact: Prog. Mgr.
PRI Contact: Bill Rahn, Sr. Prog. Mgr.
FAX: (501) 374-4797; E-mail: program_manager@wrfoundation.org or programstaff@wrfoundation.org; URL: http://www.wrockefellerfoundation.org

Incorporated in 1956 in AR as Rockwin Fund, Inc.; renamed in 1974. PRI-related activities began in 1983.
Donor(s): Winthrop Rockefeller.‡
Grantmaker type: Independent foundation
General financial activity (yr. ended 12/31/02): Assets, $118,608,401 (M); gifts received, $2,030,500; expenditures, $10,546,218; qualifying distributions, $9,183,941; giving activities include $8,077,359 for 46 grants (high: $2,550,000; low: $5,000; average: $5,000–$300,000); no PRIs paid.
Cumulative PRI activity (through 12/31/02): Since 1983, the foundation has made 8 PRIs totaling $7,564,755. The currently outstanding PRI portfolio includes 3 PRIs totaling $5,505,000 (high: $1,000,000; low: $23,000). The typical outstanding PRI has a 3- to 10-year term.
General purpose and activities: The goals of the foundation are to: 1) encourage the development of Arkansas' ability to provide an equitable, quality education for all children; 2) strengthen the capacity of local communities to break the cycle of poverty by supporting projects that promote local economic development; and 3) nurture strong, broad-based grassroots leadership through the development of community-based organizations.
General fields of interest: Early childhood education; higher education; agriculture; youth development, citizenship; civil rights, advocacy; rural development; community development; economics; public policy, research.
Program-related investment (PRI) activity: The foundation occasionally makes PRIs in the areas of rural development and small business development. PRIs have capitalized earned income ventures and financed intermediaries (e.g., loan funds and venture capital funds).
Limitations: Giving limited to AR, or for projects that benefit AR. No grants to individuals, or for capital expenditures, endowments, building funds, equipment, annual fund drives, deficit financing, general support, emergency funds, most types of research, travel, scholarships, or fellowships. The foundation accepts applications for PRIs.
Publications: Annual report, occasional report, application guidelines.
PRI program information: Submit request by E-mail to program staff@ wrfoundation.org. The foundation maintains a formal PRI program. The foundation makes PRIs occasionally.
Officers and Directors:* Bob J. Nash, Chair.; Winthrop Paul Rockefeller,* Vice-Chair.; Sybil Jordan Hampton, Pres.; Andrea Dobson, C.O.O. and C.F.O.; Ivye L. Allen, Kay Kelly Arnold, O.V. Hicks Brantley, J. Michael Jones, Al "Papa Rap" Lopez, Mary Sanchez, Martin D. Strange, Ruby Takanishi.
Number of staff: 5 full-time professional; 4 full-time support.
EIN: 710285871
PRI recipients:
210-1. Southern Development Bancshares, Arkadelphia, AR, $1,000,000. Program-related investment to strengthen overall capital structure and expand

development lending program to assist economically-depressed communities. 2000.

210-2. Southern Financial Partners, Arkadelphia, AR, $1,000,000. Program-related investment made in form of loan to support development lending by enabling Southern Financial to expand its loan portfolio. 2001.

211
Rockwell Fund, Inc.

1330 Post Oak Blvd., Ste. 1825
Houston, TX 77056 (713) 629-9022
Contact: Martha Vogt, Sr. Prog. Off.
PRI Contact: R. Terry Bell, Pres.
FAX: (713) 629-7702; E-mail: mvogt@rockfund.org; URL: http://www.rockfund.org

Trust established in 1931; incorporated in 1949 in TX; merged with Rockwell Brothers Endowment, Inc. in 1981. PRI-related activities began in 2000.
Donor(s): Members of the James M. Rockwell family.‡
Grantmaker type: Independent foundation
General financial activity (yr. ended 12/31/02): Assets, $102,024,361 (M); gifts received, $1,000; expenditures, $6,065,469; qualifying distributions, $5,370,761; giving activities include $4,833,315 for 195 grants (high: $126,000; low: $500; average: $3,000–$126,000); no PRIs paid.
Cumulative PRI activity (through 12/31/02): Since 2000, the foundation has made 2 PRIs totaling $200,000. The currently outstanding PRI portfolio includes 2 PRIs totaling $200,000 (average: $100,000). The typical outstanding PRI has a 3- to 7-year term with an average term of 5 years and earns 2 to 4 percent interest with an average of 3 percent.
General purpose and activities: Giving primarily for charitable, religious, educational, medical, arts and humanities, and civic purposes.
General fields of interest: Visual arts; museums; performing arts; theater; music; humanities; historic preservation/historical societies; arts/cultural programs; early childhood education; child development, education; elementary school/education; secondary school/education; higher education; adult/continuing education; adult education—literacy, basic skills & GED; libraries/library science; reading; education; natural resources conservation & protection; environment; animal welfare; hospitals (general); family planning; medical care, rehabilitation; nursing care; health care; health associations; AIDS; biomedicine; crime/violence prevention, youth; crime/law enforcement; food services; human services; children & youth, services; child development, services; homeless, human services; government/public administration; Christian agencies & churches; Protestant agencies & churches; minorities; disabled; aging; homeless; general charitable giving.
Program-related investment (PRI) activity: The foundation has made PRIs to renovate space for the housing of artists and to provide housing for the disadvantaged.
Types of PRI Support: Loans/promissory notes.
Limitations: Giving primarily in TX, with emphasis on Houston. No grants to individuals or for medical or scientific research projects, underwriting benefits, dinners, galas, and fundraising special events, or mass appeal solicitations; grants primarily awarded on a year-to-year basis only. The foundation accepts applications for PRIs.
Publications: Annual report, application guidelines, grants list.
PRI program information: The foundation does not maintain a formal PRI program. The foundation makes PRIs occasionally.
Officers and Trustees:* R. Terry Bell,* C.E.O. and Pres.; Margaret E. Mcconn,* V.P. and C.F.O.; Barbara Bellatti,* Secy.; Bennie Green,* Treas.; Gene Graham, Helen N. Sterling, Tr. Emerita.
Number of staff: 5 full-time professional; 2 full-time support.
EIN: 746040258
PRI recipients:

211-1. Artspace Projects, Minneapolis, MN, $100,000. Loan to renovate historical Levy Building in Galveston, Texas to be used as artist lofts. 2000.

211-2. McAuley Institute, Silver Spring, MD, $100,000. Loan to supplement Houston Revolving Loan Fund. 2001.

212
Michael Alan Rosen Foundation

c/o Geibelson, Young & Co.
16501 Ventura Blvd., Ste. 304
Encino, CA 91436-2067 (818) 971-7300

Established in 1986 in CA. Classified as a private operating foundation in 1991.
Donor(s): Tobi Haleen, Conrad Hilton Foundation, The AGR Trust.
Grantmaker type: Operating foundation
General financial activity (yr. ended 12/31/01): Assets, $2,044,412 (M); gifts received, $202,124; expenditures, $1,400,953; qualifying distributions, $553,580; giving activities include $5,450 for grants (high: $3,500; low: $40), $781,575 for foundation-administered programs and $195,347 for PRIs.
Cumulative PRI activity (through 12/31/01): Since beginning PRI activity, the foundation has made 9 PRIs totaling $613,652.
General purpose and activities: The foundation's primary activity is financing and running drug/alcohol treatment programs.
General fields of interest: Substance abuse, services; substance abuse, treatment.
Program-related investment (PRI) activity: The foundation makes PRIs to organizations that assist people who are addicted to drugs and alcohol.
Limitations: Applications not accepted. No grants to individuals.

Officers: Arlene Rosen, Pres. and Treas.; Tobi Haleen, V.P. and Secy.
Number of staff: 2 full-time professional; 7 full-time support; 6 part-time support.
EIN: 943024736

213

Pleasant T. Rowland Foundation, Inc.

3415 Gateway Rd., Ste. 200
Brookfield, WI 53045-5111
Contact: Marti Sebree, Grants Mgr.
Application address: 1 S. Pinckney St., No. 810, Madison, WI 53703

Established in 1997 in WI.
Donor(s): Pleasant T. Rowland.
Grantmaker type: Independent foundation
General financial activity (yr. ended 12/31/01): Assets, $135,100,821 (M); expenditures, $8,258,903; qualifying distributions, $6,714,295; giving activities include $6,704,173 for 106 grants (high: $869,797; low: $500; average: $5,000–$20,000) and $12,725 for 4 grants to individuals (high: $5,000; low: $1,500); no PRIs paid.
General purpose and activities: Giving primarily for arts, education and historic preservation.
General fields of interest: Historic preservation/historical societies; arts/cultural programs; education.
Program-related investment (PRI) activity: The foundation has made a PRI in the form of property leased to a nonprofit organization for $1 per year.
Types of PRI Support: Charitable use assets.
Limitations: Giving primarily in, but not limited to, WI, with emphasis on Dane County.
Officers: Barbara Thiele Carr, Walter Jerome Frautschi, Valerie Tripp, Rhona E. Vogel.
Number of staff: 1 full-time professional.
EIN: 391868295
PRI recipients:
213-1. Hoffman Institute Foundation, San Anselmo, CA, $5,839,670. Purchase of White Sulphur Springs Resort by Foundation for leasing to Hoffman Institute. 2000.

214

The Erich & Hannah Sachs Foundation

810 Austin Ave.
Sonoma, CA 95476 (707) 935-0345
Contact: Caryn P. Sachs, Pres.
FAX: (707) 933-3810; E-mail: carynsachs@hotmail.com

Established in 1997 in DE.
Donor(s): Reynold M. Sachs.
Grantmaker type: Independent foundation
General financial activity (yr. ended 12/31/01): Assets, $11,101,794 (M); expenditures, $168,172; qualifying distributions, $209,239; giving activities include $126,000 for 2 PRIs.
Program-related investment (PRI) activity: The foundation has made PRIs in the form of low-interest loans to several CA community development organizations, including a land trust and a library development fund.
Types of PRI Support: Loans/promissory notes.
PRI giving primarily in CA.
Officers: Caryn P. Sachs, Pres.; John R. Mackall, Secy.; Reynold M. Sachs, Treas.
Director: Lucy M. Sachs.
EIN: 223337781
PRI recipients:
214-1. ACCION International, Boston, MA, $80,000. Loan. 1999.
214-2. Boston Community Capital, Boston, MA, $150,000. Low-interest loan. 1999.
214-3. Cascadia Revolving Fund, Seattle, WA, $250,000. Loan, below market rate. 2000.
214-4. Libraries for the Future, NYC, NY, $26,000. Loan, below market rate. 2001.
214-5. Northern California Community Loan Fund, San Francisco, CA, $250,000. Loan, below market rate. 2000.
214-6. Sonoma Land Trust, Santa Rosa, CA, $100,000. Loan, below market rate. 2001.

215

The Saint Paul Foundation, Inc.

600 5th St. Ctr.
55 Fifth St., E.
St. Paul, MN 55101-1797 (651) 224-5463
Contact: Paul A. Verret, Pres. and Secy.
FAX: (651) 224-8123; E-mail: inbox@saintpaulfoundation.org; URL: http://saintpaulfoundation.org

Established in 1940 in MN by adoption of a plan; incorporated in 1964.
Grantmaker type: Community foundation
General financial activity (yr. ended 12/31/01): Assets, $562,096,908 (M); gifts received, $22,547,850; expenditures, $40,426,580; giving activities include $26,616,371 for grants and $377,674 for 1,098 grants to individuals (high: $1,098; low: $10; average: $10–$775); no PRIs paid.
Cumulative PRI activity (through 12/31/01): The currently outstanding PRI portfolio includes PRIs totaling $3,587,975.
General purpose and activities: The foundation actively serves the people of Saint Paul, MN, and the surrounding communities by building permanent charitable capital, making philanthropic grants, and providing services that contribute to the health and vitality of the community. This is done by working with donors to achieve their philanthropic goals; managing responsibly the foundation's assets; encouraging and participating in community initiatives and partnerships; broadening the base of effective leadership in the community; building awareness of the role

of philanthropy in meeting the needs of the community; and providing services to other charitable organizations. The foundation pays special attention to helping achieve the following outcomes through its grants from unrestricted funds: an anti-racist community, economic development for all segments of the East Metro area, strong families that provide healthy beginnings for children and youth, and quality education for all.
General fields of interest: Humanities; arts/cultural programs; elementary/secondary education; adult education—literacy, basic skills & GED; reading; education; health care; health associations; human services; children & youth, services; minorities/immigrants, centers & services; race/intergroup relations; community development, neighborhood development; economic development; minorities.
Program-related investment (PRI) activity: The foundation has made loans for energy conservation, heating plant conservations and construction.
Types of PRI Support: Loans/promissory notes.
Limitations: Giving from restricted and unrestricted funds limited to nonprofit organizations and public entities primarily serving residents of the East Metro area of Ramsey, Washington, and Dakota counties in the metropolitan Saint Paul, MN, area. No support for sectarian religious programs, except from designated funds. No grants to individuals (except from designated funds) or for annual operating budgets, agency endowment funds, and capital projects located outside the East Metro area.
Publications: Annual report (including application guidelines), application guidelines, grants list, financial statement, newsletter, informational brochure.
PRI program information: The foundation makes low interest loans to nonprofit organizations and governmental agencies for purposes considered beneficial to the community. The foundation maintains a formal PRI program. The foundation makes PRIs occasionally.
Officers and Directors:* John A. Clymer,* Chair.; Paul A. Verret, Pres. and Secy.; Jack H. Pohl, V.P. Finance and Treas.; John G. Couchman, V.P., Grants and Progs.; Marialice P. Harwood, V.P., Devel. and Comm.; Henry M. Buffalo, Jr., Robert L. Bullard, Iris H. Cornelius, Jay Cowles III, Yang Dao, James Frey, Hon. Luz Maria Frias, Phyllis A. Rawls Goff, Joan A. Grzywinski, Susan Kimberly, Molly O'Shaughnessy, Elizabeth A. Pegues-Smart, L.J. Schoenwetter, Judith L. Titcomb, Jerrol M. Tostrod, Barbara Winthrop.
Corporate Trustees: American National Bank and Trust Co., First Trust, N.A., Wells Fargo Bank Minnesota, N.A.
Number of staff: 38 full-time professional; 2 part-time professional; 19 full-time support.
EIN: 416031510

216
The San Francisco Foundation

225 Bush St., 5th Fl.
San Francisco, CA 94104-4224 (415) 733-8500
Contact: Sandra R. Hernandez, M.D., C.E.O. and Secy.
PRI Contact: Christine Searson
FAX: (415) 477-2783; E-mail: SRH@sff.org;
URL: http://www.sff.org

Established in 1948 in CA by resolution and declaration of trust.
Grantmaker type: Community foundation
General financial activity (yr. ended 06/30/02): Assets, \$672,512,115 (M); gifts received, \$51,289,503; expenditures, \$77,995,227; giving activities include \$66,179,921 for grants, \$1,129,557 for grants to individuals, \$149,925 for 88 employee matching gifts and \$2,700,000 for 3 PRIs.
General purpose and activities: Grants principally in six categories: the arts and humanities, community health, education, environment, neighborhood and community development, and social services. Technical assistance grants also made, primarily to current recipients. The foundation serves five counties of the Bay Area.
General fields of interest: Media/communications; performing arts; dance; humanities; arts/cultural programs; early childhood education; child development, education; elementary school/education; adult education—literacy, basic skills & GED; reading; education; natural resources conservation & protection; environment; family planning; health care; substance abuse, services; mental health/crisis services; health associations; cancer; AIDS; alcoholism; cancer research; AIDS research; crime/violence prevention, youth; legal services; employment; housing/shelter, development; youth development, services; human services; children & youth, services; child development, services; family services; aging, centers & services; homeless, human services; international human rights; civil rights; urban/community development; community development; voluntarism promotion; public policy, research; government/public administration; leadership development; public affairs; minorities; disabled; aging; immigrants/refugees; economically disadvantaged; homeless.
Program-related investment (PRI) activity: The foundation has made PRIs occasionally to nonprofit organizations in the areas of the environment, community improvement, employment, housing, the arts, education, health, and immigrant services. PRIs have provided interim financing, supported facility improvement, and equipment acquisition, and capitalized earned income ventures and housing development.
Types of PRI Support: Loans/promissory notes, loan guarantees.
Limitations: Giving limited to the San Francisco Bay Area, CA, counties of Alameda, Contra Costa, Marin, San Francisco, and San Mateo. No support for religious

purposes. No grants for annual campaigns, general fundraising campaigns, emergency or endowment funds, deficit financing, matching funds, or for scholarships or fellowships, except when so designated by donor. PRI applications not accepted.
Publications: Annual report, newsletter, application guidelines, program policy statement, informational brochure (including application guidelines), grants list.
PRI program information: The foundation maintains a formal PRI program. The foundation makes PRIs occasionally.
Officers and Trustees:* F. Warren Hellman,* Chair.; Leslie P. Hume,* Vice-Chair.; Sandra R. Hernandez, M.D.,* C.E.O. and Secy.; Sandi Hutchings, Cont.; Gay Plair Cobb, Stephanie DiMarco, Peter E. Haas, Jr., Rolland C. Lowe, M.D., James C. Normel, David J. Sanchez, Jr., Gladys Thacher.
Number of staff: 34 full-time professional; 1 part-time professional; 16 full-time support; 5 part-time support.
EIN: 941101547

217
The Scherman Foundation, Inc.

16 E. 52nd St., Ste. 601
New York, NY 10022-5306 (212) 832-3086
Contact: Sandra Silverman, Pres. and Exec. Dir.
FAX: (212) 838-0154; URL: http://www.scherman.org

Incorporated in 1941 in NY.
Donor(s): Members of the Scherman family.
Grantmaker type: Independent foundation
General financial activity (yr. ended 12/31/02): Assets, $68,569,283 (M); expenditures, $6,149,430; qualifying distributions, $5,224,700; giving activities include $5,224,700 for 140 grants (high: $100,000; low: $1,000; average: $5,000–$100,000); no PRIs paid.
Cumulative PRI activity (through 12/31/02): The currently outstanding PRI portfolio includes PRIs totaling $75,000.
General purpose and activities: Grants largely for environment, disarmament and peace, reproductive rights and services, human rights and liberties, the arts and social welfare. In the social welfare field, grants are made to organizations concerned with social justice, housing, public affairs, and community self-help.
General fields of interest: Performing arts; theater; music; arts/cultural programs; libraries/library science; natural resources conservation & protection; environment; family planning; legal services; housing/shelter, development; human services; international peace/security; arms control; international human rights; civil rights, minorities; reproductive rights; civil rights; community development; economically disadvantaged; homeless.
Program-related investment (PRI) activity: The foundation has made loans on a limited basis and only in special circumstances for the arts and the environment.
Types of PRI Support: Loans/promissory notes.
Limitations: Giving in NY and nationally in all areas, except for the arts and social welfare, which are primarily in New York City. No support for colleges, universities, or other higher educational institutions. No grants to individuals, or for building or endowment funds, scholarships, fellowships, conferences or symposia, specific media or arts production, or medical, science or engineering research. PRI support primarily in New York, NY. PRI applications not accepted.
Publications: Annual report (including application guidelines).
PRI program information: Applications not accepted for PRI support. The foundation does not maintain a formal PRI program. The foundation makes PRIs occasionally.
Officers and Directors:* Karen R. Sollins, Chair.; Axel G. Rosin,* Chair, Emeritus; Sandra Silverman, Pres. and Exec. Dir.; Susanna Bergtold,* Secy.; Mitchell C. Pratt, Treas. and Prog. Off.; Hillary Brown, Gordon N. Litwin, John J. O'Neil, Katharine S. Rosin, Anthony M. Schulte, Marcia Thompson, John Wroclawski.
Number of staff: 2 full-time professional; 1 full-time support; 1 part-time support.
EIN: 136098464
PRI recipients:
217-1. Classical Theater of Harlem, NYC, NY, $12,000. Loan to help make payroll. 2003.

218
786 Foundation

c/o Marshall & Ilsley Bank
P.O. Box 2980
Milwaukee, WI 53201-2980
Contact: Sharon Blank
Application address: P.O. Box 8988, Madison, WI 53708, tel.: (608) 232-2056

Established in 1990 in WI.
Donor(s): Mary M. Lamar, Matthew W. Lamar, Michael Price, N. Stewart Stone III, Sarah Mead Stone, Timothy Stone.
Grantmaker type: Independent foundation
General financial activity (yr. ended 12/31/01): Assets, $4,199,887 (M); expenditures, $219,649; qualifying distributions, $166,000; giving activities include $166,000 for 13 grants (high: $40,000; low: $3,000); no PRIs paid.
Cumulative PRI activity (through 12/31/01): The currently outstanding PRI portfolio includes a high PRI value of $100,000 and a low PRI value of $50,000. The typical outstanding PRI has a 4- to 5-year term, and earns 2.50 to 3 percent interest.
General purpose and activities: Giving primarily for human services.
General fields of interest: Natural resources conservation & protection; housing/shelter, homeless; human services; YM/YWCAs & YM/YWHAs; foundations (community); philanthropy/voluntarism.
Program-related investment (PRI) activity: The foundation has made low-interest loans to community loan funds.

Types of PRI Support: Loans/promissory notes.
Limitations: Giving primarily in WI.
PRI program information: The foundation makes PRIs on a frequent but not annual basis.
Trustee: Marshall & Ilsley Bank.
EIN: 396515741

219
The Shiffman Foundation

18135 Hamilton Rd.
Detroit, MI 48203 (313) 345-1225
Contact: Richard H. Levey, Pres.
FAX: (313) 345-1930; E-mail: ShiffmanFd@aol.com

Incorporated in 1948 in MI. PRI-related activities began in 1995.
Donor(s): Abraham Shiffman,‡ Richard H. Levey.
Grantmaker type: Independent foundation
General financial activity (yr. ended 09/30/01): Assets, $951,757 (M); expenditures, $137,721; qualifying distributions, $79,343; giving activities include $51,931 for 47 grants (high: $13,409; low: $25); no PRIs paid.
Cumulative PRI activity (through 09/30/01): Since 1995, the foundation has made 2 PRIs totaling $51,040. The currently outstanding PRI portfolio includes PRIs totaling $72,040 (high: $125,000; low: $40,000; average: $25,000). The typical outstanding PRI has an average term of 10 years and earns 0 to 4 percent interest with an average of 4 percent.
General purpose and activities: The foundation is committed to giving program-related investments for community development and economic justice through the Episcopal Diocese of MI and other suitable institutions.
General fields of interest: Arts/cultural programs; higher education; education; international human rights; race/intergroup relations; urban/community development; community development; minorities; economically disadvantaged.
Program-related investment (PRI) activity: The foundation has made PRIs in the form of equity investments in two ventures: ITI China and Physicians On-Line. The foundation has also made PRIs in the form of loans for investment in two social service organizations: Michigan McGehee Interfaith Loan Fund and Poverty & Social Reform Institute.
Types of PRI Support: Loans/promissory notes, equity investments.
Limitations: Giving primarily in MI. No grants to individuals. The foundation accepts applications for PRIs.
PRI program information: The foundation maintains a formal PRI program. The foundation makes PRIs on a frequent but not annual basis.
Officer: Richard H. Levey, Pres.
Number of staff: None.
EIN: 381396850
PRI recipients:
219-1. Poverty and Social Reform Institute, Farmington Hills, MI, $25,000. Loan. 1999.

220
Sierra Health Foundation

1321 Garden Hwy.
Sacramento, CA 95833 (916) 922-4755
Contact: Tom Bennett, Prog. Off.
FAX: (916) 922-4024; URL: http://www.sierrahealth.org

Established in 1984 in CA; converted from Foundation Health Plan of Sacramento.
Donor(s): Foundation Health Plan of Sacramento.
Grantmaker type: Independent foundation
General financial activity (yr. ended 12/31/01): Assets, $144,041,090 (M); expenditures, $9,428,159; qualifying distributions, $5,939,119; giving activities include $3,250,566 for 128 grants (high: $312,500; low: $435; average: $5,000–$50,000) and $106,500 for 141 employee matching gifts; no PRIs paid.
General purpose and activities: Giving for health-related programs that 1) will have a long-term impact on the general health of the population; 2) provide a positive change in health care systems; and 3) may cause a positive change in the use of health care resources. Support also for model projects that may be replicated by others. The foundation has an ongoing significant interest in the health of young children.
General fields of interest: Child development, education; hospitals (general); medical care, rehabilitation; health care; substance abuse, services; mental health/crisis services; health associations; cancer; heart & circulatory diseases; skin disorders; AIDS; alcoholism; biomedicine; crime/violence prevention, youth; nutrition; human services; children & youth, services; child development, services; family services; aging, centers & services; minorities/immigrants, centers & services; community development; leadership development; minorities; aging; economically disadvantaged.
Program-related investment (PRI) activity: The foundation has made a PRI to a youth center.
Limitations: Applications not accepted. Giving limited to the following CA counties: Alpine, Amador, Butte, Calaveras, Colusa, El Dorado, Glenn, Lassen, Modoc, Mono, Nevada, Placer, Plumas, Sacramento, San Joaquin, Shasta, Sierra, Siskiyou, Solano (eastern), Stanislaus, Sutter, Tehama, Trinity, Tuolumne, Yolo, and Yuba. No support for programs, activities, or organizations that are not health-related. No grants for endowments.
Publications: Grants list, newsletter, informational brochure, occasional report.
PRI program information: The foundation makes PRIs occasionally.
Officers and Directors:* Wendy Everett, Sc.D.,* Chair.; Len McCandliss,* Pres.; Dorothy Meehan, V.P.; Steve Vorous, C.F.O.; Byron Demorest, M.D., George Deubel, J. Rodney Eason, Manuel Esteban, Ph.D., Albert R. Jonsen, Ph.D., Fr. Leo McAllister, Robert Petersen, Earl Washburn, M.D., Carol Whiteside.

Number of staff: 7 full-time professional; 1 part-time professional; 6 full-time support; 6 part-time support.
EIN: 680050036
PRI recipients:
220-1. Marysville Youth Center, Marysville, KS, $175,000. Program-related investment. 2000.

221
Marty and Dorothy Silverman Foundation
150 E. 58th St., 29th Fl.
New York, NY 10155
Contact: Lorin Silverman, Secy.-Treas.

Established in 1986.
Donor(s): Marty Silverman.
Grantmaker type: Independent foundation
General financial activity (yr. ended 07/31/01): Assets, $284,894,121 (M); gifts received, $1,237,916; expenditures, $13,848,618; qualifying distributions, $16,351,310; giving activities include $13,597,795 for 156 grants (high: $1,500,000; average: $10,000–$50,000) and $2,915,000 for 7 PRIs.
General purpose and activities: Support for programs that address the special needs of indigent senior citizens, including nursing homes and hospitals. Grants may also be made to educational and cultural organizations, and health and welfare agencies.
General fields of interest: Arts/cultural programs; education, association; hospitals (general); health associations; human services; aging, centers & services; aging.
Program-related investment (PRI) activity: The foundation has made PRIs to organizations serving the aging, and for education, human services, community development, and the arts.
Types of PRI Support: Loans/promissory notes.
Limitations: Applications not accepted. Giving primarily in NY. No grants to individuals.
PRI program information: The foundation makes PRIs on an annual basis.
Officers and Directors:* Marty Silverman,* Pres.; Joan Silverman,* V.P.; Lorin Silverman,* Secy.-Treas.
EIN: 222777449
PRI recipients:
221-1. American ORT Federation, NYC, NY, $2,000,000. Program-related investment. 1999.
221-2. Central Park Historical Field Trips, NYC, NY, $100,000. Program-related investment. 2001.
221-3. Child Development Center of the Hamptons, East Hampton, NY, $30,000. Program-related investment. 2000.
221-4. Community Food Resource Center, NYC, NY, $40,000. Program-related investment. 2000.
221-5. Doe Fund, NYC, NY, $450,000. Program-related investment. 1999.
221-6. Educational Alliance, NYC, NY, $150,000. Program-related investment. 2000.
221-7. Fund for the City of New York, NYC, NY, $100,000. Program-related investment. 2001.
221-8. Fund for the City of New York, NYC, NY, $250,000. Program-related investment. 1999.
221-9. Greater Jamaica Development Corporation, Jamaica, NY, $300,000. Program-related investment. 1999.
221-10. Institute for Urban Family Health, NYC, NY, $213,500. Program-related investment. 1999.
221-11. Jewish Community Center of Cleveland, Nesiya Institute, Cleveland, OH, $45,000. Program-related investment. 2000.
221-12. Jewish Family and Life, Newton, MA, $250,000. Program-related investment. 2001.
221-13. Jewish Federation of Rockland County, New City, NY, $20,000. Program-related investment. 2000.
221-14. John F. Reisenbach Charter School, NYC, NY, $800,000. Program-related investment. 2001.
221-15. National Council on the Aging, DC, $20,000. Program-related investment. 2000.
221-16. National Council on the Aging, DC, $1,000,000. Program-related investment. 1999.
221-17. New York City Environmental Justice Alliance, NYC, NY, $10,000. Program-related investment. 2000.
221-18. Nonprofit Finance Fund, NYC, NY, $200,000. Program-related investment. 2001.
221-19. University Heights Association, Albany, NY, $1,300,000. Program-related investment. 2001.
221-20. University Heights Association, Albany, NY, $11,750. Program-related investment. 2000.
221-21. University Heights Association, Albany, NY, $1,150,000. Program-related investment. 1999.
221-22. Youth Education Support Services (YESS) of Greater Monmouth County, Monmouth, NJ, $165,000. Program-related investment. 2001.

222
Southland Charitable Trust
P.O. Box 6759
Raleigh, NC 27628

Established in 1986. PRI-related activities began in 2001.
Donor(s): Gordon Smith, Jr., Jean P. Smith.
Grantmaker type: Independent foundation
General financial activity (yr. ended 06/30/02): Assets, $1,597,215 (M); expenditures, $102,234; qualifying distributions, $66,500; giving activities include $66,500 for 3 grants (high: $65,000; low: $500); no PRIs paid.
Cumulative PRI activity (through 06/30/02): The currently outstanding PRI portfolio includes PRIs totaling $495,000.
General purpose and activities: Giving primarily for education and human services.
General fields of interest: Film/video; education; Christian agencies & churches.
Program-related investment (PRI) activity: The foundation made a loan to a cultural organization to assist in the

building and development of a museum to help expose children to different cultures.

Limitations: Applications not accepted. Giving primarily in NC and VA. No grants to individuals.

Trustees: Clark Smith, Gordon Smith.

EIN: 566268422

PRI recipients:

222-1. Exploris, Raleigh, NC, $495,000. Loan to develop museum. 2001.

223
Stark Community Foundation

(Formerly The Stark County Foundation, Inc.)
Unizan Plz., Ste. 750
220 Market Ave. S.
Canton, OH 44702 (330) 454-3426
Contact: James A. Bower, Pres., and Cynthia M. Lazor, V.P.
FAX: (330) 454-5855; E-mail: jbower@starkcf.org; Additional E-mail: cmlazer@starkcf.org; URL: http:// www.starkcommunityfoundation.org

Established in 1963 in OH by resolution and declaration of trust.

Grantmaker type: Community foundation

General financial activity (yr. ended 12/31/02): Assets, $115,000,000 (M); gifts received, $10,330,535; expenditures, $4,125,000; giving activities include $3,615,703 for grants; no PRIs paid.

General purpose and activities: To enhance the sound health and general welfare of Stark County, OH, citizens through support for civic improvement programs and educational institutions. Primary areas of interest include the arts, education, community development, health and wellness, youth, and social services.

General fields of interest: Visual arts; performing arts; historic preservation/historical societies; arts/cultural programs; early childhood education; child development, education; elementary school/education; higher education; business school/education; law school/education; education; natural resources conservation & protection; environment; health care; substance abuse, services; AIDS; AIDS research; crime/law enforcement; food services; housing/shelter, development; recreation; youth development, services; human services; children & youth, services; child development, services; family services; aging, centers & services; minorities/immigrants, centers & services; homeless, human services; urban/community development; community development; government/public administration; leadership development; minorities; disabled; aging; homeless.

Program-related investment (PRI) activity: The foundation makes PRIs on a limited basis to local community organizations to carry out their charitable purposes.

Limitations: Giving limited to Stark County, OH. No support for religious organizations for religious purposes. No grants for endowment funds, operating budgets, continuing support, annual campaigns, publications, conferences or deficit financing; no grants or loans to individuals (except to college students who are permanent residents of Stark County, OH).

Publications: Annual report (including application guidelines), program policy statement, application guidelines, financial statement, grants list, newsletter, informational brochure.

PRI program information: The foundation makes PRIs occasionally.

Officers: James A. Bower, Pres.; Cynthia M. Lazor, V.P., Progs.; Howard S. Rubin, Jr., V.P., Devel.; Patricia C. Quick, V.P., Fin. and C.F.O.

Distribution Committee: Paul R. Bishop, Chair; Nazamovia "Naz" Adams-Phillips, Lynne S. Dragomier, Jeffrey A. Fisher, Thomas W. Schervish, Candy Wallace, John R. Werren.

Trustee Banks: Bank One Ohio Trust Co., N.A., FirstMerit Bank, N.A., KeyBank, N.A., National City Bank, Northeast, Univan Bank, Sky Bank.

Number of staff: 4 full-time professional; 3 part-time professional; 1 full-time support; 3 part-time support.

EIN: 340943665

224
Steans Family Foundation

River Plz., 2E.
405 N. Wabash Ave.
Chicago, IL 60611 (312) 467-5900
Contact: Greg Darnieder

Established in 1986 in IL.

Grantmaker type: Independent foundation

General financial activity (yr. ended 12/31/01): Assets, $22,926,272 (M); gifts received, $573,482; expenditures, $4,343,543; qualifying distributions, $3,028,403; giving activities include $2,476,904 for 135 grants (high: $500,229; low: $40; average: $1,000–$40,000) and $163,851 for 14 employee matching gifts; no PRIs paid.

General purpose and activities: Giving primarily for education and youth services; support also for community services.

General fields of interest: Higher education; children & youth, services; urban/community development; community development; public affairs; minorities.

Program-related investment (PRI) activity: The foundation makes PRIs to support community development and education.

Types of PRI Support: Loans/promissory notes.

Limitations: Applications not accepted. Giving primarily in Chicago and North Lawndale, IL. No grants to individuals. PRI applications not accepted.

PRI program information: PRI support only to pre-selected organizations.

Officers and Directors:* Harrison I. Steans,* Pres.; Lois M. Steans,* V.P.; Heather A. Steans, Robin M. Steans, Jennifer Steans.

Number of staff: 1 full-time professional; 2 part-time professional; 1 full-time support.

EIN: 363486843
PRI recipients:
224-1. Lawndale Business and Local Development Corporation, Chicago, IL, $60,142. Loan. 2000.
224-2. Lawndale Christian Development Corporation, Chicago, IL, $119,993. Loan. 2000.
224-3. Manley High School, Lawndale, IL, $39,406. Loan. 2000.
224-4. North Lawndale Learning Community, Chicago, IL, $50,000. Loan. 2000.

225
The Abbot and Dorothy H. Stevens Foundation

P.O. Box 111
North Andover, MA 01845 (978) 688-7211
Contact: Elizabeth A. Beland, Admin.
FAX: (978) 686-1620; E-mail:
74722.2637@compuserve.com

Trust established in 1953 in MA. PRI-related activities began in 1989.
Donor(s): Abbot Stevens.‡
Grantmaker type: Independent foundation
General financial activity (yr. ended 12/31/01): Assets, $23,997,510 (M); expenditures, $1,222,100; qualifying distributions, $1,222,100; giving activities include $1,222,100 for 100 grants (high: $100,000; low: $100; average: $2,000–$9,000); no PRIs paid.
Cumulative PRI activity (through 12/31/01): Since 1989, the foundation has made 3 PRIs totaling $1,600,000. The currently outstanding PRI portfolio includes 1 PRI totaling $200,000. The typical outstanding PRI has an average term of 5 years, and earns an average of 5 percent interest.
General purpose and activities: Giving primarily for the arts, education, conservation and health and human services.
General fields of interest: Museums; humanities; historic preservation/historical societies; arts/cultural programs; medical school/education; education; natural resources conservation & protection; health care; health associations; domestic violence prevention; human services; children & youth, services; African Americans/Blacks; Hispanics/Latinos; disabled; aging; immigrants/refugees; economically disadvantaged.
Program-related investment (PRI) activity: The foundation has made PRIs for museum support and historic preservation. PRIs have financed facility acquisition and renovations.
Types of PRI Support: Loans/promissory notes.
Limitations: Giving limited to MA, with emphasis on the greater Lawrence area. No support for national organizations, or for state or federal agencies. No grants to individuals, or for annual campaigns, deficit financing, exchange programs, internships, professorships, scholarships, or fellowships. PRI decisions are based on regular grant applications for capital support. PRI applications not accepted.
Publications: Program policy statement, application guidelines.
PRI program information: The foundation does not maintain a formal PRI program. The foundation makes PRIs occasionally.
Trustees: Phebe S. Miner, Christopher W. Rogers, Samuel S. Rogers.
Number of staff: 1 full-time professional; 1 part-time support.
EIN: 046107991
PRI recipients:
225-1. Merrimack Valley Community Foundation, Andover, MA, $200,000. Low-interest loan. 1999.

226
The Nathaniel and Elizabeth P. Stevens Foundation

P.O. Box 111
North Andover, MA 01845 (978) 688-7211
Contact: Elizabeth A. Beland, Admin.
FAX: (978) 686-1620; E-mail:
74722,2637@compuserve.com

Trust established in 1943 in MA. PRI-related activities began in 1989.
Donor(s): Nathaniel Stevens.‡
Grantmaker type: Independent foundation
General financial activity (yr. ended 12/31/02): Assets, $17,300,773 (M); expenditures, $985,736; qualifying distributions, $974,781; giving activities include $916,135 for 136 grants (high: $150,000; low: $100; average: $2,000–$8,000); no PRIs paid.
General fields of interest: Museums; historic preservation/historical societies; arts/cultural programs; medical school/education; education; natural resources conservation & protection; hospitals (general); health care; health associations; domestic violence prevention; housing/shelter, development; human services; minorities/immigrants, centers & services; minorities; African Americans/Blacks; Hispanics/Latinos; disabled; aging; immigrants/refugees; economically disadvantaged.
Program-related investment (PRI) activity: The foundation has made PRIs for museum support and historic preservation. PRIs have supported facility acquisition and renovation.
Types of PRI Support: Loans/promissory notes.
Limitations: Giving limited to MA, with emphasis on the greater Lawrence and Merrimack Valley areas. No support for national organizations, or for state or federal agencies. No grants to individuals, or for deficit financing, exchange programs, internships, lectureships, research, professorships, scholarships, fellowships, or annual campaigns. PRI decisions are based on grant proposal applications for capital support. The foundation accepts applications for PRIs.
Publications: Application guidelines, program policy statement.

PRI program information: The foundation does not maintain a formal PRI program. The foundation makes PRIs occasionally.
Trustees: Joshua L. Miner IV, Phebe S. Miner, Samuel S. Rogers.
Number of staff: None.
EIN: 042236996
PRI recipients:
226-1. Merrimack Valley Community Foundation, Andover, MA, $200,000. Low-interest loan. 1999.

227
Lydia B. Stokes Foundation
721 Don Diego Ave.
Santa Fe, NM 87505
URL: http://www.lydiabstokesfoundation.org

Trust established in 1959 in NJ.
Donor(s): Lydia B. Stokes.‡
Grantmaker type: Independent foundation
General financial activity (yr. ended 06/30/02): Assets, $3,807,444 (M); expenditures, $193,784; qualifying distributions, $167,975; giving activities include $167,975 for grants; no PRIs paid.
General purpose and activities: Support for the environment and conservation, education, community funds, and women's and children's issues.
General fields of interest: Education; natural resources conservation & protection; environment; human services; children & youth, services; family services; women, centers & services; community development; federated giving programs; women.
Program-related investment (PRI) activity: The foundation has made a PRI in the form of a low-interest loan to a community development organization.
Types of PRI Support: Loans/promissory notes.
Limitations: Applications not accepted. Giving in the U.S., with emphasis on CO, New England, FL, and NM. No grants to individuals.
Trustees: Nancy V. Deren, Ann R. Stokes, Sally S. Venerable, Thomas R. Willits.
Number of staff: None.
EIN: 216016107
PRI recipients:
227-1. Calvert Social Investment Foundation, Calvert Community Investment Notes, Bethesda, MD, $60,000. Low-interest loan. 2001.

228
Stranahan Foundation
4159 Holland-Sylvania Rd., Ste. 206
Toledo, OH 43623-2590 (419) 882-5575
Contact: Pamela G. Roberts, Prog. Off.
FAX: (419) 882-2072; E-mail: proberts@stranahanfoundation.org; URL: http://www.stranahanfoundation.org

Trust established in 1944 in OH.
Donor(s): Robert A. Stranahan,‡ Frank D. Stranahan,‡ and others.
Grantmaker type: Independent foundation
General financial activity (yr. ended 12/31/01): Assets, $87,728,211 (M); gifts received, $1,000; expenditures, $5,759,301; qualifying distributions, $5,218,786; giving activities include $5,150,000 for 59 grants (high: $500,000; low: $1,000; average: $10,000–$50,000) and $50,000 for 1 PRI.
Cumulative PRI activity (through 12/31/01): The currently outstanding PRI portfolio includes 1 PRI totaling $50,000.
General purpose and activities: Giving largely for higher education; support also for a community foundation and a community fund, youth, social service, health agencies, and cultural organizations, including a fine arts museum and performing arts groups.
General fields of interest: Museums; opera; music, choral; ballet; orchestra (symphony); arts/cultural programs; higher education; education; health associations; human services; youth, services; business & industry; community development; federated giving programs.
Program-related investment (PRI) activity: The foundation made a PRI to an organization providing senior care.
Types of PRI Support: Loans/promissory notes.
Limitations: Giving primarily in Toledo, OH. No support for religious organizations or religious purposes, projects located outside the U.S., or government sponsored or controlled projects. No grants to individuals, or for deficit reduction, computer projects, film, television, or radio productions, or endowment funds.
Publications: Annual report, informational brochure (including application guidelines).
PRI program information: The foundation makes PRIs occasionally.
Officer and Trustees:* Stephen Stranahan,* Pres.; Diana Foster, Michael Foster, William Foster, Pam Howell, Kathy Knight, Roberta Pawlak, Marcia Piper, Duane Stranahan, Jr., Charles G. Yeager, Emeritus.
Number of staff: 1 part-time professional; 2 full-time support.
EIN: 346514375
PRI recipients:
228-1. Sunset Haven Senior Ministries, Ontario, CA, $50,000. Non-interest bearing loan for general operating support. 2001.

229
The Summit Charitable Foundation, Inc.
2100 Pennsylvania Ave., N.W., Ste. 525
Washington, DC 20037 (202) 912-2900
Contact: Victoria P. Sant, Pres.
FAX: (202) 912-2901; E-mail: info@summitfdn.org;
URL: http://www.summitfdn.org

Established in 1991 in DE.
Donor(s): Roger W. Sant, Victoria P. Sant.
Grantmaker type: Independent foundation
General financial activity (yr. ended 12/31/01): Assets, $74,439,452 (M); gifts received, $2,962,970; expenditures, $15,123,615; qualifying distributions, $14,604,977; giving activities include $12,384,151 for grants (high: $840,000; low: $250; average: $1,000–$100,000) and $8,000 for 23 employee matching gifts; no PRIs paid.
Cumulative PRI activity (through 12/31/01): The currently outstanding PRI portfolio includes 2 PRIs totaling $350,000.
General purpose and activities: The foundation is in the process of revisiting its priorities. New program priorities will be available in 2003.
General fields of interest: Environment, research; natural resources conservation & protection; environment; family planning; population studies; women.
General international interests: Caribbean; Latin America.
Program-related investment (PRI) activity: The foundation makes loans to organizations that supports small businesses.
Types of PRI Support: Loans/promissory notes.
Limitations: Applications not accepted. Giving primarily on an international basis, in the mesoamerican reef ecoregion and Atlantic Coastal Forests ecoregion, with emphasis on Latin America and the Caribbean for environmental grantmaking. No grants to individuals, or for freestanding conferences, film and video projects or basic research.
Publications: Annual report, financial statement, grants list, informational brochure, program policy statement.
PRI program information: The foundation makes PRIs on a frequent but not annual basis.
Officers and Trustees:* Roger W. Sant,* Chair. and Treas.; Victoria P. Sant,* Pres.; Shari Sant Plummer,* Secy.; J. Martin Goebel, Dan Plummer, Alexis Sant, Alison Sant, Chrissie Sant, Kristin Sant, Michael Sant, Shira Saperstein.
Number of staff: 3 full-time professional; 1 part-time professional.
EIN: 521743817
PRI recipients:
229-1. Stellar Fisheries, Philippines, $250,000. Program-related investment. 2000.
229-2. Womens Capital Corporation, DC, $100,000. Program-related investment. 2000.
229-3. Womens Capital Corporation, DC, $50,000. Program-related investment. 1999.

230
Sweet Water Trust
77 Central St., 5th Fl.
Boston, MA 02109 (617) 482-5998
Contact: Nancy Smith, Exec Dir.; or Sigrid Pickering, Prog. Dir.
PRI Contact: Nancy Smith
FAX: (617) 482-4844; E-mail: watersweet@aol.com;
URL: http://www.sweetwatertrust.org

Established in 1991 in MA. PRI-related activities began in 1995.
Donor(s): Walker G. Buckner, Jr., Foundation for the Needs of Others, Inc.
Grantmaker type: Independent foundation
General financial activity (yr. ended 12/31/01): Assets, $23,316,816 (M); expenditures, $1,470,927; qualifying distributions, $1,417,414; giving activities include $962,500 for 5 grants (high: $300,000; low: $12,500) and $165,816 for 2 PRIs.
Cumulative PRI activity (through 12/31/01): Since 1995, the foundation has made 9 PRIs totaling $698,656. The currently outstanding PRI portfolio includes 2 PRIs totaling $309,000 (high: $300,000; low: $7,678). The typical outstanding PRI has a 1-month to 1-year term with an average term of 1 year.
General purpose and activities: Support for environmental preservation through 3 programs: 1) Land Protection Program: wild land; wild water - to help purchase land and conservation easements. The trust seeks partners (land trusts, government agencies, businesses and individuals) to work toward the ecological and biotic health of New England by establishing, enlarging, and connecting reserve areas. Grants range from $1,000-$1,000,000 for land acquisition, 2) Conservation Stewardship— $1,000-$15,000 for conservation stewardship, and 3) wilderness advocacy grants; giving through this program is earmarked for nonprofits in ME, MA, NH, NY, and VT; and - Grants are awarded for projects in science and natural resource protection, ecological analysis, stewardship, endowments, management plans; projects to create more wilderness and/or to ensure areas so designated are managed as such.
General fields of interest: Natural resources conservation & protection; environment, water resources; environment, land resources; wildlife preservation & protection; biological sciences.
Program-related investment (PRI) activity: The foundation's Wildlands Program supports environmental preservation through the purchase of land and conservation easements. PRIs include loans to organizations for purchasing land and the acquisition of charitable use property and easements by the foundation.
Types of PRI Support: Loans/promissory notes, interim financing, charitable use assets.
Limitations: Giving generally limited to New England and upstate NY. No support for projects for the protection of farmland, timberlands, parks, and trails unless they are a

small part of a reserve design of a natural area which exceeds 2,000 acres. No grants to individuals.
Publications: Biennial report (including application guidelines), grants list.
PRI program information: The foundation does not maintain a formal PRI program. The foundation makes PRIs occasionally.
Trustee: Walker G. Buckner, Jr.
Number of staff: 4 part-time professional.
EIN: 043118545
PRI recipients:
230-1. Appalachian Trail Conference, Harpers Ferry, WV, $300,000. Loan at no interest. 1999.
230-2. Green Mountain Club, Waterbury Center, VT, $12,500. Loan at no interest. 2000.
230-3. Lakes Region Conservation Trust, Meredith, NH, $125,000. No-interest loan. 2001.
230-4. Sweet Water Trust Project, Boston, MA, $40,816. Purchase of Stelmok Property in Atkinson, Maine. 2001.

231
T By D Foundation
P.O. Box 1252
Morro Bay, CA 93443-1252

Grantmaker type: Operating foundation
General financial activity (yr. ended 12/31/01): Assets, $1,306,918 (M); expenditures, $33,250; qualifying distributions, $47,750; giving activities include $33,250 for grants and $14,500 for 3 PRIs.
General purpose and activities: Giving for food services, the arts, higher education, and youth services.
General fields of interest: Media/communications; higher education; food services; children & youth, services; civil liberties, advocacy.
Program-related investment (PRI) activity: The foundation has made PRIs to a fine arts academy for its performing arts school, to a university, for its performing arts program, and to a school for the handicapped, for its space camp program. The foundation also purchases video equipment and counts the cost as PRIs.
Types of PRI Support: Charitable use assets.
Limitations: Applications not accepted. Giving primarily in CA. No grants to individuals.
Officer: Robert Lane, Pres. and Treas.
EIN: 942785097

232
The Greater Tacoma Community Foundation
1019 Pacific Ave.
P.O. Box 1995
Tacoma, WA 98401-1995 (253) 383-5622
Contact: Lynne Rumball, Prog. Off.
FAX: (253) 272-8099; E-mail: lrumball@gtcf.org; URL: http://www.tacomafoundation.org

Incorporated in 1977 in WA. PRI-related activities began in 1986.
Grantmaker type: Community foundation
General financial activity (yr. ended 06/30/01): Assets, $48,000 (M); gifts received, $6,444,370; expenditures, $17,172,029; giving activities include $1,508,346 for grants and $23,464 for 1 PRI.
Cumulative PRI activity (through 06/30/01): The currently outstanding PRI portfolio includes a high PRI value of $25,000. The typical outstanding PRI has a 3-month to 3-year term, and earns 0 to 5 percent interest.
General fields of interest: Museums; performing arts; theater; historic preservation/historical societies; arts/cultural programs; child development, education; higher education; adult/continuing education; libraries/library science; education; natural resources conservation & protection; environment; hospitals (general); health care; substance abuse, services; mental health/crisis services; health associations; AIDS; AIDS research; food services; housing/shelter, development; recreation; youth development, services; human services; children & youth, services; child development, services; family services; hospices; aging, centers & services; homeless, human services; community development; voluntarism promotion; government/public administration; leadership development; disabled; aging; economically disadvantaged; homeless.
Program-related investment (PRI) activity: The foundation established the Agency Loan Fund in 1986 to provide short-term (up to one year) loans on a revolving basis to stable nonprofit agencies experiencing financial emergencies. Most loans range from $5,000 to $10,000, with an exceptional maximum of $25,000. Interest rates vary between 0 percent and the prime rate depending on the agency's financial condition, type of collateral provided, and length of time needed to repay the loan. Preference is given to agencies with annual budgets of $500,000 or less.
Types of PRI Support: Loans/promissory notes, interim financing, lines of credit.
Limitations: Giving limited to Pierce County, WA. No support for religious or political activities. No grants for annual campaigns, scholarships, fellowships, seminars, meetings or travel, or publications, unless specified by donor. Applicants must be 501(c)(3) nonprofit agencies. The foundation accepts applications for PRIs.
Publications: Annual report, informational brochure (including application guidelines), newsletter, application guidelines.
PRI program information: The foundation maintains a formal PRI program. The foundation makes PRIs on a frequent but not annual basis.
Officers and Directors:* Sally B. Leighton, Chair.; Tom Hosea,* Vice-Chair.; Margy McGroarty, Pres.; Gregory M. Tanbara,* Secy.; James P. Dawson,* Treas.; James Brown, Piper Cheney, Dick DeVine, Andrea S. Gernon, John Larsen, Barbara Skinner, Terry Stone, Pamela Transue, Michael Tucci, James Walton.
Number of staff: 4 full-time professional; 1 full-time support.
EIN: 911007459

233
T. L. L. Temple Foundation

109 Temple Blvd., Ste. 300
Lufkin, TX 75901 (936) 639-5197
Contact: A. Wayne Corely, Exec. Dir.

Trust established in 1962 in TX.
Donor(s): Georgie T. Munz,‡ Katherine S. Temple.‡
Grantmaker type: Independent foundation
General financial activity (yr. ended 11/30/02): Assets, $284,997,443 (M); expenditures, $15,149,442; qualifying distributions, $14,215,839; giving activities include $14,017,274 for 143 grants (high: $2,500,000; low: $1,000; average: $5,000–$60,000) and $64,019 for 85 employee matching gifts; no PRIs paid.
Cumulative PRI activity (through 11/30/02): The currently outstanding PRI portfolio includes 3 PRIs totaling $4,216,888.
General purpose and activities: Support for education, health, and community and social services; support also for civic affairs and cultural programs.
General fields of interest: Arts/cultural programs; elementary school/education; higher education; adult/continuing education; education; animal welfare; hospitals (general); medical care, rehabilitation; health care; substance abuse, services; mental health/crisis services; human services; hospices; community development; government/public administration; economically disadvantaged.
Program-related investment (PRI) activity: The foundation has made PRIs to health organizations, a retirement community and a college and holds PRIs in the form of real estate as part of a community revitalization effort.
Types of PRI Support: Loans/promissory notes, charitable use assets.
Limitations: Giving primarily in counties in TX constituting the East Texas Pine Timber Belt. No support for private foundations. No grants to individuals, or for deficit financing. PRI applications not accepted.
Publications: Application guidelines, program policy statement.
PRI program information: The foundation does not maintain a formal PRI program. The foundation makes PRIs occasionally.
Officers and Trustees:* Arthur Temple III,* Chair.; Arthur Temple,* Chair. Emeritus; M.F. Zeagler, Cont.; A. Wayne Corley, Exec. Dir.; Ward R. Burke, Phillip M. Leach, H.J. Shands III, W. Temple Webber, Jr., W. Temple Webber III.
Number of staff: 4 full-time professional; 2 part-time professional; 1 full-time support; 1 part-time support.
EIN: 756037406
PRI recipients:
233-1. Angelina College, Lufkin, TX, $2,100,000. Program-related investment. 1999.
233-2. Jasper, County of, Jasper, TX, $226,921. Program-related investment to purchase 28.11 acres in Jasper County. 2000.
233-3. Lufkin, City of, Lufkin, TX, $500,000. Program-related investment for animal control facility. 1999.
233-4. Methodist Retirement Services, The Woodlands, TX, $2,100,000. Program-related investment. 2000.

234
William T. Thorkildsen Trust

c/o Wells Fargo Bank West, N.A.
1740 Broadway, MAC C7300-484
Denver, CO 80274-8681

Established in 1990 in CO.
Donor(s): Blanche Thorkildsen.‡
Grantmaker type: Independent foundation
General financial activity (yr. ended 07/31/02): Assets, $2,041,433 (M); expenditures, $29,536; qualifying distributions, $471,960; giving activities include $47,188 for 2 PRIs.
General purpose and activities: Loan funds paid directly to university and colleges in CO; primary giving to the University of Colorado and University of N. Colorado, to provide college loans to students.
General fields of interest: Scholarships/financial aid.
Program-related investment (PRI) activity: The foundation has given loans to Colorado universities and colleges.
Types of PRI Support: Loans/promissory notes.
Limitations: Applications not accepted. Giving limited to CO.
Trustee: Wells Fargo Bank West, N.A.
EIN: 846233895
PRI recipients:
234-1. Aims Community College, Greeley, CO, $41,955. Loans at below-market interest rate. 2001.
234-2. Colorado State University, Fort Collins, CO, $11,000. Loans at below-market interest rate. 2001.
234-3. Colorado State University, Fort Collins, CO, $12,222. Loans at below-market interest rate. 2000.
234-4. Colorado State University, Fort Collins, CO, $16,379. Loans at below-market interest rate. 1999.
234-5. University of Colorado, Boulder, CO, $29,045. Loans at below-market interest rate. 2001.
234-6. University of Colorado, Boulder, CO, $50,465. Loans at below-market interest rate. 2000.
234-7. University of Colorado, Boulder, CO, $58,168. Loans at below-market interest rate. 1999.
234-8. University of Northern Colorado, Greeley, CO, $23,350. Loans at below-market interest rate. 2001.
234-9. University of Northern Colorado, Greeley, CO, $25,350. Loans at below-market interest rate. 2000.
234-10. University of Northern Colorado, Greeley, CO, $36,200. Loans at below-market interest rate. 1999.

235

The Tikvah Fund

1345 Ave. of the Americas
New York, NY 10036 (212) 756-4385
Contact: Roger Hertog, Chair.

Established in 1992 in NY.
Donor(s): Zalman C. Bernstein.
Grantmaker type: Independent foundation
General financial activity (yr. ended 12/31/01): Assets, $100,716,549 (M); gifts received, $5,000,000; expenditures, $6,007,067; qualifying distributions, $5,956,817; giving activities include $5,897,517 for 1 grant; no PRIs paid.
Cumulative PRI activity (through 12/31/01): Since beginning PRI activity, the foundation has made 3 PRIs totaling $2,370,298.
General purpose and activities: Giving primarily for Jewish affairs. Makes grants and program-related investments to companies located in areas of high unemployment or development in Israel, and to companies that are owned by or employ new immigrants or veteran soldiers.
General fields of interest: Religion, public policy; Jewish agencies & temples.
General international interests: Israel.
Program-related investment (PRI) activity: The foundation makes PRIs to Israeli companies located in areas of high unemployment or underdevelopment, and to Israeli companies that are owned by or employ new immigrants or veteran soldiers. Initial financial commitments range from $200,000 to $500,000 and may take any combination of debt and/or equity, not to exceed 24.9 percent of ownership.
Types of PRI Support: Equity investments.
Limitations: Giving primarily in Israel.
Officers and Directors:* Roger Hertog,* Chair.; Christina Restivo, Secy.; Arthur W. Fried,* C.F.O.; Kenneth A. Abramowitz, Mem Bernstein, Morris Smith, David Stone.
EIN: 133676152
PRI recipients:
235-1. Shalem Center, Jerusalem, Israel, $1,000,000. Loan for general support. 1999.
235-2. Shalem Center, Jerusalem, Israel, $897,000. Loan for general support. 1999.
235-3. Shalem Center, DC, $150,000. Loan for general support. 1999.
235-4. Shalem Center, DC, $55,000. Loan for general support. 1999.

236

The University Financing Foundation, Inc.

(Formerly Georgia Scientific and Technical Research Foundation)
3333 Busbee Dr., Rm 150
Kennesaw, GA 30144 (770) 420-4300
Contact: C.M. Lampman, Mgr.

Classified as a private operating foundation in 1989.
Grantmaker type: Operating foundation
General financial activity (yr. ended 12/31/01): Assets, $236,305,173 (M); expenditures, $6,782,030; qualifying distributions, $48,581,352; giving activities include $53,000 for 4 grants (high: $50,000; low: $300) and $43,030,163 for PRIs.
Cumulative PRI activity (through 12/31/01): Since beginning PRI activity, the foundation has made 15 PRIs totaling $7,917,592.
General purpose and activities: Giving primarily for education or research to public or private non-profit colleges or universities only.
General fields of interest: Higher education; public policy, research.
Program-related investment (PRI) activity: The foundation has made low-interest loans to educational institutions.
Types of PRI Support: Loans/promissory notes.
Limitations: Giving primarily in Lakeland, FL and Atlanta, GA.
Officers: J. Frank Smith, Pres.; John E. Aderhold, V.P.; James M. Sibley, Secy.; Thomas H. Hall III, Treas.; Charles M. Lampman, Mgr.
EIN: 581505902
PRI recipients:
236-1. California State University, Fresno, CA, $224,310. Low-interest loan. 2001.
236-2. California State University, Fresno, CA, $416,437. Program-related investment. 2000.
236-3. California State University, Long Beach, CA, $208,745. Program-related investment. 1999.
236-4. California State University, Dominguez Hills, Carson, CA, $119,631. Program-related investment. 1999.
236-5. Charleston Southern University, Charleston, SC, $21,130. Program-related investment. 2000.
236-6. Council for Christian Colleges and Universities, DC, $1,163,569. Low-interest loan. 2001.
236-7. Council for Christian Colleges and Universities, DC, $1,600,000. Program-related investment. 1999.
236-8. Elizabethtown College, Elizabethtown, PA, $360,000. Program-related investment. 1999.
236-9. Georgia Institute of Technology, Atlanta, GA, $1,025,618. Low-interest loan. 2001.
236-10. Georgia Institute of Technology, Atlanta, GA, $920,072. Program-related investment. 1999.
236-11. Georgia Soccer Development Foundation, Roswell, GA, $150,000. Program-related investment. 1999.
236-12. University Financing Foundation Project, Kennesaw, GA, $40,376,666. Purchase of equipment and real estate during the year by Foundation, which will be available for rent by nonprofit educational organizations. 2001.
236-13. University of Alabama, Tuscaloosa, AL, $269,000. Program-related investment for Department of Hematology. 2000.

236-14. University of Alabama, Tuscaloosa, AL, $40,295. Program-related investment for Georgia Medical System. 2000.
236-15. University of Georgia, Athens, GA, $12,065. Program-related investment. 1999.
236-16. Wesleyan College, Macon, GA, $240,000. Low-interest loan. 2001.
236-17. Wesleyan College, Macon, GA, $140,000. Program-related investment. 2000.
236-18. Wesleyan College, Macon, GA, $430,000. Program-related investment. 1999.

237
UnumProvident Corporation Foundation

(Formerly Unum Foundation)
2211 Congress St.
Portland, ME 04122 (207) 575-2211
Contact: Shelia Coyne, Community Rels. Specialist

Established in 1969 in ME.
Donor(s): Unum Life Insurance Co. of America, UnumProvident Corp.
Grantmaker type: Company-sponsored foundation
General financial activity (yr. ended 12/31/01): Assets, $144,943 (M); expenditures, $224,037; qualifying distributions, $223,952; giving activities include $104,396 for 66 grants (high: $16,831; low: $58; average: $100–$4,000) and $106,179 for 194 employee matching gifts; no PRIs paid.
General purpose and activities: Primary areas of interest include AIDS, aging, the disabled, economic development, and the arts, education (K-12), and family issues, including United Way support.
General fields of interest: Arts/cultural programs; education; AIDS; family services; economic development; disabled; aging.
Program-related investment (PRI) activity: The foundation has made loans in the areas of vocational education and recreation. Loans have also provided support for intermediaries (e.g., loan funds) that promote affordable housing, economic development, and social justice.
Types of PRI Support: Loans/promissory notes, capitalizing loan funds/other intermediaries.
Limitations: Giving primarily in Biddeford, Cape Elizabeth, Cumberlane, Falmouth, Graham, Portland, Saco, Scarborough, South Portland, Westbrook, Windham, and Yarmouth, ME. No support for political parties, religious organizations, or United Way member agencies. No grants to individuals, or for fundraising, athletic events, or goodwill advertising.
Publications: Multi-year report, grants list, application guidelines.
PRI program information: The foundation makes PRIs occasionally.
Officers and Trustees:* J. Harold Chandler,* Pres.; Robert E. Broatch, V.P.; John Lang, V.P.; Donna T. Mundy,* V.P.; Elaine D. Rosen,* V.P.; Kevin A. Healey,* Secy.; Vicki J. Gordon,* Treas.; Eugene G. Ardito, Timothy G. Arnold, Anne R. Devine, Margaret R. Downing, Eileen C. Farrar, Robert Fast, Joseph R. Foley, Douglas J. Frantzen, Matthew Gilligan, Denise Griffin, Robert K. Hecker, Keith Hickerson, Ann H. Monkhem, Charles Tarbell, Tom White, Frank Williamson, John S. Roberts.
Number of staff: 3 full-time professional.
EIN: 237026979
PRI recipients:
237-1. Woodfords Family Service, Portland, ME, $23,000. Loan to enable Woodfords to finance acquisition and improvement of single family home into living quarters for disabled adults. 1999.

238
VNA Foundation

(Formerly Visiting Nurse Association of Chicago)
20 N. Wacker Dr., Ste. 3118
Chicago, IL 60606 (312) 214-1521
Contact: Robert N. DiLeonardi, Exec. Dir.
FAX: (312) 214-1529; E-mail: asvnac@aol.com; URL: http://www.vnafoundation.net

Established in 1995 in IL; converted from the transfer of VNA-C operations to CareMed Chicago; status changed to a private foundation in July 1998.
Grantmaker type: Independent foundation
General financial activity (yr. ended 06/30/02): Assets, $41,292,161 (M); gifts received, $32,202; expenditures, $2,709,786; qualifying distributions, $2,364,546; giving activities include $2,067,101 for 47 grants (high: $125,000; low: $3,000; average: $5,000–$60,000); no PRIs paid.
Cumulative PRI activity (through 06/30/02): The currently outstanding PRI portfolio includes 1 PRI totaling $250,000.
General purpose and activities: The grantmaking goal of the foundation is to support home- and community-based health care and health services for the medically underserved in Cook and Collar counties, with a focus on Chicago. Capital and general operating grants for the purpose of home health care services, prevention and health promotion, and early intervention are available to nonprofits. Priority is given to programs in which care is provided by nurses.
General fields of interest: Nursing care; health care, home services; health care.
Program-related investment (PRI) activity: The foundation has made a PRI to an organization that provides loans and technical assistance to nonprofit borrowers.
Types of PRI Support: Loans/promissory notes.
Limitations: Giving primarily in Cook, DuPage, Kane, Lake, and McHenry counties, IL.
Publications: Annual report (including application guidelines), grants list.
PRI program information: The foundation makes PRIs occasionally.
Officers and Directors:* Janet Cabot,* Chair.; Bernadette Kelly,* Vice-Chair.; Katherine H. Miller,* Secy.; Ann Davis,*

Treas.; Robert N. DiLeonardi, Exec. Dir.; and 6 additional directors.
Number of staff: 3 full-time professional.
EIN: 362167943
PRI recipients:
238-1. Illinois Facilities Fund, Chicago, IL, $250,000. Loan. 2001.

239
Todd Wagner Foundation
3008 Taylor St.
Dallas, TX 75226

Established in 2000 in TX.
Donor(s): Todd R. Wagner.
Grantmaker type: Independent foundation
General financial activity (yr. ended 12/31/01): Assets, $4,071,769 (M); gifts received, $4,051,000; expenditures, $2,008,584; qualifying distributions, $2,645,644; giving activities include $1,569,343 for 9 grants (high: $1,000,000; low: $2,500) and $686,951 for 2 PRIs.
Cumulative PRI activity (through 12/31/01): The currently outstanding PRI portfolio includes 3 PRIs totaling $986,937.
General purpose and activities: Giving primarily to support athletic, educational and computer technology programs for young people.
General fields of interest: Education; recreation; children & youth, services; computer science.
Program-related investment (PRI) activity: The foundation created the Todd R. Wagner Equity Capital Fund (TWF Fund) to provide funding and resources to minority-owned, technology-focused businesses based in the inner-city Dallas area.
Types of PRI Support: Equity investments.
Limitations: Giving primarily in CA and TX. No grants to individuals. Organizations must be located in or willing to re-locate to the inner-city Dallas, TX, area.
PRI program information: The foundation makes PRIs on a frequent but not annual basis.
Officers and Directors:* Todd R. Wagner,* Chair. and C.E.O.; Sean Griffiths, Pres. and C.O.O.; Matthew J. Dolan, Secy.; Leslie W. Mcmahon,* Treas.; William Toates, Exec. Dir.
EIN: 912028112
PRI recipients:
239-1. Abstract Concepts, Dallas, TX, $264,929. Equity investment for start-up support of business venture. 2001.
239-2. Imaginuity Interactive, Dallas, TX, $422,022. Equity investment for start-up support of business venture. 2001.
239-3. Imaginuity Interactive, Dallas, TX, $299,986. Equity investment for start-up support of business venture. 2000.

240
The Rachel Walker Charitable Foundation
101 Main St.
Cooperstown, NY 13326

Donor(s): A. Tadgell.
Grantmaker type: Independent foundation
General financial activity (yr. ended 12/31/01): Assets, $995,197 (M); gifts received, $866,032; expenditures, $120,835; qualifying distributions, $1,116,032; giving activities include $120,835 for 1 grant and $995,197 for 1 PRI.
General fields of interest: Opera.
Program-related investment (PRI) activity: The foundation has made a PRI, in the form of the acquisition of a housing facility, for use by an opera company to provide housing for its performers and for its technical staff.
Limitations: Applications not accepted. Giving primarily in Cooperstown, NY. No grants to individuals.
Officers and Directors:* A. Tadgell,* Pres.; E. Gozigian,* Secy.-Treas.; H. Dechair.
EIN: 161585841
PRI recipients:
240-1. Glimmerglass Opera Theater, Cooperstown, NY, $995,197. Program-related investment to acquire housing facility for use by Opera company for housing performers and technical staff. 2001.

241
Wallace Global Fund
1990 M St., N.W., Ste. 250
Washington, DC 20036 (202) 452-1530
Contact: Catherine Cameron, Exec. Dir.
FAX: (202) 452-0922; E-mail: tkroll@wgf.org;
URL: http://www.wgf.org

Established in 1995. PRI-related activities began in 1998.
Donor(s): Robert B. Wallace,‡ Gordon G. Wallace,‡ Henry A. Wallace,‡ Ilo B. Wallace.‡
Grantmaker type: Independent foundation
General financial activity (yr. ended 12/31/02): Assets, $109,989,213 (M); expenditures, $6,039,936; qualifying distributions, $5,363,000; giving activities include $4,395,218 for 81 grants (high: $225,000; low: $25; average: $25,000–$100,000); no PRIs paid.
Cumulative PRI activity (through 12/31/02): Since 1998, the foundation has made 3 PRIs totaling $2,300,000.
General purpose and activities: Giving primarily for environmental, population, and reproductive health issues. The foundation also funds projects that work toward global policy change in these areas.
General fields of interest: Environment, global warming; environment, forests; family planning; youth, pregnancy prevention; international economic development.
General international interests: Europe.
Program-related investment (PRI) activity: The foundation makes PRIs to environmental organizations.

Types of PRI Support: Loans/promissory notes.
Limitations: Applications not accepted. Giving on an international basis. No grants to individuals, or for scholarships, professorships, university overhead expenses, capital campaigns, construction, debt reduction, endowment funds, land acquisition, in-kind gifts, film or video projects, travel (except project-related travel). PRI applications not accepted.
Publications: Grants list, occasional report, financial statement.
PRI program information: The foundation does not maintain a formal PRI program. The foundation makes PRIs occasionally.
Officers and Directors:* R. Bruce Wallace,* Pres. and Treas.; Catherine Cameron, Secy. and Exec. Dir.; Jonathan Lash, Richard Moore, H. Scott Wallace, Randall C. Wallace.
Number of staff: 4 full-time professional; 1 full-time support.
EIN: 521918002
PRI recipients:
241-1. Innovest Group International, NYC, NY, $400,000. Loan to Strategic Value Advisors to conduct environmental ratings. 2000.
241-2. Innovest Group International, NYC, NY, $750,000. Program-related investment to conduct environmental ratings. 1999.

242
The Wallace Research Foundation
c/o RSM McGladrey, Inc.
221 3rd Ave. S.E., Ste. 300
Cedar Rapids, IA 52401
Contact: Joe Gevock

Established in 1996 in IA.
Donor(s): H.B. Wallace, Jean W. Wallace, Robert B. Wallace, Jocelyn M. Wallace, Henry D. Wallace, Linda Wallace-Gray.
Grantmaker type: Independent foundation
General financial activity (yr. ended 12/31/01): Assets, $81,222,630 (M); expenditures, $4,578,781; qualifying distributions, $4,139,412; giving activities include $4,050,116 for 41 grants (high: $635,250; low: $7,200; average: $10,000–$200,000) and $42,000 for 1 PRI.
Cumulative PRI activity (through 12/31/01): The currently outstanding PRI portfolio includes 1 PRI totaling $42,000.
General purpose and activities: Giving primarily for education, the environment, and medical research.
General fields of interest: Higher education; natural resources conservation & protection; environment; skin disorders research.
Program-related investment (PRI) activity: The foundation has made PRIs to a swim club and to a hospital for equipment.
Limitations: Applications not accepted. Giving primarily in Tucson, AZ. No grants to individuals.
Officers: H.B. Wallace, Pres. and Secy.-Treas.; Henry D. Wallace, V.P.; Jocelyn M. Wallace, V.P.; Linda Wallace-Gray, V.P.
EIN: 426540579
PRI recipients:
242-1. Navajo Health Foundation-Sage Memorial Hospital, Ganado, AZ, $42,000. Interest-free loan to buy chemistry analyzer for use by Sage Memorial Hospital. 2001.

243
Walton Family Foundation, Inc.
P.O. Box 2030
Bentonville, AR 72712 (479) 464-1570
Contact: Buddy D. Philpot, Exec. Dir.
FAX: (479) 464-1580; URL: http://www.wffhome.com

Established in 1987 in AR.
Donor(s): Sam M. Walton,‡ Helen R. Walton.
Grantmaker type: Independent foundation
General financial activity (yr. ended 12/31/01): Assets, $948,658,074 (M); gifts received, $44,907; expenditures, $104,049,018; qualifying distributions, $97,996,619; giving activities include $101,740,343 for 538 grants (high: $22,290,000; average: $1,500–$200,000), $433,250 for grants to individuals and $1,710,000 for 3 PRIs.
Cumulative PRI activity (through 12/31/01): The currently outstanding PRI portfolio includes 8 PRIs totaling $5,207,824 (high: $5,480,124; low: $60,000). The typical outstanding PRI earns 2 to 5 percent interest.
General purpose and activities: Giving primarily for systemic reform of primary education (K-12) and early childhood development.
General fields of interest: Elementary/secondary education; child development, education; elementary/secondary school reform.
Program-related investment (PRI) activity: The foundation has made PRIs for educational purposes, economic development, and to the Presbyterian Church for building, renovation, and expansion
Types of PRI Support: Loans/promissory notes.
Limitations: Giving primarily in AR, with emphasis on the Mississippi River's delta region of AR and MS. No support for unestablished medical research programs. No grants to individuals (except for scholarship program for children of Wal-Mart associates), or for endowments for operations, church-related construction projects, travel expenses for groups to compete or perform, or start-up funds. PRI applications not accepted.
Publications: Application guidelines.
PRI program information: The foundation does not maintain a formal PRI program. The foundation makes PRIs on a frequent but not annual basis.
Directors: Buddy D. Philpot, Exec. Dir.; Carrie W. Penner, Alice L. Walton, Benjamin Walton, Helen R. Walton, James C. Walton, John T. Walton, S. Robson Walton, Samuel R. Walton.

Number of staff: 5 full-time professional; 1 full-time support.
EIN: 133441466
PRI recipients:
243-1. High Tech High, San Diego, CA, $150,000. Loan to supplment operating support until funding is received from School District. 2001.
243-2. Northwest Arkansas Aviation Technologies Center, Fayetteville, AR, $30,000. Loan toward training for avaition maintenance. 2001.
243-3. Presbyterian Church USA - National Headquarters, Louisville, KY, $3,500,000. Below-interest loan to build new churches, renovate and expand existing churches and refinance other churches' existing debt. 1999.
243-4. School Futures Research Foundation, San Diego, CA, $5,480,124. Interest-free loan to be used for operating support for charter schools. 2000.
243-5. Southern Financial Partners, Arkadelphia, AR, $1,500,000. Loan to allow recipient to fund small business in Delta area of Arkansas and Mississippi. 2001.

244
Washington Square Health Foundation, Inc.

875 N. Michigan Ave., Ste. 3516
Chicago, IL 60611 (312) 664-6488
Contact: Howard Nochumson, Exec. Dir.
PRI Contact: Katy Tyrell, Prog. Asst.
E-mail: washington@wshf.org; URL: http://www.wshf.org

Established in 1985 in IL; converted from Henrotin Hospital. PRI-related activities began in 1991.
Donor(s): Henrotin Hospital.
Grantmaker type: Independent foundation
General financial activity (yr. ended 09/30/02): Assets, $21,896,721 (M); gifts received, $8,053; expenditures, $871,262; qualifying distributions, $1,091,178; giving activities include $416,490 for 39 grants (high: $42,500; low: $150) and $300,000 for 1 PRI.
Cumulative PRI activity (through 09/30/02): Since 1991, the foundation has made 19 PRIs totaling $2,184,635. The currently outstanding PRI portfolio includes 5 PRIs totaling $1,022,977 (high: $627,000; low: $100,000; average: $309,411). The typical outstanding PRI has an average term of 5 years, and earns an average of 5 percent interest.
General purpose and activities: To promote and maintain access to adequate primary health care, through grants for medical and nursing education scholarships, medical research, and direct health care services.
General fields of interest: Medical school/education; nursing school/education; nursing care; nursing home/convalescent facility; health care; AIDS; medical research; AIDS research; domestic violence prevention; minorities; disabled; aging; women; people with AIDS (PWAs); gays/lesbians; immigrants/refugees; homeless.
Program-related investment (PRI) activity: The foundation has made PRIs in the areas of health care and aging. The PRIs made be used for construction, land acquisition, and major capital equipment.
Types of PRI Support: Loans/promissory notes.
Limitations: Giving primarily in the Chicago, IL, area. No grants to individuals, or for general operating or administrative expenses, land acquisition, or construction. The foundation accepts applications for PRIs.
Publications: Annual report, application guidelines.
PRI program information: The foundation maintains a formal PRI program. The foundation makes PRIs on a frequent but not annual basis.
Officers and Directors:* Angelo P. Creticos, M.D.,* Pres.; Mrs. Arthur M. Wirtz, Jr.,* V.P.; William B. Friedeman,* Secy.; John C. York,* Treas.; Howard Nochumson,* Exec. Dir.; Howard M. McCue III, Legal Counsel; Robert S. Kirby, Richard B. Patterson, James M. Snyder, William N. Werner, M.D., Bill G. Wiley.
Number of staff: 1.
EIN: 361210140
PRI recipients:
244-1. Casa Central, Chicago, IL, $159,057. Loan at 5 percent interest. 2000.
244-2. Family Christian Health Center, Harvey, IL, $100,000. Loan at 5 percent interest. 2000.
244-3. Norwegian-American Health System, Chicago, IL, $628,000. Program-related investment. 2001.
244-4. Samaritan Housing Services, Chicago, IL, $50,000. Loan at 5 percent interest. 1999.
244-5. Suburban Primary Health Care Council, Westchester, IL, $300,000. Program-related investment. 2002.

245
Weaver Family Foundation

P.O. Box 19409
Boulder, CO 80308-9409
Contact: Stephanie Schaffer, Opers. Mgr.
E-mail: info@weaverfoundation.org; URL: http://weaverfoundation.org

Established in 1999 in CO. PRI-related activities began in 2001.
Donor(s): Lindsey A. Weaver, Jr., Francine Lavin Weaver.
Grantmaker type: Independent foundation
General financial activity (yr. ended 12/31/02): Assets, $13,496,762 (M); expenditures, $824,816; qualifying distributions, $843,535; giving activities include $726,419 for 100 grants (high: $100,000; low: $50; average: $50–$100,000) and $120,000 for 2 PRIs.
Cumulative PRI activity (through 12/31/02): Since 2001, the foundation has made 1 PRI totaling $60,000. The currently outstanding PRI portfolio includes 1 PRI totaling $20,000 (average: $60,000). The typical outstanding PRI has an average term of 1.5 years, and earns an average of 5 percent interest.
General fields of interest: Arts/cultural programs; education; environment; health associations;

housing/shelter, development; human services; Jewish agencies & temples.
General international interests: Honduras.
Program-related investment (PRI) activity: The foundation has made a PRI, in the form of a below-market-rate loan, to an agency for Jewish education, to enable them to continue their educational program during a temporary fiscal crisis.
Types of PRI Support: Loans/promissory notes.
Limitations: Giving primarily in Boulder, CO, and Israel. No grants to individuals. PRI applications not accepted.
PRI program information: The foundation does not maintain a formal PRI program. The foundation makes PRIs occasionally.
Directors: Francine Lavin Weaver, Lindsey A. Weaver, Jr.
Number of staff: 1 full-time professional.
EIN: 841513850
PRI recipients:
245-1. Colorado Agency for Jewish Education, Denver, CO, $60,000. Loan at below-market rate to enable organization to continue educational program during temporary fiscal crisis. 2001.

246
Weeden Foundation
(Formerly Frank Weeden Foundation)
747 3rd Ave., 34th Fl.
New York, NY 10017 (212) 888-1672
Contact: Donald A. Weeden, Exec. Dir.
PRI Contact: James Sheldon
FAX: (212) 888-1354; E-mail: weedenfdn@weedenfdn.org; URL: http://www.weedenfdn.org

Established 1963 in CA. PRI-related activities began in 1993.
Donor(s): Frank Weeden,‡ Alan N. Weeden, Donald E. Weeden, John D. Weeden, William F. Weeden, M.D.
Grantmaker type: Independent foundation
General financial activity (yr. ended 06/30/02): Assets, $29,913,217 (M); expenditures, $3,106,172; qualifying distributions, $2,712,686; giving activities include $2,529,483 for 265 grants (high: $50,000; low: $175; average: $5,000–$50,000); no PRIs paid.
Cumulative PRI activity (through 06/30/02): Since 1993, the foundation has made 12 PRIs totaling $2,295,000. The currently outstanding PRI portfolio includes 7 PRIs totaling $1,837,271 (high: $598,831; low: $25,000; average: $150,000). The typical outstanding PRI has a 2- to 9-year term with an average term of 4.5 years, and earns an average of 10 percent interest.
General purpose and activities: Giving primarily to environmental organizations working to preserve biological diversity. Program interests also include organizations working to stabilize human population and organizations working to address the over consumption of the earth's resources.
General fields of interest: Natural resources conservation & protection; environment; population studies.
General international interests: Russia; Bolivia; Chile.
Program-related investment (PRI) activity: The foundation has made PRIs in the U.S. and overseas for conservation purposes and in environmental technology companies.
Types of PRI Support: Loans/promissory notes, interim financing, equity investments.
Limitations: Giving on a national and international basis, primarily in northern CA, the Pacific Northwest, Latin America (Chile and Bolivia), and Central Siberia. No grants to individuals; generally no funding for films, conferences, or scientific research. PRI applications not accepted.
PRI program information: The foundation does not maintain a formal PRI program. The foundation makes PRIs occasionally.
Officers and Directors:* Norman Weeden, Ph.D.,* Pres.; William F. Weeden, M.D.,* V.P.; John D. Weeden,* Secy.-Treas.; Donald A. Weeden, Exec. Dir.; David Davies, Christina Roux, Alan N. Weeden, Donald E. Weeden, Leslie Weeden.
Number of staff: 2 full-time professional.
EIN: 946109313

247
The Margaret L. Wendt Foundation
40 Fountain Plz., Ste. 277
Buffalo, NY 14202-2220 (716) 855-2146
Contact: Robert J. Kresse, Secy.-Treas.

Trust established in 1956 in NY.
Donor(s): Margaret L. Wendt.‡
Grantmaker type: Independent foundation
General financial activity (yr. ended 01/31/02): Assets, $118,168,880 (M); expenditures, $8,166,966; qualifying distributions, $7,677,173; giving activities include $6,611,610 for 152 grants (high: $750,000; low: $300; average: $5,000–$50,000) and $1,000,000 for 1 PRI.
Cumulative PRI activity (through 01/31/02): The currently outstanding PRI portfolio includes 2 PRIs totaling $1,239,388.
General purpose and activities: Emphasis on education, the arts, and social services; support also for churches and religious organizations, health associations, public interest organizations, and youth agencies.
General fields of interest: Visual arts; museums; performing arts; theater; history & archaeology; historic preservation/historical societies; arts/cultural programs; education, fund raising; early childhood education; higher education; libraries/library science; education; natural resources conservation & protection; hospitals (general); substance abuse, services; mental health/crisis services; health associations; cancer; AIDS; alcoholism; biomedicine; medical research; cancer research; AIDS research; legal services; crime/law enforcement; human services; children & youth, services; hospices; aging, centers & services; minorities/immigrants, centers & services; international human rights; community development; federated giving programs; political science; government/public

administration; public affairs; religion; minorities; disabled; aging; economically disadvantaged.
Program-related investment (PRI) activity: The foundation has made PRIs to support the preservation of historic buildings, the operations of arts organizations, and capital improvements to a community center.
Types of PRI Support: Loans/promissory notes, interim financing, lines of credit.
Limitations: Giving primarily in Buffalo and western NY. No grants to individuals, or for scholarships.
Publications: Application guidelines.
PRI program information: The foundation makes PRIs on an annual basis.
Officer and Trustees:* Robert J. Kresse,* Secy.-Treas.; Janet L. Day, Thomas D. Lunt.
Number of staff: 1 part-time support.
EIN: 166030037
PRI recipients:
247-1. Clarkson Center, Buffalo, NY, $85,714. Loan, non-interest bearing, for working capital operations. 2000.
247-2. King Urban Life Center, Buffalo, NY, $31,069. Loan, non-interest bearing, for working capital operations. 1999.
247-3. Martin House Restoration Corporation, Buffalo, NY, $65,000. Interest-free, demand line of credit for historic building preservation. 1999.
247-4. Sheas OConnell Preservation Guild, Buffalo, NY, $244,876. Non-interest bearing loan for working capital operations. 2001.
247-5. Sheas Performing Arts Center, Buffalo, NY, $1,000,000. Non-interest bearing loan for working capital operations. 2002.
247-6. Western New York Heritage Institute, Buffalo, NY, $20,000. Loan, non-interest bearing, for working capital operations. 1999.

248
The Whitaker Foundation
1700 N. Moore St., Ste. 2200
Rosslyn, VA 22209 (703) 528-2430
Contact: Peter G. Katona, Sc.D., C.E.O. and Pres.
E-mail: info@whitaker.org; URL: http://www.whitaker.org

Trust established in 1975 in NY.
Donor(s): U.A. Whitaker,‡ Helen F. Whitaker.‡
Grantmaker type: Independent foundation
General financial activity (yr. ended 12/31/02): Assets, $246,225,766 (M); expenditures, $73,108,146; qualifying distributions, $71,867,554; giving activities include $68,508,176 for 531 grants (high: $5,702,000; low: $2,000; average: $3,000–$70,000) and $190,327 for 77 employee matching gifts; no PRIs paid.
Cumulative PRI activity (through 12/31/02): The currently outstanding PRI portfolio includes 1 PRI totaling $479,936.
General purpose and activities: Primary areas of interest include education, medical research, and biomedical engineering. Support for projects that integrate engineering with biomedical research; grants also to human service agencies and educational institutions in the Harrisburg, PA, area.
General fields of interest: Engineering school/education; biomedicine; medical research; biomedicine research; human services; science; mathematics; engineering; biological sciences; science.
General international interests: Canada.
Program-related investment (PRI) activity: The foundation has made a PRI to a museum.
Types of PRI Support: Loans/promissory notes.
Limitations: Giving limited to the U.S. and Canada for Biomedical Engineering Research and Special Opportunity Awards Programs; Regional Program limited to Collier County, FL; other programs are limited to the U.S. No support for sectarian religious purposes. No grants to individuals, or for deficit financing, annual campaigns, emergency funds, or endowment funds. PRI applications not accepted.
Publications: Annual report (including application guidelines), program policy statement, informational brochure (including application guidelines), application guidelines.
PRI program information: The foundation does not maintain a formal PRI program.
Officers: Peter G. Katona, C.E.O. and Pres.; James A. Frost, V.P., Finance; John H. Linehan, Ph.D., V.P.
Committee Members: G. Burtt Holmes, O.D., Chair.; William R. Brody, M.D., Ph.D., Ruth Whitaker Holmes, Ph.D., Thomas A. Holmes, James E. Kielley, Harold A. McInnes, Portia Whitaker Shumaker.
Trustee: JP Morgan Bank, N.A.
Number of staff: 4 full-time professional; 5 full-time support.
EIN: 222096948
PRI recipients:
248-1. Whitaker Center for Science and the Arts, Harrisburg, PA, $1,945,755. Loan. 1999.

249
Wieboldt Foundation
53 W. Jackson Blvd., Ste. 838
Chicago, IL 60604 (312) 786-9377
Contact: Carmen Prieto
FAX: (312) 786-9232

Incorporated in 1921 in IL.
Donor(s): William A. Wieboldt,‡ Anna Krueger Wieboldt,‡ Ford Foundation.
Grantmaker type: Independent foundation
General financial activity (yr. ended 12/31/01): Assets, $277,413,407 (M); expenditures, $2,014,352; qualifying distributions, $1,946,125; giving activities include $1,596,920 for 88 grants and $40,000 for 1 PRI.

Cumulative PRI activity (through 12/31/01): The currently outstanding PRI portfolio includes 3 PRIs totaling $272,000. The typical outstanding PRI has a maximum term of 5 years.
General purpose and activities: The foundation's highest priority is the support of multi-issue community organizations that work in low-income neighborhoods, that are accountable to neighborhood residents, and through which people are empowered to have a major voice in shaping decisions that affect their lives. A second priority is given to organizations that support community organizations through training, technical assistance, legal strategies, coalition building, advocacy, and policy development.
General fields of interest: Community development; public affairs.
Program-related investment (PRI) activity: The foundation offers PRIs to support neighborhood development and revitalization in low-income neighborhoods in the Chicago, IL, metropolitan area. PRIs generally provide for housing, promote economic development accountable to local residents, create or support neighborhood-based business ventures, increase local ownership of financial resources and access to other investors, or provide employment opportunities to local residents. PRIs have financed construction predevelopment costs, supported facility improvement, capitalized housing development projects and earned income ventures, and provided interim financing. Funding is occasionally directed to intermediaries (e.g., loan funds and venture capital funds). The Wieboldt Foundation will consider PRIs in amounts up to $40,000. The term will be negotiable, but will not exceed five years. A rate of return is expected and will be negotiated on a project by project basis. Plans for repayment of the PRI must be included in the application.
Types of PRI Support: Loans/promissory notes, interim financing, loan guarantees, equity investments, capitalizing loan funds/other intermediaries.
Limitations: Giving limited to the metropolitan Chicago, IL, and IN areas. No grants to individuals, or for endowment funds, studies and research, capital campaigns, scholarships, fellowships, conferences, direct service projects, or economic development.
Publications: Annual report (including application guidelines), grants list.
PRI program information: A pre-application, available from the foundation, must be submitted and approved prior to submitting a proposal.
Officers and Directors:* John Darrow,* Pres.; John W. Straub,* V.P.; Regina McGraw,* Secy. and Exec. Dir.; Nancy Wieboldt,* Treas.; Anne W. Burghard, Jennifer S. Corrigan, Anita S. Darrow, Jessica Darrow, Phil Darrow, Bill Davis, T. Lawrence Doyle, Esther Nieves, Rita Simo.
Number of staff: 2 full-time professional.
EIN: 362167955
PRI recipients:
249-1. ACCION Chicago, Chicago, IL, $40,000. Program-related investment. 2001.
249-2. Center for Neighborhood Technology, Chicago, IL, $40,000. Program-related investment. 2000.
249-3. Chicago Community Loan Fund, Chicago, IL, $100,000. Program-related investment. 2000.
249-4. Chicago Community Loan Fund, Chicago, IL, $200,000. Loan. 1999.
249-5. Chicago Mutual Housing Network, Chicago, IL, $40,000. Program-related investment. 2000.

250
Williamsport-Lycoming Foundation
(Formerly Williamsport Foundation)
220 W. 4th St., Ste. C, 3rd Fl.
Williamsport, PA 17701-6102 (570) 321-1500
Contact: Kimberley Pittman-Schulz, Pres.
FAX: (570) 321-6434; E-mail: wlf@wlfoundation.org; URL: http://www.wlfoundation.org

Established in 1916 in PA by bank resolution. PRI-related activities began in 1997.
Grantmaker type: Community foundation
General financial activity (yr. ended 12/31/01): Assets, $46,193,175 (M); gifts received, $704,694; expenditures, $2,468,408; giving activities include $1,785,232 for 260 grants (high: $200,000; low: $50; average: $1,000–$30,000) and $20,000 for 1 PRI.
Cumulative PRI activity (through 12/31/01): Since 1997, the foundation has made 2 PRIs totaling $176,220. The currently outstanding PRI portfolio includes 2 PRIs totaling $151,000 (high: $100,000; low: $5,000; average: $11,500). The typical outstanding PRI has a 4- to 14-year term with an average term of 14 years.
General purpose and activities: The foundation exists to make Williamsport and Lycoming counties and the surrounding regions the best possible place to live. The foundation helps people find the most effectual way for "giving back" to help build vibrant communities.
General fields of interest: Arts/cultural programs; education; health care; natural resources conservation & protection; recreation; human services; youth, services; family services; economic development; community development.
Program-related investment (PRI) activity: The foundation awards low and no-interest loans to qualified area non-profit organizations.
Types of PRI Support: Loans/promissory notes.
Limitations: Giving primarily to organizations serving Lycoming County, PA. No support for sectarian religious programs. No grants to individuals, or for endowment funds. Generally no grants for ongoing operating support. The foundation accepts applications for PRIs.
Publications: Annual report, informational brochure, financial statement, program policy statement, application guidelines.
PRI program information: Applications for low and no-interest loans will be considered twice per year. The

foundation maintains a formal PRI program. The foundation makes PRIs occasionally.
Officers and Directors:* Ann M. Alsted,* Chair.; Daniel G. Fultz, Vice-Chair.; Kimberley Pittman-Schulz,* Pres.; Robert More, Thomas C. Raup, John C. Schultz, Carol Sides, John Young.
Number of staff: 4 full-time professional; 1 part-time professional; 1 full-time support; 1 part-time support.
EIN: 246013117

251
Winds of Peace Foundation

(Formerly Children's Haven, Inc.)
203 S. 6th St.
Kenyon, MN 55946-1036 (507) 789-5526
Contact: Christine B. Sartor, Exec. Dir.
E-mail: peacewinds@peacewinds.org

Established in 1978. PRI-related activities began in 1994.
Donor(s): Foldcraft, Inc.
Grantmaker type: Independent foundation
General financial activity (yr. ended 12/31/01): Assets, $4,537,591 (M); gifts received, $77,249; expenditures, $348,645; qualifying distributions, $706,939; giving activities include $165,330 for 18 grants (high: $30,315; low: $100; average: $100–$30,315) and $440,000 for 6 PRIs.
Cumulative PRI activity (through 12/31/01): Since 1994, the foundation has made 35 PRIs totaling $2,093,704. The currently outstanding PRI portfolio includes 8 PRIs totaling $565,000 (high: $400,000; low: $4,000; average: $25,000). The typical outstanding PRI has a 1- to 2-year term with an average term of 2 years and earns 4 to 9 percent interest with an average of 6 percent.
General purpose and activities: Supports organizations and programs that work for social justice.
General fields of interest: International relief; international peace/security; international human rights; civil rights.
General international interests: Central America; Nicaragua.
Program-related investment (PRI) activity: The foundation makes loans to Nicaraguan l organizations that support social justice.
Types of PRI Support: Loans/promissory notes.
Limitations: Giving in Nicaragua. No support for children's organizations. The foundation makes PRIs to Nicaragua-based community banks that support at least one of the following: indigenous, women, and rural sector. The foundation accepts applications for PRIs.
Publications: Application guidelines.
PRI program information: The foundation maintains a formal PRI program. The foundation makes PRIs on an annual basis.
Directors: Annette Bjork, Donald J. Fleugel, John T. Kisch, Harold R. Nielsen, Louise V. Nielsen, Stephen C. Sheppard.
Number of staff: 1 full-time professional.
EIN: 411343012

PRI recipients:
251-1. Conjunto de Cooperativas Agropecuarias de Jalapa (CCAJ), Managua, Nicaragua, $50,000. Loan for microcredit program in Jalapa. 2001.
251-2. Conjunto de Cooperativas Agropecuarias de Jalapa (CCAJ), Managua, Nicaragua, $25,000. Loan at 6 percent for microcredit program. 2000.
251-3. Fundacion para el Desarrollo Sustentable de Eco-Regiones (FunDeSER), Buenos Aires, Argentina, $15,000. Loan for productive economic reactivation of peasants of fifteen communities of Raan. 2001.
251-4. Hand-to-Hand Rural Bank, $15,000. Loan at 6 percent. 2000.
251-5. La Cooperativa de Servicios y Desarrollo Comunal de Tisma (COSDECOTI), Managua, Nicaragua, $25,000. Loan for microcredit program. 2001.
251-6. Nicaraguan Cultural Alliance, Hyattsville, MD, $20,000. Loan at six percent interest. 1999.
251-7. Nitlapan, Managua, Nicaragua, $250,000. Loan at 9 percent for microcredit program. 2001.
251-8. Nitlapan, Managua, Nicaragua, $100,000. Loan at 9 percent for microcredit program. 2000.
251-9. Nitlapan, Managua, Nicaragua, $400,000. Loan at eight percent for microcredit program. 1999.
251-10. Quixote Center, Hyattsville, MD, $15,000. Loan at 8 percent. 2000.
251-11. SACPROA, Matagalpa, Nicaragua, $25,000. Loan at 4 percent. 2000.
251-12. Wisconsin Coordinating Council of Nicaragua, Madison, WI, $55,000. Loan at 6 percent for Nicaraguan Credit Alternatives Fund. 2001.
251-13. Wisconsin Coordinating Council of Nicaragua, Madison, WI, $45,000. Loan for Nicaraguan Credit Alternatives Fund. 2001.
251-14. Wisconsin Coordinating Council of Nicaragua, Madison, WI, $150,000. Loan at six percent interest for microcredit program. 1999.

252
The Winslow Foundation

(Formerly Windie Foundation)
2040 S St., N.W., Ste. 200
Washington, DC 20009 (202) 833-4714
Contact: Dr. Betty Ann Ottinger, Exec. Dir.
FAX: (202) 833-4716

Established in 1987 in NJ.
Donor(s): Julia D. Winslow.‡
Grantmaker type: Independent foundation
General financial activity (yr. ended 12/31/01): Assets, $30,994,490 (M); expenditures, $1,961,876; qualifying distributions, $1,545,795; giving activities include $1,533,500 for grants and $25,000 for 1 PRI.
General purpose and activities: Giving primarily for the environment and population studies.
General fields of interest: Natural resources conservation & protection; population studies.

Program-related investment (PRI) activity: The foundation has made an interest-free mortgage loan to a local conservation organization and a management group helping women start their own businesses.
Types of PRI Support: Loans/promissory notes, equity investments.
Limitations: Giving on a national basis. No grants to individuals. PRI applications not accepted.
Publications: Application guidelines.
PRI program information: The foundation does not maintain a formal PRI program.
Officers and Directors:* Wren Winslow Wirth,* Pres.; Samuel W. Lambert III,* V.P. and Treas.; Betty Ann Ottinger.
Number of staff: 1 part-time professional; 1 part-time support.
EIN: 222778703
PRI recipients:
252-1. Wilderness Land Trust, Carbondale, CO, $50,000. Non-interest bearing mortgage loan. 1999.
252-2. Womens Capital Corporation, DC, $25,000. Investment in corporate stock. 2001.
252-3. Womens Capital Corporation, DC, $50,000. Investment in corporate stock. 2000.

253
The Winston-Salem Foundation

860 W. 5th St.
Winston-Salem, NC 27101-2506 (336) 725-2382
Contact: Scott F. Wierman, Pres.
FAX: (336) 727-0581; E-mail: info@wsfoundation.org; URL: http://www.wsfoundation.org

Established in 1919 in NC by declaration of trust.
Grantmaker type: Community foundation
General financial activity (yr. ended 12/31/01): Assets, $179,938,414 (M); gifts received, $17,573,597; expenditures, $20,280,252; giving activities include $17,531,807 for grants (high: $2,000,000; low: $100; average: $1,000–$25,000), $402,786 for 347 grants to individuals (high: $8,000; low: $250), $7,170 for 49 employee matching gifts, $121,000 for 35 loans to individuals and $20,000 for 1 PRI.
Cumulative PRI activity (through 12/31/01): The currently outstanding PRI portfolio includes PRIs totaling $1,044,093.
General purpose and activities: Student aid primarily to bona fide residents of Forsyth County, NC; support also for nonprofit organizations of all types, especially educational, social service and health programs, the arts, and civic affairs.
General fields of interest: Arts/cultural programs; education; health associations; recreation; human services; youth, services; public affairs, government agencies; government/public administration; religion; general charitable giving.
Program-related investment (PRI) activity: The foundation has made PRIs to a school, a cultural organization, and a loan fund.
Types of PRI Support: Loans/promissory notes.
Limitations: Giving primarily in the greater Forsyth County, NC, area. No grants for operating support, annual campaigns, land acquisition, publications, equipment or conferences.
Publications: Annual report (including application guidelines), newsletter, grants list, application guidelines.
Officer: Scott F. Wierman, Pres.
Foundation Committee: Richard P. Budd, Chair.; Rence Callahan, Greg Cox, Richard Janeway, M.D., James T. Lambie, Dr. Harold L. Martin, John G. Medlin, Jr., T. David Neill, L. Glenn Orr, Jr., Ann C. Ring, Vivian L. Turner, Robert C. Vaughn, Jr., Jane B. Williams.
Trustees: Bank of America, BB&T, Central Carolina Bank & Trust Co., First Citizens Bank, First Union National Bank of North Carolina, Wachovia Bank of North Carolina, N.A.
Number of staff: 12 full-time professional; 8 full-time support.
EIN: 566037615
PRI recipients:
253-1. East Winston Primary School, Winston-Salem, NC, $20,000. Loan. 2001.
253-2. Winston-Salem Enrichment Center, Winston-Salem, NC, $67,000. No-interest loan which Foundation Committee will consider converting to grant after one-year if sufficient progress toward financial stability is achieved. 2000.

254
Woods Charitable Fund, Inc.

1440 M St.
P.O. Box 81309
Lincoln, NE 68501 (402) 436-5971
Contact: Pam Baker, Secy. and Exec. Dir.
FAX: (402) 436-4128; E-mail: pbaker@woodscharitable.org; URL: http://www.woodscharitable.org

Incorporated in 1941 in NE. PRI-related activities began in 1975.
Donor(s): Frank H. Woods,‡ Nelle C. Woods,‡ Sahara Coal Co., Inc., Frank H. Woods, Jr.,‡ Thomas C. Woods, Jr.,‡ Henry C. Woods.‡
Grantmaker type: Independent foundation
General financial activity (yr. ended 12/31/02): Assets, $25,738,995 (M); expenditures, $1,891,484; qualifying distributions, $1,465,210; giving activities include $1,465,210 for 68 grants (high: $200,000; low: $2,500; average: $10,000–$25,000) and $3,810 for 1 PRI.
Cumulative PRI activity (through 12/31/02): Since 1975, the foundation has made 5 PRIs totaling $163,000. The currently outstanding PRI portfolio includes 2 PRIs totaling $80,381 (high: $50,000; low: $3,810; average: $35,850). The typical outstanding PRI has a 1- to 6-year term with an average term of 3 years.
General purpose and activities: Grants primarily to nonprofit organizations working to build a stronger community. Particular interest in projects that benefit

children, young people, families, community development and housing, education, and the arts and humanities.
General fields of interest: Visual arts; performing arts; humanities; arts/cultural programs; elementary school/education; education; domestic violence prevention; housing/shelter, development; human services; children & youth, services; family services; community development; immigrants/refugees.
Program-related investment (PRI) activity: The foundation has made no-interest loans and provided a line of credit in the areas of community development, education, housing, health services, and rehabilitation. PRIs have benefited the disabled, minorities, women, young adults, and children.
Types of PRI Support: Loans/promissory notes, loan guarantees.
Limitations: Giving primarily in Lincoln, NE. No support for religious activities, or college or university programs that do not involve students and/or faculty in projects of benefit to the Lincoln, NE, area, or for environmental programs or residential care and medical clinics. No grants to individuals, or for endowments, scholarships, fellowships, fundraising benefits, program advertising, medical or scientific research, recreation programs, individual school programs, or capital projects in health care institutions. PRI applications not accepted.
Publications: Annual report (including application guidelines), application guidelines.
PRI program information: The foundation does not maintain a formal PRI program. The foundation makes PRIs occasionally.
Officers and Directors:* Stephen Sands,* Pres.; Susan Ugai,* V.P.; Pam Baker,* Secy. and Exec. Dir.; Michael Tavlin,* Treas.; Eugene Crump, Lynn Roper, Avery L. Woods, Donna Woods.
Number of staff: 3 full-time professional.
EIN: 476032847
PRI recipients:

254-1. Day Watch, Lincoln, NE, $30,000. Cash reserve loan. 2001.

254-2. Hispanic Community Center, Lincoln, NE, $10,000. Loan for emergency support of Changing Trends and America Reads programs which will provide Americorps members to assist staff at 7 centers in Lincoln. 1999.

254-3. Madonna Foundation, Lincoln, NE, $75,000. Program-related investment to fund start-up staffing and operating costs of Supported Living Program for Young Adults facility. 1999.

254-4. YWCA of Lincoln, Lincoln, NE, $50,000. Program-related investment to stabilize financial base while implementing new long-term strategic financial plan. 2001.

255
Greater Worcester Community Foundation, Inc.

44 Front St., Ste. 530
Worcester, MA 01608-1782 (508) 755-0980
Contact: Ann T. Lisi, Exec. Dir.
FAX: (508) 755-3406; E-mail: atlisi@greaterworcester.org or conaghan@greaterworcester.org; URL: http://www.greaterworcester.org

Incorporated in 1975 in MA.
Grantmaker type: Community foundation
General financial activity (yr. ended 12/31/02): Assets, $75,867,937 (M); gifts received, $5,098,241; expenditures, $5,130,850; giving activities include $4,180,970 for 781 grants (high: $200,000; low: $100; average: $500–$30,000); no PRIs paid.
General purpose and activities: To support programs that improve the quality of life for residents of the greater Worcester, MA, area.
General fields of interest: Humanities; arts/cultural programs; medical school/education; nursing school/education; education; environment; health care; health associations; medical research; abuse prevention; housing/shelter, development; youth development; human services; children & youth, services; family services; aging, centers & services; homeless, human services; community development; government/public administration; public affairs; African Americans/Blacks; disabled; aging; people with AIDS (PWAs); economically disadvantaged; homeless.
Program-related investment (PRI) activity: The foundation has made PRIs on a limited basis to nonprofit organizations, including housing, economic development, education, and arts organizations. PRIs have provided interim financing and have financed facility acquisition or improvement and land acquisition, often through intermediary lending institutions.
Types of PRI Support: Loans/promissory notes, interim financing, capitalizing loan funds/other intermediaries.
Limitations: Giving limited to Worcester County, MA. No grants to individuals (except for designated scholarship funds); generally no grants for general operating expenses, capital improvements, or endowment campaigns. Support limited to nonprofit organizations in the greater Worcester, MA, region. PRI applications not accepted.
Publications: Annual report, application guidelines, newsletter.
PRI program information: Accepts inquiries and reviews requests for loans and other investments from all nonprofits in greater Worcester, MA, region. The foundation does not maintain a formal PRI program. The foundation makes PRIs occasionally.
Officers and Directors:* Michael D. Brockelman,* Pres.; Robert K. "Ross" Dik,* V.P. and Dist. Chair.; Robert Bachelder,* Clerk; James E. Collins,* Treas.; Ann T. Lisi, Exec. Dir.; Sara Trillo Adams, Christopher W. Bramley, P. Kevin Condron, Allen W. Fletcher, Ramon V. Frias, Lawrence J. Glick, Barbara E. Greenberg, Mary Kett,

Cynthia M. McMullen, Janet Wilson Moore, Barrett Morgan, Martha R. Pappas, Gladys Rodriguez-Parker, Paul R. Rossley. **Distribution Committee:** Pamela K. Boisvert, Ellen S. Dunlap, Susan G. Gateley, Joseph M. Hamilton, Monica E. Lowell, Donna McGrath.

Number of staff: 6 full-time professional; 1 part-time professional; 2 full-time support; 2 part-time support.
EIN: 042572276

INDEX TO DONORS, OFFICERS, TRUSTEES

Abbott, David, 108
Abell, W. Shepherdson, 1
Abell Co., A.S., 1
Abramowitz, Kenneth A., 235
Abramowitz, Morton, 190
Achtherhoft, Tim, 58
Acton, Evelyn Meadows, 169
Adams, Carmella, 133
Adams, Sara Trillo, 255
Adams-Phillips, Nazamovia "Naz", 223
Aderhold, John E., 236
Adubato, Steven, 132
Agee, John, 6
AGR Trust, The, 212
Ahmadi, Hoshang, 2
Akman, Larry, 83
Akman, Nonie, 83
Albers, C. Hugh, 55
Albrechtsen, Dennis, 58
Alcantar, Joe, Jr., 80
Aldridge, Elizabeth A., 185
Alexander, Anne M., 3
Alexander, Cynthia K., 20
Alger, Consuelo Zobel, 4
Aljian, James D., 157
Allaire, Paul A., 93
Allen, Corinne, 28
Allen, Ivye L., 210
Allen, Joan E., 84
Allen, Paul G., 5
Allen-Bradley Co., 33
Alsted, Ann M., 250
Althaus, Ruth Ann, Ph.D., 67
Alvarez, Cesar L., 151
Alving, Amy E., 7
Alving, Barbara M., 7
Alving, Carl R., 7
AMCORE Bank, N.A., 64
American Century, 70
American Financial Holdings, Inc., 9
American National Bank and Trust Co., 215
American Savings Bank, 9
Anderson, James G., 148
Anderson, Kenneth, 170
Anderson, Michael D., Dr., 200
Anglin, Jeannette, 66
Angood, Arthur W., 178
Annette, Kathleen R., 30
Apodaca, Clara R., 122
Appleby, Robert S., 91
Arader, Walter G., 208
Archbold, Armar A., 168
Archie, Willard N., 132
Ardito, Eugene G., 237
Armacost, Samuel H., 134
Armbrister, Denise McGregor, 91
Armstrong, William, 33
Arnold, Kay Kelly, 210
Arnold, Timothy G., 237
Arnston, Peter A., 179
Athearn, W. James, 154
Atlan Management Corp., 12
Auen, Joan C., 29
Auen, Ronald M., 29
Auerbach, Stuart, 170
August, Andrew, 13
August, Burton S., 13
August, Burton Stuart, 13
August, Charles J., 13
August, Elizabeth, 13
August, Jan, 13
August, Jean B., 13
August, John, 13
August, Pierre, 130
August, Robert, 13
Austen, W. Gerald, 151
Avampato, Charles M., 51
Axelson, Frances R., 80
Axworthy, Lloyd, 158

B.G. Wholesale, Inc., 125
Babcock, Bruce M., 15
Babcock, Charles H., 15
Babcock, Mary Reynolds, 15
Baca, Patricia, 56
Bachelder, Robert, 255
Bacon, Kenneth J., 88
Bader, Daniel J., 16
Bader, David M., 16
Bader, Linda C., 16
Bader, Michelle Henkin, 16
Baglivo, Daniel, 133
Baker, Pam, 254
Baldwin, James P., 23
Baldwin, Robert H.B., 73
Balgooyen, Warren, 186
Bangser, Michael R., 116
Bank of America, 70, 253
Bank of America Corp., 17
Bank One, N.A., 18, 22, 52, 64
Bank One Ohio Trust Co., N.A., 223
Bank One, Texas, N.A., 69
Banwart, Leslie S., 163
Barazzone, Esther L., 26
Barba, Stephen P., 184
Barnes, Beverly L., 88
Barnes, Leroy T., Jr., 45
Barnes, Sara, 162
Barnes, William F., 200
Barness, W.E., 168
Bartz, Karen, 110
Barwick, Kent L., 50
Bass, Edward P., 20, 206
Bass, Lee M., 20, 206
Bass, Nancy Lee, 20, 206
Bass, Perry R., 20, 206
Bass, Perry R., Inc., 20
Bass, Sid R., 206
Bates, Jeanne, 109
Bates, Leon, 201
Bates, Robert T., 21
Batyko, Richard, 52
Baugh, Eula Mae, 24
Baugh, John F., 24
BB&T, 253
Beach, Charles S., 9
Beale, R. Michelle, 53
Bean, Elizabeth N., 25
Bean, Norwin S., 25
Bean, Ralph J., Jr., 26
Beard, Peter, 88
Beard, William M., 200
Beaufait, Fred W., 132
Beckner, Jay, 173
Beckwith, G. Nicholas, 26
Beebe, Frederick S., 107
Behrenhausen, Richard A., 164
Belcher, Jennifer, 38
Belda, Alain J.P., 93
Bell, Judith M., 81
Bell, R. Terry, 211
Bellatti, Barbara, 211
Bellinger, Geraldine G., 98
Belloff, Frederick M., 40
Belloff, Mary Gretchen, 40
Bellor, Mary M., 107
Benedum, Michael Late, 26
Benedum, Paul G., Jr., 26
Benedum, Sarah N., 26
Bennett, James E. III, 52
Bennett, Jo Ann P., 75
Bensen, James, 30
Benson, James M., 174
Benson, Martha L., 169
Benson, Vickie, 137
Benstein, Diane, 59
Bentson, Linda, 188
Berger, John N., 29
Bergtold, Susanna, 217
Berkopec, Robert N., 33
Bernstein, Alison R., 93
Bernstein, Joshua B., 175
Bernstein, Mem, 14, 235
Bernstein, Zalman C., 235

Goodban, Nicholas, 164
Goodnow, Charles, 58
Goodwin, Peter, 141
Gordon, Barbara, 106
Gordon, Vicki J., 237
Gorelick, Jamie S., 88, 158
Gorman, Judith B., 61
Gother, Ronald, 44
Gough, Thomas E., 118
Gozigian, E., 240
Graham, Angela, 23
Graham, Donald E., 107
Graham, Gene, 211
Graham, Katharine, 107
Graham, Mary, 158
Graham, Patricia Albjerg, 122
Gralen, Donald J., 67
Grange, David L., 164
Grans, Sue, 64
Grant, David N.W. III, 73
Graves, Barbara, 66
Gravin, Laurence A., 41
Gray-Felder, Denise A., 209
Grebe, Michael W., 33
Green, Bennie, 211
Green, Richard C., Jr., 145
Greenberg, Barbara E., 255
Greener, Charles V., 88
Griego, Linda, 141
Griffin, Denise, 237
Griffith, Mary K., 61
Griffiths, Sean, 239
Grigsby, L. Lane, 22
Grogan, Paul S., 151
Grousbeck, H. Irving, 119
Grover, Nancy T., 116
Groza, Michael, 162
Grzywinski, Joan A., 215
Guderian, Courtney, 63
Guempel, Scot R., 62
Guillermo, Tessie, 45
Guinier, Lani, 190
Gumerson, Jean G., 200
Gund, Ann L., 108
Gund, Catherine, 108
Gund, Geoffrey, 108
Gund, George, 108
Gund, George III, 108
Gund, Llura A., 108
Gund, Zachary, 108
Gupta, Geeta Rao, 182
Gurieva, Diana M., 76
Gustin, Marie, 9

Haas, David W., 195
Haas, Frederick R., 195
Haas, Nancy B., 195
Haas, Otto, 195
Haas, Peter E., Jr., 216
Haas, Phoebe W., 195
Haas Charitable Trusts, Otto Haas & Phoebe W., 195
Hagedorn, Jessica, 137
Hagen, Wendy, 141
Halbritter, Jane A., 61
Haleen, Tobi, 212
Hall, Charles T., 98
Hall, Donald J., 109, 110
Hall, Donald J., Jr., 110
Hall, E.A., 109
Hall, Joyce C., 109
Hall, R.B., 109
Hall, Thomas H. III, 236
Hall, William A., 109, 110
Hallmark Cards, Inc., 109, 110
Halpern, Stephen, 138
Hamilton, Beverly L., 45
Hamilton, Charles H., 50
Hamilton, Joseph M., 255
Hamilton, Marilyn, 45
Hamm, Charles J., 132
Hammack, John A., 169
Hammer, Dru, 111
Hammer, Kimberly J., 198
Hammer, Michael A., 111
Hampton, Sybil J., 15
Hampton, Sybil Jordan, 210
Hangs, George L., Jr., 114
Hanna, Richard, 61
Hanrahan, Robert E., Jr., 195
Hansen, Inc., 112
Hansen, Nancy K., 112
Hansen, Timothy R., 67
Hansen, William Gregg, 112
Hansen, William S., 112
Hansmann, Ralph E., 105
Hanson, Jon F., 202
Hardin, Philip Bernard, 113
Hardin's Bakeries Corp., 113
Harmon, Claude C., 114
Harmon, John c., 198
Harmon, Julia J., 114
Harnden, Thomas L., 19
Harris, John H., 6
Harris, Paul W., 124
Harris, Ric, 52
Harris Associates, 67
Harris Bankcorp, Inc., 115
Harris Trust and Savings Bank, 115
Hart, Randy, 19
Hartman, Sid, 162
Hartnett, Edward J., 141
Harvey, Hal, 173
Harvey-Reid, Stacey, 72
Harwood, Donald W., 140
Harwood, Marialice P., 215
Haskins, Lillian Escobar, 91
Hatfield, David L., 143
Haugen, Roy, 35
Hawkinson, John, 30
Hawn, Gates Helms, 50
Hay, Thomas S., 198
Hayes, Carol, 53
Hayes, Denis, 38
Hayes, Dyanne M., 121
Hayes, Gordon M., 61
Hazel, James R.C., Jr., 23
Heald, Edward S., 46
Healey, Kevin A., 237
Healey, Thomas J., 209
Healy, John R., 12
Hechscher, Martin A., 201
Hecker, Robert K., 237
Heeschen, Paul C., 85
Heffern, Gordon E., 151
Heffner, Charlotte M., 159
Heinmann, Harry N., Jr., 3
Hellman, F. Warren, 216
Henderson, Rhoe B. III, 98
Hennessy, Marilyn, 205
Hennessy, Michael W., 55
Henrikson, C. Robert, 174
Henrotin Hospital, 244
Henshaw, G. Russell, Jr., 141
Herdt, Robert W., 209
Hernandez, Antonia, 209
Hernandez, Colleen, 88
Hernandez, Sandra R., 216
Herrick, Rhoda R., 118
Hertog, Roger, 235
Hessler, Deborah J., 40
Hettinger, James F., 23
Hewlett, Flora Lamson, 119
Hewlett, Walter B., 119
Hewlett, William R., 119
Heydon, Henrietta M., 183
Heydon, Peter N., 183
Hickerson, Keith, 237
Hilbert, Robert J., 81
Hilbrich, Gerald F., 40
Hill, Cathy, 80
Hill, J. Jerome, 137
Hill, Linda, 209
Hiller, Lisa, 16
Hilliker, Don, 8
Hilt, George, 58
Hilt, Jack, 58
Hilt, John, 58
Hilton, Barron, 121
Hilton, Conrad N., 121
Hilton, Conrad N. III, 121
Hilton, Eric M., 121
Hilton, Steven M., 121
Hilton, William B., Jr., 121
Hilton Foundation, Conrad, 212
Hinson, J.A., 197
Hirota, Sherry M., 45
Hirsch, Colette, 41
Hirsch, John B., 41
Hirsch, Steven B., 41
Hirschhorn, Barbara B., 31
Hirschhorn, David, 31
Hirschhorn, Gina B., 31
Hirschhorn, Michael J., 31
Hitachi America, Ltd., 122
Hoagland, Laurance, 119
Hobika, Joseph H., Sr., 61
Hoblitzelle, Esther T., 124
Hoblitzelle, Karl St. John, 124
Hoch, Larry H., 181
Hockaday, Irvine O., Jr., 109, 110
Hodgkin, Krista L., 150
Hodjat, Mehdi, 2
Hoffer, Walter C., 157
Holaday, A. Bart, 71
Holaday, Alberta B., 71
Holaday, Brett C., 71
Holaday, Janet L., 71
Holaday, Patrick B., 71
Holder, Eric H., Jr., 175
Holdren, John P., 158
Holm, Herbert W., 40
Holman, Rhonda, 145
Holmes, G. Burtt, 248
Holmes, Ruth Whitaker, 248
Holmes, Thomas A., 248
Hoolihan, James, 30
Hopkins, John E. "Jack", 143
Horan, Lucia, 41
Horan, Peggy A., 41
Hormel, Rampa R., 104
Hormel, Thomas D., 104

GEOGRAPHIC INDEX

For PRI providers with a history of making PRIs in another state, consult the "see also" references at the end of each state section.

LOUISIANA

Baton Rouge: Baton Rouge 22
Metairie: Brown 36

MAINE

Ellsworth: Maine 161
Portland: Libra 156, UnumProvident 237

see also 135, 227, 230

MARYLAND

Baltimore: Abell 1, Blaustein 31, Development 72
Bethesda: Alpha 7
Columbia: Columbia 57
Gaithersburg: Casey 47
Huntingtown: Doran 74
Potomac: Felder 90
St. Michaels: Knapp 150

see also 175, 195

MASSACHUSETTS

Boston: Hyams 130, Sweet 230
Framingham: CARLISLE 46, Highland 120
Marion: Island 135
North Andover: Stevens 225, Stevens 226
Worcester: Worcester 255

see also 227

MICHIGAN

Ann Arbor: Mosaic 183
Battle Creek: Battle Creek 23, Kellogg 146, Miller 178
Detroit: Shiffman 219
Elk Rapids: Northern 187
Kalamazoo: Kalamazoo 143
Lansing: Michigan 177
Muskegon: Community 58
Winn: Morey 181

see also 18, 205

MINNESOTA

Bemidji: Northwest 188
Edina: Emmerich 82
Grand Rapids: Blandin 30
Kenyon: Winds 251
Minneapolis: George 101
St. Paul: Bremer 34, Jerome 137, McNeely 168, Saint Paul 215

see also 6, 202

MISSISSIPPI

Meridian: Hardin 113

see also 36, 243

MISSOURI

Kansas City: Hall 109, Hallmark 110, Kauffman 145
Neosho: Farber 89

see also 205

MONTANA

Red Lodge: Edwards 79

see also 34, 38

NEBRASKA

Lincoln: Woods 254

NEVADA

Reno: Hilton 121

NEW HAMPSHIRE

Concord: Bean 25, New Hampshire 184

see also 227, 230

NEW JERSEY

Morristown: Community 62, Dodge 73
Newark: Prudential 202
Princeton: Johnson 141

see also 91, 195, 199

NEW MEXICO

Hobbs: Maddox 160
Santa Fe: Lannan 152, McCune 165, Stokes 227

see also 71, 114

NEW YORK

Brooklyn: Independence 132
Buffalo: Wendt 247
Cedarhurst: Garber 97
Cooperstown: Walker 240
Essex: Eddy 78
Jamestown: Gebbie 98
Liberty: Gerry 103
Millbrook: Dyson 76
Monsey: Benmen 27
New York: Alavi 2, Atlantic 12, AVI 14, Clark 50, Ford 93, Golden 105, Heron 117, Herrick 118, HKH 123, Johnson 140, Joukowsky 142, Kaplan 144, Leshkowitz 155, Media 170, Mertz 173, MetLife 174, Norcross 186, Open 190, Rockefeller 209, Scherman 217, Silverman 221, Tikvah 235, Weeden 246
Rochester: August 13
Utica: Community 61

see also 41, 43, 137, 230

NORTH CAROLINA

Charlotte: Bank 17
Greensboro: Anonymous 10, Community 60
Raleigh: Southland 222
Winston-Salem: Babcock 15, Winston-Salem 253

NORTH DAKOTA

Jamestown: Dakota 71

see also 34

OHIO

Barberton: Barberton 19
Canton: Stark 223
Chagrin Falls: Geisse 99
Cleveland: Cleveland 52, Gund 108
Columbus: Hunt 127
Dayton: Mathile 163
Okeana: Hubert 126
Toledo: Stranahan 228

see also 18, 148, 199

OKLAHOMA

Ardmore: Noble 185
Oklahoma City: Presbyterian 200
Tulsa: Harmon 114

see also 148

OREGON

Portland: Meyer 176, Pacific 192
Salem: Faith 87

see also 5, 38

PENNSYLVANIA

Bala Cynwyd: Roberts 208
Elverson: Firstfruits 92
Haverford: Presser 201
Philadelphia: First 91, Oberkotter 189, Penn 195, Pew 196
Pittsburgh: Benedum 26, Buhl 37, Hansen 112, Jewish 138, McCune 166, Mellon 171, Pittsburgh 198, PNC 199
Swarthmore: Inverso 133
Titusville: Rees 204
West Chester: Chester 48
Williamsport: Williamsport 250

see also 41, 202

RHODE ISLAND

Providence: Melville 172

see also 135, 227, 230

SOUTH DAKOTA

Sioux Falls: Alpha 6

TENNESSEE

Chattanooga: Benwood 28, Maclellan 159
Knoxville: East 77
Memphis: Jeniam 136
Nashville: Frist 96

TEXAS

Austin: Puett 203
Dallas: Hoblitzelle 124, Meadows 169, Wagner 239
El Paso: El Paso 80
Fort Worth: Bass 20, Richardson 206
Galveston: Kempner 147
Houston: Baugh 24, Rockwell 211
Lufkin: Temple 233
San Antonio: ArtPace 11
Waco: C.I.O.S. 42, Christian 49

see also 69, 110, 114, 202

UTAH

Salt Lake City: Huntsman 128

VERMONT

see 227, 230

VIRGINIA

Great Falls: Leggett 154
Lynchburg: English 84
Oakton: Moore 179
Rosslyn: Whitaker 248

see also 75, 175, 222

WASHINGTON

Eastsound: Parnell 194
Seattle: Allen 5, Bullitt 38, Gordon 106
Tacoma: Tacoma 232
Wenatchee: Community 63

see also 9, 176

WEST VIRGINIA

Charleston: Clay 51

see also 26

WISCONSIN

Brookfield: Rowland 213
Milwaukee: Bader 16, Bradley 33, Crump 69, 786 218
Plymouth: Gentine 100
Wausau: Alexander 3

see also 18, 34, 41, 205

WYOMING

Jackson: Kerr 148

PRI RECIPIENT LOCATION INDEX

PRI recipients are separated by domestic and foreign locations. Domestic recipients are listed by state, then alphabetically by city. Foreign recipients are listed by country, city if available, and alphabetically by name. Each recipient name is followed first by an entry number, then by a PRI number within the foundation entry.

Domestic Recipients

ALABAMA

Mobile: Alabama Baptist Convention, 42-1, Mobile Historic Development Commission, 88-23
Tuscaloosa: University of Alabama, 236-13, 236-14

ARKANSAS

Arkadelphia: Ouachita Baptist University, 42-18, Southern Development Bancshares, 93-31, 210-1, Southern Financial Partners, 210-2, 243-5
Fayetteville: Northwest Arkansas Aviation Technologies Center, 243-2

ARIZONA

Flagstaff: Skystone Foundation, 152-3, 152-4, 152-5
Ganado: Navajo Health Foundation-Sage Memorial Hospital, 242-1
Phoenix: Neighborhood Housing Services of Phoenix, 88-26

CALIFORNIA

Aptos: Santa Cruz Montessori School, 193-20, 193-21
Beverly Hills: Shalhevet High School, 14-13
Burlingame: Shelter Network of San Mateo County, 193-23
Carmel: Big Sur Land Trust, 193-4, 193-5
Carpinteria: Girls Inc. of Carpinteria, 129-5
Carson: California State University, Dominguez Hills, 236-4
Chula Vista: South Bay Pentecostal Church, 153-17
Concord: Calvary Apostolic Church, 153-4, 153-5
Culver City: Museum of Jurassic Technology, 152-2
East Los Angeles: Charisma in Mission, 153-7
East Palo Alto: East Palo Alto Community Alliance and Neighborhood Development Organization (EPA CAN DO), 193-10
Fallbrook: Fallbrook Land Conservancy, 78-8
Fontana: Fountain of Truth Church, 153-10
Fresno: California State University, 236-1, 236-2
Lompoc: Life Options Vocational and Resource Center, 129-7
Long Beach: California State University, 236-3
Los Angeles: Accelerated School, 68-1, Alexandria House, 39-1, Archdiocese of Los Angeles, 121-1, 121-2, 121-3, 121-4, 121-5, Camino Nuevo Charter Academy, 202-5, Immaculate Heart High School, 39-2, New Economics for Women, 88-27, Survivors of the Shoah Visual History Foundation, 207-1, 207-2, 207-3, Veterans Park Preserve, 191-2
Los Gatos: Yavneh Day School, 14-20
Menlo Park: Boys and Girls Club of the Peninsula, 193-6
Napa: Napa County Land Trust, 193-12
Newport Beach: Santa Monica BayKeeper, 85-1
Oakland: East Bay Asian Local Development Corporation, 117-8, 117-9, Low Income Housing Fund, 93-22, 117-15, 158-24, Neighborhood Housing Services of America, 93-25
Ontario: Calvary Apostolic Tabernacle, 153-6, Sunset Haven Senior Ministries, 228-1
Point Reyes Station: Coyuchi, Inc., 78-5, 78-6, Fund for Global Awakening, 94-1, 94-2
Rancho Cucamonga: Apostolic Assembly of the Faith in Christ Jesus, 153-1, 153-2, 153-3
San Anselmo: Hoffman Institute Foundation, 213-1
San Clemente: Progressive Vision, 159-1
San Diego: Church of Jesus Christ, 153-8, High Tech High, 243-1, James Hervey Johnson Truth Seeker Trust, 139-1, Light of the World Christian Community Church, 153-11, 153-12, North Park Apostolic Church, 153-13, Revival Pentecostal Tabernacle, 153-15, Saint Stephens Church of God in Christ, 153-16, School Futures Research Foundation, 243-4, Truth Seeker Company, 139-2
San Francisco: Alliance for Community Development of the San Francisco Bay Area, 93-1, Asian Inc., 88-2, Blood Research Foundation, 7-1, BRIDGE Housing Corporation, 88-3, 193-7, Independent Press Association, 193-11, Northern California Community Loan Fund, 95-4, 102-2, 214-5, Silicon Valley Community Ventures, 209-4, Trust for Public Land, 106-1, 123-5, 193-24, 193-25, 193-26, 193-27
San Jose: First United Pentecostal Church, 153-9
San Mateo: Samaritan House, 193-19
San Rafael: California Neuropsychology Services, 151-1
Santa Barbara: Alpha Resource Center of Santa Barbara, 129-1, Alzheimers Disease and Related Disorders Association, 129-2, Community Environmental Council, 129-3, Direct Relief International, 129-4, Jewish Federation of Santa Barbara, 129-6,

Mental Health Association of Santa Barbara, 129-8, Santa Barbara Rescue Mission, 129-9
Santa Monica: Saint Johns Hospital and Health Center, 121-8
Santa Rosa: Sonoma Land Trust, 214-6, World Stewardship Institute, 38-7
Spring Valley: Visions of God Christian Fellowship, 153-18, 153-19
Sunnyvale: Resource Area for Teachers (RAFT), 193-17
Van Nuys: E-Access Foundation, 191-1
Walnut Creek: Bank of America Community Development Bank, 193-2, 193-3, Save Mount Diablo, 193-22
West Sacramento: Rural Community Assistance Corporation, 45-1
Whittier: Regency Christian Center, 153-14, Young Eun Korean Presbyterian Church, 153-20

COLORADO

Basalt: HyperCar, 119-1
Boulder: University of Colorado, 234-5, 234-6, 234-7
Carbondale: Wilderness Land Trust, 252-1
Denver: Colorado Agency for Jewish Education, 245-1, Mercy Housing, 158-26, Rocky Mountain Mutual Housing Association, 158-37
Fort Collins: Colorado State University, 234-2, 234-3, 234-4
Greeley: Aims Community College, 234-1, University of Northern Colorado, 234-8, 234-9, 234-10

CONNECTICUT

Manchester: Islamic Institute of Ahl Albait, 2-10
New Haven: Columbus House, 172-1, Greater New Haven Community Loan Fund, 172-3, Mutual Housing Association of South Central Connecticut, 172-4, New Haven Homeless Resource Center, 172-6
Stamford: Mutual Housing Association of Southwestern Connecticut, 172-5
West Hartford: Jafaria Association of Connecticut, 2-13, Solomon Schechter Day School of Greater Hartford, 14-16
Wethersfield: Connecticut Coalition to End Homelessness, 172-2

DELAWARE

Greenville: Christ Church Christiana Hundred, 75-1

DISTRICT OF COLUMBIA

Advocates for Justice and Education, 175-1, African Continuum Theater Company, 175-2, Alexander Graham Bell Association for the Deaf, 189-1, Andrew Cacho African Drummers and Dancers, 175-3, Archdiocese of Washington, 74-1, Byte Back, 175-4, 175-5, Calvary Bilingual Multicultural Learning Center, 175-6, Capital Childrens Museum, 175-7, Clean and Pure Kids, 175-12, Cornerstone, 88-11, Corporation for Enterprise Development (CFED), 158-11, 158-12, 158-13, Corporation for Public Broadcasting, 93-8, Council for Christian Colleges and Universities, 236-6, 236-7, Council for Court Excellence, 175-13, Count Me In for Womens Economic Independence, 95-2, DC Central Kitchen, 175-17, DC Coalition Against Domestic Violence, 175-18, 175-19, DC SCORES, 175-20, District of Columbia Developing Families Center, 175-21, East of the River Community Development Corporation, 88-14, 88-15, East River Family Strengthening Collaborative, 175-22, Excel Institute, 175-23, Hazport Solutions, 72-24, 72-25, Housing Assistance Council, 117-13, Indian Law Resource Center, 152-1, Jobs Have Priority (JHP), 175-30, 175-31, Latin American Youth Center, 54-1, Latino Economic Development Corporation of Washington, DC, 175-32, Life Skills Center, 175-33, Manna, 117-16, Masjid Al-Islam, 2-14, Metropolitan-Delta Adult Literacy Council, 175-34, National Child Day Care Association, 175-35, 175-36, National Council of La Raza, 88-24, National Council on the Aging, 221-15, 221-16, National Housing Trust, 158-29, National Housing Trust Enterprise Preservation Corporation, 88-25, 158-30, NHP Foundation, 88-28, North Capitol Neighborhood Development, 175-37, 175-38, Sexual Minority Youth Assistance League, 175-39, Shalem Center, 235-3, 235-4, Smithsonian Institution, 209-5, Support Center of Washington, 175-42, 175-43, 175-44, Time Dollar Institute, 175-45, U Street Theater Foundation, 175-48, University Legal Services, 175-49, Washington Chamber Symphony, 175-50, Washington Parks and People, 175-51, Wellspring Ministries, 107-1, Whitelaw Housing Development, 174-6, Womens Capital Corporation, 190-3, 193-28, 193-29, 193-30, 193-31, 229-2, 229-3, 252-2, 252-3

FLORIDA

Apopka: Homes in Partnership, 88-19
Jacksonville: Episcopal Diocese of Florida, 75-4
Miami: Inter American Press Association (IAPA), 164-1, Jubilee Community Development Corporation, 88-20
Miami Beach: Talmudic College of Florida, 14-18
Naples: Solar En, 43-3, 43-4, 43-5
Orlando: Florida Community Loan Fund, 158-18, YMCA, Central Florida, 197-1
Port Saint Joe: Church of God in Christ, 75-2
Tampa: Islamic Education Center of Tampa, 2-7
West Palm Beach: Community Financing Consortium, 88-10, Local Initiatives Support Corporation (LISC), 158-23
Wewahitchka: First Baptist Church, 75-5, First Baptist Church Of White City, 75-6

GEORGIA

Athens: University of Georgia, 236-15
Atlanta: Georgia Institute of Technology, 236-9, 236-10, Reynoldstown Revitalization Corporation, 88-30
Dunwoody: Zainabia Nonprofit, 2-17
Kennesaw: University Financing Foundation Project, 236-12
Macon: Wesleyan College, 236-16, 236-17, 236-18
Roswell: Georgia Soccer Development Foundation, 236-11

HAWAII

Honolulu: Hawaii Community Loan Fund, 102-1, Ohana Foundation for Technical Development, 86-1

ILLINOIS

Chicago: ACCION Chicago, 18-1, 18-2, 55-1, 55-2, 55-3, 249-1, Ahkenaton Community Development Corporation, 18-3, Americans United for Life, 82-1, Casa Central, 244-1, Center for Neighborhood Technology, 249-2, Chicago Association of Neighborhood Development Organizations (CANDO), 18-4, Chicago Community Loan Fund, 18-5, 18-6, 88-6, 115-1, 115-2, 117-5, 158-4, 249-3, 249-4, Chicago Mutual Housing Network, 249-5, ChicagoLand Real Estate Development Institution, 158-5, Council for Adult and Experiential Learning, 93-9, Illinois Facilities Fund, 32-1, 32-2, 32-3, 32-4, 67-1, 117-14, 158-20, 238-1, Joffrey Ballet of Chicago, 8-1, Lawndale Business and Local Development Corporation, 224-1, Lawndale Christian Development Corporation, 224-2, National Community Investment Fund, 158-28, Neighborhood Housing Services of Chicago, 93-26, 158-32, North Lawndale Learning Community, 224-4, North Side Community Federal Credit Union, 18-8, Norwegian-American Health System, 244-3, Samaritan Housing Services, 244-4, Shorecap International LLC, 93-30, South Shore

Bank of Chicago, 164-2, 164-3, 164-4, United Neighborhood Organization of Chicago, 18-9, Womens Business Development Center, 18-11
Greenville: Greenville College, 42-11
Harvey: Family Christian Health Center, 244-2
Lawndale: Manley High School, 224-3
Oak Brook: Opportunity International, 99-1
South Holland: Bible League, 149-1
Westchester: Suburban Primary Health Care Council, 244-5, West Cook Community Development Corporation, 18-10
Wheaton: Wheaton College, 42-20

INDIANA

Merrillville: Lake County Economic Development Fund, 18-7

IOWA

Cedar Rapids: Mid America Housing Partnership, 88-22
Wilton: Rural Housing Institute, 88-31

KANSAS

Kansas City: Habitat for Humanity of Kaw Valley, 145-2
Marysville: Marysville Youth Center, 220-1
Overland Park: Hyman Brand Hebrew Academy, 14-3, National Association of Basketball Coaches, 109-1

KENTUCKY

Berea: Federation of Appalachian Housing Enterprises, 117-10
Bowling Green: Bowling Green Seventh Day Adventists Church, 125-2, White Stone Quarry Baptist Church, 125-29
Campbellsville: Mount Roberts Baptist Church, 125-18
Glasgow: East Barren Volunteer Fire Department, 125-6
Hiseville: Old Blue Springs Baptist Church, 125-22
Hopkinsville: Christian County Rescue Team, 125-5
Leitchfield: Bethel Fellowship, 125-1
London: Kentucky Highlands Investment Corporation, 93-19, 158-21
Louisville: Community Foundations of America, 22-3, Louisville Community Development Bank, 79-1, Presbyterian Church USA - National Headquarters, 243-3
Munfordville: Munfordville Church of God, 125-20
Salyersville: New Bethel United Methodist Church, 125-21
Smiths Grove: Cave Springs Missionary Baptist Church, 125-3
Wilmore: Asbury Theological Seminary, 42-3
zz: Shiloh General Baptist Church, 125-25

LOUISIANA

Baton Rouge: Arts Council of Greater Baton Rouge, 22-1, Baton Rouge Community College Foundation, 22-2, Louisiana State University and A & M College, 36-6, 36-7, Scotlandville Community Development Corporation, 22-4
Lake Charles: Education and Treatment Council, 36-4
Metairie: Alliance of Cardiovascular Researchers, 36-1, 36-2, Volunteers of America, 36-16
New Orleans: Fellowship of Orthaopeadic Researchers, 36-5, Methodist Home for Children, 36-8, My House, 36-9, Neighborhood Housing Services of New Orleans, 36-10, 36-11, New Orleans Mission, 36-12, Tulane University, 36-13, 36-14, 36-15
Port Allen: West Baton Rouge Foundation for Academic Excellence, 22-5

MAINE

Fort Kent: Kent, Inc., 156-3
Portland: Woodfords Family Service, 237-1, YWCA of Portland, 176-4
Presque Isle: Freshway, Inc., 156-1, 156-2
Wiscasset: Coastal Enterprises, 93-4, 117-6, 146-1, 146-2, 158-7, 158-8

MARYLAND

Baltimore: Baltimore Childrens Museum, 1-1, Baltimore Development Corporation, 1-2, Baltimore School for the Arts Foundation, 1-3, Bird 33, 72-5, Byron Desbordes, Inc., 72-9, Cherry Tomato Boutique, 72-10, Community Law Center, 1-4, Comprehensive Housing Assistance, 1-5, 1-6, 1-7, Constellation Foundation, 1-8, Cosmos Cleaners, 72-12, Cypnana, Inc., 72-13, Dogwood Video, 72-15, Donrit Corporation, 72-16, Downtown Partnership of Baltimore Foundation, 1-9, ES Holding Company, 72-19, Fabara, Inc., 72-21, Garrison Company, 72-22, Hong Phat-Saigon Remembered, 72-28, Living Classrooms Foundation, 1-11, Lordrone Athletic Club, 72-36, Lynch Manor Subway, 72-37, Maryland Center for Arts and Technology, 1-12, 1-13, Michelle L. Kirkner, Inc., 72-38, Miracles-N-More Unisex Salon, Inc., 72-39, Neighborhood Revitalization Fund, 1-14, P&R Sales, 72-40, Patriot Construction Management, 72-41, Patterson Park Community Development Corporation, 1-15, 1-16, 1-17, Petit Louis, 72-43, Repertory Theater of America, 72-47, Shoe Biz, 72-48, Simmones Balloon Gallery, 72-49, Success for All Foundation, 93-32, TMG Services, 72-50, 72-51, Ultimate Driving Academy, 72-53
Bel Air: Beths Bridal Boutique and Formalwear, 72-4
Bethesda: Calvert Social Investment Foundation, 6-1, 95-1, 117-4, 158-2, 158-3, 227-1
Brandywine: Top Banana Home Delivered Groceries, 175-47
Catonsville: Lisa Carter Insurance, Inc., 72-35
Cheltenham: Prism Auto Glass, 72-44
Chestertown: JRH Educational Services, 72-34
Churchville: Harford Land Trust, 1-10
Columbia: Blue Cow Cafe, 72-6, Enterprise Foundation, 88-17, 93-17, 158-16
Cumberland: Barnes-Powell Enterprises, Inc., 72-3
Dunkirk: Triple M Welding Service, 72-52
Fallston: Auto Intentions, 72-2
Frostburg: JH Transportation, 72-32, 72-33
Glen Burnie: Jack in the Box Toy Company, 72-30
Hanover: Eccentrics Hair Studio, 72-18
Hyattsville: Housing Initiative Partnership, 175-29, Nicaraguan Cultural Alliance, 251-6, Quixote Center, 251-10
Joppa: Rabbit Transportation, 72-45
Laurel: HealthCare Resolutions, 72-26, 72-27
Marlow Heights: Butlers Varsity Sports, 72-8, Varsity Sports, 72-54
Monkton: Jamon Foods, 72-31
Mount Rainier: World Arts Focus, 175-52
Owings Mills: Pepes, Inc., 72-42
Pasadena: H2O Tommy, 72-29
Pikesville: Hamid Taxi, 72-23
Queenstown: Everlast Tub and Tile Refinishing, 72-20
Randallstown: WW Contractors, 72-55, 72-56, 72-57
Rockville: A Dab of Muscle LLC, 72-1, Melvin J. Berman Hebrew Academy, 14-7
Silver Spring: McAuley Institute, 117-17, 211-2, Tony Powell Music and Movement, 175-46, Yeshiva of Greater Washington School, 14-24
Suitland: Suitland Family Life and Development Corporation, 175-40, 175-41
Takoma Park: Dance Exchange, 175-14, 175-15, 175-16
Timonium: Epiphany Episcopal Church, 75-3
Towson: Ransoms Boutique, 72-46
Tyaskin: Chesapeake, Inc., 72-11
Westminster: BOLM Micro Speedway, 72-7

Woolford: Easy Trucking Company, Inc., 72-17

MASSACHUSETTS

Acton: Concord Youth and Family Services of Acton, 46-5
Andover: Merrimack Valley Community Foundation, 225-1, 226-1
Boston: ACCION International, 214-1, Boston Community Capital, 130-1, 158-1, 209-1, 214-2, Boston Community Loan Fund, 117-2, 117-3, 130-2, Boston University Residential Charter School, 46-1, Housing Partnership Network, 158-19, Philanthropic Initiative, 172-7, Preservation of Affordable Housing (POAH), 158-36, Solomon Schechter Day School of Boston, 14-15, Sweet Water Trust Project, 230-4
Burlington: New Jewish High School, 14-8
Cambridge: EcoLogic Enterprise Ventures, 182-1, Organic Commodity Project, 158-34, 158-35
Carlisle: Carlisle Extended Day Care Program, 46-2, 46-3, 46-4
New Bedford: Nativity Prep of New Bedford, 120-1, 120-2
Newton: Jewish Family and Life, 221-12
South Natick: Eliot Montessori School, 142-1
Watertown: Perkins School for the Blind, 121-7

MICHIGAN

Ann Arbor: Mosaic Feline Refuge, 183-1, 183-2
Battle Creek: Guardian, Inc. of Calhoun County, 23-1, Private School Development Corporation, 178-1
Boyne City: Northern Homes Community Development, 177-11
Dearborn Heights: Islamic House of Wisdom, 2-8, 2-9
Detroit: Central Detroit Christian Community Development Corporation, 177-2, College Park Commons, 177-3, Focus: Hope, 93-18, Genesis Community Development Corporation, 177-4, Golden Oaks, 177-5, 177-6, 177-7, Kercheval Townhouses, 177-9, Northstar Community Development Corporation, 177-12, Simon House, 177-15, Southwest Nonprofit Housing Corporation, 177-16, U-SNAP-BAC Nonprofit Housing Corporation, 177-18
Farmington Hills: Poverty and Social Reform Institute, 219-1
Kalamazoo: Downtown Tomorrow, 143-1, Hollander Development Corporation, 177-8, Kalamazoo Area Housing Corporation, 143-2, Kalamazoo Aviation History Museum, 143-3, 143-4, Local Initiatives Support Corporation (LISC), 143-5, Southwest Michigan First Corporation, 143-6
Lansing: Michigan Capital Fund for Housing, 177-10, Paddock Nonprofit Housing Corporation, 177-13
Marquette: Northern Economic Initiatives Corporation, 146-3, 146-4
Muskegon: Trinity Village Nonprofit Housing Corporation, 177-17
Newaygo: Autumn Grove Housing, 177-1
zz: Riverside Estates, 177-14

MINNESOTA

Aitkin: Aitkin County Advocates Against Domestic Abuse, 34-3
Crookston: Crookston Firefighters Association, 34-18
Duluth: Northeast Ventures Development Fund, 158-33
Grand Rapids: Second Harvest North Central Food Bank, 34-55
McGregor: Aitkin County Daytime Activity Center, 34-4
Minneapolis: American Indian Housing Corporation, 34-5, Artspace Projects, 211-1, Center for Victims of Torture, 34-8, Central Community Housing Trust, 34-9, Centro Cultural Chicano, 34-10, Chrysalis, A Center for Women, 34-13, Community Loan Technologies, 93-6, 93-7, Community Reinvestment Fund, 34-16, 117-7, 158-10, East Side Neighborhood Service, 34-22, Exodus Community Development Company, 34-23, Hope Community, 34-34, Institute for Agriculture and Trade Policy, 123-1, Migizi Communications, 34-38, Opportunities Industrialization Center, American Indian, 34-46, Plymouth Christian Youth Center, 34-50, Plymouth Church Neighborhood Foundation, 101-1, Public Radio International (PRI), 12-2, Ronald McDonald House Charities, Upper Midwest, 34-54, Trust for Public Land, 30-3, Wilderness Inquiry, 34-61
Moorhead: American Red Cross, 34-6, 34-7, Churches United for the Homeless, 34-14
New York Mills: Otter Tail-Wadena Community Action Council, 34-47
Oak Park Heights: Hope Adoption and Family Services International, 34-33
Pillager: PEAKS Charter School, 34-49
Redwood Falls: Girl Scouts of the U.S.A., 34-28
Saint Louis Park: Wayside House, 34-57
Saint Paul: Acorn Dual Language Community Academy, 34-1, Advocating Change Together (ACT), 34-2, Chicanos Latinos Unidos En Servicios (CLUES), 34-11, Childrens Safety Center Network, 34-12, CommonBond Communities, 88-8, 88-9, Community Solutions Fund, 34-17, Face to Face Health and Counseling Service, 34-24, Family Tree, 34-26, Friends School of Minnesota, 34-27, Greater Minnesota Housing Fund, 34-31, Higher Ground Academy, 34-32, Minnesota Diversified Industries, 30-1, Model Cities Health Center, 34-43, Model Cities of Saint Paul, 34-44, Resources for Child Caring, 34-53, SOTA TEC Fund, 30-2, Union Gospel Mission Association of Saint Paul, 34-56, West Side Community Health Center, 34-60
Sawyer: Minnesota Indian Primary Residential Treatment Center, 34-39
Willmar: Greater Minnesota Family Services, 34-30, YMCA, Kandiyohi County Area Family, 34-63

MISSISSIPPI

Clinton: Mississippi College, 42-17
Jackson: Enterprise Corporation of the Delta, 93-13, 93-14, 93-15, 93-16, 158-15, Millsaps College, 42-16
Marks: Quitman County Federal Credit Union, 117-23

MISSOURI

Kansas City: Community Builders of Kansas City, 145-1, Jazz District Redevelopment Corporation, 145-3
Neosho: Neosho R-5 School District Charitable Foundation, 89-1, 89-2
Saint Louis: Solomon Schechter Day School, 14-14

NEBRASKA

Lincoln: Day Watch, 254-1, Hispanic Community Center, 254-2, Madonna Foundation, 254-3, YWCA of Lincoln, 254-4

NEVADA

Gardnerville: Washiw Itlu Gawgayay, 152-6

NEW HAMPSHIRE

Concord: Merrimack Valley AIDS Project, 184-2, New Hampshire Public Radio, 184-5, Northern Forest Center, 123-2, Sustainable Forest Futures, 123-3
Manchester: Neighborhood Housing Services of Manchester, 184-3, 184-4, New Hampshire Symphony, 184-6
Meredith: Lakes Region Conservation Trust, 230-3
Nashua: Granite State Ballet, 184-1

NEW JERSEY

Atlantic City: Oceanside Charter School, 202-34, 202-35, 202-36, 202-37, 202-38
Bloomfield: E and Co, 173-1
Camden: LEAP Academy Charter School, 202-24, 202-25, 202-26
Clifton: Hope Charter School, 202-23
Dover: College Preparatory Academy Charter School, 202-6
East Orange: East Orange Community Charter School, 202-7, 202-8, 202-9, 202-10
Edison: Multicultural Community Services, 202-31
Egg Harbor City: REACH Charter School, 202-42, 202-43
Elizabeth: Jewish Educational Center, 14-5
Ewing: Samuel Proctor DeWitt Academy Charter School, 202-46
Hoboken: Elysian Charter School, 202-11, 202-12, Hoboken Charter School, 202-22
Jersey City: Greenville/ACORN Charter School, 202-21, Learning Community Charter School, 202-27, 202-28, 202-29, 202-30, University Academy Charter High School, 202-48
Linwood: Ocean City Charter School, 202-33
Monmouth: Youth Education Support Services (YESS) of Greater Monmouth County, 221-22
Morristown: Family Service of Morris County, 199-1
New Brunswick: Greater Brunswick Charter School, 202-20, New Brunswick Affiliated Hospitals, 141-1
Newark: Gray Charter School, 202-19, New Community Corporation, 117-19, New Jersey Performing Arts Center Corporation, 202-32, New Jersey State Opera, 62-1, 62-2, Simon Bolivar Charter School, 202-47
Paramus: Yavneh Academy, 14-19
Paterson: Paterson Charter School for Science and Technology, 202-39, Paterson Charter School for Urban Leadership, 202-40
Plainfield: CALLA Charter School, 202-3, 202-4
Pleasantville: Pleasantville Charter School for Academic Excellence, 202-41
River Edge: Yeshiva of North Jersey, 14-25
Skillman: Early Stage Enterprises, 91-1, 91-2, 91-3
Smithville: Galloway Kindergarten Charter School, 202-17
South Belmar: Academy Charter School, 202-1, 202-2
Trenton: Emily Fisher Charter School of Advanced Studies, 202-13, 202-14, Granville Charter School, 202-18, Samuel Proctor DeWitt Academy Charter School, 202-45
Willingboro: Family Alliance Charter School, 202-15

NEW MEXICO

Albuquerque: Historic District Improvement Company, 165-1, 165-2, 165-3, Magnifico Arts Incorporated, 165-4, New Mexico Community Development Loan Fund, 117-20, Womens Economic Self-Sufficiency Team (WESST), 71-8
Dexter: Reins for Life, 160-3
Hobbs: Habitat for Humanity, Hobbs, 160-1, Opportunity House, 160-2

NEW YORK

Albany: Islamic Shia Ithna Asheri Jamaat of Albany, 2-12, University Heights Association, 221-19, 221-20, 221-21
Brooklyn: Brooklyn Youth Chorus, 132-1, Congregation Zichron Schneur, 27-1, Fifth Avenue Committee, 88-18, Greenpoint Manufacturing and Design Center Local Development Corporation, 117-11, Habitat for Humanity - New York City, 132-2, Working Today, 93-34, Yeshiva and Mesivta Toras Chaim of Greater New York, 14-21, Yeshiva Shaare Torah, 14-26, 14-27, Yeshiva Tiferes Yisroel, 14-28
Buffalo: Clarkson Center, 247-1, King Urban Life Center, 247-2, Martin House Restoration Corporation, 247-3, Sheas OConnell Preservation Guild, 247-4, Sheas Performing Arts Center, 247-5, Western New York Heritage Institute, 247-6
Cooperstown: Glimmerglass Opera Theater, 240-1
East Hampton: Child Development Center of the Hamptons, 221-3
Elizabethtown: Boquet River Association, 78-4
Essex: Black Kettle Farm, 78-1, 78-2, Boquet Mountain, 78-3
Far Rockaway: Yeshiva of Far Rockaway, 14-23
Forest Hills: Rabbinical Seminary of America, 14-9
Getzville: Jewish Heritage Day School of Buffalo, 14-6
Ithaca: Cornell University, 196-2
Jackson Heights: Jackson Heights Community Development Corporation, 132-3
Jamaica: Greater Jamaica Development Corporation, 221-9
Jamestown: Jamestown Center City Development Corporation, 98-1
Long Beach: Hebrew Academy of Long Beach, 14-2
Monsey: Keren Hachesed, 27-2, 97-1, 97-2, 97-3
New City: Jewish Federation of Rockland County, 221-13
NYC: American ORT Federation, 221-1, Audubon Society, National, 193-1, Black Rock Forest Preserve, 105-1, Central Park Historical Field Trips, 221-2, Classical Theater of Harlem, 217-1, College of Insurance, 174-1, 174-2, Columbia University, 105-2, Community Development Venture Capital Alliance, 93-5, 158-9, Community Food Resource Center, 221-4, Corporation for Supportive Housing, 88-12, Danco Laboratories, 193-8, 193-9, Doe Fund, 221-5, Educational Alliance, 221-6, Fund for the City of New York, 221-7, 221-8, Hebrew Free Loan Society, 105-3, Helen Keller International, 121-6, Innovest Group International, 241-1, 241-2, Institute for Urban Family Health, 221-10, John F. Reisenbach Charter School, 221-14, JSTOR, 12-1, Libraries for the Future, 214-4, Local Initiatives Support Corporation (LISC), 158-22, Media Development Loan Fund, 158-25, National Federation of Community Development Credit Unions, 93-24, 117-18, New York City Environmental Justice Alliance, 221-17, New York Initiative, 112-1, Nonprofit Finance Fund, 73-1, 221-18, Open Space Institute, 73-2, 73-3, 144-1, Origin, 93-27, 209-2, Orpheon, The Little Orchestra Society, 140-1, Puerto Rican Legal Defense and Education Fund, 93-28, Ramaz School, 14-10, Retail Initiative, 174-3, 174-4, Trust for Public Land, 50-1, 144-2
Phoenicia: Tongore Pines Housing Development Fund, 105-4
Poughkeepsie: Family Services of the Mid-Hudson and Harlem Valleys, 76-1, YMCA of Dutchess County, 76-2
White Plains: Solomon Schechter School of Westchester, 14-17
Woodside: Islamic Institute of New York, 2-11
Yonkers: Greyston Foundation, 117-12

NORTH CAROLINA

Boone: Northwestern Housing Enterprises, 88-29
Charlotte: Charlotte-Mecklenburg Housing Partnership, 88-4
Clarendon: Lebanon United Methoidst Church, 125-14
Durham: North Carolina Minority Support Center, 117-21, Sustainable Jobs Development Corporation, 71-5, 158-39
Greensboro: Guilford College, 10-1
Mars Hill: Mars Hill College, 42-15
Raleigh: Exploris, 222-1, Southern Rural Development Initiative, 15-1
Rocky Mount: Cedar Grove Baptist Church, 125-4
Winston-Salem: East Winston Primary School, 253-1, Winston-Salem Enrichment Center, 253-2
zz: Fairview United Methodist Church, 125-7

NORTH DAKOTA

Bismarck: Lewis and Clark CommunityWorks, 71-1, Pride, Inc., 71-4, Urban Enterprise Fund, 71-7
Fargo: Community Homes and Resources in Service to Many, 34-15, Family Health Care Center, 34-25, Lake Agassiz Regional Development Corporation, 34-36, Prairieland Home Health Agency, 34-51
Grafton: Red River Community Housing Development Organization, 34-52

OHIO

OKLAHOMA

OREGON

PENNSYLVANIA

SOUTH CAROLINA

TENNESSEE

TEXAS

Odessa: Saint Johns Episcopal Church, 69-7
San Antonio: San Antonio Alternative Housing Corporation, 88-32, Trinity University, 42-19
Southlake: Saint Laurence Episcopal Church, 69-8
The Woodlands: Methodist Retirement Services, 233-4, Trinity Episcopal Church, 69-11
Waco: American Thai Foundation for Education, 42-2, Baylor University, 24-1, 42-6, Central Texas Senior Ministry, 49-2

UTAH

Salt Lake City: Alrasool Center, 2-2

VERMONT

Montpelier: Vermont Community Loan Fund, 88-33
Waterbury Center: Green Mountain Club, 230-2

VIRGINIA

Arlington: EcoEnterprises Fund, 78-7, Environmental Enterprises Assistance Fund, 158-17, Nature Conservancy, 180-1, 193-13, 193-14, 193-15, 193-16
Falls Church: Center for Multicultural Human Services, 175-8, 175-9, 175-10, 175-11, Danie Dollar LC, 72-14
Hurt: Faith Christian Academy, 84-1
Irvington: White Marsh United Methodist Church, 75-7, 75-8
Kilmarnock: Wicomico United Methodist Church, 75-9
Richmond: Virginia Foundation for Housing Preservation, 88-34
Springfield: Housing and Community Services of Northern Virginia, 175-24, 175-25, 175-26, 175-27, 175-28

WASHINGTON

Bellingham: Northwest Ecosystem Alliance, 38-4
Eastsound: Seventh-Day Adventist Church, 194-1, 194-2
Kent: American Moslem Foundation, 2-3
Seattle: Archimedes Institute, 38-1, Cascade Land Conservancy, 5-1, 5-2, 38-2, Cascadia Revolving Fund, 214-3, Evergreen Forest Trust, 38-3, Pioneer Human Services, 71-3, 117-22, Pioneer Social Ventures, LLC, 209-3, Trust for Public Land, 38-6

WEST VIRGINIA

Charleston: McCabe-Henley Properties Limited Partnership, 51-1, River School, 189-2
Harpers Ferry: Appalachian Trail Conference, 230-1
Wheeling: Ohio Valley Foundation, 26-2

WISCONSIN

Almena: Impact Seven, 34-35
Glenwood City: West Central Wisconsin Community Action Agency, 34-58, 34-59
Madison: Wisconsin Coordinating Council of Nicaragua, 251-12, 251-13, 251-14
Menomonie: Disabled and Elderly Transportation, 34-20, Dunn County Interfaith Volunteer Caregivers, 34-21, Greater Menomonie Area Community Foundation, 34-29
Milwaukee: La Causa, 16-1, Legacy Redevelopment Corporation, 16-2, Menomonee Valley Partners, 16-3, Southeast Wisconsin Professional Baseball District, 33-1, Wisconsin Womens Business Initiative Corporation, 34-62, Yeshiva Elementary School, 14-22, YWCA of Greater Milwaukee, 16-4
Plymouth: Plymouth Coalition, 100-1
Spring Green: Sustainable Woods Cooperative, 123-4
Wausau: DAV Fixed Asset Account, 3-1, Marathon County Development Corporation (MCDEVCO), 3-2, 3-3, 3-4, Northland Lutheran Good News, 3-5, 3-6, Wausau and Marathon County Parks Foundation, 3-7

WYOMING

Jackson: National Museum of Wildlife Art, 148-1, 148-2, 148-3, 148-4, 148-5

Unspecified

Business Consortium Fund, 53-1, EcoTimber Industrial, 95-3, Faith Missionary Baptist Church, 125-8, Family Enrichment Center, 125-9, First Apostolic Church, 125-10, First Baptist Church of Woodburn, 125-11, Grace Baptist Church, 125-12, Greenmeadows United Baptist Church, 125-13, Hand-to-Hand Rural Bank, 251-4, Larch Pond, 78-9, Little Barren Baptist Church, 125-15, Little Clifty Baptist Church, 125-16, Morning Star Baptist Church, 125-17, Mount Vernon Baptist Church, 125-19, Rough Creek Missionary Baptist Church, 125-23, Servant Valley United Baptist Church, 125-24, Smith Grove Presbyterian Church, 125-26, The Recovery Center, 174-5, Tri-City Baptist Church, 92-1, Vincent Church, 125-28

Foreign Recipients

Argentina

Buenos Aires: Fundacion para el Desarrollo Sustentable de Eco-Regiones (FunDeSER), 251-3

Armenia

Yerevan: A-Up, 43-1, Armenia TV, 43-2, Armenia, Government of, 128-1, 128-2, 128-3, 157-1, 157-2, 157-3, 157-4

Bosnia-Herzegovina

Banja Luka: Reporter, 170-42
Sarajevo: Dani Civitas, 170-14
Srebrenica: Drina Press, 170-15

Brazil

Sao Paulo: Terra Capital Investors, 158-40

Croatia

Kijeka: Novi List, 170-28, 170-29
Rijeka: Rijecki List, 170-43
Zagreb: Tiskara Maslina, 170-49, 170-50, 170-51

England

Oxford: Construction Management Alliance (Europe), 190-1, 190-2

Guatemala

Guatemala City: Aldea Global, 170-1, 170-2, 170-3

Hungary

Budapest: Magyar Narancs-Magazine, 170-21, 170-22, 170-23, 170-24, 170-25

India

Gurgaon: Eda Rural Systems Private Limited, 93-12
Hyderabad: Bhartiya Samruddhi Investments and Consulting Services, 93-2

Indonesia

Jakarta: PT Media Lintas inti Nusantara, 170-40

Israel

Jerusalem: Shalem Center, 235-1, 235-2

Kenya

Nairobi: Kenya Women Finance Trust Limited, 93-20, 93-21
Wildlife Works, 78-10, 78-11

Malaysia

Kuala Lumpur: Malasyakini, Inc., 170-26

Mexico

Mexico City: Desarrolladora de Emprendedores, 93-10
Oaxaca: Union de Credito Estatal de Productores, 158-41

Nicaragua

Managua: Conjunto de Cooperativas Agropecuarias de Jalapa (CCAJ), 251-1, 251-2, La Cooperativa de Servicios y Desarrollo Comunal de Tisma (COSDECOTI), 251-5, Nitlapan, 251-7, 251-8, 251-9
Matagalpa: SACPROA, 251-11

Philippines

Stellar Fisheries, 229-1

Russia

Barnaul: AltaPress, 170-4, 170-5, 170-6, 170-7, 170-8, 170-9
Chelyabinsk: CR Manager, 170-12, 170-13
Krasnodar: Eisk TV, 170-16
Moscow: Paritet, 170-31, 170-32, 170-33, 170-34, 170-35, 170-36, 170-37
Stavropol: Commercial Broadcasting Studio Network (ATVs), 170-11
Tomsk: TV 2, 170-52, 170-53
Vologda: Premier Publishing Group, 170-38, 170-39

Slovakia

Bojnice: Beta Bojnice, 170-10

Ukraine

Kiev: Express, 170-17, 170-18, 170-19, 170-20

Yugoslavia

Belgrade: Media Works, 170-27, Radio Television B92, 170-41
Niksic: Onogost, 170-30
Podgorica: Roto-Slog, 170-44, 170-45, 170-46, 170-47, 170-48

INDEX TO PRIs BY SUBJECT

For each subject term, PRIs are listed first by foundation entry number, then by PRI number within the foundation entry. For a general subject index to the PRI purposes and activities of the foundations in this volume, see the Index to Foundations by Fields of PRI Interest.

Developing countries, food/nutrition/agriculture 158-34
Developing countries, health—specific diseases 121-6
Developing countries, international affairs/development 93-30, 99-1, 121-6, 158-17, 158-34, 173-1
Developing countries, public affairs/government 93-30
Developmentally disabled, centers & services 34-4, 107-1, 129-1, 129-7, 253-2
Developmentally disabled, debt reduction 129-1, 129-7
Developmentally disabled, loans/promissory notes 107-1, 129-1, 129-7, 253-2
Developmentally disabled, mortgage financing 129-7
Developmentally disabled, program-related investments/loans 34-4, 107-1, 129-1, 129-7, 253-2
Diagnostic imaging research, program-related investments/loans 36-1
Disabled, arts/culture/humanities 34-2
Disabled, civil rights 34-2
Disabled, community improvement/development 88-9
Disabled, education 121-7
Disabled, employment 34-42, 71-4
Disabled, environment 34-61
Disabled, food/nutrition/agriculture 34-21, 175-47
Disabled, health—general 34-25, 36-3, 160-3
Disabled, housing/shelter 88-8, 88-9, 88-12, 88-21, 158-24, 254-3
Disabled, human services—multipurpose 34-2, 34-20, 71-4, 88-8, 88-9, 88-12, 254-3
Disabled, medical research 36-3
Disabled, recreation/sports/athletics 160-3
Disabled, science 36-3
Disasters, building/renovation 34-7, 121-8, 128-1, 128-2, 128-3
Disasters, children & youth 128-1, 128-2, 128-3
Disasters, economically disadvantaged 128-1, 128-2, 128-3
Disasters, equipment 34-18
Disasters, fire prevention/control 34-18, 125-6
Disasters, loans/promissory notes 121-8, 125-5, 125-6, 128-1, 128-2, 128-3
Disasters, preparedness & services 34-7, 121-8, 128-1, 128-2, 128-3
Disasters, program-related investments/loans 34-7, 34-18, 121-8, 125-5, 125-6, 128-1, 128-2, 128-3
Disasters, search & rescue 125-5
Domestic violence prevention, building/renovation 34-3
Domestic violence prevention, children & youth 34-3
Domestic violence prevention, crime/abuse victims 34-3, 175-18, 175-19
Domestic violence prevention, interim financing (bridge loans, cash flow financing) 175-18, 175-19
Domestic violence prevention, loans/promissory notes 175-18, 175-19
Domestic violence prevention, program-related investments/loans 34-3, 175-18, 175-19
Domestic violence prevention, women 34-3, 175-18, 175-19
Drug/alcohol abusers, housing/shelter 193-23
Drug/alcohol abusers, human services—multipurpose 34-13, 34-57, 36-4, 160-2
Drug/alcohol abusers, mental health/substance abuse 34-30, 34-39, 34-57, 36-4, 160-2, 174-5, 193-23
Early childhood education, building/renovation 34-53, 114-4
Early childhood education, children & youth 34-53, 114-4, 193-2, 202-17
Early childhood education, economically disadvantaged 114-4, 193-2
Early childhood education, loan guarantees 193-2
Early childhood education, program-related investments/loans 34-53, 114-4, 193-2, 202-17
Eastern Europe, international affairs/development 190-1, 190-2
Economic development, building/renovation 93-11, 117-19, 129-3
Economic development, business startups/expansion 91-1, 91-2, 91-3, 209-1
Economic development, capital campaigns 93-5
Economic development, economically disadvantaged 18-1, 18-2, 31-1, 34-35, 34-44, 42-7, 54-2, 55-1, 55-2, 55-3, 71-5, 71-8, 83-1, 88-33, 93-1, 95-1, 95-5, 117-4, 117-19, 117-21, 158-2, 158-3, 158-7, 158-8, 158-9, 158-10, 158-11, 158-12, 158-13, 158-32, 209-1, 209-3, 209-4, 214-1, 227-1, 249-1
Economic development, equity investments 91-1, 91-2, 91-3, 156-1, 156-2, 156-3, 158-7, 158-8
Economic development, faculty/staff development 158-9
Economic development, land acquisition 26-1
Economic development, loans for loan funds 18-1, 18-2, 34-35, 54-2, 71-6, 93-1, 93-5, 102-2, 117-4, 158-7, 158-8, 158-10, 158-33, 209-1
Economic development, loans/promissory notes 16-3, 18-1, 22-4, 34-35, 42-7, 55-1, 55-2, 55-3, 71-6, 83-1, 88-33, 93-1, 93-11, 98-1, 112-1, 117-19, 117-21, 129-3, 158-10, 158-33, 214-1, 227-1
Economic development, management development 102-2, 158-2, 158-3, 158-32
Economic development, minorities 71-8, 117-19, 117-21, 158-32
Economic development, Native Americans 34-35
Economic development, program-related investments/loans 3-1, 16-3, 18-1, 18-2, 22-4, 26-1, 31-1, 34-35, 34-44, 42-7, 54-2, 55-1, 55-2, 55-3, 71-5, 71-6, 71-8, 78-10, 78-11, 83-1, 88-33, 91-1, 91-2, 91-3, 93-1, 93-5, 93-11, 95-1, 95-5, 98-1, 102-2, 112-1, 117-4, 117-19, 117-21, 129-3, 156-1, 156-2, 156-3, 158-2, 158-3, 158-6, 158-7, 158-8, 158-9, 158-10, 158-11, 158-12, 158-13, 158-32, 158-33, 209-1, 209-3, 209-4, 214-1, 227-1, 249-1
Economic development, research 158-2, 158-6, 158-9, 158-13
Economic development, seed money 71-6
Economic development, women 71-8
Economically disadvantaged, arts/culture/humanities 1-11, 145-3, 211-1
Economically disadvantaged, community improvement/development 1-5, 1-6, 1-7, 1-11, 1-14, 6-1, 15-1, 18-1, 18-2, 18-5, 18-6, 26-3, 31-1, 34-5, 34-9, 34-16, 34-35, 34-44, 34-47, 34-48, 34-52, 34-62, 42-7, 54-1, 54-2, 55-1, 55-2, 55-3, 71-2, 71-5, 71-7, 71-8, 79-1, 83-1, 88-1, 88-2, 88-5, 88-6, 88-9, 88-13, 88-14, 88-15, 88-16, 88-17, 88-18, 88-19, 88-20, 88-28, 88-30, 88-31, 88-33, 93-1, 93-2, 93-4, 93-10, 93-12, 93-20, 93-21, 93-24, 93-29, 93-30, 93-31, 93-33, 95-1, 95-2, 95-5, 102-1, 108-4, 108-5, 108-6, 115-1, 115-2, 117-1, 117-2, 117-3, 117-4, 117-5, 117-7, 117-8, 117-9, 117-11, 117-18, 117-19, 117-20, 117-21, 130-1, 143-5, 145-1, 145-3, 146-4, 158-1, 158-2, 158-3, 158-4, 158-5, 158-7, 158-8, 158-9, 158-10, 158-11, 158-12, 158-13, 158-14, 158-15, 158-16, 158-18, 158-20, 158-21, 158-22, 158-23, 158-27, 158-28, 158-32, 158-38, 158-39, 164-2, 164-3, 164-4, 174-3, 174-4, 175-32, 177-11, 195-1, 199-2, 209-1, 209-3, 209-4, 210-1, 210-2, 214-1, 214-2, 224-2, 227-1, 243-5, 249-1, 249-3, 249-4, 251-1, 251-2, 251-3, 251-5, 251-6, 251-7, 251-8, 251-9, 251-11, 251-12, 251-13, 251-14
Economically disadvantaged, crime/courts/legal services 1-4, 145-1, 175-49
Economically disadvantaged, education 1-11, 68-1, 93-9, 93-18, 93-32, 114-4, 128-1, 128-2, 128-3, 175-1, 175-4, 175-5, 175-6, 175-20, 175-23, 193-2, 243-4
Economically disadvantaged, employment 1-11, 1-12, 1-13, 34-46, 54-1, 71-3, 71-5, 71-7, 71-8, 93-1, 93-4, 93-9, 93-18, 93-27, 93-29, 93-30, 93-33, 93-34, 117-8, 117-9, 117-19, 117-22, 145-1, 146-4, 158-8, 158-14, 158-21, 158-39, 175-30, 175-31, 209-1, 209-2, 209-3
Economically disadvantaged, environment 71-5, 93-2, 158-5, 158-8, 158-39, 195-1, 251-3
Economically disadvantaged, food/nutrition/agriculture 34-48, 34-55, 34-59, 71-2, 158-34, 174-3, 175-17, 175-47, 221-4, 251-1, 251-2, 251-5
Economically disadvantaged, health—general 34-24, 34-25, 34-26, 34-43, 34-60, 93-34, 193-19, 221-10, 244-2, 244-5
Economically disadvantaged, housing/shelter 1-5, 1-6, 1-7, 1-14, 18-5, 18-6, 18-9, 34-5, 34-9, 34-16, 34-31, 34-34, 34-35,

Guatemala, arts/culture/humanities 170-1, 170-2, 170-3
Guatemala, community improvement/development 182-1
Guatemala, environment 182-1
Guatemala, international affairs/development 182-1
Health care clinics & centers, building/renovation 34-43, 34-60
Health care clinics & centers, disabled 34-25
Health care clinics & centers, economically disadvantaged 34-25, 34-26, 34-43, 34-60, 193-19, 221-10, 244-2
Health care clinics & centers, equipment 34-26
Health care clinics & centers, Hispanics 34-60
Health care clinics & centers, interim financing (bridge loans, cash flow financing) 175-21
Health care clinics & centers, land acquisition 193-19
Health care clinics & centers, loans/promissory notes 34-26, 34-43, 34-60, 175-21, 193-19, 244-2
Health care clinics & centers, minorities 34-26, 193-19
Health care clinics & centers, program-related investments/loans 34-25, 34-26, 34-43, 34-60, 175-21, 193-19, 221-10, 244-2
Health care, aging 34-45
Health care, building/renovation 34-54
Health care, capital campaigns 93-34, 139-1, 139-2
Health care, children & youth 34-54
Health care, computer systems/equipment 34-51
Health care, economically disadvantaged 93-34
Health care, emergency transport services 34-37, 34-45, 125-5
Health care, equipment 34-37, 34-45, 67-1
Health care, general and financing 67-1, 139-1, 139-2
Health care, home services 34-51
Health care, insurance 93-34
Health care, loans for loan funds 67-1
Health care, loans/promissory notes 34-54, 93-34, 125-5, 139-1, 139-2, 193-8
Health care, patient services 34-54
Health care, program-related investments/loans 34-37, 34-45, 34-51, 34-54, 67-1, 93-34, 125-5, 139-1, 139-2, 193-8
Health care, publication 139-1, 139-2
Health care, reproductive health 193-8
Health care, women 193-8
Health sciences school/education, curriculum development 138-2
Health sciences school/education, loans/promissory notes 236-14
Health sciences school/education, program-related investments/loans 138-2, 236-14
Health sciences school/education, research 138-2
Health—general, China 138-2
Health—general, global programs 34-8, 138-2, 190-3
Health—specific diseases, developing countries 121-6
Health—specific diseases, global programs 190-3
Heart & circulatory research, program-related investments/loans 36-1, 36-2, 36-6, 36-13, 36-14, 36-15
Hematology research, loans/promissory notes 7-1, 236-13
Hematology research, program-related investments/loans 7-1, 236-13
Higher education, loans/promissory notes 236-6, 236-7
Higher education, program-related investments/loans 236-6, 236-7
Hispanics, civil rights 88-24, 93-28
Hispanics, community improvement/development 54-1, 88-24, 175-32
Hispanics, crime/courts/legal services 93-28
Hispanics, education 175-6, 254-2
Hispanics, employment 54-1
Hispanics, health—general 34-60
Hispanics, housing/shelter 18-9, 88-24, 169-1, 175-32
Hispanics, human services—multipurpose 16-1, 34-11, 34-60, 175-6, 244-1, 254-2
Hispanics, mental health/substance abuse 34-10
Hispanics, philanthropy/voluntarism 254-2
Hispanics, youth development 54-1
Historic preservation/historical societies, building/renovation 52-4, 152-4, 169-3, 169-4, 169-5, 191-2, 247-3, 247-6
Historic preservation/historical societies, charitable use real estate 169-3, 169-4, 169-5
Historic preservation/historical societies, equipment 204-2
Historic preservation/historical societies, line of credit 247-3
Historic preservation/historical societies, loans/promissory notes 52-4, 88-23, 112-1, 152-4, 247-4, 247-6
Historic preservation/historical societies, program-related investments/loans 52-4, 88-23, 112-1, 152-4, 165-1, 165-2, 165-3, 169-3, 169-4, 169-5, 191-2, 204-2, 247-3, 247-4, 247-6
Historic preservation/historical societies, veterans 191-2
Historical activities, building/renovation 108-1
Historical activities, capital campaigns 108-1
Historical activities, program-related investments/loans 26-2, 52-7, 108-1
History & archaeology, loans/promissory notes 207-1, 207-2, 207-3
History & archaeology, program-related investments/loans 207-1, 207-2, 207-3
Homeless, building/renovation 117-12
Homeless, business startups/expansion 117-12
Homeless, children & youth 36-9, 129-9
Homeless, community improvement/development 34-9, 117-12
Homeless, debt reduction 129-9
Homeless, emergency funds 172-2
Homeless, employment 117-12
Homeless, health—general 34-24
Homeless, housing/shelter 34-9, 34-14, 34-56, 36-9, 36-12, 36-16, 39-1, 88-12, 129-9, 172-1, 172-3, 172-4, 193-23
Homeless, human services 36-9, 117-12, 129-9, 172-2, 172-6, 221-5, 254-1
Homeless, human services—multipurpose 34-56, 36-4, 36-9, 39-1, 88-11, 88-12, 117-12, 129-9, 172-2, 172-6, 221-5, 254-1
Homeless, interim financing (bridge loans, cash flow financing) 254-1
Homeless, loans/promissory notes 36-9, 117-12, 129-9, 172-2, 254-1
Homeless, mental health/substance abuse 34-24, 36-4, 88-11, 193-23
Homeless, mortgage financing 129-9
Homeless, program-related investments/loans 36-9, 117-12, 129-9, 172-2, 172-6, 221-5, 254-1
Homeless, women 36-9, 129-9
Hospitals (general), building/renovation 121-8
Hospitals (general), equipment 242-1
Hospitals (general), loans/promissory notes 121-8, 242-1
Hospitals (general), Native Americans 242-1
Hospitals (general), program-related investments/loans 121-8, 242-1, 244-3
Hospitals (psychiatric), capital campaigns 49-1
Hospitals (psychiatric), children & youth 49-1
Hospitals (psychiatric), loans/promissory notes 49-1
Hospitals (psychiatric), mentally disabled 49-1
Hospitals (psychiatric), program-related investments/loans 49-1
Hospitals (specialty), building/renovation 141-1
Hospitals (specialty), loans/promissory notes 141-1
Hospitals (specialty), program-related investments/loans 141-1
Housing/shelter, aging 1-5, 1-6, 1-7, 34-36, 88-8, 88-9, 88-21, 105-4, 158-36, 254-3
Housing/shelter, alliance 249-5
Housing/shelter, Armenia 128-1, 128-2, 128-3
Housing/shelter, Asians/Pacific Islanders 88-2
Housing/shelter, blacks 93-13, 224-2
Housing/shelter, building/renovation 1-6, 1-7, 1-16, 1-17, 16-2, 18-5, 18-9, 34-3, 34-5, 34-14, 34-36, 34-47, 34-56, 36-12, 36-16, 51-1, 93-3, 105-4, 117-5, 117-10, 117-16, 117-17, 117-19, 128-1, 128-2, 128-3, 143-2, 158-19, 158-20, 158-23, 158-26, 158-29, 158-30, 158-31, 158-37, 164-2, 164-3, 169-1, 172-3, 172-4, 174-6, 176-2, 176-4, 177-1, 177-2, 177-3, 177-4, 177-5, 177-6, 177-7, 177-8, 177-9, 177-10, 177-11, 177-12, 177-13, 177-14, 177-15, 177-16, 177-17, 177-18, 193-7, 193-23, 203-1, 203-2, 211-1
Housing/shelter, capital campaigns 93-17, 93-22, 93-25, 117-13, 158-23

Mental health, Hispanics 34-10
Mental health, homeless 34-24, 88-11
Mental health, immigrants/refugees 34-8
Mental health, land acquisition 129-8, 160-2
Mental health, loans/promissory notes 34-8, 34-24, 88-11, 129-8, 160-2, 163-1
Mental health, mentally disabled 88-11
Mental health, minorities 34-24
Mental health, program-related investments/loans 34-8, 34-10, 34-24, 34-30, 34-48, 34-57, 88-11, 114-6, 114-7, 129-8, 160-2, 163-1
Mental health, residential care 34-30
Mental health, transitional care 34-57, 160-2
Mental health, treatment 34-8, 34-10, 88-11
Mental health, women 34-57
Mental health, youth 34-24, 34-30
Mentally disabled, education 175-33
Mentally disabled, employment 30-1, 34-4, 114-1, 129-7
Mentally disabled, health—specific diseases 129-2
Mentally disabled, human services—multipurpose 34-4, 88-11, 107-1, 114-2, 129-1, 129-7, 237-1, 253-2
Mentally disabled, mental health/substance abuse 49-1, 88-11
Mexico, community improvement/development 93-10
Mexico, food/nutrition/agriculture 158-41
Mexico, housing/shelter 169-1
Mexico, international affairs/development 158-41
Mexico, public affairs/government 93-10, 158-41
Migrant workers, community improvement/development 45-1
Migrant workers, employment 45-1
Migrant workers, food/nutrition/agriculture 45-1
Migrant workers, health—general 45-1
Migrant workers, human services—multipurpose 45-1
Military/veterans' organizations, building/renovation 191-2
Military/veterans' organizations, program-related investments/loans 191-2
Minorities/immigrants, building/renovation 34-11, 45-1
Minorities/immigrants, centers & services 34-11, 45-1, 202-31, 254-2
Minorities/immigrants, emergency funds 254-2
Minorities/immigrants, faculty/staff development 254-2
Minorities/immigrants, Hispanics 34-11, 254-2
Minorities/immigrants, loans/promissory notes 34-11, 45-1, 254-2
Minorities/immigrants, migrant workers 45-1
Minorities/immigrants, minorities 202-31
Minorities/immigrants, program-related investments/loans 34-11, 45-1, 202-31, 254-2
Minorities, arts/culture/humanities 1-11, 93-6, 93-7, 175-52
Minorities, community improvement/development 1-11, 71-8, 88-14, 88-15, 88-19, 93-10, 93-24, 117-18, 117-19, 117-21, 145-1, 158-32, 174-3, 174-4
Minorities, crime/courts/legal services 145-1, 221-17
Minorities, education 1-11, 34-1, 68-1, 175-1, 175-20, 175-23, 243-4
Minorities, employment 1-11, 1-12, 1-13, 71-8, 117-19, 145-1
Minorities, environment 221-17
Minorities, food/nutrition/agriculture 174-3
Minorities, health—general 34-24, 34-26, 193-19
Minorities, housing/shelter 88-3, 88-14, 88-15, 88-19, 117-16, 117-19, 158-32, 177-2, 193-7, 193-10
Minorities, human services—multipurpose 145-1, 175-1, 202-31
Minorities, medical research 196-5
Minorities, mental health/substance abuse 34-24
Minorities, public affairs/government 1-12, 1-13, 93-10, 93-24, 117-18, 117-21, 158-32, 174-4, 239-2, 239-3
Minorities, recreation/sports/athletics 175-20
Minorities, science 196-5
Minorities, social sciences 196-5
Minorities, youth development 1-11
Museums (art), building/renovation 169-5, 196-4
Museums (art), charitable use real estate 148-1, 148-2, 148-3, 148-4, 148-5, 169-5
Museums (art), collections acquisition 148-1, 148-2, 148-3, 148-4, 148-5
Museums (art), loans/promissory notes 136-1, 206-1
Museums (art), program-related investments/loans 136-1, 148-1, 148-2, 148-3, 148-4, 148-5, 169-5, 196-4, 206-1
Museums (children's), building/renovation 222-1
Museums (children's), children & youth 1-1, 175-7, 222-1
Museums (children's), interim financing (bridge loans, cash flow financing) 175-7
Museums (children's), loans/promissory notes 175-7, 222-1
Museums (children's), program-related investments/loans 1-1, 175-7, 222-1
Museums (history), building/renovation 143-3, 152-2
Museums (history), loans/promissory notes 143-3, 143-4, 152-2
Museums (history), program-related investments/loans 143-3, 143-4, 152-2
Museums (marine/maritime), building/renovation 1-8
Museums (marine/maritime), economically disadvantaged 1-11
Museums (marine/maritime), loans/promissory notes 1-8
Museums (marine/maritime), minorities 1-11
Museums (marine/maritime), program-related investments/loans 1-8, 1-11
Museums (marine/maritime), seed money 1-11
Museums (marine/maritime), youth 1-11
Museums (natural history), building/renovation 152-2
Museums (natural history), loans/promissory notes 152-2
Museums (natural history), program-related investments/loans 152-2
Museums (science & technology), building/renovation 34-19
Museums (science & technology), capital campaigns 248-1
Museums (science & technology), loans/promissory notes 248-1
Museums (science & technology), program-related investments/loans 34-19, 248-1
Music, building/renovation 145-3, 201-1
Music, children & youth 132-1
Music, choral 132-1
Music, economically disadvantaged 145-3
Music, equity investments 201-1
Music, interim financing (bridge loans, cash flow financing) 175-46
Music, loans/promissory notes 93-23, 132-1, 175-46
Music, program-related investments/loans 93-23, 132-1, 145-3, 175-46, 201-1
Native Americans, arts/culture/humanities 34-38, 152-6
Native Americans, civil rights 152-1
Native Americans, community improvement/development 34-5, 34-35, 34-38
Native Americans, crime/courts/legal services 152-1
Native Americans, education 152-6
Native Americans, employment 34-46
Native Americans, health—general 242-1
Native Americans, housing/shelter 34-5, 34-35
Native Americans, mental health/substance abuse 34-39
Native Americans, public affairs/government 34-38
Natural resources conservation & protection, building/renovation 93-11, 129-3
Natural resources conservation & protection, economically disadvantaged 93-2, 158-8, 251-3
Natural resources conservation & protection, equity investments 158-8, 158-40
Natural resources conservation & protection, land acquisition 180-1, 193-1
Natural resources conservation & protection, loans for loan funds 93-2, 158-8, 182-1
Natural resources conservation & protection, loans/promissory notes 38-4, 38-7, 93-2, 93-11, 129-3, 182-1, 193-1, 214-6, 230-1, 230-2, 230-3, 241-1, 251-3
Natural resources conservation & protection, program-related investments/loans 38-4, 38-7, 78-5, 78-6, 93-2, 93-11, 129-3, 158-8, 158-40, 180-1, 182-1, 193-1, 214-6, 221-2, 230-1, 230-2, 230-3, 241-1, 241-2, 251-3
Natural resources conservation & protection, research 241-2

170-33, 170-34, 170-35, 170-36, 170-37, 170-38, 170-39, 170-52, 170-53
Safety/disaster relief, Armenia 128-1, 128-2, 128-3
Safety, automotive safety 72-53
Safety, business startups/expansion 72-53
Safety, loans/promissory notes 72-53
Safety, program-related investments/loans 72-53
Scholarships, education 49-3
Science, building/renovation 105-1, 114-3, 114-5
Science, children & youth 202-39
Science, curriculum development 196-5
Science, fellowships 196-5
Science, formal/general education 105-1
Science, interim financing (bridge loans, cash flow financing) 243-1
Science, loans/promissory notes 105-1, 243-1
Science, minorities 196-5
Science, program-related investments/loans 105-1, 114-3, 114-5, 196-5, 202-39, 243-1
Science, youth 114-5
Sculpture, building/renovation 169-5
Sculpture, charitable use real estate 169-5
Sculpture, program-related investments/loans 169-5
Secondary school/education, building/renovation 114-3, 114-5
Secondary school/education, capital campaigns 202-2, 202-33, 202-42, 202-43
Secondary school/education, interim financing (bridge loans, cash flow financing) 243-1
Secondary school/education, loans/promissory notes 14-8, 14-13, 39-2, 202-2, 202-33, 202-42, 202-43, 224-3, 243-1
Secondary school/education, program-related investments/loans 14-8, 14-13, 39-2, 114-3, 114-5, 202-1, 202-2, 202-33, 202-42, 202-43, 202-48, 224-3, 243-1
Secondary school/education, seed money 202-2, 202-33, 202-42, 202-43
Secondary school/education, youth 114-5
Senior continuing care community, aging 228-1
Senior continuing care community, loans/promissory notes 228-1
Senior continuing care community, program-related investments/loans 228-1
Single parents, community improvement/development 34-52
Single parents, housing/shelter 34-52
Slovakia, arts/culture/humanities 170-10
Social sciences, capital campaigns 139-1, 139-2
Social sciences, interdisciplinary studies 139-1, 139-2
Social sciences, loans/promissory notes 139-1, 139-2
Social sciences, program-related investments/loans 139-1, 139-2
Social sciences, publication 139-1, 139-2
Space/aviation, building/renovation 143-3
Space/aviation, faculty/staff development 243-2
Space/aviation, loans/promissory notes 143-3, 143-4, 243-2
Space/aviation, program-related investments/loans 143-3, 143-4, 243-2
Student aid, education 42-2, 42-3, 42-8, 42-10, 42-11, 42-12, 42-13, 42-14, 42-15, 42-16, 42-17, 42-18, 42-19, 42-20, 93-9, 93-18
Student aid, employment 93-9, 93-18
Students, building/renovation 1-2
Students, program-related investments/loans 1-2
Students, sororities/fraternities 1-2
Substance abuse, building/renovation 34-30, 34-39, 36-4, 193-23
Substance abuse, economically disadvantaged 34-39
Substance abuse, homeless 36-4, 193-23
Substance abuse, loans/promissory notes 34-39, 36-4, 174-5, 193-23
Substance abuse, Native Americans 34-39
Substance abuse, program-related investments/loans 34-30, 34-39, 36-4, 174-5, 193-23
Substance abuse, treatment 34-30, 34-39, 36-4, 174-5, 193-23
Substance abuse, women 193-23
Substance abuse, youth 34-30, 34-39, 36-4
Telecommunications, blacks 239-1
Telecommunications, blind 191-1
Telecommunications, business startups/expansion 239-1, 239-2, 239-3
Telecommunications, capital campaigns 170-41
Telecommunications, children & youth 86-1
Telecommunications, collections management/preservation 12-1
Telecommunications, computer systems/equipment 52-3
Telecommunications, curriculum development 86-1
Telecommunications, economically disadvantaged 93-27, 209-2, 239-2, 239-3
Telecommunications, electronic media/online services 12-1, 34-17, 34-38, 52-3, 86-1, 191-1
Telecommunications, electronic messaging services 12-1, 12-2, 34-17, 52-3, 93-8, 170-41, 191-1, 239-1, 239-2, 239-3
Telecommunications, equipment 86-1
Telecommunications, equity investments 239-1, 239-2, 239-3
Telecommunications, loans/promissory notes 12-1, 12-2, 34-17, 86-1, 93-8, 93-27, 170-41
Telecommunications, minorities 239-2, 239-3
Telecommunications, Native Americans 34-38
Telecommunications, program-related investments/loans 12-1, 12-2, 34-17, 34-38, 52-3, 86-1, 93-8, 93-27, 170-41, 191-1, 209-2, 239-1, 239-2, 239-3
Television, charitable use real estate 170-11, 170-16, 170-53
Television, equipment 170-11, 170-16, 170-52, 170-53
Television, equity investments 43-1, 43-2
Television, loans/promissory notes 93-8, 170-52
Television, program-related investments/loans 43-1, 43-2, 93-8, 170-11, 170-16, 170-52, 170-53
Thailand, education 42-2
Theater, blacks 175-2, 217-1
Theater, business startups/expansion 72-47
Theater, interim financing (bridge loans, cash flow financing) 175-2
Theater, loans/promissory notes 72-47, 136-2, 136-3, 175-2, 217-1
Theater, program-related investments/loans 72-47, 136-2, 136-3, 175-2, 204-1, 217-1
Theological school/education, endowments 42-6
Theological school/education, loans/promissory notes 14-9, 14-18, 42-3, 42-6, 42-10, 49-3
Theological school/education, program-related investments/loans 14-9, 14-18, 42-3, 42-6, 42-10, 49-3
Theological school/education, scholarships 49-3
Theological school/education, student aid 42-3, 42-10
Transportation, business startups/expansion 72-37
Transportation, equity investments 119-1
Transportation, loans/promissory notes 72-17, 72-23, 72-32, 72-33, 72-37, 72-45
Transportation, program-related investments/loans 72-17, 72-23, 72-32, 72-33, 72-37, 72-45, 119-1
Ukraine, arts/culture/humanities 170-17, 170-18, 170-19, 170-20
Ukraine, international affairs/development 170-17, 170-18, 170-19, 170-20
University, loans/promissory notes 42-2, 42-12, 42-14, 42-18, 42-19, 234-2, 234-3, 234-4, 234-5, 234-6, 234-7, 234-8, 234-9, 234-10, 236-1, 236-2, 236-3, 236-4, 236-5, 236-9, 236-10, 236-15
University, program-related investments/loans 24-1, 42-2, 42-12, 42-14, 42-18, 42-19, 234-2, 234-3, 234-4, 234-5, 234-6, 234-7, 234-8, 234-9, 234-10, 236-1, 236-2, 236-3, 236-4, 236-5, 236-9, 236-10, 236-15
University, student aid 42-2, 42-12, 42-14, 42-18, 42-19
Urban/community development, aging 1-6, 1-7
Urban/community development, Asians/Pacific Islanders 88-2, 117-8, 117-9
Urban/community development, blacks 224-2
Urban/community development, building/renovation 1-2, 1-6, 1-7, 1-16, 1-17, 18-5, 108-1, 108-2, 108-3, 117-5, 117-12, 145-3, 158-23, 164-2, 164-3, 165-4, 166-2
Urban/community development, business startups/expansion 93-33, 117-11, 117-12

INDEX TO FOUNDATIONS BY FIELDS OF PRI INTEREST

Arts/media/historic preservation

California: Berger 29, Gerbode 102, Hammer 111, Marin 162, Righteous 207, San Francisco 216, T By D 231
District of Columbia: Meyer 175
Florida: Dade 70, Phillips 197
Illinois: Alphawood 8
Louisiana: Baton Rouge 22
Maine: Maine 161
Maryland: Abell 1, Felder 90
Massachusetts: Stevens 225, Stevens 226, Worcester 255
Michigan: Community 58
Minnesota: Jerome 137
Missouri: Hallmark 110
New Hampshire: New Hampshire 184
New Jersey: Community 62, Dodge 73
New Mexico: Lannan 152
New York: Atlantic 12, Herrick 118, Independence 132, Johnson 140, Kaplan 144, Media 170, MetLife 174, Rockefeller 209, Scherman 217, Silverman 221, Walker 240, Wendt 247
North Carolina: Southland 222, Winston-Salem 253
Ohio: Gund 108
Pennsylvania: Hansen 112, McCune 166, Pew 196, Presser 201, Rees 204, Roberts 208
Tennessee: Frist 96, Jeniam 136
Texas: ArtPace 11, Bass 20, El Paso 80, Kempner 147, Richardson 206, Rockwell 211
Virginia: Whitaker 248
Washington: Community 63
Wisconsin: Alexander 3
Wyoming: Kerr 148

Civil rights

Maine: UnumProvident 237
Minnesota: Emmerich 82, Winds 251

Community improvement/economic development

Arkansas: Rockefeller 210, Walton 243
California: California 44, California 45, Community 65, Gerbode 102, Global 104, Marin 162, Sachs 214, San Francisco 216
Connecticut: Hartford 116
District of Columbia: Butler 41, Cohen 54, Hitachi 122, Meyer 175, Moriah 182, Summit 229, Winslow 252
Florida: Knight 151
Georgia: Coca-Cola 53
Hawaii: Alger 4
Illinois: BANK 18, Coleman 55, Community 64, Community 67, MacArthur 158, McCormick 164, Steans 224, Wieboldt 249
Iowa: Bates 21
Louisiana: Baton Rouge 22
Maine: Libra 156, Maine 161, UnumProvident 237
Maryland: Abell 1, Blaustein 31, Development 72
Massachusetts: Hyams 130, Island 135, Worcester 255
Michigan: Community 58, Kalamazoo 143, Kellogg 146, Northern 187
Minnesota: Bremer 34, George 101, Northwest 188
Missouri: Hall 109, Hallmark 110, Kauffman 145
Montana: Edwards 79
Nebraska: Woods 254
New Hampshire: Bean 25
New Jersey: Prudential 202
New Mexico: McCune 165, Stokes 227
New York: Atlantic 12, Community 61, Eddy 78, Ford 93, Gebbie 98, Gerry 103, Heron 117, HKH 123, Independence 132, Mertz 173, MetLife 174, Rockefeller 209, Silverman 221, Tikvah 235, Wendt 247
North Carolina: Babcock 15
North Dakota: Dakota 71
Ohio: Barberton 19, Cleveland 52, Geisse 99, Gund 108, Mathile 163, Stark 223
Oklahoma: Noble 185
Oregon: Pacific 192
Pennsylvania: Benedum 26, Buhl 37, Chester 48, McCune 166, Penn 195, Pittsburgh 198, PNC 199, Williamsport 250
Rhode Island: Melville 172
Tennessee: East 77
Texas: El Paso 80, Meadows 169, Temple 233
Wisconsin: Alexander 3, Bader 16, Bradley 33, Gentine 100, 786 218

Education

Arkansas: Walton 243
California: Berger 29, Burns 39, California 44, Crail 68, Everlasting 86, Hammer 111, Layne 153, Marin 162, Sachs 214, San Francisco 216, T By D 231
Colorado: Thorkildsen 234, Weaver 245
District of Columbia: Hitachi 122, Meyer 175
Florida: Phillips 197
Georgia: University 236
Illinois: Steans 224
Louisiana: Baton Rouge 22
Maine: UnumProvident 237
Massachusetts: Highland 120, Island 135, Worcester 255
Michigan: Miller 178, Morey 181
Mississippi: Hardin 113
Missouri: Farber 89
Nebraska: Woods 254
Nevada: Hilton 121
New Mexico: Lannan 152
New York: Alavi 2, AVI 14, Ford 93, Garber 97, Golden 105, Leshkowitz 155, Silverman 221
North Carolina: Anonymous 10, Winston-Salem 253
Oklahoma: Harmon 114
Pennsylvania: Buhl 37, Oberkotter 189, Pew 196
Texas: Bass 20, Baugh 24, C.I.O.S. 42, Christian 49, El Paso 80, Temple 233
Utah: Huntsman 128
Wisconsin: Alexander 3, Bader 16

Employment/jobs

Arkansas: Rockefeller 210
California: San Francisco 216
District of Columbia: Cohen 54
Illinois: BANK 18, Wieboldt 249
Maine: Libra 156
Maryland: Abell 1
Minnesota: Blandin 30
New York: Ford 93, Rockefeller 209, Tikvah 235
North Dakota: Dakota 71
Pennsylvania: First 91

Environment

California: Environment 85, Foundation 94, Gerbode 102, Global 104, Hewlett 119, Marin 162, Moore 180, Packard 193, Sachs 214, San Francisco 216
District of Columbia: Wallace 241, Winslow 252
Florida: Cafesjian 43
Illinois: MacArthur 158
Maryland: Abell 1, Knapp 150
Massachusetts: Island 135, Sweet 230
Michigan: Community 58, Mosaic 183
Minnesota: Blandin 30, Saint Paul 215
New Hampshire: New Hampshire 184
New Jersey: Dodge 73
New York: Clark 50, Eddy 78, Gerry 103, Golden 105, HKH 123, Kaplan 144, Mertz 173, MetLife 174, Norcross 186, Scherman 217, Weeden 246
Pennsylvania: Mellon 171, Penn 195
Texas: El Paso 80
Washington: Allen 5, Bullitt 38, Community 63, Gordon 106
Wisconsin: Alexander 3

Food/agriculture

New York: Eddy 78

Health

California: California 44, Gerbode 102, Hutton 129, Johnson 139, Marin 162, Oppenheimer 191, Packard 193, Rosen 212, San Francisco 216
District of Columbia: Meyer 175
Illinois: Blowitz 32, Washington 244
Iowa: Wallace 242
Louisiana: Brown 36
Maryland: Abell 1, Alpha 7, Columbia 57
Minnesota: Bremer 34
Nebraska: Woods 254
Nevada: Hilton 121
New Hampshire: New Hampshire 184
New Jersey: Johnson 141, Prudential 202
New Mexico: Maddox 160
New York: August 13, Ford 93, MetLife 174
Ohio: Mathile 163
Oklahoma: Presbyterian 200
Pennsylvania: Inverso 133, Jewish 138
Texas: Christian 49, El Paso 80, Richardson 206, Temple 233
Wisconsin: Bader 16

Housing/shelter

California: Berger 29, Brookmore 35, Burns 39, California 44, Gerbode 102, Marin 162, Packard 193, San Francisco 216
District of Columbia: Butler 41, Community 59, Fannie 88, Meyer 175, Moriah 182
Florida: Knight 151
Hawaii: Alger 4
Illinois: BANK 18, MacArthur 158, Retirement 205, Wieboldt 249
Louisiana: Brown 36
Maine: Maine 161, UnumProvident 237
Maryland: Abell 1, Casey 47
Massachusetts: Hyams 130, Worcester 255
Michigan: Community 58, Kalamazoo 143, Michigan 177
Minnesota: Bremer 34
Missouri: Hall 109, Hallmark 110
Nebraska: Woods 254
New Jersey: Johnson 141, Prudential 202
New York: Ford 93, Gerry 103, Golden 105, Heron 117, Independence 132, Kaplan 144, MetLife 174, Walker 240
North Carolina: Community 60
Ohio: Cleveland 52, Gund 108, Hubert 126
Oklahoma: Presbyterian 200
Oregon: Faith 87, Meyer 176
Pennsylvania: Benedum 26, First 91, McCune 166
Rhode Island: Melville 172
Tennessee: East 77
Texas: Meadows 169, Puett 203, Rockwell 211
Utah: Huntsman 128
West Virginia: Clay 51
Wisconsin: Bader 16

Human services—multipurpose

California: Burns 39, California 44, Hutton 129, Marin 162, Packard 193, T By D 231
Connecticut: American 9
District of Columbia: Meyer 175
Florida: Phillips 197
Illinois: Blowitz 32
Maryland: Abell 1
Massachusetts: CARLISLE 46
Minnesota: Bremer 34
New Hampshire: New Hampshire 184
New York: Dyson 76, Gebbie 98, Heron 117, Kaplan 144, Silverman 221
Ohio: Stranahan 228
Oklahoma: Harmon 114, Presbyterian 200
Pennsylvania: Pittsburgh 198, PNC 199
Texas: C.I.O.S. 42, El Paso 80, Temple 233
Wisconsin: Bader 16, Rowland 213

International affairs and development

District of Columbia: Hitachi 122
Florida: Cafesjian 43
Minnesota: Winds 251
New York: Media 170, Tikvah 235

Philanthropy

California: Irvine 134
Kentucky: Houchens 125
Louisiana: Baton Rouge 22
Maryland: Blaustein 31
New York: Norcross 186
South Dakota: Alpha 6
Texas: Hoblitzelle 124
Washington: Tacoma 232

Public affairs/society benefit

California: Hewlett 119, Lincy 157, Oppenheimer 191
Minnesota: Blandin 30, Bremer 34
New York: Atlantic 12, Heron 117
North Carolina: Winston-Salem 253
Ohio: Hubert 126
Wisconsin: Bradley 33

Recreation/leisure activities

California: T By D 231
District of Columbia: McIntosh 167
Iowa: Wallace 242
Maine: Maine 161, UnumProvident 237
Maryland: Abell 1
Missouri: Hall 109
Oregon: Meyer 176

Religion/church support

Arkansas: Walton 243
California: Hammer 111, Johnson 139, Layne 153
District of Columbia: England 83, Graham 107
Florida: duPont 75
Illinois: Immanuel 131, Khesed 149
Kentucky: Houchens 125
Nevada: Hilton 121
New York: Alavi 2, AVI 14, Benmen 27, Garber 97, Leshkowitz 155
Ohio: Hunt 127
Pennsylvania: Firstfruits 92
Rhode Island: Melville 172
Tennessee: Maclellan 159
Texas: C.I.O.S. 42, Christian 49
Virginia: English 84
Washington: Parnell 194
Wisconsin: Crump 69

Safety/disaster relief

Colorado: Colorado 56
Florida: Bush 40
Illinois: Community 64

Science

California: Hewlett 119
Oklahoma: Noble 185
Texas: Wagner 239

Social sciences

California: Johnson 139

Youth development

California: Berger 29, Hutton 129, Packard 193, Sierra 220
New Mexico: Maddox 160
New York: Dyson 76, Garber 97
Oregon: Meyer 176
Tennessee: Jeniam 136
Texas: Christian 49
Virginia: Moore 179

INDEX TO FOUNDATIONS BY PRI TYPES OF SUPPORT

Loan guarantees

Loans/Promissory notes

Mortgage Financing

FOUNDATION NAME INDEX

RECIPIENT NAME INDEX

A Dab of Muscle LLC, MD, 72-1
A New Leaf, OK, 114-1
A-Up, Armenia, 43-1
Abstract Concepts, TX, 239-1
Academy Charter School, NJ, 202-1, 202-2
Academy Theater Foundation, PA, 204-1
Accelerated School, CA, 68-1
ACCION Chicago, IL, 18-1, 18-2, 55-1, 55-2, 55-3, 249-1
ACCION International, MA, 214-1
Acorn Dual Language Community Academy, MN, 34-1
Adena Ventures, OH, 117-1
Advocates for Justice and Education, DC, 175-1
Advocating Change Together (ACT), MN, 34-2
African Continuum Theater Company, DC, 175-2
Ahkenaton Community Development Corporation, IL, 18-3
Aims Community College, CO, 234-1
Aitkin County Advocates Against Domestic Abuse, MN, 34-3
Aitkin County Daytime Activity Center, MN, 34-4
Al Zahra Islamic Center, TN, 2-1
Alabama Baptist Convention, AL, 42-1
Aldea Global, Guatemala, 170-1, 170-2, 170-3
Alexander Graham Bell Association for the Deaf, DC, 189-1
Alexandria House, CA, 39-1
Alliance for Building Communities, PA, 88-1
Alliance for Community Development of the San Francisco Bay Area, CA, 93-1
Alliance of Cardiovascular Researchers, LA, 36-1, 36-2
ALMONO, LLP, PA, 26-1
Alpha Resource Center of Santa Barbara, CA, 129-1
Alrasool Center, UT, 2-2
AltaPress, Russia, 170-4, 170-5, 170-6, 170-7, 170-8, 170-9
Alzheimers Disease and Related Disorders Association, CA, 129-2
American Indian Housing Corporation, MN, 34-5
American Moslem Foundation, WA, 2-3
American ORT Federation, NY, 221-1
American Red Cross, MN, 34-6, 34-7
American Thai Foundation for Education, TX, 42-2
Americans United for Life, IL, 82-1
Andrew Cacho African Drummers and Dancers, DC, 175-3
Angelina College, TX, 233-1
Apostolic Assembly of the Faith in Christ Jesus, CA, 153-1, 153-2, 153-3
Appalachian Trail Conference, WV, 230-1
Aramgah Memorial Garden Foundation, PA, 2-4
Archdiocese of Los Angeles, CA, 121-1, 121-2, 121-3, 121-4, 121-5
Archdiocese of Washington, DC, 74-1
Archimedes Institute, WA, 38-1
Armenia TV, Armenia, 43-2
Armenia, Government of, Armenia, 128-1, 128-2, 128-3, 157-1, 157-2, 157-3, 157-4
Arts Council of Greater Baton Rouge, LA, 22-1
Artspace Projects, MN, 211-1
Asbury Theological Seminary, KY, 42-3
Ascension Orthopedics, TX, 36-3
Asian Inc., CA, 88-2
Association for Retarded Citizens of Washington County, OK, 114-2
Audubon Society, National, NY, 193-1
Auto Intentions, MD, 72-2
Autumn Grove Housing, MI, 177-1
Baltimore Childrens Museum, MD, 1-1
Baltimore Development Corporation, MD, 1-2
Baltimore School for the Arts Foundation, MD, 1-3
Bank of America Community Development Bank, CA, 193-2, 193-3
Baptist General Convention of Texas, TX, 42-4, 42-5
Barnes-Powell Enterprises, Inc., MD, 72-3
Baton Rouge Community College Foundation, LA, 22-2
Baylor University, TX, 24-1, 42-6
Beta Bojnice, Slovakia, 170-10
Bethel Fellowship, KY, 125-1
Beths Bridal Boutique and Formalwear, MD, 72-4
Bhartiya Samruddhi Investments and Consulting Services, India, 93-2
Bible League, IL, 149-1
Big Sur Land Trust, CA, 193-4, 193-5
BioEnterprise Corporation, OH, 52-1
Bird 33, MD, 72-5
Bishop Kelley High School, OK, 114-3
Black Kettle Farm, NY, 78-1, 78-2
Black Rock Forest Preserve, NY, 105-1
Blood Research Foundation, CA, 7-1
Blue Cow Cafe, MD, 72-6
BOLM Micro Speedway, MD, 72-7
Boquet Mountain, NY, 78-3
Boquet River Association, NY, 78-4
Boston Community Capital, MA, 130-1, 158-1, 209-1, 214-2
Boston Community Loan Fund, MA, 117-2, 117-3, 130-2
Boston University Residential Charter School, MA, 46-1
Bowling Green Seventh Day Adventists Church, KY, 125-2
Boys and Girls Club of the Peninsula, CA, 193-6
Bradford Church of Christ, OH, 127-1, 127-2
BRIDGE Housing Corporation, CA, 88-3, 193-7
Brooklyn Youth Chorus, NY, 132-1
Brooks Museum of Art, TN, 136-1
Brownsville Housing Finance Corporation, TX, 42-7
Bryan College, TN, 42-8
Bryn Mawr College, PA, 196-1
Buckeye Christian Church, OH, 127-3
Buckner Adoption and Maternity Services, TX, 42-9
Business Consortium Fund, ZZ, 53-1
Butlers Varsity Sports, MD, 72-8
Byron Desbordes, Inc., MD, 72-9
Byte Back, DC, 175-4, 175-5
California Neuropsychology Services, CA, 151-1
California State University, CA, 236-1, 236-2, 236-3
California State University, Dominguez Hills, CA, 236-4
CALLA Charter School, NJ, 202-3, 202-4
Calvary Apostolic Church, CA, 153-4, 153-5
Calvary Apostolic Tabernacle, CA, 153-6
Calvary Bilingual Multicultural Learning Center, DC, 175-6
Calvary Episcopal Church, TX, 69-1

East River Family Strengthening Collaborative, DC, 175-22
East Side Neighborhood Service, MN, 34-22
East Winston Primary School, NC, 253-1
Eastside Renaissance, OK, 185-1
Easy Trucking Company, Inc., MD, 72-17
Eccentrics Hair Studio, MD, 72-18
EcoEnterprises Fund, VA, 78-7
EcoLogic Enterprise Ventures, MA, 182-1
EcoTimber Industrial, ZZ, 95-3
Ecotrust, OR, 93-11
Eda Rural Systems Private Limited, India, 93-12
Education and Treatment Council, LA, 36-4
Educational Alliance, NY, 221-6
Eisk TV, Russia, 170-16
El Paso Collaborative for Community and Economic Development, TX, 88-16
Eliot Montessori School, MA, 142-1
Elizabethtown College, PA, 236-8
Elysian Charter School, NJ, 202-11, 202-12
Emily Fisher Charter School of Advanced Studies, NJ, 202-13, 202-14
Emmanuel Episcopal Church, TX, 69-4
Enterprise Corporation of the Delta, MS, 93-13, 93-14, 93-15, 93-16, 158-15
Enterprise Foundation, MD, 88-17, 93-17, 158-16
Environmental Enterprises Assistance Fund, VA, 158-17
Epiphany Episcopal Church, MD, 75-3
Episcopal Church of the Holy Spirit, TX, 69-5
Episcopal Diocese of Florida, FL, 75-4
ES Holding Company, MD, 72-19
Evergreen Forest Trust, WA, 38-3
Everlast Tub and Tile Refinishing, MD, 72-20
Excel Institute, DC, 175-23
Exodus Community Development Company, MN, 34-23
Exploris, NC, 222-1
Express, Ukraine, 170-17, 170-18, 170-19, 170-20
Fabara, Inc., MD, 72-21
Face to Face Health and Counseling Service, MN, 34-24
Fairview United Methodist Church, NC, 125-7
Faith Christian Academy, VA, 84-1
Faith Missionary Baptist Church, ZZ, 125-8
Fallbrook Land Conservancy, CA, 78-8
Family Alliance Charter School, NJ, 202-15
Family Christian Health Center, IL, 244-2
Family Enrichment Center, ZZ, 125-9
Family Health Care Center, ND, 34-25
Family Service of Morris County, NJ, 199-1
Family Services of the Mid-Hudson and Harlem Valleys, NY, 76-1
Family Tree, MN, 34-26
Federation of Appalachian Housing Enterprises, KY, 117-10
Fellowship of Orthaopeadic Researchers, LA, 36-5
Fifth Avenue Committee, NY, 88-18
Financial Foundation for Texas Charter Schools, TX, 202-16
First Apostolic Church, ZZ, 125-10
First Baptist Church, FL, 75-5
First Baptist Church Of White City, FL, 75-6
First Baptist Church of Woodburn, ZZ, 125-11
First United Pentecostal Church, CA, 153-9
Florida Community Loan Fund, FL, 158-18
Focus: Hope, MI, 93-18
Fort Worth Art Association, TX, 206-1
Fountain of Truth Church, CA, 153-10
Freshway, Inc., ME, 156-1, 156-2
Friends School of Minnesota, MN, 34-27
Frist Center for the Visual Arts Foundation, TN, 96-1, 96-2
Fund for Global Awakening, CA, 94-1, 94-2
Fund for the City of New York, NY, 221-7, 221-8
Fundacion para el Desarrollo Sustentable de Eco-Regiones (FunDeSER), Argentina, 251-3
Galloway Kindergarten Charter School, NJ, 202-17
Garrison Company, MD, 72-22
Genesis Community Development Corporation, MI, 177-4
Georgia Institute of Technology, GA, 236-9, 236-10
Georgia Soccer Development Foundation, GA, 236-11
Girl Scouts of the U.S.A., MN, 34-28
Girls Inc. of Carpinteria, CA, 129-5
Glimmerglass Opera Theater, NY, 240-1
Golden Oaks, MI, 177-5, 177-6, 177-7
Goodrich-Gannett Neighborhood Center, OH, 52-6
Grace Baptist Church, ZZ, 125-12
Grand Lake Mental Health Center, OK, 114-6, 114-7
Granite State Ballet, NH, 184-1
Granville Charter School, NJ, 202-18
Gray Charter School, NJ, 202-19
Greater Brunswick Charter School, NJ, 202-20
Greater Jamaica Development Corporation, NY, 221-9
Greater Menomonie Area Community Foundation, WI, 34-29
Greater Minnesota Family Services, MN, 34-30
Greater Minnesota Housing Fund, MN, 34-31
Greater New Haven Community Loan Fund, CT, 172-3
Green Mountain Club, VT, 230-2
Greenmeadows United Baptist Church, ZZ, 125-13
Greenpoint Manufacturing and Design Center Local Development Corporation, NY, 117-11
Greenville College, IL, 42-11
Greenville/ACORN Charter School, NJ, 202-21
Greyston Foundation, NY, 117-12
Grove City College, PA, 196-3
Guadalupe Economic Services Corporation, TX, 169-1
Guardian, Inc. of Calhoun County, MI, 23-1
Guilford College, NC, 10-1
Habitat for Humanity, OR, 87-4
Habitat for Humanity - New York City, NY, 132-2
Habitat for Humanity of Kaw Valley, KS, 145-2
Habitat for Humanity of Portland, OR, 176-2
Habitat for Humanity, Hobbs, NM, 160-1
Hamid Taxi, MD, 72-23
Hand-to-Hand Rural Bank, ZZ, 251-4
Hardin-Simmons University, TX, 42-12
Harford Land Trust, MD, 1-10
Hawaii Community Loan Fund, HI, 102-1
Hazport Solutions, DC, 72-24, 72-25
HealthCare Resolutions, MD, 72-26, 72-27
Hebrew Academy of Long Beach, NY, 14-2
Hebrew Free Loan Society, NY, 105-3
Helen Keller International, NY, 121-6
High Tech High, CA, 243-1
Higher Ground Academy, MN, 34-32
Hispanic Community Center, NE, 254-2
Historic District Improvement Company, NM, 165-1, 165-2, 165-3
Historic Gateway Neighborhood Corporation, OH, 52-7, 108-1
Hoboken Charter School, NJ, 202-22
Hoffman Institute Foundation, CA, 213-1
Hollander Development Corporation, MI, 177-8
Holy Family Church, OR, 87-5
Homes in Partnership, FL, 88-19
Hong Phat-Saigon Remembered, MD, 72-28
Hope Adoption and Family Services International, MN, 34-33
Hope Charter School, NJ, 202-23
Hope Community, MN, 34-34
HOST Development, OR, 176-3
Housing and Community Services of Northern Virginia, VA, 175-24, 175-25, 175-26, 175-27, 175-28
Housing Assistance Council, DC, 117-13
Housing Initiative Partnership, MD, 175-29
Housing Partnership Network, MA, 158-19
Hyman Brand Hebrew Academy, KS, 14-3
HyperCar, CO, 119-1
H2O Tommy, MD, 72-29
Illinois Facilities Fund, IL, 32-1, 32-2, 32-3, 32-4, 67-1, 117-14, 158-20, 238-1
Imaginuity Interactive, TX, 239-2, 239-3

My House, LA, 36-9
Napa County Land Trust, CA, 193-12
National Association of Basketball Coaches, KS, 109-1
National Child Day Care Association, DC, 175-35, 175-36
National Community Capital Association, PA, 158-27
National Community Investment Fund, IL, 158-28
National Council of La Raza, DC, 88-24
National Council on the Aging, DC, 221-15, 221-16
National Federation of Community Development Credit Unions, NY, 93-24, 117-18
National Housing Trust, DC, 158-29
National Housing Trust Enterprise Preservation Corporation, DC, 88-25, 158-30
National Museum of Wildlife Art, WY, 148-1, 148-2, 148-3, 148-4, 148-5
Nativity Prep of New Bedford, MA, 120-1, 120-2
Nature Conservancy, VA, 180-1, 193-13, 193-14, 193-15, 193-16
Navajo Health Foundation-Sage Memorial Hospital, AZ, 242-1
Neighborhood Capital Corporation, OH, 158-31
Neighborhood Housing Services of America, CA, 93-25
Neighborhood Housing Services of Chicago, IL, 93-26, 158-32
Neighborhood Housing Services of Manchester, NH, 184-3, 184-4
Neighborhood Housing Services of New Orleans, LA, 36-10, 36-11
Neighborhood Housing Services of Phoenix, AZ, 88-26
Neighborhood Progress, OH, 52-8
Neighborhood Revitalization Fund, MD, 1-14
Neosho R-5 School District Charitable Foundation, MO, 89-1, 89-2
New Bethel United Methodist Church, KY, 125-21
New Brunswick Affiliated Hospitals, NJ, 141-1
New Community Corporation, NJ, 117-19
New Economics for Women, CA, 88-27
New Hampshire Public Radio, NH, 184-5
New Hampshire Symphony, NH, 184-6
New Haven Homeless Resource Center, CT, 172-6
New Jersey Performing Arts Center Corporation, NJ, 202-32
New Jersey State Opera, NJ, 62-1, 62-2
New Jewish High School, MA, 14-8
New Mexico Community Development Loan Fund, NM, 117-20
New Orleans Mission, LA, 36-12
New York City Environmental Justice Alliance, NY, 221-17
New York Initiative, NY, 112-1
NHP Foundation, DC, 88-28
Nicaraguan Cultural Alliance, MD, 251-6
Nitlapan, Nicaragua, 251-7, 251-8, 251-9
Nonprofit Finance Fund, NY, 73-1, 221-18
North Capitol Neighborhood Development, DC, 175-37, 175-38
North Carolina Minority Support Center, NC, 117-21
North Lawndale Learning Community, IL, 224-4
North Park Apostolic Church, CA, 153-13
North Side Community Federal Credit Union, IL, 18-8
Northeast Ventures Development Fund, MN, 158-33
Northern California Community Loan Fund, CA, 95-4, 102-2, 214-5
Northern Economic Initiatives Corporation, MI, 146-3, 146-4
Northern Forest Center, NH, 123-2
Northern Homes Community Development, MI, 177-11
Northland Lutheran Good News, WI, 3-5, 3-6
Northstar Community Development Corporation, MI, 177-12
Northwest Arkansas Aviation Technologies Center, AR, 243-2
Northwest Ecosystem Alliance, WA, 38-4
Northwestern Housing Enterprises, NC, 88-29
Northwood Deaconess Health Center, ND, 34-45
Norwegian-American Health System, IL, 244-3
Novi List, Croatia, 170-28, 170-29
Ocean City Charter School, NJ, 202-33
Oceanside Charter School, NJ, 202-34, 202-35, 202-36, 202-37, 202-38
Ohana Foundation for Technical Development, HI, 86-1
Ohio City Near West Development Corporation, OH, 108-2
Ohio Valley Foundation, WV, 26-2
Oil Creek Railroad Historical Society, PA, 204-2
Oklahoma Life Sciences Fund, OK, 185-2, 185-3
Old Blue Springs Baptist Church, KY, 125-22
Onogost, Yugoslavia, 170-30
Ontario Christian Church, OH, 127-7
Open Space Institute, NY, 73-2, 73-3, 144-1
Opportunities Industrialization Center, American Indian, MN, 34-46
Opportunity House, NM, 160-2
Opportunity International, IL, 99-1
Organic Commodity Project, MA, 158-34, 158-35
Origin, NY, 93-27, 209-2
Orpheon, The Little Orchestra Society, NY, 140-1
Otter Tail-Wadena Community Action Council, MN, 34-47
Ouachita Baptist University, AR, 42-18
P&R Sales, MD, 72-40
Paddock Nonprofit Housing Corporation, MI, 177-13
Paritet, Russia, 170-31, 170-32, 170-33, 170-34, 170-35, 170-36, 170-37
Pars Academy, TX, 2-15
Partners in Progress, ND, 34-48, 71-2
Paterson Charter School for Science and Technology, NJ, 202-39
Paterson Charter School for Urban Leadership, NJ, 202-40
Patriot Construction Management, MD, 72-41
Patterson Park Community Development Corporation, MD, 1-15, 1-16, 1-17
PEAKS Charter School, MN, 34-49
Pepes, Inc., MD, 72-42
Perkins School for the Blind, MA, 121-7
Petit Louis, MD, 72-43
Philadelphia Museum of Art, PA, 196-4
Philanthropic Initiative, MA, 172-7
Pioneer Human Services, WA, 71-3, 117-22
Pioneer Social Ventures, LLC, WA, 209-3
Pittsburgh Gateways Corporation, PA, 166-1
Planned Parenthood of Eastern Oklahoma and Western Arkansas, OK, 114-8
Playhouse Square Foundation, OH, 108-3
Pleasant Run Church of Christ, OH, 127-8
Pleasantville Charter School for Academic Excellence, NJ, 202-41
Plymouth Christian Youth Center, MN, 34-50
Plymouth Church Neighborhood Foundation, MN, 101-1
Plymouth Coalition, WI, 100-1
Poverty and Social Reform Institute, MI, 219-1
Prairieland Home Health Agency, ND, 34-51
Premier Publishing Group, Russia, 170-38, 170-39
Presbyterian Church USA - National Headquarters, KY, 243-3
Preservation of Affordable Housing (POAH), MA, 158-36
Pride, Inc., ND, 71-4
Prism Auto Glass, MD, 72-44
Private School Development Corporation, MI, 178-1
Progressive Vision, CA, 159-1
Project Home, TX, 203-1, 203-2
PT Media Lintas inti Nusantara, Indonesia, 170-40
Public Radio International (PRI), MN, 12-2
Puerto Rican Legal Defense and Education Fund, NY, 93-28
Quitman County Federal Credit Union, MS, 117-23
Quixote Center, MD, 251-10
Rabbinical Seminary of America, NY, 14-9
Rabbit Transportation, MD, 72-45
Radio Television B92, Yugoslavia, 170-41
Ramaz School, NY, 14-10
Ransoms Boutique, MD, 72-46
Raymond and Ruth Perelman Jewish Day School, PA, 14-11
REACH Charter School, NJ, 202-42, 202-43
Red River Community Housing Development Organization, ND, 34-52
Regency Christian Center, CA, 153-14
Reins for Life, NM, 160-3
Repertory Theater of America, MD, 72-47
Reporter, Bosnia-Herzegovina, 170-42
Research Park Project, OK, 200-1, 200-2, 200-3, 200-4, 200-5, 200-6, 200-7, 200-8, 200-9, 200-10, 200-11
Resource Area for Teachers (RAFT), CA, 193-17

Vincent Church, ZZ, 125-28
Virginia Foundation for Housing Preservation, VA, 88-34
Visions of God Christian Fellowship, CA, 153-18, 153-19
Volunteers of America, LA, 36-16
Washington Chamber Symphony, DC, 175-50
Washington Parks and People, DC, 175-51
Washiw Itlu Gawgayay, NV, 152-6
Wausau and Marathon County Parks Foundation, WI, 3-7
Wayside House, MN, 34-57
Wellspring Ministries, DC, 107-1
Wesleyan College, GA, 236-16, 236-17, 236-18
West Baton Rouge Foundation for Academic Excellence, LA, 22-5
West Central Wisconsin Community Action Agency, WI, 34-58, 34-59
West Cook Community Development Corporation, IL, 18-10
West Side Community Health Center, MN, 34-60
West Side Ecumenical Ministry, OH, 52-9, 52-10
Western New York Heritage Institute, NY, 247-6
Wheaton College, IL, 42-20
Whitaker Center for Science and the Arts, PA, 248-1
White Marsh United Methodist Church, VA, 75-7, 75-8
White Stone Quarry Baptist Church, KY, 125-29
Whitelaw Housing Development, DC, 174-6
Wicomico United Methodist Church, VA, 75-9
Wilderness Inquiry, MN, 34-61
Wilderness Land Trust, CO, 252-1
Wildlife Works, Kenya, 78-10, 78-11
Wilson Historic Block District Project, TX, 169-3, 169-4, 169-5
Winston-Salem Enrichment Center, NC, 253-2
Wisconsin Coordinating Council of Nicaragua, WI, 251-12, 251-13, 251-14
Wisconsin Womens Business Initiative Corporation, WI, 34-62
Womens Business Development Center, IL, 18-11
Womens Capital Corporation, DC, 190-3, 193-28, 193-29, 193-30, 193-31, 229-2, 229-3, 252-2, 252-3
Womens Economic Self-Sufficiency Team (WESST), NM, 71-8
Woodfords Family Service, ME, 237-1
Working Today, NY, 93-34
World Arts Focus, MD, 175-52
World Stewardship Institute, CA, 38-7
WW Contractors, MD, 72-55, 72-56, 72-57
Yavneh Academy, NJ, 14-19
Yavneh Day School, CA, 14-20
Yeshiva and Mesivta Toras Chaim of Greater New York, NY, 14-21
Yeshiva Elementary School, WI, 14-22
Yeshiva of Far Rockaway, NY, 14-23
Yeshiva of Greater Washington School, MD, 14-24
Yeshiva of North Jersey, NJ, 14-25
Yeshiva Shaare Torah, NY, 14-26, 14-27
Yeshiva Tiferes Yisroel, NY, 14-28
YMCA of Cleveland, OH, 52-11
YMCA of Dutchess County, NY, 76-2
YMCA, Central Florida, FL, 197-1
YMCA, Kandiyohi County Area Family, MN, 34-63
YMCA, Minot Family, ND, 34-64
Young Eun Korean Presbyterian Church, CA, 153-20
Youth and Family Services of Washington County, OK, 114-9, 114-10, 114-11
Youth Education Support Services (YESS) of Greater Monmouth County, NJ, 221-22
YWCA of Greater Milwaukee, WI, 16-4
YWCA of Lincoln, NE, 254-4
YWCA of Portland, ME, 176-4
Zainabia Nonprofit, GA, 2-17